Industrial Design

Reflection of a Century

Industrial Design

Reflection of a Century

Edited by Jocelyn de Noblet

Director, Centre de Recherche sur la Culture Technique

Publication sponsored by:

A.F.A.A., Association Française d'Action Artistique,
Ministère des Affaires Etrangères.

Ministère de la Culture et de la Francophonie,
Délégation aux Arts Plastiques (FIACRE).

Flammarion/APCI

Published in conjunction
with the exhibition
Design, miroir du siècle
at the Grand Palais, Paris,
19 May to 25 July 1993.

The translation of this volume
was made possible by a grant
from the A.F.A.A.,
Association Française d'Action
Artistique, Ministère des
Affaires Etrangères.

Photographic research
Françoise Icikovics,
Centre de Recherche
sur la Culture Technique
Anne Gelli

Editor
Bernard Wooding

Copy-editor
Christine Schultz-Touge

Publication co-ordinator
Stacey Ealy

Translations from the French
John Goodman:
– Prefaces and Postface
– Abolish Bric-à-brac
– The Bauhaus and the Theory of Form
– Beyond a Semiology of Objects
– CAD and the Conception of Objects
– Colour, Design and Mass Production
– Comfort
– Dandyism
– Design for Everyday Objects
– Design in the First Machine Age
– Design for the Happy Days:
  The 1950s
– Design in Progress
– The Great Utopia
– New Materials in the Industrial Age
– Time-Objects: Beyond Form
– The Voice of Things
David Howell:
– Car Design
– The Process of Car Design

**Translation and adaptation
of the chronology from the
French**
Bernard Wooding

**Translations from the
Italian**
David Howell:
– Italian Radical Architecture
– New Questions

**Translation from the
German**
Samuel Danzig:
– Modernity and the Ulm
  School

Design
Agence Comme ça, Paris

Typesetting
Octavo, Paris

Photoengraving
Bussière, Paris

Film
Leyre, Paris

Jacket printed by
Mussot, Paris

Printed by
Imprimerie Clerc S.A.,
Saint-Amand-Montrond

Bound by
Ateliers Diguet-Deny,
Breteuil-sur-Iton (Eure)

Flammarion
26, rue Racine, Paris 75006
Copyright © Flammarion
All rights reserved.
No part of this publication may
be reproduced in any manner
without written permission from
Flammarion.

Copyright © ADAGP, Paris
1993, for the works by Herbert
Bayer and Marcel Duchamp
Copyright © SPADEM, Paris
1993, for the works by René
Lalique, Le Corbusier,
Fernand Léger, Piet Mondrian,
Jacobus Johannes Pieter Oud,
Pablo Picasso, Jean Puiforcat
and Vladimir Tatlin

ISBN 2-08013-539-2
N° d'édition: 0 645

Dépôt légal: May 1993

Printed in France

Association Française d'Action Artistique A-AA
Ministère des Affaires Étrangères

E x h i b i t i o n

Design, Miroir du Siècle

The Grand Palais, Paris

19 May to 25 July 1993

Presented under the patronage of
François Mitterrand, President of the French Republic

Production

Ministère de la Culture et de la Francophonie
Délégation aux Arts Plastiques
François Barré, *Director*
Jérôme Bouët, *Assistant Director*
Joëlle Malichaud, *Design Co-ordinator*

Exhibition organizers

Agence pour la Promotion de la Création Industrielle
Anne-Marie Boutin, *President*
Myriam Provoost, *General Secretary*

Exhibition curators

Marianne Barzilay
Sylvain Dubuisson

Executive curators

BL Associés SA:
Jean-Jacques Bravo
Jacques Lichnerowicz

Exhibition designer

François Seigneur

Sponsorship

Serge Kirszbaum
Huguette Meyran

In collaboration with

Centre National d'Art et de Culture Georges Pompidou (Musée National d'Art Moderne/Centre de Création Industrielle) – Paris

With the participation of

Vitra Design Museum – Weil am Rhein
Musée des Arts Décoratifs – Paris
Bibliothèque Nationale, Département de la Phonothèque et de l'Audiovisuel – Paris
Musée National des Techniques, Conservatoire National des Arts et Métiers – Paris
Musée d'Orsay – Paris
Direction des Musées de France

Executive committee

Co-ordination
Jacqueline Febvre
Curatorial assistance
Thomas Klug
with the collaboration of
Sido Hennequart-Perrottet
Marie-France Monstin

Curatorial committee

Selection of objects
Claire Fayolle
Brice d'Antras, *consultant*
Registrar
Sophie Rogier, *assisted by*
Caroline Cesbron
Exhibition officer
Jack Nouet
Technical co-ordinators
François Champeau, *architect*
Sophie Roulet, *architect*
Alain Micaelli, *architect*
Claude Malaplate, *architect*
Production assistant
Fatiha Zeggaï
Documentation
Éric Mézil

Exhibition design

Agence François Seigneur:
Catherine Bonnier, *architect*
Héléna Solé, *architect*
Aldric Beckman, *assistant*

Consultants

Raymond Guidot
Lucette Lombard-Valentino
Jocelyn de Noblet

Vehicle research and selection

Centre de Recherche sur la Culture Technique
Centre International de l'Automobile de Pantin

Selection of office interiors

Huguette Meyran

Stage soundtrack

Sound Director
Louis Dandrel – Diasonic
Production
Éric Bonnard – Diasonic
Sound illustration
Émilie Pianta
Acoustics
Jean-Pascal Monin – Diasonic

Sound
Denis Fortier et Daniel Bujon – Diasonic
Sound effects
Phonothèque Nationale

Soundtrack for headsets

Development
France Culture/INA-Phonothèque
Production
Jacques Taroni – France Culture
Frank Dufour – Institut National de l'Audiovisuel
Recording
Michel Créis – Radio France
Sound illustration
Linda Simhon – Institut National de l'Audiovisuel
Production assistance
Noëlle Luciani – France Culture

Audiovisuals

Research and co-ordination
Claire Davanture
Technical facilities
Centre National d'Art et de Culture Georges Pompidou (Audiovisual Service)
Bakelite Installation

Photographic documentation

Dominique Alfonsi

Graphic design

Doumig Le Cuziat
Edith Devaissier and Anne Barcat

Lighting

Grandeur Nature

Communications and public relations

CCC (Claudine Colin Communication):
Claudine Colin
Anne-Sophie Decronumbourg
Julie Goëlff
Corinne Martin
Amélie von Leithner

Poster design

Shigeo Fukuda

Conferences and debates

In collaboration with
Centre National d'Art et de
Culture Georges Pompidou
(Département du
Développement Culturel -
Les Lundis du CCI)

Educational tour of the exhibition

Centre National d'Art et de
Culture Georges Pompidou
(Département du
Développement Culturel,
Atelier des Enfants, Pédagogie
du CCI)

Acknowledgements to sponsors

This exhibition received the
collaboration of
Association Française d'Action
Artistique, Ministère
des Affaires Étrangères
Centre International de
l'Automobile de Pantin
Centre National des Archives de
la Publicité

active support

BMW
Danish Design Centre
Gaz de France
ICE – Italian National Foreign
Trade Institute
McDonald's France
Renault
RATP
Scholtès
Swatch
3 Suisses

participation

the following sponsors provided
production assistance
Aéroports de Paris – ADP
Algéco
Apple
Aubry Nogueira
Bose
Canon France
CNIM
Equipole
Féralco
Isoroy
Layher
Placoplâtre
Print
Saint Frères
Scanachrome
Sitraba

Thomson
Tollens
Thyssen

Media partners

France Culture
Institut National de
l'Audiovisuel

with the participation of

Affichages Giraudy
Elle
France Info
Intremuros
Le Figaro
M6
Métrobus

Lenders to the exhibition

Museums and institutions:

GERMANY
Die Neue Sammlung – Munich
Städtliche Kunst Sammlung –
Darmstadt
Stadt Ulm HFG Archiv – Ulm
Vitra Design Museum –
Weil am Rhein
Werkbund-Archiv – Berlin
Museum der Alltagskultur des
20 Jahrhunderts

CANADA
Musée des Arts Décoratifs –
Montreal

DENMARK
Museum of Decorative Arts –
Copenhagen

UNITED STATES
The Museum of Modern Art –
New York
Philadelphia Museum of Art

FRANCE
Bibliothèque Nationale,
Département de la
Phonothèque et de l'Audiovisuel
– Paris
Centre International
de l'Automobile de Pantin
Centre National d'Art
et de Culture Georges
Pompidou (Mnam-CCI) – Paris
Cité des Sciences et de
l'Industrie – Paris
Écomusée de Saint-Quentin-en-
Yvelines

Fonds National d'Art
Contemporain (FNAC) – Paris
Fonds Régional d'Art
Contemporain (FRAC) Nord-
Pas-de-Calais
Musée des Arts Décoratifs –
Paris
Musée d'Art et d'Industrie –
Saint-Étienne
Musée d'Art Moderne –
Saint-Étienne
Musée National des
Techniques,
Conservatoire National des
Arts et Métiers – Paris
Musée d'Orsay – Paris
Musée de Radio France – Paris
Musée Français de la
Photographie – Bièvres

SWITZERLAND
Design-Sammlung, Museum für
Gestaltung – Zurich

CZECH REPUBLIC
National Museum of
Technology – Prague

Collectors and private corporations:

AEG – Germany
AG Distribution – France
Airborne – France
Alcatel Business Systems –
France
Alessi – Italy
Alias – Italy
Altras – France
Anthologie Quartett – Germany
Apple – France
Arflex – Italy
Arteluce Flos – Italy
Artemide – Italy
Artifort – France
Automobile Citroën, Direction
de la Communication – France
Automobile Peugeot, Direction
du Plan – France
Collection Asenbaum – Austria
Association 'Hier à Demain' –
France (AFEGAZ, François
Daveau and Lycée Pierre de
Coubertin, Meaux
Jean-Pierre Gabriel, Jeanne and
Jean-Pierre Guélon
Jean Plateau and the Institut
pour l'Histoire de
l'Aluminium,
Magasin 'Lumière de l'œil',

Société Noirot, Patrimoine
Histoire et Étude du Repassage,
Société Primagaz)
Jean Aubert – France
Au Vieux Campeur – France
Bang & Olufsen – Denmark
Albrecht Bangert – Germany
Jean-Pierre Beltoise – France
Bertone – Italy
Birkenhead Collections – Great
Britain
BMW – Germany
Bodum – France
Braun – France

Calor – France
Richard Camus – France
Georges Candilis – France
Canon – France
Alain Carré Design – France
Cassina – Italy
Centre Historique de
l'Automobile Française – France
The Conran Shop – France
Corning-Pyrex – France

Danese – France
Philippe Decelle – Belgium
Design Plan Studio – France
Disform – Spain
Domodinamica – Italy
Driade – Italy
Eileen and Richard Dubrow –
United States
Du Pont de Nemours – France
Darrel and Luan Ellsworth –
United States

Eos Corporation – United States
Erik Mangor – Denmark
Natacha Endt – France
Ex Design – Japan

Fermob – France
Fulvio Ferrari – Italy
Nunzio Ferrari – Italy
Fiat Auto, Division Alfa Roméo
– Italy
The Fine Art Society,
Andrew McIntosh Patrick –
Great Britain
Fondation Arts Ménagers,
Jacques Rouaud – France
Formes Industrielles, François
Quirin – France
Forum Diffusion – France
France Telecom, Historical
Collection, CNET – France
Fredericia Stolefabrik –

DENMARK
Fritz Hansens – Denmark

Galic – France
François Guilhaume – France

Haslam & Whiteway London
Ldt – Great Britain
Historical Design Collection –
United States
Honda – France
Marc Hotermans – Belgium

Takenobu Igarashi – Japan
Ital Design – Italy

Jensen – Denmark
Johannes Hansen – Denmark
Philippe Jousse, Galerie Jousse-
Seguin – France

Kartell – Italy
Kenwood – France
Knoll – France
Ursula and Hans Ulrich Kölsch
– Germany
Kyocera – Japan

Lagostina – Italy
Laguiole – France
Lauren G. – France
Lego A/S – Denmark
Le Klint – Denmark
Lexon – France
Louis Poulsen – Denmark

Magimix – France
Matsushita Electric Industrial –
Japan
Ingo Maurer – Germany
Eric Mangor – Denmark
Megalit – France
Memphis – Italy
Collection Ménard-Dewindt –
Belgium
Meubles et Fonction MFI –
France
François Meyer – France
Norman Mizuno – United
States
Philippe Moch – France
Groupe Moulinex – France
Musée de l'Automobile de
Lugano – Switzerland

NEC Corp. – Japan
Necchi – Italy
Donald Neuburger –
Switzerland

Marc Newson – France
ninaber/peters/krouwel –
Netherlands

Oceano-Oltreluce – Italy
Olivetti – France

A.E.T., Paliotto's Art Collection
Italy
Parker – France
Pentagram – Great Britain
Nestor Perkal – France
Perobell – Spain
Peugeot PSA – France
Gilles Peyroulet, Paris – France
Philips – France
Pininfarina – Italy
Plus Corp. – Japan
PPMøbler – Denmark
Prodir – Switzerland
Protis – France
Punt Mobles – Spain

RATP, Département
du Patrimoine – France
Paul Reeves – Great Britain
Renault, Département
Patrimoine et Innovations –
France
Renault, Direction de la
Communication – France
Roset – France
Rosenthal AG – Germany
Rover SA – France
Royal Copenhagen – Denmark

Denis Santachiara – Italy
Savinel & Rozé – France
Scholtès – France
Seb – France
Sedec -France
Seymour, Powell – Great Britain
Sharp Corp. – Japan
Singer – France
Soca Line – France
Sony – France
Stelton – Denmark

Tebong – France
Tecno – France
Techniland – France
Tefal – France
Terraillon – France
Thomson Electroménager –
France
William Threadwell –
Switzerland
Jacques Tissinier – France
Torben Holmbäch – Denmark

Emmanuelle Torck et
Emmanuelle Noirot – France
Toshiba Corp. – Japan
3 Suisses – France

U.R.L.A., Blusson, Dandine,
Glusker, Meyer – France

Venini – Italy
Vespa Diffusion, Groupe
Piaggio – France
Vitra – France
Vitrac Design – France
VAG – France

XO – France

Zanotta – Italy
Zanussi – Italy

Audiovisual documents
Archi-Productions
DEMD Productions
Ministère de l'Equipement – SIC
Pathé Cinéma
Sygma
Prony Productions
Doc Reporter

Sound effects
Institut National de l'Audiovisuel
Radio France

Acknowledgements to
individuals

– Gilles Amado
– Barry Artwood
– Bernard Baissait
– Jean-Paul Barray
– Arlette Barré-Despond
– Jacques Barsac
– Marc Bascou
– Yves Beauvalot
– Maryse Bender
– Thierry P. Benizeau
– Gaëlle Bernard
– Nuccio Bertone
– Sylvie Blanchet
– Isabelle Boisseau
– Sylvie Bourrat
– Jean Robert Bouteau
– Andrea Branzi
– Alain Braun
– Claude Braunstein
– Yvonne Brunhammer
– Michel Butor
– Marie-France Calas
– David Caméo

– Humbert Carcel
– Hélène Carentz
– Josée Chapelle
– Philippe Charbonneaux
– Marie Chauveau
– Roman Cieslewicz
– Didier Coudray
– Guillemette Delaporte
– Mireille Delbeque
– Robert Delpire
– Gilles Devincre
– Jean Digne
– Murielle Dos Santos
– Judith Dupasquier
– Jean Duvignaud
– Marsha Emanuel
– Evert Endt
– Claude Eveno
– Paolo Fabbri
– Luigi Ferrarrizi
– Dominique Ferriot
– Denis Fortier
– Jean-Charles Gaté
– Christian Germain
– Cyrille Giorgini
– Danièle Giraudy
– Giorgetto Giugiaro
– Agnès de Gouvion Saint-Cyr
– Jean-Pierre Guélon
– Rosalie Guernier
– Olivier Guichard
– Cécile de Guillebon
– Véronique Hahn
– Gisèle Halimi
– David Hanks
– Laurent Hériou
– Alexandre Hotton
– Bruno Jacomy
– Danièlle Janton
– Anne-Marie Jensen
– Françoise Jollant-Kneebone
– Nicolas Joly
– Philippe Jousse
– Marie-Laure Jousset
– Peter Koefoed
– Raymond Lachat and the
Atelier de Recherche et de
Création, Mobilier National –
CNAP
– Olivier Lagadec
– Laure Lefébure
– Jean-Philippe Lenclos
– Véronique Leprette
– Nicole Letourneur
– Laurent Leyva
– Henri de Looze
– Yves Macaire
– Pierre-Yves Madeline
– Pierre Maillet

– Luisella Majewski
– Yves Mamou
– Ezio Manzini
– Serge Mauduit
– Laurence Maynier
– Vittorio Meloni
– Bernard Michel
– Isabelle Moins
– Jean-Pierre Mohen
– Pierre Monnet
– Edgar Morin
– Véronique Morvan
– Mosco
– Tomoko Murakami
– Brigitte Naulot
– Nathalie Naylor
– Michel Nicolle
– Odile Nouvel
– Jean-Luc Olivié
– Christian Paligiano
– Gian Beppe Panicco
– Maryline Passini
– Pierre Perrigault
– Gaetano Pesce
– Gilles Peyroulet
– Elise Picard
– Jean-Paul Pigeat
– Jacques Pigout
– Sergio Pininfarina
– Catherine Plantard
– Josée Playoust
– Jean-Pierre Poggi
– Danièle Portaz
– Evelyne Possémé
– Andrée Pouderoux
– Nathalie Proust
– Philippe Puicouyoul
– Andrée Putman
– François and Simone Quirin
– Jean-Eudes Rabut
– Robert Réa
– Stéphanie Real del Sarte
– Marie Rezaï
– Jacques Riboux
– Lionel Richard
– Marie-Christina Roasenda
– Jean Robert
– Georges Rosevègue
– Jacques Rouaud
– Jean-Loup Roubert
– Michel Rougé
– Clément Rousseau
– Corinne Rozental
– Anne Saint Dreux
– Yves Savinel
– JSM Scott
– Marie-Paule Serre
– Claudette Sèze
– Ettore Sottsass

– Chantal Soyer
– Ronald Cecil Sportes
– Philippe Starck
– Richard Ugolini
– Fredi Valentini
– Gilles Varet
– Hélène Vassal
– Simone Veil
– Eliane de Vendeuvre
– Michel Vernes
– Germain Viatte
– Patrick Volson
– Roger von Barry
– Alexander von Vegesack
– Michael Whiteway
– Henri Zuber
– Agence pour la Promotion de
la Création Industrielle
– École Nationale Supérieure de
Création Industrielle (Ensci-Les
Ateliers).

Corporations

Algéco: *construction site mobile
office*
Ateliers Chatet: *partial installation
of the sales and reception area*
Aubry-Nogueira: *placoplâtre
partitions*
C.A.R: *insurance*
CNIM: *escalator*
Coffral Belgium: *stays*
Défi: *fire escapes*
Entrepose: *scaffolding*
Equipole: *builder's hoist*
Expo Surveillance: *security*
FID: *transportation*
Forclum-Saunier Duval:
lighting and electricity
Gidel: *floor coverings
and painting*
Gras Savoye: *insurance*
Hasenkamp: *transportation*
La Panthère: *maintenance*
Layher: *scaffolding*
LDA: *insurance*
LME: *stage
construction*
LP Art: *shipping*
Møbeltransport: *transportation*
Ponticelli: *lifting*
Ranno: *carpeting*
Saint Frères: *facade net*
Scanachrome: *screen printing*
Sitraba: *locksmithing, metal frame,
woodworking, furnishings*
Texen: *sound*
Thyssen: *gangways*

Industrial Design from 1851 into the 21st Century

Sir Terence Conran

Every single thing made by man or woman since the beginning of time has been designed. In other words, some thought, usually combined with basic instinct, has occurred in the decision-making process to decide how the object should work and how it should look.

The history of the world can be documented by the design of objects and the study of these objects gives a clear message about the changes that were taking place in society. Indeed, it is reasonable to conclude that in many instances, especially in the 20th century, it is the very design and innovation of products that induced change in society.

But what is 'design'? Its very name causes confusion to many people and certainly means different things to them depending on their age, race, creed, socio-economic position and occupation.

A great many people have tried to define its meaning, some with great erudition, some with simple good intentions and recently some with malice, describing design as if it was the work of the devil, designed (here we go again) to lead us down the path of wanton consumerism.

For my part, I believe design can best be described as '98 per cent common sense and 2 per cent aesthetics'. It is a skill, in the right well-trained, talented hands, that brings together experience, innovation, craft and art.

The results of this process are objects of desire which are a pleasure to own, a pleasure to use and a pleasure to behold. They bring a quality to life that is often sadly lacking in this largely man-made world we inhabit.

It is interesting to consider why it is that the Church and the State have, over the years, recognized the symbolic power of design – cathedrals, pyramids, triumphal arches, crowns, crosses and swastikas are the result – but have failed to comprehend that the economic and social well-being of the people they rule can also be enhanced by the application of intelligent design to the everyday things they use.

It would be such a simple and, in these days when economists rule the world, cost-effective thing to do to see that every single product the State procured was designed to the highest standards.

In this way a national culture which educated its people would emerge. We should never forget that taste is formed by what people are offered and if they do not have the chance to observe, feel, own and use well designed products, how on earth can they discover whether they would like them?

The by-product of all this (and this should appeal to economists) is, of course, that industry would, with help from the State, produce products that not only satisfied the desires of its domestic customers, but would stand a very much better chance of reaching world markets.

The arguments so often heard against the intelligent application of good design come from cynical industrialists who frequently do not have a passion for the products they make. Their sole concern is for profit and the balance sheet and their cosy life in the reproduction splendour of the suburbs.

They have no vision and very little taste for the modern world that is in their hands to fashion. Their cry goes out 'it's our job to give the people what they want, it's not our job to educate them'. They need guidance and education and it is the role of governments to give it to them.

In Britain an ambitious programme to unite commerce with art began when William Shipley founded the Society of Arts in 1754. Its objectives were 'to embolden enterprise, to enlarge Science, to refine Art, to improve Manufactures and extend Commerce', thus summarizing the material and metaphysical aims of Britain's Industrial Enlightenment. It was established in imitation of the more exclusive Royal Society, an elected academy of distinguished scientists, but with more democratic, popular and practical aspirations. As such it gave Britain an institution which did justice to her role as international industrial leaders, and the Society set about administering the Industrial Revolution and regulating its aesthetics.

However, the Society of Arts' results were, sadly, more cerebral than practical. Some 80 years after the Society was founded, Great Britain's arts might have been doing well enough, and her manufacturing industry and commerce were well established, but her products were not setting standards which provided for future generations. Sadly, the situation is much the same today.

Looking back in history to the beginning of the Industrial Revolution it becomes easier to understand why industry did not, on the whole, encourage the co-operation of contemporary designers with modern ideas. Despite the tremendous innovation and aesthetic beauty of much of the machinery of mass production – a perfect example of form following function – it was easy to emulate and bastardize the handmade products of the rich at a price the poor could afford, so why look further? It is always cheaper in the short term to copy somebody else's ideas and short termism is the curse of much of industry. This process of reproduction has continued more or less unhindered to the end of the 20th century. It is only products with a high technological content such as transport, power generators and communication systems that have broken the mould of antiquity. When modernity in domestic products does rear its head, it is usually in the province of the affluent, thus giving the impression that if an object is well designed it must be expensive, which quite often it is because it is made in very small quantities for a very limited market.

Perhaps the Industrial Revolution will turn full circle in the 21st century and the modern 'objects of desire' of the elitist few will be produced for the mass market.

This is the moment to study the achievements of the designers of the past and with this knowledge go forward optimistically into the future using the amazing skills and intelligence that we have at our disposal to create a man-made world of contemporary beauty which is available to all in society.

Design in Question

François Barré

It has been quite some time, in France at least, since a design exhibition set out, like the present one, to carry out a historical survey of the discipline. When François Mathey and I founded the CCI (Centre de Création Industrielle) in 1969, very few people talked about design, but those who did knew exactly what it was. Today, the word is familiar to many, but most do not understand what it means. It is widely used, cropping up in fashion magazines as well as casual conversation, a kind of semantic badge, fascinating and derisory by turns. Because it can designate anything, it ends up signifying nothing. Perhaps a new word should be found for the original meaning, assuming this is still current.

Jack Lang has always had a special interest in design and has been determined that it should play a major role in the culture of our era. The opening of the ENSCI (Ecole Nationale Supérieure de Création Industrielle), directed first by Anne-Marie Boutin and then by Evert Endt, testifies to this commitment and the decision to organize a design exhibition at the Grand Palais has lent further weight to it. When Dominique Bozo was a delegate in the ministry department concerned with the visual arts, Margo Rouard and Christian Dupavillon were appointed to head the project. When I succeeded Dominique Bozo, and Christian Dupavillon was named Directeur du Patrimoine, a decision was taken to form a new organizing committee. Sylvain Dubuisson and Marianne Barzilay were put in charge of the exhibition, and subsequently the architect and exhibition designer François Seigneur and Jocelyn de Noblet, editor of the catalogue, were brought on board. It was decided early on that the APCI (Agence pour la Promotion de la Création Industrielle), headed by Anne-Marie Boutin, would be responsible for implementing the project and Jean-Jacques Bravo and Jacques Lichnerowicz were subsequently appointed as executive commissioners. Thanks are due to all of them for their time and talent.

But let us return to the shifts in the meaning of 'design'. Design has undergone considerable changes over the last 30 years. At the end of the 1960s, when the CCI opened its doors, it was something of a rarity. The CCI set out (sometimes without success) to locate corporations whose commitment to design was exemplary. Braun, Olivetti, Leica, IBM, Mobil, Merlin-Gerin, Knoll, Citroën, Poclain, Herman Miller and a few others were the exceptions that proved the rule. The Bauhaus and Ulm Hochschule remained the standard models. France had some difficulty in coming to terms with the complex heritage of the decorative arts and industrial design. Formes Utiles lacked the admirable vigour of the UAM (Union des Artistes Modernes), and industry responded with some reluctance to the repeated appeals of Henry Vienot (who followed in the footsteps of his father Jacques, its founder, at the Institut d'Esthétique Industrielle), Roger Tallon ('our' industrial designer), and Jean Sargueuil. We were all dressed in Schreiber-Hollingtons and kept our eyes out for signs of innovation: institutional in Great Britain with Sir Paul Reilly and the Design Council; creative and industrial in Italy with Joe Colombo, Gia Ponti, Domus, the Milan Triennale, the Danese, Enzo Mari, Nizzoli, Bellini, Sottsass. . .

The situation has since all but reversed itself. Design has, it would seem, undergone a double transformation. Industry has become increasingly interested in it. As a result, design and designers play an increasingly prominent role in industry and in many cases have been taken to its bosom. Products for general consumption are better designed, and less distinguishable from one another. This does not represent a triumph of *gute form* and its ideal of consistency, because 'marginal differences' continue to count for much in the market-place. It does indicate, however, that genuine functional criteria have gained general acceptance. White products (kitchen appliances) and black ones (audio-visual appliances) have largely lost their symbolic status, becoming no more than the 'discreet servants' which Dr Braun dreamed of. Even cars, though invested with fantasies of mobility and power, have evolved in accordance with the dictates of economic considerations and industrial rationalization, coming to look very much the same.

In the face of this growing tendency towards conformity, a new agenda has taken shape which acknowledges the symbolic and expressive power of design. It is leaving its mark on household objects, furniture, and domestic ornament, on the countless fetishes (clothing, pens, watches, bedding, lighting...) of a cocoon society preoccupied with everything close to the body. This kind of design functions like a signature, entailing a return to fine craftsmanship and limited series.

This takes us a long way from Adolf Loos' denunciation of ornament as a crime. Self-image, self-presentation and self-affirmation (and the affirmation of others complicit in the related sign games) have all become inseparable from art and fashion.

The aesthetic of the Machine Age was structural, and thus natural. The work of art remained the archetype. Its stays, braces, and piers rendered visual a construction (a figure) as well as a function. The watch with its wheels, the steam locomotive with its pistons, the crane with its boom and lifting gear, the bicycle. . . all are self-explanatory objects expressing with exemplary clarity a structure and its operation, a working aesthetic. The spread of electronics and computers, along with the increasing miniaturization of their components, is creating a universe of occultation in which things are no longer visible, no longer readily accessible to understanding. This occult design ('hidden beneath a kind of mystery', according to the Littré dictionary) generates abstractions such that nothing which moves or functions assumes discernable

form. Form, which in the founding, progressive movement was destined to follow function, no longer follows anything, not even for Philip Johnson. It has become autonomous. It doesn't play second fiddle, it leads.

It is no accident that the debates over the function of design and designers have been so heated. This exhibition sets out to demonstrate how design has always been a key factor in theories about the role of industry, the supposed empire of reason, the system of objects, and the meaning of our collective undertakings. The representative of the consumer within the production process, the industrial designer has always believed (sometimes ingenuously) in the coherence of the world and his own active role in creating it. But the disappearance of ideologies and the increasing predominance of a generalized liberal model, together with the evolution of society and technology, have blurred these boundaries, raising doubts about the relevance of such a perspective.

It is becoming difficult for us to imagine emerging from the 20th century. Some of the many exit routes seem to have been blocked. All indicators suggest that we must undertake to find that which is shared, which is common to us all – a suitable mission indeed for this millenium's end, dominated as it is by near panic, pervasive narcissism, the most extreme brands of nationalism, concern over the ozone layer, a marked disparity between rich and poor countries, and great hopes for a better world. The temptation is real in these waning days to seek out a few saviours equipped to undertake historic missions, to take on simultaneously the mantles of citizen, politician, and master thinker. From dessert spoons to entire cities, design has often been the vehicle for a kind of architectural ambition claiming as its province nothing less than the great Whole, which it sets out to inventory with a view to synthesizing all that is human. We must be wary of such universalist notions, which would transform engineers into accountants of the innumerable and designers into redeemers. Confronted, like every one of us, by the enigmas of progress and social disfunction, the designer is not equipped to address them unaided. He is discovering that the boundaries of the tangible object are disappearing, that displacements and dematerializations are throwing hallowed borders into confusion and sowing doubts about the nature of the body and the separation between function and materials.

It is the intention of this exhibition to stress the important role of design and the object in our daily lives, by viewing them from a historical perspective. It makes no claims to extrapolating from this history determinist predictions about future developments. The possibilities are too numerous, the interactions are still unfolding. Designers are becoming more and more successful at addressing the questions put to them, but these questions are not always the right ones. Must we learn to ask the proper questions? Must we take lessons in complexity?

Design, Mirror of the Century

François Seigneur

Since the era when the Salons abandoned the Grand Palais for quarters on the outskirts of Paris, the building's interior architecture has tended to be forgotten, frequently concealed behind awnings and curtains.

Many people do not realize just what an extraordinary place the Grand Palais is. For the present occasion, it seemed indispensable to install a structure which would be on the same scale as the architecture. And since it was a matter of travelling backwards in time, the general idea was to display the Grand Palais as it has always been, to initiate a great voyage there, to induce a sense of vertigo and to create an atmosphere of celebration.

Outside the Grand Palais, two telescoping passageways (like those used to access planes from airport waiting lounges) greet visitors at the foot of the steps, conduct them under the broad blue banners hanging in front of the colonnades and deposit them at the ticket counters. This all takes place some seven feet above the floor, which will not be touched again until the exhibition has been completed. After the visitor has bought his ticket, there is nothing: a grey, nondescript, scaleless space, without shadow and without sound. It is a kind of decompression chamber, a mute and monochrome air-lock that leads us, surreptitiously and gropingly, toward the exhibition. After one final turn, we pass through a small, narrow doorway. Suddenly, the Grand Palais opens out before us, unencumbered, immense.

Emerging from the semi-darkness, one has to blink. A few moments are needed to take in the gigantic scaffolding which occupies the entire length of the nave and rises, on one side, up to the glazed roof almost 60 feet above the floor. One might be in a port, on a quay or at the foot of a great ship. Everything is happening above one's head. An exhibition city in suspended time, enclosed in a sound environment which reminds us that design was born not of rural but of urban, industrial concerns.

A few prehistoric, pre-design objects arranged at the foot of the scaffolding evoke the realities which form the foundations for the world toward which one is about to rise. The visitor takes the escalator beside the scaffolding and, heading backwards in time, emerges onto a small platform attached to the great inclined floor. Here, at the top of the escalator, one is just below the glass roof.

A few steps further the visitor arrives at the platform and there, finally, at one's feet, extends the exhibition, spanning, on a gentle incline, the entire length of the nave. A century and a half of history visible at a single glance.

The 'ship' – 57 feet wide by 492 feet long – is like an aircraft carrier. Its surface is not a closed space, but a sequence opening both backwards and forwards. The floor is a neutral, dark grey, punctuated by luminous panels indicating important names and dates. The objects themselves are placed on this floor. At the opposite end of the nave, an immense tilted mirror reflects the Grand Palais and the exhibition in a disorientating, tilted perspective.

The concept for the design of the exhibition was shaped by five basic concerns and objectives:

1. Designed objects are not art objects but objects intended for use.

This is not a principle of disqualification, but I see no reason why design should be exhibited in the same way as art. Hence the inclining floor on which the objects are also inclined. Hence the absence of stands: the objects are placed directly on the floor and are presented in an unbroken sequence. All the objects are laid out in a vast collection that has been labelled and rigorously and chronologically inventoried. The exhibits move from the urban, collective object to the private object; from the large to the small. A determined effort has been made to avoid museological and artistic associations, which are too categorical and/or uncertain.

2. Objects and information should become progressively more concentrated.

The intention is to evoke the idea that as space extends and the impression of liberty grows, the number of objects and propositions will increase to fill and channel it. At the top end, in 1850, there are few objects, and while they are large, one can circulate freely around them. At the bottom end, in 1993, the mass of objects and information is much greater, and while the exhibits are sometimes small-scaled or miniaturized, circulation is impeded and all pathways explicitly indicated. Correspondingly, the sound effects will become denser as one descends.

3. There should be cross views from different angles.

At the inner edge of the inclined floor and along its entire length will be a raised ledge, reached by steps, where visitors can rest and stroll about freely; a kind of gangway in the form of a balcony, inclined at the same angle as the exhibition floor. Here, raised up and slightly detached from the main level, the visitor, seated or standing, can enjoy views across the exhibition in which objects and images become superimposed in dated sequences.

Headphones, telephones and monitors provide information about the period spread out before one. Tripods with telescopes allow for long or close-range viewing.

4. There should be a backdrop in the form of a picture gallery. Opposite the ledge and separate from the exhibition floor are 29 photographs, 13 by 20 feet and printed on fabric, which provide images of successive periods. They are accompanied by complementary documents (buildings, events, texts, individuals) illustrating relevant facts and evoking the time and place in which the objects were created.

5. Light and lighting.

Aside from 'star' objects identified with a particularly important innovation, which will be spotlit, there is to be no directed lighting. Only daylight, lots of daylight.

By night, there will be a nocturnal lighting scheme of an orange-pink hue. The light of the city should modify the spectrum, reintegrating forms and colours into a familiar, monotone monochrome.

Sound.

From beginning to end, the exhibition's sound design is organized around 'mute' and 'video' chambers. Mute chambers, by cutting out ambient sound, provide a transition from natural to remastered noises, noises which can be considered as 'designed'. The video chambers feature the binary sounds that are invading contemporary life and are shaping the sound environment of tomorrow. On the main level, there are eight sound programmes corresponding to different periods. Certain objects also have their own sound effects. Texts, music and commentary are available by means of telephones and earphones placed on tables along the central gangway.

Mirror, chamber, video, end.

Upon arrival at the bottom of the inclined floor, the visitor crosses a footbridge 23 feet long leading to a balcony which is attached to the mirror with its tilted, distorted reflection of the Grand Palais. Here the visitor can take one last backward look at the exhibition and its 150 years of history, before passing in front of the mirror, exchanging one world for another.

Beyond the mirror, there is a video viewing room evoking our growing mastery of the electron, a development which has already begun to reshape the future. Legible computer screens and illegible television monitors form a space of glossy surfaces. The final door provides access to the descending passageway which leads to the exit. Here the visitor is on the other side of the exhibition, behind and beneath its scaffolding, in an area where the principal sponsors of the exhibition have set up information booths.

The word design is a generic term, a portmanteau word

covering everything concerned with the shaping of

industrially produced material culture over the last

140 years. At this point, it would be as well to define more

closely both the scope of this volume and its lines of enquiry.

As this is a catalogue for an international retrospective

exhibition, I have decided to offer the reader five

complementary approaches to its subject.

First of all, it seemed appropriate to call on authors

working in disciplines at the frontiers of design, so as to

establish the links between design and the factors that shape

it. I would like to thank them for the quality

of their contributions.

To enable a clearer appreciation of the formal evolution of

design, we have included notes on a number of key objects

that we regard as indispensable. These design classics are

landmarks in the history of our everyday environment.

In conjunction with the essays and their notes, quotations

and historical texts offer parallel readings and open a window

on the past.

A chronology forms the backbone of the historical section

of the work, linking developments in design to significant

social, cultural and political events.

Finally, the illustrations have been treated as the raw material

of the work and serve to interlink all the texts. Without

Françoise Icikovics, choosing and gathering them together

would have been impossible.   *J. d. N.*

CONTENTS

The Realm of Objects

Marianne Barzilay and Sylvain Dubuisson,

curators of the exhibition

We were entrusted with the task of giving meaning to things which initially appear all but devoid of it. An object's form, the way it works, the materials used and the process by which it becomes part of a culture, these things, in themselves, seem to signify very little. It is clear that design produces signs before it produces meaning, and this is doubtless its principal characteristic. Aside from the ambiguous market value of what we are showing (from a collector's point of view, higher than what the shops would charge; from that of the Grand Palais, much less than what is usually exhibited there!), we were confronted with the problem of how best to give form to a vision and with the question of what exhibiting an object means, or what we want to say by exhibiting an object. How can we facilitate the play of meaning and emotion such that the objects would take on a resonance that design, considered in isolation, could not give them. We decided to concentrate on the historical perspective in order to make the objects easier to 'read'. We resolved to illuminate design using criteria other than formal ones, through references borrowed from outside the field proper: industrial production, consumer trends, use... In this exhibition, objects are not treated like freestanding works: their development processes, modes of manufacture, numbers sold, and so on are all indicated. A multitude of interrelated elements have been included to aid in interpreting them, measuring their impact and recovering the emotions they once prompted: sounds that date the objects or strengthen our memories of them, photographs of people from different periods, images of a city to remind us of the dominant role played by this or that country, others of buildings.

The exhibition design by François Seigneur allows for the objects to be treated in ways which accord with the 'demystifying' aims of the exhibition: placed on the floor, deprived of their use value, they convey unexpected messages about what they once were. The designs displayed in the exhibition often represent the last stage of a consumer object. It might even be maintained that this exhibition allows the objects to escape their predestined end as junk, that it sublimates the waste cycle in which they would otherwise be swallowed up. Here they are fitted out with discourse. In effect, our joint intention has been to adopt a social approach to design: not merely to assign labels and work within a narrow definition of 'design', but to think in broader terms, to encourage objects to tell us all they can about a society and way of life influencing their development – to the point that they can be seen to embody the social aim of Western nations: the production of large quantities of objects to increase comfort, which is the material side of a collective aspiration for happiness. Certainly the image of our societies might be legitimately summed up in such terms.

The exhibition as it has been conceived raises the question of the place occupied by the designer. By creating, on this grand stage, an abbreviated view of a 150-year period, beginning with the first industrially-produced objects and ending with those of today, we can see the clash of tendencies, projects and prejudices, some of them quite virulent, and all with roots in the past. Who could adequately define the current stakes in design? Firstly, it must be admitted that objects are becoming increasingly numerous and increasingly well designed; there are very few products whose design seems in need of improvement. This should be interpreted as a battle won: the process of design has now been fully integrated into the industrial system on a global level. Formalism is no longer the name of the game, or only marginally so. The aesthetic approach seems outdated in view of the new functions performed by the object, unimaginable even ten years ago, and the enormous impact these have had on the way we live and work.

In addition, one thing is immediately striking upon entering the realm of objects: most of the thinkers who have reflected on them have been critical of the consumer ideology, as if the material side of our culture merited only contempt, even though our manufacture and consumption of products proceeds on an ever more massive scale. After Marxist, situationist, and left-wing versions, the most recent formulation of this critique is that of the ecologists, who sometimes seem to have embarked on a sort of crusade against the very foundations of modernity, with this difference, however, that they question the centrality of man's position. But their devaluation of objects and consumption, linked as it is with a challenge to humanism, demonstrates just how delicate a matter is the distinction of man from merchandise. The exhibition takes no position in relation to these debates, but allows us to read – through objects – the different phases of modernity, up to that of today, in which the omnipresence of machines that are increasingly compact, fast and efficient proves that society is transferring much that is most essential in human production and exchange to objects of communication.

Marc Augé

From what perspective might the question of industrial design interest an anthropologist? That of his discipline's traditional interest in material culture? The fact that material culture cannot be abstracted from culture in general and consequently expresses values and references which tell us things about society? The way product styling can infer gestures and postures, actions of the body, a subject which, at least since Mauss, has been an important focus of anthropological study? The answer is: all of the above, in addition to others that might be worth dwelling on.

It is generally agreed that industrially produced objects are today subject to several constraints: technical ones associated with their function, aesthetic ones associated with users' perceptions of them, and cultural ones determined by various traditions and, again, by the supposed feelings of their users. It isn't easy to establish the precise nature of the relationship between these three constraints, especially given that each of them remains problematic in itself. The nature of the link between form and function varies considerably according to the kind of object in question; the taste of the public changes, and it can sometimes seem both desirable and profitable to try and keep one step ahead of it, to not only satisfy expectations but surprise them and create new ones. Exoticism has its charms and even the intimate relationship one has with one's own culture can be given a different nuance or modified: if Japanese cars today succeed in seducing many French drivers, as American ones did in the past, this is partly because they're less expensive, but it is also because something about their design captures the attention.

Jocelyn de Noblet writes in the introduction to his book *Design* that this term is used by all sorts of people 'to express value judgements about a family of goods which in their eyes produce meaning'. The key word has been uttered: if the art of industrial design stands apart from art for art's sake, this is not so much because of its functional role (there is sometimes a marked discrepancy between form and function) as its claim to generate meaning. But what, exactly, is at issue in this production of meaning? For anthropologists, meaning is social meaning and an object invested with meaning is an object that can be read as indicating or implying something about virtual social relations. This virtuality and necessity of the social goes by another name: the symbolic. A symbolic object is one that can bring human beings together or that can serve as a basis for reflection about human relations. It is worth noting parenthetically that the objects we call 'fetishes' (which Christian missionaries stressed were adored for themselves) are eminently 'symbolic', steeped in social meaning: cult objects, without doubt, but as such – by means of the figure of the deity simultaneously represented and incarnated by them – serving to mediate between men.

The objects of the industrial world are not so far removed from 'fetish' objects. Perhaps they are not cult objects, unless metaphorically, as, for example, when a car is made the object of jealous attention. But they are manifestly symbolic, carriers of social meaning, if only because most of them are intended for circulation, communication (Molière's pedantic women already spoke of their chairs as 'conversational aids'), distribution and recording. In short, they are destined to affect our relationships with one another.

The conditions shaping their aesthetic are changing. The world in which they proliferate is a world in which history moves at an accelerated pace, a shrinking world in which inhabitants of the most distant lands feel they have a stake, a world, finally, in which cultural differences are under constant pressure from the forces of economic liberalism and the ideal of individualism is affirmed. Such is the setting for the creative process associated with mass production. If the aesthetic in question is to retain a symbolic value, it must be responsive to both the desire for individual affirmation and parameters that are becoming increasingly universal. The situation provides opportunity as well as challenge: contacts multiply and traditions intermingle, while the boundary between the social and the cultural grows less and less pronounced. Design must find some way of translating this universalism without betraying meaning: and designers a way of creating recognizable signs capable of establishing, for the first time in world history, a complicity encompassing the entire planet.

The Evolution
of Industrial Design

Design in Progress

Jocelyn de Noblet

In the first quarter of the 19th century, the decline of a production system based on specialized craft industries, which had prevailed for several millennia, had come to seem inevitable. Its replacement by a new system allowing for the mass production of objects was to be rapid and the construction of the Crystal Palace for the Great Exhibition – the first of its kind – in London, in 1851, symbolized the point of no return.

In 1908, the mass production of cars by Ford in the United States marked a new phase. From that point on, it was not technological problems that posed the biggest challenge to the new mode of production, but rather the economic and cultural evolution that would foster the development of the necessary infrastructure.

In all cultures prior to the Industrial Revolution, both technical expertise and the manufacture of objects were in the hands of a single individual: the craftsman. The craftsman received traditional training and underwent an apprenticeship, after which he was equipped not only to reproduce models, but also to make objects according to specifica-

tions provided by the client (church, lord, or private individual) establishing the general parameters and, in certain cases, creating appropriate ornamentation. But there remains something aphasic in the work of craftsmen and it was manual skill that allowed the most adept to distinguish themselves. Their abilities are difficult to characterize in words, since they were the product of experimentation and cumulative experience as much as of training. Artisanal knowledge of this kind differs radically from more conventional, readily transmissable bodies of knowledge, like that of science.

After the Industrial Revolution, when machine tools had replaced hand tools, a new figure appeared on the scene – the engineer – who gradually pushed the craftsman off the stage of production.

If an object is to be mass-produced, the following four conditions must be met:

1) One must have at one's disposal a considerable range of machine tools, and a reliable and efficient source of power.

2) One must be capable of producing elements that are standardized, prefabricated, and interchangeable (SPI).

3) One must be able to organize the workplace scientifically, rationalizing the production chain.

4) One must master a descriptive geometry sufficiently precise and efficient to serve as the basis for designing individual components.

With regard to this last point, we might invoke what Gaspard Monge wrote in his *Traité de géométrie descriptive* (1779): 'This art has two principle aims. The first is to represent with exactitude, in two-dimensional drawings, objects of three dimensions susceptible of rigorous definition. From this perspective, it is a language equally necessary to the man of genius who conceives a project, those responsible for implementing it, and the artists charged with executing its various elements. The second aim of descriptive geometry is to deduce from the precise description of bodies everything necessarily entailed by their form and relative position. Thus it would prove advantageous to the national education if we were to familiarize our young artists with the applications of descriptive geometry and the graphic constructions which are necessary to most of the arts, teaching them how to use this geometry to represent and define machine components'.

It was only after the unprecedented transformation in the system of production that the question of the formal development of industrial products arose. It rapidly became clear that their forms could not be determined purely and simply by technical considerations. If engineers had been able to master such formal questions satisfactorily, if they had received an education equipping them to tackle the complex relations between objects and the cultural system shaping their production, it wouldn't have been necessary to invent the designer.

The word 'design' designates both conception and formal definition; it should be preceded by a qualifying adjective specifying its meaning. The subject of this volume is chiefly industrial design, but the term 'designer' can designate both the conceiver of a metal bridge and the creator of a piece of jewellry. In an English handbook on meal preparation published in 1893, there is a chapter entitled: 'Designs for Dinner Menu Cards'.

The objects which resulted from this new mode of production could be divided into three categories:

1) New objects conceived, for the most part, by inventive, self-taught mechanics such as Samuel Colt, Elisha K. Roth, Henry Leland and Henry Ford, as well as numerous producers of machine tools in England and the United States. This new elite would play a fundamental role, initiating the mass production of sewing machines, typewriters, cameras, and, a bit later, cars.

2) Works of art and, especially, metal bridges, created by civil engineers of genius with superior educations, extremely protective of their prerogatives.

3) Pre-existing objects initially shaped by craft traditions, such as domestic furniture, but modified to facilitate their mass production.

Initially, a controversy developed around this last category over the respective responsibilities of artist and engineer within the new production system. On the one hand, William Morris, John Ruskin and the members of the Arts and Crafts Movement viewed industrialization solely in terms of a cultural shipwreck, such that Ruskin could write in *The Stones of Venice*: 'The great clamour, louder than the roar of steam engines, rising from these factory cities reminds us that they manufacture everything save men'. As for William Morris, he believed that liberty, as necessary to human survival as food, could only come from the crafts. Thus it was only logical for him to condemn industrial production. In the matter of artistic education, the Arts and Crafts Movement would prove enormously influential: in key respects both Art Nouveau and Jugendstil followed its example (see the article by Gillian Naylor).

In France, in 1889, construction of the Eiffel Tower was opposed by Zola, de Maupassant, Garnier, Meissonnier and Sully Prudhomme, all of whom signed an open letter in the newspaper *Le Temps*, in which we read: 'And for 20 years we shall see the odious shadow of this odious column of bolted iron spread like an ink stain'.

In the opposite camp were all those committed to 'enlightenment', who believed that the symbolic unity of the world should give way to a different vision: that of a physical universe, an ordered cosmos subject to a determinism governed by laws man could decipher. The word 'determinism', which was legitimized by the functionalism of the 1920s, first entered general use in around 1820, when it was understood to designate the complete explanation of a machine's workings: 'The universe is an automaton whose movements are mechanically determined', wrote marquis Pierre Simon de Laplace in 1796.

The functionalist aesthetic, which would be at the origin of the first definition of industrial design, made its first appearance in superb metal-framed works constructed by the engineers of the Ponts et Chaussées, the department overseeing French bridges and roads. But we have to wait until the architects of the Chicago school for a definition generally and dogmatically applicable to all forms. In 1896, Louis Sullivan wrote:

'All things in nature have a form, an exterior aspect that tells us what they are, what it is that distinguishes them from ourselves and from one another...It would seem that life and form make an inseparable whole and that the meaning of the accomplishment is situated in this mutual correspondence. Whether it's a question of an eagle soaring through the air or an apple tree in bloom, of a fatigued workhorse or an alert swan, of the waters of a meandering river or a stolid oak, of passing clouds or the movement of the sun, form always follows function and such is the law. There's no changing form without also changing function. The law prevailing over everything that's organic and inorganic, all things physical and metaphysical, human and superhuman, all

Far left:
Gaspard Monge
(1746-1818).

Armoured car
used during the
siege of Paris in
1870. Plate from
*Nouvelles
conquêtes de la
science*, 1883-1885.

Taon motorcycle,
designed by Roger
Tallon for Derny,
1957.

Honda motorcycle
NR 750, 1992.

Below:
Gramophone and
telegraph,
original drawings
by Thomas
Edison, 1888.

Ford model T
assembly line at
the Ford factory
in Highland Park,
1923.

affective manifestations of head, heart, and soul, is that life is decipherable through its expression, that form follows function. Such is the law.'

Between 1907 and 1914, a debate unfolded within the Deutscher Werkbund[1] over the role of the artist in defining forms for mass production. Henry van de Velde did not subscribe to the functionalist views of Hermann Muthesius, who affirmed that 'only standardization resulting from reasoned collaboration will allow us to rediscover a taste that's reliable and shared by all'. For van de Velde, there was no way to reconcile the artist's creative work with the rules and aesthetic canons imposed by mass production. In his view, the artist should not adhere to any pre-set model. These two opposed tendencies would coexist until the great Werkbund exposition in 1914.

From 1920, there was an evolution from organic functionalism to a more mechanical conception of form. The architects and designers of this period thought it would be possible to devise an ideal society that would satisfy the greatest number, on three conditions:

1) There must be a break with tradition, leading to the development of abstract forms purged of all ornament and figuration.

2) Functions must be made readily apparent, leading to a utilitarian beauty consistent with a machine aesthetic.

3) Finally, the public must be educated so it has a better grasp of a society shaped by scientific and technological progress.

The educational programme of the Bauhaus made a major contribution to the formation of the modern industrial designer, in particular thanks to the establishment of a preliminary course which featured an active apprenticeship in the evolution of form intended to develop students' creative abilities. The Bauhaus's espousal of principles devised by the post-Cubist avant-garde movements fostered geometric formalism and the use of primary colours. Walter Gropius and many of the other of its teachers shared a conviction that it would be pos-sible to use this new language to shape a material culture that would be responsive to aesthetic considerations as well as to the exigencies of mass production.

The influence of the Bauhaus was considerable and long-lived, both in Europe and the United States. In 1936, France Jourdain, one of the founders of the Union des Artistes Modernes (UAM) in France, wrote: 'It's not by surrendering everyday objects to the fantasies of ornamentalists that we'll be able to renew them. By embellishment we need not necessarily understand the addition of superfluous, supposedly artistic elements. Isn't embellishment rather a purification, achieved through the revision of form and the rigorous adaptation of these to their functions; a process of purification, revision and adaptation realizable by the artist only to the extent he takes into account the demands of the technician as well as the user?'

After 1954, the teaching of the Bauhaus was continued in a more radical form at the Hochschule für Gestaltung in Ulm. It was Thomas Maldonado, the former rector of this school, who formulated the first definition of industrial design, one that was officially endorsed in 1969 at the meeting of the International Council of Societies for Industrial Design (ICSID): 'Design is a creative activity which consists of determining the formal properties of an object to be produced industrially. In referring to an object's "formal properties", we mean not only its external characteristics, but above all the structural relations which make an object (or a system of objects) a coherent unity, from the producer's point of view as well as that of the consumer.' Even today, orthodox neo-functionalist designers remain faithful to this definition.

Functionalist design represents a tendency that was dominant only in the development of certain categories of objects in the context of a supposedly ideal society.

In the United States between 1919 and 1929, industrial production doubled and purchasing power increased by 20 per cent. It was during this period that the Ford model

– namely adherence to a single design – was replaced by Sloanism,[2] which entailed the association of mass production with a broad range of products. American industrial design evolved in accordance with a principle different from that of functionalism. In effect, when Raymond Loewy said that 'ugliness doesn't sell' he was only paraphrasing a remark made by the Spanish Jesuit Baltasar Gracián in 1648: 'It serves no purpose whatever to be right with a face that declares one to be wrong.' To seduce consumers, the publicists of Madison Avenue and a few designers thought it indispensable to develop an explicit brand of modernity. Aerodynamics appealed to them as the visible symbol of speed and before long a formalist mode of aerodynamics had been christened as the streamline style. This came to dominate the car industry and was a feature of the design of countless domestic products until 1959. At this same time, the industrial aesthetic provided a French equivalent of industrial design, a logical extension of the modernist goals of the founders of the Union des Artistes Modernes (UAM) in 1930. On the initiative of Jacques Viénot, one of the first design agencies was established, Technès (headed for 12 years by Roger Tallon), as were the Institut Français d'Esthétique Industrielle and the *Revue d'esthétique*. It was in this magazine that Viénot published the charter of design: 'Design is the science of the beautiful in the domain of industrial production. Its concern is with the environment and conditions of the workplace, means of production, and end products.' If functional industrial design 'functioned' well, this was largely because the mechanical products themselves imposed their own irrevocable laws. Machine technology can easily be given form, and, in most cases, products inevitably express their function and mode of operation. It might be said that mechanical components provide a general basis for forms which functional design expressed in so many stereotypes. In the 1980s, material culture began to be

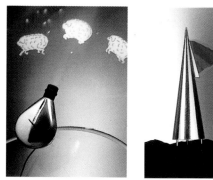

Portafrutta wall lamp: fruit cup mural and lamp designed by Denis Santachiara, 1989.

Notturno italiano lamp, designed by Denis Santachiara for Yamagiwa, 1988. Aluminium bulb projecting images of sheep.

Maestrale lamp, designed by Denis Santachiara for Dilmos, 1987. Heat produced by the lamp causes a piece of cloth to move.

Far left: Soudain le sol trembla lamp, designed by Philippe Starck, 1981.

shaped by several new elements which implied as yet undetermined conceptions of form.

– Where possible, machinery has been replaced by electronics.

– An increasingly complex and diffuse information system supported by new technologies is fostering a search for alternatives to the self-contained 'black box'.

– The progressive replacement of traditional materials by plastics, composites and ceramics, as well as by 'intelligent' materials, is allowing for greater flexibility in the process of industrial production.

These innovations tend to render many existing apparatuses obsolete. This inevitably entails a loss of meaning that must be compensated for by the development of new symbolic connotations. In addition, our post-modern society is no longer dominated by a single ideology, and in this sense, too, the meanings associated with functionalism have become diluted. This new situation, along with the generalized use of the word 'design', can only tend to encourage the emergence of many different styles. There isn't *one* design, but rather a multitude of situations, places, political orientations and cultures that claim our attention but have no discernible common thread. This crumbling of meaning gives new currency to a statement made by Benjamin Constant in 1790: 'God died before completing his work; we are like watches without faces whose wheels, gifted with intelligence, continue to turn until they're completely worn down.' For all that, it cannot be said that the development of a form is an aleatory, entirely unpredictable phenomenon. Many families of objects are subjected to such rigid external and internal constraints that we may legitimately speak of an unavoidable determinism: high speed vehicles, for example, and exposed metal structures like bridges. And yet, while there's no denying that objects consisting of electronic components are functional, it is none the less true that this functionality does readily find expression. An emerging tendency towards greater expressivity in industrial design has been encouraged by a need to facilitate the process of identification and reappropriation in a society of increasing complexity. It is indispensable to give functional objects, when mute, a semiological value that will ease their integration into the culture, even if the only way to do this is by resort to metaphor.

As currently practised, design is an intermediary art governed by few laws and fracturing into multiple tendencies, under pressure exerted by a consumer society demanding from it a wide array of objects. Designers work not with universals but with particulars and their working procedures remain various. How could it be otherwise? But in the best circumstances, the design of everyday objects involves their representation in linguistic form, which is a tall order.

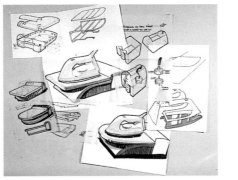

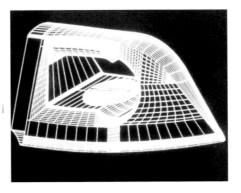

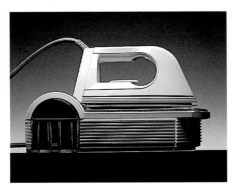

The Thonet chair

Michael Thonet was born in 1796 in Boppard, a small town on the Rhine surrounded by forest, where the principal activity was carpentry. In 1830, Thonet, a cabinet-maker, began to experiment with ways of assembling sections of furniture and on the bending of wood. He succeeded in applying the steaming technique used by boat builders and coopers to furniture construction. He glued bundles of thin sheets of wood together and heated them to produce the desired elasticity. Held in wooden clamps until they were dry, the bunches of wood kept their form and became tougher. In 1851, Thonet signed his first important order, which was to furnish a famous café of the time owned by Mme Daum with his No. 4 chair. In the same year, he decided to exhibit at the first Great Exhibition in London.

The problems that Thonet encountered trying to export his chairs led him to simplify his technique. With the aid of strips of tin-plate, which he fixed to the wood, he was able to bend solid stems of beech beyond the natural elasticity of the wood. The tin-plate prevented the wood from stretching and bursting during bending. With this invention, Thonet paved the way for mass production of bent wood. In 1858, the first No. 14 chair, which had a round seat, was made in his factory. Manufacture of the chair would eventually reach several million.

The passage from craft to industrial production was made possible by the rationalization and simplification of the various models into four detachable and interchangeable parts. The firm's production and distribution methods had a number of advantages: simple assembly (Thonet was the precursor of furniture delivered in kits); employment (women were able to do the caning at home, something which was almost unprecedented – caning is still done by hand today); packaging for export to North and South America (35 chairs, unassembled, took up no more than one square metre of space); the modest price (the chair cost £3). Overseas marketing helped establish the firm's image in places as far apart as Vienna, Paris, London, Berlin and Budapest.

Thonet's furniture represents a rare example of continuity and formalism before its time. The manufacturing process made possible completely new forms, that have been continuously popular for more than a century. Le Corbusier, who furnished all of his buildings with Thonet furniture, wrote in 1920: 'For elegance of conception, purity of execution and efficacity of use, no one has ever surpassed it.'

E. M.

The first Great Exhibition
of the industrial products
of all nations. London, 1851

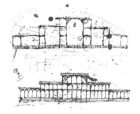

The Crystal Palace

This exhibition was the first great media event to mark the advent of a new material culture, one based on the industrial production of objects.

In terms of architectural style and structural principle the Crystal Palace, built to house the exhibition, represents a rupture between the European architectural tradition and the new industrial aesthetic made possible by scientific and technological progress. On 11 June 1850, during a railway trip, an English horticulturist Joseph Paxton made the first two sketches for what would become the Crystal Palace. How did this design evolve? And why was a horticulturist chosen?

In 1850, the committee organizing the exhibition, which was actively headed by Prince Albert,[1] received 245 architectural submissions, a number which testifies to the great interest of the profession in this project. But the results of this competition were distressing: none of the projects were acceptable. In desperation, the committee accepted the proposal of an outsider who had not participated in the competition.

Joseph Paxton was not unknown and was considerably more than a simple craftsman. He was, in fact, an exceptional man who had perfected, between 1840 and 1850, several kinds of metal construction frames which he used to build numerous greenhouses.[2] Paxton was also on friendly terms with the great English engineers and entrepreneurs of the period, who helped him design the building.

Construction of the Crystal Palace began as soon as the proposal was accepted, on 26 July 1850: its erection on the site at Hyde Park in London, using prefabricated components, was unprecedented and took only 17 weeks. The Great Exhibition opened its doors on the day announced, 1 May 1851.

The Crystal Palace was innovative in a number of respects: standardized modular construction, flat roof, the use of glass on a massive scale (400 tons, which was one third of England's annual production), facing portals, its prefiguration of the curtain wall, the visibility of its structural frame, and use of cast iron components.

To all this must be added the mechanization of the construction process: motorized winches and hoists were used, as were interchangeable screw-nuts and bolts. In 1852, the Crystal Palace was disassembled and rebuilt on the western slope of Sydenham Hill near London, where it became an exhibition centre (it was destroyed by fire in 1936).

The objects and products exhibited in the Crystal Palace were organized into six sections: primary materials, machines, textiles, manufactured products, applied arts and miscellaneous. This breakdown reflected the contradictions of the period, for it led to the side-by-side display of functional objects, like machines and tools, and highly decorative, domestic objects.

As Mario Praz remarked in his History of Interior Decoration: 'The furnishings section of the exhibition evidenced the high level of national prosperity and gave clear indication of the wealth and domestic refinement of those for whom these objects were intended'.[3]

J. d. N.

Vignettes:
Original design by Joseph Paxton, Derby, 11 June 1850.

Interior view of the Crystal Palace, 1851.

Background:
Detail of original drawing by Paxton.

1. Queen Victoria's husband, who was the president of the commission for the organization of the exhibition.
2. Legend has it that Joseph Paxton's framework for the Crystal Palace was inspired by the leaf structure of the Victoria Regia, a giant water lily for which he had constructed a greenhouse in Chatsworth, in 1849.
3. Mario Praz, An Illustrated History of Interior Decoration, London, 1987.

Machine tools

In his book Future of Technics and Civilization, *Lewis Mumford wrote that the greatest sculptors of the 19th century were the engineers responsible for the construction of modern machine tools.[1] The advent of machine tools marked a crucial advance in the mechanics of transforming matter, but its history is not widely known.*

Before they could be introduced into the production line, two conditions had to be met. Firstly, there had to be tools capable of cutting and shaping metal, especially iron: mastery of manufacture using tempered carbon steel was essential. Secondly, precision measurement had to be possible: 'vernier'[2] measurement instruments and micrometers would be necessary. These two conditions were satisfied for the first time in the first quarter of the 19th century.

Basically, machine tools are used either to alter primary materials (stampers, folders, punchers, machines for fabric-ating sheet iron) or to remove metal (lathes, drills, milling cutters, borers, planing machines, etc.).

The Englishman, John Wilkinson, was the first to adapt the machine drill for boring the cylinders of steam engines. And the first manufacturer of machine tools was Henri Maudslay (1771-1831), who built many machines designed by Marc I. Brunel.

In 1843 James Nasmyth invented the steam-driven pile-driver, laying the foundations for a mechanical functionalism that would subsequently become the basis for an aesthetic. In 1841 he wrote: 'If we consider, from an abstract point of view, the different elements of which each machine tool is composed, we realize that it is possible to regroup them in accordance with six primary geometric forms: the line, the plane, the circle, the cylinder, the cone and the sphere. However complicated, a machine is always the result of a more or less complex com-bination of these six elements'.

The lathe is rightly held to be the mother machine tool, from which were derived all subsequent machines (it seems the Scythians and the Germans used wooden lathes that were more evolved than those of the Romans). However that might be, it was around 1900 that the American, Gridley, created a multiple automatic lathe capable of working eight spindles on a single mount. This design had been inspired by the Gatling machine gun used in the American Civil War.

Toward 1910, the Americans devised Natco multiple drills for piercing the crankcases of the gearboxes in the celebrated Ford model T. That same year, a specially hardened steel perfect for compact tools was introduced. Today, from a central computer it is possible to control programmable robotized and digital machines of all kinds. But that's another story.

J. d. N.

Background:
Mortising machine for cutting six pieces of sheet metal (3 cm thick) for locomotive sideframes, manufactured by Établissements Derosne & Cail. From *Grandes usines* **by L. Turgan, 1866.**

Vignette: Wagon wheel lathe Model No. 5. Engraving taken from the *Catalogue de machines-outils,* **Niles-Bement-Pond Cy, 1921.**

1. Lewis Mumford, Future of Technics and Civilization, New York, 1934.
2. Vernier: a short scale made to slide along the divisions of a graduated instrument (as the limb of a sextant or the scale of a barometer). Named after its inventor, Pierre Vernier, mathematician (1580-1637).

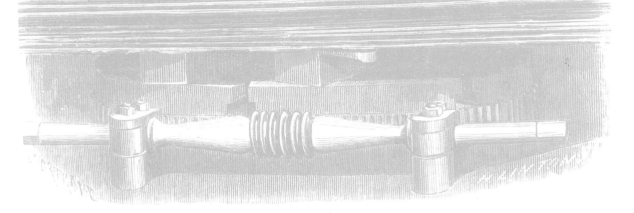

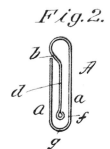

Fig.2.

When we travel from one country or continent to another, it is hard to resist making comparisons between different cultures. For me, it has become a reflex. For several years I was head of an American design office in Paris which had clients in both Europe and the United States and oversaw programmes on both sides of the Atlantic. I was constantly brought up short by the absence of a single, shared definition of design. This was something which, despite the increasing internationalization of the marketplace, tended to complicate the interaction between cultures. A response to the quandary presented by these divergent views of design, however, can be formulated by looking at the history of design. Historically, there are two important and opposing currents, a European one and an American one, and each is shaped by different factors. The European view of design grew out of cultural tradition, while the American approach evolved as a response to economic pressures.

The European intellectual tradition accords ideas and reflection a privileged place,

Pencil sharpener, designed by Raymond Loewy, 1933-1934. A classic example of streamlining.

Top: **Drawing of a paper clip (anonymous).**

Design

for Everyday Objects

Evert Endt
with **Sabine Grandadam**

sometimes to the detriment of the concrete. The pre-eminence accorded to abstract thought in education favours the elaboration of concepts, encouraging people to approach problems intellectually rather than pragmatically.

At the beginning of this century, confronted by social inequalities brought about by the excesses of capitalism, which did not spare the artistic elite, European intellectuals woke up and attempted to redefine their role. The result was a mission to produce products that would democratize the aesthetic and cultural realms, thereby improving the quality of life. Design, which was in its infancy, progressed hand-in-hand with this movement, adapting itself to the demands imposed by industrial criteria for careful, rational planning. It rejected the applied arts and the use of excessive ornamentation, effacing everything that might function as a social marker. Beauty of form became inextricable from functional considerations and was made accessible to the greatest number. It was the dawn of the age of the mechanical paradise. The history of western societies turned a decisive corner at the beginning of the 19th century. In the wake of the French Revolution new priorities came to the fore, fostering a more acute self-consciousness about the human condition. Roles were redistributed, and the culture of craft gave way to one of mechanical production. Numerous products of this period bear witness to the difficulty of formulating a conceptual approach appropriate to the new means of production. Most of these products in fact featured forms and decorative elements devised in response to artisanal needs and capacities.

The era's creators believed that human intelligence would triumph by imposing existing concepts and ideals on the new products of modern technology. Despite economic pressures in the opposite direction, in many respects the forces of European industrialization still obeyed priorities shaped by a far-flung network of craftsmen. Their skills had been developed for the production of high-quality, individually crafted objects. Such methods, together with the pronounced taste of the privileged public for 'fine workmanship', were difficult to reconcile with industrialization. Industrial products were seen as 'vulgar', of inferior quality. It was in this context that intellectuals' questioning of the social contract led to a programme for the adaptation of industrial design to social and cultural requirements.

Non-institutional design in the United States

By contrast, American design developed in an environment largely free of the aristocratic traditions and customs of Europe. The challenges faced by successive waves of American emigrants instilled in them a genuine spirit of enterprise, which they used to solve the most basic problems of daily life. Their resourcefulness was a crucial factor in the country's growing industrial capacity. In less than two centuries, the United States was transformed into a modern industrial state, and the course of its design history was shaped by its emergence as a nation. 'A new world calls for new methods' would seem to have been the motto of America's founding fathers. Benjamin Franklin, who was a statesman, humanist, inventor, scientist, and diplomat, offers a striking example

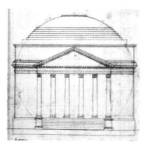

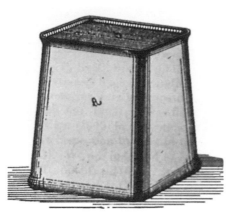

of this approach. So does Thomas Jefferson. Politician, writer, spare time architect, and a passionate student of the natural sciences, his home, Monticello, in Virginia, is now a museum full of objects and inventions bearing witness to his open-minded, creative intelligence. Their design was not the result of a philosophy put into practice by architects, artists, or other such professionals. Rather it reflected the non-institutional approach typical of any entrepreneur confronted by specific circumstances. This resulted in a characteristic industrialist profile: a born inventor, ingenious and imaginative, he channelled his intelligence into the development of new products to be manufactured as inexpensively as possible so as to put them within the reach of as many as possible. Reacting as a businessman, the industrialist was acutely aware that survival in a competitive marketplace depended upon new ideas.

In the United States, it soon became essential to find a means of reconciling products with mass production. The objects in question had to be adapted and distributed quickly. Firmly established European ways of doing things were swept away by new designs lending themselves to streamlined industrial production. Many of the resulting products, such as Gillette razors and Yale locks, still figure in our daily lives. American industry was totally oriented towards the democratization of production, while in Europe the middle class and the aristocracy resisted innovation and the functionalist aesthetic in the name of a deeply-entrenched cultural tradition.

If the French Revolution established the principles of liberty, equality, and fraternity in Europe, sectarianism was not completely eliminated, and many Europeans were forced to seek refuge in the United States, the new country open to all. A small group of English emigrants elected to settle on this continent, so full of promise, to establish what they called 'God's earthly realm'. This Christian sect, the Shakers, was completely self-governing and had set its sights on founding a just society. The community functioned in accordance with strict rules which were rooted in fundamental spiritual principles. It rejected all ornament, all profane decoration, as useless. Only what was useful and functional conformed to the sect's religious ideals of purity, simplicity, and unity.

The Shakers offer a striking example of the compatibility of artisanal know-how and mechanization. They developed a mode of artisanal production that was co-operative and collectivist. Respectful of their environment, they made sure their ways of producing everyday, utilitarian objects harmonized with their beliefs. The objects that resulted were of an admirable rigour and had

an aesthetic quality rare in such everyday articles, even by pre-industrial standards. Everything about Shaker objects set them apart from contemporary European artisanal production, which was characterized by an opulence designed to appeal to an aristocratic sensibility. The Shaker objects were strictly but superbly crafted to meet the vital human needs for lodging, furniture, clothing, and tools, for the kitchen and the field. Their furniture bears witness to the appropriateness with which they used materials and forms, marrying technical ingenuity and stripped-down personality. The famous Shaker rocker was one of the first chairs to be manufactured in series. It represented a novel response to collective needs that had unconsciously been given a 'trademark' look, though one reflecting the group's ethic.

Later, the vastness of America's farmlands would necessitate the mechanization of agriculture, resulting in its transformation into an industry. The use of machinery and fertilizer engendered a new phenomenon: agricultural over-production. The response was the conservation of produce, first in jars then in tins. The technique was pioneered in Europe by Nicolas Appert, but it was not immediately adopted there on a truly industrial scale.

Up until the Civil War the American population essentially consisted of peasants, trappers, and farmers. The development during the war of a technology for the construction of steel-plated ships' hulls marked the start of the industrial era. This transitional period also saw the beginning of non-institutional design, characterized by objects which bear no relation to similar hand-crafted items and are conceived for mass consumption. Amazing objects made their first appearance in these years, like George Eastman's Kodak camera, which could be had, film and all, for the affordable price of a dollar. Its straightforward design, easy operation and small format made photography accessible to amateurs and families. Eastman's camera helped create a fabulous new marketplace and Eastman Kodak, Gillette, Westinghouse, and Bell Telephone, the new knights of industry, went after their share of it.

A little later, Henry Ford devised the assembly line for the manufacture of his famous Model T car. This car openly declared its function, in contrast with the European competition, which were designed to resemble motorised coaches. Black, functional, relatively inexpensive, it remained in production for 20 years with little notable change. Blue jeans are another archetypal example of the American approach to design, a product for the greatest number that has been perfectly adapted to the down-and-dirty realities of daily life.

Towards industrial design

The 1929 depression destroyed many fortunes, but it also spawned new dreams. The 1930s saw the implementation of Roosevelt's New Deal as well as the birth of the industrial design profession in the United States. The resourcefulness of the first industrialists found itself confronted by a new and difficult challenge: over-production was changing the dynamics of the market, which previously had seemed limitless. Now a concentrated effort had to be made to sell products and these therefore acquired a new dimension. For them to find their place in the market, they had to be made to stand out in some way and this relentless economic pressure was the main reason for the birth of design as a specialized profession.

Under the leadership of pioneers such as Bel Geddes, Dreyfuss, Loewy, Teague, and Van Doren, who were simultaneously advertising specialists, theatre decorators, and experts at display, the profession took shape. Industry, impressed by the 1925 Art Deco exhibition in Paris, turned to them for help. Regarded as magicians, the first industrial designers contributed a crucial inventive dynamism to the enterprise of redefining and reconquering the various markets. To achieve their goals they used a new formal language: that of streamlining.

This style quickly became dominant, for it expressed the speed and optimism of the

Above left: Project for a transatlantic liner designed by Norman Bel Geddes, 1932.

Above right: 1930s transatlantic liner.

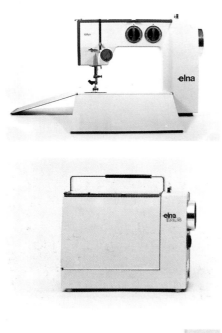

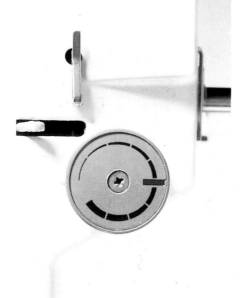

machine economy. And aerodynamic forms lent themselves perfectly to the new assemblage techniques, and so were cost-efficient. Housing a mechanism in a single, easily maintainable body proved beneficial to both customers and manufacturer. The old Gestetner duplicator, whose complicated form was a veritable dust trap, was rendered obsolete by Raymond Loewy. His alternative, covered by a plastic hood – quite an innovation at the time – caused a stir among the public and launched the designer's career. Passionately interested in the problems of transport and mobility, Loewy made them the focus of his energies. Locomotives, cars, buses, helicopters, motorboats (such as his classic streamline model): there wasn't a single type of vehicle that remained untouched by his creative genius. Walter Dorwin Teague's cash register also provided a fine example of how one might set about purifying the form of a familiar object. He collaborated with Eastman Kodak over a period of many years. In addition to his contribution to styling, he influenced product development and became involved in mechanical design (many of his ideas were patented). From 1930, Henry Dreyfuss and his associates worked on perfecting the design of the telephone for the Bell company. In 1929, the visionary designer Norman Bel Geddes conceived a futurist boat whose aerodynamic form was a precursor of today's jumbo jets.

Between 1930 and 1948 these new designers acquired growing reputations, but it was in 1939, on the occasion of the New York World's Fair, that they were allowed to give free rein to their conception of the future. Norman Bel Geddes's 'Futurama' was incontestably the exhibition's most spectacular attraction. With superb foresight, he gave concrete form to his vision of New York City *circa* 1960 in a huge model, replete with highways, peripheral routes, pedestrian zones, and satellite airports.

The influence of the designer continued to increase, and sometimes he found himself overseeing not just an isolated product but an entire product line – witness the 40-year collaboration between the Dreyfuss organisation and Bell Telephone. Another equally remarkable example was Eliot Noyes' global design concept for Mobil, which gave an unmistakable visual signature to its buildings as well as its product. The association of industrialist and designer that culminated in the fifties was born of the need to 'stand out' in the marketplace. Initially, their association tended to take the form of a close, man-to-man collaboration shaped by a common interest: the timely anticipation of future human and cultural needs.

The convergence of the American and European approaches

Eventually, the European and American currents converged as design began to respond in both continents to economic as well as to social and cultural imperatives. New fields were thrown open to designers' creative abilities: Nasa, for instance, consulted with them when designing the living quarters for their Skylab spacecraft.

In the past, artisanal production had fostered an anonymous mode of design and an ideal of perfection whose focus was increased skill, with the conceptual being downplayed. Fundamental questions about the object and the techniques for its manufacture were never posed.

All that changed with the collapse of the European empires at the beginning of this century. Genuine hope for a new society gave birth to movements of various kinds, such as the Deutscher Werkbund, De Stijl, Futurism, and Russian Constructivism. With the establishment of the Bauhaus school, European design became a dynamic force that was to help shape a new generation of creators. The Bauhaus was the most important single factor in the history of modern European design and it was in Europe that form-givers such as artists and architects developed an innovative formal language linked to function. Under the banner of 'form and function', industrial products designed for daily use contributed to the creation of a new aesthetic.

Although modern design in Europe was conceptual (so at odds with Art Deco) and obeyed cultural dictates, as opposed to technological and industrial ones, it was none the less pitched to appeal to the greatest number as in the United States. But design in Europe had arrived at its preoccupation with the democratization of the industrial product by a different route. From now on, in Europe as in the United States, the two trends meet. Design must address economic necessities as well as social and cultural ones.

Until the fifties, design was a matter for relatively informal discussion between the head of an enterprise and a creative personality (as is still often the case in Italy today). Subsequently it came to be seen as an economic tool to be exploited by industrialists as part of their market strategies. None the less, the profiling of a product remained secondary to the development process overseen by engineers, being largely a matter of materials and detailing – in short, of hardware. Techniques were developed for defining the product and adapting it to suit market conditions, and allow the mounting of a successful publicity campaign. The advent of the age of cyberspace, however, would once again reshuffle the designer's cards.

The design of intelligence

The eighties marked a recentering of the industrial world and saw the emergence of new approaches, at the managerial as well as the individual level. After years of prosperity during which criticism had been muted, consumers became more demanding with regard to product quality, durability, and safety. Technology rapidly became obsolete and was losing its inherent attractiveness. The desire for social expansion was replaced by the need to 'manage' progress, to rethink it in strategic terms.

During these years 65 per cent of Japan's great corporations established their own design departments, some of which had as many as 150 to 200 designers distributed throughout a network of decentralized offices. The rapid development of new technologies brought about a profound transformation in the cultural landscape and the professional environment. Electronics and computer science introduced multiple-use product categories which had previously been unimagineable in the market. Individual products gave way to 'systems'

Pasta designed by Nemo for Panzani, 1987.

designed to accommodate evolution, each of their components interacting with others, functioning as a link in an integrated, multi-purpose chain, in a multi-media network. This development marked the beginning of the software revolution and of a new determination to develop design projects predicated less exclusively on technological performance and functionalist criteria. This approach also had to take account of nology and performance marketing. From this point forward, design involved a great deal more than stylistic indicators: it would operate at the very heart of product evolution. Its job would be to formulate a product 'philosophy' and to assure the coherence of the whole. In itself, the product, however technologically advanced, had no meaning and so no use unless designed to function within a global communications network.

Disposable gloves designed by the agency Cent Degrés for Mappa, French prize for product design 1992. A new image for a new function.

the human element in the 'man-machine' dialogue, as well as the cultural factors involved in changes of such magnitude. The Sony Walkman is a telling example. This product, born of an intuition of genius, materialized at just the right moment to rejuvenate a declining audio market. It was an immediate success because it responded to the previously unexpressed desires of individualist consumers. Another example is the Apple Macintosh mouse, which totally altered the relationship between man and machine, bringing it closer to an interactive model as opposed to the binary one that had previously held sway.

These transformations modified the very foundations of the enterprise. It was no longer a matter of simply 'producing' systems. It was now a question of developing a 'communications strategy' around these products, and of privileging values distinct from the established ones associated with tech-

If it is to succeed, a product must be based on a strong idea. Product development requires the collaboration of the managing director of the company, the designer, technicians, marketing specialists and manufacturing experts. Objects produced by artisans bear the stamp of their individual makers, but today the scale and complexity of production and marketing structures demands a pooling of expertise. The designer's role is to evaluate the proposed product in terms of the user's needs.

So design performs an essential function in assessing a product's suitability for the human environment and in anticipating the future needs of users. These were also the goals of the first manufacturers, inventors, and industrialists. Modern management should be trying to reactivate the impulses behind the actions of their predecessors, with a view to shaping a better world for the greatest possible number of consumers.

The Gestetner duplicator

The duplicator before (background) and after (top) Raymond Loewy's redesign, 1929.

Up until 1930, the mechanization of office work was an American phenomenon. The major concern was with increased productivity. The tertiary sector was in full expansion and machine manufacturers of all kinds found themselves confronting a demand they had difficulty satisfying. The exterior appearance of early office machines was the result of chance and necessity, for the industrial aesthetic had not yet been born. But from 1929, the Great Depression made competition particularly fierce.

That year Raymond Loewy, a Frenchman who had arrived in the United States in 1919, was working to modify the appearance of the Gestetner duplicator. This project marked the beginning of American industrial design, whose first objective would be to attract a clientele through an aesthetic of seduction. This aesthetic would be sensation-based rather than rational. It proposed to soften forms by making them 'aerodynamic'.

In his book Never Leave Well Enough Alone (1951), Raymond Loewy provides an account of this episode which describes the sculptural approach he took for redesigning the duplicator's form: 'The Gestetner duplicator wasn't superior to other products on the market, and what's more it was much uglier. I began to make a plaster model of the machine. In this way, I gradually managed to shape a case enclosing everything that could be hidden. I perfected its lines until it seemed to me simple, practical and agreeable to the eye...After a few other minor adjustments, the duplicator was ready. I had worked for three days, and the result was received with enthusiasm.'

This text, naive but objective, demonstrates very precisely what the economy of the American market expected of industrial design when it commissioned the reworking of a product intended for sale; it also makes clear how marketing and publicity networks dealt with competition.

It has to be said that this opportunism did not always lead to poor results. According to the logic of the marketplace, many talented designers succeeded, despite the constraints, in affirming a style and designing handsome products.

J. d. N.

In our highly competitive system, few products are able to maintain any technical superiority for long . . . they must be endowed with richness of associations and imagery; they must have many levels of meaning, if we expect them to be top sellers, if we hope that they will achieve the emotional attachment which shows up as brand loyalty.

Pierre Martineau, *Motivation in Advertising: Motives that Make People Buy*, New York, 1957

The Shakers

'Hands to work, heart to God', 'The best is that which functions best', are two of the proverbs formulated by the Shakers. One century before Louis Sullivan's famous phrase 'form follows function', the Shakers anticipated the future principles of functionalism when they affirmed: 'All forms breed force'.

The first Shaker community was founded by a British woman named Ann Lee, who was born in 1736 in Manchester. At the age of 22, she joined the Quakers, who at the time were being persecuted in England. In order to escape oppression she and her followers fled to America in 1774.

Shaker communities were based on equality between the sexes, with men and women living together as 'brothers' and 'sisters'. They pronounced a vow of chastity in accordance with Christ's word: 'In the resurrection they did not marry nor give themselves in marriage, but are as angels in the heavens.' In order to perpetuate themselves, the communities relied on the arrival of new members and adopted orphans. This very simple puritan philosophy calls for a community organization reinforced by clearly defined rules.

Friedrich Engels cited the Shakers as proof that communism was viable.

In Deutsches Bürgerbuch für 1845, he praised them as 'the first in America and in the entire world to have effectively created a society based on common sharing of property.' He rapidly passed over their 'very strange beliefs...'

The Shakers succeeded in integrating their convictions with their physical environment and developed a co-operative private industry. On a creative and aesthetic level, their designs are remarkable. Their earliest objects were imbued with a purity and simplicity of form, whether made from metal, like the 'Shaker stoves', or wood, like their rocking chairs or famous hat boxes made from wood shavings.

Industrial 'production' only started when the needs of the community were satisfied. They started to make objects and furniture in New Lebanon from 1849 up until 1947. Curiously, fashion has led to the reappropriation of the Shaker style, which is characterized by a rigorous honesty and sobriety of form. There are only two Shaker communities in existence today, one in Maine and the other in New Hampshire. The few remaining sisters who still live there do not accept any new members. The Shakers will disappear with them.

E. M.

Right: Machine for preparing pills, manufactured at New Lebanon, New York, beginning of the 19th century.

Vignettes, from top to bottom: Quakers in Canterbury, New Hampshire, c.1915.

Chair manufactured in New Lebanon, New York, c.1840.

Writing desk created by a Shaker brother, from Harvard, Massachusetts, 19th century.

A room in the family home in Hancock, Massachusetts.

Fig. 1.

The Kodak camera

In 1887 George Eastman began work on a new photographic device that would be easy to use; he intended to devise 'a system…that leaves all the difficulties to the manufacturer, placing in the hands of the user an apparatus that could be used by any six-year-old'.

In the specifications of the patent he registered for his new amateur camera, Eastman noted that some of its elements were intended to facilitate 'ease of manufacture and simplicity of construction'. He invented the name Kodak in 1887. The 1888 Kodak was a modern device; its 'black box' form anticipated by more than 60 years the aesthetic promulgated by the Hochschule für Gestaltung at Ulm and applied by the Braun company from 1960.

This device, loaded with a strip of film allowing for a hundred exposures, was sold for $25. The novice photographer had only to direct it toward his subject and press a button. When he had taken a hundred shots, he returned it to the factory where, for about $10, the film was removed and the camera reloaded. The system's simplicity was perfectly conveyed by Eastman's famous publicity slogan: 'Push the button, we do the rest.'

The experience of the principal investor in the company, Henry A. Strong, was probably typical of thousands throughout the world. Eastman described it as follows: 'I gave one of these devices to Mr Strong, who a few weeks ago took it with him on a trip to Tacoma. It was the first time he'd taken a photographic apparatus with him, and he was as excited as a child with a top. I've never seen anyone derive so much pleasure from a few photos. Apparently he'd thought he would never be able to take photos himself.'

The success of the Eastman Kodak company was the result of a solid knowledge of the interrelationship between technology and the market. This knowledge served as the basis for Eastman's modification and reorientation of his business on both the technological and commercial level, acknowledging the existence of a mass market, which he successfully exploited.

The example of the Kodak camera is significant because it illustrates the passage from a professional market to a largely amateur one, which necessitated mass production.

While approximate, statistics of the period indicate a substantial increase in sales between 1880 and 1904, with annual profits growing from $.25 million to $13.2 million.

J. d. N.

Background: George Eastman's patent application for the camera, 4 September 1888.

Vignettes: First Kodak camera, 1888.

George Eastman on the boat to Europe.

Right: George Eastman and Thomas Edison, inventor of the kinetograph, photographed in front of Eastman's home in Rochester, 1928.

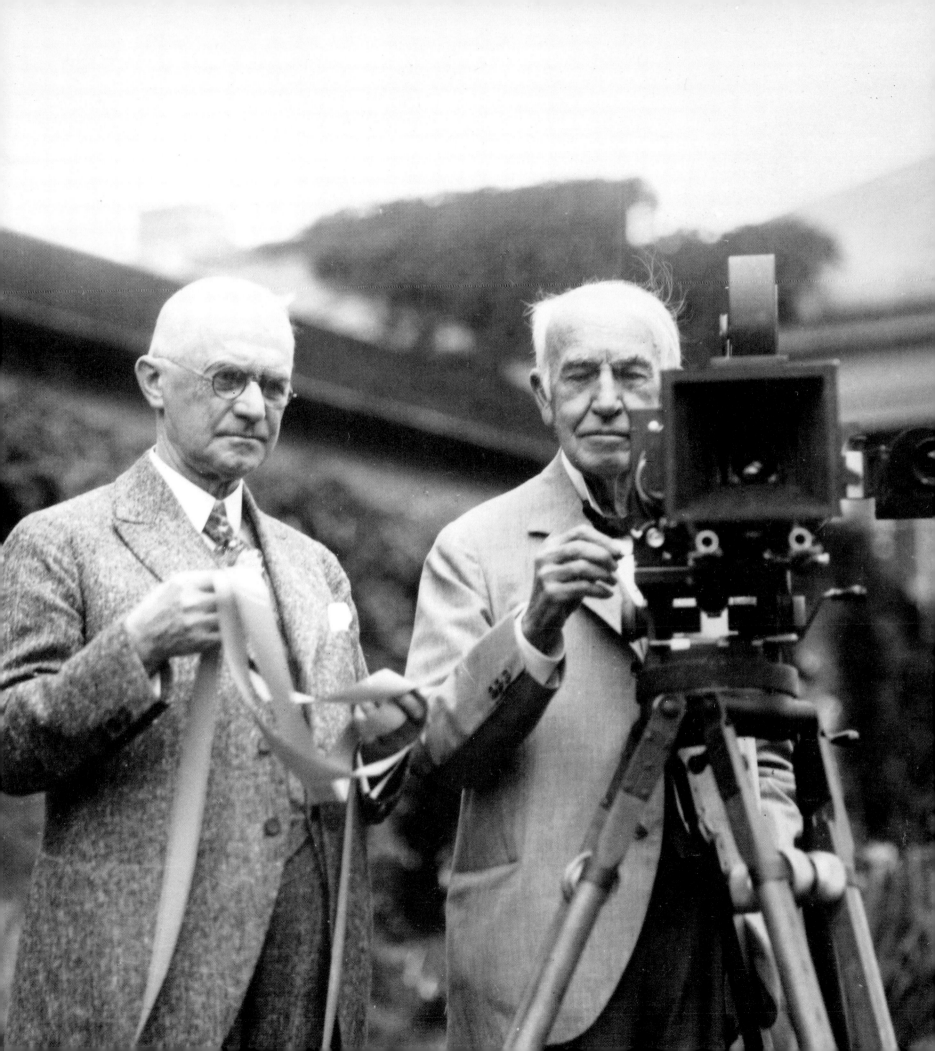

In 1886, the pharmacist John S. Pemberton invented the magic formula for Coca-Cola. Working in the back room of his shop, he was trying to create a new thirst-quenching drink. He mixed cola nut extract, sugar, de-cocainized cocaine leaves, caffeine and vegetable extracts whose composition still remains secret. The first advertisement for the drink, which appeared in the daily newspaper The Atlanta Journal, consisted of the simple slogan 'Delicious and refreshing'. Six years after inventing his soda, Pemberton, unable to raise the funds necessary to promote it, sold his shares to Asa G. Chandler,

The Coca-Cola bottle

who formed the Coca-Cola company. Thanks to a perfectly orchestrated publicity campaign, which included calendars, posters, wallpapers, trays, clocks and vending machines, the brand became highly successful at the beginning of the century. Business grew at an incredible rate. In 1901, the annual publicity budget was set at $100,000. Ten years later it was fixed at $1 million (in 1948 the budget had risen to $20 million and in 1959 $40 million). The bottle was restyled, with the logo moulded into the glass. Shortly after the bottle was given what was virtually its definitive form. The new design, pro-

posed by Alexander Samuelson in 1913, was accepted two years later by a committee of members of the company. During the Second World War, the various products were grouped under the new name of 'Coke'. The most famous design agency of the period, managed by Raymond Loewy, was hired: 'I did not design the Coca-Cola logo, but I redesigned the red vending machines that are installed in the lemonade bars, cafeterias, drugstores, snack bars etc. Coca-Cola also asked us to redesign the bottle in order to give it a more refined silhouette, An interesting project consisted of designing

a delivery truck, where heavy boxes of cans or bottles had to be handled quickly, efficiently and with a maximum of security. Coca-Cola has been our client for more than ten years.'
Since then, the marketing budget has continued to increase and new products are launched in publicity campaigns. In 1983, Coca-Cola created a decaffeinated Coke. Diet Coke, which contains no added sugar, was launched at the same time. More than two thousand million bottles of Coca-Cola in its various forms are sold every year.

E. M.

1851-1879

by

Jocelyn de Noblet

From an economic point of view, the 19th century is characterized by the appearance of a plethora of new products, the fruit of the gradual mastery of science and technology by engineers. These included not just the machine tools, steam engines, tools and measuring instruments which make up the infrastructure of a new production system, but also means of transport (railways and steamships) and new forms of architecture marked by metal construction.

Once standardization had made possible prefabrication and the interchangeability of parts, mass production could begin. New domestic products, such as the Remington typewriter, would be devised thanks to the industrial infrastructure of the munitions factories. It was not until 1870 that this system of production was extended to other objects, such as the camera, as well as to a wealth of domestic hardware.

With a few exceptions, all these products belong to a first generation functionalism and their form reflects the culture of engineers (the oft-quoted example of stationary steam engines with pillars in the form of Doric columns remains an exception).

Moreover, the objects designed with the middle class domestic interior in mind lost their neoclassical Restoration elegance and were a heterogeneous and eclectic group. In 1836, in *Les Confessions d'un enfant du siècle*, Alfred de Musset had a premonition of their lacklustre evolution: 'Our century has no forms of its own. We have stamped the mark of our time neither on our homes, nor on anything else. The apartments of the wealthy are like curiosity cabinets: Greek and Roman, Gothic, Renaissance style, Louis XIII – everything is jumbled together… Our taste is eclectic, we grab whatever we can find [...] such that we only live on debris, as if the end of the world was near…'

Thus, the new society which emerges from the Industrial Revolution cannot be considered a homogeneous entity, but as a place of endless confrontations, of rifts between rapidly evolving technical and industrial parameters, and of bruised, wounded mentalities which have still not had the time to heal. A culture, wrote the French philosopher Sylvain Auroux, 'is the set of symbolic, technical and statutory mediations which a particular human group, in order to satisfy its needs, has set up between itself and its natural environment'. This definition, however, does not suit periods of rapid and unpredictable upheaval. The split between humanist and techno-scientific culture in western civilization is the corollary of the complexity of its material culture: the growth of disorder is somehow the consequence of the poorly managed development of technology and its applications.

It was William Morris and the followers of the English Arts and Crafts Movement who, from 1860 on, instigated both a new aesthetic and a radical critique of industrialization.

Life in the forge, Great Britain, c.1857.

Preceding double page: **The metal span of the Lessart viaduct is put into position, France, 1879.**

1769

- Sir Richard Arkwright: water-powered spinning frame

1779

- Abraham Darby III: Coalbrookdale bridge, River Severn, England, the first cast iron bridge

1782

- Immanuel Kant: *Critique of Pure Reason*
- James Watt: steam engine (the first patents date from 1769)

1789

- French Revolution
- Eli Whitney originates mass production of guns

1792

- Edmund Cartwright: steam-powered loom

1796

- Edward Jenner discovers smallpox vaccine

1799

- decimal system devised in France
- Eli Whitney: cotton gin

1807

- gas street lights, London

1808

- independence movements in Spanish and Portuguese America
- Madame de Staël: *On Germany*, greatly influences European thought and letters

1812

- first commercial tinned foods using the technique of vacuum storage invented by Nicolas Appert in 1775

- cylinder printing press invented, adopted by *The Times* (London)
- Pierre Simon, marquis de Laplace : *Analytical Theory of Probabilities*

1819

- first gas street lighting, Paris

1822

- José Nicéphore Niepce: first photographic image

1825

- first passenger railway, England

1829

- **George and Robert Stephenson: The Rocket steam locomotive**

1834

- mechanical reaper (USA)
- Louis Braille invents the Braille system of writing for the blind

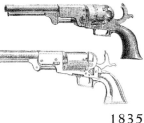
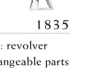

1835

- **Samuel Colt: revolver with interchangeable parts**

1837

- start of Queen Victoria's reign in Great Britain
- Pitman's shorthand invented

1840

- first postage stamp (Great Britain)
- Charles Goodyear discovers vulcanization of rubber
- José Nicéphore Niepce and Jacques Daguerre: daguerreotype, the first practical photographs

1844

- Samuel Morse sets up electric telegraph between Washington and Baltimore

1847

- Johan Edvard Lundström (Sweden) invents safety matches

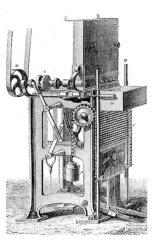

1848

- James Bogardus: first buildings using cast iron skeleton made from prefabricated sections (United States)
- Dante Gabriel Rossetti and William Holman Hunt found the Pre-Raphaelite movement
- Nathaniel Hawthorne: *The Scarlet Letter* (40,000 copies published)
- Karl Marx and Friedrich Engels: *The Communist Manifesto*

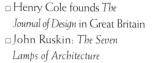

- Henry Cole founds *The Journal of Design* in Great Britain
- John Ruskin: *The Seven Lamps of Architecture*
- Charles Fourier: workers' housing estates

1850

- deck chair
- Richard J. Gatling: machine gun

- development of semi-finished products in laminated steel
- in Great Britain, half the population live in towns
- Rudolf Clausius formulates second law of thermodynamics and kinetic theory of gases

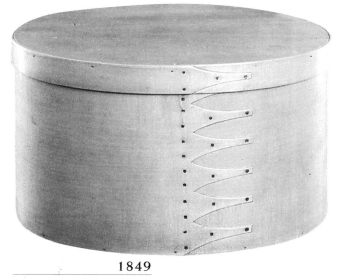

1849

- **Shaker community produces tools and furniture (USA)**

1851

- Isaac Singer: first sewing machine
- James T. King: first drum washing machine
- Cyrus McCormick: agricultural machinery (automatic reaping machine)
- Sir Joseph Paxton builds the Crystal Palace for the Great Exhibition in London

- Herman Melville: *Moby Dick*
- Léon Foucault demonstrates the rotation of the earth in an experiment with a pendulum in the Panthéon
- in France, law protecting working children: minimum age is raised to ten years and the working day shortened
- William Thomson, later Lord Kelvin: laws of conservation and dissipation of energy

1852

- Emile Loubat: first tramway, New York

- Henri Giffard: motorized dirigible

- construction of King's Cross, Paddington and St Pancras railway stations, London (1852-1853)

1853

- Baron Haussmann starts the urban transformation of Paris
- Abraham Bréguet mass-produces watches
- vaccination against smallpox compulsory in Great Britain
- Louis Pierre Baltard: start of construction of Les Halles, Paris

1854

- Henri Sainte-Claire-Deville devises method of obtaining pure aluminium starting with cryolite

- George Andemars: patent for production of rayon
- Franz Koller develops tungsten steel
- David Hughes invents the printing telegraph
- R. S. Lawrence constructs turret lathe
- first iron Cunard steamer crosses the Atlantic
- Florence Nightingale introduces hygienic standards into military hospitals during the Crimean War

1855

- François Coignet: reinforced concrete house, Saint-Denis, France
- Universal Exposition, Paris

- Cyrus Yale Jr: safety lock
- Robert Wilhelm Bunsen: gas burner (Bunsen burner)

1856

- Henry Bessemer's blast furnace permits mass production of steel
- Jean-Marie Le Bris flies an unmanned glider

1857

- Elisha Graves Otis: first public lift (New York)
- Charles Baudelaire's *Les Fleurs du Mal* is published and censored
- Gustave Flaubert: *Madame Bovary*

- Louis Pasteur discovers that fermentation is due to the action of micro-organisms

1858

- Michael Thonet: Bistrot No.14 chair

- Sail Bornen produces condensed milk using Appert's method
- Henri Labrouste: Bibliothèque Nationale, Paris
- Nadar: first aerial photographs taken from a balloon

1859

- Gaston Planté: first practical storage battery
- Edwin Laurentine Drake drills first oil well in Titusville, Pennsylvania

- Jean Baptiste Godin founds the industrial cooperative le Familistère de Guise

- Ferdinand de Lesseps: start of the Suez Canal
- Edouard Manet: *Le Buveur d'Absinthe*
- Richard Wagner: *Tristan and Isolde*
- Charles Darwin: *On the Origin of Species*

1860

- Etienne Lenoir builds the first practical petroleum-burning internal-combustion engine
- Ferdinand Carré: refrigeration machine using ammonia

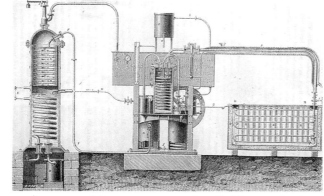

- construction of the London underground (Metropolitan Railway)
- in Paris, some streets are paved in asphalt

- development of artificial lighting for photography using magnesium wire
- Abraham Lincoln elected president of the United States

1861

- universal milling machine by Brown & Sharp
- Michaux père et fils: the first pedal bicycle
- Ernest Solvay patents a new process of producing soda
- Jean Dollfuss: workers' housing estates, Mulhouse

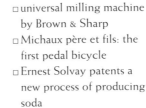

- Charles Garnier designs the Opéra in Paris

- William Morris forms Arts and Crafts company
- Louis Pasteur evolves germ theory of disease
- American Civil War

1862

- Alphonse Beau de Rochas: theory of the four-cycle engine
- London International Exhibition

1863

- William Bullock: rotary printing press
- Albert Nobel uses nitroglycerine for the first dynamite
- first Salon des Refusés, Paris
- Jean Henri Dunant founds the Red Cross in Geneva
- Jules Verne begins publishing *Fantastic Voyages in Known and Unknown Lands*

1864

- Karl Wilhelm Siemens develops the open-hearth method for steel furnaces using pig iron and iron ore
- Edouard Manet: *Olympia*, rejected by the Salon

1865

- laying of the first transatlantic cable by the Great Eastern

- mechanical washing machine (American patent)
- **George Mortimer Pullman: sleeping car (United States)**
- Gregor Mendel: the principles of heredity
- Claude Bernard: *L'Introduction à l'Etude de la Médecine Expérimentale*
- James Clerk Maxwell: electromagnetic theory

1866

- Fyodor Mikhailovich Dostoevsky: *Crime and Punishment*

1867

- Christopher Latham Sholes, Samuel Soule and Carlos Glidden patent typewriter (United States)
- Félix Léon Edoux: hydraulic lift
- Leo Tolstoy: *War and Peace*
- Universal Exposition, Paris
- Karl Marx: *Das Kapital* (first volume)

1868

- discovery of Cro-Magnon man
- Ernst Haeckel institutes ecology as a scientific discipline

1869

- William F. Sempel patents chewing gum
- Ives W. McGaffey: vacuum cleaner (United States)
- Louis Ducos du Hauron: *Les Couleurs en Photographie; Solution du Problème*
- compressed air jack (Westinghouse)
- Gustave Flaubert: *L'Education Sentimentale*
- first transcontinental railway, United States

- Dmitri Ivanovich Mendeleyev: periodic classification of chemical elements

1870

- John Wesley Hyatt: method of manufacturing celluloid
- John Davison Rockefeller founds Standard Oil Co.
- Heinrich Schliemann discovers the presumed site of Troy at Hissarlik
- co-operation agreements between Havas, Reuter and Wolf press agencies

- Napoléon III capitulates at Sedan, the Third Republic is proclaimed in Paris on 4 September

1871

- Zénobe Gramme invents the dynamo (dynamoelectric generator)

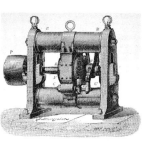

- Jules Saulnier: first building of skeleton construction at Noisiel-sur-Marne, France

- Henry Fuseli: *The Nightmare*
- Arthur Rimbaud: *Le Bateau Ivre*
- proclamation of the German empire by Otto Bismarck
- Germany annexes Alsace-Lorraine

1872

- Friedrich von Hefner-Alteneck: first efficient electrical generator

- Claude Monet: *Impression, Sunrise*
- Eugène Viollet-le-Duc: *Lectures on Architecture* (1863-1872)

- Friedrich Engels: *The Housing Question*

1873

- Universal Exposition, Vienna
- Philo Remington manufactures typewriters (designed by Christopher Latham Sholes)

- Jean Charcot writes *Leçons sur les Maladies du Système Nerveux*
- Gustave Tissandier founds the publication *La Nature*

1874

- first electric tram (New York)
- first Impressionist exhibition, Paris

1875

- Carl Klietsch: photogravure printing
- **Thomas Edison invents the incandescent lamp, the phonograph and the microphone (1875– 1876)**

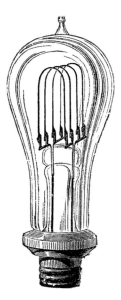

1876

- Karl Heinz invents Tomato Ketchup
- Alexander Graham Bell invents the telephone

- Nikolaus Otto: four-cycle engine

- International Exhibition Philadelphia
- Auguste Renoir: *Le Moulin de la Galette*

1877

- Charles Tellier designs the ship Le Frigorifique and frozen meat is transported for the first time (Argentina to Europe)
- Gustave de Laval uses centrifugal force to skim milk
- Claude Monet: *Gare Saint-Lazare*
- Leo Tolstoy: *Anna Karenina*
- Emile Zola: *L'Assommoir*
- Jules Guesde founds the first socialist newspaper *L'Egalité*

1878

- Werner von Siemens: industrialization of the alternator
- first electric street lighting, London
- Universal Exposition, Paris

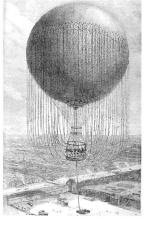

- George Eastman: gelatin silver bromide photographic plate

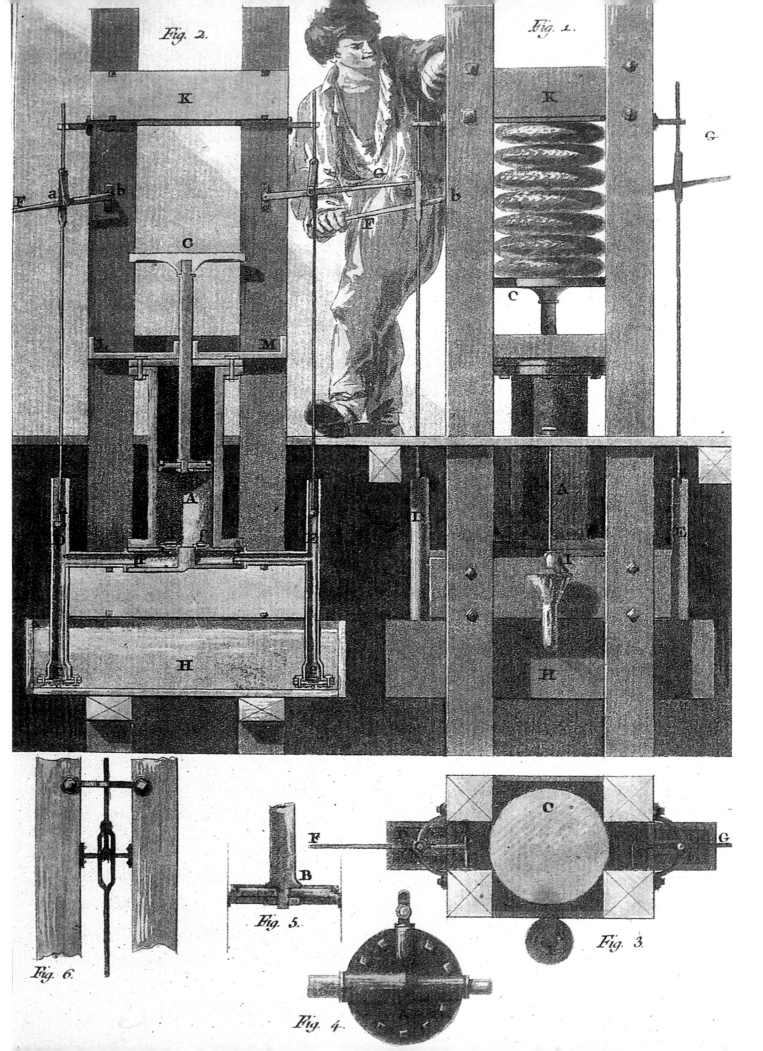

Hydraulic machine by Joseph Bramah, 1796.

Far right, from top to bottom:
1. Universal fixed head, Jahn system, for polishing screws.
2. Fixed head with device for grinding and polishing metals, woods, etc.
3. Fixed head with saw.
4. and 5. Complete head for grinding, polishing, and sawing.
6. and 7. Interchangeable accessories for precision lathes. Illustrations taken from the catalogue of the *Établissements, Fisseau et Cochot*, Paris, c.1930.

Design in the First Machine Age

Jacques Guillerme

Some have tried to make a case for design as both the sign and instrument of modernity, a modernity that carefully weathers successive fashions and finds in innovation the principle of a presumed freshness. It is well known that for over a century industrial production has borne the imprint of stylization – constantly changing for sure, but adapted to the intertwined requirements of machining and economic calculations, of the art of manufacture and corporate profits.

Producers set out to impose on the market – as large a share of it as possible – an abundance of mass-produced articles said to respond to the 'needs' of the consumer. If it happens that one of these articles enjoys a monopoly through protectionist legislation or some other means, its appearance in the world of objects comes to seem increasingly natural, until one day an ingenious competitor threatens its position as market-leader. Sometimes the crisis results from a novel appearance, from a new form of styling which eclipses a style which has dominated the market for a while. The new product will succeed in finding its mar-

ket niche only with the combined effect of a set of heterogeneous factors not always easy to predict, namely economics, public taste and the conditions of industrial manufacture. Working within this compound of influences the designer, with varying outcomes, uses his ingenuity to imagine and plan the form (structure and appearance) of a prototype which will be mass-produced once the experts in feasibility and marketing have given their endorsement. These basics are widely known, and I mention them here in order to summarize the current situation in an unfolding history: that of the conditions, moral and material, shaping the emergence of the developmental discipline which, in France, has recently been termed 'design' but was earlier known as *'esthétique industrielle'*, though strictly speaking these terms do not mean the same thing.

The phrase *'esthétique industrielle'* is a syntagma which was first employed in 1819, but it was not used again for quite some time. It appears at the end of the *Plan de technonomie* by Gérard-Joseph Christian, then director of the Conservatoire Royal des

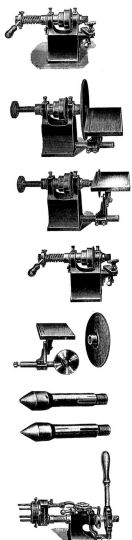

Arts et Métiers (Royal Conservatory of Arts and Crafts). Christian thought that the function of this aesthetic was to serve an industry that had 'reached quite an advanced state', developed enough to have a 'powerful effect on consumption', by dictating taste. The precise means? The instilling 'of order and a prudent reserve in the art of varying product form'.[1]

This desire for 'prudent reserve' was very much in the spirit of the times, if we can leave to one side the upheavals of society. Geometrical drawing and the outlines of descriptive geometry are cited as exemplary methods for capturing form, whether natural or artificial. As early as 1766, Bachelier, the promoter of the Ecoles Gratuites de Dessin, denounced 'the ineptitude of a multitude of workers, persons without taste, without principles, without precision... given to a routine of operations which degrades the best-conceived projects'.[2] He further noted that 'education begins with geometry: it alone can stop the deviations of the imagination, containing it within the limits of reason and forcing ideas to follow...regular channels'.[3] This high regard for 'regularity' anticipates the advent of a taste we would subsequently designate as 'neo-classical'. But it would be mistaken and chauvinistic to claim that France was its point of origin. The exaltation of regularity originated in the United Kingdom in this period. In his *Select Architecture*,[4] Robert Morris described regularity as an 'essential ingredient' in building composition; it results from 'a uniformity of parts that are justly proportioned and disposed', for the mind is agreeably affected by the fit arrangement of distinct elements. Slightly later, Priestley, in his *A Course of Lectures on Oratory and Criticism*, analysed with brio the felicitous properties relating to the contrast of uniformity and variety in the forms of products, and he linked them to appreciation of their use: 'The pleasure we derive from that which we call the just proportions of objects is derived by association from the idea of the utility of such proportions'.[5]

This way of intuiting space, also a factor in the manipulation of objects, falls far short of the pretentions of descriptive geometry: its programme' purports without blinking to be 'well suited to exercising the intellectual faculties of a great people and contribute thereby to the perfection of the human species'.[6] Vain hope: the species, though it may well have the intention of perfecting itself, delegated the task of cultivating Gaspard Monge's beautiful geometric theorems and their applications to a small elite. It is perhaps worth recalling that during the 19th century only two kinds of industrial drawing were current in the studios of the industrious English nation. Firstly, there were the traditional geometric figures known as plan, section and elevation – all derivatives of orthogonal projection. Subsequently, the more synthetic isometrics of William Farish were introduced, which were based on the configuration of an encompassing cube seen from the top of one of its diagonals.

Isometric Perspective, which appeared in 1822 in the *Transactions* of the Cambridge Philosophical Society, was to establish the popularity of axonometric perspective, which made possible the simultaneous illustration of the interior and exterior of composite structures. It made it possible to fix, among other things, exploded configurations showing fittings – useful to mechanics. These exploded views were plagiarized shortly after in publicity images.

When all is said and done, save for its usefulness in dealing with the singular problems presented by stereotomy (the science of measuring stones for complex structures like oblique pendentives), we still tend to think of descriptive geometry as a school exercise. Yet most graphic documents relating to industrial manufacture are in a geometric idiom, sometimes complicated by the relevant illustrational conventions relating to the materials and their assembly. Hence the techniques used for representing objects bear witness, through their graphic style and their associated conventions, to their place of origin and the industrial culture which held sway there.

The book by Peter Jeffrey Booker, *A History of Engineering Drawing*,[7] makes this perfectly clear. Although the zealots of descriptive geometry in France have often celebrated its supposed suitability for the design of manufactured forms that are simple, pure and smoothly finished, it would be incorrect, Booker suggests, to suppose in every case a marked reciprocal interrelationship between techniques of illustration and techniques of manufacture. A case in point: when a certain simplicity is observed in manufactured forms, it is usually due to an economy in the machine tools used in their manufacture, as will be discussed below.

To return to Gérard-Joseph Christian, when he recommends a prudent restraint in the art of varying forms, he goes on, logically, to establish a catalogue of standardized components. His *Plan de technonomie* recommends a uniform classification system for items of furniture and construction elements: 'If we presuppose...large, separate factories for production of each specific object...a dozen different sizes and a dozen different levels of luxury should more than suffice to satisfy all needs and all tastes'. Such regulation of diversity would result, in the eyes of our technomat, in 'an increase in user-friendliness' and 'a more perfect, and assuredly more economical production system'.[8] It would seem, then, that Christian's industrial aesthetic accords pride of place to the standardization of component elements and, as a consequence, to the standardization of assembled products as well.

This programme would be taken up again in 1828 by Jean-Baptiste Say, in the second volume of his *Cours complet d'économie politique pratique*. In it he extols 'standardization in manufacture', in other words a 'mode of manufacture in which large quantities of a given product are manufactured in accordance with a uniform model'. He cites coffee mills and artillery wheelmaking as specific examples, but he makes it clear that 'most of the products we use could be standardized'.[9] He takes from Christian the scheme for a set of dimensions based on twelve standard door-frame dimensions, while, in addition, advocating the use of cast iron, in imitation of the English, though he has no illusions about the obstacles vanity and fashion pose to the adoption of standardized housing. To be sure, he neglects to point out another, very different obstacle, namely resistance to the metrical system of measurement adopted by the republican legislature 30 years before. Habits die especially hard when they're rooted in the projection of one's own body and limbs onto practical dimensions.

Napoleon was a partisan of the new system of measure, but even he spoke on occasion in favour of the old system, which had the merit of allowing for a greater number of complete units. A systematic adoption of the decimal system would entail a 'reworking of all the regulations of public administration, all artistic standards'; work that 'alarms reason', we read in the emperor's *Mémoires*, where he also remarks

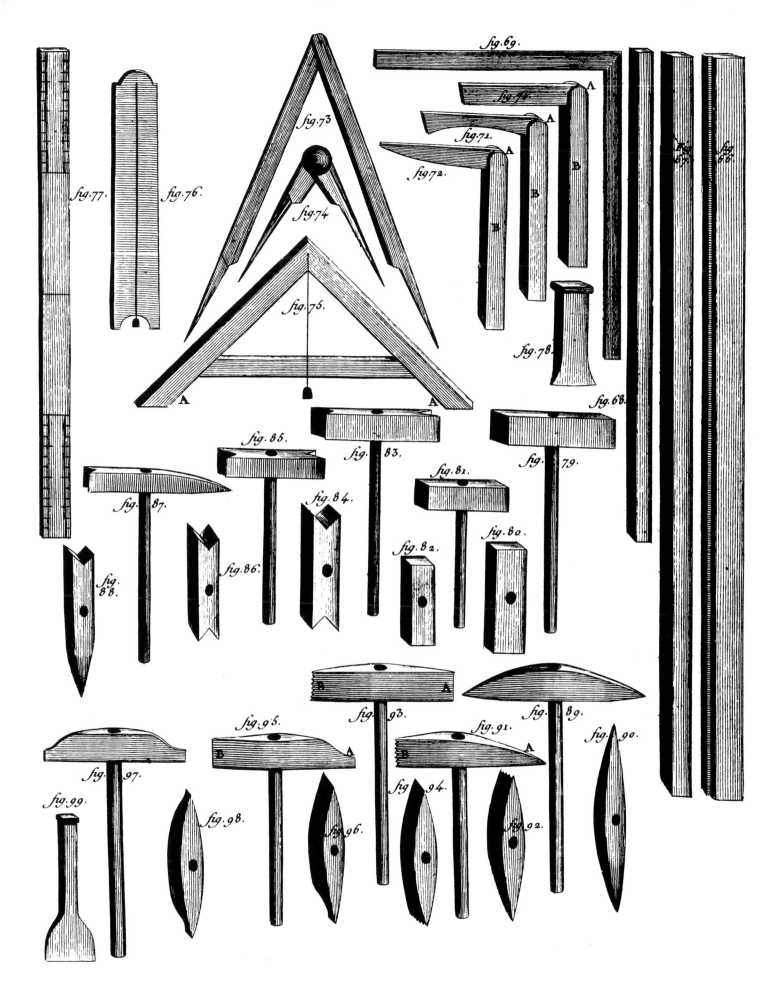

'Architecture-Masonry' plate taken from Diderot and d'Alembert's *Encyclopédie*, second half of the 18th century. Scissors, hammers, chisels, and tools for piercing and cutting are presented here with measuring instruments and templates.

'all instruments, all machines have been conceived and calibrated in accordance with the old nomenclature, and are expressed in simple numbers, which conversion would only render into numbers composed of five or six figures'. In conclusion, 'The new system of weights and measures will create inconvenience and difficulty for several generations'; what was worse, 'the first commission charged with verifying the measurement of the meridian will have to make corrections'.[10]

That was an astute assessment. The legal status of the metric system led to its increasing acceptance, but this did not prevent the old units of measurement from continuing to be used in certain professions, while successive attempts to verify the geographic reference point would lead, in the middle of the present century, to the selection of an entirely different standard, namely the radiation frequency associated with two electronic orbits of a rare gas!

But to return to the practical domain of industrial standardization, we should not be surprised by the vigorous survival of the traditional units in most Anglo-Saxon manufacture and in the many industries involved with it. Idiosyncracy, certainly. On the other hand, just think of the enormous expense that would be entailed simply by converting screw cutting in American mechanical industry and everything that depends on it.

It would be impossible to exaggerate the perceptiveness of Jean-Baptiste Say when, in his *Cours*, he stressed the advantages which would follow from the introduction of standardization into the manufacture of artillery. This had been fully understood since the adoption, during the reign of Louis XVI, of the 'system' of Gribeauval, which not only limited the number of calibres but facilitated replacement of parts. Here and there, implementation of the reform was criticized, as for example in *La Correspondance de deux généraux*;[11] such is the lot of all innovation. But the basic principles behind Gribeauval's conception,

whose only weak point was the presumed decline of artisanal ingenuity, increasingly met with acceptance.

In the second edition of their *Théorie des affûts* (*Theory of Mountings*), the engineers Jean Migout and Claude-Lucien Bergery sang the praises of the interchangeability of parts from a vast stock of material, which would facilitate their use in all sorts of circumstances and locations: 'Uniformity demanded extreme precision in the execution of each piece and rigorous exactitude of assemblage. These qualities were prescribed and obtained; as a result, construction attained such a degree of perfection that any given piece, whether wood or iron, of a certain model of vehicle, from any arsenal whatever, could be used as a replacement in any vehicle of this model fabricated in any other arsenal...The complete interchangeability of analogous pieces, which was as necessary for solidity and speed of repair as for reducing the need for replacements, was the fruit of construction tables for each model which were established with the greatest care'.[12]

The advantages resulting from these standardizing procedures proved so great 'that some wanted to push them much farther and apply them to still larger systems of elements used in campaign material, including complete products'; but this project, which required greater technical sophistication, 'remained imperfect', according to our engineers. Yet a relative failure did nothing to lessen the significance of standardizing procedures, which presupposed more exacting standards of precision upon which efficiency depended. The matrix of all quality industrial production was coming into being, subordinated to a network of metrological controls, which are only meaningful with the help of a thorough knowledge of the materials being used. The inevitable result was the establishment of testing procedures, a standardization of tests which is tuned to standard samples and aims at a standardized quality of product.

There is no denying, all the same, that the

idea of standardization predated the knowledge required for its realization. Each technology carries in its memory a kind of prehistory of standardizing codes. Artillery provides one example; the art of shipbuilding might well offer an earlier one, whether in models made for hulls, rigging, details of trimming cargo, or even simple treenails. Here one particularly eloquent example will suffice: the running of the Venice arsenal, where in the 16th century Nicolo Zen ordered the numerical labelling of spare parts for reserve armaments, thereby assuring greater speed of reassembly. Better yet, in 1568 he decided to set up a central lumber warehouse in which wood was classified in accordance with a set of samples, an 'admirable order' anticipating later prefabrication programmes.[13]

Such classification and numbering systems led to increased speed and efficiency, there being a presumed correlation between means and ends. The integrating of assembly operations is an ideal schema which could be corrected in shipbuilding or building construction by caulking or the use of mortar; in short, by means of rather coarse finishing work, which allowed for the correction of flaws, whether in the original materials or in their sizing. Such is not the case with factory machinery, where the acceptable threshold of formal precision and productive capacity is much higher. From the ancient practice of casting bricks to the shaping of cathode tubes, the entire history of industrial prefabrication is made up according to a scale of degrees of dimensional tolerance; they are correlated with the 'play' permitted by diverse types of assembled structures between their component elements. Knowledge about tolerances, added to knowledge about materials and to the calculations of constraints in proposable buildings form the very basis of the engineering expertise of engineers for both design and manufacture. Newly acquired mastery of an industrial product, for example cast iron, can be a stimulus to production. In 1826, Gérard-

Joseph Christian noted in *L'Industriel* that 'the mere replacement of wood and hand-worked metal by cast iron' must be counted as 'one of the principal causes of the remarkable changes brought about in the products of the art of building', in view of the 'great facility' made possible by 'the use of a very solid material, which almost invariably retains throughout its life the forms originally given it, and upon which one can have forged, at nominal expense, any design a composition might require, and even repeat these same forms, after a single model, as many times as one likes'.[14]

Steel building construction did indeed flourish in a radically new way, but manufacturing equipment was also totally transformed. Christian advocates the use of casting in the manufacture of 'machinery frames', which would thereby gain in stability and uniformity: precious advantages, to be sure, but ones that cannot be extended to the machining of most of the moving parts of a machine, and, *a fortiori*, to their

operators. Ease of movement, consistency, a capacity to continue operating normally when jolted, a certain delicacy in the handling of surfaces: all demanded attention to determine the morphological and physical characteristics of the instruments activated by the machine. One result was the creation of special kinds of steel, suited to various manoeuvres, whose hardness gives tools an appropriate leading edge as well as a controllable degree of wear and tear.

The phenomenon in question here is not so much a question of the invention of instruments of precision mechanics than its spread to industry through the machine tool. From the beginning of the 18th century, clock-making, the construction of scientific instruments, and the development of optics had given an impetus to knowledgeable craftsmen; the Conservatoire des Arts et Métiers has since displayed their marvellous works, above all their lathes, whose instrument-bearing plates were capable of ingenious decentrings. Marx

held the invention of the steam engine to be of only secondary importance: 'On the contrary, it was the creation of machine tools that made possible the revolutionized steam engine', that is to say a motor capable, in its function as a kind of 'centralized robot', of moving a number of distinct machines simultaneously.[15] In the wake of this development, it became inappropriate to refer to a set of machine tools all working together in a production system tending towards automatism in terms of 'manufacture'. So in 1867 the great engineer Franz Reuleaux put forward, in his *Offiziel Bericht uber die Pariser Weltausstellung* (*Official Report on the Paris Universal Exposition*), the neologism 'machinofacture'; he continued to support its use in his *Cinématique*, where he states that 'it is to machinofacture that we are indebted…for the spread of sewing machines' as well as for 'all manufactured products where it is a question of establishing a great many machines after a single model, or, at least, in accordance with a fairly limited number of

Far left: Diagram of ship's mast. Plate taken from Traité élémentaire de la mâture des vaisseaux pour les élèves de la Marine by Pierre Alexandre Forfait, 1788.

Woolf beam-engine. Plate taken from Études sur l'exposition de 1878, Annales et Archives de l'industrie au xixe siècle.

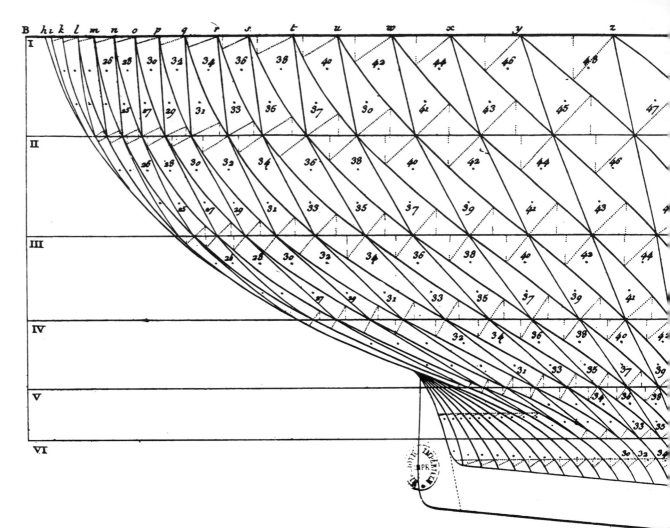

types'.[16] This was an acknowledgement of the success of the programme for standardization of 'systems of parts' called for, a generation earlier, by the artillery-specialists Migout and Bergery.

It is difficult for us today to comprehend the impact on the industrial economy of the possibility of producing, in large quantities, identical parts which you could be sure of being able to assemble wherever you were. All sorts of schemes resulted, including some which set a precedent for our present multinational corporations. The standards by which workers' skills were judged changed radically, and, of course, from a more general point of view the advances of what soon came to be denoted by the ambitious syntagma 'the scientific organization of work'.

It would be presumptuous to attempt to describe in a few pages, even in broad outline, the physiognomic changes brought about in the expanding network of production and consumption, whose activities, by turns increasing, declining and displaced, express the more polemical aspects of competition and changing commercial prospects, factors which influence formal innovation. Since our inquiry is more particularly focused on the factors affecting product aesthetics, we must return to the question of products and their relation to perceived value. One of the most powerful stimuli of customer appreciation is quality, and even robustness, evident in certain metal forms of structure. But this is already less visible in the masts assembled from many precisely-tooled elements (the ingenious assemblages of which were praised by Pierre Alexandre Forfait in his *Traité de la mâture*)[17] and which proved indispensable when a shortage of long northern logs deprived the imperial navy of its customary raw materials. Even more concealed from prying eyes are the linkages of components obtained by metal stamping, or, in more recent times, moulds by extrusion.

In all circumstances, a material dictates the forms into which it can be shaped and the way it is assembled. But in the realm of de-

sign aesthetics, we move very quickly from appreciating the quality of assemblage to passing judgement on a harmony between form and function supposedly embodied in the product. To put it another way, the connoisseur's gaze seeks out that beauty of 'fitness' designated and celebrated by Archibald Alison in his *Essays on the Nature and Principles of Taste*.[18] The speculations of Scottish philosophers on form, composition, and complexity have provided one of the most sure and solid roots for the term and the idea of 'design'. Symmetry and intricacy play a role in the definition of the beautiful so that, from the end of the 18th century, machines seen in operation became aesthetic objects.

To be sure, the spread of this sensibility was frequently met with sourness. In France, in particular, where an academic rigour, which

was turned into an inflexible doctrine by Quatremère de Quincy, long held sway; witness his disapproval of any aesthetic response to industrial products: 'Man...gives being to the objects he multiplies, by reproducing them, to satisfy society's needs'; such objects 'resemble one another, without, for all that, giving birth within us to the impression or the pleasure which, in imitation of the fine arts, results from the resemblances which it gives'. This passage is drawn from his *Essai sur la nature, les buts et les moyens de l'imitation* (*Essay on Nature, Ends and Means of Imitation*),[19] which appeared at a time when there was a marked interest in France in exhibitions of industrial products, which enjoyed considerable official support (one need only think of the heterogeneous display installed in the Louvre's 'Salon des Grands Hommes' in 1819). In truth, manu-

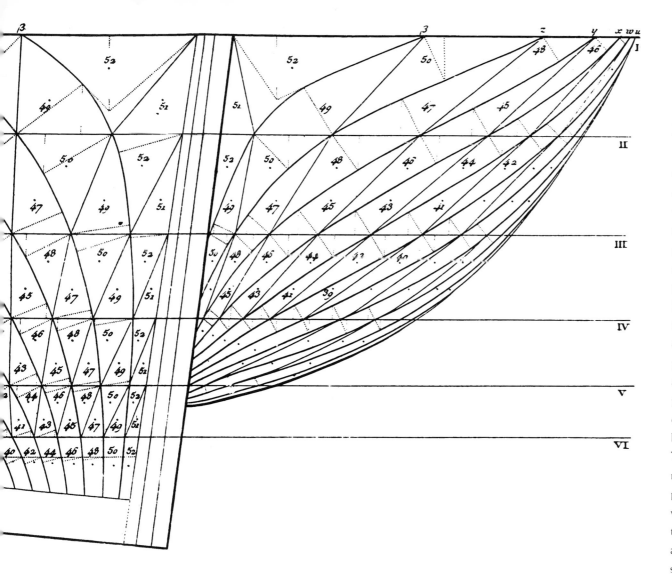

though it finally led to the establishment of the Musée des Arts Décoratifs, inspired in many respects by the Victoria and Albert Museum in London, founded by Richard Wallace. In the meantime, a Société de l'Art Industriel had been created in Paris, on Guichard's initiative. From this moment, differing views took shape over the question of just how widely the term 'industrial art' should be applied, with some holding it should be used exclusively to designate traditional crafts while others supported mass production. It was generally admitted that large-scale production was capable of invention, though some condemned it for contributing to 'the ignominiously shoddy pastiches introduced into the marketplace' and the 'deplorable imitations filling the display cases in Bon Marché and the [Magasin du] Louvre', which Joris-Karl Huysmans berated in 1886, with good reason.[21]

Thus, from competing exhibitions, to museum windows and department store displays, the manufactured object was everywhere on display, but the problem of continuity with craft objects, themselves not always marked by a taste for 'fine workmanship', remained unresolved. What is most striking about the enormous production of the 19th century, in France as well as in the other industrialized nations, is the considerable range of quality reflected in commercial articles. From this point on, the market tended to become stratified, reflecting a hierarchy of customers based on a divergence of tastes and financial means. But such an assertion must be qualified somewhat. While no single taste can be ascribed to the dominant class, the contours of which evolved, it is also true that the equivocal effects of philanthropy must be taken into account. 'The political and Christian idea of a public exhibition of those products necessary or useful for the simplest domestic life' was celebrated in 1858 by the marquis de Bausset-Roquefort, who was, like many others, anxious to 'moralize' the working class. While 'the bringing together of the masterpieces of industry of all peoples

facturers who exhibited in hopes of winning a medal were reaping, under the Restoration, the fruits of initiatives first sponsored by previous governments; this is documented in a large body of literature, the rhetorical double of the growing number of requests for patents for inventions and improvements.

Despite, or because of, economic crises periodically having an adverse effect on business and living conditions up until the Second Empire, government encouraged competition between industrialists. The temporary exhibitions intensified their competitive spirit; it wasn't long before a group of established industrialists sought a permanent forum for the celebration of their products. An initial idea was put forward by Auguste-François Silvestre in his *Essai sur les moyens de perfectionner les arts économiques* (Essay

on the Means of Perfecting the Economic Arts). He called for the creation of an 'Economic Museum' which would contain 'the series of diverse forms assumed by all natural productions prior to their being used in the arts and delivered over to commerce'.[20] A quarter of a century later, Rey, in his *Annales mensuelles de l'Industrie*, pleaded the necessity of constructing 'a building specially devoted to general exhibitions of the products of industry'; in his view, this would be a 'kind of sanctuary' bearing witness to the 'exalted rank' occupied by manufacturers 'in the public esteem'. An abandoned hôtel on the Quai d'Orsay seemed to him admirably designed for this purpose, and the idea became reality when the decree of 28 January 1830 designated the site 'for the exhibition of the products of industry'. But this project was to have a complicated history,

Planking of a ship's hull. Plate taken from *Architectura Navalis mercatoria* by E. Chapmann, pl. XVII, Stockholm, 1775.

Ammunition. Extract from the *Catalogue de la Manufacture française d'armes et de cycles de Saint-Étienne*, 1903.

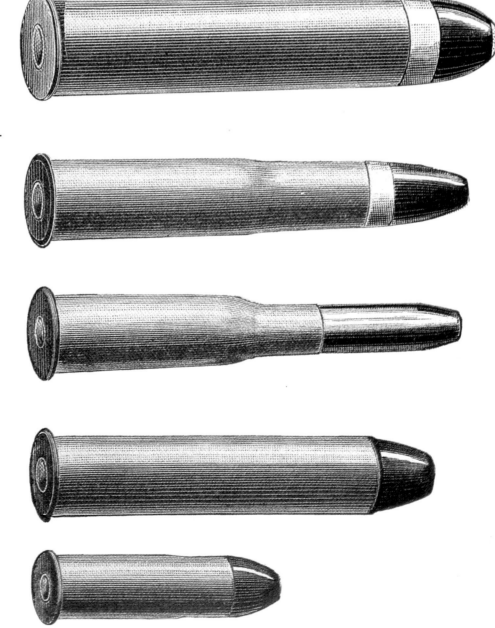

was not a project designed to save money', the quality/price criterion figured in the judgements of that class which the jury felt looked for 'the greatest utility, high quality, and the lowest possible price'. The article welcomed virtuous projects. Also the *Note sur la galerie de l'Economie domestique* expressed the desire that 'each nation [should] create a permanent museum of prototypes offering a guarantee of quality, with an indication of prices and retail outlets', with a view to 'improving the material conditions of the poor'.

A century elapses: the *économie domestique* (domestic economy) gives way to the *arts ménagers* (domestic science), which henceforth had their own annual Salon, even their own pavilion in international exhibitions. A part of the moral programme of the marquis de Bausset-Roquefort had been realized: the more secure members of the working class had gained the status and the access to consumerism previously restricted to the middle class, a development which deprived the project for a 'permanent museum of prototypes' of its innocence... In approaching a popular clientele, the industries producing household products created a market tainted with the constraints and turpitude common to all other markets. Subject to the rumours and seductions of advertising and fashion, to say nothing of 'incorporated obsolescence',[22] the production of household appliances was marked, starting in 1925, by the arrival of 'designers', principally in America. Far from the display cases, there emerged a 'scientific' organization of assembly line procedures and mass production rationales, all of which was subordinate to choices made by specialists in the stimulation of desire, haughty 'iconocrats' masterminding the domination of a given set of stylistic markers in the realm of fashion.[23]

Thus prior to the forties a gap opened – never to be closed – between the design of production tools, synonymous with technological rationality, and the design of products, which involves, to varying degrees, the requirements of stylization. The delicious and irrational streamlining of the thirties still offers specimens of the fanciful conjunction of 'art' and 'function'... And this same period saw the complicity of two technical fields in the enterprise of designating everyday products: the art of formal modelling, which aims to give expression to the modernity of the moment; and the arts of economical manufacture and distribution.

In both cases – giving form to a prototype, and its industrialization – it is a question of devising satisfactory solutions to problems that were impossible to formulate fully. Acknowledgement of this confusion opened the way towards a 'scientific' approach to design which was intended to replace the intuitive, 'artistic' approach of the American pre-war generation, though without going so far as to embrace the functionalist 'scientism' of the Russian Constructivist school whose members, both famous and unknown, strove very hard to 'calculate' the minimum 'dimensions' of socialist comfort. A reasoned prudence was displacing the determined quest for the optimum, as the wise Nobel prize-winning author Herbert A. Simon has pointed out.[24] This

goal of calculated sufficiency fostered the emergence of the tempered functionalism which has since become the general rule in most industrial projects.

None the less, it is perhaps worthwhile for us to question the possibly pathological character of an industrialism dominated by the dogma of growth, so beloved of financial technocrats in their hazardous manipulations of budget deficits. More generally, from a phenomenological point of view, how can we fail to see that an abundance of objects available for consumption changes the tone and values of a society? Jean Baudrillard expressed this well in his *Système des objets*: 'Previously, it was man who imposed his rhythm on objects; today, it is objects which impose their discontinuous rhythms on men, their discontinuous and sudden way of being there, of breaking down or of replacing one another without aging'; hence the theorem: 'The status of an entire civilization changes...with the mode of presence of its everyday objects and the nature of the pleasure derived from them'.[25] If we wanted to seek out a technological cause behind this characteristic of our society, already perceived and criticized by thinkers as diverse as Oswald

Spengler, Paul Valéry, J. Lafitte, and André Leroi-Gourhan, we might do well to examine the economy of labour resulting from the automation of assembly lines, with its considerable impact on the way we see work, leading to the dissolution of those virtues attributed to thrift by an over-prudent middle class.

If we allow ourselves to free-associate, we can 'see' very clearly that 'streamlining', which coincided with a period of grave social crisis, was perfectly suited to colour the fragility of fortunes and the instability of enterprises. Does this mean that an emblematic morphology of a quasi-catastrophic period is sufficient to account for the intrinsic duplicity of 'design', fixated on the 'uselessly' expensive appearances of products sold for their 'utility'? Alternatively, as suggested by Alain Findeli, could we not draw comfort from a more optimistic analysis, acknowledging that at least industrial design performs the salutary task of softening the blow of technological change on the social body?[26] But wouldn't this then oblige us to view rapid design change not as the ploys of amoral prop men, but rather as the fortunate result of responsible hygienist leadership?

Section of the Idéal hunting rifle without hammer with two shots and centre fire, made by the Manufacture française d'armes de Saint-Étienne. Extract from the 1891-1892 catalogue.

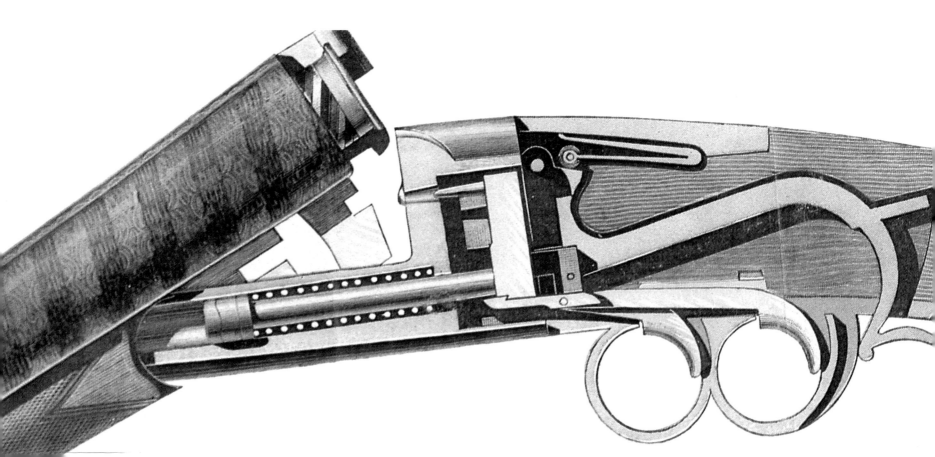

The Singer sewing machine

The first practical sewing machine was invented by the Frenchman Barthélemy Thimonnier in 1830. His design had all the features found on today's sewing machines. Fifteen years later, Thimonnier applied for a second patent for a machine capable of two hundred stitches a minute and in 1848 he developed a metal machine which could do chain stitches. In parallel with these developments in France, the American Walter Hunt designed a machine with two threads and a shuttle in 1834. In 1846, Elias Howe replaced the shuttle's hook by a needle with an eye in it and the invention of the sewing machine was complete.

In 1851, at the Great Exhibition in London, due to an extraordinary piece of bad luck, Thimonnier's machine reached the stand two days late. The prizes had already been awarded by the jury to Isaac Singer who, as a result, became much more famous than Thimonnier. That same year, Singer produced the first domestic sewing machine. The needle used was an exact copy of the one invented by his compatriot Elias Howe, another brilliant inventor, who, like Thimonnier, died ruined. Two years before his death, Thimonnier did have the consolation of finally presenting his machine at the Universal Exposition in Paris, but the general public had already chosen Singer's sewing machine. The success of Singer's machine was more due to commercial skill than his talent as an engineer. Today, it is recognized that the invention of the sewing machine was due to Elias Howe and Barthélemy Thimonnier.

There were many stories similar to this one in America and Europe at the end of the 19th century: it was no longer enough to be a brilliant inventor, as it was at the beginning of the Industrial Revolution. It was also necessary to take account of the new principals of the economic market. The use of publicity and advertising presaged marketing. Isaac Singer was one of the first industrialists to propose sale by credit to his clients. The system of payment in several monthly instalments revolutionized the purchasing of mechanical objects by the American middle class. It was so successful that the Singer, millions of which were manufactured, flooded the European market.

In around 1890, at one of the Singer factories in New Jersey, the workshops were turning out 1,500 machines every day. The journal La Nature wrote in 1892: 'They are making two and a half machines every minute, the working day being ten hours long. Supposing that there are 300 working days per year, this factory therefore produces 450,000 sewing machines in a year, and the company which owns it possesses a large number of other establishments.'

E. M.

Samuel Colt's revolver

There are several reasons why Samuel Colt's revolver is one of the most significant devices to have appeared during the Industrial Revolution. Marking the functional adaptation of the six-charge handgun, it had the advantage of using a single barrel and a turning breech holding several charges. It was patented in 1835. The first revolvers, manufactured between 1836 and 1845, were part hand-operated and part mechanical; they were used successfully in the Florida Indian War.

From 1847, Samuel Colt decided to standardize his production and turned to machine tools. He engaged talented engineers, such as Elisha K. Roth, who oversaw implementation of the project, including design, organization and setting up of the new factory. Roth installed one thousand four hundred machine tools, some of which were designed by himself. He conceived, for example, a machine to trim the components, an intricate operation that had previously been done by hand. All the revolver's pieces were manufactured separately and were made to be interchangeable.

The mass production process developed by Samuel Colt allowed for continuous refinement and adjustment. In 1847, he introduced the 44 calibre Walker Colt and in 1848 the Dragoon Colt, which became the first regulation revolver of the American army. Toward 1860, the Colt facilities emerged as the most important, most advanced arms factory in the world. In 1935, many of the original machines, having been well maintained, were still functioning perfectly.

After the death of Samuel Colt in 1862, the success of his enterprise was assured. The Peacemaker and Frontier Colts, which sold in large quantities from 1873, are still available today in versions that have been only slightly improved. It was with a Peacemaker that Sheriff Pat Garrett shot Billy the Kid in 1881 – the Colt revolver is also the preferred weapon for characters in westerns and mysteries.

Finally, it was the Colt revolver that inaugurated the principle of distinctive, personalized product lines. It was possible to obtain all kinds of models, with short or long barrel, decorated with damascene or other incrustations on the metal parts. Certain models were veritable works of art sold in boxes made of precious woods.

J. d. N.

Left: Colt single action 44 calibre pistol, c.1880.

Vignette: Dragoon Colt, c.1880.

The standard metre

From the end of the 17th century, a period which saw important scientific discoveries, and this when men of science still called themselves 'philosophers', the idea of universal standard measurements began to receive attention: the advent of electricity, magnetism, steam power and the development of manufacturing made it increasingly apparent that there was a need for such standards of measurement. But it would take an important event to overcome the inertia of established usages: the French Revolution.

Mechanization of the system of production, permitting the mass production of objects, could only proceed with the aid of precise instruments of measurement. It was for this reason that metrology, whenever possible, was based on universal standards.

It was the French Academy of Sciences that decided, in 1792, to adopt a definition specifying that a metre equalled one ten-millionth of a quarter of the earth's meridian running from the North Pole to the Equator. Two astronomers, Méchain and Delambre, were charged with calculating as precisely as possible the length of the metre using the meridian arc stretching from Dunkirk to Barcelona as the basis for their calculations.

In 1796, the Convention decreed that 16 standard metres in marble be placed in highly frequented places throughout Paris. Two of these can still be seen today: the first is to the right of the entrance of number 36, rue de Vaugirard; the second is at number 13 in the Place Vendôme, to the left of the entrance to the Ministry of Justice.

It wasn't until 1889 that the famous standard metre in iridium was deposited in the Breteuil pavilion in Sèvres. Today, this platinum metre is a relic and the standard is established in reference to the distance travelled by light in a billionth of a second.

In 1989, during a ceremony commemorating the establishment of standard measurements on the occasion of the bicentenary of the Revolution, it was verified that the standard metre measures, with a margin of error of half a millimetre, 1.002 metres.

Marcel Duchamp was perfectly aware of the symbolic importance of this universal measurement standard. That is why he took the first step towards conceptual art with his three 'stoppage-étalons' in a croquet box, thus drawing attention to the singularity of the artist in relation to the universalist pretentions of science and technology.

J. d. N.

The typewriter

The wooden prototype of the first viable typewriter resulted from the joint research of Christopher Latham Sholes and Joseph Farwell Glidden. Collaborating in a Milwaukee workshop, they developed a machine that numbered the pages of books.

It was Glidden who first became interested in the possibility of adapting their invention into a machine that could print letters. With the help of the printer Samuel Soule, Sholes and Glidden succeeded in making a prototype in 1872.

A first handmade machine was produced with the aid of two financiers, James Densmore and George Washington Newton Yost. On 1 March 1873, Sholes and Densmore signed a contract to mass produce an efficient version of the machine. It was only in 1876 that the machine, fitted out with metallic characters, was baptized the Remington No. 1. Its initial sale price was $125.

Success was long in coming; early sales figures remained at less than a thousand per year. It might be worth noting that Mark Twain was among the first to purchase a Remington, seduced by publicity claiming it was possible to type 57 words a minute. The main reason they sold so badly at first was the poor quality of the aniline inks then available.

The first machine capable of writing in lower case as well as capital letters was the Remington No. 2, which became available in 1878.

In 1885, when it became possible to manufacture permanent ink ribbons, sales increased. But prior to 1890 there were less than 60,000 typewriters in use in the United States.

It was only in 1902 that the first electric typewriter appeared and it functioned according to the same principle as the later IBM golfball model, in which typographic characters are engraved in relief on a plastic sphere.

At the end of his life, Sholes felt that his invention had led to the production of the first machine to further the emancipation of women. In a report to the French workers' delegation to the Chicago World's Fair of 1893, he wrote: 'To qualify as a "type-writer", one must have two essential qualities: one must be able to write quickly, and one must know stenography, but the occupation is well paid and almost exclusively reserved for women.'

Despite their subsequent ubiquity, typewriters did not immediately catch on in offices; they were first used to transcribe speech to the written page.

It was in the 1950s that designers first became interested in typewriters. In Italy, Olivetti commissioned Marcello Nizzoli to design, successively, the Lexicon 80 (1948) and the Lettera 22 (1954). Beginning in 1959, Ettore Sottsass Jr., continued in his footsteps. In the United States, IBM's typewriters were designed by Eliot Noyes.

Finally, mention should be made of the services rendered the blind by these new machines. Issue 114 of the magazine Cosmos (2 April 1887) reported the following remarks made by a lawyer in the appeals' court: 'Having gone blind some months ago, I found in the typewriter a means of keeping up with my friends without need of a secretary, and I am indebted to it as the most powerful distraction in my life as an invalid. After several weeks I was able to use it all by myself, and now I write rather quickly and much more legibly than in the past; I can thus maintain a correspondence with both friends and colleagues; I don't think Mr Remington was thinking of the blind when he invented his excellent machine, but he undoubtedly rendered them a great service, and I consider him to be one of the benefactors of these unfortunates'.

J. d. N.

Remington No. 1, 1876.

Vignette: Remington typewriter. Engraving from *La Nature*, 1877.

Right-hand page: Atget, *Photograph of interior belonging to M. B., collector, rue de Vaugirard, 1910.*

This page, main picture: Atget, *Photograph of interior belonging to M. R., dramatic artist, rue Vavin, 1910.*

Right, top to bottom: Baccarat crystal candelabrum (over 16ft high).

Aviary, designed by M. Cornu, exhibited at the Universal Exposition, Paris, 1855.

Sideboard, carved by Liénard, exhibited at the Great Exhibition in London, 1851.

Louis XVI book-case, exhibited at the Universal Exposition, Paris, 1855.

Illustrations taken from the *Dictionnaire des arts et manufactures* by Charles Laboulaye, Paris, 1868.

Abolish

Profusion and Confusion in

Bric-à-brac

19th-century Industrial Art

Michel Vernes

For Joëlle Letessier

The history of 19th-century urban dwellings is that of a progressive intensification of pain and pleasure. In an expanding world, the middle-class man created for himself a home with no boundaries, more internalized than any dream. Closed in on himself and his family, his home became an extension of his conscience. What the home environment lost in simplicity it gained in romanticism. The ideal of comfort, imported from England in the romantic era, favoured well-being while stirring up the passions of the soul. Convinced that he was different from other people, the middle-class man surrounded himself with quantities of personal objects he believed to be unique, whereas in fact they had been manufactured in bulk for people like himself.

Abundantly furnished, such homes offended common sense even as they sacrificed at the altar of the most rigid conventions. It soon became impossible to distinguish amid their furniture between what was useful and what was fantasmagorical. The often precarious state of the fittings, the frequent replacement of furniture,[1] and the growing ascendancy of memory, which prompted the purchase of all sorts of fashionable 'antiques', only added to the confusion. Movable decorative elements, multiplied by industry and enriched by a multitude of stereotypical objects, helped obscure architectural irregularities and simulated a universe apart. The accessory became essential and architectural *bors-d'oeuvres*, initially intended only to temper the severity of the architecture, gradually took its place. Framing elements which were supposed to link architecture and furnishings became fake. On top of all this, there was a confusion of styles. Having been inadequately trained, decorators committed unknowing heresies. Sculptors, ornamentalists, upholsterers, metalworkers, jewellers and workers in mosaic did not always have a very clear idea about the different styles. As a result, flats were invaded by 'hybrid, unwholesome products without precise signification, without unity, without harmony, which rightly offend the taste of true amateurs'.[2] This state of affairs would continue until the eve of the 20th century. 'Look in detail at our interiors', wrote Henry Havard in 1890, 'everywhere you'll find the most curious mixture of ideas of every conceivable origin, ornaments in every conceivable style, inspirations drawn from every period.'[3] In vain, he reminded readers that the decoration of a room should be of a piece with its architecture. Irresistibly, fluctuating tastes transformed this decoration into a picturesque, sentimental reverie. In salons, nothing accurately matched anything else: they were fitted out with 'everything that might charm the most various, the most delicate tastes'.[4] Having become veritable *cabinets de curiosité*, they were counterparts to the Street of Nations and the History of Human Dwellings, attractions at the Universal Exposition of 1889 which announced a triumphant eclecticism. Their contents also mirrored the architectural eclecticism characteristic of the new neighbourhoods to the west of Paris, where the medieval castle rubbed shoulders with a Renaissance palace and a house in a vague Louis XIV style.

Frequently, heterogeneous designs were crammed onto a single piece of furniture. At the Universal Exposition of 1855, a monumental sideboard was laden with historical and symbolic figures of all sizes, from life-size to minuscule. The sculptor Auguste Poitevin squeezed into a single one of its panels 500 figures in a round lump representing 'all the celebrated great men from the dawn of time to the 18th century: philosophers, mathematicians, legislators, prophets, historians, commentators, philologists, poets, alchemists, inventors and doctors'.

In his essay 'The Modern Idea of Progress Applied to the Fine Arts', written in 1855, Charles Baudelaire indicted the sworn professors who had decreed the rules of the 'philosophic art' then reigning unchallenged in the field of decoration. He said that if these rules continued to prevail beauty itself could disappear, 'because all types, all ideas, all sensations would merge into a vast unity, monotonous and impersonal, immense as boredom and the void. Variety, the condition *sine qua non* of life, would be expunged from life'.

The universal expositions provoked in each visitor 'a duel between the determination to see everything and forget nothing, and the memory faculty, which has become accustomed to enthusiastically taking in general colour and shape'. At the Universal Exposition of 1855, works by Dominique Ingres and Eugène Delacroix testified to these two dispositions: to either see what is new in the world, or list all its riches. The honesty of line in their paintings contained form and recorded information, while the flashing colours spoke of the movements of life and its transitory beauty. When they recounted the history of mankind in ebony, bronze or silver, the industrial arts embraced the discipline of line, with an aim that was both pedagogic and speculative. Like the universal expositions in which they were accorded such prominence, these arts broke up and formed a thesaurus of the beauty of the world without being genuinely affected by it. Their masterpieces were displayed as so many compendia and catalogues, as inexhaustible reservoirs of theories and allegories. By their excess they satisfied the enterprising middle-class person's demand for minutiae and universality.

As such, they participated in the project, typical of 19th-century European culture, to draft an intellectual map of time and space. 'The true French worker is the art worker, and, it has to be said, whatever his faults, he is the Parisian worker', wrote the economist Adolphe Blanqui on returning from the Great Exhibition of 1851 in London. Like his predecessors, in the capital he acquires the taste and skill necessary to realize these structures of knowledge – the pompous items of furniture and large centrepieces. The teaching of draughtsmanship instilled a sense of detail, allowing him to exploit every possibility suggested by the designs in ornamental pattern books.

The persistance of the true nourished the progress of the false. The creations of the period in metal and wood, which, some claimed, bore comparison with works of the Renaissance, provided industry with ennobling models. Thus an aesthetic legitimized by historical knowledge managed to thrive right through the Industrial Revolution.[5] Despite new processes of multiplication and reduction, substitute materials, evolution and the temptation of increased profits, there was no dethroning it. To artists asserting that 'the arts become decadent as a direct result of their extension', Léon de Laborde responded in 1856 by saying that by becoming 'generally available to all, the culture of the arts will bring the producer and the consumer together'.[6] Respectful of the hierarchy established by the Royal Academies, he advised industrialists to commission models from artists rather than from 'mere practitioners without initiative or ideas'. While the polytechnician Charles Laboulaye, for his part, admitted that 'industrially reproduced sculpture ceases to belong to the fine arts proper', he went on to add that it still retained the beauty of the original. Only reduction in size diminished its quality, but this was an inevitable consequence of 'its exploitation as isolated decoration or industrially produced ornament'.[7]

When Edouard Didron ascribed responsibility for the 'decadence of industrial applications of art' to the division of labour and over-production, it was to bemoan the loss of liberty in artistic practice. And, while admitting that 'we must live in a way reasonably consistent with modern society', he lamented the fact that 'our artisans are not as creative as their predecessors',[8] and that 'the sense of the true and the beautiful' seemed to have disappeared even from the most privileged.

By permitting their industrial replication and multiplication, art was democratized. Fine furniture exercised a considerable influence over the designers of more affordable commodities, such as those in the 'articles de Paris' series. To use language employed by Philippe Burty, we might say that 'a certain cachet of pure and distinguished origins'[9] trickled down to even the meanest emblems of middle-class prosperity. 'Imitation metalwork', which used metal plate, nickel silver, and silver-plating, commenced its conquest of lower middle-class households under the Second Empire. Likewise, the more prosperous sections of the middle class were learning from specialized publications and museums to love relics of the past. When assembled into collections in their salons, such relics enhanced their prestige and bore witness to their culture. Their success gave birth to the curio market, which in turn generated a bric-à-brac industry. Old art diffused in this way provided the most recent arrivals into urban society with signs of their integration. That said, the cultural capital of the nobility and the upper middle class 'functions as a kind of advance (in the double sense of an initial advantage and a financial credit) which, by providing an initial example of a culture realized after familiar models, allows the newcomer [to high society] to begin, in the least conscious, least self-aware way possible, to acquire the basic elements of legitimate culture – and to minimize the work of deculturation, reformation and correction necessary to rectify the

effect of an improper apprenticeship'.[10] The development of archaeological knowledge brought with it a progressive slackening of the rules governing the decorative arts. The result was eclecticism, an empirical way of assimilating the most diverse styles, of combining them, then fusing them. In 1830, Du Sommerard, founder of the Musée de Cluny, 'restored' a spinet with fragments from various pieces of furniture in order, he said, to 'bring it into harmony with the sculpted ebony furniture in his old salon'.[11] This piece, a model of academic impurity and a protoype for the industrialized curio, inspired novel associations. A half-century later, an entrepreneur did not hesitate to dismantle a Renaissance chateau in order to sell its various elements. The chateau at Montal, in the Lot region, was transported to Paris stone by stone. 'Its venerable remains, windows, fireplaces, medallions, friezes, gables etc. were dispersed under the auctioneer's hammer on 31 April 1881,' recounts the architect Ernest Bosc, who recalled a particular dormer window 'sold for 15,000 francs to M. Edmond Foule, who used it as a door in the town house he has just had built at the Trocadéro'.[12] Less wealthy owners decorated the walls of their rooms with prefabricated elements that were just as anomolous.

Decorators engaged in a maze of ever more daring aesthetic experiences. Whether artistic or sentimental, interiors became totally chaotic despite a recall to order issued by the 'grammarians' of domestic furnishings. Some handbooks prescribing what was and was not acceptable flattered the snobism of *nouveaux riches* by proposing they adopt a mode of existence that was both bohemian and aristocratic. The baron de Mortemart-Boisse cited the example of the 'retreat' belonging to the comte d'Orsay, a garret that the celebrated dandy had transformed into a 'pavilion from the thousand and one nights' under the July Monarchy. He 'began by amassing pell-mell a quantity of marbles, bronzes, plasters, canvases, drawings, books, statuettes, arms and curiosities of every variety. Then a fairy's wand, perhaps, transformed this chaos into an encampment worthy of a prince. Then this encampment became a bedroom, a salon, a gallery, a temple, the whole adorned with the name studio.'[13] There follows a detailed description of the collection of rare objects and the account of the transformation of the 'hall' into a 'palais à la Sommerard'. This studio-palace, a model of architecture prized by wealthy bachelors and unfaithful husbands, had a middle-class equivalent in the 'young man's apartment', which Gustave Flaubert characterized as being 'in constant disorder, with feminine trinkets scattered about and an odour of cigarettes. One must find extraordinary things there.'[14]

During the Second Empire, the boudoir was a similar, if watered down, version of the same thing for high society women. That of Mme de la Panouse was famous for her collection of Saxon porcelains, which included chandeliers, clocks, small tables and mirrors. The *petits salons* of the Third Republic were just as encumbered. Less playful because more middle class, they were filled with those 'elements of vain sumptuousness that industrial art, in its innumerable branches, prodigally placed at the disposition of modern society'.[15] The knick-knacks business set about reproducing authentic souvenirs within the reach of everyone.

In the final decades of the century, the middle-class mind recognized itself as much in the proliferation of bric-à-brac as in the extent of its conquests. It sometimes seemed to become conscious of its excessive interiority. In such moments it sensed that the possession of too many things paralyzed it, that in its desire to possess everything, it ended up being possessed by things. Futility, if allowed to luxuriate, can lead to more distant interiors such as exile or revolt. In *A Rebours* (Against the Grain), Joris-Karl Huysmans posits a correspondence between inner space, that of dreams and abode combined, and outer space, that of travel and conquest. His hero, the chevalier des Esseintes, creates in his home an interior landscape that procures 'the rapid, almost instantaneous sensations of an ocean voyage, and the pleasure of being in transit that exists, in the end, only in memory and almost never in the present, when it's actually happening'.[16] The correspondence between the physical interior and the ethical interior fulfils a need for comfort which is tainted with fetishism. Inhabitants and bric-à-brac can exchange confidences. 'Furnishings are our friends. Works of art are extensions of us. When I was near them my personality was ennobled', noted Cécil Sorel. 'All of this was a representation of myself. It was as though I rediscovered my previous existences in it.'[17]

At one time they were children's toys, but in the second half of the 19th century knick-knacks evolved into objects for display and women's trinkets. Baubles whose only value was sentimental, they prolifer-

ated in corners and bedrooms. Henri de Noussanne recommended that in the corner of the salon there be placed 'a fantasy room[18] containing a few curious knick-knacks: Japanese ivories, jades, Chinese quartzes, an Ibis lamp with a multi-coloured Tonkinese shade on which brilliant pearls sparkle, and a small table covered in old material with a book rack, an ivory or old silver letter opener and a graceful vase from which a branch of orchids spreads its bizarrely elegant blooms'.[19] A kind of surrogate boudoir, this haven behind an oriental screen provided asylum for whispered confidences. A few furtive memories, a bamboo settee and two or three ingeniously-placed cushions were sufficient to reassure the indecisive and mobilize the intimate. A carefully chosen obstacle and a selective violation of the prevailing order mark the exit from the official stage dominated by man and entry to the wings, where affectation was no longer necessary.

At the heart of her house on the rue Trudon, the celebrated actress Rachel conceived a mysterious retreat closed off by tapestries and hangings. She called it her 'parlour' or 'little waiting room', reserving it for her most intimate friends. On an ebony table were daggers 'not one of which was classic in form'. Within another sanctuary, behind partitions covered with crimson Andrinople cotton, an effeminate young man, des Esseintes, gave free reign to his unavowable sufferings. 'Frightful prints illustrating all the tortures invented by the madness of religion, prints from which the spectacle of suffering screamed out,'[20] decorated his solitude and intensified it. In its rigorous confinement, the boudoir became a clandestine space well suited to aesthetic transgression. Generally speaking, the 1880s witnessed a fusion of erudite memory and feeling. Unstable and multiform, beauty became a stranger to itself. Salons became filled with exotic objects that challenged the 'customary mental tone'. Egotism seemed to order this evolution,

Left: A living-room, 1919.

Right: Interior, c.1900.

with its insatiable appetite for the singular. 'In augmenting our faculty to perceive diversity, are we shrinking our personalities or enriching them? Are we depriving them of something or making them more various? There can be no doubt: we are abundantly enriching them with the whole universe,'[21] asked and replied Victor Segalen at the beginning of the next century.

Between the grand salon where one cultivated one's appearance and the small one where one cultivated one's originality, there is a kind of masking relationship that also applies to the relationship between pompous pieces of furniture, symbols of social legitimacy, and knick-knacks, signs of individualism. The impossible boldness of these last resulted from their role as accessories. In so far as they derived from architecture and large furniture, they retained something of the latter's authority and immutable beauty. While this profusion, a result of the vertiginous course on which art and industry had embarked, brought confusion to the point of fusion necessary for the renewal of design, it also determined a lasting malaise by weakening the authority of architecture, the very figure of universal order and a body of moral prescription. Along with Emile Guichard, a number of architects and decorators wondered, in the middle of the century, how they might 'change the prevailing discord into harmony'.[22]

By returning to those principles that guaranteed the architectural coherence of interiors prior to the Industrial Revolution, replied scholars. Periodically, it was proposed that the teaching of drawing should be strengthened and the number of museums, whose superior authority would be recognized by everyone, increased. 'Study of the older arts, which were practised in accordance with a rational method, is the only thing that can once more instill in us the habit of using, first and foremost, the dose of reason with which nature has supplied us,' wrote Eugène Viollet-le-Duc, who called for the establishment of a museum of sculpture. The memorizing of ornaments could thus progress without necessarily meaning that they were understood any better. What commonly prevailed was 'education through the eyes' with the help of directories and museological catalogues. Their abundant iconography aided the development of industrial art while sowing confusion in the mind. The prodigality of eclecticism, its bold juxtapositions shook the most solid aesthetic convictions. And, finally, the capriciousness of industrial imitations gave birth to a

the art book amplified it by unwittingly encouraging craftsmen to mix their borrowings. 'Conservators of the basics of good architecture,' acknowledged Viollet-leDuc, 'view with dismay the invasion of documents gathered from everywhere, the evils of archaeology.'[24]

Maintaining that 'numerous heresies have become standard in the contemporary idiom',[25] the partisans of a legislating aesthetic published, after 1860, a mass of dictionaries and grammars for the use of inter-

surfaces and the way the decoration has been executed. Upholsterers and decorators applied these visual formulas, which authorized the accumulation of as many objects in a room as possible without compromising its welcoming character.

The need for restraint was the dominant note in all the propositions of the academic Charles Blanc. Believing that architecture 'generated' its decoration, he wanted the latter to reflect the former. To check the increasing insubordination of household

'cosmopolitan and restrospective taste' consistent with the conquering spirit of the 19th century. Though lacking in logic and intelligence, the syncretism of decorators favoured industrial expansion by diversifying markets. Before long, informed curiosity turned into covetousness. Shop windows came to seem like extensions of archaeological cabinets, and manufacturers' catalogues increasingly resembled those of museums. 'Since industry, by lowering the price of all objects of basic necessity, has accustomed everyone to well-being and interior comfort, the multiplication of works of art of all kinds has itself become an industry of the first order,' concluded the engineer Oppermann.[23]

Far from slowing down this movement,

ior design professionals. For 'without art, in other words without adherence to the rules containing it and without the taste that directs it, luxury is but a nameless thing, a pitiless effect of vanity'.[26] These books taught them how to impose form on the inflationary domestic universe, how to contain its excesses. Towards the end of the century, the proliferation of rooms, furniture, drawers, boxes and shelving facilitated the collection and display of an inexhaustible harvest of bagatelles. Henry Havard, Charles Blanc and a few others set down conventions governing the exact relationship between a decorative scheme's general arrangement and the proportions of objects or decorative surfaces, between the nature and intended purpose of these objects or

furnishings, he wanted them put in the right position, with 'each one occupying the place assigned it by the division of walls and partitions'. Diversity would be integrated by softening the harmonies. Reliefs of all kinds were to be reduced. The idiosyncratic was to disappear.

When respect brings together the rules of architecture and the rules of civility and when ornaments are restored to their primary source and society to its innermost essence and is all of a piece, the interior finally follows the same law and its occupants become indistinct. That is when, wrote Marcel Proust, 'only imagination and belief are capable of differentiating certain objects, certain beings from others to create an atmosphere'.[27]

Comfort

Roger-Henri Guerrand

T he word 'comfort' apparently derives from ecclesiastical Latin of the first centuries of the Christian era. It comes from *confortare*, which means 'to consolidate, to reinforce, to fortify'. This first usage prevailed throughout the Middle Ages, when corporal pleasures were renounced in the valley of tears preceding the entry into Paradise. Medieval man had no concept at all of what we would regard as minimum comfort today with regard to either the urban (streets and buildings) or the domestic environment (furnishings, with the exception of bedding). This poverty contrasts starkly with the rich clothing of the period, some of which was so extraordinarily refined that it is tempting to see it as a form of compensation.

In the course of the 16th century, which was marked by the advent of capitalism and a secure middle class, certain items of furniture were introduced that would prove to be long lived. They included the fixed table, the wardrobe and the cabinet. In the 17th century the first armchairs appeared, but the general spirit of the period remained that of previous centuries. Jansenism, which gained

many adherents among the provincial clergy and bourgeoisie, rejected the material comforts of life, with the notable exception of the commode, which was much easier to use than the chamber pot and became widespread among the more prosperous classes under the reign of Louis XIV. In this context, the term 'comfort' retained its original meaning of 'assistance', as is evidenced by the *Dictionnaire universel* published by Antoine Furetière (1690), a knowledgeable observer of the social life of his time.

At the beginning of the century of the Enlightenment, or, to use Talleyrand's phrase, the century of the *douceur de vivre*

(the easy life), the urban landscape boasted no more amenities than it had in the past, apart from a small number of prestige projects such as royal squares, and even these were a continuation of urban forms inherited from the Middle Ages. A certain decline in the architectural *grand genre* was making itself felt and there was a mounting desire for intimacy which was reflected in a growing taste for small living spaces (Louis XV was especially fond of them).

In furniture, the chest of drawers became ubiquitous. Entire families of chairs and movable furniture appeared; the sofa became an obligatory feature for every living room. In the matter of hygiene, the introduction of the English W.C. with its flushing system, complemented by the bidet (so appreciated by the French), marked a decisive advance. It would be more than a century, however, before these new conveniences became widespread in most European nations.

Well before 1789, the British adopted the term 'comfort' to designate everything to do with material and physical well-being. Chateaubriand and Balzac used the word in this sense, something confirmed admirably by Charles Nodier: 'This anglicism is a readily intelligible and even necessary addition to our language, in which there is no equivalent; this word expresses a state of ease and well-being similar to pleasure and to which all men aspire quite naturally, and which carries no implications of moral laxity or slackness.'[1]

Doubtless the librarian of the Arsenal was aware that the *Dictionnaire de l'Académie française* (1823 edition) endorsed only the long-established definition of *succour* or *assistance*. It did not even include the adjectival form *confortable*, though this became current before the French Revolution: as a noun, it meant an armchair. Obviously the 40 academicians were as yet unaware that industrial society, stimulated by scientific advances, from now on constantly demanded growing numbers of engineers and technicians who were unconcerned about the future.

The utopian socialists provided evidence of this new state of mind, especially Charles Fourier, theoretician of the Phalanstery, an innovative building providing unprecedented creature comforts for all the inhabitants, including central heating, hot and cold running water, large communal kitchen, and spaces for gatherings and leisure activities.[2] In the same period, the coal magnate Henry de Gorge, owner of the Grand Hornu mine near Mons and a precursor of those continental European industrialists who were to oversee the lodgings of their workers, made Fourier's dream a reality by building a set of pavilions intended to give his employees 'an unprecedented sense of well-being'.[3] In this era of the victorious middle class, was quotidian happiness on the verge of becoming available to everyone?

A time of cushions and frills

The dominant class began by rationalizing the spatial disposition of its living accommodation, organizing it according to function, in contrast to the confusion which had prevailed under the *ancien régime*. As regards interiors, since it was unwilling to develop a style of its own (the task of 'disenchanting' the world required all its energies), the middle class resorted to bric-a-brac, made up stylistically of a mixture of diverse periods and civilizations.

Renaissance dining rooms rubbed shoulders with Louis XVI bedrooms, while Moorish billiard rooms opened onto verandas 'in the Japanese style'. There was an overabundance of fabrics, wall-hangings, silks and carpets covering every square inch of unoccupied surface. The prestige of the upholsterer increased by leaps and bounds: this craftsman, the faithful interpreter of prevailing sexual restrictions, went so far as to mask the 'legs' of pianos. Lace-making was at its height, while fringes and tassels proliferated wildly. Adeline Daumard has put forward an interesting explanation for this curious attitude.[4] Throughout the 19th century, members of the middle class, especially in Paris, were terrified of popular uprisings. They sought to create welcoming, reassuring domestic environments: 'A symbolic division was effected between interior space (associated with security and the family) and exterior space (associated with the unknown and danger).' The refusal to allow any exposed wall or flooring such as was common in the dwellings of the poor became an obsession. An editor of *L'Illustration* – a magazine widely read by the middle class – offered the following description of these new interiors on 15 February 1851: 'We assemble in a salon whose windows are hermetically sealed by curtains, silk cushions, and lined drapes...There's a fine carpet under our feet...A profusion of material adorns the windows, covers the mantelpiece, obscures the woodwork. Cold marble and bare wood are hidden beneath velvet hangings.'

In 1885, 30 years later, Guy de Maupassant, in his novel *Bel-Ami*, describes the flat of the journalist Forestier in similar terms: 'The walls were covered with old fabric of faded violet, peppered with little flowers the size of flies. Door curtains of blue-grey cloth, military material on which red silk carnations had been embroidered, hung over the

Above: The show *Sex Appeal* 1932 at the Casino de Paris: 'The modern mistress of the house demonstrates the virtues of her new vacuum cleaner to the maid.'

Left: Electric hob and oven. Extract from *L'Art ménager*, 1931.

doors; the chairs of all shapes and sizes were scattered haphazardly through the room, reclining chairs, enormous armchairs, poufs and stools, were all covered in Louis XVI silk or fine Utrecht velvet with a garnet pattern on a cream background.'

This kind of voluptuous decor had already aroused the indignation of moralists. During the Second Empire, the famous Monseigneur Pie, Bishop of Poitiers and

Top: Revolving
kitchen, designed
by Ilana Henderson,
1968.

From left to right:
'A practical method
for home
laundering: The
lavatory-laundry
room for low-cost
housing – the
washtub also
serves as a
shower.' Extract
from *L'Art
ménager*, 1932.

Técalémit vacuum
cleaner, 1933.

'Tomorrow's
electric kitchen'.
Extract from *L'Art
ménager*, 1935.

champion of montanism, denounced 'this comfort which weakens character, which devours like a parasitic plant the life force of the soul, which stunts intelligence and concentrates one's whole being on the meticulous arrangement of the boudoir...on the thousand trivialities that today have come to be regarded as indispensable'.[5] The ecclesiastic then proceeded to pose his central question: who among us fails to sense a cer-

tain vulgarity in the act of surrendering oneself to a welcoming armchair? There can be no doubt about the diabolical character of comfort. Through it, we want to return to the paradise which existed before original sin. All aspirations of this kind are mortal sins: 'For comfort is for the glorious resurrection, not before. We must be parsimonious with comfort here on earth, we must jettison this burden so that the soul might live, so that

one day its joy might radiate from its transfigured flesh.' A role model is proposed for the faithful, namely Benoît Labre, who voluntarily lived in perpetual squalor: he was beatified in 1860 and the Catholic church used the moment of his sanctification to criticize, yet again, a century excessively preoccupied with 'utilitarianism and comfort'. Such statements suggest that the spirit of Port-Royal continued to inspire a segment of the French clergy; but Ernest Renan, who in this regard had embraced the views of his new social class, voiced identical sentiments when ranting against the 'imbecility' of women: 'Instead of spurring men on to great things, to challenging tasks, to heroic deeds, they require of him only riches, as a means of satisfying their vulgar taste for luxury. Petty household anxieties have thus been transformed into grave concerns and the tendencies prevailing in the world made to serve the female instinct, not the great instincts reflective of our divine nature, but inferior instincts which form the least noble part of our vocation.'[6] Let us hope that the august professor at the Collège de France never learned that the most brilliantly successful department stores – the first commercial endeavours to aim at making comfort available to all – have to be put down to two exceptionally harmonious couples: Aristide Boucicaut and Marguerite Guérin (Bon Marché), and Ernst Cognacq and Marie-Louise Jay (La Samaritaine).

Monseigneur Pie and Ernest Renan – irreconcilable adversaries in most respects, though they joined forces in defence of male supremacy – need not have worried. It would be some time before the secondary, non-public spaces of middle-class households – to say nothing of those of the one-room lodgings of the popular classes – were equipped with the same degree of comfort as the public rooms, namely the living room and the dining room. Oddly, when it was a question of direct contact with the body there was a worrying attitude of indifference. Enamoured of eating but repulsed by material tasks, the 19th-century bourgeois preferred not to know how his meals were prepared. The kitchen, relegated to a back corner of his flat, seemed like a place of chaos filled with acrid smoke and odours, permanently heated by an enormous stove. Perhaps we shouldn't stay too long in the dressing room, encumbered by jugs and washbasins in the absence of running water, and should pass even more quickly through the bathroom – a rarity – for the delights of

In organic architecture...
it is quite impossible to consider
the buildings as one thing, its furnishings
another and its setting and environment
still another. The spirit in which these
buildings are conceived sees all these
things together at work as one thing...
The very chairs and tables, cabinets
and even musical instruments, where
practicable, are of the building itself
and never fixtures upon it.

Frank Lloyd Wright, An American Architecture,
New York, 1955

washing easily take on a sexual character (in boarding houses, young women wore long robes while taking their weekly baths, a custom that persisted until 1945 in certain particularly reputable provincial establishments). Neither will we linger in the public lavatories, places still more suspect and the object of close surveillance in schools. It was only at the very end of the 19th century that these facilities began to be equipped with toilets, which by that time had been perfected by British plumbers.[7]

It should be remembered, then, that in this period the preoccupation with comfort quickly reached moral limits. If the dominant class did not put heating, lighting and running water at the head of its concerns (even though technical advances now made it easy to install them in private dwellings), this was because of its scruples about all things concerning the body, its determination not to give way to the laxity that had brought down the aristocracy.

What ensured that comfort became established as a part of everyday life was the need to keep diseases at bay through good hygiene. Cholera had disappeared (the last outbreak in Paris occured in 1894), but it had been replaced by tuberculosis, for which no effective treatment would be found before the mid-20th century. In any case, thanks to the advance of 'materialism', those who regarded everyday comforts with contempt found themselves outflanked. In 1869, Catherine Beecher, sister of the author of *Uncle Tom's Cabin*, published *The American Woman's House*, which marked the advent of the 'domestic arts'. At the same time, Pierre Larousse devoted three columns of his *Grand dictionnaire universel du XIXᵉ siècle* (1866-1879) to the history of comfort and concluded his entry with the following sentence: 'Comfort, the offspring of wealth, speaks favourably of any society able to acquire it.'

Democratic hedonism

On the eve of the First World War, the problem of the residential interior became a matter of passionate public debate. This is borne out by the appearance of journals with revealing titles. For example *Mon chez moi* (My Home, 1909-1911), which dealt with both decoration and hygiene, and *L'Intérieur* (The Interior, 1911-1912): both these publications had short lives because they failed to target their potential readerships, but the idea of 'rational' home furnishings was in the air. Francis Jourdain was among the first to express this clearly in France, when he exhibited the living-room of his flat in the stepped building designed by Henri Sauvage on the rue Vavin, at the Salon of 1913. It consisted of an ensemble of stripped-down furniture totally lacking any 'application of art', which provoked a scandal among traditionalists.

In any case, it was newly-developed machinery, gradually introduced into each household thanks to electricity, that finally put domestic comfort within reach of the public at large. Here the pioneer was the German-born Peter Behrens (1868-1940), a jack of all trades who was initially devoted to the curves of Art Nouveau. Behrens came fully into his own as artistic advisor to AEG, which, prior to 1914, was the world's most powerful electrical appliance firm. Beginning in 1907, Behrens designed most of AEG's products, including arc lamps, fans, clocks and especially electric kettles and teapots (1909) which number among the most beautiful household objects of the 20th century.

AEG set an influential precedent for contemporary design, revealing the basic parameters of the quest for 'modern' comfort: the desire to create household objects – in this instance, electrical products, which still frightened many people – characterized by a utilitarian ease of operation resulting from rational study as well as a pleasing appearance devoid of embellishment.

The Modern Movement's 'machines for living in', which were scattered over the European landscape from the twenties, included the first room to be structured expressly to accommodate objects perfected by the developers of household appliances:

the kitchen. Even before 1914, its transformation from a dark to a luminous space was under way. In women's magazines,[8] there was talk of walls painted white or covered in faïence tiles. Following an example set by the Germans, stoves were made of white enamel and equipped with hoods of cathedral glass, while aluminium or nickel cooking pots began to be preferred to copper ones.

But the archetypal rational cooking workshop of the era was the so-called 'Frankfurt kitchen', invented by the young Austrian architect Margarete Schütte-Lihotzky, the first woman to graduate from the School of Applied Arts in Vienna. Firmly committed to the improvement of workers' housing, she collaborated with the architects of the Rote Wien group before being noticed by Ernst May, who was in charge of new building in Frankfurt under the Weimar Republic. There she conceived the 'kitchen space' that was precisely calculated and equipped like a laboratory. Rectangular in form, well lit by an immense window, it featured a stool which could be adjusted to the height required by the different work surfaces and the electric cooker, and each of its walls was covered with hanging utensils. Everything was placed within easy reach and the ceiling lamps were mounted on rails so that light could be directed wherever it was needed. This was Taylorism applied to the family kitchen and the invention of this young Austrian, a militant socialist, was to have considerable influence throughout Europe (witness the Cubex kitchen developed in Belgium).

In France, after the events of 1914-1918, two remarkable personalities, a man and a woman, were behind the establishment of the powerful Arts Ménagers (domestic science) movement. The first, Jules-Louis Breton (1872-1940), was a chemical engineer, a socialist member of parliament and a disciple of Dr. Edouard Vaillant – leader of the 'extreme' left of the early 20th century. Under-secretary of state for inventions during the war and an advocate of the tank, he was largely responsible for a great deal of social legislation and was passionately interested in household appliances. On his initiative, on 18 October 1923, the first international show of household appliances opened its doors on the Champ de Mars in Paris. It attracted 100,000 visitors. Three years later, in 1926, this exhibition, now dubbed the Salon des Arts Ménagers (Salon of Domestic Science), moved to the Grand Palais, where it would be held until 1939 – drawing 608,646 visitors that year. The term *arts ménagers* was coined by Breton: before him, the French spoke only of housework or household education (*travaux*

Cover of *L'Art ménager*: 'the simple bathroom', illustration by Joe Brigde, June 1931.

Cover of *L'Art ménager* illustrating Paulette Bernège's article 'The bathroom for everyone', illustration by Mory, July 1932.

Advertisement for AEG lamps, 1907.

Range of toilet bowls made in Great Britain by the firm Doulton & Co Ltd., 1890-1895.

Above right: Electric iron *à coques*, for ironing loops of ribbon, Babeth, 1955.

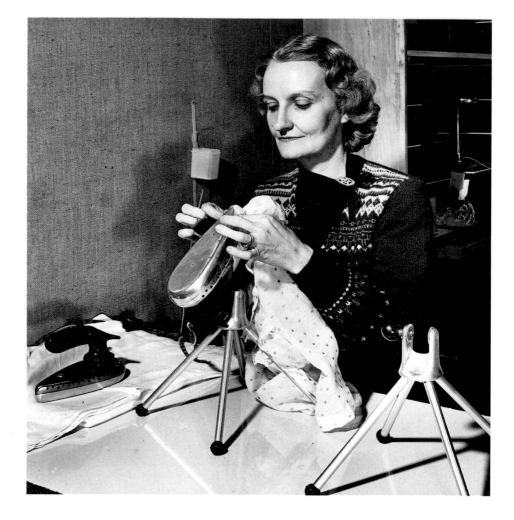

ménagers, enseignement ménager). The new designation, which broadened the application from domestic tasks alone to the whole house – its appliances, fittings and decoration – was given the imprimatur of the *Larousse* in 1950.

The Salon des Arts Ménagers was an extraordinary display of objects of all kinds intended to bring the comforts made possible by the provision of water, gas and electricity into every household. Its role was decisive. At the Grand Palais, the public was educated through lectures, slides and thematic exhibits: retrospectives and displays of 'useful forms' focusing on specific appliances or other household objects such as irons, casseroles, children's furniture, and so on. Founded in 1927, the journal *Arts ménagers* joined in the campaign and it quickly became a source of information for women's magazines.

Now for the woman in question, who worked to achieve many of the same

goals as Breton and who often had the opportunity to collaborate with him. The holder of a degree in philosophy – an exceptional achievement for a woman at this time – Paulette Bernège founded, in Nancy, the same year as the first Salon at the Grand Palais was held, the Institut d'Organisation Ménagère (Institute for Household Organization) as well as the associated journal *Mon chez moi*, which was published until 1930. Two years later, as part of the programme of the Musée Social, which, since the late 19th century had fostered many important initiatives, including feminist ones, Bernège helped establish the Ligue d'Organisation Ménagère (League for Household Organization) and became its secretary general.

Having learned of the work of Christine Frederick, the dominant force behind household Taylorism in the United States,[9] Paulette Bernège, in her determination to

'seek to improve the living conditions within each family dwelling', lectured widely in France as well as abroad and published many books and pamphlets in which she developed a 'physiology of the home'. She articulated this project fully in her finest book – dedicated to Louis Loucheur – *Si les femmes faisaient les maisons*,[10] which falls quite comfortably within the tradition established by the school of Charles Fourier. Beginning with the principle that 'pipes are an essential element of civilization', she predicted that each flat – her preferred form of housing – would soon be equipped with a battery of odd devices: a *bouche d'ozone* (ozone opening) to purify and disinfect the air; a *bouche de vide* – a sort of vacuum cleaner; a rubbish chute; a chute for dirty laundry going directly into the building's laundry room, outfitted with electric washing machines, wringers, and driers; and a mail chute communicating directly with the building's central mailbox.

Here electricity ruled. Paulette Bernège was certainly the first person to maintain that five-amp meters were no longer sufficient for modern households. Power circuits were essential and each room should have a minimum of four sockets.

The campaigns of Paulette Bernège and Jules-Louis Breton were not waged in vain. Their influence, direct and indirect, on the growing acceptance of the Arts Ménagers agenda was considerable: comforts derived from technological progress, far from encouraging indolence, helped make possible the full development of human potential by liberating the individual from the constraints of manual chores.

None the less, certain social milieux continued to resist this truth: one final moralizing crusade against comfort was mounted after the Liberation. Influential figures took part, notably Georges Bernanos: 'In short, this world seeks nothing but comfort, which it will obtain at any cost, and to deceive others as well as itself it declares this comfort to be nothing other than Justice.'[11] This elegant, hollow statement doesn't take any account of the realities of the time. Most of the French population was poorly housed and in Paris there were some 200,000 people crowded into 17 Parisian blocks.

The Swiss essayist Frédéric Hoffet[12] blamed Protestantism for the invention of comfort and this 'accusation' was taken up by the architect and urbanist Gaston Bardet,[13] whose outrageous formulations exceeded all bounds. He maintained that the appearance of the bathroom, emblem of the 'superiority of the body', signalled a civilization's entry into a decadent phase, a thesis he tried to justify by citing historical precedent. He pointed out that Abraham had left Ur before its fall and that excavations had revealed numerous bathrooms throughout that city. More than a hundred had been counted in the palace of the Aztec ruler Montezuma. And in the United States, he maintained, there was a growing realization that daily washing led to degeneracy. In short, the 'roots of secular, obligatory comfort are situated in a mystique of action that led to a mystique of manufacture, which in turn prompted a mystique of consumption'. In this way the hierarchy of values was turned upside down, with the earth displacing heaven.

But it was too late to indulge in such prophetic nonsense when the housing crisis had reached a peak in France, something which didn't make the sale of household appliances any easier. Over the 12 months of 1955, 250,000 housing units were constructed; that same year, the Salon des Arts Ménagers received 1,402,299 visitors and more than 200,000 issues of the journal *Arts ménagers* were published each month. Throughout Europe, the domestic sciences were shaking off their inferior status, and institutes specializing in relevant research proliferated. Neither France nor Great Britain established centralized institutions, but study of the 'vile details of housekeeping' was not neglected. France, in particular, profited from the theories of a new social thinker, the engineer Jean Fourastié.[14] For him 'comfort prevents the sterile dissipation of physical strength in the execution of insignificant tasks while favouring maximal development of the proper human faculties'.

Its biggest economy was that of time, the modern era's most precious commodity. To which Lucien Febvre added that the Arts Ménagers implied a new social ethic regarding women, 'the will to continue the process of their emancipation, to make available to them all the career opportunities which men, to this point, have so jealously guarded as their sole province'.[15]

The percentage of French households with bathrooms rose from 30 per cent in 1962 to 93 per cent in 1992, and the 'moralizers' no longer dared to show themselves. But they might, however, have attacked the 'perversion' of aerodynamic styling – originally devised for functional reasons, to facilitate the rapid passage of fast-moving vehicles through the air, but which was subsequently appropriated for all kinds of domestic products, such as cocktail mixers and children's cars. Or they might have thundered against electric nail varnish driers, not to mention toilet seats covered in mink. Comfort and kitsch will never be incompatible. It is impossible to contain human aspirations within the boundaries of unchanging schemas, as the avatars of design will always be eager to demonstrate.

Open spaces and rural belts

After the common, the chief feature of the spaciousness of the garden city is its rural setting. The town is set in open fields like a jewel in its setting. Two-thirds of the entire area of the estate are kept as farms, orchards, parks and smallholdings. This rural belt surrounds the town like the walls of the medieval city. . . . In all the modern Utopias, town and country are pictured as being in happy relations, in contrast to the existing state of our society, in which agriculture and industry are isolated as they were never before in history. In News from Nowhere, it is said 'The town invaded the country; but the invaders, like the warlike invaders of early days, yielded to the influence of their surroundings, and became country people; and in their terms, as they became more numerous than the townsmen, influenced them also; so that the difference between town and country grew less and less; and it was indeed this world as the country vivified by the thought and business of town-bred folk which has produced the happy and leisurely but eager life. . . 'And in Mr [H. G.] Wells's Modern Utopia we read 'As one walks out from the town centre one will come to that mingling of homesteads and open country which will be the common condition of all the more habitable parts of the globe.'

The idea of new conditions in which country life would be remade with the remaking of town life is one of the most attractive notions of these two books, and the Garden City is interesting, if nothing else, as the first organized attempt to bring about that revolution. The cry of 'Back to the land' has been raised many times, and many half-hearted efforts have been made to repeople the starved countryside, but not until the foundation of the Garden City was there any promising means of bringing new life into agriculture. It was not merely to build a healthy town that the promoters of the Garden City set out, but to bring new interests and new developments to the farm.

C. B. Pardon,
The Garden City: A Study in the
Development of a Modern Town,
1913

The Edison lamp

Thomas Alva Edison was born in Ohio in 1847, of modest origins. While selling newspapers on the Detroit railway, an employee of the railway company taught him how the telegraph worked, and Edison became fascinated by it. At 21, working for the Western Union Company in Boston, he began various electrical experiments. He moved to New York, where he made his mark as a specialist in telegraphic systems with the 'multiplex' telegraph, which allowed the transmission of several messages simultaneously. After a stint working for the stock exchange, in 1876 he decided to set up an 'invention factory' of his own in Menlo Park, between New York and Philadelphia.

In 1878 Edison developed an electrical system and made the first incandescent lamps using a loop of carbonized thread. 'It was at this time that I wanted to move on to something new. That's when Professor Barker suggested I try to break down electric lighting into small units, as was done with gas. It was not a new suggestion, for a year earlier I had already conducted several experiments with electric lighting. I had temporarily abandoned them for photography'.

The idea was simple and was based on Joule's principle. A glass bulb enclosed a wire that, when an electrical current was passed through it, became hot and gave off light. But how could the effect inside the bulb be made to last?

With the help of his assistants, Edison experimented with long, thin wires and low voltage levels. On 21 October 1879, a carbonized piece of Japanese bamboo was used, achieving for the first time, an effect similar to that of the electric bulb as we know it. Subsequently other vegetable substances and then metallic ones were substituted.

On the other side of the Atlantic, at about the same time, the Englishman Sir Joseph Swan was developing a similar system. He never ceased claiming that he was the true father of this invention. After a series of trials over copyright violation (Edison was used to this sort of thing), the two inventors joined forces in 1883. A typically European feature distinguished Swan's light bulb: it was chased or engraved, as if this new technological invention had to be given some sort of decorative appeal.

In 1882 the first complete system for distributing electrical current became operative, on a small scale, in Menlo Park. Then the first central power station was installed in the vicinity of New York's Wall Street. Initially Edison provided current to select customers free of charge, the better to convince them of its convenience.

Within a year eight thousand Edison lamps were fed by a 110 volt distribution system. This first power station burned down in 1890, but by that time the Edison system was already widely in use. In 1892 the Edison General Electric Corporation changed its name to General Electric.

E. M.

Background: Edison lamp, 1879, Washington Smithsonian Institution, National Museum of American History.

Far left: Cross-section of the Edison lamp and its base, showing the connection between the platinum wires of the lamp and the copper circuit wires. Engraving from Nouvelles Conquêtes de la Science, L. Figuier, 1883.

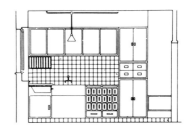

The laboratory kitchen

In Germany, between 1925 and 1930, several architects proposed model kitchens for workers' housing. In 1923, Walter Gropius had organized an exhibition of works executed by professors and students at the Bauhaus in Weimar. On this occasion an individual house, Das Haus am Horn, was constructed, and a functional L-shaped kitchen was installed in it. 'What strikes the observer about this model kitchen in which organization is allied with form, is the careful coordination of counters and areas for preparation, cleaning and cooking, with work surfaces and appliances being situated at the same height and wall-mounted cabinets in the corners of the room.'

The most influential of these models was the so-called 'Frankfurt kitchen', the first kitchen realized under the guidance of Ernst May, the official architect of the city of Frankfurt. Residential construction had practically ceased in Frankfurt during the First World War and the situation became still worse during the economic depression in the years following the war. In order to address this situation and reabsorb the shanty towns that had grown up, Ernst May assembled a team of architects and designers, which included Adolf Meyer, Ferdinand Kramer, Mart Stem, Franz Schuster, and Margarete Schütte-Lihotzky. They set about conceiving and building a set of standardized lodgings as quickly as possible.

In particular, it was Margarete Schütte-Lihotzky, architect and close collaborator of Ernst May, who oversaw the design of the kitchen. As Ferdinand Kramer subsequently noted The New Housekeeping, a book by Christine Frederick, served as her guide in developing the project.

In 1933, the Dutch company Bruynzeel asked the architect Peet Zwart to design modular, standardized kitchen furniture. The resulting furniture, the first of its kind in Europe appeared in around 1936.

Before the Second World War the theoretical concept of the functional kitchen had come to be widely accepted, and annual exhibitions such as Ideal Home, in Great Britain, and the Salon des Arts Ménagers (created by Jules-Louis Breton in 1923), in Paris, were extremely successful. Unfortunately, the war would delay for more than a decade the programmes for the construction of low-cost housing planned from 1936 in Europe.

Variants of the functional kitchen which appeared in the Germany of the Weimar Republic around 1925 came to be regarded as the models of reference and would be imitated in blocks of flats after the Second World War. They seemed to offer the best synthesis of hygienic principles and theories of domestic economy, all integrated into a functionalist architectural frame.

J. d. N.

Left-hand page and vignette: Drawings of the Frankfurt kitchen.

Background: Spice drawer for the Frankfurt kitchen.

Dandyism:
from Luxury
to Immateriality

Françoise Coblence

Luxury associates taste with

excessive comfort in the social life of a community

(it works against its prosperity).

When it is not accompanied by taste, this sort of excess

is outward pomp. As for their effects on the economy,

luxury is an unnecessary expense that impoverishes,

while pomp makes it sick.

Immanuel Kant, Anthropologie in pragmatischer Hinsicht

English and French excesses

In Great Britain after 1810, there emerged a satirical literature mocking the 'dandy mania' that was all the rage in elegant circles. It represents the dandy as a rather stiff figure in muslin jabot who is prone to excess and bombast, a prisoner of the starch of his cravat and the tightness of his clothing. François René de Chateaubriand described him awkwardly sitting astride a horse, 'carrying a cane like a taper, indifferent to the animal chance had placed between his legs'.[1] A creature of exaggeration, of fastidious and ostentatious dress, does the dandy exemplify the taste which Kant, in the best of cases, discerned in luxury?

Was the dandy an arbiter of good taste or a heretic born of the elegant life, as Honoré de Balzac thought? The descriptions which began to accumulate in the early 19th century are inconsistent: in some the dandy is presented as a model of sobriety and refinement, while in others his eccentricities are said to have transformed him into a dummy for the display of outrageous attire, a walking sign of privilege in a world of blurred social distinctions where it was nonetheless important to maintain a certain tone. Both the social history of the period of the July Monarchy (established after the revolution of 1830) and contemporary literature tend to validate the latter image. The dandy was ridiculously obsessed with England; he spent two hours at his toilet and made a spectacle of his fatuity and vain mediocrity along the boulevards and in cafés. Dandies were 'ninnies who know nothing but how to put on a cravat and make an elegant impression in the Bois de Boulogne'.[2] Balzac shows us Lucien de Rubempré arriving in Paris, rushing to the Tuileries and spending two cruel hours coming to realize the ugliness of his clothing. Later, Lucien would pass for a dandy the day he had 'marvellous walking sticks, a charming lorgnette, diamond buttons, jewellery for his morning cravats, signet rings, and finally, enough splendid waistcoats to be able to vary the colour scheme of his attire'.[3]

Under Louis-Philippe, the dandies paraded at the Chantilly derby. Many wore the dress prescribed by a commission in 1832: suits cut *à la française*, in olive green material with gold buttons. Sports were fashionable; (it was at this time that Lord Seymour launched boxing): 'The dandies most passionate about the sport are on the course, racing. They wear scabious outfits buttoned up the front, with small pockets on the chest for silk neckerchiefs. . . They would regard it as unsightly to carry a riding crop; instead they hold small metal canes or "little-sticks", the latest English fashion.'[4] As the goal was to set oneself apart in an increasingly conformist society, dandyism manifested itself in the choice of rare objects and accessories, the frequenting of fashionable places, and ostentatious spending unjustified by rank, title, or even personal financial resources. The life of the dandy was a matter of show and showing oneself.[5] Such display encouraged the inventorying of the objects with which the dandy surrounded himself, scrutiny of his clothing, careful notation of the places he visited and assessment of how he spent his days. After having devoured with his eyes the marvellous canes decorating the antechamber of novelist Paul Bourget, which distracted his attention from the fine paintings hung nearby, Eugène Marsan assigned to each cane a specific purpose, sorting them into groups according to the hour of the day or the colour of the outfit in question.[6] Dandyism was precious, sophisticated and prescriptive.

In the wake of Charles Baudelaire, a tradition developed that saw dandyism as 'the last flash of heroism through decadence',[7] a new kind of aristocracy that was a response to the rising tide of democracy and was staunchly opposed to middle class ugliness. Dandyism countered these developments with precious stones, opium-inspired sensuality and rare perfumes, with environments in which artifice triumphed but in the end exhausted itself. Des Esseintes, the hero of Joris-Karl Huysmans' novel *A Rebours*, was the quintessence and funereal culmination of the tradition: 'Des Esseintes acquired

the reputation of an eccentric, which he encouraged by dressing in suits of white velvet and orphrey waistcoats, by inserting, like cravats, Parma violets into the open collars of his very low-necked shirts, by giving extraordinary dinner parties. . . In the dining room draped in black, which opened onto a strangely metamorphosed garden, its paths powdered with charcoal, its small basin now edged by a thin border of black basalt and filled with ink, and its usual shrubs replaced by cypresses and pines, the dinner had been laid out on a black table cloth, decorated with baskets of violets and scabiosae, illuminated by candelabra in which tall tapers burned.'[8]

And yet, though Baudelaire bestowed letters of nobility on any nostalgic reading of dandyism that saw it in terms of aristocratic reaction, he was the first to emphasize the sobriety, the quasi-monastic rigour of the dandy's toilet. In a world still decked out with ribbons, wouldn't dandyism consist of setting oneself apart precisely by the absolute simplicity of one's appearance?

The sobriety of the first dandy

Certainly George Bryan Brummell was not exempt from exaggeration and impertinence. His extravagant gambling and alcohol consumption were notorious. However, the exquisite discretion of his dress was as distinct from the flashy chic of the foppish puppets who were his Epigones as from the exaggerated refinement of the decadents. Jacques Boulenger wrote that in the evening he invariably wore 'a blue jacket with linked buttons, white vest, flawlessly-tailored black trousers buttoned at the ankle, striped silk stockings and a cocked hat'.[9] The cravat alone – metres of white muslin the adjustment of which required a prolonged, precise, but always aleatory ceremonial – escaped the constraints of this quasi-uniform: of all the component elements of such attire, only the cravat showed individuality. The dandy arranged his cravat on his own, without aid. 'The laundress delivers a piece of starched batiste; one deals with it as skilfully as one can: it is a block of marble that has fallen into the hands of either a Phidias or a stonecutter.'[10] 'Brummell was one of the first who revived and improved the taste for dress; and his great innovation was carried out on neck-cloths... The collar, which was always fixed to his shirt, was so large that, before being folded down, it completely hid his head and face, and the white neckcloth was at least a foot in height. The first coup d'archet was made with the shirt collar, which he folded down to its proper size; and Brummel, then standing before the glass, with his chin poked up towards the ceiling, creased the cravat by gradually lowering his lower jaw until the right balance between the volumes of shirt and cravat had been found.'[11] In the person of Brummell, ostentation and distinction were separated. The dandy reigned over the court and opinion as the 'arbiter of elegance', but ultimately he did not see himself as well dressed. He proscribed perfumes, ostentatious colours, costly-fabrics, ribbons and lace. The most important thing about clothing was its line, its sobriety. It was pure form, and purity, as was pointed out by Kant, who of course would never have associated it with clothing, signified in the simple mode of sensation that 'the uniformity of this mode is not troubled or destroyed by a sensation of a different kind'.[12] To his contemporaries, Brummell was a disconcerting mixture of cutting insolence and subtle humour deploying words, objects and elegance with both detachment and a mastery of litotes. Objects seem to have been more than a matter of décor for the dandy: they represented the only source of stability in a changing world. But the dandy had something of the collector about him: he, too, detached objects from their utilitarian relations, inserting them into open-ended series that never reached completion. 'His passion for snuffboxes was extreme: he had one which only he could open, and some friend of his, while he was at Belvoir, tried it with his knife, with the intention, no doubt, of purloining his snuff, which was always

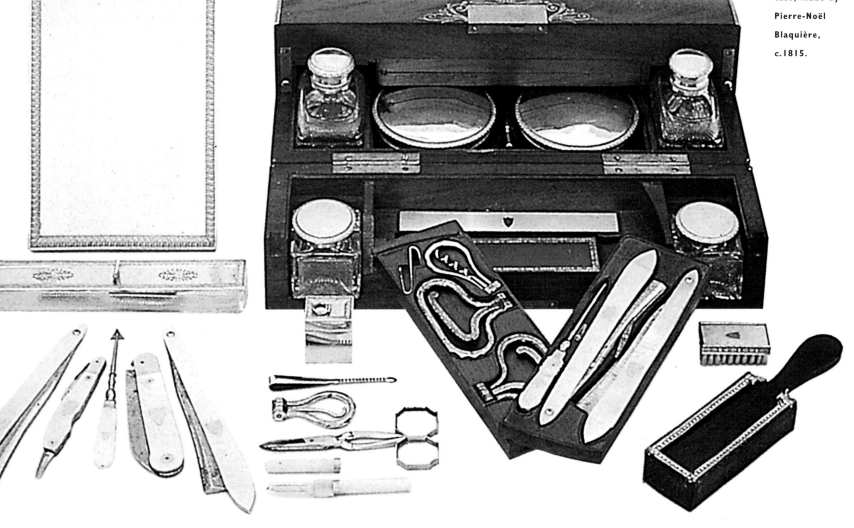

excellent. Hearing of the outrage, Brummell said: "Confound the fellow, he takes my snuffbox for an oyster".[13] A famous anecdote recounts how Brummell, when asked by the Duke of Bedford what he thought of his new coat, replied: 'You call that thing a coat?' The spirit of the dandy disconnected articles of clothing from their use. This was a form of aestheticism, without doubt, which held utility to be the antithesis of beauty. But the essential thing was the asceticism of the dandy's relation to objects. Brummell, wrote Jules Amédée Barbey d'Aurevilly, 'had the home of a woman aspiring to be a poet'.[14] His dinners were celebrated for their refinement, delicacy and lightness. 'Once I ate nothing but a single pea', Brummell answered when asked about his taste for vegetables. In matters of love, his moderation bordered on abstinence, suggesting that no passion could retain his attention as fully as the construction of his own person. His jokes and witticisms were all but nonexistent, tending to be inaudible, monosyllabic and extremely concise. An ephemeral object, the dandy's intelligence exhausted itself in the very instant of its enunciation. Reports of these utterances record their most vivid moments. But isn't this precisely the nature of the dandy's special relationship to things? Objectifying himself through coolness and apathy, the dandy impresses initially as a mere marionette. To luxury, which would be an exaggeration of aristocratic opulence, he opposes an economy of moderation and discretion that transforms the brilliant, unique individual into a banal being, a readily reproducible exemplar.

From this viewpoint, elegance precludes ornament. The principles of dress are not without resemblance to those formulated by Edgar Allan Poe in his *Philosophy of Furniture*. Poe deplored the fact that in America, a society lacking an aristocracy of birth but possessed of an 'aristocracy of dollars', taste was often drowned in 'pure ostentation', and beauty and sumptuousness were often confused. He favoured carpets and

hangings decorated with simple arabesques, in other words with forms 'without any meaning', and his opposition to bombast of all sorts led him to condemn the exaggerated brilliance and indiscretion of mirrors and bright lights. 'Glare is a leading error in the philosophy of American household decoration. . . We are violently enamoured of gas and of glass. The former is totally inadmissable within doors. Its harsh and unsteady light offends... Never was a more lovely thought than that of the astral lamp. . . with its original plain ground-glass shade, and its tempered and uniform moonlight rays. The cut glass shade is a weak invention of the enemy. . . It alone is sufficient to mar a mass of good effects in the furniture subjected to its detestable influence.' Baudelaire noted in a commentary accompanying his translation, in 1852, that the description of an ideal room subsequently proposed by Poe as a model of simplicity might strike many as extremely sumptuous. The 'oriental' imagination of the poet here prevailed over the spirit of the dandy. For the dandy who is only a dandy maintains an absolute sobriety that is all the more difficult to describe because it seems self evident. Once completed, his toilet is forgotten. Baudelaire stressed a tension in him that was more spiritual than material. One could not become a dandy by training or imitation. 'One doesn't make oneself into a Brummell. One either is one or one isn't.'[15]

Modernity and the posterity of the dandy

The Prince of Wales spent many hours observing Brummell at his toilet, but in vain: he was never able to equal this commoner. Far from being indistinguishable from an aristocratic extravagance, dandyism implied, in the words of James Laver, 'a conspiracy against the aristocracy'.

'Instinctively, Brummell had grasped that the era of aristocracy was over and that that of gentility had arrived. There would be no more peers proudly bearing their orders on their brocaded coats, only gentlemen

Detail from the engraving, page 87.

Below: Kelly handbag, designed in 1956, Hermès, 1993. At the beginning of this century, the 'high bag with straps' was used to carry saddles. In around 1930, Hermès had the idea of reducing it in size to make a lady's handbag. The bag was used by Grace Kelly and Hermès paid homage to her in 1956 by calling it Kelly.

wearing co-ordinated suits and immaculate linen. There would be no more three-cornered hats with feathers and braid, only well-brushed top hats. Top hats were in effect the symbol of this new state of things. Their flat but elevated surfaces seemed to say that all gentlemen were equal, even if one of them was named George, the Prince of Wales, and the other George Brummell. And in truth, nothing distinguished the one from the other, save that Brummell's cravat was more carefully knotted and his clothing suited him better.'[16]

The refinement of the dandy emerged and found appreciation only in societies once dominated by 'aristocracies of birth', to use Poe's phrase. By his rigour and impassivity, the dandy pursued the process of the interiorization of constraints and prohibitions that, in the view of Norbert Elias as well as Freud, constitutes what we call civilization. However, and herein lies his modernity, he broke with the subtle game of *ancien régime* elegance, with the model of the *'je ne sais quoi'* and the *'presque rien'*. He set out to codify elegance in a society in which 'the natural son of a millionaire banker and a man of talent have the same rights as the son of a count'.[17] Brummell's impeccable attire, his mastery of the pose, his control of his emotions could no longer be measured by the standard of classic taste and *honnêteté*. Walter Benjamin likened these qualities to the composure and rapidity of response needed by stock market speculators. Nervous tics would then be awkward but faithful manifestations of this.[18] Stiff or, to use Baudelaire's terms, 'tensed like an extravagant', the dandy, with his cravat and polished boots, incarnated the pressure of urban life, its flux and anonymity.

'However, doesn't it have a beauty and charm all its own, this much-derided attire? Isn't it the appropriate dress for our suffering era and also a symbol, with its black, thin shoulders, of perpetual mourning? Note that the black suit and the frock coat not only have a certain political beauty, but also a poetic beauty which expresses the soul of the public – an immense procession of undertakers, amorous undertakers, middle-class undertakers. We are all of us celebrating some burial or other.'[19]

In a world in which tradition no longer offered points of reference, in which heroism had shifted venues from the public to the private scene, Brummell, who was often compared to Napoleon, was the first to take charge of his own person, to invent it from top to bottom and, in a manner of speaking, hold it up to public scrutiny. To a greater degree than the *élégants* and *mondains*, whose strategies functioned within the field of distinction, he cleared the way for artists, for those who issue a challenge to modernity by risking everything in their own selves.

It was said of the first dandy that he seemed to have been hatched in his frock coat. His clothing was a second skin, or the skin itself, inseparable from the figure behind it, or, if such language is permissible, the material body striving to attenuate itself. Brummell, whose close-fitting gloves were made by three different artisans to guarantee a superior standard of workmanship, and who couldn't turn his head when his cravat was knotted around his neck, was a walking demonstration of how dress was crucial to the dandy. There was nothing beyond it, nothing behind its surface. But Brummell also demonstrated that, more than the clothing itself, it was the way it was worn and the preparation of one's toilet, the time invested in getting this perfect, that made the dandy. In him, the temporality that is part and parcel of the human condition – of what Hannah Arendt called the fragility of human affairs – appeared as the very stuff of dress.

'One can be a dandy with wrinkled clothing... Can you believe it? One day the dandies let their fantastic notions go so far as "threadbare apparel". This was during Brummell's time. They had reached the limits of impertinence, they couldn't figure out what to do next. Then they settled on the incredibly dandyish idea (I can't think of another word to express my meaning) of shredding their clothing before donning it,

every part of it, until it had become a kind of lace – a cloud. They wanted to walk on the clouds, these gods! The operation was extremely delicate and prolonged, and they used a piece of sharpened glass to accomplish it. Well then! Here's a true fact of dandyism for you. The clothing counts for nothing. *It almost ceases to exist.*'[20]

'The Prince of Kaunitz was not a dandy when he wore a satin corset like the Andalusian one worn by Alfred de Musset, but he was one when, to give his hair just the right touch, he walked through a series of rooms, whose size and number he had carefully calculated, in which valets armed with puffs sprinkled powder over him for as long as it took him to walk past them!'[21]

Brummell frequented fashionable venues, or rather the ones he frequented immediately became fashionable. So striking was his appearance that he had only to pass through a doorway or relax in the famous bay window of White's, the dandy's club, to produce an effect. There was in dandyism a tendency toward sobriety and neutrality that was opposed to flounce and fussy fashionability, just as it was to the romantic pining of aristocratic heroism. Under its aegis, in the era of photography and mechanical reproduction, fashion became 'a kind of uniform of elegance'.[22] As used by the dandy, black became a colour of infinite nuance. Yves Saint Laurent expresses a similar idea when he says: 'The most beautiful thing for me, in fashion, is to manage to make a piece of clothing that works just like a sweater or a black skirt, that's nothing and yet everything. Such is the essence of our craft: rigour, humility, gravity, timelessness.'[23]

But, beyond concern over rigorous lines and the reproducibility of a type, and beyond the opposition – always puritanical – to excess and ornament, the dandy shows, through his person and in the objects with which he surrounds himself, a tendency to immateriality and dematerialization: 'clothing almost ceases to exist'. In the starched rigidity of his impersonal, hieratic toilet, Brummell was transformed into a subject

And it is to be noted that it is the fact that Art is this intense form of Individualism that makes the public try to exercise over it an authority that is as immoral as it is ridiculous, and as corrupting as it is contemptible. It is quite their fault. The public has always, and in every age, been badly brought up. They are continually asking Art to be popular, to please their want of taste, to flatter their absurd vanity, to tell them what they have been told before, to show them what they ought to be tired of seeing, to amuse them when they feel heavy after eating too much, and to distract their thoughts when they are wearied of their own stupidity. Now Art should never try to be popular. The public should try to make itself artistic.

Oscar Wilde, 'The Soul of Man Under Socialism', The Fortnightly Review, 1890

devoid of interiority, of sensibility; he was devitalized. The world in all its density was a matter of indifference to him: he had no preferences. Flesh and the body were outside his purview. The dandy became an automaton, a 'ready-made', a transparent surface, pure energy. Having become impersonal, he accepted the loss of all uniqueness: As Marcel Duchamp wrote, 'There's nothing unique about ready-mades. . . The replica of a ready-made conveys the same message; in fact, almost none of the ready-mades in existence today are originals in the accepted sense.'[24]

But above all, his clothing, his person and his witticisms, in the end, signified only the space and time they occupied – in other words, speed, ephemerality and dispossession. 'We will be able, for example, to first examine all the possible results of an envisaged act, all the market possibilities of a conceived object, only to then cast them aside and set about divining something more intense or more precise than the thing given, having discovered we have the power to snap out of a thought that's lasted too long.'[25] 'At the extreme limit of anguish, nothing remains', wrote Friedrich Hölderlin, 'but the conditions of time and space.'[26] Dandyism recognized the truth of these statements and, more than on objects themselves, focused on the forms and conditions of their presentation: on space and time. The fascination dandyism exerted (and exerts) derived not from any kind of aura, from some irreducible singularity to which it adhered for better or worse in a prosaic world. It derived, rather, from its engagement – simultaneously nonchalant and deeply committed – with technical and aesthetic transformations, with what Paul Valéry in 1928 called the 'conquest of ubiquity', traceable as far as the latest technology, which Jean-François Lyotard[27] sees as substitutes for mental operations. 'I think that the infinite, mysterious charm of contemplating a boat, and especially a moving boat, derives, in the first instance, from the regularity and symmetry which are among the primal needs of the human spirit, to the same degree as complication and harmony; and in the second instance, from the successive multiplication and generation of all the imaginary curves and figures operated in space by the real elements of the object'.[28]

Dandyism, which stands apart from all ideology and especially from the belief in progress, will never be transformed into a cult of the machine, of speed and of power. It made do with display of the fragile and the ephemeral, a taste for lightness and the generation of curves and forms, an attempt to wrest, specifically by means of fashion, the new and contingent away from reproduction and reiteration – a dimension of modernity it knew to be irremediable and inclined toward 'catastrophe'. It is, then, the boat that Baudelaire enjoyed contemplating, imperceptibly balancing on waters that will never be calm, as the poet must have known.

Perfume bottles

Opposite:
Glass
perfume
bottles
by René
Lalique,
1910-1930.

Vignettes,
from left
to right:
Jicky,
Guerlain,
1889.

Shalimar,
Guerlain,
1925.

Opium,
Yves Saint
Laurent,
1977.

At the end of the 18th century bathing spas emerged as the preferred meeting place for a society increasingly attentive to cleanliness. It wasn't long before this development prompted the establishment of perfume companies, the semi-industrial production of bottles made of moulded glass and the formation – made possible by the development of railways and steamships – of an efficient distribution network.

To differentiate these various new products the illustrated, coloured label was invented. Technical advances (notably alembic distillation) and the development of synthetic substances (artificial musk was created in 1888, and heliotrope in 1896) favoured the development of the perfume industry. At the Universal Exposition of 1900 a crowd of perfume companies presented a broad array of product lines, most of them bearing suggestive names and evocative labels. They were marketed much like haute couture clothing. Fashion changes quickly, which makes the continued commercial viability of certain 'classic' perfumes, such as the famous Jicky devised by Aimé Guerlain in 1889, rather extraordinary.

In 1910, François Spoturno, better known as Coty, revolutionized perfume packaging by asking the jeweller and glassmaker René Lalique to create quality containers that would be generally affordable; eventually tens of millions of them would be distributed worldwide. In 1917, Paul Poiret became the first couturier-parfumeur, extending his revamping of the feminine image with a perfume he called Chypre (Cyprus), and in 1925 Coco Chanel followed suit and launched her famous No. 5. That same year, at the Exposition des Arts Décoratifs, René Lalique was placed in charge of a perfumers' booth. It was about this time, too, that Guerlain introduced Shalimar and Patou commissioned Louis Süe and André Mar to design the bottles for his famous perfumes.

In the fifties, in a phenomenon paralleling the return to hand-crafted luxury items given such prominence by Dior and Baccarat, the automation of perfume bottle production developed on a new scale. The growth of industries such as Desjonquère (which became Saint-Gobain) and the Masnières glassworks (BSN) attest to this. This automation of glass-making technologies, which initially limited the range of forms and colours, has recently evolved in ways that allow for a new richness of palette and a greater precision in casting.

For more than 20 years the designers Serge Mansau and Pierre Dinand have dominated the production of the perfume bottle. The sculptural qualities of Mansau's work are evident in designs as varied as those for Lancôme's Climats, Guy Laroche's J'ai Osé and Montana's perfumes. Among the most notable of Dinand's designs are those which celebrate the marriage of glass and plastic, such as Paco Rabanne's Calandre, Givenchy 3, and Yves Saint Laurent's Opium. C'est la Vie by Christian Lacroix extends the tradition linking couturiers and designers. In 1990, after having decorated Lacroix's offices and showrooms, Garouste and Bonetti were commissioned to design his perfume bottles.

E. M.

Pullman sleeping cars

In the United States, which encompasses an area about ten times larger than that of Europe, it was not until 10 May 1869, when the Atlantic and Pacific railway lines were joined at Promontory Point, that the country could be crossed by train.

Ten years earlier, in Chicago, the entrepreneur George Mortimer Pullman (already famous for having moved inconveniently-placed buildings by mounting them on railway trucks), annoyed at the prospect of the discomfort he would suffer during prolonged train trips to neighbouring states necessitated by his expanding business, decided to borrow two of the twelve cars of the Chicago Alton & St. Louis Railroad in order to make them more comfortable.

Pullman, a self-made, self-taught businessman, did the bulk of the work himself because he couldn't find any working drawings or plans suffi-

ciently refined for his taste. Seat backs that could be adjusted to a horizontal position were installed, such that when lowered they formed small beds.

The American patent for sleeping cars was registered in 1864. A year later the first luxury Pullman car, the Pioneer, made its inaugural trip as part of the funeral train of Abraham Lincoln. In 1867 Pullman established the Pullman Palace Car Company to manufacture luxury sleeping and restaurant cars. He set the standard of quality service to be enjoyed by rich Americans heading to conquer the west, an achievement that would make him world famous. Some businessmen even rented entire trains of 'hotel cars' or purchased their own Pullmans to guarantee their travel comfort.

The success of Pullman's enterprise was prodigious. When setting up his new factories, the inventor constructed an entire city on the outskirts of

Chicago to house his workers, naming it after himself (it was one of America's first industrial cities). By 1930 some 9,000 cars had been produced, carrying 30 million travellers each year.

Today only three Pullman trains remain: the Manchester Pullman (London-Manchester), the Merseyside Pullman (London-Liverpool), and the Yorkshire Pullman (London-Leeds), the last two having been brought back into service on 13 May 1985.

Pullman's research and innovations had a direct influence on the design of limited-space facilities (American kitchens and bathrooms, for example) in the thirties. New procedures for conserving and preparing food developed by the company, initially for use exclusively in restaurant cars, stimulated the development of all sorts of novel cooking methods that are now part of our daily lives.

E. M.

The history of watches

At the end of the 18th century, when American timepieces were made entirely by craftsmen trained in the tradition of French, Swiss and English master clockmakers, Eli Terry conceived the idea of mass producing them by standardizing their components and replacing the engraved face with one printed on paper. By 1809 he was producing 3,000 clocks a year.

Due to the use of interchangeable pieces, a simple manufacturing process and mechanization, the price of these clocks had already gone down substantially when, towards 1830, Chauncey Jerome produced what he called the One Day Brass Clock. Produced at a rate of 1,500 per day and priced at a mere $1.50, the clock was also marketed in Europe.

In 1876, at the American Centenary Exposition in Philadelphia, and then in 1878, at the Paris Universal Exposition, the American Watch Company of the town of Waltham caused alarm among its English and Swiss compet-itors with the excellence of its products and their amazingly low prices. Its One Dollar Watch could not be surpassed, either in terms of quality or economical manufacture.

Miniaturization and the use of metal in the works of pocket watches exemplify the transition from artisanal to industrial production that characterized late 19th-century America. In Europe during this same period clockmakers adhering to the teachings of Bréguet, an influential master of their craft, continued to perfect their own models and increase their precision. Only Georges Frederick Roskopf, an industrialist from Chaux-de-Fonds, proposed in around 1870 what he called the 'proletariat watch'.

The wristwatch as we know it was introduced at the beginning of the present century, its design, like that of many everyday objects, having been shaped by the requirements of sports. Hans Wilsdorf of Switzerland established the Rolex company and in 1927 invented the waterproof watch, which he had tested during a swim across the English Channel. In 1904 the French-man Louis Cartier devised a wrist-watch for the aviator Santos-Dumont. Throughout the 20th century, watches have kept up with the fashionable styles and trends of the moment. Thanks to Swatch, in the last 15 years they've taken on vivid colours. Swatch's proto-types were designed in the early seventies by three engineers: Ernst Thonke, Jacques Müller and Elmar Mock. The Delirium was the first of its many models which now dominate the market, and was the first integrated watch in which the action was not a separate element. Then came the quartz watch which, whether made of plastic or some other material, offered very high quality. Composed of 51 pieces (as opposed to more than 90 in traditional watches), the Swatch could make its workings fully visible, becoming a celebration of transparency.

E. M.

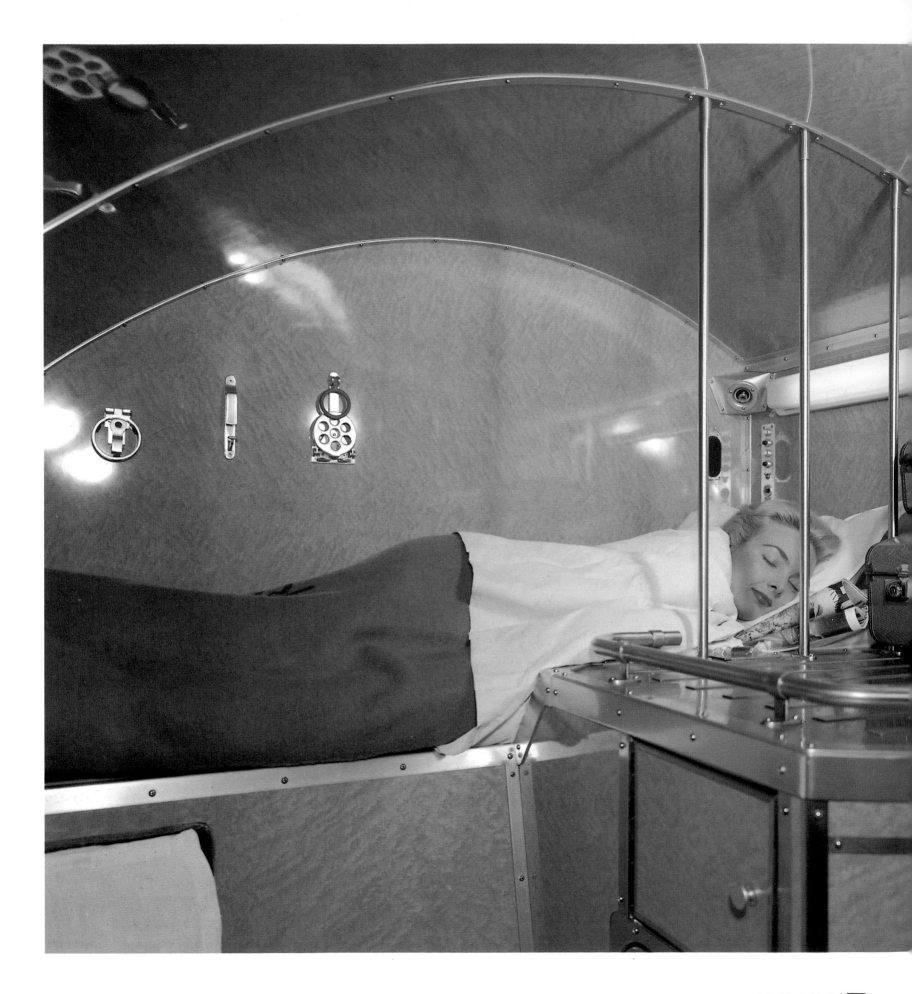

From the trunk to the suitcase

Top: Wardrobe
cabin trunk
made from
rigid Monogram
canvas and
hat box,
Louis Vuitton.

Centre: Cabin
trunk MC 2000
made from
leather and
carbon fibre,
Hermès, 1988.

Bottom:
Spectrum
suitcase
with wheels,
featuring
patented
braking system
and made
from ABS,
designed by
Giugiaro Design
for Samsonite,
1991.

At a time when travel was still an adventure, 'a veritable expedition', when Phileas Fogg required 80 days to make his circuit of the globe, Louis Vuitton was designing travel articles which embodied a certain ideal of comfort and a specific aesthetic of manufacture. Skilled workers cut, sewed, glued and assembled each piece of luggage by hand. Time-intensive techniques worthy of the luxury craft tradition were employed. The end product was a symbol of solidity and refinement.

Louis Vuitton (1821-1892) was the founder of the famous business. His son Georges (1857-1936) designed its now-familiar patterned cloth and Gaston (1883-1970), his grandson, created the company's image and collected all kinds of travel articles, from trunks made of precious woods to old engravings. He put the Vuitton stamp on the great expeditions of the 20th century, designing, for example, the trunks packed in the half-track vehicles used by André Citroën for the Croisière Noire, the long-distance car trek to Africa in 1924-1925.

The word 'luggage' denotes the ensemble of effects and objects we take with us when we travel. Trunks, suitcases, bags and packages are all associated with itinerancy, and each period, each variety of transport, ends up with objects adapted to its specific needs. As jets have become the prevalent mode of long-distance travel, luggage has become lighter. While over the centuries an abundance of chests and trunks has been synonymous with grandeur and wealth, today it would be considered the height of luxury to

travel without any baggage at all. The prestige of Vuitton luggage remains unchallenged, but new means of travel have dictated the development of lines that are both light and sturdy. Accordingly this company, so closely associated with French luxury products throughout the world, now offers not only its traditional models but also new ones better suited to present day circumstances.

As luggage is now relegated to the baggage holds of aeroplanes and handled hurriedly in the course of flight changes and arrivals – in other words, battered and dragged about – suitcases have had to be modified. The Samsonite Company, founded in 1910 in Denver, Colorado by Jesse Shwayder, reached its leading position in the field by tackling these new conditions. 'Strong enough to stand on' was the company's slogan when it advertised the first wooden suitcases for gold-rushers. The corporate name derives, of course, from that of Samson, the ancient hero renowned for his extraordinary strength.

Samsonite was the first manufacturer to offer rigid luggage, to place wheels on suitcases and to use new materials such as magnesium and ABS. In the early eighties the company introduced a line of luggage with a high tech look that it named Ultralite (the name speaks for itself) made of dull enamelled metal. And there is reason to hope the trend toward such innovation in luggage design will continue: it seems the number of passengers travelling by air is likely to double between now and the year 2000. . .

E. M.

1880-1917

by

Jocelyn de Noblet

Do aesthetic contradictions always arise at the end of a century? It would certainly seem to be true of the 19th century. It seems difficult to reconcile the symbolic and aesthetic decadence proposed by Joris-Karl Huysmans and personified by the character of Des Esseintes in his novel *A Rebours*, with the enthusiasm shown by Gustave Eiffel for metal construction.

Huysmans was writing about an aesthetic of pure sensation: 'For a long time, he (Des Esseintes) was an expert in the sincerity and dissembling of hues. Formerly, he had created a boudoir for receiving women, where, amidst small pieces of furniture carved in pale Japanese camphor wood, under a kind of tent made of pink satin from India, flesh would take on the subtle colours of the changing light which filtered through the material.'

For Gustave Eiffel and numerous other civil engineers, on the other hand, 'aesthetics resides entirely in the resistance of materials, established according to mathematical formulae which make it possible to calculate exactly the smallest of pieces, to work out the most advantageous arrangement and to thereby arrive at the lightest, strongest structures.'

These different ways of thinking led to simultaneous but divergent developments in form. The first was bound up with Art Nouveau, whose principle practitioners were Hector Guimard, Victor Horta, Antonio Gaudí and the glassmakers at Nancy under the aegis of Emile Gallé. Characterized by a style of ornamentation based on organic forms, Art Nouveau soon spread to the whole of Europe. The other tendency was crystallized in the 1899 Universal Exposition in Paris, which was dominated by the vast metal structure of the Galerie des Machines by Dutert and Contamin. At the same time, the Eiffel Tower and the Forth Bridge, designed by Benjamin Baker, were being built.

At the beginning of this century, these two tendencies were overtaken by developments in technology and the emergence of radical artistic movements. Cubism (1908) and Futurism (1909) gave rise to a new language of form. At that same time, mass production of cars was beginning with the Ford model T (1908). The first car races were organized, helping the model T to become a dream object. In 1909, Louis Blériot flew across the English Channel. Speed captured the imagination of artists, intellectuals and the general public. In the Futurist manifesto published in *Le Figaro* on 20 February 1909, Filippo Tommaso Marinetti declaimed: 'We declare the world's splendour to be enriched by a new beauty, the beauty of speed. A racing car, its bonnet decorated with large pipes like serpents with explosive breath . . . a roaring car, its engine sounding like a machine gun, is more beautiful than the *Victory of Samothrace*.' This new dynamicism was epitomized by Umberto Boccioni's sculpture *Unique Forms in the Continuity of Space* (1913).

In Germany, between 1909 and 1914, industrialists, architects and artists joined forces in the Deutscher Werkbund, where they sought to define their respective roles in the process of giving form to industrially produced objects. The Werkbund enabled German products to find a consistent functionalist style.

Woman working on a collodionizing machine for the manufacture of incandescent mantles.
Preceding double page: **Scale model of Deperdussin's aeroplane, built by Deperdussin and presented to the Conservatoire National des Arts et Métiers in 1912.**

1879

- William Le Baron Jenney: First Leiter Building, Chicago

- Auguste Rodin: *Le Penseur*
- Ferdinand Cheval, known as Facteur Cheval: Palais Idéal (Hauterives, Drôme, 1879–1912)

- F. W. Woolworth opens first 'five and ten cent store'

1880

- mass production of the pocket watch the One-Dollar-Watch by the American Watch Company
- Christopher Dresser: tea service silver-plated by electrolysis
- Hermann Hollerith: electromechanical tabulating machine

- Werner von Siemens: electric lift
- Gustave Eiffel: Garabit viaduct (1880–1884)

- International Exhibition, Melbourne

1881

- Henry Seely: electric iron
- Werner von Siemens: direct linking of a steam engine to an electric dynamo
- John Augustus Roebling: Brooklyn Bridge (481m), opened 1883
- the tsar Alexander II assassinated in Russia

1882

- Thomas Edison: world's first power station, New York
- Thomas Edison: first hydro-electric plant, Wisconsin, United States
- Etienne Marey: photographic gun, chronophotography

- Universal Exposition, Moscow
- Viennese physician Joseph Breuer uses hypnosis to treat hysteria

1883

- Gottlieb Daimler and Wilhelm Maybach: petrol engine
- start of Orient Express rail service
- William Le Baron Jenney: Home Insurance Company Building, Chicago (1883–1885)
- work starts on Antonio Gaudí's Sagrada Familia, Barcelona
- Universal Exposition, Amsterdam
- Friedrich Nietzsche: *Also Sprach Zarathustra* (1883–1891)

1884

- Lewis Edson Waterman: the Waterman Regular, first fountain pen

- Hiram Stevens Maxim: first recoil-operated machine gun

- Charles Algernon Parsons produces first steam turbine
- Hilaire Bernigaud, comte de Chardonnet: cellulose, first artificial fibre
- Paul Nipkow develops his perforated disk, origin of television
- George Eastman patents photographic film

- Georges Seurat: *Baignade à Asnières*

1885

- Mannesmann brothers produce steel tubing without soldering
- James Kemp: Rover Safety, first bicycle using a chain
- Gottlieb Daimler and Wilhelm Maybach: motorcycle
- Karl Benz builds single-cylinder engine for motor car
- completion of Canadian Pacific railway

1886

- John Pemberton invents Coca-Cola (Atlanta)
- Carl Zeiss invents an optical glass, forerunner of Pyrex
- Charles M. Hall (United States) and P. L. T. Héroult (France) independently produce aluminium by electrolysis
- Frédéric Auguste Bartholdi: *Statue of Liberty* (made by Gustave Eiffel) dedicated in New York

- first Sears, Roebuck and Co. catalogue, United States
- Jean Moréas: Symbolist manifesto
- Auguste Villiers de L'Isle-Adam: *L'Eve Future*, science fiction novel

1887

- Tolbert Lanston: monotype typesetting machine
- Edward Muybridge: animals in movement
- Augustus Désiré Waller carries out the first human electrocardiogram (London)

1888

- George Eastman: Kodak box camera
- John Dunlop: pneumatic tyre
- Universal Exposition, Barcelona
- Heinrich Hertz proves the existence of magnetic waves in the air

□ Gustave Zédé: electrically-propelled submarine The Gymnote

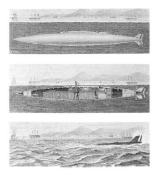

1889

□ Emile Gallé: development of the Art Nouveau glassworks at Nancy, France

□ Gustave Eiffel: three hundred-metre tower, Paris
□ Ferdinand Dutert and Victor Contamin: Galerie des Machines, Universal Exposition, Paris, featuring the widest iron vaulting to date

1890

□ Whitecomb Judson invents the zip
□ mass production of bicycles in the United States
□ first execution using the electric chair, invented by Harold Brown, in Auburn prison, New York
□ Clément Ader: Eole aeroplane
□ Otto Lilienthal makes his first flights in a glider

□ reinforced concrete comes into widespread use in France and in the United States
□ Vincent van Gogh: *Crows in the Wheatfields*
□ Paul Cézanne: *The Cardplayers*
□ William James: *The Principles of Psychology*

1891

□ **American Express cheques**

□ construction of the Trans-Siberian railway begins (5,800 miles, 1891–1907)
□ Claude Monet: *Water-lilies*

□ Oscar Wilde: *The Picture of Dorian Gray*
□ Ivan Petrovich Pavlov: studies on conditioned reflexes
□ Panama financial scandal

1892

□ Lingmer Wirke: Odol bottle

□ first automatic telephone switchboard introduced
□ François Hennebique: first reinforced concrete building in Paris
□ Emile Reynaud Optical Theatre, Musée Grévin, Paris

□ Henry Ford builds his first motor car
□ Hendrick Antoon Lorentz discovers electrons

1893

□ Rudolf Diesel develops prototype Diesel engine
□ Victor Horta: Tassel house, Brussels
□ Universal Exposition, Chicago
□ in Great Britain, William Lethaby founds Central School of Arts and Crafts
□ Emile Durkheim: *The Division of Labour in Society*
□ Julius Elster and Hans Friedrich Geitel study photoelectric cells

□ in Great Britain, James Keir Hardie forms the Independent Labour Party

1894

□ Emile Berliner invents gramophone disc
□ Victor Contamin and Anatole de Baudot: reinforced concrete church Saint-Jean-l'Evangéliste, Montmartre

□ Henri de Toulouse-Lautrec: posters featuring La Goulue
□ Claude Debussy: *Prélude à l'après-midi d'un faune*
□ in France, start of the Dreyfus affair

□ Rudyard Kipling: *The Jungle Book*

1895

- King C. Gillette invents the safety razor

- Brown & Sharp: automatic turret lathe
- Carl von Linde: refrigeration by compression
- Konstantin Tsiolkovsky formulates theory of rocket propulsion
- Auguste and Louis Lumière make their first films
- Wilhelm Conrad Röntgen discovers x-rays

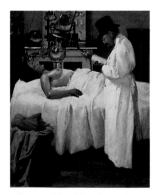

- first public film show, Paris
- Aleksander Stepanovich Popov: antenna
- Guglielmo Marconi invents radio telegraphy

- opening of Siegfried Bing's Art Nouveau gallery in Paris
- Otto Wagner: *Moderne Architektur*
- spread of Art Nouveau (Austrian Secession, Liberty style, Jugendstil)
- Edvard Munch: *The Scream*
- Emile Verhaeren: *Les Villes tentaculaires*
- Josef Breuer and Sigmund Freud: studies on hysteria

1896

- Victor Horta: Maison du Peuple, Brussels
- Hermann Muthesius visits Great Britain and writes a report on the principles of industrial design
- Alfred Jarry: *Ubu Roi*
- Anton Chekhov: *The Seagull*
- Theodor Herzl: *Jewish State*, birth of the Zionist movement
- Henri Becquerel discovers radioactivity
- Baron Pierre de Coubertin revives the Olympic games at Athens

1897

- Charles Rennie Mackintosh: Argyle chair

- Karl Ferdinand Braun: cathode ray tube
- Charles Rennie Mackintosh: Glasgow School of Art library
- Hector Guimard: Castel Béranger
- International Exposition, Brussels
- foundation of the Secession in Vienna
- foundation of the Vereinigte Werkstätte für Kunst und Handwerk in Munich
- James Ensor: *Masks and Death*
- Louis Lumière: *L'Arroseur arrosé*
- Stéphane Mallarmé: *Un Coup de Dés n'Abolira Jamais le Hasard*

1898

- Valdemar Poulsen: tape recorder, the Telegraphon (Denmark)
- Paris métro opens

- Josef Maria Olbrich: Secession art gallery, Vienna
- Henrik Berlage: Amsterdam Stock Exchange
- Pierre and Marie Curie observe radioactivity and isolate radium
- Paul Cézanne: *Bathers* (1898-1905)
- Georges Méliès invents the fade out

1899

- Bayer markets aspirin
- Louis Henry Sullivan and Dankmar Adler: Carson, Pirie and Scott department store, Chicago

- Camille Jenatzy: electric car La Jamais-Contente sets world speed record

- Maxime Laubeuf: the Narval submarine
- Ernest Rutherford discovers alpha and beta rays in radioactive atoms
- Paul Gauguin: *Where do we come from? Who are we? Where are we going?*

- Ebenezer Howard's *Garden Cities of Tomorrow* initiates modern city planning
- first popular cartoon strips in the American press
- beginning of the Boer War

1900

- Charles Rennie Mackintosh: Ingram chair
- George Eastman: Kodak Brownie camera
- Antonio Gaudí: Güell park, Barcelona (1900–1914)
- Josef Hoffmann: Secession room at the Universal Exposition, Paris
- Hector Guimard: métro entrances, Paris

- R. A. Fessenden transmits human speech via radio waves (United States)
- Ferdinand, count Zeppelin: first flight of the LZ1 zeppelin airship which flew for 20 minutes

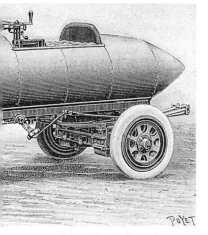

- Max Planck: formulates quantum theory
- Sigmund Freud: *Interpretation of Dreams*
- Boxer uprising in China

1901

- Charles Robert Ashbee: silver sugar bowl
- **Frank Hornby: Meccano construction toy**

- David E. Kenney: vacuum cleaner (United States)
- Frank Lloyd Wright: Martin House, Oak Park (United States)
- Tony Garnier: Cité Industrielle project
- Ecole de Nancy (Art Nouveau movement including Emile Gallé and Victor Prouvé) forms a company
- Guglielmo Marconi transmits telegraphic radio waves across the Atlantic
- Pablo Picasso: *Self-portrait*, blue period
- August Strindberg: *A Dream Play*
- death of Queen Victoria
- Theodore Roosevelt elected president of the United States

1902

- Kolo Moser: furniture

- Auguste Perret: reinforced concrete apartment block, rue Franklin, Paris
- Otto Wagner: *Die Zeit* telegraph office

- Claude Debussy: *Pelléas et Mélisande*
- Georges Méliès: *Le Voyage dans la Lune*
- Vladimir Ilyich Lenin publishes *What Is To Be Done?*

1903

- C. H. Stearn and F. Topham: industrial manufacture of viscose
- J. C. Beidler: photocopying machine
- Wilbur and Orville Wright fly a powered aeroplane, the Flyer (Kitty Hawk, United States)
- Wilhelm Einthoven perfects the electrocardiograph

- Wilhelm Maybach makes the first Mercedes cars
- Georges Claude invents the industrial process of liquefaction of air

1904

- Josef Hoffmann: silver cutlery for Lilly and Fritz Waendorfer, made by the Wiener Werkstätte (1904–1908)
- W. Rubel: offset printing
- the first ultraviolet lamps
- J. P. L. Elster devises the first practical photoelectric cell
- Otto Wagner: Postal Savings Bank, Vienna (1904–1906)
- Adolf Loos: Villa Karma, Montreux
- Universal Exposition, St. Louis
- Paul Cézanne: *Montagne Sainte-Victoire*
- with *Luxe, Calme et Volupté*, Henri Matisse exhibits at Ambroise Vollard

- Raymond Unwin and Barry Parker: first garden city, Letchworth, Great Britain
- foundation of the Wiener Werkstätte by Koloman Moser and Josef Hoffmann

- Anton Chekhov: *The Cherry Orchard*
- work begins on the Panama Canal
- in Paris, first congress on hygiene in the home
- war breaks out between Russia and Japan

1905

- Sir John Ambrose Fleming: diode
- Josef Hoffmann: Palais Stoclet, Brussels
- Robert Maillart: Tavanasa bridge, Switzerland, using reinforced concrete
- rayon yarn manufactured commercially through viscose process
- Universal Exposition, Liège
- first neon light signs appear
- first motor buses in London
- in Munich, foundation of the Expressionist group Die Brücke
- at the Salon d'Automne in Paris, the term 'fauve' first applied to work of Matisse, Braque, Marquet, Camoin…
- Gustav Klimt: *Hope*
- Paul Cézanne: *Les Grandes Baigneuses*

- Max Linder: *Sauvé par Rover*
- Sigmund Freud: *Three Contributions to the Theory of Sex*
- Albert Einstein: theory of relativity
- first Russian revolution

1906

- Sir James Dewar: Thermos bottle
- International Exposition, Milan

1907

- Leo Hendrik Baekeland: bakelite, synthetic resin

- Pablo Picasso: *Les Demoiselles d'Avignon* (the start of Cubism)

- foundation of the Deutscher Werkbund by Hermann Muthesius and Henry van de Velde
- Louis Lumière: process for colour photography
- Ross Harrison develops tissue culture techniques
- slow motion effect invented by August Musger
- Ferdinand de Saussure: course on general linguistics, Geneva

1908

- Henry Ford: Model T, first mass-produced motor car (assembly line starts 1913)

- Peter Behrens: electric kettle
- General Motors Corporation formed
- Henry van de Velde builds the Kunstgewerbeschule at Weimar
- Frank Lloyd Wright: Robie house, Chicago
- Peter Behrens: AEG turbine factory, Berlin
- first Hollywood film studio established
- Adolf Loos: *Ornament and Crime*
- Henri Matisse: *La Desserte*

1909

- the American Robert Edwin Peary reaches the North Pole (6 April)
- Georges Braque and Pablo Picasso: analytical cubism
- Sergei Diaghilev presents his Ballets Russes for the first time in Paris
- Filippo Tommaso Marinetti: Futurist manifesto
- Henri Matisse: *La Danse*
- Gustav Mahler: *Symphony No. 9*
- Sigmund Freud: *Introduction to Psychoanalysis*
- Louis Blériot crosses the English Channel in an aeroplane

1910

- Henri Fabre: first successful seaplane flight
- Universal Exposition, Brussels
- Adolf Loos: Steiner house, Vienna
- Le Corbusier, Ludwig Mies van der Rohe and Walter Gropius work in Peter Behren's practice
- Wassily Kandinsky, Frantisek Kupka, Robert Delaunay: beginnings of abstract art
- first Michelin road map

- Herwarth Walden founds the journal *Der Sturm*
- Igor Stravinsky: *The Firebird*
- Mexican Revolution

1911

- radio transmitter placed on top of the Eiffel tower
- Italian war planes carry out first bombing raids during the conquest of Libya
- Perret brothers: Champs-Elysées theatre
- foundation in Munich of the Blaue Reiter group (Kandinsky, Marc, Macke…)
- Georges Braque: *Man with a Guitar*
- Igor Stravinsky: *Petrushka*
- Walter Gropius and Adolf Meyer: Fagus factory at Alfeld an der Leine

- Roald Amundsen discovers the South Pole (14 December)
- Chinese Revolution

1912

- first Futurist exhibition in Paris
- Marcel Duchamp: *Nude Descending a Staircase*

- Arnold Schönberg: *Pierrot lunaire*
- Wassily Kandinsky: *Concerning the Spiritual in Art*
- Franz Kafka: *Metamorphosis*
- Balkan wars

1913

- Domerle, first commercial refrigerator sold in United States
- Hans Geiger: device capable of counting individual alpha rays
- Henry Ford uses a conveyor belt assembly line for the production of the model T car
- industrial manufacture of acetate
- Carlo Castagna: Alfa Romeo 20/30 for count Mario Ricotti

- Leica camera
- Cass Gilbert: Woolworth building, skyscraper (242m) in New York
- Universal Exposition, Ghent
- Armory Show: 1,200 Post-Impressionist works shown in New York, Chicago and Boston
- Kasimir Serevinovich Malevich: *Black Square on White Ground* (birth of Suprematism)
- Alexander Archipenko: *Cubist Nude*
- Umberto Boccioni: *Unique Forms of Continuity in Space*
- Marcel Duchamp: *Bicycle wheel*, first 'readymade'

- Igor Stravinsky: *The Rite of Spring*
- Thomas Mann: *Death in Venice*

- Niels Bohr formulates his theory of atomic structure
- suffragette demonstrations in London

1914

- first traffic lights, Cleveland, United States
- Walter Gropius and Adolf Meyer: model factory displayed at the Deutscher Werkbund exhibition, Cologne
- Walter Gropius: sleeping car compartment for Deutsche Reichsbahn
- Antonio Sant'Elia: drawings for the città nuova and *Futurist Manifesto of Architecture*

- Le Corbusier: project for Domino house
- Marcel Proust: *A la Recherche du Temps Perdu* (start of publication)
- Docteur Hustin carries out the first blood transplant with the donor absent
- Panama Canal opens

- First World War

1915

- Junkers make airframes using Duralumin
- the Design and Industries Association set up (England)
- San Francisco World's Fair
- Robert Delaunay: *Homage to Blériot*
- **Alexander Samuelson designs the Coca-Cola bottle**

- Marcel Duchamp: *The Bride Stripped Bare by her Bachelors, Even* (1915–1923)
- D. W. Griffith: *Birth of a Nation*
- Sir Patrick Geddes: *Cities in Evolution*
- Alfred Wegener enunciates theory of continental drift

1916

- Gabrielle Chanel, known as Coco Chanel, founds her fashion company

- Frank Lloyd Wright: Imperial Hotel, Tokyo
- birth of the Dada movement, Zürich
- Robert Andrews Millikan measures the charge of an electron
- first birth control advice centre opened in New York
- Oswald Spengler: *The Decline of the West* (1916–1920)

1917

- **Gerrit Thomas Rietveld: red and blue armchair**
- Theo van Doesburg founds the group and the journal *De Stijl*
- the Ballets Russes perform *Parade* (plot by Cocteau, music by Erik Satie, sets and costumes by Pablo Picasso)
- Charlie Chaplin: *The Immigrant*
- first jazz records (United States)
- October Revolution in Russia
- the United States enters the war on the allies' side

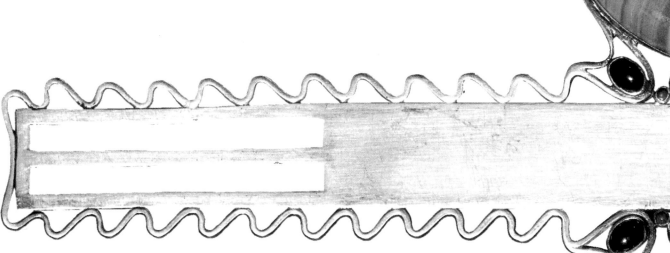

T he ideals and achievements of the
British Arts and Crafts Movement
are now well documented, and
detailed studies of its major protagonists
have contributed to its wider interpretation.[1]
My aim in this essay is to consider subsequent transformations of the craft ideal,
concentrating on European developments
in the first decades of the 20th century.
In the 19th century, the campaign of John
Ruskin and William Morris and their followers promoted the crafts as agents of
social, moral and aesthetic reform. In

The Survival of the
Craft Ideal

Gillian Naylor

The Arts and Crafts Movement means standards,

whether of work or life; the protection of standards,

whether in the product or producer,

and it means that these things must be taken together.

Charles Robert Ashbee, Craftsmanship in Competitive Industry, *London, 1908*

Craftsmanship in Competitive Industry, published in 1908, C. R. Ashbee wrote: 'The Arts and Crafts Movement means standards, whether of work or life; the protection of standards, whether in the product or producer, and it means that these things must be taken together.' The survival of the crafts came to be associated with the survival of humanism and standards – in an industrial society the only viable alternative to the futility of that 'useless toil', which, as far as Morris was concerned, culminated in the production of 'tons and tons of unutterable rubbish'.

These convictions were obviously persuasive – craft revivals were celebrated in Europe and America, as well as in Britain – and they came to serve a variety of causes. The 'craft ideal', for example, could sanction experiment in the interests both of individualism and the collective; it embraced the claims of tradition as well as those of the avant-garde; it promoted concepts of regional and national identity, and above all it established designing and making as a democratic process – so much so that at least one of the first historians of the Arts and Crafts achievement was convinced that William Morris and his followers had 'pioneered' the Modern Movement.

Before one can assess what survived of the Arts and Crafts ideals and achievements, therefore, one must first confront Nikolaus Pevsner's conviction that William Morris and his followers were proto-modernists. In *Pioneers of Modern Design* (first published as *Pioneers of the Modern Movement* in 1936),[2] Pevsner set out to demonstrate that 'the phase between Morris and Gropius is a historical unit'. According to Pevsner 'Morris laid the foundation of the modern style; with Gropius its character was ultimately determined.'

Such statements were obviously problematical, and their ambiguity was evident in Pevsner's text. In order to sustain his argument, Pevsner was obliged to distinguish between Morris the artist and Morris the thinker: Morris the artist, according to

Top:
Suite of
furniture,
designed by
Louis Sparre
and A. Willy
Finch,
manufactured
by Iris,
c.1900.

Bottom left:
Silver and
glass carafe,
designed by
Archibald Knox
for Liberty,
c.1900.

Bottom right:
Armchair,
designed by
George Jack,
manufactured
by Morris &
Co., c.1895.

Pevsner 'may in the end not have been able to reach beyond the limits of his century; Morris the man and the thinker did'.[3] Pevsner, therefore, was unable to reconcile the conservatism of the achievements of Morris and his followers with the radicalism that inspired their work, so that while the ideals which inspired these 19th-century design reforms were, in his opinion, 'politically correct', most of the objects that demonstrated these ideals were misguided. One had to wait until the advent of the Bauhaus to see the glorious reformation of Arts and Crafts reforms.

Nevertheless, as Pevsner had correctly stated: 'We owe it to him [Morris] that an ordinary man's dwelling house has become once more a worthy object of the architect's thought, and a chair, a wallpaper or a vase a worthy object of the artist's imagination'.[4] In other words, the practice of design, especially the creation of everyday household objects, became a social as well as symbolic activity.

To his contemporaries, therefore, and to the majority of his successors in the early years of the 20th century, Morris preached a message of hope as well as action. In the first place, 'design' became a viable occupation for the educated and socially committed classes – it was dignified, rather than deplorable, to create objects and to work as an artisan. And in the second place, Morris established an aesthetic for design which, in theory, substituted 18th-century (and therefore aristocratic) concepts of taste for a new basis of 'distinction' – a means of distinguishing between 'genuine' and commercial or expedient production. In other words, the emphasis in making shifted from commodity to symbolic production.

Nevertheless, this belief in a democracy of craft-based design that would bring 'joy to the maker and the user' had its disadvantages. Without the assistance of some form of machine-aided production, the craft product remained expensive and exclusive, and the survival of Morris-inspired craftsmanship depended on wealth and patron-

age. The dilemma of his position led Morris to radical political commitment, and his successors in the 20th century had to choose between exclusivity (the Viennese model), 'beauty for all' (the Scandinavian model), or the 'new spirit' of Modernism.

The Vienna Werkstätte

When Josef Hoffmann and Koloman Moser announced plans to establish craft workshops in Vienna in 1903, they made their intentions clear. Their aim, according to their working programme was 'to establish intimate contact between public, designer and craftsman, and to produce good, simple domestic requisites'.[5] And they intended to do this without the aid of machine production: 'We are aware', they wrote, 'that a mass-produced object of a tolerable kind can be provided by means of the machine; it must, however, then bear the imprint of its method of manufacture. We do not regard it as our task to move into this area as yet.' It is obvious, therefore, that from the outset the workshops rejected any Arts and Crafts ideal of egalitarianism, and that their chief targets – for sales, as well as reform – were the affluent bourgeoisie: 'We neither can nor will compete for the lowest prices,' they wrote. 'Our middle class is as yet very far from having fulfilled its cultural task. Its turn has come to do full and wholesale justice to its own evolution.'

The Vienna workshops, therefore, provided a cosmopolitan, urbane and essentially urban version of the craft ideal. Their designers were not primarily concerned with tradition, nor with the preservation of artisanal skills. They were stylistic innovators, and their products were intended for a wealthy, fashion-conscious avant-garde who could appreciate (and pay for) sophisticated simplicity and individuality in design and making. In the early years of their experiment, the Werkstätte designers contributed to those transformations of form and space that are now associated with the aesthetic of Modernism (in the Palais Stoclet, for example), and it is no coincidence that the work of Charles Rennie and Margaret Mackintosh was more appreciated in Vienna than it was in London. For the 'craft' in the Mackintosh achievement lay in the refinement and purity of form and surface. 'Building in his hands becomes an abstract art', wrote Pevsner,[6] and it was this abstraction, this seemingly wilful denial of the materiality, as well as of the vernacular traditions, of designing and making that so incensed the English Arts and Crafts crusaders and so delighted the Viennese, who, as one contemporary critic pointed out, 'were already a little bored with the eternal solid goodness of the English interior'.[7]

In the years leading up to the First World War, therefore, the Viennese challenged the social, moral and vernacular associations of craftsmanship, and championed its elitism – 'craft', according to Josef Hoffmann, could only survive as a luxury and he fought a bitter rearguard action in the post-war years to preserve the aura of Werkstätte production. When one of his managers secured lucrative licensing agreements with manufacturing firms in the early 1920s, Hoffmann was incensed: 'When our things are on view in every shop in the Mariahilfestrasse,' he is reported as saying, 'it will be all up with us'. [8]

In the Depression years, however, it was neither financially, socially nor politically correct to pursue policies of elitism, especially in Central Europe. 'Austria must come to terms with the demands and necessities arising from its social upheaval,' wrote one critic of the Austrian contribution to the 1925 Paris exhibition; and Adolf Loos – the so-called 'Wrathful Anti-Christ of the Wiener Werkstätte' – was even more emphatic: 'I warn the Austrians against identifying themselves with the Wiener Werkstätte movement,' he declared in a speech in 1927. 'The modern spirit is a social spirit, and modern objects exist not just for the benefit of the upper crust, but for everybody.'[9]

The crafts, it seemed, could only become 'modern' (or democratic, or egalitarian) if and when the 'modernism' of contemporary production methods was accepted. It is interesting that those British designers who did not entirely reject machine production succeeded in producing 'modern' design in the Pevsnerian sense: Christopher Dresser's metalwork, for example, with its simple geometric forms and its undecorated surfaces, was designed for production – it was not handmade. Dresser always prided himself on being a 'commercial' designer, and he was, of course, admired in Vienna. Again, W. A. S. Benson, a metalworker, a director of Morris's firm, and a founder of the Art Workers' Guild, established a factory in Hammersmith, London, in order to produce his work. His light fittings were marketed through wholesale and retail outlets, as well as sold to private clients, and they could also lay claim to 'modernity', not necessarily because of their formal simplicity, but because Benson welcomed the opportunities that mechanized production, as well as the introduction of electricity, brought him.

Craft and production

In the early years of the 20th century, therefore, the democratic idealism associated with craftsmanship went through several transformations. It survived, for example, in furniture production in Germany, where groups like the Munich and Dresden Werkstätte supported experiments in machine-assisted workshop production, which involved the introduction of standardized and interchangeable components. In Munich, Bruno Paul, a self-taught designer, pioneered the concept of *Typenmöbel* – or 'type' furniture – that could be produced using semi-mass production techniques, and in 1908 he introduced a range of domestic furniture – cupboards, cabinets, chairs and tables – that were made from standardized components in a variety of woods and finishes. These standardized ranges could be used throughout the house, and, according to Paul, they

Silver chalice,
designed by
Archibald Knox
for Liberty,
c.1900.

When, then, will you disencumber yourselves of the lymphatic ideology of your deplorable

Ruskin. . .with his hatred of the machine, of steam and electricity, this maniac for antique

simplicity resembles a man who in full maturity wants to sleep in his cot again and drink

at the breasts of a nurse. . .in order to regain the carefree state of infancy.

Filippo Tommaso Marinetti, Lecture to the Lyceum Club in London, March 1912

demonstrated an admirable ideal of domestic order and unity (rather than uniformity) that was related to middle class rather than elitist requirements.

Similarly Karl Schmidt, a cabinet-maker and carpenter who had visited England, set up the Deutsche Werkstätte in Hellerau, near Dresden in the early years of the century, where he commissioned well-known designers to produce reasonably priced furniture for the middle class market. Deutsche Werkstätte *Typenmöbel*, also using standardized components, were designed by his brother-in-law, Richard Riemerschmid, and this furniture was much admired by the visiting British when it was exhibited in the Deutscher Werkbund exhibition in Cologne in 1914: 'The great economic mode of this type of production,' wrote a contributor to the *Studio Year-Book* of that year, 'is that all these single parts, of which there are about 800 different kinds, can be made in large quantities and with the most advantageous employment of machine labour, while the extensive range of combinations ensures to the complete article an individuality and character of its own, without betraying the use of machinery in its production.'[10]

A similar ideal of individuality and character, as well as traditions, was pursued by Gustav Stickley in the United States – the country which was to pioneer the fact, as well as the ideology, of mass production and mass consumption. In Europe, however, prior to the First World War, the conviction that the use of machinery must be concealed, especially in designs for the domestic market, persisted until economic realities and the ideologies associated with Modernism and the Modern Movement challenged the aura surrounding craft and craftsmanship. Modernist idealism, as Pevsner's approach indicates, absorbed the social concerns of the earlier generation and related them to the collective rather than individual endeavour; it rejected tradition in its promotion of the new, and celebrated

Silver bowl, designed by Charles Robert Ashbee, c.1893.

formal rather than emotive qualities in design. The aesthetic of the machine and the machine age absorbed theories of the avant-garde in fine arts, but it banished craftsmanship and all the traditional associations of craftsmanship as relics of a bygone age. If the crafts were to survive, they were to be channelled into the greater service of industrial design, and in the internal battles of the Bauhaus, for example, that very public arena for debate about the contrasting claims of craft and industry, 'handiwork', in theory at least, was only permitted to survive in the production of prototypes (or typeforms) for industry.

The Bauhaus, craft and industry

In *The New Architecture and the Bauhaus*, Walter Gropius wrote: 'The Bauhaus represents a school of thought which believes that the difference between industry and handicraft is due, far less to the different nature of the tools employed in each, than to subdivision of labour in the one and undivided control by a single workman in the other. Handicrafts and industry may be regarded as opposite poles that are gradually approaching each other. The former have already begun to change their traditional nature. In the future the fields of handicrafts will be found to lie mainly in the preparatory stages of industrial production.'[11]

The history of the Bauhaus (like that of the Arts and Crafts Movement) has been told and re-told.[12] What is significant in this context, however, is the re-interpretation of the role of the designer that Gropius's changing philosophies implied. He may have established the school as a cathedral of the crafts (as seemed appropriate to the pre-war Weimar), but in Germany during the inter-war period industry and industrial production was essential to economic survival and industrial production implied standardization of parts and components, together with the introduction of Fordist principals of manufacture.

Gropius absorbed the lessons of Fordism – like Ashbee, he believed in 'standards,

whether of work or life', but he also believed that these standards could only be maintained through standardization. At Dessau, therefore, the students were to use their skills in craftsmanship and making to produce prototypes (or typeforms) for industrial production. The workshops were transformed into laboratories. Marianne Brandt, for example, has described how, under the direction of Moholy-Nagy, the students from the former metal workshops concentrated on the production of lighting fitments. 'Gradually,' she wrote, 'through visits to the industry and inspections and interviews on the spot, we came to our main concern – industrial design. Moholy-Nagy fostered this with stubborn energy…We tried to create a functional but aesthetic assembly line, small facilities for garbage disposal, and so forth.' She adds, somewhat caustically, 'considerations which in retrospect seem to me no longer prerequisite for the production of a first-class lamp'.[13]

Nevertheless, although the new directions in the Bauhaus attempted to eliminate craft and craftsmanship as determinants for form, they did not challenge the role of art in the design process. Gropius's slogan for the Dessau school was 'art and technology – a new unity', and 'artists' (like Moholy-Nagy) remained central to the teaching programmes. These artists, however, were transformed into designers – and just as Moholy-Nagy had once produced a 'painting' without applying brush to canvas, so the designer could conceptualize his work through understanding, rather than participating in the production process. At the same time, however, the artist or designer maintained full control of the appearance (or the 'look') of the end product, and provided what Gropius described as the 'meaning in design'.

The conviction that there could and should be a relationship between art and industry was a potent one in Europe in the 1920s and 1930s. It was fundamental to De Stijl and

Constructivist philosophies, and it contributed to transformations of the craft ideal in Britain. In his seminal book *Art and Industry* (first published in 1934), the poet, art and social critic Herbert Read wrote: 'In every practical activity, the artist is necessary to give form to material. An artist must plan the distribution of buildings within a city; an artist must plan the houses themselves, the halls and factories and all that makes up the city; an artist must plan the interiors of such buildings – the shapes of the rooms, down to the smallest details, the knives and forks, the cups and saucers and the door handles. And at every stage we need the abstract artist, the artist who orders materials until they combine the highest degree of practical economy with the greatest measure of spiritual freedom.'[14]

Now, apart from one word, this statement could summarize the ideals of the Arts and Crafts Movement. The 'form-giver' in both programmes was the artist, and 'art', in 19th-century interpretations, encompassed both craft and architecture; for Read, however, the form-giver was the abstract artist, 'abstraction' providing a universal aesthetic for art, architecture and design. 'Design' in Read's (and therefore Modernist) interpretation related to design for manufacture, or industrial design, and craft no longer had a role to play in any creative or productive process.

Nevertheless, the ideal of craft and industry in peaceful and productive wedlock was a persuasive one, and it continued to survive in 20th-century programmes for design reform, especially in Scandinavia, where a 'modernist' aesthetic, encompassing both traditional, regional and national values, was demonstrated in both architecture and design.

Swedish grace

'… Always, when we buy something for our homes, we should ask ourselves if it fulfils the most vital requirement – namely, that everything should answer the purpose it is intended for. A chair should be comfortable to sit on, a table comfortable to work or eat at, a bed good to sleep in. Uncomfortable chairs, rickety tables, and narrow beds are, therefore, automatically ugly. But it does not follow that comfortable chairs, steady tables, and broad beds are beautiful. Things must, as everywhere in nature, fulfil their purpose in a simple and expressive manner, and without this they do not achieve beauty even if they satisfy practical requirements.'[15]

In her book *Beauty for All*, Ellen Key, a Swedish sociologist and social reformer, was campaigning for standards of domestic simplicity, utility and order that were already well established in Nordic interpretations of the British craft ideal. In Sweden, the Svenska Slöjdföreningen (now known as Svensk Form), with its motto 'Swedish handicraft is the father of Swedish independence', had been founded in 1845 to encourage self-sufficiency in local industries. In the early years, Svensk Form promoted evening training for workmen, published patterns and prototypes for various products, and throughout the century organized exhibitions, especially in local workers' institutes. Surviving traditions in local and vernacular craftsmanship were studied and encouraged, so that by the 1890s, when the renaissance associated with the Arts and Crafts was spreading throughout Europe, the Swedes had well-defined programmes of teaching and reform to draw on.

Fundamental in these programmes, however, was the conviction that design was a democratic process. 'Beauty,' as Ellen Key expressed it, was 'for all', and reforms that resulted in exquisite, expensive and elitist products were meaningless. Svensk Form, therefore, became the custodian of egalitarian standards, and, from the 1880s and 1890s, it focused its attacks on industries that concentrated on the production of exclusive rather than 'everyday' goods. In 1914, for example, when Sweden took part in a Baltic exhibition in Malmö, Eric Wettergren, Svensk Form's spokesman, wrote: 'Our furniture manufacturers have marked time … simple and inexpensive pieces for the industrial and farm worker still do not exist, and our more modest town homes still lack furniture specially designed to meet their needs.'[16]

The policies that were established in this period helped to promote the prestige of Swedish design in the 1930s, and in the 1950s, when Scandinavia seemed to have succeeded where Britain had failed, in 'democratizing' craftsmanship by relating it to industrial production. As early as 1917 the Swedish ceramics manufacturers Gustavsberg and Rörstrand appointed artists to advise on their design production. Wilhelm Kåge, a young painter and poster designer produced the Worker's Service for Gustavsberg in that year, while Edward Hall, a painter who had trained with Matisse, worked for Rörstrand, and for Orrefors, the glass manufacturers. As well as working on the production ranges, these and other artists were given their own studios where they could experiment, so that they benefited from the freedoms associated with craft, as well as from the disciplines inherent in the production process. Sweden (and the other Scandinavian countries), therefore, established a seemingly ideal model for maintaining the spirit of craftsmanship within industrial production. 'Make an inspection of a [Swedish] modern factory,' wrote one contributor to the British journal *The Architectural Review* in August 1930, 'and you will see mass products turned out with the precision and beauty of the silversmith.' William Morris could not have asked for more.

C h r i s t o p h e r   D r e s s e r

Christopher Dresser, born in 1834, was first employed as a botanical draughtsman. Plans and Elevations of Flowers, one of several works published by him in 1860 that were well received by English specialists, proved invaluable to decorative artists working with natural forms in the decades prior to Art Nouveau. After having presented his dissertation and failed to obtain a chair at London's University College, he turned his attention from plant life to the design and making of metal objects. Dresser incorporated botanical metaphors into his designs, formulating an elegant, minimal style. His training as a botanical artist left its mark on all his theories. Influenced by Owen Jones's The Grammar of Ornament, he himself published two works in 1862, The Art of Decorative Design and The Development of Ornamental Art, in which he argued an affinity between natural forms and those of design.

The first Dresser tea services made their mark through the restraint of their forms. Purity of line and simplicity of shape were at the heart of this designer's work and these same principles would be honoured through the first decades of the 20th century.

In 1877, on returning from a trip to Japan, Dresser simplified his forms still further. For the first time a designer renounced decorative ornament altogether in favour of sobriety. Having been thoroughly initiated into the world of industrial production, now fully conversant with metals and their potential, Dresser gave his designs a resolutely modern profile, as can be seen in his celebrated riveted metal teapot of 1898.

The great English firms of the late 19th century were interested in producing limited editions made not of silver but of electrolyzed metals. The Elkington and James Dixon & Sons companies set up experimental laboratories to perfect the production of objects made of silver plate and alloys with decorations applied to their surfaces. Dresser exploited every available advanced technique (otherwise used at the time primarily to make less expensive copies of models initially produced in solid silver), combining inexpensive materials with more luxurious ones such as ebony and mahogany.

The only things that mattered were functionality and cost. Like the members of the Arts and Crafts Movement, Christopher Dresser always rejected the label 'artist', preferring to consider his activity in terms of industrially-oriented experiment.

E. M.

Top, from left to right: Bonbonnière, 1889.

Silver-plated teapot, made by Hukin & Heath.

Silver-plated carafe, made by Hukin & Heath, 1879.

Silver sugar bowl, made by Hukin & Heath.

Silver carafe, made by Hukin & Heath, 1881.

Background: Silver-plated carafe, made by Elkington & Co.

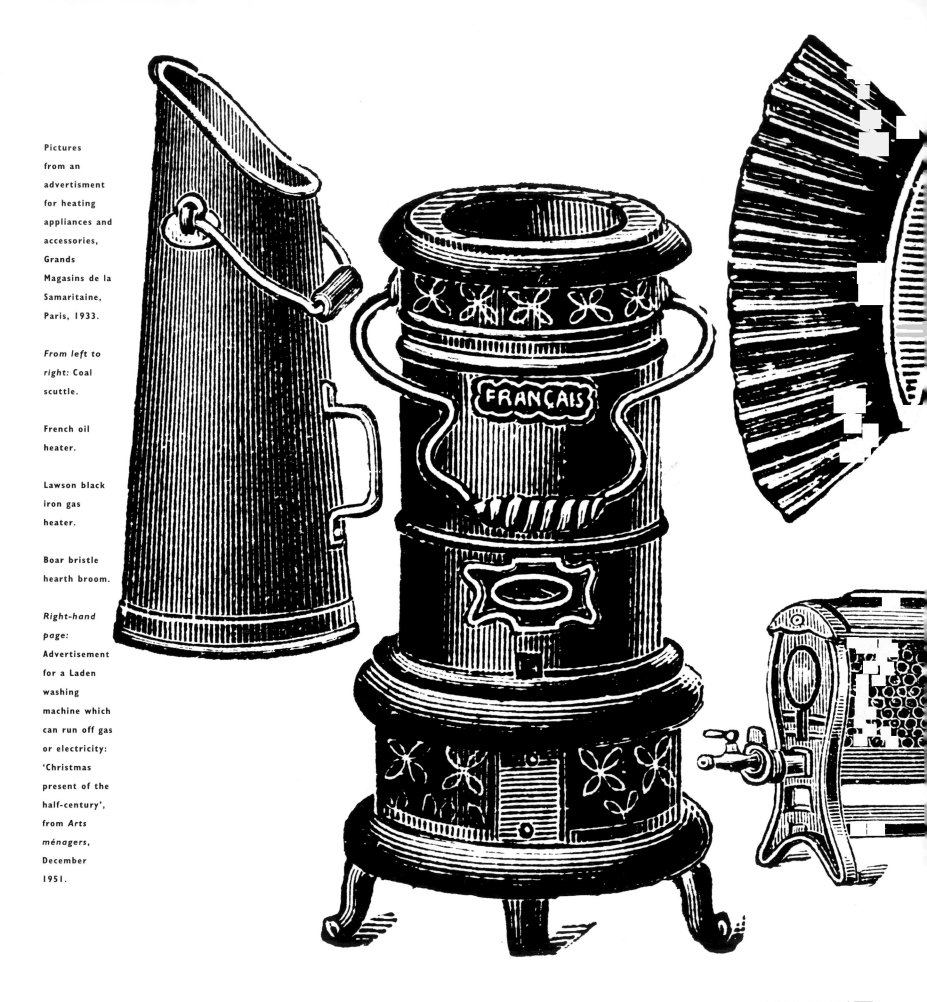

Pictures from an advertisment for heating appliances and accessories, Grands Magasins de la Samaritaine, Paris, 1933.

From left to right: Coal scuttle.

French oil heater.

Lawson black iron gas heater.

Boar bristle hearth broom.

Right-hand page: Advertisement for a Laden washing machine which can run off gas or electricity: 'Christmas present of the half-century', from *Arts ménagers*, December 1951.

FRANÇAIS

Art for Everyone

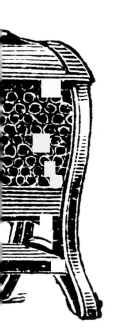

The attempt to change the everyday environment in France at the turn of the century

....

Lionel Richard

The end of the 19th century in Europe was marked by an exaggerated faith in the capacity of science to improve the daily lives of all social classes. A spirited analyst of *The Contemporary Scientific Spirit*,[1] Foveau de Courmelles voiced sentiments shared by all those who claimed to support 'progress' when he stated that thanks to Science (as he wrote it) well-being in both the city and the home had been increased. He noted admiringly that luxury, instead of being limited to 'the tiny minority of the old days', had spread widely, thereby producing 'a more just distribution of wealth'.

With the exception of a small fringe of determined sceptics firmly attached to the past and a few rebels under the sway of anarchist ideas, the contemporaries of Pasteur were enthusiastic about the technical innovations that had abruptly and substantially changed their daily existence. In Parisian department stores, those temples of the marvellous, all the utilitarian objects that industry had begun to produce in such immense quantities were regularly brought together for what was now democratic

consumption. Life in the capital was changing on any number of fronts: central heating had made it possible for new buildings to have running hot water, lifts were becoming increasingly commonplace and electric lighting, while expensive, had begun to replace gas lamps.

The imagination of dreamers responded with excitement to these astonishing developments. Jules Verne was not alone in fabricating, in his head and on paper, a prodigious future for machines. After all, the machines were already there; they only needed to be perfected. Albert Robida,[2] anticipating the *Electric Life of the 20th Century*, was not mistaken about the consequences of the development of electricity: with great prescience he foresaw gramophones and cinematographs in every home, interphones, remote control, and the transformation of cooking and eating habits.

The riches promised to everyone were not only material but intellectual, too, for the time saved could be used to educate oneself. The popularization of knowledge was one of the ideas embraced and fought for by those adhering to the faith in scientific progress. It would develop the inventive genius of each individual and reveal to him the meaning of Beauty, instilling in him aesthetic standards. Science and its applications were considered natural allies of the arts:[3] in the words of Foveau de Courmelles, 'Art should be learned like science, by observation if not by instruction; the two hold together, like science and poetry, by the indissoluble alliance of the true and the beautiful previously affirmed by Plato.'

Industry to art's rescue?

Would the broad dissemination of science throughout society necessarily entail art becoming available to everyone? Foveau de Courmelles thought so, and he attempted to prove this thesis. It was his view that specialists in the applied arts, whether potters, porcelain painters, upholsterers, sculptors or engravers, all stood to gain from the new industrial processes. Furthermore, these technical innovations would make it possible for their works to be popularized, 'for the pleasure of the eyes and the artistic edification of all'.[4]

This generous, liberating vision – which prophesied a collective perfecting of taste and an ongoing embellishment of man's everyday environment through the creation of objects of high artistic quality – was characteristic of the era. *L'Art pour tous* (Art for everyone) was a monthly magazine founded in Paris in 1860 by Emile Reiber, and its subtitle was 'An encyclopaedia of the industrial and decorative arts'. It set out to present the masterpieces of civilization – from painting to architecture and furniture – to the new sections of the population that were gaining access to the realm of culture. Thanks to modern reproductive techniques, numerous plates and illustrations were used to implement this programme.

But it was not by accident that *L'Art pour tous*, in anticipation of the forthcoming Universal Exposition, in May 1899 devoted several pages to publishing the rules of the competition for products organized by the Union Centrale des Arts Décoratifs. For it

Interchangeable furniture, designed by Francis Jourdain, 1912-1913.

Every real tectonic constructional form has an absolute nucleus, to which the decorative embellishment, which within certain limits is changeable, lends a varying charm. First, however, the absolute element has to be found, even if as yet in an imperfect, rough form.

Hans Poelzig, Essay on the Third German Exhibition of Applied Art, *Dresden 1906*

Illustrations from a furniture catalogue, Galerie Barbès, c.1930.

From top to bottom: Neo-rustic dining room made from solid, waxed, weathered oak.

Chiffonnier writing desk; chest of drawers and gramophone cabinet; chiffonnier semainier; chiffonnier.

Chest of drawers and chiffonnier.

had resolved to be at the forefront of the radical changes being introduced into daily life by the techniques of industrial design. Changes endorsed more than 40 years earlier by Count Léon de Laborde who, after visiting the 1851 Great Exhibition in London, bitterly observed that in France the only consequences of industrial manufacturing for the decorative arts had been 'a half-century of abdication, impotent copying, and the ridiculous grimaces of apes', and called for the establishment of a union of industry and the arts.[5] And in fact it was the pathetic importunings of Laborde that

led to the founding of the Union Centrale des Arts Décoratifs. Thus it is not surprising that entrants in the competition organized by it in 1899 were exhorted to always bear in mind the motto it had adopted as its own: 'Beauty in Utility'. The competition in question was intended to encourage 'artists seeking to give decorative art objects forms that are both beautiful and original, especially those in everyday use, which they will send to the exposition of 1900'.

Potential competitors had two options. They could submit projects relating to interior design, furniture and everyday

utensils – in the words of the organizers, to 'fixed or movable elements of domestic decor'. Or they could focus exclusively on 'bodily ornament', that is to say on clothing and jewellery. And one particular tendency received a strong endorsement: 'It is the goal of the Union Centrale to stimulate new ideas that might not only further the embellishment of luxurious residences, but also and above all bring Art into the lives of the greatest number. Consequently, competitors are warned against the too-pervasive tendency in such competitions to create, instead of objects which are affordable and

The master saddler

Once upon a time there was a master saddler. He was a good and skilled master. He made saddles that had nothing in common with traditional saddles, and nothing to do with Turkish or Japanese saddles. They were modern saddles. But he did not know this. He only knew that he made the best saddles that he could. Then the town became prey to a strange movement. It was called 'Secession'. This movement demanded that from now on only modern objects be made. When the saddler heard this, he took one of his best saddles and went to find a leader of the Secession.

He said, 'Professor,' for the leaders of this movement had been immediately promoted to the status of professor, 'Professor, I heard about your demands. I am also a modern man and I would like to do modern work. Tell me, is this saddle a modern one?' The professor looked at the saddle and gave a long speech from

which the saddler retained the most frequent words: art and crafts, individuality, modern, Hermann Bahr, Ruskin, applied arts, etc.,etc.

One thing was clear: the saddle was not modern. The saddler left covered in shame. He pondered, started working again and thought some more. But even though he worked hard to satisfy the demands of the professor, he only ended up re-making his old saddle.

Heartbroken, he returned to see the professor to tell him his troubles. The professor looked at the saddler's attempts and said: 'My dear Master, the thing is, you have no imagination.' Yes, it was true. Obviously, he had no imagination! But he had not known that imagination was necessary for making saddles. If he had had any, he would certainly have become a painter or sculptor or a poet or composer. The professor said, however, 'Come back

and see me tomorrow. We are here to stimulate industry and create new ideas; I am going to see what we can do for you.' Back in his class, the professor proposed this theme: a project for a saddle.

The saddler came back the next day. The professor was able to show him 49 saddle projects. There were only 44 students, but five projects were his own, which created a good atmosphere in the studio.

The saddler studied these designs for a long time and his eyes became more and more light. Then he said, 'Professor, if I knew as little as you to do about horse-riding, horses, leather and labour, I would surely have as much imagination as you.'

The saddler now lives a happy and contented man. He makes saddles. Modern? He does not know. He makes saddles.

Adolf Loos
(1870-1933), fable written for the journal
Das Andere, 1903

useful, exceptionally lavish-looking works that are costly to produce.'

Thus the Union Centrale's intentions here coincided with those of *L'Art pour tous*, both of them in favour of embellishing the everyday environment of ordinary people. They both aimed to rejuvenate the forms of practical objects in general use, as opposed to furthering the production of luxury items. Furthermore, these new everyday objects were to be sold at low prices, while being of high quality.

Given the inferior status of women in society, and also given the special brand of contempt reserved for those choosing to pursue careers in teaching and the arts, it is hardly surprising that these same people, in the cause of emancipation, proposed a separate competition 'open to women'. But the themes reserved for this demonstration of feminine capabilities can hardly be considered today as audacious. Apart from the fact that submissions had to be made only in the form of sketches, it being assumed that women would have difficulty completing fully realized projects, the rules enclosed them within a closeted domestic sphere. They were asked, for example, to imagine the furnishings for a studio-salon with fireplace, mirror, lamps, couch and cushions, desk and armchair, as well as a space for the mother of the family with cradle, basket for baby clothes, toys, pictures on the walls, and night light.

All these elements are typical of the evolution of urban society in the second half of the 19th century and of the aspirations of an emergent lower middle class for greater comfort and greater individual well-being. In order to capitalize on and fulfil the needs of this 'average clientele', the agitators of lucrative ideas took their models from the recent middle-class past. One example for them to follow was set by the bourgeoisie of the Restoration which withdrew into an apartment-refuge protected from the assaults of the exterior world by a proliferation of curtains, tapestries and fabrics.

These calls for Art and Beauty for everyone

Top and centre: Interchangeable furniture, designed by Francis Jourdain, 1912-1913.

Below: Advertisment for a washing machine, c.1920.

Left-hand page: Dining-room furniture, designed by Francis Jourdain, manufactured by Abel Motté, c.1920.

issued in two kinds of response. On the one hand, a tendency to bow down before machines as if they were idols and to declare their products to be generators of Beauty because they were adapted to the needs of modern life; on the other hand, the copying and dissemination of models borrowed from past epochs, which led to a frenzied imitation of earlier styles.[6]

The decoration of objects

A rival publication to *L'Art pour tous*, which also appeared every month, *L'Art décoratif*, 'an international magazine of art and decoration' founded in Paris in 1898, was attentive to this bending of noble aesthetic aspirations to commercial ends[7] – recourse to abundant ornamentation being one of its manifestations. According to Fernand Weyl in 1899, the introduction of a bit of art, or of what was misleadingly presented as art, into the daily environment had become the standard recipe. In the name of 'Modern Style', he wrote, we are threatened to the point of absurdity, with inconsistent lines, 'artifical curves', and 'uncertain ellipses', without any attention being paid to the qualities of the materials used. What was important for the 'middle classes' was a facade of bric-à-brac. As for the upper middle class, it aspired 'to wallpaper with regular patterns and artistic salt cellars'.

The idea of decorating objects, with the intention of injecting Art into them, was for *L'Art décoratif* the principal evil which needed to be fought. One of its regular contributors, G.-M. Jacques, denounced this idea repeatedly, seeing in it the cause of trashy goods which, manufactured and sold in huge quantities, was corrupting the sense of the Beautiful in thousands of unsuspecting consumers. He thought ornament should be present 'in inverse proportion to an object's utility, to its fulfilment of our genuine material needs'. In making such remarks he was registering his opposition to the excesses of the Modern Style and anticipating the violent attacks of the Viennese architect Adolf Loos against excessive use of ornament, synthesized in 1910 in his work *Ornament and Crime*, on the basis of a philosophy that would soon become that of the partisans of functionalism. According to this philosophy it is necessary to determine an object's function in order to give it a form that is both appropriate and beautiful. This beauty could only be a 'geometric beauty, like that which nature has given all her works, from crystals to mountains, from cells to flowers.'

Thus Jacques praised English furniture of the 1890s and expressed regret that the supposed ugliness of these pieces kept them from being popular with the French public. Neither the work produced by the Arts and Crafts workshops nor the theories of William Morris had met with much success in France. And in fact Jacques didn't refer to them directly. What he was defending through the image of furniture from across the English Channel was a type of furniture which, in his opinion, represented a 'return to truth, to the nature of things, to simplification, to an aesthetic as well as material adaptation of the object to its function'.

Louis Lumet and the Société de l'Art pour Tous

But *L'Art pour tous* was not only the name of a periodical founded by Emile Reiber. An organization unconnected with the journal bore this name at the beginning of the 20th century, also publishing a journal with this title. Edited by Louis Lumet, it was under the sway of socialist ideas, following in the wake of the popular universities, and was committed to the cause of the artistic education of the people. Lumet understood it to be 'an aesthetic propaganda group'. In an account of his activities in the period 1901-1904, he states there were 2,300 individual members as well as many affiliated organizations, unions and cooperatives.[8]

The Société de l'Art pour Tous had its principal base in Paris among craftsmen, workers and teachers. It ran a theatre, promoted literary gatherings and debates, and offered lectures and museum visits. With

regard to artistic problems, its programme did not limit itself to increasing the people's familiarity with masterpieces but aimed to place Beauty within their reach in the form of new everyday objects, and especially to stimulate them to exercise their own creative faculties.

Lumet was one of a small number of people who disseminated William Morris's ideas in France, (although he criticized them in certain respects), and he looked to the Arts and Crafts Movement as a model when formulating his own programme. This is made clear at the end of his preface to a 1904 anthology of lectures given to the Société de l'Art pour Tous: 'We must set up co-operatives for the production of art objects as well as communal shops outside the mercenary circuit of shopkeepers; we must transform dress, decorate the family interior, guide taste in the selection of furniture and accessories towards simplicity, towards a sober, light harmony, and destroy the prejudice that luxury objects are art objects; we must decorate the schools, public buildings, the streets; we must embellish secular ceremony and ennoble national celebrations'.[9]

What became of these projects? Some experiments were indeed carried out, and in some instances public institutions became involved in popular artistic activities. But in the end it was the conditions of industrial production that determined the nature of objects available to the mass of potential consumers. The notion of art for everyone was perverted by the omnipotence of the industrial arts and the purportedly artistic industries. Even if in this domain France was unable to catch up with Germany and Great Britain, it none the less resolved to combat foreign competition by applying the advice given by Marius Vachon in an 1885 report commissioned by the Ministry of Public Instruction and the Fine Arts: 'Despite all the attempts made by foreign countries, our works still remain the most beautiful, the most original. The grace and elegance of their forms, the brilliance and delicacy of their colours, and their overall sense of taste

Decorative panels for cast iron, enamelled stoves. Taken from the Godin catalogue, 1934. The stylized 'rose' decoration is typical of Art Deco in its most traditional form.

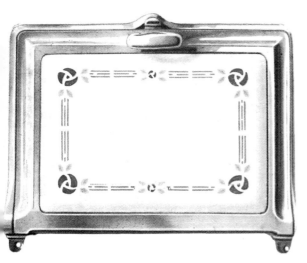

set them brilliantly apart from all the products of competing industries. But this superiority will not be a source of benefit to national prosperity if we do not adapt our genius to the new circumstances of contemporary society. Art must descend from its elevated pedestal and mix with the crowd.'[10]

Routine is preferable to creation

In this connection, too, the arguments of a personality such as Foveau de Courmelles are symptomatic. In his blissful devotion to scientific progress, he saw only the positive aspects of the transformations worked on the home. But what of the increasing uniformity of lifestyle, household decor and everyday objects? In his view large-scale industry was deserving of unmitigated praise for manufacturing products that could be sold at affordable prices. He held it to be responsible for peasants and workers' being able to move from hovels to agreeable lodgings. As he saw it, this evolution was so obvious that he did not take seriously the criticism that every home was being furnished just like every other, since the daily lives of the humblest among us had been considerably improved: 'In the country, [modest farmers now have] slate-roofed houses with chromolithographs on the wall, high mahogany beds with bases, mattresses and eiderdown, wardrobes in which formal clothes and linen are stored, sideboards filled with coffee, salt, spices and seasonal foods, both meat and vegetables. City workers. . .have one or two small rooms that are furnished and decorated, often with the traditional wardrobe with mirror, curtains, and sometimes even with wallpaper simulating tapestries.'[11]

Were chromolithographs sold in department stores and industrially-manufactured furniture really a panacea for the hardship of these people's daily lives? Did the provision by industry of identical everyday objects to masses of consumers preclude, in the name of increased comfort and the satisfying of needs, any attention being paid to the forms of these objects? If so, wouldn't it be better to encourage craft skills instead? Such were the terms of a debate that, born of industrialization, would continue for decades amid a seemingly eternal 'crisis of the decorative arts' in France.

There have been numerous attempts to approach everday objects creatively, pointed out Camille Mauclair in 1906, but by and large these efforts had been aimed at millionaires, with simple forks going for an exorbitant price well beyond the means of most consumers.[12] As a result, shoddiness reigned. Imitation was the rule, to such an extent that the Modern Style was imitated in the shops of the faubourg Saint Antoine, those 'citadels of Louis-Philippe taste', where chairs with 'twisted'[13] backs normally held sway.

According to Mauclair, responsibility for this unhealthy situation fell squarely on the shoulders of the members of the Union Centrale des Arts Décoratifs, by and large composed of tradesmen little concerned with the 'genius of the people'.[14] They were out to defend their own interests: 'To provide lowly employees as well as the people with glasses, forks, wardrobes and curtains no more expensive and more delicately formed than the ugly objects offered them by the department stores, is so much nonsense that won't improve one's year-end accounts, that might haunt the brain of some naïve socialist but certainly not that of any self-respecting, well-off businessman. The creation of models is an expensive proposition. Labour, in this case, must entail research and initiative. By contrast, the imitation of older styles leads to ready sales and is easy to produce. One has only to copy, and any worker unable to invent even the smallest moulding can produce a wonderful reproduction of an Henri II sideboard or a Louis XVI chair.'

As a consequence, those charged with coming up with models for manufacture gradually lost their desire to invent new forms: 'Even the most gifted young man, the one most anxious to create new models, is, from the moment he's obliged to make a

Electromatic electric coffee-maker, c.1950.

Right-hand page, from top to bottom: Cadillac electric coffee-maker, c.1960.

Utentra electric coffee-maker, c.1960.

Krups T10 Aroma electric coffee-maker, 1987.

living for himself, reduced to the servile imitatation of older styles. He earns a better living that way than by risking to submit models no one will want and that he hasn't the means to execute.'[15]

This servility attains the height of ridicule with, in certain Parisian apartment buildings, electric lifts modelled on sedanchairs! As for ordinary hardware such as radiators and stoves, cast iron (fashionable since the beginning of the 19th century thanks to the industrialist André) made possible the popularization of the most anachronistic forms and shapes. One notable example of such 'innovatory' castiron production was the Louis XIII electric candelabrum.

Everyday objects ill-adapted to the modern world

In 1916, in order to compete with Germany in the wake of the First World War, and particularly to thwart the Werkbund, by taking it as a model, the under-secretary for the fine arts created the Comité Central Consultatif Technique des Arts Appliqués. The declared aims consisted of organizing the defence of French industry and fostering a return to that 'regional' art which had once been at the origins of French grandeur, so that French homes would not be lit by 'Nuremburg lamps' and and heated by 'Leipzig radiators'. Ten years later, this ambiguous programme intended to favour a synthesis between industrial modernism and tradition had produced little in the way of tangible results.

In 1925 the same problems still prevailed. On the eve of the Exposition Internationale des Arts Décoratifs in Paris of that year, Waldemar George[16] criticized the inability of French furniture-makers to formulate a new aesthetic other than through artifice: 'A lamp with a giant stand topped by a shade in the form of a cupola, a round table, a few black and orange cushions, such is the public's idea of a "modern" interior, an assemblage of futile accessories imposed by the taste and fashion of the day.' Aside from

Francis Jourdain and Pierre Chareau, whom he judged to be strong and original personalities possessing, like Adolf Loos, a certain rigour, he saw evidence only of minds lacking both method and practical sense, and thus ill-suited to address the material problems of the century: 'They have gained nothing from modern technology. Their furniture for workers' housing consists of vulgar replicas of luxury furniture mass produced using ordinary wood. They ignore the triple principle of economy – economy of money, economy of place, economy of time – that should govern all their efforts. Their reforms are focused on furniture's lines as opposed to its vital function.'

The director of the Ecole des Beaux-Arts himself, Paul Léon, was far from contradicting such assertions. He publicly acknowledged, during the inauguration of this exhibition, that the scientific discoveries of the preceding century had completely transformed the conditions of human existence, while the 'arts of life' remained stuck in the rut of tradition. And he spoke ironically about the persistence of political regimes after their end: 'From beds with columns that would have been recognizable to Henry II to bedrooms evocative of Madame de Pompadour or dining rooms ready to receive the First Consul, we relive in the acts of our everyday existence the various stages of our history.'[17]

None the less, obliged by his position, Paul Léon announced that all this was in the process of changing, that French manufacturers had finally come to realize 'the necessity of creating a truly modern house consistent with our needs and customs', and that customers, too, were growing tired of the Valois and the Bourbons. The director of the Beaux-Arts proclaimed that a new era was dawning: 'Thanks to the new spirit, to the enlightened eclecticism of the large trade unions, the question of the relation between the creators and the producers of models seems to have been resolved. We can march into battle sure of meeting with success.'[18]

His limitations as a prophet are only too evident from the kinds of furniture and everyday objects that were in fashion in later years. In the end, it would seem that only two phenomena have led to the modification of the forms of everyday objects: the invention of new materials and technological progress. Both these developments have been all the more effective for having been applied not to pre-existing objects but to newly created ones. This observation holds even with regard to form: the shape of the fork, for example, has changed very little in comparison with that of the electric coffee-maker, which has gone through myriad substantial design changes in a relatively short time.

As to the fine-sounding calls for art for everyone, they met with failure. Over a half-century period, from the 1873 Vienna exposition (where industrially-produced everyday objects were presented to the public in such circumstances for the first time) to the 1925 Exposition Internationale des Arts Décoratifs in Paris, European industrial production intended for mass consumption consisted almost exclusively of shoddy, inferior goods. Was this due to the omnipotence of tradition in society, to difficulties inevitably faced by human groups trying to break with old habits for the sake of creative dynamism, to the preeminence necessarily accorded economic considerations? In closing, it might be appropriate to cite the conclusion drawn in 1913 by Francis Jourdain's father, the decorator Frantz Jourdain, a participant in, and witness to, the applied arts adventure from the end of the 19th century into the twenties: 'Instead of raising the humble up to the level of Art, we contented ourselves with lowering Art to the level of the crowd.'[19]

Meccano

The Englishman Frank Hornby, the inventor of Meccano, used to pore over the biographies of famous men. The father of two children, he made toys for them and, at Christmas 1899, decided to build them a crane. Unable to find the necessary components, he resolved to make them himself. He later wrote: 'I was dismayed at the thought of the terrible loss of time and effort...I saw that only interchangeable pieces could remedy this state of affairs. This would require a new principle of standardization allowing for the assemblage of pieces in the system in multiple combinations. Then, happily, I realized that pieces perforated with tiny holes of like diameter at regular intervals would do the trick admirably.'

On 9 January 1901, Frank Hornby registered his patent (thanks to a £5 loan from his employer) under the name Mechanics Made Easy. In 1907, the first Meccano factory opened its doors at 10 Duke Street, in Liverpool. The system of basic norms has not changed since, but now, instead of just nine types of component there are several hundred available today.

The Meccano set is an educational toy and it was perhaps not altogether by chance that it first appeared in 1900. The so-called 'active' teaching theories were formulated at about the same time, notably by John Dewey and Marie Montessori. They advocated not only the use of educational games, but the creation of a new system of education informed by the spirit of play, with all its spontaneity and efficiency.

The Meccano set is also a system that illustrates perfectly the principles of standardization, prefabrication and interchangeability that underlie all mass production. The different metal elements making up the set are sufficiently varied to form a coherent system with which all sorts of objects can be constructed. Play with Meccano sets prepared little boys for active participation in a rational society.

The design of the various pieces imposes a high tech aesthetic and is reminiscent of the metal constructions of engineers in the second half of the 19th century.

J. d. N.

The pavilion of
le Bon Marché
department
store at the
Exposition
Internationale
des Arts
Décoratifs et
Industriels
Modernes,
Paris, 1925.

*Right-hand
page*: Detail
of an armchair
by Louis Süe
and Paul
Huillard, 1912.

Art Deco

Nostalgia and Post-Modernism during the First Machine Age

Suzanne Tise

It should hardly come as a surprise that for the last three decades, domestic designs in the Art Deco style have remained objects of avid collection and speculation, a more lucrative object for copyists than any of the French Louis styles have ever been, and the epitome of sophistication, pleasure and elegance for the décors of television commercials, films and decorating magazines. Probably no other style of the 20th century has appealed so directly to the Post-Modern sensibility and to our cultural stereotypes about a profound unity of expression that we imagine to have existed in the past. Art Deco was 'rehabilitated' as Post-Modernism was beginning to emerge, by a retrospective held at the Musée des Arts Décoratifs in Paris in the mid-sixties. Ten years later, in 1976, it was apotheosized by a *cinquantenaire* at the same institution, at the height of the post-rationalist crisis of the 1970s.

Both ideologically and stylistically, Art Deco can be compared to the definitions laid out by the pundits of Post-Modernism. Pastiche was one of its central features. Art Deco was self-consciously retro: its subject was the history of art and design. The style affirmed definite, but threatened, values and often relied on the mimesis of historical ornament in an ironic manner. Its appeal then and now lies in the fact that it was at once professionally based (that is, it was deliberately and methodically invented by an elite group of Parisian designers), while retaining a popular appeal. Art Deco combined new techniques with old patterns while maintaining a distinctly modern sensibility. More often than not, Art Deco can be distinguished by a dominating classicism.[1] And like the best definition by Post-Modernism's defenders, it was nostalgic without (necessarily) being reactionary. Perhaps it is possible to imagine Art Deco as the Post-Modernism of the First Machine Age.

Dozens of books and articles have been

devoted to the artifacts of the Art Deco style and the appellation has been used to designate almost anything from Georges Lepape's decorative fashion illustrations, to the productions of the Bauhaus, bakelite jewellery and Hollywood film decors of the 1930s. This discussion focuses on the French Art Deco style – which took its name from the Exposition Internationale des Arts Décoratifs et Industriels Modernes, held in Paris in 1925 – and the specific conditions in which it evolved from 1910 onwards. Criticism of modern design today stems from the increasing modernization of industry, the threat of unemployment, the diminishing need for skilled labour and the feeling that technology is out of control. In this context, it is worthwhile re-examining Art Deco's origins.

1900: 'Il faut absolument être moderne'

The style known as Art Deco evolved as though to circumvent the spectre of the rationalization of design production in France and the manifestation of its rationalization in Germany. The decorative arts had long been big business in France and a linchpin of the Parisian economy. The French domestic design industries stagnated, however, after the Paris Universal Exposition of 1900, as a result of the overproduction and banalization of the Art Nouveau style. During the 1890s, reformers and artists alike had hoped that Art Nouveau, whose structural logic and ornamentation were inspired by an intense study of nature, would be a new departure for the decorative arts in France, which had relied for too long on the success of its historical styles. Instead, Art Nouveau was condemned by critics soon after 1900 and was apparently a commercial failure.[2] Even the style's most ardent supporters began to recognize its failure to respond to the needs of a broad clientele and criticized its decorative formalism and symbolist references as elitist art that appealed only to dilettantes and neurotic aesthetes.[3]

Reformers like Roger Marx (1859-1913), the friend of Gallé and champion of design reform, began calling for a 'social art' that was simple and modern in style, and which could be produced on a massive scale by the machine.[4] Convinced that non-mechanized craft production was utopian in an age of competitive world markets, Marx encouraged French artists to accept the machine and the division of labour. Mass production, he believed, rather than elite craftsmanship, was the only way to ensure the victory of good taste and to provide a base from which France could restore its competitive edge in design production.[5]

It was in this context that the first project for an Exposition des Arts Décoratifs was imagined in 1906. Radical-Socialist deputy Charles Couyba (1866-1931) proposed the first project for an international exhibition of decorative arts to the Chamber of Deputies as part of his annual budget project for the Ministry of Fine Arts.[6] An international exhibition of decorative arts, he argued, would foster new research and encourage artists and manufacturers to provide works for unlimited production from which all classes of society could benefit.[7] Couyba's project for an international exhibition of decorative arts was elaborated by Roger Marx. In 1909, he published an article entitled 'De l'art social et de la nécessité d'en assurer le progrès par une exposition', in which he explained that design was the perfect embodiment of the notion of an *art social*.[8] His international exhibition devoted strictly to the arts of the home, street and city would include only works that were specifically modern.[9] Marx maintained that economists rather than artists should define the specific programme of the exhibition; it would be their task to re-unify art with nature, life and science. Only then would the machine be given its rightful place, not as something to be despised and feared, but as an agent of the dissemination and democratization of beauty. This desire to redirect French design towards machine production was rendered

urgent by the threat of serious competition from Germany revealed at an exhibition of the Munich Vereinigten Werkstätte für Kunst und Handwerk within the Paris Salon d'Automne in 1910.[10] The work by the Munich designers, led by Bruno Paul and Richard Riemerschmid, was vaguely inspired by the Biedermeier style and on the whole was not particularly innovative, but it demonstrated a sobriety, unity of design and urbanity that were completely unexpected by the Parisian public. Elegant, spare and modern, each uncluttered interior featured a tasteful arrangement of furnishings, and the sophisticated adjustment of architectural proportions for effect. The simple furnishings were produced by semi-mass production techniques.

Although the displays were admired by the public and most critics, the Munich designers' demonstration of a model of design directed towards mass production techniques and modern commerce immediately planted the seeds of a negative reaction in Paris. One of the most significant commentaries on the German display was made by Guillaume Apollinaire, poet, critic and impresario of the avant-garde, who was particularly concerned about the implications of commerce's control over creativity and the artist's lack of references to artistic traditions:

'If it is true that these pieces of furniture were designed by artists and professors, it is also true that the designs were bought and executed by commercial firms who are financing this exhibition and who have already received some very large orders since their arrival in Paris. . . . But the real danger is not in the commercial harm that this exhibition is doing to France, it is in the confusion that will certainly be sown in the minds of our artisans, who are already so far removed from the tradition they never should have abandoned. The gracious and comfortable furnishings that adorned the homes of the 17th and 18th centuries are the finest works ever produced by the domestic arts. . . .Today's artisans want to start from scratch, without owing anything to the past. It is conceivable that such an ambition can revolutionize the major arts, when the artists involved possess genuine culture. But in the productions of artisans, only the details must be left to their fancy. And if they are allowed to see the follies of foreign peoples, they will be utterly confused. . . . It is true that in France the decorative arts are undergoing a crisis of ugliness. That is not a reason, however, for exposing our miseries to the incurable defects of the Germans. We still have at least a residue of good taste that provides some basis of hope.'[11] This commentary is interesting for several reasons. Apollinaire must be counted among the most open-minded observers of the 1910 Salon, yet his views on design were conservative and quite typical of the differences between the French and German approaches to interior design. His remarks confirm that if French designers were looking for a new style of decorative arts to compete with the developments taking place in Germany, they did not intend to find it through industry and modern commerce. He refused the notion that commercially-produced furniture could be worthy of a place in a Salon, and lamented unhealthy cosmopolitan influences on French artisans, which he seemed to think were responsible for the loss of the 17th and 18th-century traditions that had made French furnishings so great. Most important, he could not accept the notion that a new style could be born that refused references to tradition, except when an artist was completely familiar with the great works of art from the past.

The impressively organized display by the Munich designers at the Salon d'Automne in 1910 nevertheless led the progressive factions of the French arts administration to rehabilitate the project for the international exhibition of decorative arts proposed by Couyba and Marx, in order to counter the lead taken by Germany in modern design. After discussions among representatives from the major Paris organizations involved in the decorative arts,[12] they submitted a project for an international exhibition of exclusively modern decorative arts to be held in Paris in 1915 to the Commission of Commerce and Industry of the Chamber of Deputies. Its supporters insisted that the exhibition was necessary for the defence of national interests – both artistic and economic – and that it should be considered an urgent obligation by the Republic.[13] The project was ratified in July 1912.

Le Nouveau style

In Apollinaire's reaction to the Munich designers, an alternative model of design modernity was indicated, one in which the concepts of nation and tradition were seen as the only true sources of creativity and innovation. The constituent elements of a new style of decorative arts began to be explored in art reviews by 1910, when *L'Art décoratif* opened an inquiry into whether a modern style could be born of the 'spirit of the age' or from the efforts of a few individuals working in isolation. Particularly revealing was the pervasive *fin-de-siècle* sentiment of detachment from eternal values reflected in the editor's affirmation on the opening page of the inquiry, 'Notre époque est une époque de désarroi,' and his doubt as to the meaning and value of modern art.[14] The responses echoed this sense of malaise. Frantz Jourdain wrote of a 'vertigo that had annihilated the national energy and creativity,' while an anonymous writer contended that the previous ten years had been characterized by an aesthetic anarchy, distinguished from all past epochs by their total break with tradition and the collective ideals that were reflected in a unified style.[15] Other art and literary reviews dating from 1910-1914 carried articles that condemned individualism in art and announced a new era of classicism in art and design. The new classicism, however, was rigorously distinguished from

From top to bottom: Michel Dufet, design for a salon, 1919.

Bar of the Hôtel de Paris, designed by Molinié and Nicod, 1925.

Lady's bedroom, designed by Charlotte Chauchet-Guilleré, made by Primavera, 1925.

Smoking room, designed by Maurice Matet, made by the Studium-Louvre, 1925.

academicism and was only occasionally based on a Greek model. It signified rather a nostalgia for a kind of idealism and organization that would give a new sense of order and meaning to art.

To be classical, then, meant more than a style, but a certain *état d'esprit*; it meant rigour, discipline and order. In design reviews, articles appeared on artists like Maurice Denis and Puvis de Chavannes and proposed that the decorative quality of their work, and their tendency to purify form, could provide the model for 'a generation that was once again posing the question of classicism'.[16]

Nowhere was this dialectic among tradition, nationalism and modernity more plainly articulated than in an article intended as a kind of manifesto, heralding a new style of domestic furnishings, entitled 'Le Nouveau style,' published by the landscape artist and theorist André Vera (1881-1971) in the January 1912 issue of *L'Art décoratif*.[17] Vera believed that the design salons of the previous year had featured two modern styles – one dying and one in the process of being born. The fading modern style was Art Nouveau, an art that could not be truly modern because it appealed to sensibility rather than to reason. The phenomenon of Art Nouveau was not an isolated one, but symptomatic of an entire generation that, in its desire to be original and its search for the unexpected, had lost sight of tradition. Vera also lamented the undesirable effects of industrial society and the mediocrity it had engendered.

An art founded on reason, Vera contended, naturally led one to the 17th century, the greatest moment of glory in French art and the period that demonstrated most eloquently the discipline that artists were looking for. At the same time, it was necessary to pick up the threads of the true French tradition that had been dormant since the Revolution of 1848. He recommended, therefore, that artists draw on the Louis-Philippe style for inspiration, the last true French style to manifest itself before the onslaught of historicism: 'We are looking for the qualities of clarity, order, and harmony that we found as a whole in the 17th century, and at the same time, we would like to revive the tradition that was stopped around 1848.'[18] Vera even specified the decorative form-language that the new style was to employ: baskets and garlands of flowers would become the hallmarks of the new style as the torch, the bow and arrows had been the iconography of 17th-century decoration.

Vera's text is significant both because it provided an ideological basis for the work of an entire group of young designers trying to find their way out of the impasse of Art Nouveau to create a modern style, and because it illustrated the ambiguous position towards progress held by many artists and intellectuals who tried to reconcile tradition, and even a certain elitism, with a striving for modernity. His paradigm of modernity, however, with its components of nationalism, traditionalism and humanism, had little to do with a concept of design centered on notions of function or an *art social*. He believed that the modern domestic environment should be imbued with meaning, a highly coded space composed of symbols that reflected a cultural renaissance on a national scale.

Vera's article was illustrated by ornamental motifs and drawings for furniture created by a group of young designers who collaborated on the architect Louis Süe's (1875-1968) design workshop, the Atelier Français.[19] Süe founded the design studio in 1912, and united some established artists and decorators around the notion of creating a modern style of design based on the French tradition. Among his collaborators were the painters André Mare (1885-1932), Roger de La Fresnaye and Paul Vera (the brother of André), and designers André Groult and Jean-Louis Gampert.[20] The ornamental motifs by André Mare that accompanied Vera's article illustrated the way in which nature

Top to bottom: Silver service, designed by Michael Graves for Alessi, 1983. One of the 11 services from the series 'Tea & Coffee Piazza', each produced in a limited series of 99.

Hexagonal vase, designed by Jean Puiforcat, 1927.

Sideboard, designed by Djo Bourgeois, 1925.

Table and armchair, designed by Lucie Renaudot, produced by P.-A. Dumas, 1925.

was to be represented in the 'New Style.' Diametrically opposed to the twisting, climbing plant forms characteristic of Art Nouveau, Mare opted for a more static decorative concept, abandoning tendrils and stems in favour of stylized rose blossoms, gathered up and tied, as Vera had suggested, into symmetrical arrangements of baskets and garlands. An armchair by Süe, displayed a carved flower basket as part of the back support, conforming to the new decorative repertoire called for by Vera; it was topped by a large volute terminated by carved tassels in wood. However, the most original aspect of his design – and highly uncharacteristic of French furnishings – was the use of colour: the various decorative elements of the chair were delineated in bold colours – red for the roses and green for the basket and tassels.[21]

The group presented the new style at the Salon d'Automne in 1912. Painter and designer André Mare (1887-1932) organized an ensemble of elements from the decorative arts, painting and sculpture, with a dozen artists and craftsmen, including Raymond Duchamp-Villon along with his brother Jacques Villon, *férronnier* Richard Desvallières, decorator Jean-Louis Gampert, glassmaker Maurice Marinot, and the painters Paul Vera, Roger de la Fresnaye and Marie Laurencin.[22] The ensemble that they were planning deliberately challenged Art Nouveau, as well as the work of the Munich decorators, whose presentation at the 1910 Salon d'Automne had remained very much on the minds of French designers and critics. It was Mare who gave the artistic and intellectual direction to the group and he hoped to encourage his friends to create something both modern, but at the same time explicitly and strikingly French. Clearly he had Vera's article 'Le Nouveau style' in mind when he wrote the following letter to the glassmaker Maurice Marinot in February 1912:[23]

'Above all, we should do something very *French*. Stay in the tradition, let yourself be guided by your instinct that compels you to react against the errors of 1900. . . .

1. Return to lines that are simple, pure, logical and even somewhat cold, since the period that preceded us was horribly tortured

2. Return to very fresh colours, even if the same preceding period contented itself with washed out, discoloured, anaemic tones. Let your drawing be vigorous and naïve, render the detail amusing, be gauche rather than skilful. For decorations, take up and develop the motifs that have not changed from the Renaissance to Louis-Philippe; give them a new life, adapt them to forms . . . according to our way of feeling – the bouquet of flowers, fruits, the garland, the rose, the carnation, the tulip. And for ornaments . . . the volute . . . . Take up novelty within sensibility rather than in invention. . . .'.[24]

The results of the collaboration were presented at the Salon d'Automne of 1912, in a collection baptized by the press as the Maison Cubiste.[25] Visitors to the Salon d'Automne passed through Duchamp-Villon's façade into the entrance hall fitted out with furniture and objects by André Mare, Richard Desvallières and Duchamp-Villon. The hall opened onto what the group named somewhat sarcastically Un Salon Bourgeois. Paintings by Fernand Léger, Marcel Duchamp, Jean Metzinger, Albert Gleizes and Roger de la Fresnaye completed the interior.[26] The title Un Salon Bourgeois was only partially a joke; the furnishings hardly seemed as daring as Duchamp-Villon's façade had promised, or as the Cubist paintings placed on the walls. For the most part, the collection fulfilled the decorative prescriptions laid out by Vera and Mare. Deliberately making references to past French styles, the furniture and woodwork, lacquered a light colour, recalled the comfortable, bourgeois Louis-Philippe style as well as French provincial furnishings.

Mare employed large simple forms, such as the big volutes that composed the backs of the chairs, enlarged to such an extent that they became almost comical. La Fresnaye was responsible for the sculpted woodwork comprising volutes and flower baskets – the decorative elements proposed by Vera and Mare. The salon opened onto a small bedroom where the bed was placed in an alcove – typical of the Louis-Philippe period. Perhaps the most striking aspect of the collection lay in the way Mare and his colleagues applied their training as painters to decoration, first in the general colour scheme – lemon yellow, cobalt blue and red – and then in the treatment of the woodwork and furniture, whose decorative mouldings were heavily outlined in a dark colour and often composed of exaggeratedly large motifs, like the painted or carved volutes.[27]

Except for Duchamp-Villon's façade and the palette of strident colours employed in the interior, there was nothing particularly revolutionary about the Maison Cubiste, and judging from Mare's letter to Marinot, that was precisely his idea. Their friend and champion Apollinaire underlined this when he remarked on the eve of the opening at their Salon d'Automne: 'There is already talk of a new style continuing the old traditions.'[28] Clearly an artist like Duchamp-Villon, creator of powerful Cubist sculptures such as *Baudelaire* (1911) and *The Horse* (1914), was deeply committed to the modern experience, but he could also write about his apprehension in a modern world that seemed to lack meaning and cohesion with the past. He hoped to find a means of joining tradition with innovation, since the latter could only find its true validity through a continuity with the former. The sculptor described his experiment with the decorative arts as an attempt to fill an artistic void as well as a question of national prestige:

'We suddenly realized that we were living in the poorest epoch of our artistic history from the point of view [of design]. It is an undeniable fact that for the last 50 years no contribution has been made

that can be qualified as useful. . . People are talking about opening an exhibition of modern decorative art in Paris in 1915. An event of this kind is a true contest in which the supremacy of taste is in question; we must be able to defend our reputation, which until now has been unassailable.'[29]

The big exhibition of modern decorative arts scheduled for 1915, however, never took place. It was postponed several times due to lack of organization and rendered impossible by the outbreak of the war.

Modernity and Modernism: towards the 1925 exhibition

In an essay published in 1925, the poet Paul Valéry posed the following question: 'But how will a style be made? That is, how will it be possible to acquire a stable type, a general formula of construction and decoration . . . when impatience, rapidity of execution and abrupt transformations in technique, speed the works along and when for a century the condition of novelty has been a requisite of all production in every domain?'[30]

With the signing of the armistice, the creation of a modern style appropriate to the post-war era dominated discussions about modern design and once again encouraged new speculation on the role of the artist in society. In these intense aesthetic debates, the calls for order, discipline and collective action that had begun to develop before 1914 were given a new urgency by the war. Valéry and others who examined the issue after 1918 were still yearning for a unified style, but understood that a fundamental ontological change had occurred. The world was no longer constructed in quite the same way and the incoherence of the modern experience might prevent the development of this ideal style.

The calls for unity that dominated post-war debate on art in France have been discussed in recent scholarship dealing with the then prevalent notion of a *rappel à l'ordre*, essentially a revision of the concept of modernity that took place in the domains of painting and sculpture between 1918 and 1925. The *rappel à l'ordre* was also a dominant theme in the discourse on design. If 19th-century reformers had believed that a modern style could liberate itself from the past, after 1918 few still believed this to be a viable solution. Certainly, the artistic discourse of the post-war years blurred the distinction between reactionary and avant-garde positions: nearly all artists working in the 1920s claimed to be 'modern'. At the same time, many of those who called for a return to national traditions in art, were not neces-

sarily reactionary, but rather expressed deep convictions about cultural values that they considered to be the very essence of national identity. Writers like Valéry or designers like André Vera and Louis Süe sought legitimacy, the constants of a trans-historical tradition that permitted them to look to the past for new sources of inspiration without abandoning their faith in their previous innovations. They maintained that modernity preserves a secret tie with the classical and that a reliance on norms could re-establish an ethic of discipline in art and society in general.[31] For them, progressiveness could be incorporated into pronouncements on tradition and the past was perceived as the wellspring from which all new creation would flow.

Examining the contributions to the October 1919 Salon d'Automne, one would never have known that there had been a war during which hundreds of thousands of homes were destroyed. Few interiors displayed simple, unadorned models designed for series production and in fact most resembled the interiors of the years 1912-1914. Among the most elaborate salons and boudoirs were Michel Dufet's fantasy rooms with blue-lacquered walls highlighted with silver motifs evoking

Above, left to right: Exposition des Arts Décoratifs, 1925:

Hôtel du collectionneur, designed by Pierre Patout and Jacques-Émile Ruhlmann.

View from the Pavillon de Sèvres.

The fountain on the *cours La Reine* designed by Michel Roux-Spitz and Raymond Delamarre.

Left-hand page: Salle des fêtes at the Grand Palais, designed by Louis Süe and André Mare, Exposition des Arts Décoratifs, 1925.

clouds and fountains. The co-ordinated furnishings were lacquered black, with silver highlights and floral decorations painted in free style.

In his review of the Salon, Jean-Louis Vaudoyer, editor of *Art et décoration*, proclaimed that the post-war leader of the decorative arts would be like Dufet, an *ensemblier*.[32] Vaudoyer praised the participants in the Salon d'Automne for their adherence to tradition and even compared the *ensemblier* to a mythological hero who had made the correct choice between eternal values and ephemeral fashion: 'The *ensemblier* often makes one think of the Greek hero, rich with the power and aspirations that destiny has maliciously placed in his path at a crossroad to put him to the test, and telling him: "Now you must commit yourself to one or the other of these paths – choose".'[33]

Master cabinet-maker Jacques-Emile Ruhlmann was certainly the 'Greek hero' to whom Vaudoyer was referring. He contributed what was to be the *clou* of the Salon of 1919: a buffet in macassar ebony that was a masterpiece of *ebenisterie*. Elegant, majestic in its proportions, the design was based on 18th-century models and yet completely modern. Its broad, smooth surfaces were unadorned; only a central motif in ivory marquetry, representing Apollo in a chariot drawn by horses, disrupted the flow of its broad, polished surfaces.

This trend towards the re-establishment of the pre-war craft order was made official in the resurrection of the project for the international exhibition of decorative arts in Paris. In the spring of 1919, deputy Marc Réville submitted a new project to the Chamber of Deputies inviting the government to take steps to organize the exhibition for 1922.[34] The justification for the exhibition provided by Léon Riotor, Conseiller Municipal de Paris, shows how important the maintenance of highly skilled labour, here equated with *le goût français*, was to the national economy and how the

exhibition could help in its development: 'Our concern for our industry, for our national prosperity urgently calls for the defence of French taste. The arts applied to industry (improperly called decorative arts), are from now on the basis for our efforts. Since we are no longer big producers, let's at least be producers of taste. It is in this way that we can resist foreign over-production and give to our highly esteemed but rarified skilled labour, the benefits it deserves.'[35]

Although the opportunities for design renewal left by the ruins of the war were

great, the desire to restore the pre-war craft order proved to be more compelling. The reaffirmation of the artist's role in post-war society through the exhibition would confirm the status quo and form the foundations for a sense of national community.

The decorative doctrine for tomorrow

In a 1918 essay entitled 'La Doctrine décorative de demain', André Vera commented on the need to preserve French tradition and craftsmanship in the post-war era. Vera's essay was one of the earliest post-war

declarations on the future of the decorative arts in France. Its message must have been appealing in the climate of reconstruction because it was reprinted in five major journals and newspapers over the course of the following year.[36] His ideas on a post-war style provided the intellectual *raison d'être* for the organization of a new design group by Süe and Mare in 1919 called the Compagnie des Arts Français. Although Vera's new article abandoned some of his pre-war aesthetic advice, it upheld the demand of the pre-war tract for the creation of a modern, unified style based on the French tradition. Vera announced that the war had swept away the confusion in artistic and national life that had characterized the years before 1914. He reminded artists of their duty, which was to provide a model for a material and moral reconstruction after the disaster of the war.

Vera called upon designers to follow the lead of architects in order to fulfil their roles as 'artisans of the indispensable intellectual and moral reform' of the post-war era, by providing clear symbols of a new and unified post-war epoch. He emphasized the

View of the Exposition des Arts Décoratifs, 1925.

importance of the patient work of craftsmen in this reform:

'The next style will not be charged with nonchalance, but with an obstinate and male vigour: superficiality, precipitation and fickleness will no longer be in fashion. Patient works can be finished before the desire has passed: you will see, for example, tapestry come back into favour.'

Vera's views on geometry and craftsmanship must be understood within the broader context of the debate on a *rappel à l'ordre* taking place contemporaneously in other artistic domains. For Vera, adhering to the skills of a craft meant adhering to national traditions.[37] The exaltation of *métier*, then, was a means of returning to a common base of eternal values that had withstood the test of time, of rejecting the individualism of Art Nouveau for what amounted to an almost Ruskinian celebration of handicraft. Only painstaking craftsmanship could instil creative work with meaning and spirituality. The second important issue in Vera's article, and one closely linked to the emphasis he placed on *métier*, is the relationship he established between the idea of modernity and that of respect for tradition. For all that his ideas might seem reactionary, he used his pronoucements on tradition and *métier* to back up an essentially progressive argument. In a second article entitled 'Modernity and Tradition' (1919), for example, he stressed that only tradition could give artists the necessary tools for innovative work. Each epoch had had its own modern style, he argued, each based on tradition, yet equally new: 'No modernity without tradition,' he admonished, and 'no tradition without modernity'.[38]

Following the prescriptions of Vera, the team of artists working with Süe and Mare designed furnishings relying on arabesques contained within an ordering grid of lines. In his decorative compositions, Paul Vera let this grid show, as in the frontispiece for a book in which the ordering scheme of triangles remains clear. Evidently they hoped that their compositional systems, which in

their two-dimensional designs added a decorative, Cubist touch, would provide a structure on which a modern style could be founded, one that could rival the quality of the great French styles of the past.

The Compagnie des Arts Français made a conscious attempt to create a modern style on which a national consensus could be based. They attempted to re-establish an all-encompassing world view and guaranteed the continuation of the cultural values of classicism in French art.[39] At the same time, however, the artists involved attempted to construct a coherent edifice which would make of classicism an avant-garde current. Not only was geometry declared modern, but modernity was measured with respect to the classical tradition.

The Exposition Internationale des Arts Décoratifs et Industriels Modernes finally opened in Paris on 28 April 1925. Nearly 20 years had passed since the project was first announced and with them successive governments and a world war. Inaugurating a new era of peace and stability, the event was unique in its intention to exercise a definitive influence on artistic development in France and throughout the world. With its specific requirement of 'modernity', the exhibition provided an extraordinary showcase for each nation to project a specific image of itself and to compare this image with those of the other participating nations. In spite of the celebration of 'modernity', little in the event reflected the machine iconography featured in contemporary paintings by Fernand Léger or films by Abel Gance and Marcel L'Herbier.[40] In this dream world of modernity, industry was engulfed in a perfect environment of art and elegance, an ideal world that reassured the public that the havoc and destruction of the war had been supplanted by the *douceur de vivre* of the pre-war years.

The inauguration speech made by the Minister for Commerce, left no doubt as to the exhibition's anti-industrial ideology or to the administration's position on the

rationalization of the design process and the introduction of mass production into the decorative arts:

'Certainly we admire the continual advances made by the sciences applied to industry. We are grateful to them for the daily ameliorations in our well-being and comfort. But industrial organization, as it develops and turns increasingly to mechanization, as it reduces the role of human labour, and as the worker himself becomes a kind of mechanism, this organization takes away the personal touch of the maker and everything of his soul that he could put into his work. Series production is incompatible with Art.'[41]

The profusion of domed white plaster structures that dominated the exhibition's central axis lent a vaguely neo-classical atmosphere to the overall look of the exhibition, but the traditional architectural orders were everywhere transformed by a kind of commercial Cubism – bold geometric motifs in the form of flowers, triangles and waterfalls replaced the doric, ionic and corinthian, while the wood and plaster pavilions were low and constructed of simple compact forms, many with an all-over surface motif in bas-relief highlighted with gold or silver. Jacques-Emile Ruhlmann's Hôtel d'un Riche Collectionneur corresponded most clearly to the offical image that the exhibition was to project.[42] Ruhlmann knew just how to use the French classicist tradition to create a distinctly modern, albeit elitist style. Visitors were greeted on the garden side by a large statue of the *Three Graces* by Alfred Janniot, highly elongated figures enveloped in garlands of stylized flowers. The pavilion's architecture, by Pierre Patout, made discreet references to 18th-century masterpieces like Bagatelle. The interiors were total works of art that featured the beautifully crafted furnishings in ebony and ivory that had made the cabinet-maker's name and which vied in quality with pieces from the 18th century. Delicate, sober and highly distinctive, they consisted of large smooth masses on slender curving mounts.

In the Salon de Musique, the wallpaper was decorated with a stylized garland design and the marble mantelpiece was subtly defined by an egg and dart motif. The ensemble was dominated by *Les Perruches*, a giant canvas by Jean Dupas depicting a group of perversely elongated women, both dressed and undressed, treated in an eccentric style that made references to the Ecole de Fontainebleau.

Louis Süe and André Mare named their pavilion representing the Compagnie des art français, the Musée d'Art Contemporain, in criticism of what they considered to be the over-utilization of the word 'moderne'. To emphasize the continuity between tradition and modernity, they displayed a selection of works that they had created over the past five years rather than designing new models especially for the exhibition. In their Musée d'Art Contemporain there could be no doubt as to their bid to manufacture tradition. They tried to impose a certain legitimacy on their enterprise by associating their commercial pavilion with a museum and its function of preservation.[43] Süe and Mare succeeded in creating a kind of official French style – one that was decidedly luxurious and highly palatable – by calling on forms and techniques that were unmistakably French. They combined something of Louis XV voluptuous curves and gilding with the solidity and simplicity of the Louis-Philippe style, as in the desk in ebony and bronze that formed one of the centrepieces of their pavilion. Its bronze mounts recalled the mixture of materials common to 18th-century French *ébénisterie*. They were not copyists, however: their references to traditional styles were powerful cultural signs. This approach was apparently adequate for official perceptions of modernity, because the two artists were asked to design one of the most important rooms at the exhibition: the Salle des Fêtes in the Grand Palais, where official receptions were held. Here, the dominant decorative motif consisted of a typically classical element – an exaggeratedly large, stylized palmette – which was employed in an iconic fashion.

Those who remembered the original ideals of the exhibition were profoundly disappointed in the results and the event unleashed a storm of criticism that would have seemed unthinkable only a few months earlier. For a designer like Francis Jourdain, who had fought for the ideals of an 'art for the people' since the beginning of his career, the exhibition was a failure that provided no genuine solution to the real problems of modern domestic furnishing:

'This exhibition is inconsequential. It has no meaning, it teaches no lesson and it resolves no problem. It has not even posed one. At the most it has permitted us to meditate upon the problem of figuring out if the fruit basket constitutes a more "modern" ornament than the chestnut leaf of 1900, or if the great ornamental conquest of the period was not, in fact, the fan shape. I admit to being one of those whose sleep is not troubled by such solutions.'[44]

Yet from another point of view, the exhibition achieved much of what its planners wanted: to find new applications for a wide range of traditional luxury crafts, to re-establish Paris as the world centre of style and taste, and to create a new and uniquely French style of decorative arts that would rival those of the past.

The exhibition did have the effect of breaking the hold that historicizing styles had over the general public. The next two years witnessed the explosion of the Art Deco style, especially in the United States, where a travelling exhibition of works from the event was shown at Macy's department store in New York, at Lord and Taylor's department store and at the Metropolitan Museum of Art.[45] As a large display, which was intended to promote French luxury goods throughout the world, then, it worked perfectly.[46]

Two historians of 1920s France have recently written that the crux of that period resided in the dialectic between the desire to return to the past and the impossibility of doing so.[47] The outcome of the exhibition of 1925 clearly illustrates their point. If France could not return to the past, it could manufacture a new tradition. The consequences of this attempt to cloak the realities of the modern world in the shroud of the past would be revealed just a few years later when the world economic crisis shook the foundations of French society.

The Art Deco style, like Post-Modernism today, was an equivocal model of modernity, contrived of a complex corpus of symbols that responded to the conflicting forces unleashed by industrialization and the social and economic upheavals engendered by the reconstruction. Art Deco was long in developing and carefully promoted by designers and critics; it was criticized by the functionalist avant-garde as retrograde, and indeed its forms, iconography, materials and craftsmanship firmly upheld French traditions and confirmed the status quo. The Art Deco style still appeals today because of the message of nostalgia it contains, its evocation of memory, and the glorification of the body through luxury. By pretending to the universalism of classicism, it became a stylistic 'mask' of modernity that hid the ugly realities of an industrial world and the emergence of consumer society.

E s p r i t   N o u v e a u

A great epoch has begun. There exists a new spirit. Industry, overwhelming us like a flood which rolls on towards its destined end, has furnished us with new tools adapted to this new epoch, animated by the new spirit. Economic law unavoidably governs our acts and our thoughts. The problem of the house is a problem of the epoch. The equilibrium of society today depends upon it. Architecture has for its first duty, in this period of renewal, that of bringing about a revision of values, a revision of the constituent elements of the house. Mass production is based on analysis and experiment. Industry on the grand scale must occupy itself with building and establish the elements of the house on a mass production basis. We must create the mass production spirit. The spirit of constructing mass production houses. The spirit of living in mass production houses. The spirit of conceiving mass production houses. If we eliminate from our hearts and minds all dead concepts in regard to the houses and look at the question from a critical and objective point of view, we shall arrive at the 'House-Machine', the mass pro-

duction house, healthy (and morally so too) and beautiful in the same way that the working tools and instruments which accompany our existence are beautiful. Beautiful also with all the animation that the artist's sensibility can add to severe and pure functioning elements.

Le Corbusier,
Towards a New Architecture,
1927

The Pavilion Esprit-Nouveau was one of the buildings of the International Exhibition of Decorative Arts and represents a cell of the Villas-Apartment Block.
The programme: to reject decorative arts. To affirm that architecture extends from the smallest furnishing to the house, to the street, to the city and beyond. To show that industry creates pure objects by selection (by means of the standardized series). To demonstrate the radical transformation and new freedom inherent in reinforced concrete and steel for the conception of urban habitation. To show that an apartment can be standardized to sat-

isfy the needs of a 'series-man'. The practical, habitable cell, comfortable and beautiful, a veritable machine for habitation, grouped in large colonies, both in height and breadth.
A new term has replaced the word furnishing; this term embodies accumulated traditions and outdated usage. The new word is the equipment of a house. In analysing the problem, equipment means the classification of the various elements necessary for domestic operations. In replacing the innumerable furnishings of all shapes and sizes, standard cabinets are incorporated in the walls or set against the walls, so located within the apartment as to best serve its exact daily function (clothes, linen, dishes, bookcase, etc.): they are constructed not of wood, but of metal, in the shops where office furniture is fabricated. The cabinets constitute, in themselves, the sole furnishing for the house, thus leaving a maximum amount of available space within each room.

Le Corbusier,
'Pavilion Esprit-Nouveau, Paris',
Œuvres Complètes 1910-1965

Right-hand page: Esprit-Nouveau pavilion, designed by Le Corbusier and Pierre Jeanneret, Exposition des Arts Décoratifs de Paris, 1925.

Background: Chaise longue in chrome steel, designed by Le Corbusier, Pierre Jeanneret and Charlotte Perriand, 1928.

Vignette: Villa Savoye, designed by Le Corbusier and Pierre Jeanneret, Poissy, 1928-1931.

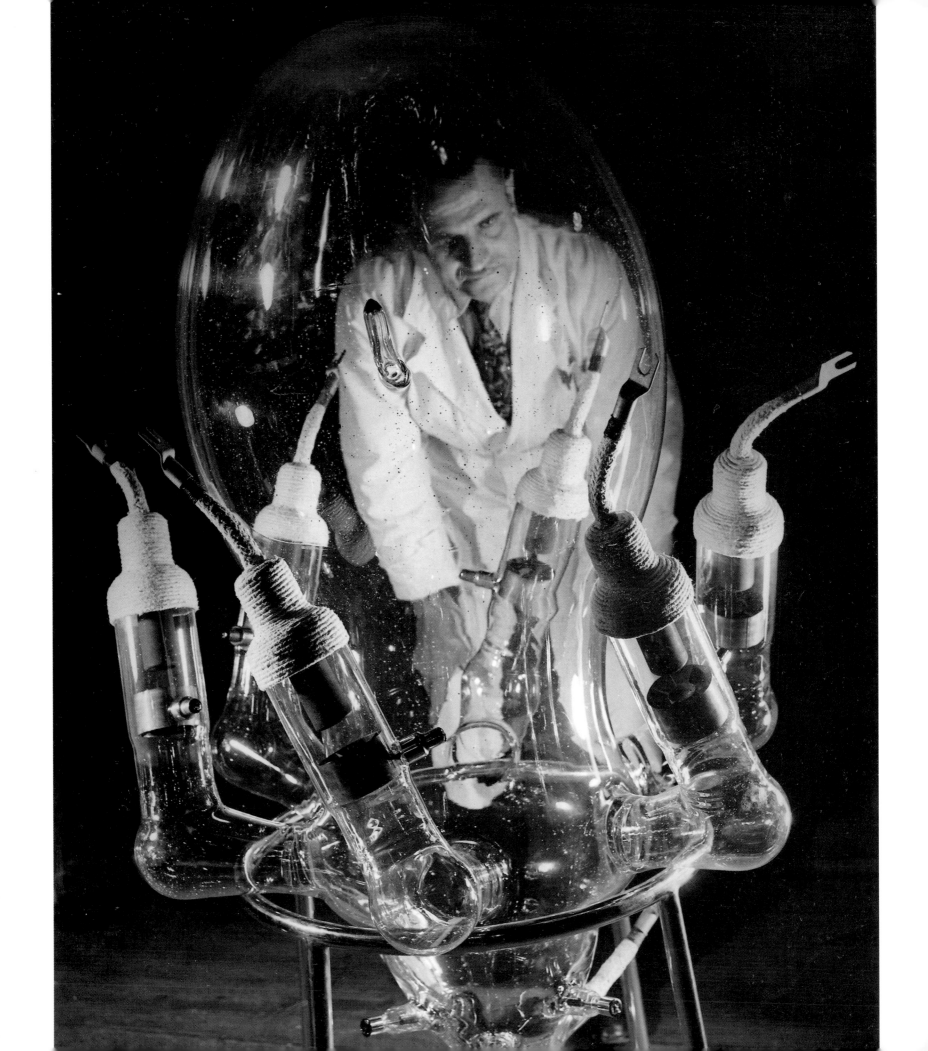

1918-1945

by

Jocelyn de Noblet

After the First World War, the more progressive members of the European elite grasped the fact that scientific and technological progress had profoundly transformed the production process, but that material culture had evolved much more rapidly than people's lifestyles. Le Corbusier, when asked what architecture was, replied laconically: 'It is tidying up.' He added that it was important to sift the past and its memories through the sieve of reason and to address problems in the manner of aeronautic engineers, creating 'machines for living in'. In a similar vein, Georges Braque made his famous comment: 'I love the rule which holds emotion in check.'

Faced with the necessity of building a new world in tune with modernity, several solutions were envisaged and applied differently according to the country.

In 1919, on the initiative of Walter Gropius, a school of a wholly new kind – the Bauhaus – was created in Weimar. Its guiding principle was that scientific and technical progress should lead society to abandon its traditional notions and follow those who urge a radical introduction of originality into the existing order. Director of the Bauhaus from 1928 to 1930, Hannes Meyer summed up the aim well when he wrote, in 1926: 'Each period has its own forms. Our job is to renew our world with present day means. Our knowledge of the past, however, weighs us down, and we are tragically held back by our education. The acceptance of the present leads to the rejection of the past.' The Bauhaus, whose influence is felt to this day, was in fact the first modern school of design to totally overhaul artistic education.

According to Art Deco designers in France in the 1920s, one should be modern by following tradition and not by breaking with it. The trend is represented by decorative artists as varied as Jacques-Emile Ruhlmann, René Prou, Clément Rousseau, André Groult, Clément Mère and Dominique.

In the United States, where the development of consumer society was facilitated by easy credit and the hard sell, early industrial designers chose to offer, through mass-produced artefacts, an aesthetic of sensation. From 1930, streamlined forms became the unifying force in American material culture, resulting in a formal consistency which was accepted by the vast majority of consumers.

However, the start of the Second World War put a stop to the effervescent creativity on both sides of the Atlantic. Formal concerns then moved away from the civilian sector to the military domain, where intensive design research absorbed everyone's energy. The resulting innovations proved decisive and, by 1945, the transfer of the new technologies to civilian society gave an enduring impetus to a number of industrial sectors.

Mercury-vapour ion rectifier, made by Cooper Hewitt Corp.

Preceding double page: Silver soup tureen (detail), designed by Jean Puiforcat, 1925. Musée des Arts Décoratifs, Paris.

1918

- Charles Rennie Mackintosh: Sedia chair
- General Motors markets the Frigidaire domestic refrigerator in the United States

- first air service between Washington and New York
- Giorgio De Chirico participates in the Epoca exhibition, Rome
- Piet Mondrian: *Composition No. 2*
- start of the Vkhutemas (Higher State Art Training Centre) in Moscow
- armistice, end of the First World War
- in Russia, Leon Trotsky organizes the Red Army

1919

- Jean Patou opens his fashion house
- Walter Gropius: the Bauhaus at Weimar opens
- Citroën Type A motor car
- Robert Wiene: *The Cabinet of Dr Caligari*
- André Breton and Philippe Soupault: *Les Champs Magnétiques*
- Ernest Rutherford splits the atom
- J. W. Alcock and A. Whitten Brown make the first non-stop transatlantic flight
- prohibition in the United States
- Third International founded in Moscow
- first meeting of the League of Nations

- Benito Mussolini founds fascist movement in Italy

1920

- first electric hairdriers (United States)
- Le Corbusier and Amédée Ozenfant found the journal *L'Esprit Nouveau*
- Vladimir Tatlin: project for the *Monument to the Third International*

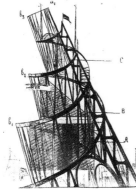

- Constructivist exhibition in Moscow
- first general radio broadcasts begin in Great Britain and the United States

1921

- Coco Chanel launches her perfume Chanel No. 5

- Erich Mendelsohn: Einstein observatory at Potsdam
- Adolf Loos: *Spoken into the Void*
- Ludwig Josef Wittgenstein: *Tractatus Logicophilosophicus*
- British Broadcasting Corporation founded

- Albert Calmette and Camille Guérin experiment with the BCG vaccine
- creation of the Chinese Communist Party

1922

- launderette in the Karl Marx Hof, Vienna
- Citroën 5CV motor car
- Adolf Loos: The Chicago Tribune Column (project)
- Kazimir Malevich: architectural models
- El Lissitzky: catalogue for the Van Diemen gallery
- James Joyce: *Ulysses*
- T. S. Eliot: *The Waste Land*
- Thomas Hunt Morgan experiments with the hereditary mechanisms of fruit flies
- Stalin elected general secretary of the Central Committee
- Mussolini takes power in Italy

1923

- Citroën half-track vehicle

- first Salon des arts ménagers in Paris
- George Gershwin: *Rhapsody in Blue*
- László Moholy-Nagy joins the Bauhaus
- Le Corbusier: *Towards a New Architecture*
- Hitler's *coup d'état* in Munich fails

1924

- Wilhelm Wagenfeld and Carl J. Jucker (Bauhaus): metal and glass lamp
- Barker and Skinner invent Plexiglas (registered trademark in 1934)
- Victor and Alexander Vesnine: project for La Pravda building in Leningrad
- Gerrit Rietveld: Schröder house (with furniture), Utrecht
- first winter Olympic games, Chamonix

- Constantin Brancusi: *The Beginning of the World*
- Oskar Kokoschka: *Venice*
- André Breton: *Surrealist Manifesto*
- Erich von Stroheim: *Greed*
- René Clair: *Entr'acte* (in collaboration with Francis Picabia)
- patent application for iconoscope (TV) filed by Vladimir Kosma Zworikin
- Louis de Broglie publishes study concerning wave theory of matter
- death of Lenin

- **Marcel Breuer: Wassily chair, made from tubular steel**

- industrial manufacture of Leica cameras
- Pieter Oud: facade for De Unie café, Rotterdam
- Exposition Internationale des Arts Décoratifs et Industriels Modernes, Paris
- the Bauhaus is moved to Dessau, buildings designed by Walter Gropius; Josef Albers becomes head
- Le Corbusier and Pierre Jeanneret: Plan Voisin for Paris
- Sergueï Eisenstein: *The Battleship Potemkin*
- Charlie Chaplin: *The Gold Rush*
- Georg Wilhelm Pabst: *The Joyless Street*
- Francis Scott Fitzgerald: *The Great Gatsby*
- Franz Kafka: *The Trial*
- Adolf Hitler: *Mein Kampf*

1926

- Marianne Brandt (Bauhaus): ceiling lamp
- John Logie Baird: experimental television transmissions
- Adolf Loos: Tsara house, Paris
- Ernst May: construction of fifteen thousand houses in the suburbs of Frankfurt (with fully fitted interiors)
- Alexander Calder: wire sculptures

□ Fritz Lang: *Metropolis*
□ Alban Berg: *Wozzeck*

□ Franz Kafka: *The Castle*

1927

□ Le Corbusier: Maison de Monzies, Garches
□ Charles Lindbergh flies The Spirit of St Louis from New York to Paris

□ Alan Crosland: *The Jazz Singer*, first sound film
□ Kasimir Malevich: *The World Without Object*
□ Hugo Häring: publication on the reorientation of applied arts
□ quantum mechanics accepted by phycisists at the Solvay congress
□ Duke Ellington's band plays at the Cotton Club in Harlem, New York
□ Nicolas Sacco and Bartolomeo Vanzetti executed (United States)

1928

□ Richard Buckminster Fuller: Dymaxion house
□ Richard G. Drew invents adhesive tape, marketed by the company 3M
□ **Jacob Schick: electric razor (United States)**
□ **Opel Rak II, first rocket-propelled car**

□ Graff Zeppelin LZ 127
□ Le Corbusier: Villa Savoye, Poissy (1928–1931)
□ Luis Buñuel: *Un Chien Andalou*
□ Carl Theodor Dreyer: *The Passion of Joan of Arc*
□ Erich Maria Remarque: *All Quiet on the Western Front*
□ Georg Wilhelm Pabst: *Lulu*
□ Bertolt Brecht and Kurt Weill: *Die Dreigroschenoper*
□ Gio Ponti founds the design journal *Domus* in Italy
□ Alexander Fleming discovers penicillin
□ first five-year plan in USSR
□ Chiang Kai-shek becomes president of China
□ in Japan, start of emperor Hirohito's reign

1929

□ Ludwig Mies van der Rohe: Barcelona furniture
□ Alvar Aalto: stool 60
□ Josef Albers: collapsible chair
□ Raymond Loewy: Gestetner model 66 office duplicator
□ Le Corbusier, Pierre Jeanneret and Charlotte Perriand: housing facilities
□ Warren Alvin Morrison: first quartz-crystal clock
□ International Exposition, Barcelona

□ Alvar Aalto: Paimio sanatorium (Finland, 1929–1933)
□ second congress of the CIAM (international congress of modern architecture) in Frankfurt: Housing for a Minimal Existence
□ in New York, inauguration of the Museum of Modern Art (MOMA), first museum entirely devoted to modern art
□ foundation of the Union des Artistes Modernes (UAM) in Paris
□ Djiga Vertov: *Man with a Camera*
□ Walt Disney: *Steamboat Willie* (Disney's first sound cartoon)
□ Pathé: His Master's Voice gramophone model 02

□ Hergé begins publication of *Tintin*
□ William Faulkner: *The Sound and the Fury*
□ first appearance of the term 'science fiction' (United States)
□ Wall Street Crash precipitates world depression
□ Trotsky is expelled from the USSR

1930

□ Wilhelm Wagenfeld (Bauhaus): Pyrex service
□ Ludwig Mies van der Rohe: Brno chair

□ Frank Whittle: first turboreactor
□ Pier Luigi Nervi: Florence stadium
□ end of Constructivism in USSR
□ Theo van Doesburg first uses the term 'art concret'
□ André Breton: second manifesto of Surrealism
□ in the Soviet Union, start of Stakhanovism

1931

□ the Bell laboratories use the telex nationwide (United States)
□ Harold Edgerton applies the electronic flash to photography
□ Fritz Lang: *M*
□ in Germany, rise of Nazism

1932

□ Jean Mantelet, founder of Moulinex, invents the food mill

□ Karl Guthe Jansky: experimental radiotelescope
□ Otto Kuhler, Henry Dreyfuss, Raymond Loewy, Norman Bel Geddes: aerodynamic steam locomotives (United States 1932–1938)

□ foundation of the Black Mountain College in North Carolina
□ Alexander Calder: mobiles
□ Howard Hawks: *Scarface*
□ Aldous Leonard Huxley: *Brave New World*
□ Louis-Ferdinand Céline: *Voyage au Bout de la Nuit*
□ in India, Ghandi leads a campaign of non-violence

1933

- Guerlain creates the perfume Vol de Nuit

- Max Braun: combined radio-record player
- Wuff develops polystyrene (Germany)
- **Volksempfanger, popular radio set used for Nazi propaganda (based on a 1928 design by Walter Maria Kersting)**
- Ernst Friedrich Ruska and Max Knoll: electronic microscope (based on theories developed by Hans Busch in 1926)
- J. Strauss: Golden Gate Bridge, San Francisco (1933–1937)
- ChicagoWorld's Fair: A Century of Progress
- the federation of German architects (BDA) pledges allegiance to the national socialist regime
- Bauhaus at Dessau closed by the Gestapo, and the staff flee to America
- fourth CIAM congress: The Functional City (elaboration of the Athens charter, published in an article by Le Corbusier in 1943)
- Hitler becomes chancellor of Germany, first concentration camps erected by the Nazis
- Franklin D. Roosevelt launches the New Deal in the United States

1934

- Gerrit Rietveld: Zig-Zag chair

- Hans Ledwinka: Tatra V8 motor car, based on the ideas of Paul Jaray
- Citroën 11CV *traction avant* (using front-wheel drive) motor car

- Carl Breer, Owen Skelton and Fred Zeder: Chrysler Airflow motor car
- **Ferdinand Porsche: Volkswagen prototypes (1934–1936)**
- George Carwardine: anglepoise lamp
- exhibition of graphic design by Hans Schleger
- Norman Bel Geddes: *Horizons*
- Jean Vigo: *L'Atalante*
- Night of the Long Knives in Germany
- in China, Long March by the partisans of Mao Tse-tung

1935

- Gabriele Mucchi: chaise longue

- **Adolph Rickenbacker: electric guitar (United States)**
- Braun builds first battery-operated portable radio
- Hermes Baby typewriter

- IBM markets first commercially successful electric typewriter
- first parking meters in use (Tulsa, Oklahoma)
- **Pierre-Jules Boulanger and André Lefèbvre: prototype of the 2CV motor car**
- **Douglas DC-3 Dakota aeroplane**
- Sir Robert Alexander Watson-Watt invents radar
- Universal Exposition, Brussels
- Rouben Mamoulian: *Becky Sharp*, first feature film in technicolor
- Le Corbusier: *La Ville Radieuse*

1936

- Raymond Loewy: Coldspot refrigerator for Sears Roebuck
- Walter Dorwin Teague: Kodak Brownie camera
- Olivetti commissions Marcello Nizzoli to design its offices
- Frank Lloyd Wright: Falling Water (Kaufmann House), Bear Run, Pennsylvania
- in Rio de Janeiro, Lucio Costa and Oscar Niemeyer direct the construction of the ministry of education and culture
- Meret Oppenheim: *Déjeuner en fourrure*

- Charlie Chaplin: *Modern Times*

- France: Front Populaire is elected to govern, with Léon Blum as president

- Nikolaus Pevsner: *Pioneers of the Modern Movement from William Morris to Walter Gropius*
- first regular public television transmissions (BBC, Great Britain)
- start of the Spanish Civil War
- China declares war on Japan

1937

- Frank Lloyd Wright: Barrel chair
- Walter Zapp: Minox camera for VEF in Riga
- Wallace Hume Carothers patents nylon (for the Dupont company)

- Henry Dreyfuss: Bell telephone
- **Hobast Manufacturing & Co: the 10A, first electric coffee grinder**
- Walter Gropius becomes professor at the Harvard School of Architecture
- Lewis Mumford: *The Culture of Cities*
- International Exposition: Arts et Techniques dans la Vie Moderne (Paris)
- Pablo Picasso: *Guernica*
- in London, Penguin books are launched

1938

- László Biro: ballpoint pen
- Hans Coray: stacking chair
- in the United States, Orson Welles' adaptation of *War of the Worlds* causes widespread panic
- Walt Disney: *Snow White and the Seven Dwarfs*
- Marcel Carné: *Le Quai des Brumes*

- John Logie Baird: experimental television programmes in colour
- Germany annexes Austria
- Munich conference, Germany occupies Sudetenland

1939

- Isamu Noguchi: low table with glass top
- Messerschmidt Me 209 aircraft establishes a speed record
- Ernst Heinkel develops the Heinkel 178 jet plane
- Igor Sikorsky: helicopter
- Golden Gate exhibition, San Francisco
- New York World's Fair: Building the World of Tomorrow

- Marc Chagall: *Time has no Shore*
- Jean Renoir: *La Règle du Jeu*
- John Ford: *Stagecoach*
- Victor Fleming: *Gone with the Wind* (after the novel by Margaret Mitchell, published in 1936)
- James Joyce: *Finnegans Wake*
- Germany agrees nonaggression pact with USSR
- Germany invades Poland
- Britain and France declare war on Germany

1940

- Achille Castiglioni: work table and Phonola radio
- start of commercial television in the United States
- Walter Dorwin Teague: Texaco service station
- **Willys Overland Inc. and the American Bantam Co. produce prototypes of the jeep**
- John Ford: *The Grapes of Wrath* (based on the book by John Steinbeck, published in 1939)

- Charles Eames and Eero Saarinen are prizewinners in Museum of Modern Art furniture competition, New York
- Raymond Loewy: Lucky Strike cigarette packet

- Orson Welles: *Citizen Kane*
- Charlie Chaplin: *The Great Dictator*
- Walt Disney: *Fantasia*
- discovery of the caves at Lascaux, France
- Winston Churchill becomes prime minister of Great Britain
- defeat of France, Pétain government concludes armistice with Germany

1941

- John Huston: *The Maltese Falcon*
- Siegfried Giedion: *Space, Time and Architecture*
- Germany invades USSR
- Japanese attack on Pearl Harbor (7 December)

1942

- Paul Arzens: the Egg electric car

- Enrico Fermi constructs the first nuclear reactor (Chicago)
- Wernher von Braun: V2 rocket
- Le Corbusier creates modulor system of proportion which he will use after the war
- Ludwig Mies van der Rohe: Illinois Institute of Technology, Chicago (of which he becomes head in 1938)
- Ludwig Mies van der Rohe: Farnsworth house (Illinois)
- exhibition Artists in Exile organized by André Breton at the Pierre Matisse Gallery (New York)
- Peggy Guggenheim founds the gallery Art of this Century in New York
- opening of the Musée des Arts Modernes in Paris
- Orson Welles: *The Magnificent Ambersons*

1943

- first electromechanical computer Colossus is built based on the calculations of Alan Mathison Turing (England)
- Henry John Kaiser: mass production of Liberty Ships (United States) which were to be used in the allied landings in Normandy

- Le Corbusier: unités d'habitation, Marseille
- creation of a ministry of town planning in England
- Le Corbusier publishes *Urbanisme des CIAM, la Charte d'Athènes*
- Piet Mondrian: *Broadway Boogie-Woogie*
- Jackson Pollock's first one-man show
- Howard Hawks: *Air Force*
- Robert von Musil: *The Man Without Qualities*
- in Italy, Mussolini is forced to resign

1944

- death of Edvard Munch, Piet Mondrian, Wassily Kandinsky
- Otto Preminger: *Laura*
- D-Day: landings in Normandy

- Sergeï Eisenstein: *Ivan the Terrible*
- Art Concret exhibition, Basle (Arp, Kandinsky, Klee, Mondrian, Henry Moore)
- Selman Abraham Waksman discovers streptomycin which acts on tuberculosis

1945

- Percy le Baron Spencer invents the microwave oven (marketed in 1947)
- Vélosolex moped

- operational postcombustion turboreactor, Rolls Royce
- Jacob Robert Oppenheimer and his team develop the nuclear bomb (A bomb)
- Jean Dubuffet develops the concept of *art brut*
- Marcel Carné: *Les Enfants du Paradis*
- Roberto Rossellini: *Rome, Open City*
- David Lean: *Brief Encounter*
- Billy Wilder: *The Lost Weekend*
- Charlie Parker and Dizzy Gillespie make the first bop recordings
- German capitulation
- atomic bombs dropped on Hiroshima and Nagasaki
- the United Nations is created by United Nations charter, signed at San Francisco on 26 June
- independent republic of Vietnam formed

The Bauhaus
and the Theory of Form

....

Elodie Vitale

Below: **Official emblem of the Bauhaus from 1922, designed by Oskar Schlemmer.**

Opposite: **The study of materials: corrugated cardboard foldings and cut-outs, Josef Albers's preliminary course.**

When, in April 1919, the architect Walter Gropius created the Bauhaus, the school of arts, crafts, and architecture, he summoned only painters to come and teach there because he was convinced, as were many others, that 'painting is the art which for decades has marched at the head of all artistic movements and fertilized all the other arts, especially architecture.'[1] It was the responsibility of these painters not to give painting courses or educate artists, but rather to teach about form, and to teach it in a way connected to activity in the studio. Gropius felt that such an education would be valuable for all the arts and would provide the best foundation for those who subsequently decided to become architects. The painters he chose all belonged 'to artistic circles opposed to academicism and interested in the analysis of the structure of works and the search for the rules governing the world of form and colour. Their research into space went beyond the academic representational mode inherited from the Renaissance and based on Albertian perspective'.[2] According to Gropius, they were to encourage the students to experiment with the language of the plastic arts, thereby creating a climate in which 'artistic gifts' could flourish. He called them 'masters of form' (*Formmeister*), as opposed to the 'master craftsmen' (*Werkmeister*) in charge of the practical studio work. He hoped in this way to produce students who had not only the ability to give form or 'soul' to a work, but also the technical expertise to execute their ideas, thereby abolishing the 'class separation amounting to a wall of disdain between artist and craftsman.'[3]

But the painters Gropius summoned to the Bauhaus, while they agreed with him about the necessity of rehabilitating the crafts and unifying the arts, thought (perhaps without expressing it in so many words at the beginning) that each art has its own specific techniques and that the crafts should not be made to serve as a common base for all the arts. The difficulties faced by these painters in attempting to integrate their teaching about form with the practical work in the studios indicates that there was a contradiction at work, and when Gropius sought to integrate art and technology the contradiction intensified.

In reality, while their art was an influence in the studios they directed, most of the professors failed to develop a genuine theory about form. Only the preliminary courses run by Johannes Itten, László Moholy-Nagy and Josef Albers, and the teaching of Paul Klee and Wassily Kandinsky, held such theories, but none of them would be elaborated on the basis of craft practice.

Johannes Itten's preliminary course

A contemporary text, published on the occasion of the first public exhibition of work by Bauhaus students in April – May 1922, offers a precise description of the goal of the preliminary course: 'To liberate the students' creative forces, to help them understand the materials found in nature, and to teach them the fundamental laws of visual creativity.'[4] The great interest of Itten's preliminary course lay in its mixture of this novel pedagogic programme with an artistic education.

Partial to mystic conceptions redolent of Platonism, Itten was drawn to the idea of 'archi-forms', which for him meant geometric forms, especially the elementary forms of the circle, the square, and the triangle, which he thought contained all possible forms, 'visible to seers, invisible to non-seers'.[5] They 'are characterized by their different spatial orientations. Thus the square is horizontal and vertical, the triangle diagonal, and the circle circular.'[6]

For Itten, it was essential that the students learn from their own experience. Consequently, he encouraged them to try and feel the character of different forms by doing corporal exercises. He then got them to represent, through drawing or some other means, these characters as they had interiorized them, multiplying the basic parameters through contrast, combination, and repeated or opposing proportions, thus varying the forms infinitely.

According to this approach, the only way to gain access to a work was through 'empathy' (*Einfühlung*), experiencing the form in an interiorized way in order to grasp its spiritual content. The presupposition here was that forms have only one possible content, which is perceived similarly by different individuals through all of space and time. Thus, the historical and cultural dimension of a work, which is present in the form itself, was completely forgotten. But this 'formalism' is dangerous, for it courts a new academicism.[7] Certain approaches to artistic training based on Itten's preliminary course are now in use throughout the world – many are those who have retained only the formalist aspect of the approach, which is easily reducible to formulaic prescriptions – and some students succumb to this academicism.

Itten's teachings about colour

As a painter and art teacher Itten was interested in 'the effect of colours' and not the 'reality of colours', which is the domain of physicists and chemists. He limited himself to an analysis of the aesthetics of colours 'born of a painter's experience and intuition'.[8] By linking his theory to intuition, Itten relativized its implications. He felt that the teaching of colour should refine and enrich his students' sensibilities. His was an activist education, teaching the student to relive through his own experience 'the position of colours in relation to one another, their orientation, their clarity, their luminosity, or their mute tonality, the quantitative relations, structure, and rhythmic interaction of colours',[9] and finally, colour harmony and spatial effect. But for Itten, the basis for the aesthetics of colour lay in 'the effects of colour contrast and arrangement'.[10] He borrowed from the painter Philipp Otto Runge the idea that the sphere is the most useful form for representing colour classification. As for colour harmony, Itten regarded this as a simple matter of psychophysical equilibrium. He believed, as did Kandinsky, that the tension produced by discordant colour combinations, which when mixed do not produce grey, could be used as a constructive element in artistic composition.

Even if for Itten, the laws of colour, like those governing other representational devices, were eternal and absolute, 'as valid in any other time as they are now' – and these laws formed the body of transmissible knowledge that he wanted to pass on to his students – he was convinced that the real essence of colours 'remains hidden from our reason and only intuition is capable of grasping it'.[11]

The study of materials

Itten asked his students at the Bauhaus to arrange long 'chromatic' series of materials and then had them run their fingers over them, their eyes closed, in order to improve their sense of touch. Exercises such as these were without doubt the most original part of his teaching programme. Students not only studied the nature of materials, but also exploited texture and rhythm, refining the sense of touch as well as the eye. The exercises were intended to familiarize the students with materials in a creative way and help them decide which studio would be best suited to them.

László Moholy-Nagy: the shift towards industry

From 1922, the orientation of Bauhaus teaching changed from crafts to industry, a response as much to the pressure of social and economic developments as to correlative shifts in artistic movements. This change resulted in Itten's departure and the appointment of Moholy-Nagy, and caused friction between the advocates of different approaches within the school. With hindsight, it is possible to say that the battle was won by the defenders of industrial art the moment Itten was replaced by Moholy-Nagy. None the less, until the end of the Weimar period there would be no clear Bauhaus position on the question of the relationship between art, craft and industry. It was only with its move to Dessau in 1925 that this question was definitively resolved.[12] In Weimar, difficulties encountered in setting up a genuine exchange with

Life is not given to the work by fashioning the object, the building, according to a viewpoint alien to it, but by awakening, fostering, and cultivating the essential form enclosed within it.

Hugo Häring, 'The House as an Organic Structure', Innendekoration, *1932*

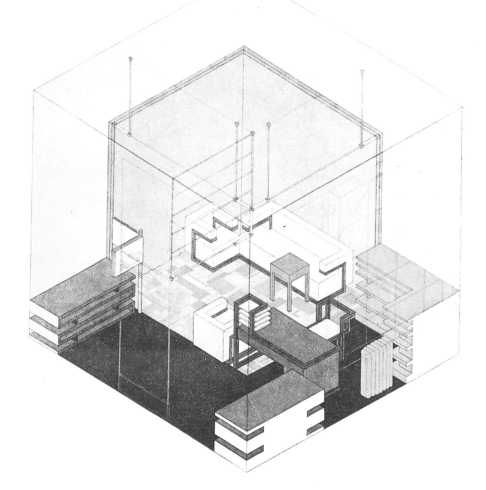

industry, the necessity of making concessions in official pronouncements to the social and economic realities of Thuringia (where artisanal culture was still deeply embedded), and the internal conflicts at the school all played their part in shaping the Bauhaus's ambiguous attitude towards the crafts.

In 1922, Gropius still wanted a confirmed artist belonging to expressionist circles when he called on Kandinsky, but he was hoping to replace Itten with an artist who, through his work as well his theory, might help the Bauhaus shift its sights from the crafts to industry and further the integration of art and the machine.

Moholy-Nagy's preliminary course

When he arrived at the Bauhaus, Moholy-Nagy's artistic practice and his theoretical ideas were somewhat at odds with those of most of the other teachers. The differences were most pronounced over the question of integrating art and technology. When he took charge of the preliminary course, however, his approach was not opposed to that of Itten but simply sought to give it a more rational, socially-grounded basis. While he was aware that a professionalized education was now unavoidable, his approach to instruction remained very similar to that of Itten and the other teachers.

Materials: tactile and optical exercises

While Moholy-Nagy continued to use Itten's exercises for developing the senses in his preliminary course, he sought to objectify the students' tactile impressions, which were necessarily subjective, by asking them to monitor their impressions by making 'tactile diagrams'. He also tried to develop a more precise vocabulary – 'structure', 'texture', 'composition', 'accumulation', and so on – to describe the various conformations of materials.

Aside from the attempt to systematize and objectify sensory experience, Moholy-

Nagy also attempted to link these exercises with the art of the time – something which played no part in Itten's programme, which tended to reinforce what was unique to each individual. Apart from these differences, the investigation of materials carried out in Moholy-Nagy's preliminary course was an extension of work initiated by Itten.

Sculpture and space

For Moholy-Nagy the 'new painter becomes the creator of relations of light', and the 'new sculptor will be the creator of relations of volumes and movement'.[13] The architect, then, is the creator of spatial relations. Thanks to technological developments, these relations had become kinetic rather than static, and architecture had become open rather than closed.

The studies of equilibrium made by Moholy-Nagy's students during the preliminary course were primarily intended to sharpen their understanding of structure, static and dynamic phases, and spatial balance. With these exercises, which Moholy-Nagy based on the most modern examples of recent architecture, the Bauhaus took a decisive step towards the integration of art and technology.

Josef Albers's preliminary course

By concentrating his teaching programme on materials, Josef Albers reinforced the work of Itten and Moholy-Nagy. His exercises were not fundamentally different from theirs. He placed great emphasis on the distinction between matter and material. His exercises dealing with matter were like those of Itten and Moholy-Nagy, but those focusing on materials, on the other hand, were new. They tested their capacity of resistance, 'their reaction to simultaneous tension and flexion, their [means of] assembly, their weak points', thereby making it possible to assess their capabilities and 'the limits of their efficacity' (for example, 'an assemblage of the bottom part of matchboxes tightly fitted together, can support the weight of several men').[14]

Essentially, Albers's teaching, which advocated a practical apprenticeship rather than the passive assimilation of an elaborated theory, was not very different from that of the other teachers. But he criticized Itten's aim of liberating the student's personality. He felt it was not the responsibility of the school to do this and that only individuals themselves could achieve self-development. The school should simply make sure it did nothing to impede this process. Nor did he seek, like Moholy-Nagy, to help the student find a 'biological' equilibrium as an aid to creative development.[15] He set out instead to liberate the student from individualism through a quest for 'economical form' (in both work and materials) – a rational approach aiming at a marriage of form and function. For Albers the confrontation with form began with the study of materials.

Such an approach is better suited to the technological and economic requirements of industry than to aesthetic concerns. Even more than the teaching of Moholy-Nagy, which was influenced by Constructivism and was still dominated by a 'romantic' view of technology, Albers's rational and systematic teaching marked the decisive shift of the Bauhaus towards the integration of art and industry.

Paul Klee: the teaching of form

According to Klee, art's aim was not to render as faithfully as possible the impressions received from natural phenomena. Rather it 'makes visible' the laws underpinning this 'art of another' that is nature. For Klee, it was necessary to analyse the specific artistic elements out of which a work, as an autonomous organism, is made, but without the elements losing their identity. This last specification is very important, for Klee was inspired more by the model of atomistic association prevalent in 19th-century thought than he was by Gestalt theory, as has often been claimed.[16] This theory assumed importance at the Bauhaus only after Hannes Meyer became its director.[17] In his

Left: Tubular metal chair made by PEL, 1946. This chair is directly inspired by the tubular steel furniture designed by Marcel Breuer at the Bauhaus from 1925.

Right: Kubus stackable glass service, designed by Wilhelm Wagenfeld for Lausitzer Glasverein, 1938.

Below: Portrait of Walter Gropius, 1920.

The ultimate aim of all visual arts is the complete building!

The ultimate aim of all visual arts is the complete building! To embellish buildings was once the noblest function of the fine arts; they were the indispensable components of great architecture. Today the arts exist in isolation, from which they can be rescued only through the conscious, co-operative effort of all craftsmen. Architects, painters, and sculptors must recognize anew and learn to grasp the composite character of a building both as an entity and in its separate parts. Only then will their work be imbued with the architectonic spirit which it has lost as 'salon art'.

The old schools of art were unable to produce this unity; how could they, since art cannot be taught. They must be merged once more with the workshop. The mere drawing and painting world of the pattern designer and the applied artist must become a world that builds again. When young people who take a joy in artistic creation once more begin their life's work by learning a trade, then the unproductive 'artist' will no longer be condemned to deficient artistry, for their skill will now be preserved for the crafts, in which they will be able to achieve excellence.

Architects, sculptors, painters, we all must return to the crafts! For art is not a 'profession'. There is no essential difference between the artist and the craftsman. The artist is an exalted craftsman. In rare moments of inspiration, transcending the consciousness of his will, the grace of heaven may cause his work to blossom into art. But proficiency in a craft is essential to every artist. Therein lies the prime source of creative imagination. Let us then create a new guild of craftsmen without class distinctions that raise an arrogant barrier between craftsman and artist! Together let us desire, conceive, and create the new structure of the future, which will embrace architecture and sculpture and painting in one unity and which will one day rise toward heaven from the hands of a million workers like a crystal symbol of a new faith.

Walter Gropius,
Programme of the Staatliches
Bauhaus in Weimar, *April 1919*

writings, Klee seems to favour a mechanistic conception according to which an organism is an association of elements linked together by mathematical laws, rather than a single integral entity, as was suggested by contemporary Gestalt theory. But one also finds in Klee a much more dynamic view, which sees the organism as both an entity and a collection of smaller component parts constantly interacting with one another. For Klee, in effect, nature's basic equilibria are not static but dynamic. Likewise, the work of art 'is above all a process of creation, it cannot be comprehended as a mere product'. Klee's stress on process is consistent with modern notions of physics, according to which the essence of matter cannot be separated from its activity, as the two of them are different aspects of a single reality in which time and space are united.

Thus in Klee's view painting is born of movement, being motion held in suspense by an equilibrium of forces. He used phrases such as 'the simultaneous unification of forms', 'the use of contrasts between divided colours', and so on. All this constitutes 'the science of forms' but is still not 'art in the highest circle'. Just as we cannot decipher the ultimate mystery of nature, we cannot solve the riddle of art, for 'in the play of art we imitate the forces that created and are creating the world'.[18] None the less, the artist manifests himself through form, in one way or another, according to the general state of human evolution which has instilled in him a particular vision of the world. Klee held it to be essential that he have at his disposal the formal elements suited to his expressive needs, but his overall approach was anything but formalist.

Klee's contribution to the theory of plastic form

Klee's first lesson begins with study of the line, 'there where creative form begins: at the point animated by movement'.[19] From the line he moves on to perspective, which is for him simply an instrument of control without intrinsic value. He then deals with the problem of equilibrium, transposing this existential concept directly into the visual domain. The equilibrium to be sought out is that between two areas, tonalities, or colours. Thus light grey and dark grey covering identical fields can be brought into equilibrium with one another by adding a black square to the first. In some cases it is difficult to determine which of the two elements is the 'heaviest', especially when one must compare a quantity (size) with a quality (tonality). Here one must rely on intuition to know when equilibrium has been reached. By analyzing many cases, you can refine your sensory perceptions and educate your eye. The most important thing to grasp is the central importance of relations between the various elements.

Klee then studied the problem of the structural formations obtained by means of the regular repetition of a given element, which can be either simple or complicated. Such repetition produces a rhythm which obeys a measure. Klee represented this measure, which was for him the structure of time, in a plastic, spatial image.

Combining the notions of structure and rhythm, he broached a new subject: movement. Beginning with a phenomenon known to everyone, namely the various movements linked to gravity, Klee conceived an exercise which did not consist in copying reality, but rather of an analysis of the structure of movements and their different rhythms.

According to Klee, images are built up bit by bit over time, not only when they are made but also when they are perceived. He poetically compared the eye which perceives an image by tracing various paths across it, to a grazing animal. When looking at a work which features strong contrasts, however, 'the eye proceeds by leaps and bounds, like an animal that is hunting'. The eye's course through the work is guided by visual markers, consisting of poles of energy which influence the movement of perception. These energy poles drawing the eye to them are always relative in nature. Klee

Café De Unie, Rotterdam, designed by Jacobus Johannes Pieter Oud, 1925:

Far left: View of the façade, 1925.

Left: Colour scheme for the façade of the café, 1924. The façade exemplifies the De Stijl movement's aesthetic creed and shows the influence that the movement exerted on the creators of the Weimar Bauhaus and, in particular, on Herbert Bayer, a student who went on to become tutor of typography and advertising at the Bauhaus in 1925.

represented the orientation and duration of this movement with arrows. The problem of orientation can find true resolution only in infinite movement. The psychological importance of orientation for Klee finds expression in the prevalence of arrows in his own work. A hidden meaning, a symbolic element is always present in his lectures on form; in his view, form could not be understood without it.

Colour theory

Klee felt that the chromatic circle allowed one to grasp the relations between colours as well as the movements of colours – 'the number of these oriented movements being determined by the circle's diameter' – and peripheral movement, which is the most original part of his theory.[20] Colours situated opposite one another on the circle's perimeter are, for Klee, true colour pairs, but there are also what he calls 'mismatches' between colours linked together by a segment and which, when blended together, do not produce grey. They do not constitute a totality, but by this very fact can produce new conflicts that enrich a work. These mismatches are an important resource, and participate in the dynamic unfolding over time of artistic creation.

In this connection, Klee warned his students against an overly schematic application of this law and the temptation to construct for construction's sake. For example, to maintain that one must never use anything but the three primary colours, because they contain all the others, would be legalistic pedantry. This line of reasoning would soon lead one to use nothing but basic grey, which contains all the primary colours as well as black and white. The consequence would be 'the world as pure grey, as nothingness. It would be possible to push simplification to this absurd point and, if one wanted, to the extreme of total poverty, even the loss of life.'

Here Klee's opposition to the theories of the Dutch De Stijl group, which advocated the exclusive use of primary colours, is

Essential criterion for modern, creative people: The capacity to think and fashion elementally. The school for the new creation of form is: to elucidate the elements of every creative domain radically and unimpeachably. And: to live the modern world view in its most extreme implications.

Werner Gräff,
'The New Engineer is Coming',
G, July 1923

obvious. In Klee's view such an attitude betrays a confusion between law and application. Laws exist to provide a foundation. They are but 'the common basis of both nature and art'. For this reason teaching at the Bauhaus stressed student participation and the analysis of formal elements as opposed to the transmission of a body of knowledge, which might become obsolete. According to Klee, the goal of artistic education should be to teach students how to read a painting as an active being, capable of development in various ways. In other words, to clear a path for them to the creative process.

Wassily Kandinsky and the teaching of form

As early as 1912 Kandinsky wrote an article for the *Blaue Reiter Almanach* about the 'question of form' in which the word was used in the sense of the 'formation' (*Gestaltung*) of a content. In an article on 'the fundamental elements of form' published on the occasion of the 1923 Bauhaus exhibition, he made a clear distinction between form 'in the narrow sense of the term' and form 'in the larger sense of the term'. The latter was equivalent to that of 'formation', while in his book *Point, Line, Plane*, which served as the basis of his Bauhaus teaching, he dealt with form in the narrower sense, in other words as a plastic element.

In his attempt to establish a science of art Kandinsky resorted to a linguistic model. The basic elements of painting, which are not always easy to define, provided the vocabulary. In the case of forms, the basic elements consisted of point, line, and plane; in the case of colours, of the chromatic range. A grammar should govern the combination of these various elements.

The interaction of form and colour

In Russia Kandinsky had analysed the interaction of the various arts in the theatre. Now he studied the interaction of form and colour. For him, each form had an inner content. Certain forms heightened the values of certain colours, while others shackled them. In *Point, Line, Plane* he explained that the combination of vertical and horizontal in the square was favourable to red, while the sum of active and passive lines in the circle, which is a curved line, implied blue. But these analogies were not self-evident. Oskar Schlemmer, who directed the Bauhaus theatre workshop at the time, noted in his journal, among the words of famous contemporaries: 'Kandinsky = the circle is blue; Schlemmer = the circle is red'. In fact, Schlemmer's view was founded in nature: the circle exists in nature (the red sun, the red apple), whereas the square is an abstraction 'or something metaphysical, whose colour is blue'. For Kandinsky, on the other hand, the circle was a symbolic image with ties to the cosmos, which for him corresponded to the colour blue.

The symbolic value of the artistic elements

Like Goethe, Kandinsky attributed symbolic value to colours. According to him 'yellow is the typical earthly colour', but in association with certain inner states 'it may be paralleled in human nature by madness'. Blue, by contrast, 'draws man towards the infinite' and is 'the typical heavenly colour'. The 'mixture of these two diametrically opposed, totally different colours' produces green, 'the ideal point of equilibrium'. He none the less remarks that 'these statements have no scientific basis, but are founded purely on spiritual experience',[21] but, as he himself admits, 'the new science of art can only be achieved by changing signs into symbols'.

Thus the 'point' is not defined as a mathematical element but as 'the ultimate and unique union of silence and speech'. He maintains that the eye cannot travel over it, which effectively excludes the element of time from it, and concludes that the point is often an indispensable compositional element for this very reason.

While tension is the sole determining element of the point, in the line tension is

Project for a newspaper kiosk, Herbert Bayer, 1924.

augmented by direction. The most extreme opposition is found, according to Kandinsky, between straight and curved lines. As with colour, he distinguishes between straight lines on the basis of their 'temperature', using this analogy to indicate their corresponding colour. Just as there are three primary colours, there are three primary lines: horizontal, vertical, and diagonal.

The process for analysing the 'original plane' – the 'material surface called upon to support the work' – is the same as that for the point and the line, and the analysis itself always includes observations of a more general nature. For Kandinsky, the 'original plane' is a living being which is subject to limitations above, below, to the right, and to the left. By reversing an image or turning it upside down, the effects of those limitations can be studied, but here one must 'beware of first impressions, for the sensibility tires quickly, opening the way for the imagination'.

While the square is the most 'objective' form, relativization is none the less necessary, for the absolute is unattainable. It is essentially a mental construct and does not exist in reality. Hence perfect calm belongs only to the isolated point, but the isolated point does not exist. It is always in some sort of relation, and it is this which must be established.

As for the circle, it is both simpler and more complicated than the rectangular plane due to the absence of corners. Corners 'imperceptibly transform the top into right and left, just as right and left progressively merge into the bottom', which increases the pressure on these limits. For Kandinsky, the sensations expressed by an 'original plane' can be felt only by spectators with practised eyes.

Kandinsky's entire treatise was written with one goal in mind: to exercise the eye and make it more receptive. It should be clear that Kandinsky's teaching coincided in many respects with that of the other professors, notably Klee's. None the less, he laid greater emphasis than Klee on the definition of rules, as he was convinced of the need to establish a science of art. Klee's approach was much more intuitive. For him forms symbolized ideas or sensations, while for Kandinsky the sensations conveyed to us by forms belonged to the forms themselves. Hence the need to analyse them.

The Bauhaus style

Was the theory of form taught at the Bauhaus behind what has come to be called the 'Bauhaus style'? To answer this question we must look briefly at the evolution of Bauhaus production.

The initial quest for elementary forms at the Bauhaus was inspired by popular art and aimed at a return to the origins of 'craft'. This quest was gradually transformed into a search for simple forms of mathematical precision. The school's orientation towards industrial manufacture effectively required it to focus on forms reproducible by machine. Towards the end of the Weimar years and at the beginning of the Dessau period, models intended for mass production were strongly influenced by the Constructivist efforts of the Dutch De Stijl movement, as well as those of Russian and Hungarian groups. At the beginning especially, enthusiasm for the scientific and mathematical side of constructivism was so great that many studios employed geometric forms in objects for manufacture in a purely formalistic way. The result was a style that, as Georg Muche pointed out in 1926, attempted to apply the laws governing abstract art to industrial production. This led, he wrote, 'to a new style in which ornament, as an anachronistic expression of the artisanal culture of the past, has no place, but which none the less remains a decorative style'.[22]

It was in the pottery and metalwork studios that this influence was most apparent. Marianne Brandt, who was a student at the time – she became director of the studios after the departure of Moholy-Nagy – recounts that at this time there was such an obsession with elementary forms at the Bauhaus that she devised an ashtray in the form of a half-sphere with a triangular opening, and only subsequently came to realize that an eccentrically-positioned oval opening worked better. She explains this obsession as a reaction against their environment, which was still impregnated with the sort of kitsch that had prevailed under the empire.[23]

In 1927, when Hannes Meyer entered the Bauhaus to establish an architecture studio there,[24] he reproached the school for its formalism, and went as far as to deny the value of artistic creativity in industrial design and architecture.

While art was never a goal in itself for Walter Gropius at the Bauhaus, he regarded experiment in this domain as useful, believing that through practical work and theoretical analysis it could prove an invaluable aid to understanding the perceptual problems specific to the spatial experience of the time. In any case, he was not about to replace one kind of academicism with another, and staunchly opposed Theo Van Doesburg when he sought to introduce the dogma of pure form advocated by the De Stijl group into the Bauhaus. Thus the teaching of form – which even Hannes Meyer, though he introduced scientific subjects, did not eliminate from the curriculum – was oriented towards active stimulation of the student and the analysis of formal elements as opposed to the transmission of immutable rules. In training its students, the Bauhaus stressed analytic thought and the education of the eye above all else.

All the Bauhaus teachers insisted on the relativity of the rules they proposed, even Kandinsky, despite his desire to find a grammar for the 'language' of forms and colours. Klee, more than any of the others, emphasized the relativity of each rule, stressing that their meanings were determined by the context of specific systems. As Giulio Carlo Argan wrote in his book *Gropius and the Bauhaus*, within the framework of the rationalist, concrete programme at the Bauhaus, 'so set upon instilling the values of "quality" in industrial mass production, it is Klee who must get the credit for having explored more thoroughly than anyone else the meaning and value of a "quality" which could not be defined within the terms of the new proportional systems or a canon of golden rules'.[25]

The theory of form taught at the Bauhaus did not lead to the 'Bauhaus style', or to any brand of purely rational and mechanical functionalism, but the constant incitement to experimentation at the centre of this body of theory can still inspire us today.

Interior of a
sleeping car,
designed by
Walter Gropius
for Deutsche
Reichsbahn,
1914.

A chair made of high-grade steel tubing (a highly elastic material) with tightly stretched fabric in the appropriate places, makes a light, completely self-sprung seat which is as comfortable as an upholstered chair, but is many times lighter, handier and more hygienic, and therefore many times more practical in use. *Marcel Breuer, 'Metal Furniture' in Werner Gräff, Innenraume, 1928*

Marcel Breuer's Wassily Chair

Like many architects and designers who originally came from Eastern Europe, the young Hungarian Marcel Breuer was drawn to the Bauhaus. He entered the Bauhaus as a student in 1920 and rapidly became one of the most famous members of the school. He was director of the furniture section from 1925 until 1928. One of the school's fundamental principles was that a clean slate be made of the past. From this first idea came the laws of interchangeability, standardization and mass production.

From 1921, Breuer started to design chairs in the style of Gerrit T. Rietveld, and he gave his designs to his students as construction projects. A few years later, he began to use tubular steel and created chairs which broke completely with all the research carried out until then. This material was to become a significant emblem of the Modern Movement.

History has it that Breuer got the idea of using steel after studying the shape of the handlebars of his bicycle. But it was probably the proximity of the Junkers Aircraft factory, where they had mastered the use of tubular steel and frequently used the material, exerted a key influence on the professor. The first designs combined metallic tubing and sewn cloth, but had no tubular structure to support the back, which made them totally impracticable for actual use.

Breuer's club chair, made from steel tubing and leather, dates from 1925. Known later under the name 'Wassily chair' in honour of Kandinsky (it was designed for his house), the chair illustrates the Bauhaus ethos perfectly, in that the structure determines the external appearance. Its open form reflects the theories of functionalism and the school's preoccupation with the manipulation of space.

This famous chair is closely related to the cantilevered chair made from steel tubing and leather by Ludwig Mies van der Rohe at the Bauhaus in the same period. It is probably the best known formal design produced by the school. The harmony of its gentle curves and the way the elements fit together make it one of the classic designs of the century, as well as a perfect illustration of industrial design.

Simultaneously, the Dutch architect Mart Stam designed a tubular steel chair which was made by Thonet Frères. This firm, which had been experimenting with bent wood for 70 years, used their skill to make tubular steel furniture whose form evolved very little, but whose materials demanded a new industrial structure.

Marcel Breuer's famous B3 chair was manufactured by Standard Möbel in 1926, then by Thonet Frères from 1930. The chair is now produced by Knoll International. For the past 20 years it has also featured in the Habitat range.

E. M.

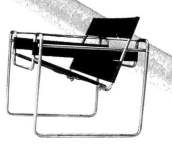

The Volksempfanger radio

The industrial rationalization that took place under the Third Reich embraced everyday objects, as well as architecture, art and armaments.

The National Socialist regime used form in a very precise way and applied its aesthetic ideas to all areas of production, using them as instruments of political and cultural propaganda. The radio receiver, like other products, was closely studied to see how it could best fulfil its role at the heart of totalitarian government: namely to infiltrate every house in the Reich.

Walter Maria Kersting was one of the pioneers of German industrial design. In The Living Form, published in 1932, he described how the task of the designer was to create 'simple and cheap objects, which must not appear to be more than they are. . . and which can be bought anywhere'. Their mechanisms must be obvious so that they can be understood by people 'who do not have a technical mind', and should be designed such that they are 'foolproof in the event of mistreatment'.

Kersting didn't realize how pertinent his comments were: in 1928 he designed a radio receiver several hundred thousand of which had been manufactured within five years. His original design only underwent one modification before mass production started: the

addition of the swastika on the front. The radio was designed according to Kersting's functionalist principles, which led to what was at the time an innovatory fusing of concept, form and materials. An ancestor of today's 'black box' hi-fi designs, its cubic cabinet, moulded from plastic, incorporated the radio's components. The buttons had

been so well thought out in the initial design that the same configuration was adopted for the manufactured version. The set was 'foolproof' to use and Hitler was careful to ensure that its range was limited to Nazi frequencies, fearing that English, French and Bolshevik transmissions would be picked up and interfere with his political broadcasts.

What was, during 15 years of Nazi rule, a formidable Nazi propaganda device, was transformed, at the end of the war, into a terrible trap for the Germans, who were unaware of the advance of allied troops through their already devastated territory.

After the Second World War, Walter Maria Kersting denied the fact that he had designed his radio receiver for political ends, despite the fact this standard and very cheap product (it was subsidized by the government) had been of enormous service to the Nazi regime for propaganda purposes.

The idea of mass producing radio receivers in which all foreign transmissions were censored was subsequently taken up by East European countries. For 25 years in Czechoslovakia the Telsa company manufactured radios whose only frequency spread communist propaganda and whose form was reminiscent of the Volksempfanger.

E. M.

Ferdinand Porsche's Volkswagen

Born in 1875, Ferdinand Porsche had a precocious passion for cars and at the 1900 Universal Exposition in Paris the Lohner-Porsche car, equipped with electric motors installed in the hubs of its wheels, created a sensation. Beginning in 1920, Ferdinand Porsche worked on a project for a popular vehicle. He took inspiration from both the Ford model T and the Citroën 'Trèfle'. In 1931 he built three prototypes for the Zündapp motorcyle company. In 1933 he submitted another project to NSU. This was the Type 32, whose form already anticipated the experimental vehicle V3 that successfully came through a 30,000-kilometre trial in 1936.

Quite audacious for the period, the forms of the first Volkswagen prototypes took their inspiration from the aerodynamic research with cars carried out by Paul Jaray. His research, which began in 1919, was patented and published in 1927.

Ferdinand Porsche was not the only person to be inspired by Paul Jaray's work, which also influenced the design of the Chrysler Airflow and that of the Peugeot 402 'Légère' in 1934.

The prototypes for popular cars that Porsche proposed to several manufac-

turers were not accepted, however. In the face of this setback, Ferdinand Porsche decided in 1934 to take his case to the government authorities in Berlin, in the hopes of getting official support. Thus it was that Hitler[1] became aware of his memoire entitled The Construction of a German Popular Car and decided to support the project. On the personal orders of the Führer, a contract was made between the study firm of Ferdinand Porsche and the Federation of the Car Industry. In 1936 three prototypes were up and running and it was evident that this would be a revolutionary vehicle for the period.

The four-cylinder engine was situated at the back and was air-cooled. The four wheels each had independent suspension. The aerodynamic body design resembled that of the Tatra V8 of 1934. Between 1936 and 1938, 60 preliminary vehicles were built and a factory was set up in Stuttgart. The war interrupted production, which would recommence only in 1945.

In 1972 the Volkswagen passed the record established by the Ford model T in 1927, becoming the world's most popular car.

J. d. N.

1. The Bauhaus was closed down by the Nazis in 1933 and its teachers were forced into exile. Thus, while condemning 'degenerate' art, Hitler supported projects with a populist aesthetic which went along with his National Socialist ideology.

The machine is neither the coming paradise in which technology will fulfil all our wishes – nor the approaching hell in which all human development will be destroyed. The machine is nothing more than the inexorable dictator of the possibilities and tasks common to all our lives.

Hans Schmidt and Mart Stam, ABC – Beiträge zum Bauen, *1928*

The Opel Rak 2

On 23 May 1928, an experimental car propelled by black powder rockets and driven by Fritz von Opel reached a speed of 175 mph on the Avus racecourse in Berlin.

This exploit, which received a good deal of attention in the German press of the day, was the climax to research by specialists in rocket propulsion who had formed an organization called the Verein für Raumschiffahrt (VFR – the Society for Space Travel).

In 1923 Hermann Oberth, a German scientist of Transylvanian origin, published Die Rakete zu den Planetraümen, a theoretical work on rockets and space travel. More than just a mathematical analysis of the question, it argued that given the current state of scientific research, it would be possible to construct economically viable space vehicles capable of transporting passengers.[1]

Max Valier, a gifted popularizer, had already contacted Oberth, and the result was the VFR organization. Members included Opel, Fritz Lang and the young Wernher von Braun, who was famous for having developed the V2 and, later, became a major figure in the American space programme in its early years.

Fritz von Opel created the Rak 2 for publicity reasons. As no one had yet mastered liquid fuel propulsion as envisioned by Oberth, he opted for a more traditional solution and the vehicle was equipped with 28 Sander black powder rockets. Its form was quite elaborate by standards of the period. With its small stabilizing wings it resembled a long-range missile from the 1970s. The speed record was broken only after numerous experiments without a pilot. In 1929 Fritz von Opel made a successful flight in a rocket-propelled glider. That same year, Fritz Lang completed his film Frau im Mond and was preparing to shoot Metropolis.

J. d. N.

1. The American Robert Hutchings Goddard and the Russian Konstantin Tsiolkovsky had already published serious works on this subject prior to 1920.

Kazimir Malevich, *Suprematist Composition*, c.1915. Graphite on squared paper, 13.8 x 11.4 cm. Musée National d'Art Moderne, Centre Georges Pompidou, Paris.

Right-hand page: El Lissitzky, costumes for *I Want a Child*, 1929. Watercolour, pencil and collage on pasteboard, 35.5 x 52.9 cm. Central State Theatre Museum of A. A. Bakhrushin, Moscow.

The Great Utopia

Éric Mézil *and* Brice d'Antras

The dawn of our century revealed a landscape destabilized by the growth of industrialization. In a world whose cultural foundations were being questioned, man was coming to understand that he needed to invent new values. The artist was to figure importantly in this project. If the world was to be saved, art would have to imbue the realm of the material with a new spirituality. An iconoclastic mysticism prevailed in the artistic manifestos of Piet Mondrian, Kazimir Malevich and Wassily Kandinsky, whose *Concerning the Spiritual in Art* established parameters for the lyric and geometric abstraction to come. The artist's aim was to achieve liberation by rejecting all figurative art. The creative process would be centered on itself ('art for art's sake' is the still-current tautological formulation of this position) or would declare its intention to serve a society in search of new points of orientation. Simultaneously, various avant-garde movements were to spring up across Europe – each with its own characteristics, to be sure, but with shared radical intentions. The artist descended from his academic Olympus to participate in a recasting of

One is an artist

only if one responds to what

non-artists call 'form' as content,

as 'the thing itself'.

The result being that one effectively inhabits a

topsy-turvy world; for all content

is reduced to pure form – including our own lives.

Friedrich Nietzsche, Joyful Wisdom, *1882*

daily life. The Impressionists, having left the studio to paint the reality of the world around them, washed their hands of representation. Adherents of the avant-garde movements associated themselves with the great transformations of their era and implanted the creative act at the heart of society. The status of the artist changed as he embraced the humanist mission of harmonizing the universe. From the late 19th century, when he began to understand the power of the object over individual and communal behaviour, he was already implicated in production: one need only think of the Pre-Raphaelites in Victorian England and the Viennese artists affiliated with the Secession.

The Russians and the Italians symbolically joined forces under the generic name Futurism, by which they meant a determination to participate as early as possible in the new industrial and technological society. They infused art with a revolutionary strength and dynamism which it had never had before. By desanctifying artistic creation through derision and the abolition of a traditional stylistic vocabulary, the Futurists contributed to a destabilization of the established order. Catcalls, laughter and indignation were their everyday currency. The Italians were quite familiar with Alfred Jarry, a Futurist *avant la lettre* and a complete nonconformist. Filippo Tommaso Marinetti admired him so much that he wrote his *King Revel* immediately after having read the *Ubu* cycle. But, as a handful of letters attest, Jarry was amused by this farce and in 1902 himself published *Surmale* (Supermale), whose triumphantly virile hero couples with a machine, which in turn becomes smitten and falls in love with him.

In 1909, after their initial audacities had met with success, the Italian Futurists drafted, under Marinetti's guidance, their manifesto, which was published in Paris in *Le Figaro* on 20 February. 'We intend to sing the love of danger, the habit of energy, and fearlessness.' Lauding the noisy city in ferment, in the grip of speed and the liberating machine, became the goal of a pictorial grammar inspired by the Cubism of Braque and Picasso and the sequential photography of Marey and Muybridge. Balla, Severini, Carrà and especially Boccioni found ways of communicating movement by means of new forms.

The idea of a better world was conveyed by *découpage*, the interpenetration of forms and a general recasting of the universe in a Cubo-Futurist mould. 'We declare the world's splendour to be enriched by a new beauty: the beauty of speed. A racing car, its bonnet decorated with large pipes like serpents with explosive breath...a roaring car, its engine sounding like a machine gun, is more beautiful than the *Victory of Samothrace*.' These excerpts from the first manifesto, characterized by a self-conscious embrace of decadence and marked symbolism, resonated in Russia.

In 1912, in Kazan, the young student Alexandr Rodchenko, who was a witness and then a participant in a provincial cultural battle, discovered three Futurist poets, Vladimir Mayakovsky, Bourliouk with his painted face, and Vassili Vasilevich Kamenski holding aloft a gigantic chrysanthemum,

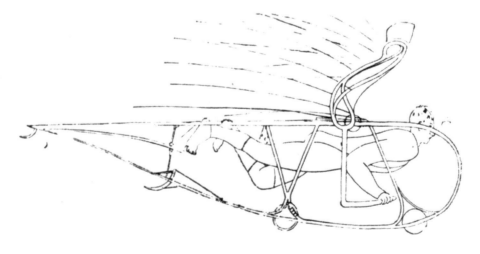

Freedom from ornament is a

sign of spiritual strength.

Adolf Loos, Ornament and Crime, *1908*

Left: Yakov Chernikhov, *Composition,* c.1920. Gouache on paper, 29.8 x 24.5 cm. Yakov Chernikov International Foundation.

Right: El Lissitzky, Design for the Lenin Tribune, 1920. Watercolour, India ink and gouache on paper, 63.9 x 48 cm.

Bottom: Vladimir Tatlin, sketch showing position of the pilot on Letatlin, 1929-1932, pencil on paper, 32.5 x 54.8 cm. Central State Theatre Museum of A. A. Bakhrushin, Moscow.

Right: Vladimir Tatlin, *Monument to the Third International,* 1920. Pencil drawing for the book *The Monument to the Third International,* by Nikolai Punin. State Tretyakov Gallery, Moscow.

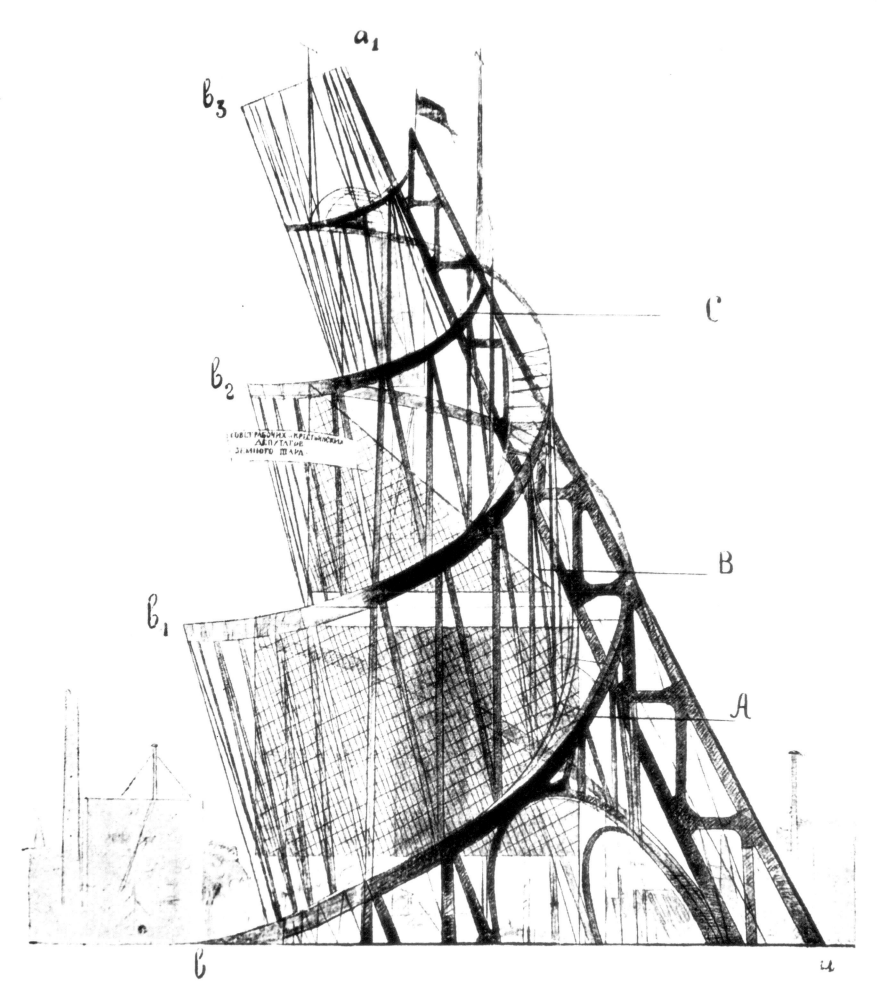

declaiming: 'It is I, it is I, Futurist soldier of song and pilot-aviator, Vassili Kamenski!' Their union was charged by a shared will to mock the world, to answer it with provocation and masquerade. Deciding to join forces in their creative work (painting, writing, graphic design), they collaborated on itinerant Futurist spectacles announcing to the people that the world was reaching boiling point. Similar intentions were behind the production of Igor Stravinsky's *L'Histoire*

York is itself a work of art, an unfinished work. And I think you've had the right idea in demolishing old buildings, souvenirs of the past. It is consistent with the manifesto – still misunderstood – of the Italian Futurists, who called for the destruction, symbolic in fact, although they've been taken literally, of museums and libraries. The dead must not be allowed to overpower the living. We must learn to forget the past, to live our own lives in our own time.'

passive deification of nature, and is against reverie; it is in favour of technology, scientific organization, the machine, planning, will, courage, speed and precision; it believes that the new man should be armed with all these things.' Contrary to the Soviets, the Italians remained faithful to an individualist approach to their art. The furniture of Giacomo Balla, which seems to announce the jubilant fantasy of Alessandro Mendini, reveals above all the right of the

du soldat in Geneva: it was necesssary to deliver the message of modernity to the public . Artists in exile had been drawn to Switzerland because of the country's neutrality in the First World War. From the beginning of the war, a circle of rebellious, non-belligerent anarchists settled in Zürich, gathering at the Cabaret Voltaire: 'I announce the Dada world! I laugh at science and culture, those miserable crutches of a society in its death throes', wrote Raoul Hausmann in *Der Einzig*. These tracts, written in quicksilver, are all characterized by the same wild determination to reject the bourgeois way of life as well as all historical precedent. In 1916, in the magazine *Arts and Decoration*, Marcel Duchamp justified his choice of his newly-adopted city: 'New

While the Dadaists refused to take part in the war, the Futurists glorified warfare as 'the only treatment for the world'. The apology for destruction and 'ideas that kill' in the founding manifesto might induce smiles if it were no more than an adolescent provocation, but it becomes chilling when considered within the historical context of the rise of totalitarianism in Italy, Russia and Germany, and even in Spain and Hungary. If they were to become the constructors of a new order, the Futurists would have to begin with acts of destruction, wiping the slate clean of traditional values. Their enthusiastic rejection of the past and, above all, the prestige they accorded the machine seduced Leon Trotsky, who noted in 1917: 'Futurism is opposed to mysticism and the

artist to express himself fully in a personal idiom. The 50 or so Italian manifestos which appeared between 1909 and 1916 seem more like an exercise in style than a genuine attempt at collective mobilization. Hesitating between a total overthrow of society and fleeting taunts directed at paternalistic authority, they unashamedly exploited the gains of the bourgeois revolution to elaborate their vision of modernity. They claimed to have discovered what they had merely co-opted, namely mass production and the speed of a new world. Two spectacular events, Mussolini's march on Rome and the 1917 revolution in Moscow, would be required to transform their adolescent indulgence into a project for society. While William Morris was admitted to the

Soviet pantheon, this was as much because of his role as the founder of the English socialist movement as for his textiles, which were none the less comparable to those by Malevich, Tatlin and Rodchenko. Vladimir Tatlin's call for 'art in life' was an echo of that issued by Morris 20 years earlier for 'an art made by the people and for the people'. The members of the Arts and Crafts Movement had also grasped the revolutionary potential of art in the mass-produced object, but their rejection of industrialization prevented them from crossing the threshold into modernity.

The Germans, on the other hand, in a period of remarkable economic expansion, would, between 1890 and 1914, manage to assert full control over the new industrial possibilities. But the Deutscher Werkbund, a simple expression of indigenous capitalism, tended to obscure any tendencies towards social revolution. In 1907, the theorist Hermann Muthesius declared, after a London sojourn undertaken for purposes of observation (a practice which would become well known a half-century later under the label 'industrial espionage'): 'More is at stake than domination of the world, more than financing, educating and inundating it with products. It's a matter of giving it a face. The people which grasps this will lead the world. Germany ought to be that people.' Acting on sentiments such as this, which resonate with a determination for western cultural hegemony, Muthesius brought together artists, craftsmen and engineers (Peter Behrens, Henry van de Velde, Richard Riemerschmid and Joseph Maria Olbrich). They were charged with creating new products that would further the development of an industrial culture capable of dominating the world market. Peter Behrens's statement, in 1910, that 'technological progress has created a civilization but not, at least to the present day, a culture', clearly indicates the extent of the questions underlying this will to link artistic and industrial disciplines, whether with a view to orienting them towards decorative

or functionalist aims. The design style that resulted would subsequently be denounced by Tatlin as perverse. Despite diametrically opposed social and political environments, the Russians, following the lead of the Germans, recognized the need to give form to an industrial culture. The theoretical debates between Tatlin and the productivists bear a resemblance to those in which Muthesius opposed van de Velde. Behrens's role as a precursor of collective organization was far from negligeable: the modestly priced electric kettle he designed for the AEG company, which was premised on technological progress (electricity for everyone), and had a form that was stripped-down and rationalized, seemed to be encouraging social homogenization.

In Petrograd in 1915, the exhibition 0-10, organized by Ivan Puni, would be the last manifestation of the Russian Futurists. The apology for chaos and the arbitrary, embraced by the formal vocabulary of the Cubo-Futurists and endorsed a year earlier, when Marinetti visited Moscow, was already a thing of the past. Mayakovsky, the charismatic visionary, proclaimed: 'We consider the first point of our programme, destruction, to be fully achieved. So don't be surprised if today you no longer see us with hatchets in our hands but rather builders' plans.' That same year, Tatlin declared: 'To innovate is always to respond to the needs and efforts of a collectivity and not an individual.' Whereas the Italian Futurists continued to increase the number of manifestos they produced, Russian artists, stimulated by their political engagement, transformed their revolt into an avant-garde movement. They would be the builders of the Great Utopia. Crystallizing the aspirations of their era, they devised rules and mechanisms intended to serve as standard reference points for a tomorrow in which the future was still written in the conditional tense. As in every period of social, economic and cultural restructuring, the determining idea was that of construction using primary geometric forms. Thus there developed a universal

language of modern classicism, the fruit more of industrial and technological revolutions than any political one. In 1920, Nikolai Punin defined Russian modernism as: 'a classicism that is the fruit not of a renaissance but rather of invention'. The collaborative efforts of Gerrit Rietveld and Theo van Doesburg, inspired by the radical works of Piet Mondrian, exemplify this international strain of rationalized form. It should be noted here that a divergence from the initial Cubist-inspired geometric idiom gradually emerged. An embrace of the oblique line, which entailed a reconfiguration of compositions on canvas, dynamized a new aesthetic. Thus the static, geometric formal vocabulary endorsed by the teachings of the Bauhaus started to oppose the more open, dynamic structures favoured by the Cubo-Futurists and the Constructivists.

Kazimir Malevich, through his extraordinary Supremacist emblems (red crosses or black squares against a white ground), proclaimed the death of traditional painting. As if adhering to Nietzsche's startling prophecy, he attained the zero degree of form and colour: monochrome. After formulating these extreme reductionist statements, the focus of his work shifted from canvas to everyday life. He set out to bring about a synthesis of the arts through the development of a new language to be used in producing consumer objects, graphics, architecture, and propaganda. From 1919 to 1922, Suprematism was at the centre of a group dynamic within the framework of the ephemeral institution UNOVIS (College for New Art) in Vitebsk. El Lissitzky acted as liaison between Malevich and the Constructivists. In his 'Prouns' (an acronym for Projects for Affirming the New) he undertook to explore the discrepancies resulting from two-dimensional depictions of three-dimensional space. On the basis of geometric explorations undertaken beneath the Supremacist banner, Malevich conceived his architectons. They influenced the design for the Bauhaus buildings in Dessau and, 50 years later, still inspire deconstructivist architects. For Malevich, architecture was the ultimate medium: 'We would like to build the world in accordance with a non-objective system, detaching ourselves more and more from the object, like the creation of the world by the cosmos.' Suprematism cast the artist in a central role. He would determine the relations between volumes and surfaces. Ceramics by Suetin, textiles by Varvara Stepanova and Liubov Popova, posters and other graphic designs by El Lissitzky, as well as the Lenin tomb he built in 1924 (based on designs by Chashnik dating from 1920): these are so many vindications of the importance of artistic creativity in a revolutionary popular culture.

Vladimir Tatlin, the spiritual godfather of Constructivism, advocated a 'culture of materials' or *factura*. The title he gave his consumer goods. The model for his Monument to the Third Communist International, completed in 1920, was conceived as a symbol of revolutionary modernity. But constant references to materials and engineering must not be allowed to obscure the humanist dimension of Constructivism. These artists' emotional and metaphysical convictions inform each of their creations, whether in the projects undertaken (chairs, the flying machine known as the 'Letatlin', clothing), in allusions to tradition (the profile of a kettle suggestive of an *isba*), or in the skilful manipulation of cosmic metaphors (the axis of the tower was inclined, paralleling that around which the earth rotates, its 400-metre height equalled one hundred-thousandth of the equator and the dynamic of its ascend-

of bourgeois culture. The terms 'to create' and 'creation' were systematically replaced by 'to produce' and 'production'. An object's sole justification was to be its social utility. Its form was no more than the consequence of its function and construction. Alexeï Gan, in *Constructivism*, published in 1922, explained the new orientation: 'The time had come for a pure applied art. An era of social experiment had arrived. We set out to introduce the utilitarian object with a form proper to it and suitable for all. Nothing would be left to chance, nothing would be gratuitous. Art is dead. There is no place for it in the universe of human activity. Work, technology and organization!'

This movement, whose presiding moral authority was Vladimir Mayakovskÿ, was defended by the leftist artists of the maga-

-----

To the factory where a gigantic trampoline is being created for the leap into universal human culture – the name of the way is Constructivism.
The great corrupters of the human race, the aesthetes and artists, have destroyed the stern bridges along that way and replaced them with a huge dose of sugar-sweet opium – art and beauty.
It is uneconomical to expend the essence of the world, the human brain, on reclaiming the marshes of aestheticism.
After weighing the facts on the scales of an honest attitude to the earth's inhabitants, the Constructivists declare art and its priests illegal.

K. Medunetsky, V. Stenberg, G. Stenberg. Moscow, January 1922

-----

course at Vkhutemas (Studios for the Advanced Study of Art and Technique), 'Construction, Volume, Materials', gives a clear indication of the orientation of his teaching. Having a greater affinity for engineering than Malevich, he involved himself with the industrial process without abdicating his role as an artist. His relief sculptures reveal a determination to synthesize painting, sculpture and architecture. He rejected the doctrine of art for the people in favour of one endorsing the integration of art into life, its involvement in the production of ing spiral was intended to express the future of humanity).

One of the first goals of the Russian avant-garde was to downplay the individual quest for material goods in favour of intellectual and social development. Objects, stripped of their more or less in-built obsolescence and market-determined idiosyncrasies, were to be designed to discourage consumerist materialism in which the object became an end in itself. The 'productivists' represented the most radical phase of Constructivism. They decreed the death of art as the last relic zine *Lef*, with Alexandr Rodchenko, Varvara Stepanova and Alexandra Exter leading the way. Their work, which they set out to purge of all individual emotion, would blossom in the development of multifunctional objects easily adaptable to changing circumstances. These advocates of 'production art' designed practical clothing that could be made to suit various kinds of bodily motion (that of work or leisure) by various additions or alterations (pockets, flaps, stapled or superimposed elements). They were active in every conceivable

Left: Vladimir
Mayakovsky,
photographed by
Alexandr Rodchenko,
c.1929.

Below: Workers'
Club, Soviet pavilion,
Exposition des Arts
Décoratifs, Paris,
1925.

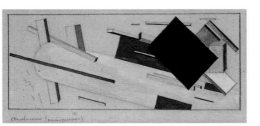

Top: Pablo Picasso, *Bottle of Bass, Packet of Tobacco, Visiting Card*, 1914. *Papier collé* and pencil on paper, 24 x 30.5 cm. Musée National d'Art Moderne, Centre Georges Pompidou, Paris.

Centre: *Study for a Proun*, c.1920. Graphite and gouache on paper, 9 x 22.6 cm. Musée National d'Art Moderne, Centre Georges Pompidou, Paris.

Below: Fernand Léger, *Mechanical Elements*, 1924. Musée National d'Art Moderne, Centre Georges Pompidou, Paris.

domain: Rodchenko founded a kind of public relations firm – Advertisement Constructors – with Mayakovsky, who abandoned poetry to compose slogans, while the filmmaker Dziga Vertov abandoned fictional films in favour of committed documentaries (*Soviet! Forward!* in 1926 and *The Man with a Film Camera* in 1929). The financial hardship that prevailed in the early years of the revolution, and a certain distrust on the part of politicians and industrialists, would eventually dampen the enthusiasm of these avant-gardists. They reacted by returning to the theatre, which had been their first field of investigation: Vsevelod Meyerhold renounced conventional sets in favour of a dynamic construction intended to evoke the studio of the worker-actor. The audience was arranged to minimize hierarchical distinctions – when, that is, these didn't disappear altogether for performances in which the spectators could intervene in the action.

Such interpenetration of the arts and the social domain was typical of early 20th-century avant-garde movements. According to the philosopher and musicologist Theodor Adorno: 'Jeremiads attacking the supposed intellectual terrorism of modernism are pure deception: they obscure the terrorism of the world which art rejects.' The real 'terrorists' are those who cannot abide the new, who cannot associate benevolence with anything other than 'the debility of official culture'. Associating his own critical and intellectual project with that of Walter Benjamin (who in the very title of his essay 'The Work of Art in the Age of Mechanical Reproduction' had summed up something essential about modernity), his philosophical message was clear: according to Adorno, the work of art is the seat of all antagonism, its form being nothing other than 'sedimented social content'.

One year after Stalin initiated the first Five Year Plan, the economic crisis of 1929 was the second drum roll announcing the end of a world of idealist, humanist progress. When in 1930 Marinetti exchanged his gaudy vest designed by Fortunato Depero for an academician's suit Mussolini had had specially tailored for him, it was clear that the Great Utopia was no longer what it had been. That same year, Mayakovsky's suicide marked another turning point: the end of the avant-garde movements. By then Europe was in the grip of totalitarianism. In April 1933, the Gestapo definitively closed down the Bauhaus. Judged undesirable and 'degenerate' by the newly-installed architects of chaos, its artists, designers and theorists sought refuge in the United States. Only the streamline style, purified of all political implications, conformed to the dynamist ideal advocated by the Futurists. Raymond Loewy, in a famous phrase summing it up – 'a well-designed aerodynamic vehicle seems to be in motion even when it's at rest' – reveals himself to be doing nothing other than straightforwardly applying the pictorial principles inscribed in the works of Balla, Boccioni, Carrà, Archipenko and Larionov.

Modernity's death knell was sounded in 1937, at the Paris Universal Exposition. The pavilions of the Soviet Union and the Third Reich gave material expression to the incredible tension prevailing prior to the outbreak of world conflagration. The space between these two structures, in which a swastika-bearing eagle surveyed a Communist couple brandishing emblems of the revolution, was palpably charged. One dares not imagine the discussions between their respective architects, each determined to make sure that *his* building would be the more dominant presence. The chasm opening between these two pavilions would become a no man's land of barbarity. In 1938, Antonin Artaud, in the preface to *The Theatre and its Double*, wrote: 'Never, in the face of so many lives being snuffed out, has there been so much talk of civilization and culture.' Then came Adorno's declaration: 'Historically, Cubism anticipated a reality, the aerial views of cities bombed during the Second World War. Thanks to it, art demonstrated for the first time that life is not alive.'

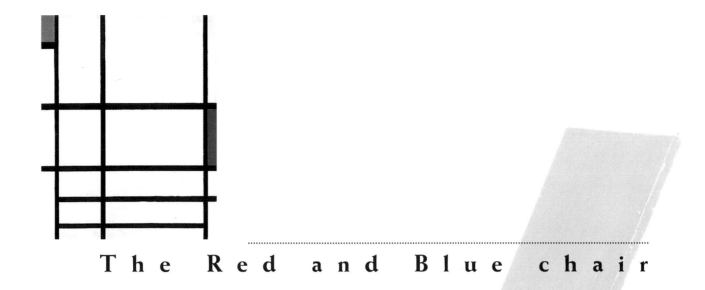

The Red and Blue chair

Born in 1888 in Utrecht, the young cabinet-maker Gerrit Thomas Rietveld became aware of the Dutch avant-garde group De Stijl, founded by Piet Mondrian and Theo van Doesburg, when the first issue of the magazine of that name appeared in 1917. The movement advocated 'elementarism', a term meant to evoke the use of a minimal number of elements, and formulated a basic lexicon to be used by artists and designers in communicating 'universal truths' to the world. Purism and mysticism also played a role in this abstract grammar.

In 1918 Rietveld designed a manifesto-chair, radically geometrical and uncompromising in form, that already gives some idea of the famous red and blue model to come. This chair, made entirely of wood (an attempt at 'structural' seating), was initially painted grey and black. Subsequently Rietveld, who wanted to accentuate its construction through the use of bright tints, painted it in volume-colours consistent with the De Stijl aesthetic. Primaries were used in accordance with rules governing the spatialization and geometricization of form, which led to the chair's red seat and blue back. The arms and legs remained black, while yellow was used to accentuate the extremities. This last colour, applied to the sections, emphasized all the planes.

The chair was essentially a translation into three dimensions of the paintings of Mondrian, which explored horizontal-vertical relationships and colour juxtapositions within asymetrical grids. The rigorous language of these works is here transformed into furniture-as-theorem; the overlapping of planes in this remarkable assemblage of colours and forms was also intended to 'graph' the various forces involved in being seated. By demonstrating that its external form was determined by construction, the designer added a poetic dimension to functionalism and a personal visual code to the industrial aesthetic. The theoretical reflection given form in this chair was to influence Dutch students, who also had privileged contact with the new Bauhaus school.

In 1923 Rietveld built the Schröder house in Utrecht, which was also characterized by a geometric approach to space manifest in the use of simple forms (notably strong vertical-horizontal contrasts) and primary colours (red, yellow, and blue for the volumes; black and white for structural elements). Volumes were articulated by fields of colour establishing spatial limits and boundaries.

In 1934 Rietveld introduced another chair that would also become a symbol of modernity: the famous Zig-Zag. It realized a dream of every furniture-maker aiming to revitalize the form of the chair: here geometry serves a form so light as to attain a quasi-metaphysical status.

E. M.

Composition 2, Piet Mondrian, 1937. Oil on canvas, 75 x 60.5 cm. Musée National d'Art Moderne, Centre Georges Pompidou.

Streamlining

1930-1955

Jeffrey L. Meikle

American design after the First World War experienced an unprecedented transformation. A strong resurgence of nationalism yielded a determination to create uniquely American idioms reflecting an expansive machine age. In the late 1920s, New York became the source of a jazzy 'new American tempo' that seemed to infect the entire nation.[1] Every Midwestern city soon boasted a lone skyscraper rising from the prairie in imitation of the towers of Manhattan. Released from dependence on Sears Roebuck's mail-order catalogues, farmers took their families to town in Ford model T's to purchase modern goods advertised in slick magazines. Rural electrification brought a host of new appliances ranging from washing machines to toasters and radios. The emergence of national broadcasting networks consolidated public opinion, unified consumption patterns and provided a flow of information about new goods and ever-changing styles. All this ended with the Wall Street Crash of 1929, but people of all walks of life trusted businessmen to restore the flow of goods by balancing production

and consumption. Out of desperation, but also with appreciation for the way design had expressed the upbeat jazz age of the 1920s, businessmen turned to commercial artists to redesign products in order to stimulate consumption and revive the economy. These industrial designers, as they became known, created in streamlining a style for the Depression decade of the 1930s – a style that reflected not perceived reality but a vision of a smooth, frictionless, machine age future.

Viewed from the present, the utopian optimism of the 1930s appears almost serene. A documentary film entitled *The World of Tomorrow*, for example, released ironically during 1984, portrayed the streamlined New York World's Fair of 1939 in a profoundly elegiac manner, implying nostalgia for an innocent vision of coherence. In fact, the Depression experience hardly suggested anything so comforting as coherence for those who lived through it. Economic hardship and inequality, hopeless migrations, unprecedented political experiments, and looming threats of totalitarianism and war contributed to a sense of uncertainty that

approached the trauma of a national identity crisis. The fate of the American experiment seemed to hang in the balance. Many Americans looked not to the future but to the past for confirmation of national purpose. The popularity of *Gone with the Wind* (1936), Margaret Mitchell's novel of agrarian loss, the establishment of such pre-industrial outdoor museums as Henry Ford's Greenfield Village and John D. Rockefeller Jr.'s Colonial Williamsburg, and the historical themes of state guide books and courthouse murals funded by the federal government's Works Progress Administration all testified to a need to find meaningful continuity with the past. Americans of the Depression years perhaps experienced less coherence and expressed less faith in technological utopia than some of their descendants, living in a far less coherent world, would like to think.

But if that is so, it then becomes difficult to make sense of the artifacts in image and in material reality of an optimistic, machine age streamline style that have been inherited from the 1930s – all those gleaming, smooth-shrouded locomotives, rounded

Opposite:
Raymond Loewy
photographed in
a reconstruction
of his office,
presented to the
Metropolitan
Museum of Art
of New York in
1934.

Left: Locomotive
for the '20th
Century Limited'
train, designed
by Henry
Dreyfuss for the
Pennsylvania
Central
Transportation
Company, 1938.
One of the most
successful
examples of the
streamlining
style, it had a
considerable
influence on the
spirit of the
times.

cars with teardrop fenders, radio cabinets with glossy black bakelite curves, 'clean-lined' washing machines and refrigerators, all those bus terminals, petrol stations, cinemas and restaurants with their curving marquees and smooth horizontal facades of stucco or enamel-steel. One must try to reconcile them with the expressions of despair and celebrations of the past that also marked the decade. Did the visual coherence and utopian promise of the streamline style truly embody the aspirations of many Americans, or did streamlining reveal little more than consumer capitalism coming to maturity with a self-conscious awareness of how to stimulate desire and manipulate behaviour? From across a gulf of 60 years it is possible to document the style, its sources, its development and its continuation into the post-war period, but we cannot now recover the emotion stirred by the sight of the Burlington Zephyr locomotive streaking along the track, nor trace the causes and results of that emotion.

American design between 1920 and 1940 revealed a quantum leap. While the designers of 1940 looked ahead to the present, those of 1920 had looked back to the late 19th century. Most designers in 1920 had emerged from art schools that emphasized handiwork and tended to work in styles reminiscent of Art Nouveau or Arts and Crafts. Few trained designers worked on mass-produced appliances or machines, which received their forms as an afterthought from engineers whose main concerns were mechanical function and ease of manufacture. As a result, clumsily integrated forms proliferated, sometimes overlaid with pre-industrial ornamentation if it could be had at no additional cost. Historical eclecticism reigned. The first hint of a new style for the jazz age came from the 'Cubist dream city' of the Paris exposition of 1925, as an American journalist referred to it.[2] For the French, the exposition's precise stylizations of Art Nouveau represented the culmination of a tradition. For Americans, on the other hand, it re-

vealed the possibility of a design style synchronized with machine rhythms. The new idiom, which might be called Machine Deco to distinguish it from French Art Deco, spread quickly as architects like Raymond Hood and Harvey Wiley Corbett adopted it for ornamenting the new skyscrapers of Manhattan. The skyscraper itself became a stylistic influence on the jagged, set-back outlines of Paul Frankl's custom-made skyscraper furniture. Frankl was only one of many immigrant designers, including Kem Weber, Joseph Urban, and William Lescaze, who spread Machine Deco through luxury furnishings, interiors and decorative objects. Although such designers provided the wealthy with jazz age environments, the new style did not penetrate the realm of less expensive mass-produced goods until economic necessity had stimulated the vision of 'an America in which beauty would become an integral part of refrigerators, vacuum cleaners, wallpaper, houses'.[3] Dramatic evidence of the economic benefit of designing for mass production came in 1927, when Henry Ford abandoned production of his beloved model T, a car that had transformed American life, and spent $18 million on the newly designed model A. This 'most expensive art lesson in history,' as someone called it, offered proof to manufacturers that visual appearance had become critically important in marketing ordinary consumer goods.[4] As the business recession of the late 1920s expanded into fully-fledged economic depression, manufacturers turned to product redesign, at first as a tool for overcoming competition in their own industries, but later as a panacea for restoring the nation's economic health.

Seeking guidance in an unfamiliar area, executives naturally turned to their advertising agencies. The most active promoter of the new field of industrial design was an advertising executive, Ernest Elmo Calkins. As head of the Calkins & Holden agency, he had advocated high-quality illustrations in advertising for 20 years, not only to imbue

Cream separator, designed by Raymond Loewy in 1937, based on a 1926 model for International Harvester.

Bus (1931) and cars (1934) with teardrop-shaped streamlining, designed by Norman Bel Geddes. Many copies were made of these models, which were used in the Futurama display designed by Bel Geddes for the 1939 New York World's Fair.

products with satisfying images but also to improve public taste. In a series of articles for businessmen, Calkins argued that they should hire commercial artists to improve product appearance. His goal went beyond improving sales. Calkins predicted that business patronage of the arts would spark a new renaissance by giving industrial civilization a measure of visual coherence – a trait it had lacked since the early Industrial Revolution. His vision reflected the idealism of early 20th-century progressive reformers, but one of his associates, Egmont Arens, added a distinctly modern slant to the emerging philosophy of industrial design. As director of an Industrial Styling Division at the Calkins & Holden agency, Arens had created such innovative designs as a series of coffee and tea packages for the A & P grocery chain – some of which were still in use 60 years later. In 1932 Arens co-authored a book titled *Consumer Engineering: A New Technique for Prosperity*. According to his interpretation of the Depression, the nation's manufacturing techniques had become so efficient that production had overrun consumption. He argued for efficient engineering of consumption to bring it into balance with production. The industrial designer, or consumer engineer, applied principles of behavioural psychology to make products so desirable that they would sell themselves. Designers should strive, he thought, 'not only to fit the product and the promotion to the existing market…but to create new needs and stimulate consumption by every possible means.'[5]

Similar thoughts appeared in most trade journal articles written by, and about, industrial designers during the Depression. In the early years, however, few appeared quite so conscious of their work's larger implications. In fact, most designers entered the new profession by chance as they gradually became aware of industry's need for visual novelty. Norman Bel Geddes, for example, had worked as an advertising illustrator at Detroit and had enjoyed success in New York as an avant-garde stage designer when

a meeting with the president of the J. Walter Thompson advertising agency propelled him into industrial design. During a brief period in 1928 and 1929, Geddes designed products for the agency's advertising clients – metal beds for Simmons, cars for Graham-Paige, and scales and a factory for the Toledo Scale Company. Of the product designs, only the furniture reached manufacture, and the factory was never built, but the experience convinced Geddes that his future lay in designing for industry.

Walter Dorwin Teague, who became America's leading industrial designer in the years prior to the Second World War, had worked as an advertising illustrator for 20 years, starting out with Calkins & Holden, before accepting his first design commission for Kodak cameras. His advertising background made him attractive to manufacturers who worried about entrusting the success of their companies to long-haired artists. Another convert from advertising was Raymond Loewy, a Frenchman who had come to New York in 1919. Loewy's first design comission, for the housing of a mimeograph machine, was awarded to him by an Englishman impressed by Loewy's remarks on the poor design of London taxi cabs. After serving as Westinghouse's art director for radio cabinets from 1929 to 1931, Loewy began a career as independent consultant by creating car bodies for the Hupp Motor Company. Only Henry Dreyfuss, the final member of the quartet of leading New York designers of the 1930s, had no connection with advertising. Around 1930 he shifted his major focus from stage design, an occupation he had learned as an apprentice of Norman Bel Geddes, to the design of products.

Industrial design flowed naturally from advertising. But executives soon learned to distrust designers who offered only flashy sketches. Each of the four major designers inspired confidence while displaying a unique personality. Teague, for example, seemed a consummate businessman with a serious concern for moral reform inherited

from his mentor Calkins. Loewy consciously styled his life to reflect the popular image of a French designer. Of the four, Dreyfuss appeared most seriously concerned with the fit of product to user and pioneered the applied science of ergonomics. Geddes, on the other hand, provided the public with flamboyant, streamlined visions of the shape of things to come. Despite these differences, they evolved a common design process that brought them a success denied to those who offered manufacturers nothing

more than very pretty pictures to look at. A typical successful industrial designer's staff consisted of a couple of associates trained in engineering or architecture, two or three draughtsmen, a model-maker, a secretary, a business manager and a public relations expert entrusted with keeping the designer's name in the news. When the firm received a commission for a product design, the designer himself toured the manufacturer's plant and met with executives, product engineers and the marketing staff. After collecting samples of competing products, conducting market surveys and sometimes observing the behaviour of consumers, the designer and his associates evaluated the problem. Draughtsmen then prepared scores of preliminary sketches, three or four of which yielded formal renderings for presentation to a client. After a final design was

Coca-Cola drinks machine, designed by Raymond Loewy for Dole Deluxe, 1947. Its streamlined form is very close to that of Evinrude outboard motors.

selected, a presentation model was prepared, precise enough to use as a source of blueprints. As a final step, the design team sometimes prepared suggestions and advertising campaigns. Although this common design process evolved in a haphazard manner, only those designers who adopted it enjoyed a high volume of commissions. Publicity in business magazines in 1932 revealed that industrial design appealed to many businessmen as a Depression panacea. At that point the angular precision and skyscraper lines of Machine Deco dominated most products that benefited from a designer's touch. All the same, it was not a style that proved easy to apply to such large appliances as stoves, washing machines and refrigerators. This area was especially significant because it marked the spread of the machine into the home. For such appliances, designers concentrated on creating volumetric forms that integrated the operating mechanisms within a single housing. This new mode of 'clean-lined' appliance design, which eliminated visual complexity and emphasized simplicity of operation, prepared the way for public acceptance of streamlining as a style that promised to eliminate complexity and friction from society in general. More than anyone else, Geddes popularized streamlining as a design style by means of his book *Horizons*, which was published in 1932 at the height of business infatuation with industrial design. Filled with fantastic visualizations of teardrop cars and buses, a sleek tubular train, a torpedo-shaped ocean liner and a vast flying wing with teardrop

Model of a railcar propelled by rear propellor, (never built), designed by Raymond Loewy, 1932. Lewis Mumford (*Technics and Civilization*, 1963) considered this project to be a naïve and romantic attempt to apply the principles of air transport to ground transport.

pontoons, *Horizons* struck a responsive chord in executives receiving promotional copies and in ordinary people who saw its visions reproduced in newspapers and magazines. Along with automotive engineers of his day, Geddes considered the teardrop – the shape taken by a drop of water sliding down an inclined surface – as the form of least resistance for a vehicle moving through the air. Engineers at Chrysler had been working on prototypes of teardrop cars for several years and Geddes's book finally convinced marketing executives to proceed with the Airflow car. Its flowing, parabolic silhouette marked the car as more radical in design than any previous production car. Introduced in 1934, the Chrysler Airflow contributed to an ever growing furore over the streamlining aesthetic.

The impact of *Horizons* on American railways was even more important. Hoping to win passengers away from the car, railway executives sought to imbue rail travel with an image of modernity. Within months of the publication of Geddes's book, the Union Pacific and Burlington lines announced plans for the first passenger streamliners. Completed early in 1934, the UP's M-10,000 and the Burlington Zephyr were intended as fast commuters trains. Their technically innovative designs incorporated internal combustion engines and lightweight bodies of aluminium or stainless steel, but it was their sleek aerodynamic forms that attracted public attention. During the spring and summer of 1934, both trains toured the nation and attracted thousands of sightseers. Some people went

through the trains during brief stops in small towns. Those in rural areas crowded to local crossings as the trains came sweeping by at times announced in advance. Farm wives made blurry Kodak snapshots as their husbands held up babies for a glimpse of the shape of things to come. Thousands more saw the two trains as star attractions of the second season of the Century of Progress Exposition at Chicago. Surrounded by the fair's Machine Deco structures, many of them designed by New York's leading skyscraper architects, the two streamliners heralded a commercial design style more in harmony with Depression attitudes than was jazzy Machine Deco. Given the central role of the railways in settling the American Midwest, it was not surprising that people adopted the word 'streamliner' to refer to a

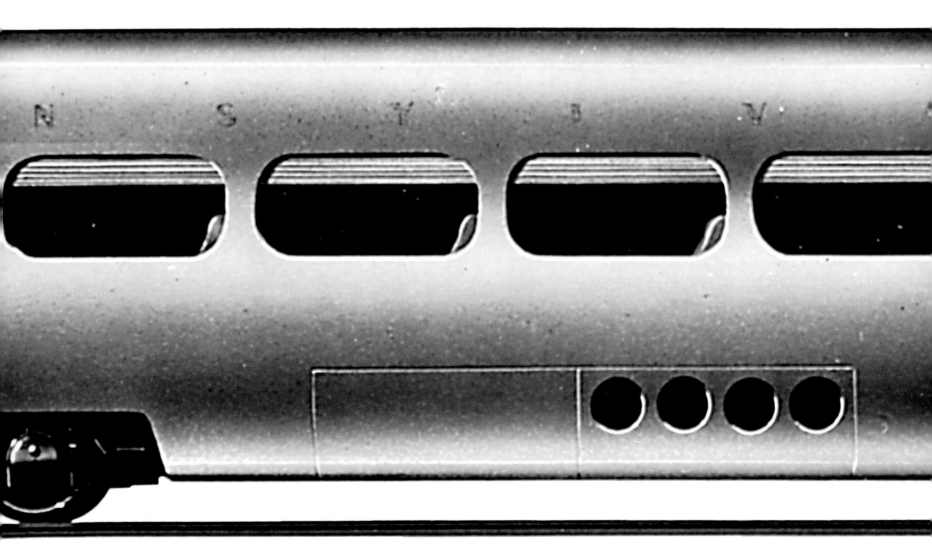

train rather than to a car or to an aeroplane, either of which more fully represented the future for which the streamline style stood as symbol. Bridging past and future, the streamliner suggested smooth, frictionless progress – exactly what the American people wanted as they struggled through the Depression.

When Egmont Arens went on a public tour in the autumn of 1934 with a lecture entitled See America Streamlined, he discovered an 'amazing response… in all parts of the country to the suggestions contained in the word "streamlining".' Although this 'welling up of national enthusiasm' seemed genuine, it was also a 'rather intangible thing'. Arens believed, however, that it might have 're-markable results' if 'used as a selling tool'.[6] Unusual attention paid by the public to streamlining suggested that it fulfilled a genuine cultural need, but the streamline style also lent itself to commercial manipulation. Even though the style evolved originally from the science of aerodynamics, it quickly passed into the more emotional realms of commerce and culture. Within a short time – no more than a couple of years – streamlining had spread to non-vehicular design on every scale – from pencil sharpeners and household fans to store fronts and petrol stations. The new style and the industrial designers who had developed it came under frequent attack from critics associated with the Museum of Modern Art, who had singled out Bauhaus designers and architects of the so-called International Style as the only sources of pure modern design. Responding in 1934 to an overture from popularizer Geddes, for example, the museum's director Alfred H. Barr Jr. denounced streamlining as 'an absurdity in much contemporary design', the result of a 'blind concern with fashion' that made it 'difficult to take the ordinary industrial designer seriously'.[7] Ardent design nationalists retorted that streamlining marked 'the emergence of an American style' boldly expressive of a vigorous modern civilization, a style that avoided both the austerity of the International Style and the hothouse excess of Art Deco.[8] In fact, they could have defended it on more practical grounds. Products of sheet metal, for example, did need rounded edges for strength and ease of assembly, while moulds for making plastic appliance housings had to be rounded to permit machine polishing of the mould, to

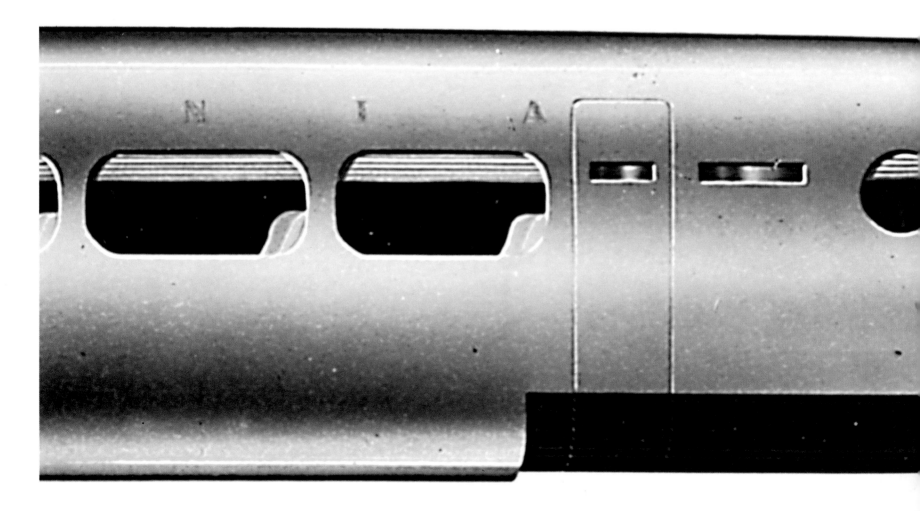

facilitate smooth flow of molten plastic to all parts of the mould and to give products a degree of strength not possible with rectilinear forms.

But most arguments for streamlining had nothing to do with manufacturing processes. Teague, the most philosophic of the designers, often asserted that streamlining provided a coherence the built environment had lacked since the beginning of the Industrial Revolution. More in touch with the mood of the public, Loewy suggested that streamlining 'symbolizes simplicity – eliminates cluttering detail and answers a subconscious yearning for the polished, orderly essential'.[9] The most telling defence of the new style came from a design publicist who echoed Aren's philosophy of consumer engineering by maintaining in 1938 that 'streamlining a product and its methods of merchandising is bound to propel it quicker and more profitably through the channels of sales resistance'.[10] Beneath all these formulations lay a common assumption that society's larger processes had to be rendered smoother, less complex, more frictionless in operation. Streamlining – whether of vehicles, appliances, or the interiors of government buildings – visually expressed this utopian desire. The style's association with aerodynamics and speed suggested a faith in technological progress, but at the same time its rounded, enclosing forms, particularly when applied to architecture, suggested a need for protection and stability. Above all else, streamlining did reveal an obsession with control.

This cultural concern came into sharpest focus at the New York World's Fair of 1939. Held on the eve of a war that soon revealed the dark side of the urge for control, the fair was dedicated to an optimistic theme of 'building the world of tomorrow,' a concept suggested by Teague. Enthusiastic critics observed that the fair's curvilinear forms, created mostly by industrial designers rather than by architects, indicated acceptance of streamlining as a uniquely American design style. Flowing effortlessly on escalators, revolving platforms, conveyor belt chairs, and on foot through one-way, flow-lined exhibits, visitors marveled at a projected future world of television, robots, neo-Le Corbusian cities, transcontinental highways, intercontinental rocket travel and a good number of currently available appliances. Implicit in

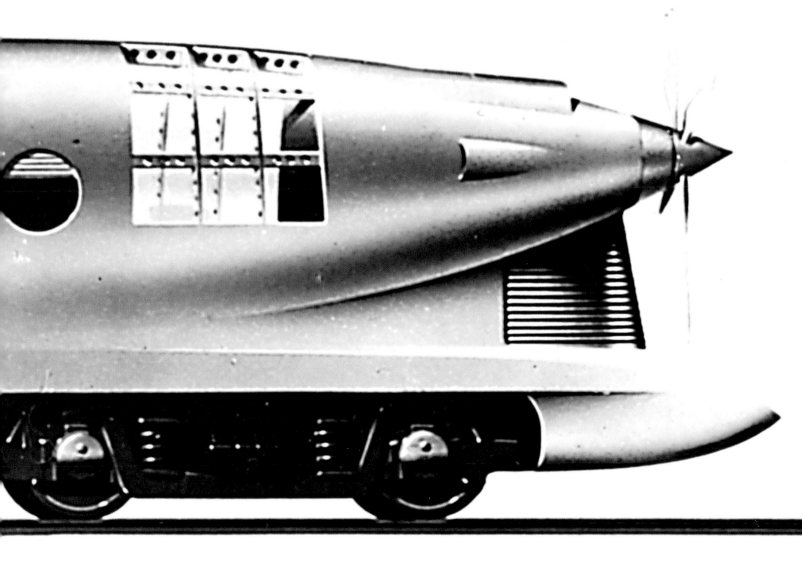

many of the more commercial exhibits of the fair, which one observer dismissed as 'looking at Tomorrow and arriving mostly in the middle of Today,' was the fact that industrial designers were soon to shift their attention from projecting utopian visions to lubricating the wheels of industry – the motive that had brought their profession into being in the first place.[11] With the post-war return to prosperity, the first that Americans had known since the 1920s, the industrial design profession became institutionalized as an adjunct of marketing. Even the founders lost not only an exhilarating sense of being at the centre of an evolving national culture but also the celebrity generated by popular recognition of their expansive role.

A more dramatic fate awaited streamlining, the exuberant style that designers had imposed not only on vehicles and consumer products but on much American commercial architecture as well. With streamlining consciously admitted as a matter of 'designing for eye resistances rather than wind resistances,' as Arens phrased it as early as 1936, forms of products of all sizes, from staplers to cars, were free to evolve toward the baroque extremes eventually reached during the 1950s.[12] During the immediate post-war years, as production shifted back from military hardware to consumer goods, most designers continued the trends of the late 1930s, leading toward a bulbous streamlining that abandoned sleek, aerodynamic lines for a reassuring sense of oversized solidity and stability. The Internationalist historian Siegfried Giedion rightly criticized commercial design of the late 1940s as being marked by 'artificial swelling of volumes.' Consumer goods were becoming so 'increasingly bloated' each year that he considered the trend as evidence of a return to the overstuffed taste of the late Victorians.[13] This trend appeared in such objects as Loewy's Studebaker Champion car and his Coca-Cola soda fountain dispenser, both from 1947, and in dozens of washing machines, refrigerators and similar domestic appliances by other designers.

Industrial design. . . is a serious profession which combines good taste, technical knowledge, and common sense. In the case of my own organization, it is taken seriously by over 75 corporations. . . Their conception of aesthetics consists of a beautiful sales curve shooting upwards.

Raymond Loewy,
'Industrial Design – The Aesthetics of Salesmanship – An American View'
The Times, 1945

Within a few years, however, American commercial design moved beyond this period of post-war bloat – a natural response to the return of material plenty after a time of economic famine – to a new variant of streamlining inspired more directly by current trends in aerodynamics. Borrowing from the shark-like noses of Second World War fighter planes, and from their vertical stabilizing fins, Harley Earl and his studio of designers at General Motors developed car designs that led in a few years to the classic American dreamboat of the mid-to-late 1950s, with its wraparound windshield, its defiant, chrome-plated radiator grill and bumpers, its electric, two-tone paint job outlined in chrome, and, above all, its soaring butterfly tail-fins, described by marketing departments with tongue firmly in cheek as essential for stabilizing such a powerful car at high speeds. Just as transportation had led the way during the 1930s, so too in the 1950s. Objects as varied as cameras, radios, hamburger stands, and even petrol pumps took on sharply flared silhouettes, ultimately in imitation of the jet fighters of the era, but so far removed from that context as to exist in a realm of their own, reinforcing each other by their presence, yet destabilizing each other by their continuous minor stylistic adjustments. Such objects suggested not, as in the 1930s, a future society of stable coherence, but instead a society continuously transcending itself so quickly as to stimulate a vertigo that would have been disorientating had not the nation seemed to be riding the crest of an American century.[14]

Oddly enough, as this design trend continued into the late 1950s, designers themselves, perhaps because their role had devolved into the routine supply of superficial 'packaging' in sheet metal and plastic, became less visible. The utopian vision that had motivated and sustained them during the 1930s dissolved into a concern for business as usual, which Gordon Lippincott expressed well in 1947 when he asserted that there was 'only one reason for hiring an industrial

191

designer... to increase the sales of a product'.[15] For several decades this attitude held sway. Only the most influential designers, such as Eliot Noyes, George Nelson, and Charles and Ray Eames, enjoyed the visibility that had blessed the profession during the 1930s, mostly because they received high-end commissions and rarely designed goods truly intended for mass production for ordinary consumers. Most designers, by contrast, fell into an anonymous obscurity from which it was difficult even to project a vision, much less to realize it. This unfortunate situation did not begin to resolve itself until the 1980s, under circumstances similar to those that had sparked the design renaissance of the 1930s. In the first place, the United States had entered a precarious state of global competition from which design promised potential escape. Far more importantly, however, the personal computer and related microchip developments affected the shapes of dozens of different types of products. Just as designers of the 1930s had given effective expression to the machine age, those of the 1980s gave expression to the miniaturized, dematerialized technologies of the digital age. Design – and culture – were poised for another quantum leap brought about this time not by transportation but by a revolution in communications.

Hairdrier, HMV (Thorn EMI), 1946.

Steam locomotives

On 6 October 1829, The Rocket, a locomotive designed by George Stephenson, emerged victorious in a competition organized by the new Liverpool and Manchester Railway. It was capable of pulling a carriage with passengers at a speed of 24 mph. Within ten years, nearly 5,000 miles of track had been built throughout the world.

In the 19th century, locomotives had come to symbolize the power of industry whose expansion they facilitated. Rarely have mechanics and aesthetics been so harmoniously combined as they were in the steam locomotive. As it evolved, the elongation of the cylindrical body and the integration of additional elements led to fluid lines that were independent of changing fashion, but that were the visible expression of progress, of increasing power.

The determination of companies and nations to forge their own identities led to the development of a great many types of locomotive and considered as a group they form one of the most important manifestations of the industrial aesthetic. Technical improvements and aesthetic choices allow us to distinguish four different categories:

– The English benefited from their head start and the quality of their metallurgy. Their 'school' was characterized by a preference for single expansion chambers and by a constant striving for functional simplicity and purity of design.

– French engineers have always attempted to combine high performance with economy, and this led to a preference for double expansion chambers. In 1935, André Chapelon developed this principle, obtaining maximal power in relation to mass.

– The Germans, led by the engineer R. Gralal, abandoned the double expansion chamber in favour of a single one with a superheater unit.

– The Americans distinguished themselves by their determination to increase traction, which necessitated bigger and more solid locomotives. Mallet articulated locomotives had as many as twelve axles, eight or ten of which were drivers.

Until the First World War, the railway, as yet unchallenged by the car and the aeroplane, enjoyed a de facto transport monopoly. But in the United States, it lost half its passengers between 1920 and 1930 to the car, and 60 per cent of urban transport went by road from 1930.

In their deliberations about how this haemorrhage might be stopped, railway companies concluded that they had to modernize their material and improve their service. The idea of giving locomotives an aerodynamic form had as much to do with publicity as with function, as Raymond Loewy himself conceded: 'A well-designed aerodynamic vehicle gives the impression of movement even when it's standing still.'

The aerodynamic locomotives were designed by the most famous American designers of the thirties and stimulated the development of the 'streamline aesthetic', which dominated the country's product design for years. In addition to Raymond Loewy's, we should cite the contributions of Norman Bel Geddes, Henry Dreyfuss, Otto Kuhler and Norman F. Zapf. In France, the most famous steam locomotive was the 241-101 Mountain type, designed in 1931 by the engineer Henri Pacon.

J. d. N.

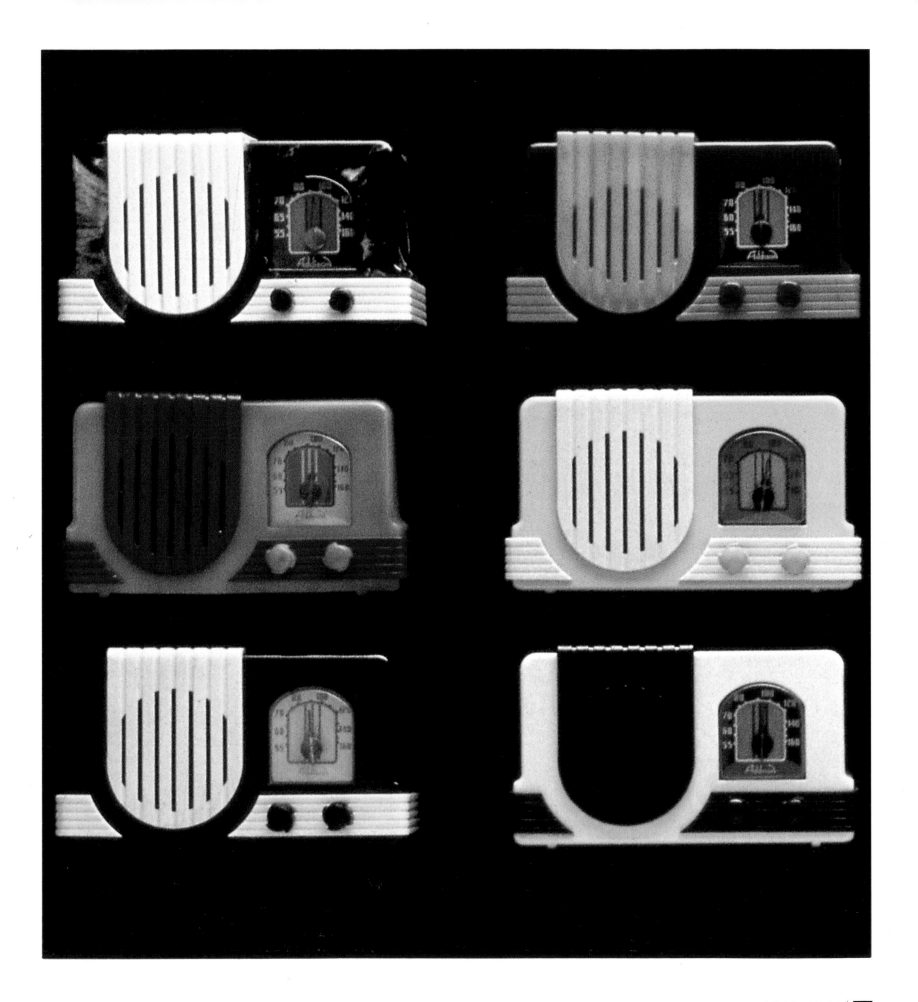

Today it is no longer possible to deny the aesthetic importance of radio cabinets. Radio buffs are, and with reason, increasingly demanding about this aspect. What they want from a receiver is that it can harmoniously blend into the décor of their living-room, office or bedroom. . . In this respect, the radios from the symphonic series are really pleasing to the eye, and their low, streamlined design marks the beginning of a new style.

Philips publicity brochure, c.1938

The golden age of American radios

'Every day industry creates objects that possess an incontestable aesthetic value: it is the spirit of this production that dominates our era.'
Fernand Léger, 1945

By 1933, conditions in the United States could hardly have been more favourable to everyone having a radio receiver of his own. First of all, there were numerous broadcasts devoted to news and music (this was the period in which jazz became popular). Furthermore, radio components had become reliable and sufficiently miniaturized to permit cabinets of small dimensions.

The years after the 1929 crash were rich in design initiatives of all sorts and American industrialists understood that if they were to seduce a large public, products such as radios and cars would not only have to function well but also have to be symbols of progress.

The radio set was a device whose internal technology imposed very few constraints on the external form. This meant that designers had considerable freedom in shaping their design.

The possibility of using the phenol-based, thermoplastic resin known as Catalin, which could be cast directly after having been coloured, facilitated many formal innovations.

In 1933, Harold Van Doren designed the model 52, a brightly-coloured radio in a late Art Deco style for Air King. It was made of a plastic called Plaskon and was marketed in several versions. From 1936 the Sears Roebuck catalogue (the most important mail-order enterprise of the period) sang the praises of radios with Catalin cases and in 1940 the Fada Radio and Electric Company introduced a model with an aerodynamic form, the Bullet 115 Streamliner, that would prove astonishingly successful. The most perfect of designs was probably the one created by Norman Bel Geddes in 1940 for the Emerson Radio Corporation: the Patriot Aristocrat 400.

Pop artists would be seduced by the colours of radios in Catalin; Tom Wesselmann even incorporated one into a painting. The aesthetic qualities of radios from this period are now generally recognized and the most beautiful models are avidly sought by museums and collectors.

J. d. N.

Left-hand page:
Addison radios,
c.1940.

Right, from top
to bottom:
Belmont model
6D120, 1947
(front and back).

Sparton model
517, designed by
Walter Dorwin
Teague, 1936.

Air King radio,
designed by
Harold Van Doren
and J. G. Rideout,
1935.

The Douglas DC-3

'The DC-3 is, to my eyes, the most perfect example of modern design, and I wouldn't know where to look to find its equal.'

Walter Dorwin Teague, 1940

The first resolutely modern aeroplane, the DC-3, known as the DST (Douglas Sleeper Transport), made its inaugural flight on 17 December 1935 (the 32nd anniversary of the Wright brothers' first flight).

Work on the DC-1 and DC-2, which preceded it, began in 1932. The project was initiated by Jack Northrop, who oversaw the structural design. Aerodynamic research was carried out by two engineers, Millikan and Klein. The plane began making commercial flights in August 1936.

The DC-3 is to aviation what the Ford model T is to the motor car. The DC-3's design, however, still seems modern, while that of the Ford model T now appears archaic.

A version adapted for military use, known as the C-47, or the Dakota, was used in the Second World War. More than 13,000 were constructed and 1,500 were still being used for short commercial flights in 1983.

The longevity of the Dakota was due to three factors: its solidity, its performance (it can carry more than 30 passengers at a speed of 200 mph, with a range of 1,600 miles) and its aerodynamic form, which made its design seem perpetually fresh.

In a book that was widely read in the United States after its publication in 1942, Design This Day, Walter Dorwin Teague wrote: 'The Dakota has a form that is perfectly realized, one that makes it comparable to a Doric statue. It owes its aesthetic quality to rigorously-calculated proportions: the engine cases integrated into its wings are proportionate with the shape of its fuselage; likewise for its tail wings, which were designed as reductions of the main wings.'

The designers of the forties and fifties all had photographs of the Dakota on the walls of their studios and specialized magazines never stopped praising its virtues. General Dwight D. Eisenhower considered it to be the most important piece of military material used in the war. Today the Dakota is still held up as an example for design students throughout the world.

J. d. N.

The Willys Jeep

The Jeep was the result of a set of requirements drawn up by the American army, which, in July 1940, issued
a call for design projects to 133 companies. Only two submissions were
found to be acceptable, those proposed
by Willys-Overland, Inc. and the
American Bantam Company. The
brief posed a considerable challenge,
stipulating that a working prototype
be ready within 60 days of the initial commitment. It called for a
light-framed vehicle with four-wheel
drive capable of transporting 600-
pound loads and on which it would be
possible to mount a machine gun.

The vehicle devised by Karl Probst for
American Bantam was the only one
ready within the prescribed time
period. But while this version enjoyed a short-lived success, it was
the Willys design that eventually carried the day because of the better performance of its motor. In truth, its
success was also shaped by the prag-
matism and cynicism of army offic-
ials, who had limited confidence in
the industrial capacity of Bantam.
They allowed engineers from Willys
and Ford[1] to examine the Bantam

prototypes, thus enabling them to by-
pass certain basic studies and focus
on the improvement of key details.

More than 630,000 Jeeps were
constructed between 1941 and 1945,
including 280,000 produced by Ford
under licence from Willys. After some
years of pleading his case, Karl
Probst of Bantam was vindicated: the
Federal Business Commission acknowledged that the basic design had
resulted from joint efforts by Bantam's
engineers and US army technicians.

The Jeep owes its success to, among
other things, the perfect standardization of its components: it could be built
at Willys, Ford, or one of their sub-
licensees, as all of its constituent elements were totally interchangeable.

This vehicle has become a legend for
both symbolic and aesthetic reasons. It
will always be associated with the presence of American GI's in the European
war theatre. Its functional aesthetic,
reminiscent of a technical drawing,
inaugurated a new style: the 'military
look'. The current fashion for four-
wheel drive vehicles provides evidence
of the Jeep's continuing attraction.

J. d. N.

**Background:
An American
Jeep from the
Second Armored
Division.
Summer 1944,
France.**

**Vignette:
Jerrycans for US
Air Force planes
based in France
in 1944.**

1. Ford, which had
not responded to the
call for designs, was
brought into the
project by the US
army.

1946-1973

by

Jocelyn de Noblet

This period is characterized, both in the United States and western Europe, by an unprecedented increase in living standards and by the development of the idea of the consumer society. Three trends, more contradictory than complementary, dominate the evolution of form during this period.

In Europe, from 1946, the neo-classic style, linked with the growth of totalitarianism, makes its reappearance. It was more a product of the period that was coming to an end than a genuine attempt to breathe new life into a bygone age. Once the Marshall Plan had begun to have an effect, unrestrained and colourful forms, symbols of a new *joie de vivre*, emerged after the years of deprivation and rationing.

This 'fifties style' continued to develop until the 1958 Universal Exposition in Brussels. Among the most significant objects of the period were the Citroën DS19, the Atomium, the Vespa scooter, Serge Mouille's lighting and Jean Royère's interiors. The same exuberance was felt in the US with the proliferation of cars with Dionysian forms, like the Cadillac and the Plymouth Fury. As regards domestic furniture, graduates from the Cranbrook Academy, like Charles Eames, Eero Saarinen and George Nelson reigned over design, producing a great variety of organic forms.

From 1959, the rationalist Ulm School — the Hochschule für Gestaltung — exerted a strong influence over German manufacturers such as Braun, Krupp and AEG. A new generation of functionalist designers appeared and their influence dominated in numerous sectors of industry. In 1962, the entrepreneur Dino Gavina, who described himself as an 'ultra-rationalist', started to manufacture furniture designed by Marcel Breuer in 1925.

In Italy, a radical reaction against functionalism started in 1966 through groups like Archizoom and Superstudio. At the same time, in America, the architect Robert Venturi wrote a theoretical work, *Complexity and Contradiction in Architecture* which marked the onset of Post-Modernism.

Venturi's critique and the growing awareness of the environment give rise to alternative design.

Sunday in Nogent, France, 1947.
***Preceding double page:* Prototype of the Citroën 2CV, developed between 1936 and 1939, and presented at the 1948 Salon de l'Automobile.**

1946

- more than fifty-six thousand 1015 jukeboxes sold by Wurlitzer
- Jacques-Yves Cousteau and Emile Gagnan: autonomous diving vessel
- Jackson Pollock develops his drip painting technique
- Chester Carlson: xerography process
- **Renato Piaggio: Vespa scooter**

- prototype Renault 4 CV motor car

- Charles Eames is the first designer to have his work displayed at MOMA, New York
- Frank Capra: *It's a Wonderful Life*
- Howard Hawks: *The Big Sleep*
- first Cannes film festival
- peace conference of 21 nations held in Paris
- in Argentina, Juan Domingo Peron is elected president
- Viet-Minh insurrection in Indochina

1947

- **Christian Dior: 'New-Look' style**
- Chuck Yeager breaks the sound barrier in his plane Bell X 1A 'Glamorous Glennis'
- Raymond Loewy: Studebaker Champion motor car

- in Great Britain, start of programmes for construction of new towns and schools
- Richard Joseph Neutra: Tremaine House, Santa Barbara, California
- Ecole de Paris, Hans Hartung exhibition at Lydia Conti's
- invention of carbon14 dating
- Marshall Plan for European recovery (adopted in 1948)
- partition of Palestine
- start of the Cold War
- India is proclaimed independent

1948

- **Ole Kirk Christiansen: Lego toy building blocks (Denmark)**
- Marcello Nizzoli: Lexicon 80 typewriter for Olivetti
- John Bardeen, Walter Brattain and William Shockley, engineers at the Bell laboratories, invent the transistor
- Francis Melvin Rogallo: prototype delta wings (basis for the development of the delta plane in 1960)

- Walter Bird: development of inflatable architectural structures designed by F. V. Lanchester in 1917
- Pier Luigi Nervi: vault, exhibition centre, Turin
- **Edwin Herbert Land: Polaroid model 95, first camera providing instant development**

- Giovanni Battista Pininfarina: Cisitalia type 202 saloon (displayed at MOMA, New York in 1951)
- Richard Buckminster Fuller builds his first geodesic domes
- start of the Cobra Expressionist movement
- Arshile Gorky commits suicide
- Satyajit Ray: *Pather Panchali*
- Roberto Rossellini: *Germany Year Zero*
- Orson Welles: *The Lady from Shanghai*
- Vittorio de Sica: *The Bicycle Thief*
- in India, assassination of Mahatma Gandhi

- state of Israel becomes independent
- Berlin blockade begins

1949

- Jean Prouvé works on different systems for prefabricated houses
- in Great Britain, Peter and Alison Smithson create the first 'brutalist' building
- Mark Rothko: first colour field paintings
- Arthur Miller: *Death of a Salesman*
- Akira Kurosawa: *Stray Dog*
- George Orwell: *1984*
- Communist People's Republic of China proclaimed under Mao Tse-tung
- North Atlantic Treaty signed
- Apartheid system established in South Africa

1950

- Marcello Nizzoli: Lettera 22 typewriter for Olivetti

- Reynolds ballpoint pen
- **Ralph Scheider creates the first credit card company**
- first colour television broadcasts in the United States
- Willem De Kooning: *Woman 1*
- John Huston: *The Asphalt Jungle*
- Vincente Minnelli: *An American in Paris*
- Carol Reed: *The Third Man*
- Akira Kurosawa: *Rashomon*

- start of the Korean war

1951

- **Caddie supermarket trolley (United States)**
- **Braun S50 electric razor**

- Arne Jacobsen: Ant chair
- first international congress on industrial design in London
- Raymond Loewy: *Never Leave Well Enough Alone*
- Elia Kazan: *A Streetcar Named Desire*
- Jean Cocteau: *Orphée*
- in the United States, Julius and Ethel Rosenberg condemned to death
- peace treaty between the United States and Japan

1952

□ Harry Bertoia: Diamond chair in steel wire

□ explosion of the first hydrogen bomb
□ Twentieth Century Fox make first film in CinemaScope based on the anamorphic system developed by Professor Henri Chretien
□ Louis I. Kahn: Yale University Art Gallery, New Haven
□ Jean Renoir: *Le Carosse d'Or*
□ Stanley Donen: *Singing in the Rain*
□ Eugène Ionesco: *The Chairs*
□ General Mohammed Naguib seizes power in Egypt, King Farouk abdicates

1953

□ **Samsonite suitcase**
□ IBM 701 computer
□ first flight of the Boeing 707
□ Marcel Breuer, in collaboration with Pier Luigi Nervi and Bernhard Zehrfuss, directs the construction of the UNESCO building in Paris
□ Hochschule für Gestaltung at Ulm organizes its first courses
□ Francis Crick and James Watson determine molecular structure of DNA
□ Kenji Mizoguchi: *Ugetsu Monogatari*
□ Yasujiro Ozu: *Tokyo Story*

□ SEB pressure cooker

□ Alain Robbe-Grillet: *The Erasers* (birth of the nouveau roman)
□ Samuel Beckett: *Waiting for Godot*
□ death of Stalin, succeeded by Khrushchev

1954

□ the Nautilus, first American nuclear submarine
□ Gregory Pincus, Min-Chueh Chang and John Rock invent the contraceptive pill (first clinical tests)
□ G. Rehklau: Ampex 600 portable tape recorder

□ in Italy, creation of the Compasso d'Oro award for good design
□ Push Pin Studios co-founded by Milton Glaser
□ Elia Kazan: *On the Waterfront*
□ Frederico Fellini: *La Strada*
□ Akira Kurosawa: *The Seven Samurai*
□ Bill Haley records his first hit: *Rock around the Clock*
□ speech by Khrushchev to the conference of builders, architects and building industry workers in Moscow
□ first seminar by the psychoanalyst Jacques Lacan
□ Indo-China armistice signed in Geneva

1955

□ first McDonald's restaurant opens in Des Plaines, Illinois

□ Hans Gugelot launches the new Braun design programme
□ **Flaminio Bertoni: Citroën DS 19 car**

□ start of Pop Art

□ Disneyland opens (California)
□ Beatnik movement
□ first appearance of teddy boys in England
□ Nicholas Ray: *Rebel Without a Cause*

□ Robert Rauschenberg: *Monogram*
□ Robert Aldrich: *Kiss Me Deadly*
□ Charles Laughton: *The Night of the Hunter*
□ Warsaw pact

1956

□ Eero Saarinen: furniture collection for Knoll

□ Gino Valle: electric clocks for Solari (Compasso d'Oro)
□ **Charles Eames: chair and ottoman for Herman Miller**
□ Gino Valle: digital clock programme for Solari (1956–1966)
□ Achille and Pier Giacomo Castiglioni: REM vacuum cleaner (Compasso d'Oro, 1957)
□ Mary Quant opens her first fashion shop, designed by Terence Conran, in London

- Renault Dauphine motor car

- Frank Lloyd Wright: Solomon R. Guggenheim Museum, New York

- atomic power station opened at Calder Hall, Great Britain
- Jørn Utzon and Ove Arup: Sydney Opera House
- Lionel Schein: experimental plastic house
- Eero Saarinen: TWA terminal, Idlewild Airport
- Lucio Costa: plan for Brasilia
- Alain Resnais: *Nuit et Brouillard*
- de-Stalinization in USSR
- Soviet troops enter Hungary

1957

- Achille and Pier Giacomo Castiglioni: Cella 200 stool
- portable Zenith radio
- Gerd Alfred Muller: food processor KM 31 for Braun
- Ettore Sottsass Jr works for Olivetti
- Raymond Loewy: Alouette helicopter for SNCASE
- Le Corbusier: Tokyo Museum of Art
- launch of the first Sputnik satellite

- foundation of the ICSID (the International Congress of the Societies of Industrial Design)
- foundation of the Groupe d'Etudes d'Architectures Mobiles (GEAM)
- start of the Situationist movement
- Leonard Bernstein: *West Side Story*
- independence of Ghana, beginning of de-colonialization in Sub-Saharan Africa
- Rome Treaty, beginning of the Common Market

1958

- Richard Gordon Gould invents the laser
- Peter Chilvers: windsurfer
- Ingvar Kamprad opens the first IKEA shop (Sweden)
- **Harley Earl: Cadillac Eldorado 'Brougham' motor car**

- Nicolas Esquillan (engineer), Robert Camelot, Bernard Zehrfuss and Jean de Mailly: the CNIT at La Défense, Paris
- Eero Saarinen: Dulles International Airport, near Washington DC
- Universal Exposition, Brussels (height of the Atom style)
- Fritz Hundertwasser publishes his *Mould Manifesto against Rationalism in Architecture*
- first stereophonic recordings
- Jasper Johns exhibits at the Leo Castelli Gallery, New York
- Christo Javacheff, known as Christo: first wrapping projects
- Satyajit Ray: *The Music Room*
- Alfred Hitchcock: *Vertigo*

- Ingmar Bergman: *Wild Strawberries*
- Jacques Tati: *Mon Oncle*

- Merce Cunningham: *Artic Meet* ballet (music by John Cage, sets by Robert Rauschenberg)
- The Beatles appear at the Cavern in Liverpool
- in France, General De Gaulle returns to power
- in the United States, Supreme Court makes schooling for black children obligatory

- Ake Senning invents the pacemaker
- NASA set up (United States)

1959

□ Carlo Mollino: Fenis chair for Zanotta

□ **Mattel launches the Barbie doll**
□ IBM 401 computer
□ Xerox photocopying machine
□ Dante Jiacosa: Fiat 500 car
□ **Alec Issigonis: Austin Mini Minor car**
□ Alan Kaprow: first happenings (United States)
□ Arman: first accumulations
□ Federico Fellini: *La Dolce Vita*
□ Jean-Luc Godard: *A Bout de Souffle* (birth of the Nouvelle Vague)
□ François Truffaut: *Les Quatre Cents Coups*
□ Alain Resnais: *Hiroshima Mon Amour*
□ Günther Grass: *Die Blechtrommel*
□ in Cuba, Fidel Castro takes power

1960

□ Clarence L. Johnson: U2 spy plane

□ foundation of the group Art Visuel in France

□ The world's longest liner the SS France is launched
□ Nouveau Réalisme movement
□ Yves Klein: Anthropometries
□ Le Corbusier: monastery at La Tourette, France
□ Michelangelo Antonioni: *L'Avventura*

□ Ornette Coleman: *Free Jazz* album (start of free jazz)
□ Reyner Banham: *Theory and Design in the First Machine Age*
□ Kevin Lynch: *The Image of the City*
□ John Fitzgerald Kennedy is elected president of the United States

1961

□ USSR: first manned spacecraft, Yuri Gagarin orbits the earth

□ Kenzo Tange: Tokyo stadium
□ formation of Archigram, start of the journal *Archigram* (Great Britain)
□ Jane Jacobs: *The Death and Life of Great American Cities*
□ François Truffaut: *Jules et Jim*
□ Henry Miller: *Tropic of Cancer*
□ Joseph Heller: *Catch-22*
□ South Africa becomes independent republic
□ creation of Amnesty International in London
□ construction of the Berlin wall
□ increasing United States involvement in Vietnam

1962

□ Achille and Pier Giacomo Castiglioni: Arco lamp for Flos
□ Hans Gugelot: carrousel for Kodak

□ **Colin Chapman: Lotus 25 (Formula One car)**
□ Seattle World's Fair: Man in the Space Age
□ birth of the Fluxus movement on the initiative of George Maciunas (international Fluxus festival in Wiesbaden)
□ Andy Warhol: *Campbell's Soup Cans*
□ Stanley Kubrick: *Lolita*
□ Cuba missile crisis
□ Algeria becomes independent

1963

□ Roger Tallon: Téléavia television
□ Joe Colombo: mobile kitchen
□ Philips minicassette
□ Kodak Instamatic 100 camera
□ foundation of ICOGRADA (International Council of Graphic Design Associations)
□ first attempts at holograms, University of Michigan
□ Claes Oldenburg: *Soft Light Switches*
□ Stanley Kubrick: *Dr Strangelove*
□ Joseph Losey: *The Servant*
□ Federico Fellini: *Eight and a half*
□ Iannis Xenakis: *Musiques Formelles*
□ civil rights demonstrations in the United States, Martin Luther King arrested
□ John Fitzgerald Kennedy assassinated in Dallas, Texas

1964

□ **Mary Quant launches the mini skirt in London**
□ Olivier Mourgue: Djinn chair

□ **Terence Conran: first Habitat shop opens in London**
□ Eliott Noyes: petrol pump for Mobil Oil
□ Ferrari 275 GT B4
□ Robert Rauschenberg wins the prize for painting at the Venice Biennial
□ Nelson Mandela is condemned to life imprisonment and South Africa is excluded from the Olympic games because of its apartheid policy
□ escalation of war in Vietnam
□ Khrushchev removed from office

1965

□ Cricket disposable lighter, Dupont

- Achille and Pier Giacomo Castiglioni: Allunaggio stool
- Willie Landels: Throw-Away sofa
- Richard Sapper and Mark Zanuso: TS 502 portable radio for Brionvega and Grillo folding telephone for Italtel
- Gaston Juchet: Renault 16 motor car
- Ieoh Ming Pei: extension of the Hyde Park area in Chicago
- Louis Kahn: National Assembly Building, Dacca (Bangladesh)
- Jean-Luc Godard: *Alphaville* and *Pierrot le Fou*
- Bridget Riley: *Arrest I*

1966

- Ettore Sottsass: experimental furniture

- Gian Carlo Pinetti: Plia 106 chair
- Vico Magistretti: Eclisse lamp for Artémide

- start of Archizoom and Superstudio (Italy)
- Luna IX spacecraft lands on the moon (USSR)

- Primary Structures exhibition at the Jewish Museum, New York
- start of Land Art (Richard Long)
- Andy Warhol: *Chelsea Girls*
- Eric Rohmer: *La Collectionneuse*
- first concerts by the Velvet Underground
- cultural revolution in China
- in the United States, demonstrations against American bombardments in South Vietnam

1967

- Wernher von Braun: Saturn rocket for NASA
- Expo '67, Montreal: Moshe Safdie designs Habitat 67, Richard Buckminster Fuller the American pavilion and Frei Otto the West German pavilion
- Germano Celant coins the expression 'arte povera' (exhibition in Genoa)
- shows by Buren, Mosset, Parmentier and Toroni (BMPT)
- Jacques Tati: *Playtime*
- Ingmar Bergman: *Persona*
- Michelangelo Antonioni: *Blow Up*
- Roger Vadim: *Barbarella*
- Luis Buñuel: *Belle de Jour*
- Gabriel Garcia Marquez: *One Hundred Years of Solitude*
- Dr Christiaan Barnard performs the first human heart transplant (South Africa)
- Six-day War between Israel and Arab nations
- execution of Che Guevara, Cuban revolutionary leader

1968

- Jacob Jensen directs Bang & Olufsen's hi-fi design programme
- Christopher Cockrell: British Hovercraft
- Ulm Hochschule für Gestaltung, closes
- exhibition: Art and the Machine (New York)
- Sol LeWitt: graphite wall drawings
- Mario Merz: *Giap Igloo*
- Jesús Rafael Soto: first penetrables
- **Gatti, Paolini, Teodoro: Sacco chair**

- Stanley Kubrick: *2001, A Space Odyssey*
- Pina Bausch: first choreographies (*Fragments, Im Wind der Zeit*)

- in France, student revolt
- assassination of Martin Luther King
- assassination of Robert Francis Kennedy
- Czechoslovakia invaded by Warsaw Pact troops

1969

- first flight by Concorde, built by British Aerospace and Aérospatiale

- Livio Castiglioni: Boalum lamp
- **Ettore Sottsass Jr and Perry King: Valentine portable typewriter**
- Archizoom Associati: Mies chair
- foundation of the CCI (Centre de Création Industrielle) on the initiative of François Mathey and François Barré
- Gaetano Pesce: Up series

- Enzo Mari: reversible vases
- Vittel plastic maxi bottle
- Bauhaus retrospective, Paris
- Harald Szeeman: exhibition When Attitudes become Forms, Bern
- start of body art in France and Austria
- Dennis Hopper: *Easy Rider*
- Pier Paolo Pasolini: *Teorema*
- Luciano Berio: *Sinfonia*
- Woodstock festival, United States
- Kurt Vonnegut: *Slaughterhouse-Five*

- Apollo 11 and 12 (NASA, United States): first men to walk on the moon (landing in the lunar module)

- in France, General De Gaulle resigns and Georges Pompidou is elected president
- in West Germany, Willy Brandt is elected chancellor
- in Libya, Moamar al Gaddafi takes power
- first United States troops withdrawn from Vietnam
- start of the SALT negotiations

1970

- Superstudio: Quaderna console and seat
- Shiro Kuramata: asymmetric storage units
- Telefunken: first videodisc
- Ricardo Bofill: buildings in Spain
- first Universal Exposition in Asia (Osaka)
- start of photo-realism in the United States
- Support/Surface movement
- Philip Guston: Ku Klux Klan paintings
- Duane Hanson: *Supermarket Lady*
- Robert Altman: *MASH*
- Alexander Solzhenitsyn wins Nobel Prize for Literature
- war in Vietnam spreads to Laos and Cambodia

- Roland Barthes: *L'Empire des Signes*
- death of Gamal Abdel Nasser
- in Chile, election of Salvador Allende

1971

- Transac automatic ticket machine by Bull
- Richard Sapper and Marco Zanuso: Terraillon kitchen scales

- Roger Tallon: corail train for the SNCF
- Godfery Newbold Hounsfield: scanner
- Joe Colombo: Birillo stool

- David Hockney: swimming pool paintings

- Michel Boué: Renault 5 motor car

- Daniel Buren is censored at the sixth Guggenheim Museum International
- Stanley Kubrick: *A Clockwork Orange*
- Federico Fellini: *Roma*
- China admitted to the UN

1972

- Richard Sapper: Tizio lamp
- Texas Instrument: pocket electronic calculator
- Scholtès: vitroceramic hot plate
- Christo: Running Fence (40 km long, Sonoma and Marin counties, California)
- Ralph Goings: *Airstream Trailer*
- Bernardo Bertolucci: *Last Tango in Paris*
- Gaetano Pesce: Moloch Floor lamp

- Francis Ford Coppola: *The Godfather*
- Ingmar Bergman: *Cries and Whispers*
- Italo Calvino: *Invisible Cities*
- Richard Nixon visits communist China

1973

- Archizoom Associati (Paolo Deganello): 'AEO' seating system
- first commercial fax machines
- Jean-Pierre Raynaud designs his white ceramic house
- first oil crisis
- Mario Bellini: Divisumma 18 calculator for Olivetti

- Victor Papanek: *Design for the Real World*
- Alexander Solzhenitsyn: *The Gulag Archipelago*
- major recession in the United States
- United States forces withdraw from South Vietnam
- fourth Arab-Israeli war
- Britain, Ireland and Denmark join the EEC

Jocelyn de Noblet

The war is over, and the Marshall Plan is beginning to have a tangible effect on the economies of the western world. The war against germs also seems to have been won: penicillin and streptomycin are available to all. The sanatoria, of which popular fiction even now retains an obsolete image stamped by eroticism, discreetly close their doors; those who would have numbered among their patients restore their health at Club Méditerranée, bathing in a liberated sexual atmosphere in which the decadent symbolism of *La Dame aux Camélias* plays no part. According to Christian Dior, 'The war is over, a revolution is needed. Women have acquired a taste for uniforms. We must put an end to this and re-feminize them, whatever the cost.' A new look featuring calf-length hemlines, pulled-in waists, and bare shoulders took shape in France at a time when ration cards and year-long waits for telephone service and new cars were the norm.

The fifties were marked by the cold war, the Korean War, and decolonization, but what concerns us here is the period's material culture, its style, its patterns of consumption, and its preferred leisure activities. In a sense, it was during the fifties that the 20th cen-

tury definitively severed its ties with the past and assumed its own formal identity. A new style of life was made possible by increased prosperity as well by profound changes in ethical standards. The advent of a European and American youth calling for a culture of its own and a total break with the most firmly established traditions; the emergence of feminism: these are among the most significant developments of the period, because they brought about profound and enduring change. The advertising poster for the Vespa scooter, in which a figurative representation of the singer Gilbert Bécaud is juxtaposed with a generalized evocation of the School of Paris, captures the tone of the decade.

It is difficult to analyse the tremendous explosion of form that occurred during this era. It was as if things that were not *a priori* destined to blend found themselves fortuitously thrown together. In the wake of the war they accumulated to such an extent that the result was a critical mass and a coherent expression. This coherence is not synonymous with unity and, to some extent, an era's vitality can best be measured by the quality of the polemics that shape its evolution. The consumer society fell

Design

for the Happy Days

The 1950s

into place in a disorderly way, and very differently in the United States and Europe. American 'Populux'[1] consisted of motor cars designed by Harley Earl for General Motors, drive-ins, drugstores, supermarkets, Frigidaires, Levitte houses for GI's, and entertainments devised by Walt Disney, not to mention the neon extravaganzas of Las Vegas.

In France and the rest of Europe this was a time of reconstruction, and the rebuilding went hand-in-hand with increased consumerism. In 1949, only one Frenchman in twenty-eight owned a car; by 1956 this figure had grown to one in thirteen. Confronted with a general increase in spending power, longer paid annual leave, and a growing predilection for tourism, the rebuilders came to understand the need to produce large quantities of popular cars within the means of all French families, cars such as the Renault 4CV, the Citroën 2CV, and lastly the Renault Dauphine 5CV.

The 1950s in Europe are the prelude to a period of prosperity that Jean Fourastié called 'the thirty glorious years'.[2] In the United States, the pleasures of consumerism were enjoyed with the same enthusiasm and abandon as in Europe. To understand the meaning of the products of this period, it is necessary to examine the various parameters which governed their design and which explain why they still make us dream today.

A taste for free, organic forms

Towards 1935, largely as a result of Surrealist influence, new forms began to appear which had nothing to do with the geometric forms and primary colours favoured by the Post-Cubist avant-garde. By Surrealism I mean that non-figurative current which, headed by Jean Arp and Joan Miro, included artists such as Alexander Calder and, in particular, Wassily Kandinsky, whose late work pictures an embryonic universe in which forms seem to be evolving before our eyes, as in a process of cell division. Kandinsky's development

bears witness to a profound and rather sudden cultural shift that marks a break with the aesthetic of the twenties. It is significant that Kandinsky taught at the Bauhaus for ten years, and that he is one of the founding fathers of geometric abstraction.

In France, designers like Elsa Schiaparelli were influenced by Surrealism. Just before the war she sought the advice of Salvador Dali when designing dresses and hats. Other artists, such as Henri Matisse, Henry Moore, and Yves Tanguy, also produced work whose forms would be imitated, more or less directly, by designers and decorators, while Isamu Noguchi's 1938 sculpture *The Heart of a Hundred Thousand Hairs* had a considerable influence in the United States. As a counterpoint to this evolution from the mechanical towards the organic, we should not underestimate the marked neo-classical element in Art Deco, which had a considerable impact through the intermediary of the movies.

In another register, the streamline aesthetic conceived by Norman Bel Geddes was influenced by the organic forms of imaginary projects designed by the Austrian architect Erich Mendelsohn. The central theme of the 1939 New York World's Fair was 'Building the World of Tomorrow'. Bel Geddes, Henry Dreyfuss, Walter Dorwin Teague, and Raymond Loewy were put in charge of its overall conception and principal attractions, and the results made them famous. The fair's futurist conceit provided an ideal occasion for the use of aerodynamic forms, and it is not surprising that they met with great success.

All these aesthetic tendencies left their mark on consumer products, but their influence was deferred by the economic crisis and the freeze in the development of civilian technology resulting from the war. In the fifties, however, circumstances favoured their dissemination. The ideology of progress stimulated technological innovation, and its application to a vast array of consumer products.

Technological innovation

When the Second World War began military technology was still shaped by the lessons of the First World War. Planes and tanks were used, as were 75 mm cannons drawn by horses. It was brought to a close, however, by the nuclear apocalypse of Hiroshima. Most of the advanced technologies that were to transform our daily lives in the sixties – including television, transistors, automation, nuclear power, and new plastic materials – first became available in the fifties. The period saw the conquest of

the world by the United States and, from a technological perspective, this was essentially the American decade.

In his important book *Technologie ou l'Enjeu du siècle* (*Technology, or What Is at Stake in Our Century*), published in 1954, Jacques Ellul argued convincingly that technical capacity is not simply a means to an end like any other. On the contrary, it affects all areas of human activity, making possible their complete integration. He explained how technology had become autonomous and that through it, 'a unitary, totalizing world is constituting itself. Any attempts to check this evolution will prove vain, as will efforts to master and direct it'.

It was also in 1954 that Martin Heidegger published his famous lecture *The Essence of Technology*. The importance of both these works is now generally acknowledged, but when they first appeared their influence was restricted to a small circle of specialists. This is symptomatic of the fifties when there was a considerable discrepancy between the enormous importance of technology and its insignificant role in contemporary ideological debates. The adaptation of military technologies to meet civilian needs was a preoccupation of the period. With the appearance of the jet engine, medium and long distance commercial aviation became a reality. The Boeing 707 and the Caravelle made their first flights in 1953 and 1955. Marcel Dassault's Mirage quickly conquered the market, and in 1958 the atomic reactor in Marcoule went into operation.

The invention of the transistor in the United States by John Bardeen, Walter

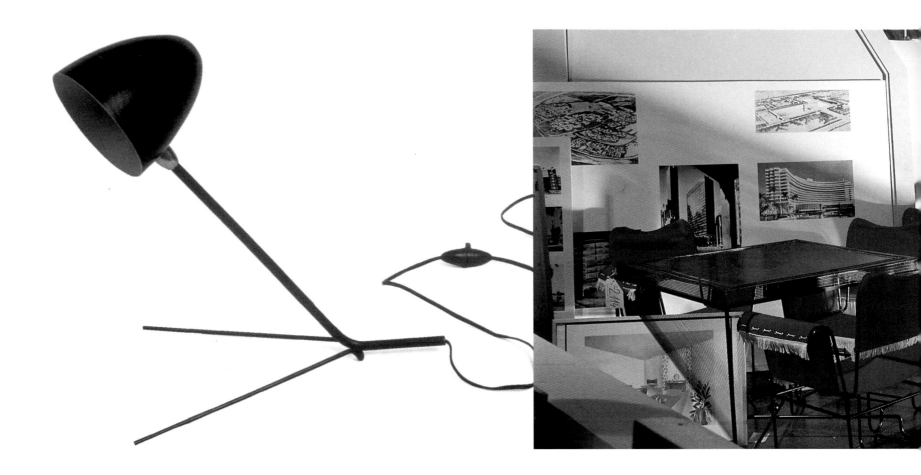

brattain, and William Schockley, in 1948, inaugurated the era of telecommunications, computers, and the media. The transistor allowed, among other things, for the miniaturization and cheaper manufacture of radio receivers, a crucial factor in the development of pop music in the United States. Between 1952 and 1962, the annual production of radios increased from 26 to 59 million.

The rapid establishment of television had an enormous impact on both individual and collective mentalities in the industrialized world. Here again, the United States led the way, as national statistics clearly indicate. Between 1947 and 1961 the total number of television sets increased from 30 thousand to 34 million. In 1959, there were 300 sets for every 1,000 inhabitants, whereas in France there were only 45. And the American pre-eminence in the field of television was not solely quantitative, it was also manifest in the quality of the programmes. Their undeniable showbiz know-how was

used with great intelligence to develop programmes which covered the full spectrum of the nation's mass culture – American television was the product of great self-confidence arising from recent victory in the war, something Europe would not have been able to achieve without American help.

Plastic materials were so widely used that the fifties have been called the 'age of plastics'. Polyvinyl chloride (PVC) was one of the most widely used, its suppleness lending itself to the creation of artifical leathers and polysterene, thanks to which most household objects could be given any shape desired. This new ease in moulding, coupled with a masterly use of bright colours, gave free rein to every fantasy and stylistic impulse. It was a derivative of PVC that made it possible, from 1950, to manufacture records in large quantities, another key factor in the development of popular music.

The introduction of antibiotics, which have since become medical mainstays, allowed for effective treatment of infections; the

'brilliant white' of household linen, a symbol of cleanliness, gave way to brilliantly-hued towels and sponges, which rendered beachside holidays even more joyous and exotic. In Europe, which in this respect was 20 years behind the United States, the fifties also saw the introduction of domestic electric appliances.

New youth, new culture

A study published in 1959 by the English sociologist Mark Abrams, *The Teenage Consumer*, revealed that 90 per cent of the money spent by English youths between the ages of 13 and 25 came from the pockets of working-class teenagers. These four million youngsters found themselves in an economic environment in which unemployment was non-existent and they were to play an important role in the development of a new mass culture. This culture had a different aesthetic, one which offered escape from depressing childhood circumstances and the chance to create a specific identity.

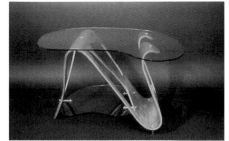

For these youngsters the cultural stereotypes underlying middle-class aspirations were part of a tradition that was completely foreign and, in any case, inaccessible to them. Contemporary design such as that presented and encouraged by the Council of Industrial Design in London was pitched to appeal to the established taste of the middle class, lower as well as upper. Essentially representing a homogenized, more 'comfortable' variation on modernist themes, it was manifestly out of sync with the aspirations of this social class which was still in the process of formation.

This new youth was determined to signal its disassociation from the adult world as emphatically and provocatively as possible, as can be seen in the emblematic example of the Teddy boys. American mass culture provided the young with new icons. They listened to the music of Bill Haley and Buddy Holly on the juke box, and those that could afford to rode motorbikes. James Dean, Elvis Presley, and Marlon Brando, hero of

The Wild One, were their idols. One of their best-known hangouts was the bar on Old Compton Road called The Two I's. Later, in the sixties, Chelsea became the fashionable neighbourhood.

In 1956, Bill Haley's first tour and the showing of the movie *Rock Around the Clock* caused more sparks and moved the phenomenon into a new phase. The *Daily Mirror* organized car pools and chartered a special train to bring fans to Haley's first concert in Southampton. Allan Sillitoe's novel *Saturday Night and Sunday Morning,* which was made into a film, treated the contemporary evolution of English working class youth as an indicator of important changes in our way of life. Its main character, Arthur Seaton, is an angry young man with a bit of money, a television, and a few suits in his cupboard. His rebellion is cultural. With great intelligence, Sillitoe delineates the coexistence within his protagonist of a realism inherited from the preceding century and a modern day penchant for anarchism. The cultural revolution brought about by English youth in the fifties was to have a strong though delayed influence on the behaviour of young people in the rest of Europe.

The English critic Reyner Banham grasped from the beginning of the 1950s that American mass culture was providing the foundations for a new popular youth culture, and that the products of consumer society were becoming symbolically charged, functioning in much the same way as Hollywood films, science fiction novels, radio, television, and pop music. Banham's theory can be broken down into four main points. First, the neo-classic aesthetic is inappropriate for products designed for mass consumption; second, a product's styling should have a built-in obsolescence; third, the aesthetic of the consumer society should not depend upon an 'eternal', abstract notion of quality, but should rather exploit an iconography of easily read symbols; fourth, these symbols should be conspicuously featured and linked to the use and nature of the product.

Banham was one of the many founders of the Independent Group, which included artists such as Richard Hamilton, Eduardo Paolozzi, and the designer Theo Crosby. This group was a crucial stimulus to the emergence of English Pop Art and met regularly between 1953 and 1956 at the Institute for Contemporary Art in London.

The members of this small group shared an interest in the burgeoning consumer society. They were convinced that our perception of the world was being fundamentally transformed by the constant bombardment of signs and colour issuing from the mass media. In 1956, they organized a large exhibition called 'This Is Tomorrow' at London's Whitechapel Art Gallery which was conceived as a kind of panorama of the icons of mass culture: a Marilyn Monroe film poster, a giant beer bottle, and a decor used in publicity shots for the film *The Forbidden Planet* were displayed within a carnivalesque installation featuring trick perspectives, shifting floor levels, and black lighting. It

was for this exhibition that the painter Richard Hamilton produced the small collage (26 x 25 cm) with the tantalising title *Just What Is It That Makes Today's Home So Different, So Appealing?* The term Pop Art was coined to describe this work.

But what exactly is 'fifties style'? We might be able to obtain some elements of an answer to this question by paying a retrospective visit to the Brussels Universal Exposition of 1958. This optimistic, idealistic event, conceived like a Belgian comic strip, was intended to dress a global balance sheet preliminary to the construction of a more humane environment. The exhibition sought to demonstrate that an ideology of science and technology triumphant had replaced the more doubtful ones of the inter-war period; that the earth was marching towards a terrestrial paradise in which the imbalances generated by the Industrial Revolution would be counterbalanced by scientific breakthroughs; in short, that the scientists of the world were working in concert to prepare our future. Jean Cocteau wrote the scenario for, and narrated, a propaganda film vaunting the peaceable uses of nuclear energy, while the magazine *Science et Vie* held forth in favour of a progress without either end or inconvenience.

One visitor to the exhibition, Winston Spriet, wrote: 'The most complete example of fifties decoration at the fair is without doubt the American pavilion . . . where everything is laid-back: no machines, no statistics . . . just drugstores, hi-fis, soda fountains, ice cream, and ultra-modern design; everything there is soft and seductive. Toasters and colour television sets are on display. The visitor falls into a delicious consumerist trap. The main attraction is the circarama, on whose circular screen all of America is laid out before one's eyes'.[3]

Another visitor, Pierre Loze, reflected that 'this was perhaps one of the last great moments of optimism. The future was before us, imminent, proximate, holding out a marvellous prospect. A euphoric wind blew over the West newly recovered from the war, the ideology of progress was at its peak, a colonialism on the verge of collapse was living its last days, and everywhere there was a persistent faith in the future'.[4]

A Francophobic visitor described the French pavilion – 'A superb example of pretentious architecture, the pavilion by the architect Gillet, with the assistance of Jean Prouvé, was structurally extraordinary. Inside, the accumulation of exhibits made it resemble a Salon of Household Appliances. Solitary and majestic, the DS 19 soared above the mêlée on its pedestal. A piquant detail: from the top of the tower beside the building, every hour an electronic carillon played "Auprès de ma blonde".[5] *Science et Vie* wrote, 'French pavilion: $z = k \, x \, y \, sin. \, alpha$'.

The exhibition was criss-crossed by every conceivable mode of transportation: cable cars, buses, motorbikes, three-wheelers. The devastating impact of pollution had not yet been understood. A principal attraction was the famous Sputnik III, which exerted great fascination over visitors.

The decorators in charge of conveying this vast programme conceived for the purpose the 'atomic style' whose emblem was the Atomium, which still exists today. Visitors took it seriously, though today it strikes us as an awkward enlargement of a comic-book image. One observer remarked at the time that 'The Atomium is typically Belgian because it's completely round, brilliant, and clean, while the Eiffel Tower has an authentic Parisian awkwardness, like that of a long-legged coquette not overly scrupulous about cleanliness. At the top of the Atomium one eats; at the top of the Eiffel Tower one dreams.'

The Atomium was conceived by the architect André Polak and the engineer André Waterkeyn. 'Waterkeyn, with what must be described as great naivety', wrote Pierre Loze, 'settled upon a crystalline metal molecule whose configuration was cubic and centered, because mechanically this made for the most solid construction.' It functioned not only as a symbol of the new possibilities opened to man by science and

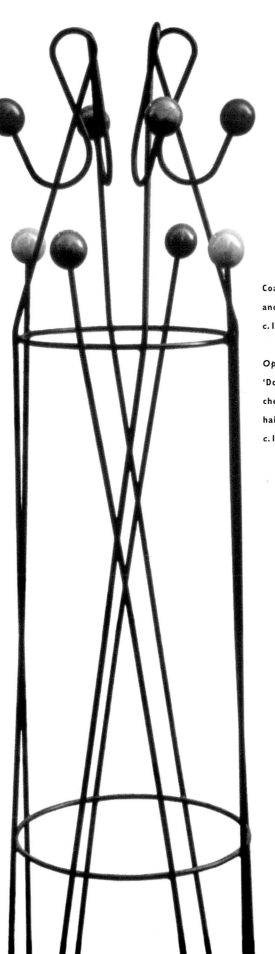

Coat stand, anonymous, c.1950.

Opposite: Calor 'Douche à cheveux' hairdrier, c.1950.

Left:
Cone chair,
designed by
Verner Panton,
1959. Nathalie
Seroussi
Collection.

Right:
Living-room
with abstract
decor, c.1950
(France).

technology, but also as a symbol of the metallurgical industries which fabricated it, and a symbol of Belgium, as the Atomium's nine spheres corresponded to the country's nine provinces.

The atomic style, which did not outlive the exhibition, eludes the categories of art and architecture. It is best to see it as a decor, a style based on a concoction of recipes and artifice, but none the less interesting for that. The light sculptures by Paz and Silva for the Claude corporation and the fresco by Jesús Rafael Soto were prefigurations of sixties Pop Art.

The Philips pavilion seemed perfectly at home in this array of exploding forms. Its designer, Le Corbusier, promised, 'I won't make you a pavilion with facades, but an electronic poem and a bottle to contain it. I won't have you create any new instruments of physics, but will organize a symphony using your own instruments.'⁶ In fact, Le

Corbusier produced a giant sculpture rather than a work of architecture, thus conforming totally to the rules and the prevailing spirit of the exhibition.

The atomic style, strikingly graphic and luminous, was the equivalent of a final burst of fireworks marking the closure of a celebration. A curiosity-seeker determinedly visiting every pavilion would have encountered all the most characteristic objects of the fifties. He would have come to understand that his difficulty in isolating a common denominator allowing for precise definition of the style resulted from its lacking a coherent formal vocabulary, from its resolutely heterogeneous character. Had it been otherwise, the concept of 'free forms' would not have existed. It would be impossible to find a language common to Carlo Molino, Charles Eames, Werner Panton, Serge Mouille, and Jean Royère, yet all of them were equally representative of their

era. What united them was a state of mind, a vitality, a certain *joie de vivre*. Much the same could be said of Harley Earl's Cadillac designs: they were shaped by a different culture, but they embodied a certain conception of happiness.

This state of affairs was too fragile and wasteful to last, however. In the United States a crisis was looming. In 1958, half as many cars would be sold as in 1955. When Harley Earl retired in 1959, his successor, Bill Mitchell, inaugurated a return to neo-classicism. The year 1959 also marked the recovery of the nations defeated in the war. The Japanese economy was being restructured. Germany, which produced 2.5 million Volkswagens in 1958, selling 100,000 of them in the United States, elected to embrace a no-nonsense, functionalist idiom to characterize its products. The Braun corporation spearheaded this reactive trend, placing its production design team under

the direction of Dieter Rams, a spiritual child of the Bauhaus. Thomas Maldonado, who succeeded Max Bill as head of the new German design school, the Hochschule für Gestaltung in Ulm, delivered a lecture at the Brussels exhibition in which he criticized American car styling. His critique of Reyner Banham's enthusiasm for American mass culture culminated in a whimsical joke: 'There's one decision that's irrevocable: Raymond Loewy must be consigned to hell for all eternity.'

This new brand of functionalism quickly drew radical critical fire in the form of a polemical text by the Viennese painter Friedrich Hundertwasser, a professor at the School of Applied Arts in Hamburg. In his *Mould Manifesto against Rationalism in Architecture*, published in 1958, he proclaimed: 'When rust appears on a razor blade, when a wall becomes mouldy, when moss grows in the corners of a room and rounds off its

corners, we should rejoice at seeing life introduce itself into the house along with microbes and mushrooms, and avow that we are witnessing architectural changes which we can learn a great deal from.' The same Hundertwasser invented, among other marvels, the rainbow ribbon for typewriters, which allowed us to give a more idiosyncratic look to commercial correspondence.

The electric guitar

The oldest surviving traditional guitar was made by the Portuguese Belchior Dias in 1581 (now in the collection of the Royal College of Music in London) and the form of the instrument has changed little since that time.

In 1935 Rickenbacker produced the first solid-bodied electric guitar in bakelite, but it was only after 1950 that different product lines were introduced and the object emerged as a prevailing symbol of pop music.

Adolph Rickenbacker, with the help of the engineers and technicians in his company, understood that the true electric guitar would be amplified solely by electromagnetic microphones. As a result, the sound-box of the traditional guitar would no longer be needed and could be replaced by a solid structure, variable in form.

As far as form is concerned, the passage from the acoustic to the electric guitar brought about a fundamental change of orientation. It signified the evolution from an instrument whose form derived from function to an object whose shape was determined exclusively by aesthetic considerations.

The electric guitar offers an exemplary illustration of the way microelectronics can transform an object to such an extent that it can assume a form which bears little relation to its original function.

In the sixties, pop music became a major social phenomenon, a passion for young people throughout the world. The electric guitar was developed because of the need for amplification: the instrument was capable of delivering sound to hundreds of thousands of spectators.

These concerts are spectacles and electric guitars have become important props. Their form can be adapted to suit the style of any group. Electric guitars are also prominent objects in televised performances, where they become prosthetic extensions of the bodies of the musicians.

J. d. N.

Background: Jimi Hendrix and his Fender Stratocaster guitar.

Top left: Black Hawk Stutz electric guitar designed by Seymour Powell, 1986.

Top right: Gibson ES 775 guitar.

The Vespa scooter

The Vespa was the first well designed product conceived for both utilitarian and leisure use to appear after the war in Italy. In 1945 Enrico Piaggio had to face up to the necessity of converting his military operations into civilian ones; thus when he summoned the aeronautics engineer Corradino d'Ascanio to his Pontedera factory, he asked him to explore the viability of producing a new type of two-wheeled vehicle that would be extremely simple and economical, both to manufacture and to use.

Piaggio began by studying a scooter, the Paperino, invented by a Pontadera technician who had himself been inspired by a vehicle designed by the engineer Belmondo and constructed in Turin in 1940.

The idea for the scooter was not a new one. A few such vehicles had been introduced in the years between the wars, rather unsuccessfully due to the marked contempt of traditional motorcyclists and the distrust of a public reluctant to accept such a small engine, with its absence of virile associations. Notable among the first scooters, were the French Velauto and the English Unibus (both 1920), as well as

a German model for Krupp and the English Autoglider (both 1929).

In 1956, on the occasion of Vespa's tenth anniversary, which coincided with its one millionth sale, Ascanio declared: 'I was familiar with the sporty, speedy external structure of the motor scooter, but as I was involved with aviation I had never considered the scooter from a construction point of view. In any case, I had observed many operational flaws in it, which were the reason for its lukewarm reception by consumers. . .Having freed myself from the technical tradition associated with the motorcycle, I was able to consider the problem afresh and shape this mode of transport according to my intuitions. . .It was necessary to make the vehicle more practical, and this meant finding a way of making it easy to mount, a problem that had already been solved for women's bicycles.'

This unisex aspect of the Vespa – the ease with which one could straddle it, the protection it provided against splashes from the front, and its ease of handling – made it ideal urban transport. Billy Wilder's Roman Holiday, (1953), contained the memorable

image of Audrey Hepburn and Gregory Peck riding through Rome on a Vespa. Another important feature of the Vespa was its appropriation of concepts first used in aeronautics and car construction. It had a forward single-tube fork, a wheel suspension which was borrowed from aviation, and its body of moulded and welded sheet iron was based on car manufacturing techniques.

The Vespa was a success in the sense that it anticipated an evolution in our mode of living, in particular the increasing emancipation of women.

In form, the Vespa was almost perfect at birth, which enabled it to evolve technically without there being any need to change its semantic value. It inspired confidence immediately, unlike the motorcycle with its more aggressive image. It was discreet and light, its seat was comfortable and the total enclosure of its engine made it reasonable for its drivers to wear normal street clothes.

More than seven million Vespas have been produced and today fashionable young women as well as delivery boys continue to ride them.

J. d. N.

125cc Vespa, 1951.

Christian Dior's New Look

Right from the outset of his career, Christian Dior occupied a place similar to that of Charles Worth during the Second Empire or Paul Poiret at the beginning of the century. After the Second World War, he launched the New Look fashion, which was immediately adopted by the women of café society, the forerunners of the jet set of the 1960s. Dior succeeded in capturing the spirit of the times in France. After the war, people discovered films like Gone with the Wind and Les Enfants du Paradis, which they had been prevented from seeing during the Occupation, and admired new actresses like Martine Carol and Audrey Hepburn. The weddings of Grace Kelly and Prince Rainier of Monaco, Elizabeth of England and the Duke of Edinburgh were shared with the rest of the world through the pages of Paris-Match and Life Magazine.

In his first collection in 1946, Dior's creations were imbued with a new spirit, completely different from that prevalent in fashion during the war years. 'We were emerging from a period of uniforms, of women soldiers with wide boxer's shoulders; I was designing women-flowers, with delicate shoulders, full busts, waists as fine as lianas and wide corollas. But we know that such fragile appearances are only had at the cost of rigorous construction.' Dior's account is a perfect description of the New Look: long, full skirts; the high-lighting of the bust through the use of the wasp-waisted corset. Among Dior's creations, the most famous is the 'Bar' model, whose skirt fabric was made up of a strip of material 14 metres long. The designer admitted to having used 200 metres of faille to make one particular afternoon dress. . .But the fullness of these dresses enabled the designer to develop, and from 1949, he started to create 'cocktail dresses', short and low-cut evening dresses, worn with taffeta capes and court shoes designed by Roger Vivier.

For an entire decade, women who could not afford the original dresses made copies from patterns printed in the recently created women's magazines, such as Elle, Marie-Claire, Vogue, Harper's Bazaar and Fashion Garden, for whom women represented a new consumer target. In 1948, Christian Dior opened an office in New York and created designs aimed specifically at American women. Hollywood used his new image of the woman in its best films. In 1950, the Dior fashion house accounted for 55 per cent of France's fashion exports.

Christian Dior died in 1957. After his death, Yves Saint Laurent, his young associate, ensured the continuity of design and production, and the following year presented a line called Trapeze, which was acclaimed in the international press.

E. M.

Right-hand page: Christian Dior adjusting a dress on a model.

Top, left to right: Diorama dress, autumn-winter 1947.

Zig-Zag range, drawing by Blossac, spring-summer 1949.

Dress, drawing by Blossac, autumn-winter 1949.

The Eames chair

Charles Eames was born in Saint Louis, Missouri in 1907. In 1936, after studying at the architecture school of Washington University, he enrolled at the Cranbrook Academy of Art where he met Eero Saarinen. In 1940, the pair entered a competition organized by the designer Eliot Noyes under the auspices of the Museum of Modern Art in New York. They took first prize in the category 'Organic Design in Home Furnishings' with chairs made of moulded plywood. In 1946 Eames was the first international designer to be honoured with a one-man show during his lifetime at the Museum of Modern Art.

Eames's furniture designs use plywood and steel spindles for the legs. The solidity of their seating elements, carefully adapted to the shape of the human body, contrasts strikingly with their slender flared supports. This preoccupation with the body found another outlet in 1942, when he designed splints for use by the US Navy. From his earliest experiments Eames entrusted his designs to Herman Miller, a manufacturer based in Michigan. A specialist in plastic moulds, it was he who attached the one-piece shells to their steel supports. The culmination of their collaboration in the manipulation of contemporary materials was the lounge chair and ottoman, made of metal, rosewood and leather.

The first of these chairs, made in 1956 for the film director Billy Wilder, instantly came to symbolize a new style of design. The comfort of the chair was unprecedented: the tilting back and headrest gave it an individual character perfectly suited to the expectations of the period. Its materials, at once noble and industrial, ensured it was at home in even the most high tech residences. Its single leg and its structure, which combined a moulded shell with padded upholstery, transformed the traditional image of the lounge chair. In 1958 Eames devised stackable chairs and a double seat using similar principles of construction. The latter design was commissioned for Dulles International Airport outside Washington, D.C., whose architect was none other than Saarinen, his friend of 20 years. Aided throughout his career by his wife Ray, his first collaborator, Charles Eames became the most famous designer of his generation and was often asked to lecture at universities, corporations and museums.

In the sixties, Eames progressively abandoned design in favour of film directing, making short films such as Powers of Ten, which was shot in the house he had built for himself in Santa Monica. After Eames's death in 1978, both this film and the house in which it was set became cult objects for young designers throughout the world.

E. M.

The shopping trolley

The history of the shopping trolley is linked to that of mass consumerism beginning, in Europe, just after the early years of post-war reconstruction. It wasn't until 1949 that ration tickets and restrictions became no more than a bad memory for an entire generation. The baby boom gave Europe a younger face. It found itself confronted with industrial growth and consumerism, progress and prosperity, population shifts and accelerated urban development. Whereas in the United States modern industrial production had been in full swing since the thirties, European industry had only just begun, in response to the war, to perform with maximum efficiency. Mass production became the dominant ideology and the Marshall Plan of 1947 was intended to catalyze this evolution towards consumerism. The 'old continent' was eager to master the principles of 'the American way of life'.

Europeans gradually adopted practices of distribution, commercialization and credit financing that had already been assimilated into American culture. The year 1949 was a milestone in France: Edouard Leclerc launched the first French supermarket and the wholesalers Duval and Lemonnier were introduced, at seminars in Baltimore, to the basics of large-scale distribution. They even decided to manage their stocks with new IBM computers. International seminars in modern sales techniques offered by the National Cash Register company in Dayton, Ohio, fostered the development of a common language appropriate to the new consumer society; for example: 'No parking, no business'; 'Display cases are the commercial equivalent of coffins'.

While there was an exodus from the French countryside, townspeople were discovering on the outskirts of their towns new urban complexes which often lacked any commercial infrastructure. Growing purchasing power, however, soon led to the establishment of American-style shopping centres — dubbed 'selling factories' and 'aircraft carriers' by the French. The first of these opened in a Parisian suburb in 1963, and since then every city has acquired its own supermarkets, the new temples of the consumer 'religion'.

The shopping trolley first appeared in the early fifties in the car parks of American supermarkets. A symbol of mass consumerism, it established a link between stores and vehicles. Rendered necessary by the new way of life, it in turn proved capable of modifying the form of the motor car: the boot of the R5 was specially designed for the Saturday ritual of supermarket shopping.

These trolleys, which have come to symbolize excessive consumption, have served as the basis for a line of improvised furniture. Often scattered about the no-man's-land between the supermarket and the block of flats, shopping trolleys have been taken apart and reconstructed in accordance with a Post-Modern aesthetic: seats with soldered or uncomfortable arms and chairs on wheels – the elements of an ephemeral furniture for a rebellious youth.

E. M.

Top left:
Supermarket
Lady, Duane
Hanson, 1970.

Top right:
Shopping
trollies designed
by the Burdick
Group for the
Esprit de Corps
shops, United
States, 1987.

The Barbie doll

Identity Profile

Name: Barbie
Date of birth: 9 March 1959
Profession: model
Marital status: single
Address: El Segundo,
Los Angeles, United States
Height: 11 inches
Hair: blonde
Eyes: blue
Astrological sign: Pisces
Distinguishing features:
a social phenomenon

Barbie, like the TV series Dallas, has become a significant phenomenon of mass culture, which can be defined as the distribution of products on a massive scale to a wide range of individuals considered regardless of their social class and profession.

More than 650 million Barbies have been sold throughout the world since 1959, which means we are dealing with a prime mass-consumption product. By 'consumption', we do not mean the passive assimilation of products, but rather the subtle, negotiated play between supply and demand which results in continual reinterpretations.

Barbie, the queen of 'Populux', is the perfect stereotype in that her importance stems not so much from what she is, but from what is added to her. In 1959 Barbie was born a celebrity. Standing eleven inches tall, she looked at America with her blue eyes, her platinum hair and her blinking eyelashes. All she lacked was a fuschia Cadillac. Her sex appeal shocked America, then Europe. But very quickly Barbie came to be accepted as a star, because she embodied the idealized media-driven stereotype of these cultures.

As the Mattel company unblushingly affirmed: 'In 1959 Barbie was created in the company's design and development department in Los Angeles.

Today this department includes some 200 designers, stylists, sculptors, engineers and psychologists charged with conceiving, designing and modelling Barbie dolls over a year-long period prior to their introduction on the market. It was they who made it possible for Barbie to become a dancer, a rock star, an aerobics teacher, a businesswoman, etc.'. This broad range of occupations allows little girls to project themselves into the future by means of Barbie and to identify themselves with jobs they would like to perform as adults.

The development of Barbie and her accessories was carefully plotted, like that of Dallas, in the course of countless meetings and creative sessions held with marketing specialists. Significantly, Mattel maintains close ties with companies (like Promostyle) who make it their business to anticipate stylistic trends, and so offer invaluable guidance to the creative and marketing teams. As with fashion generally, the jewelry and fabrics to be used in Barbie's clothing and accessories are selected by stylists.

A new Post-Modern Barbie remains to be invented, but is such a thing really conceivable? And would she still be an object of consumption?

J. d. N.

Modernity

and the Ulm School

Bernd Meurer

The Ulm Hochschule für Gestaltung in Germany, which was officially opened in 1955 and existed for 13 years, acquired its reputation thanks in particular to the success of its design work for the Braun company. In comparison with other institutions of its kind, the school's record appears meagre: it had a total of 640 students, of whom only 215 received the school's diploma.

The Ulm school's declared objective was the humanization of everyday life. Design was regarded as something that existed to further the process of civilization. No one, in spite of certain differences of opinion at the school, disagreed with this fundamental assumption. The school developed amid continual and at times fierce debates over the content and method of design practice as well as the structure of the institution itself. Thanks to the staff's capacity to continually call into question both their ideas and the school's existence, the Ulm school managed to resemble a forcefield for experimental and critical modernization. In short, the school saw itself as a kind of project, something which from the beginning made it a thorn in the flesh of the ministry of education and cultural affairs of Baden-Württemburg. There are two reasons why this essential aspect of the school has been obscured: the myth attached to its name; and the categorization of art history.

The Ulm school is commonly associated with a particular 'Ulm' style, a style which follows specific aesthetic guidelines. In fact, design at Ulm went beyond normative notions of form, attempting to respond directly to a particular problem or situation. Good examples of this, from the early fifties, are the school's washbasin installation, posters for the Ulm adult education centre, and the school buildings. These designs did not follow any canon of norms or forms. Rather they were the answers to concrete questions: what is needed? what is missing? The Ulm school was, however, influenced by Bauhaus ideas about form during its first years. Nothing could be more striking than

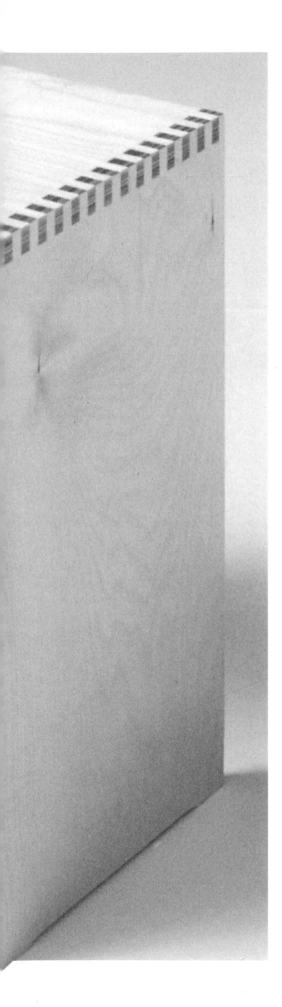

Today we demand utilitarian objects without adornments, not disguised as something else, free from masking, incrustations. They may nevertheless be noble and exquisite objects, highly valuable products; exquisite quality can be attained without senseless twisting and bending, impressed patterns and the like, which only infringe against the object's essential rights.

Hugo Häring, 'Formulations towards a reorientation in the applied arts', lecture, 1927

the contrast between the school's designs, on the one hand, and the conservative period furniture, American styling, kidney-shaped tables, and paper lampshades of the fifties, on the other. This is what gave rise to the belief that differences in design were merely a question of form. Unfortunately, this view was one that the Ulm school held to some extent. Yet, from the beginning, the channelling of aesthetic forms into design styles was considered a corruption of objective thought and planning.

Objectives of the Ulm school

Design at the Ulm school was guided by the following question: how can needs be shaped into form, and with what means, materials, techniques, procedures? The aim was to correlate the various social, technical, and aesthetic aspects of a given problem. Of major importance were the concern for social responsibility, the principle of doubt, the attempt to coordinate science and design, and, towards the end of the fifties, the concept and development of design as design of the environment. In accordance with the strong commitment to critical thinking, even rather far-fetched design ideas were seriously examined.

Art historians categorize the Ulm school as functionalist. Function was a central theme at Ulm: use function, information and communication function, social function, cultural function, technical function, and so on. Art historians, however, use the term functionalism to denote mutually exclusive principles of design: design that bases its formal laws on elementary geometry; design which regards function as the relationship between cause and effect; or, design that interprets function as the dynamic interdependence of facts and processes. Art historians place these three definitions in the same category. The first of these definitions was of no importance whatsoever at Ulm, the second remained in conflict with the third, which was the dominant interpretation of function in the school. The confusion over the concept of function

Ulm school stool, designed by Max Bill and Hans Gugelot, 1954.

Background: Project for urban lighting by Peter Hofmeister, Thomas Mentzel and Werner Zemp, under the direction of Walter Zeischegg, 1965-1966.

architecture as 'an emotional act of the artist' has no justification.

architecture as 'a continuation of the traditions of building' means being carried along by the history of architecture. this functional, biological interpretation of architecture as giving shape to the functions of life logically leads to pure construction: this world of constructive forms knows no native country.

it is the expression of an international attitude in architecture. internationalist is a privilege of the period.

pure construction is the basis and the characteristic of the new world of forms.

Hannes Meyer, 'Building', bauhaus, Year 2, No. 4, 1928

Ypso office furniture, designed by ninaber/peters/krouwel for Aspa, 1991. This functional design makes a prominent feature of the wiring necessitated by computer technology.

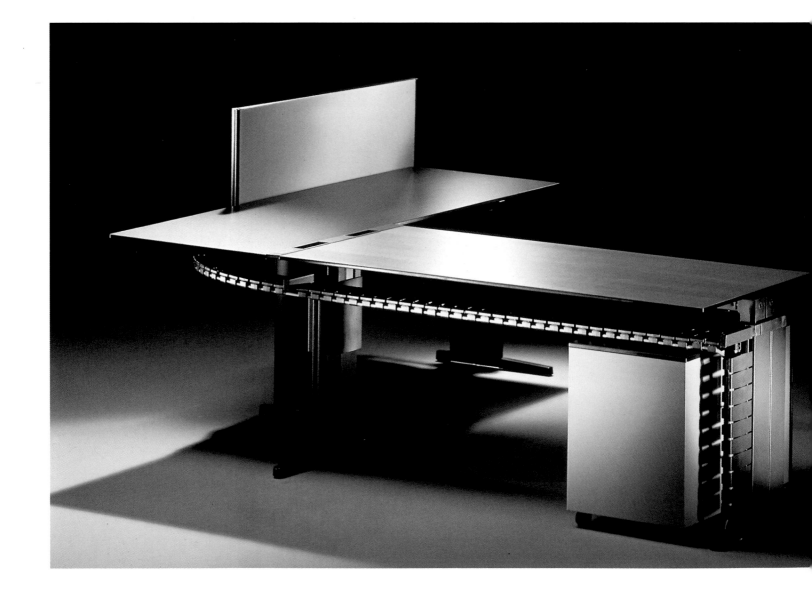

explains the idea that the school was strictly adhering in its designs to a particular formal canon.

The beginnings of the Ulm school took place under the sombre shadow of post-war Germany. Its principal instigators were Inge Scholl and Otl Aicher. They were looking to change the political and cultural attitudes, which were still perceptible in the post-war years, of a people who had supported or at least tolerated Nazism. Inge Scholl's brother and sister, Hans and Sophie Scholl, had been members of the famous anti-Nazi group White Rose, and were executed by the Nazis in 1943. During the initial planning stage, the school to be was named after them. Nazism had shown that civilization produces barbarism and this formed the background to the international centre that Inge Scholl, Otl Aicher, and Hans Werner Richter wanted to found. Their aim was to intervene critically as well as constructively in the process of civilization. The school was conceived as an alternative to the German universities which had reorganized after the end of Nazism with hardly any changes in personnel, claiming the humanist heritage of the 19th-century educated classes.

An early draft of the school programme reads as follows: 'The Scholl School... wants to form politically responsible students who can think for themselves. The school wants to help produce a democratic elite. As heir to the Scholls' resistance movement, it wants to support the politically progressive forces of this country. The school's international staff will promote cultural exchange with other peoples. As a school for the young it wants to help the new generation find the path of political activism. It wants to train its students in subjects that permit constructive contribution to the political process. The Scholl school aims at being a *universitas* well adapted to today's needs. Technical know-how, general knowledge, and social responsibility will be combined to create an integral unity. It wants to help bridge the

rift between intelligence and culture on the one hand, and everyday life on the other, by training students to be creative in practical matters of every-day life. It wants, above all, to influence the design of society's common goods... The school wants to remain independent. The school shall be ruled by democratic self-government.'[1]

The first discussions with Max Bill about the school's future programme took place in 1948. During the following years the idea of dividing the school into the following departments evolved: urban development, architecture, product design, visual communication, and radio and press. In 1950, Hans Werner Richter withdrew from the project. From 1951, the planned institution was called the Hochschule für Gestaltung, following the name used for the Dessau Bauhaus. The department of radio and press was renamed information studies. In the mid-fifties, urban planning and architecture were fused into a single department.

The Ulm school was established as a private institution in order to prevent any intervention from the ministry of education and cultural affairs of Baden-Württemburg and the school was funded by the Scholl Foundation, which was established in 1950. In 1953, the first courses were given in a few hastily found rooms. In the same year construction of the school buildings, designed by Max Bill, got under way. During this first period, the Bauhaus principle of applying forms from modern art to design was taken for granted. The founding director of the school, Max Bill, explained in 1952:

'The designer of new forms is influenced, be it consciously or unconsciously, by modern art as the purist expression of the spirit of the times. We consider art as the highest expression of life and we shall, consequently, aim to turn our lives into works of art. We want, not unlike Henry van de Velde, to combat the ugly with the help of the beautiful, the good, the practical. The Bauhaus, as heir to van de Velde's Weimar

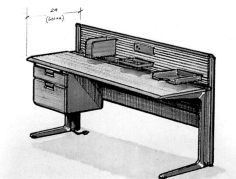

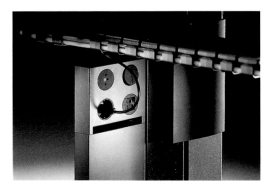

From left to right: Transrapid 06 monorail train, with linear motor and magnetic levitation, designed by Alexander Neumeister, 1985. Prototype built by Thyssen, photographed on an experimental track at Labhen, Germany.

Prototype of an electro-magnetic train, made by MBB Messerschmidt-Bölkow-Blohm SARL, designed by Alexander Neumeister, 1971-1972.

Television, designed by Bernd Meurer, 1985. Ventilation is provided for by the joints at the back of the set (see detail on the right-hand page).

Institute of Art, was pursuing the same aim. In response to the needs of our time, we must go further than our predecessors: we must attribute more importance to the design of objects, widen our notions of urban planning, update the department of visual design, and, last but not least, add the department of information studies.'2

The idea of combining art, design, and science seems to have been too ambitious a project. In the beginning, the following scientific subjects were being taught: sociology, economy, political science, psychology, philosophy and the history of

and technology, which later came to be known as the Ulm model, began taking shape. It was described by Tomás Maldonado as follows: 'Product designers will be operating at the neuralgic cross-points of our industrialized civilization. . . What will determine their success under these circumstances? To begin with, their inventiveness, of course; but more importantly, their more or less refined way of thinking in general and their working methods in particular; the extent of their scientific and technical knowledge; and, demanding great subtlety, their capacity to interpret

tecture was renamed the department of construction.

The experimental nature of design work at the school, combined with the science-oriented education, made it impossible to classify, within a common system of reference, the various professions for which students were being trained. What profession was one to take up after having studied in departments such as industrialized building, visual communication, or information studies? Yet schools are supposed to prepare their students for a future profession. Given the Ulm school's rather particular

consciousness. In addition, a research centre, a department of technology, as well as a department for social research and statistics were planned in order to help bridge the gap between scientific studies and experimental work.

The school was finally inaugurated in 1955. Its aim was not only to be an educational experiment but also a social experiment. In a remote place on the outskirts of the city of Ulm, teachers, students, employees and their families were all to live together on the campus. The school's international population was another striking feature of the experiment: about half the teaching staff as well as 40 per cent of the students were foreigners.

Between 1955 and 1956 the productive, pedagogical correlation of design, science,

the most hidden processes of our civilization.'3 The number of scientific subjects was increased substantially and theoretical courses made up half of all courses offered. What remained of the Bauhaus idea that design and the crafts were to form an integral whole was abandoned. Max Bill left the school in 1957 in response to the debates over these developments.

In the beginning, objects of rather limited complexity were designed at the school. This was to change in the mid-fifties and a major representative of this change was Konrad Wachsmann who joined the department of architecture in 1954, where he remained until 1957. Industrialization of architecture was to be the answer to the problem of industrialized life. Under Herbert Ohl the department of archi-

objectives the only solution was to invent hitherto unknown professions. Towards the end of the fifties, the designer was regarded as a co-ordinator, someone who could successfully work in collaboration with professionals from very diverse fields.4

Not only was the designer to be capable of co-ordination and integration, but the products as well were to be very flexible regarding their function and performance. The department of construction was looking for ways of replacing narrow-minded functionality by a user-friendly, constructive capacity to integrate and co-ordinate. The new system building design revised and made problematic the technological divisions of outside and inside, upstairs and downstairs, ceiling and

floor, wall, window, door, light, climate, and so on. The development of technological options was to free architecture from its academic constraints and grant total liberty to the consumer. Buildings were not considered as something finished, but as something variable.

The declared intention to correlate design and science brought about an ongoing controversy concerning the nature of science and design. The debate led to polarization, with methodological, practical, technocratic and ideological exaggerations. The ambitious idea suffered from a double problem. Firstly, science was only normally used as a secondary tool in design work, and secondly, vice versa, design was only attributed representational value in scientific analysis. The following declaration was drafted in order to lift the positivistic and deterministic veil shrouding this controversy:

'[The Ulm school] affirms that design is to play the role of a cultural imperative in today's society – but rejects the glorifying of design as messianic work. The school affirms the praxis of competition within a capitalist economy – but rejects the degradation of design for the sake of commercial success. The school affirms design as a tool of technical and scientific progress – but rejects design as a scientific and technical end in itself. The school affirms the importance of the artistic dimension in design work – but rejects design as art substitute. The school affirms that design may under certain circumstances be considered as a critique of consumer society – but rejects the idea that this society may be changed in whole by the alteration of its consumer goods. The school affirms the intervention of critical consciousness within the world of industrial commodities as well as within the universe of the communication industry – but maintains that these phenomena of our technical civilization should be approached with more than just a passive (and resigned) consciousness.'5

This period saw the design of products for private use, products for public use and the workplace, and products dealing with social problems.

In the mid-sixties, the discrepancy between affirmative and reflexive design became all too evident. Functionalism was called into question as a completely ambivalent term; in consequence, the idea that functionalism as such was a value in itself was completely abandoned: 'The term function has been misused to justify oppressive cultural mediocrity. . .The ambitious plans for industrial building came to nothing more than the clumsy and schematic use of the curtain wall, which, to make things worse, was used, with the help of advanced technology, in the construction of homes whose pathetic and empty architecture is unprecedented in the history of mankind. In the field of product design, the search for an immutable and comprehensive concept of function led to the exact contrary of what had been expected: to products whose formalism was as refined as it was sterile.'6

The 'doubt about whether the sum of well-designed objects may add up to a well-designed environment'7 transformed itself more and more into a feeling of certainty that the existing definition of design no longer sufficed when it came to confronting the problems of society and the environment. During the last phase of the school's existence the idea of seeing design as design of the environment and developing it into an interdisciplinary framework grew:

'A school for the design of the environment ought to be teaching all activities which endow our environ-ment with structure and form. The curriculum of the school that we envisage is not to consist of a conglomeration of independent disciplines divided up into separate compartments, but to be structured around themes that would be investigated within the various disciplines. To achieve this, it will require a great deal of courage to give up the widely held belief in the value of the departmentalism in which

we find ourselves hermetically enclosed, and, in particular, to do away with the traditional departments that are to be found now-adays in almost all design schools.'8 Just before the school closed, an experiment was begun to transform the course into a programme for the study of interdisciplinary projects. But the discussion about the content, method, and structure of studies at the school was overshadowed by the government's attack on the independence of the school. Thus, its final attempt to transform itself was cut short by the state-imposed closure of the school in 1968.

The aftermath

In the 25 years since the Ulm school was closed, the following themes have successively dominated debates on the rationality of design: the critique of product aesthetics, the critique of functionalism, the discourse on modernity, the question of ecology, and, last but not least, the whole range of problems stemming from the radical industrial, technical and socio-cultural changes brought about by the microchip.

In the sixties, criticism of the capitalist economy and the consumer society formed the main focus of debate about design.9 The critique of product aesthetics10 was formulated during the course of the 1968 student revolution and became, in the early seventies, an instrument of design analysis and a subject of critical reflection.11 The contradiction between use value and exchange value created a feeling of helplessness among teachers and students at the school; work even came to a complete standstill at times. Attempts, however, were also made to bring out the contradiction between use value and exchange value through the design work itself, instead of the usual covering up of any conflicts that might arise. Such design work extended from contributions to the transformation of the workplace to visual representations of rebellious social theorizing.

In the seventies two conflicting theories of design arose from this functionalist critique

Eclipse spotlight, designed by Mario Bellini for Erco Leuchten, 1986.

of the technocratic design, architecture, and urbanism which held people and the environment in contempt.

According to the first of these two theories the process of continual modernization was not to be understood as the linear development and progressive extrapolation of preceding achievements in modernization, but, instead, was to be itself the object of modernization. What in fact was being applied to design was the realization of the ambivalent nature of rationality and functionalism, triggered off by Theodor Adorno's decisive analysis of the latter in 1965.[12] Two important examples from this period were the architectural designs for the Munich Olympic games of 1972 and the Centre Pompidou built between 1971 and 1977. In both instances the problems and contradictions encountered during the design process had been incorporated into the final designs, which resisted the traditional demands of representation. In both cases the architectural idea that formally finished buildings were immovable, static real estate, untouchable property was refuted. Architecture had become process, transformation. The design for the Munich Olympic games achieved its aim by emphasizing the thematic structural principles involved, the one for the Pompidou Centre by drawing attention to the user-oriented structural possibilities.

The second of these theories criticizing functionalism opposed the notion of modernity altogether and, bidding the past farewell, proclaimed the era of Post-Modernism. The resulting movement, still alive today, aestheticized the environment as it was instead of continuing 'the incomplete project of modernism'[13] to resolve the ecological, technological, and socio-cultural contradictions manifest in the design process.

Influenced on the one hand by the humanities, and on the other the natural sciences, and in particular applied physics, functionalist ideology found itself caught in a double bind between two opposed ways of think-

ing. In architecture and design deterministic and complex, causal and reflexive modes of thinking were found to be inextricably intertwined. Newtonian physics had seemed for a long time completely satisfactory in the solving of design problems, especially since the deterministic clarity of Newtonian physics appeared to correspond perfectly with modern notions of beauty While architecture and design were posing socio-cultural questions appropriated from social theory that had all along been calling into question the validity of a total determinism applied to the world, Newtonian theory remained attractive in the technical areas of design, where all questions, it seemed, could be answered in terms of the fundamental law of cause and effect. For those rare cases where Newtonian physics did not seem applicable, Pascal had invented the probability calculus that was, in the course of the 1950s, happily incorporated into the methodology of architecture and design.[14] Yet, since the middle of the 19th century, science had started to go far beyond Newton and Pascal: the law of thermodynamics, the theory of relativity, and quantum mechanics had completely done away with the concept of determinism in physics. The full extent of those scientific revolutions was, however, not realized for a long time. Only during the past two decades has it become more normal to conceive the world not as a state of things, but as a coming into being which demands complex, multi-disciplinary thought processes and co-operative activity.

Environmental issues

In the seventies, the public at large was becoming more and more aware of ecological issues. Environmentally influenced re-evaluations, which played an increasingly central role in design thinking, were made of forms of mass transportation, the transformation of the workplace, innovations in communications technology and the organization of information. In 1971 Alexander Neumeister developed an environment-

friendly magnetic railway. In 1979 Frei Otto, in collaboration with other institutes, designed the Airfish. This 'flying tyre', over 200 m long, was meant to replace the outdated modes of freight and passenger transportation. The flexible, lighter-than-air, pneumatic craft has an almost unlimited flying range and can operate on the shortest runways, offering a highly economical as well as ecological alternative to aeroplanes. The Raisting radio station, which took 12 years to build from 1969 to 1981, exposed the contradiction between countryside and communications technology. The visually synchronous representation of the diachronic process of production from 1981 made transparent socio-political facts that would have gone unnoticed in the usual deluge of information. In 1978-1979 Richard Rogers designed the Third Generation Office for Knoll International, which consisted of an ensemble of integrated working terminals that could be regulated and modulated independently of each other by the office workers themselves according to their own individual needs. Thus, the traditional functions of table, chair, and shelves, as well as air conditioning, light regulation, noise reduction, visual protection, media and communication systems, all came under the personal control of the workers. The extremely complex working terminal, electronically interconnected with the building's infrastructure, gave the workers total control over their working environment. The television telescope, designed in 1985, openly revealed its internal functions to the interested consumer. These examples show that reflexive design recognizes the differences between the technical and visual aspects of objects, which it develops in conjunction with each other as well as in consideration of the external factors involved.

In the mid-eighties it became strikingly clear that it was no longer possible to respond to the ever new challenges of constantly changing technologies with the usual means, no matter how often those had

Adjustable spotlight, designed by Knud Holscher for Erco Leuchten, 1990. With the aid of the sextant, the light beam can be adjusted to the required angle.

been revised and refined. Not only the whole industrial infrastructure – products, means of production, communication structures and environmental conditions – but also the entire social fabric had undergone fundamental change. Industrial economy and industrial society, which since the Industrial Revolution had made up two sides of one and the same coin, were no longer developing side by side: while industry was growing more and more complex, the social system was, at the same time, progressively dissolving. The socio-economically defined character of what work was supposed to be had been radically altered. Social identities as well as the social ties binding those identities together had both waned. New forms of life emerged. In addition, the situation in eastern Europe had radically changed, forcing western Europe to reconsider most of its cherished ideas as well. The context in which design operated was no longer the same. This situation provoked opposing reactions: those hostile towards modernity reacted by cooking up the usual recipe of aesthetic transformation. When launching new products on the market, innovations took the form of new surface design, rather than radical inner structure. The representatives of this approach spoke of both a crisis of modernity and of rationality. But design had suffered not from too much rationality, but from too little rationality – from a naïve, intuitive, irrational definition of rationality, not from self-critical, reflexive reasoning.

There are two radically different approaches to design: affirmative design considers change an end in itself; reflexive design calls itself, its very own foundations, into question. Its central question is how to identify and discuss what the significant problems of the world are – independently of any established rules or classifications. The domain of reflexive design is both the physical and the social environment, and in particular, the forms and means of communication affecting the latter. It is born of critical analysis

and analysis is its mode of being. The tram design by Wolfgang Hasenauer from 1988 tackled the question of how to reduce travel time and at the same time increase passenger comfort. The single most important factor in cutting travel time is to minimize the amount of time passengers spend getting on and off the tram. Hasenauer's solution envisaged wheel-less passenger cars suspended from tower-like structures, interconnected by passageways housing the technical units. This design made it possible to lower the passenger platform almost to street level, something which would not only speed up the process of boarding, but also facilitate access for wheelchairs and pushchairs. In addition, the passenger car would be completely isolated from all sources of noise and vibration.

The narrow-minded fragmentation of design into architecture, industrial products and communication systems is totally obsolete. The terminal designed for Stansted airport by Norman Foster dissolves all traditional boundaries between architectural and technological infrastructures. Architecture becomes communication; appliances design space. The roof, supported by towering, tree-like pillars, embraces the whole network of air conditioning systems, lighting installations, indicator boards, monitors, signposts, fire-fighting equipment and other machinery. Daylight and artificial light interact. Space is defined in terms of light.

We experience the environment for real when using it. Objects for use are not something finished. They should rather be seen as fragments of a process in continual need of revision, which contradicts the usual notion of use in architecture and design. The economically miniaturized notion of use as well as the corrupt concept of user-friendly design liberate the consumer from thinking and acting. The passive user of functioning objects seems outdated: use has to be rethought as creative use, reflexive use, self-realizing use.

'Design implies that function should be the first priority. The form of Braun products should be modern and elegant, but simple. Their colour should be essentially neutral. The beauty of a Braun product should result from the perfect adaptation of form to use.'

This text appears in helvetica font, without signature or commentary, on the otherwise blank cover page of the Braun catalogue. Hans Gugelot, professor of industrial design at the Hochschule für Gestaltung in Ulm, was the first designer to work for Braun in the 1950s and the text exemplifies perfectly the rationalist, functionalist programme that served as a foundation for the teachings of the Ulm school. The Braun brothers were sufficiently astute not only to place their full confidence in designers such as Hans Gugelot and Fritz Eichler, and later Dieter Rams, but also to use their enterprise to foster the development of an overall design strategy. This strategy had two objectives:

– To design products that functioned well and expressed the idea of an advanced technology completely under control. In pursuit of this goal, Braun designs had to satisfy three criteria: order, harmony, and economy. Principles such as these encouraged the development of new aesthetic values basically consistent with the rationalist aesthetic of the Bauhaus, which stressed formal purity, the use of elementary geometric shapes, and truth to materials. 'The user of this product is a person of quality': such was the message that should be conveyed.

– To establish clear formal links between Braun's various products. The objects were to become elements of a cultural identity, in which the potential purchaser was to be encouraged to invest.

From 1960, Braun had a bombshell effect on the market for home appliances and almost all manufacturers in this sector (with the exception of Bang & Olufsen and Brion Vega) copied the Braun model, down to its products' smallest details. Even today the front of Japanese microwave ovens offers an almost perfect imitation of Braun graphics circa 1960. It is no exaggeration to say that home appliances have adopted the Braun image, which has now become a banal international stereotype.

Ever since it was established in the mid-fifties, the directors of Braun have stuck rigidly to the company's design policy. Braun, however, has recently been absorbed by the Gillette group, and it will be interesting to see whether an attempt will now be made to adapt the product line to current market trends.

J. d. N.

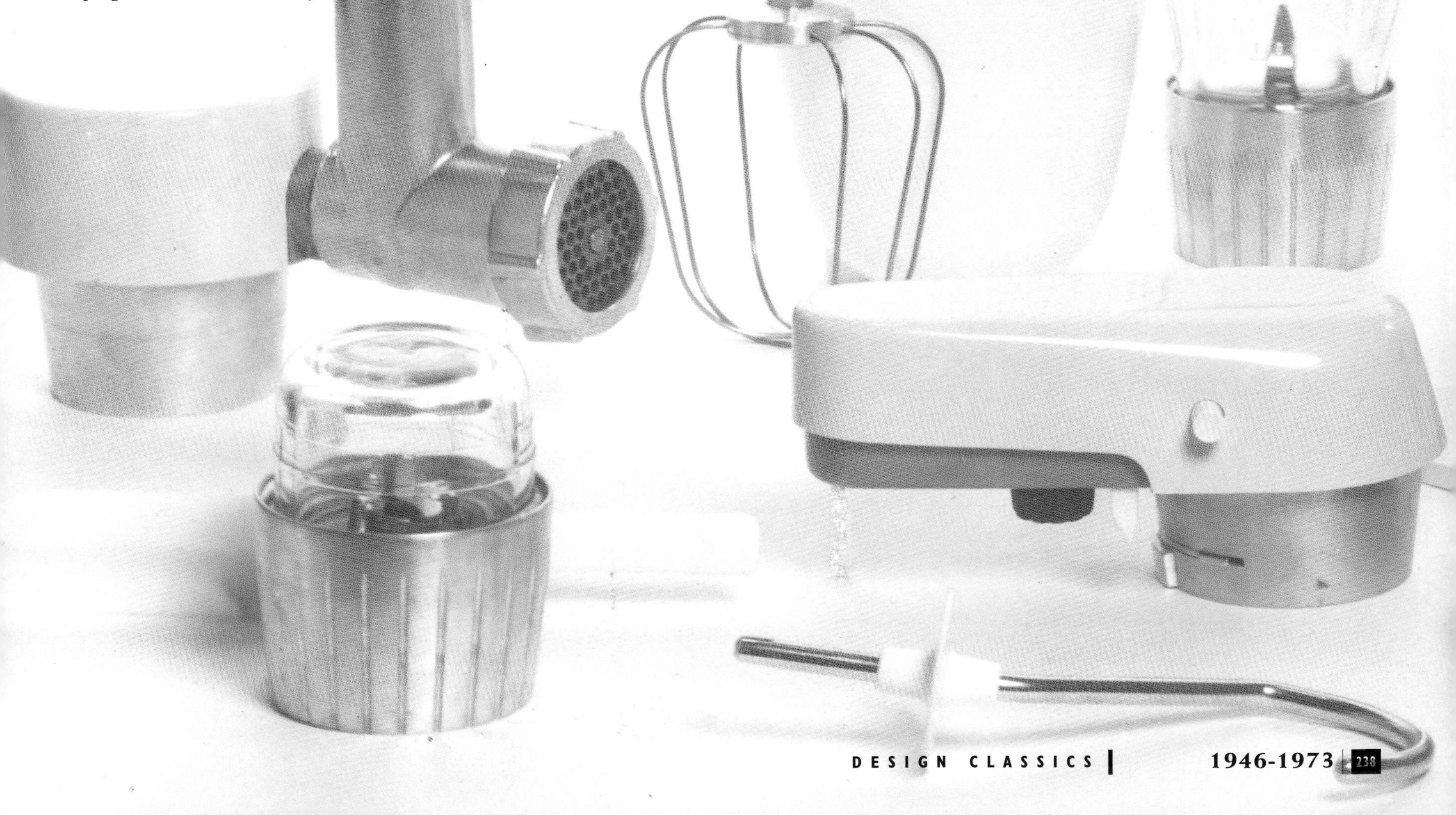

You will only apprehend the form and construction of objects in the sense of their strictest elementary logic and according to their raison d'être. These forms and constructions will accord with, and be subject to, the needs of the material used. And if you should be seized with the desire to embellish these forms and constructions, you will not give in to this need for refinement towards which you are pushed by your aesthetic sensibility or your taste for ornamentation - whatever it may be - except where you will be able to respect and conserve their logic and essential appearance.

Henry van de Velde, Kunstgewerblichen Laienpredigten, *1903*

KM 31 multi-function food processor, 1951

No. 775,134.

PATENTED NOV. 15, 1904.

K. C. GILLETTE.
RAZOR.
APPLICATION FILED DEC. 3, 1901.

NO MODEL

The razor

Background: Patent for the Gillette razor.

Vignettes, from left to right: Braun's Sixtant 6006 electric razor, designed by Richard Fischer, 1970.

Braun's Flex Control Universal electric razor, designed by Roland Ullmann, 1991.

King Kamp Gillette.

First a shell or a shark's tooth was used and later a bronze blade: the evolution of the razor has followed that of man's technological development. At the end of the 18th century, steel razors were manufactured in Sheffield, England. The design permitted the blade to be withdrawn into the handle after use. It was mostly used by professional barbers, since at that time most homes lacked the appropriate facilities (the profession disappeared with the rise of the modern bathroom).

It wasn't until 1895 that the American King Kamp Gillette patented the safety razor – a mechanical model with interchangeable, double-edged blades. In 1901, in Boston, Gillette founded the Gillette Safety Company, which soon became famous throughout the world.

The electric razor was also an American invention. Jacob Schick patented and marketed his first device in 1928. The evolution of the razor followed the evolution of American society: the modern man was a man in a hurry and the electric razor made it possible to dispense with shaving cream, following the trend for the mechanization of everyday objects.

In Europe, Braun and Philips had designed prototypes by the late thirties, but it wasn't until after the end of the Second World War that their first electric razors went on sale. In 1951, Max Braun created in his Frankfurt factory the prototype of the Braun S50, which is still regarded as a seminal design by specialists. Its robust, tapering shape, as well as its rechargeable oscillating motor, made it a model for the genre. At about the same time Philips launched the electric razor with two pivoting heads and Alan Irvine designed the Super 60, with a body made from two pieces of moulded plastic, for Remington. Since then there has been little significant progress in the design of electric razors.

As for the mechanical razor, it took a radical step forward in 1975, when baron Bich succeeded in making a complete razor for the price of a single blade. Baron Bich observed that half a blade would do the job just as well and with the money saved he was able to manufacture a plastic handle for it. Gillette, whose products are nowadays used by a billion customers, invented the first razor with a pivoting head in 1972, the first with a lubricating blade (Contour Plus) in 1986, and the first with blades which respond to every curve of the chin (Gillette Sensor) in 1990.

Currently, mechanical and electric razors share the market about equally, a market increasingly inundated with products linked to the new masculine image being peddled by marketing. Male consumers long resisted the lure of such marketing, but there are now no consumer taboos (these products are no longer seen as compromising men's virility), and they are now prime targets in campaigns for beauty products, shaving creams, after-shaves and lotions.

E. M.

Lego

In 1932, the Dane Ole Kirk Christiansen abandoned his profession as a carpenter to devote himself to the making of toys. He founded his own business in his native town of Billund, working with his son Godtfred.

The introduction of plastic at Billund marked the beginning, in 1947, of a real fairy tale, with the purchase of the first machinery and tooling required to start manufacturing products. Without abandoning the manufacture of wooden toys, Lego became the first Danish factory to enter the age of plastics.

The name Lego derives from the Danish phrase leg godt, which means 'play well'. In 1949, a plastic tractor, designed so that children could take it apart and put it back together, prefigured the products to come, and the Lego bricks were launched. 'Plastic will never take the place of true quality toys in wood,' an author wrote in the trade magazine Le Journal du jouet after a visit to the Lego factory.

Lego is an educational construction toy consisting of different coloured plastic bricks that can be joined together thanks to small round tenons. There are two kinds of brick, one with four tenons and the other with eight, together with a flat piece which serves as a base or foundation. Although the number of elements in Lego is small, they allow for the construction of a wide range of models and offer unlimited possibilities for play in every season, for boys and girls of all ages.

Lego embodies, in toy form, the various building techniques and skills which were in such heavy demand in the postwar period of reconstruction. When the child plays with these little bricks, he can take part in the recomposition of the world and so identify with adults. The multiplicity of possible forms and colour combinations stimulates the imagination, the manipulation of the pieces improves dexterity, and the possibility of reproducing objects helps children to understand the world around them.

There are basically two different kinds of Lego: creative ones (the basic set), which have a universal character; and thematic sets, which, in addition to the basic bricks, contain functional pieces linked to themes such as the car, the house or the train. Different sets have been introduced over the last 40 years, some reflecting trends of the day, some relating to other toys, but the basic form of Lego has remained unchanged. Today, the Lego group is one of the world's top ten toy manufacturers.

E. M.

Industrial design is neither an art nor a mode of expression, but rather a methodical creative procedure that can be applied to all problems of conception.

Roger Tallon, 1961

....

The Téléavia television

Right-hand page: Madame Bridoux, first television announcer in France on 180-line television, c.1934.

'Téléavia, aesthetics count as well.' This advertising slogan gave a new image to everyday objects at the beginning of the sixties, when consumerism was hitting its stride. Up until then, television sets had been assessed purely in terms of their technical performance. In France, the proliferation of the television set owed much to the industrial designer Roger Tallon, who was the first to study questions of styling.

Roger Tallon has described the reasons for the success of the set: 'We wanted to make a strong impression. As most sets in this period were square-shaped, it was necessary to find a formula for making them as compact as possible, and the sphere was the obvious shape because of the tube itself and the internal structure. But I thought that portable sets could be seen from any angle, and everything was treated in the same way throughout. This was the first set that didn't have that dead eye when it was turned off. The knobs were protected, everything was integrated. The general shape was very popular, I think because the fluid forms it inspired had not yet really been widely developed. And I also think it marked the acceptance of plastic on a new, higher level. The form/colour relationship was stressed, thus the basic elements of function, form and material were completely merged.'

The television set was a success from the moment it was launched in 1963. This was largely due to new methods of distribution introduced by the Fnac, which sought out products suitable for a clientele of young executives with disposable income, for whom the design was as important as the technical side. The Téléavia is an example of a product perfectly adapted to a new, image-oriented market. It was at this time that the mass production of televisions started in Europe. Thanks to its design and to successful marketing, it became a model whose commercial lifespan considerably exceeded the expectations of its distributors. Fifteen years later, the set was still being manufactured and sold, while most plastic objects of similar vintage had become obsolete.

And yet Roger Tallon confided to a French journalist: 'When objects like the Téléavia and so many other products become symbols, I don't think they can be regarded as successful. The designer is caught in a trap. They say, "Well done, at last we have a beautiful television!", but my only concern was to integrate the tube. For me, the demonstration was a failure.'

E. M.

The miniskirt

In the sixties, the baby boom generation reached adulthood. Young people, eager to live, became emancipated at a time when economic growth authorized optimism in all its guises. They rejected the established structures of the world in which they lived. The new society brought change and fashion became a significant force.

The interplay between designers and consumers began to work for the first time to the benefit of the customers. Popular culture was in perfect harmony with the dominating tendencies of intellectual and artistic life. More importantly, it dictated the course of fashion. The change in morals gave birth to a new concept of clothing: ready-to-wear. The miniskirt, which made its appearance at the beginning of the sixties, is undeniably the physical manifestation of a radical change, a sign of provocation and sexual freedom. Young British girls did not want to look like their mothers or conform to any model and opted for clothing which made no reference to the past. In response to 'street style' which started to influence fashion, the designer Jacques Delahaye launched an idea for a miniskirt in 1963, but he was too early and his innovation was totally unsuccessful. When the British

designers Mary Quant and Joan Huir proposed their models one year later, they were immediately taken up.

André Courrèges, after having worked for a few years at Balenciaga, opened his own fashion house in 1963. Aware of the new trends, he used them in a precise way, in which nothing was left to chance. In Great Britain, the miniskirt was only a shortened dress, but Courrèges created a separate piece of clothing. In 1965, he presented a collection which represented a complete break from the past. The fashion show was flashy and futuristic; miniskirts and minidresses were worn with white leather boots; the models had their hair in bunches or pony tails and sported fake eyelashes and freckles. This was the reign of the woman-child, incarnated by the star model Twiggy.

The miniskirts in Courrèges' show came as such a surprise to journalists that they devoted all of their attention to them to the detriment of the rest of the collection. They failed to draw attention to the fact that his designs for evening wear ('bell-bottom' jumpsuits, embroidered celluloid flowers, red or black vinyl dresses, strips of shiny mica, metallic jersey) were equally novel.

E. M.

**Background:
André Courrèges
Collection,
summer 1965.**

**Above: Drawing
by Mary Quant.**

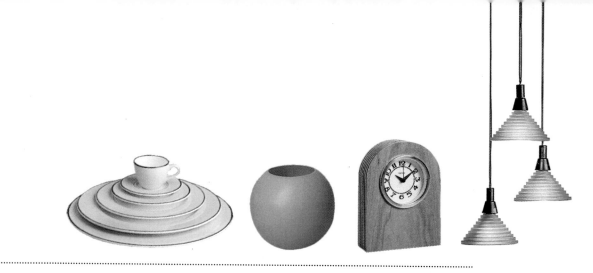

Habitat

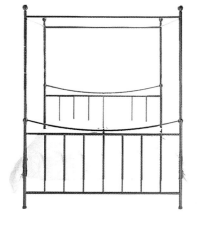

In London, the sixties, a time of opulence, pulsating to the beat of pop music, gave way to a period in which creativity and productivity slowed. The stances taken first by the hippies and later by the punks went against the current of consumerism. It was in this context that the second post-war generation reached adulthood, aspiring to furniture with a clean-lined look that they could identify with.

Terence Conran, born in 1931, responded by offering them a new look for the interior. After having opened a café called The Soup Kitchen in 1955 and then designing The Bazaar Boutique for his friend the fashion designer Mary Quant, he drew inspiration from his 1956 travels through France to create kitchens which he introduced in his first Habitat shop, opened in 1964.

The Conran business expanded greatly in the seventies with the successive opening of twelve shops throughout the world, including one in Paris and one in New York. The Habitat image, disseminated through glossy mail-order catalogues, targeted young, relatively high income couples anxious to enrol in the new society. A journalist, writing in Design magazine, described how their ideal was to enter a shop on a Saturday afternoon, choose a chair kit and walk out with it in a box immediately afterwards so that they could assemble it at home and sit in it to watch television that same night. Habitat offered quality products at competitive prices that could be delivered quickly or carried home in flat cartons.

While they recognized themselves in the Habitat style, the young shoppers also had the option of purchasing objects in limited editions, as well as re-editions skilfully selected by Conran from the great names in 20th-century design. The spectacular success of Habitat al-lowed its founder to open the Design Museum, the first in the world.

But Habitat started to run into difficulties in 1986. With the recession deepening, it became necessary to close 20 of the 76 shops. Habitat was also faced with competition from Ikea who, by selling furniture at discount prices, targeted a younger, less prosperous clientele. Since Ingvar Kamprad opened the first shop in Sweden in 1958, Ikea has come a long way. Today there are 118 world-wide and in October 1992 this other inventor of take-away furniture bought Habitat's European network from the British company Storehouse.

Frequently copied, the concept behind Habitat has become commonplace and the young people of the 1990s have abandoned the standard. Who will invent the new type of shop with which they can identify now?

E. M.

Products from the 1992-1993 Habitat catalogue.

1974-1993

by

Jocelyn de Noblet

'There is no model for he who is looking for what he has never seen.'

Paul Éluard, *Donner à voir*, 1939

The crisis for modernity reached its height when the experts proved incapable of finding satisfactory solutions to the problems thrown up by the oil crisis of 1973. Today, contemporary material culture no longer stems from a commonly held vision of society, as was the case in the past. The resulting vacuum of meaning can only be filled by the fragmentation of the systems of cultural representation.

Three basic factors, whose practical and theoretical influence has been decisive, have shaped the course of design in recent years.

The acceptance of the concept of complexity has led us to question the limits of reality and to redefine the role of design in an uncertain world. There is a feeling of absurdity and powerlessness, illustrated by the 'punk' style of a designer like Ron Arad, or by the work of the German group Pentagon. It is now acknowledged that it is impossible to design a tech-nical product without taking into account the context in which it will function. The difficulty of reconciling our on-going fascination with the motor car with the problems of pollution and traffic is a case in point.

The growing importance of electronics signals the decline of a period during which the preponderance of mechanical parts was the main ethical and aesthetic justification for the functionalism of the Modern Movement. Electronic components, which form the basis of all communications appliances, are the reason for the gradual disappearance of the functional aesthetic based on volumes. This new phenomenon takes the form of an aesthetic of platitudes. Furthermore, the interconnection of numerous modules – another characteristic of electronic appliances – results in a deconstruction of form, creating another new aesthetic and affecting various areas of design, including architecture and interior design.

The era of Post-Modernism has brought many contradictions to our daily lives. These contradictions, which designers like Ettore Sottsass and Andrea Branzi were quick to grasp, have led to the appearance of movements such as the Memphis group.

The invasion of our television screens by advertising and the constant demand for new images has yielded the most unexpected 'collages': the pleasure of looking at all sorts of unbridled forms, freed from direct reference to the message or to the meaning they are supposed to communicate, has given new inspiration to creators.

Post-Modernism is a symptom both of a transitional period and the fragmentation of the major categories of the past.

Manipulation by remote control in a nuclear power station, The Hague, 1991.
Preceding double page: Cockpit of the Airbus A340, designed by Plan Créatif, based on an ergonomic specification by Aérospatiale.

1974

□ Roland Moreno invents the smart card for storing and processing computer data

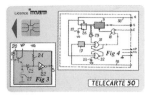

□ Joseph Beuys: *I Love America and America Loves Me*
□ Heinrich Böll: *The Lost Honour of Katharina Blum*
□ Solzhenitsyn is stripped of Soviet citizenship and expelled
□ triumphant reception for Yasser Arafat at the UN
□ end of dictatorship in Portugal
□ Richard Nixon resigns after the Watergate affair

1975

□ **Bic disposable razor**

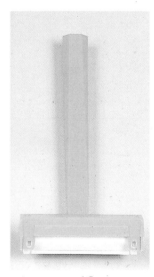

□ American and Soviet spacecraft link up in space
□ Mario Botta: Ligornetto house, Italy
□ Charles Jencks coins the term 'Post-Modern'

□ Benoît Mandelbrot develops the theory of fractal images
□ death of Franco, end of dictatorship in Spain
□ Khmer Rouge take Phnom Penh (Cambodia)
□ start of the civil war in Lebanon
□ Portugal grants independence to Mozambique and Angola

1976

□ Jakob Jensen: Beogram 600 record player and Beogram 1900 tuner for Bang & Olufsen
□ Mario Bellini: Break armchair

□ Cray 1 super-computer which carries out one hundred and fifty million operations a second
□ Nagisa Oshima: *Empire of the Senses*
□ Milos Forman: *One Flew Over the Cuckoo's Nest*

□ Jimmy Carter is elected president of the United States
□ Mao Tse-tung dies and a coup attempt by the Gang of Four is crushed by Deng Xiao-ping who is supported by the army

1977

□ **Studio Alchimia (set up in 1976) presents its first furniture collection, which includes Alessandro Mendini's Proust chair**
□ Hewlett-Packard portable microcomputer
□ first telephone links using optic fibres
□ Japan launches its first geostationary satellite
□ space probes Voyager I and II (United States) are launched to explore the outer solar system

□ start of *Dallas* television soap opera
□ George Lucas: *Star Wars*

□ inauguration of the Centre Georges Pompidou, designed by Richard Rogers and Renzo Piano
□ in England, the slogan 'no future' unites the punks
□ Walter de Maria: *Lightning Field*

1978

□ Nam June Paik: *Video-Garden*
□ Georges Perec: *La Vie Mode d'Emploi*
□ Michael Cimino: *The Deer Hunter*
□ Charles Jencks: *Post-Modern Architecture*
□ birth of Louise Brown, first baby born through *in vitro* fertilization (Great Britain)
□ in Italy, assassination of Aldo Moro, president of the Christian Democrats, by the Red Brigade
□ Camp David agreements between Israel and Egypt, Anwar Sadat and Menahem Begin receive Nobel Peace Prize
□ tragedy of the boat people in Vietnam

1979

□ Peter Noever: small table
□ Gae Aulenti: table 2652
□ Richard Sapper: 9090 expresso coffee machine
□ Emilio Ambasz: Vertebra chair
□ Gaetano Pesce: Sunset in New York couch

□ **Akio Morita (managing director of Sony): Sony Walkman**
□ Philips and Sony develop the compact disc
□ IBM presents the first laser printer-copier
□ nuclear accident at Three Mile Island, near Harrisburg, United States
□ Transavantgarde at the Venice Biennial (Francesco Clemente, Enzo Cucchi...)

- Ben: *Je me sens seul*
- Rainer Werner Fassbinder: *The Marriage of Maria Braun*
- Woody Allen: *Manhattan*
- Francis Ford Coppola: *Apocalypse Now*
- in Great Britain, Margaret Thatcher becomes prime minister
- fall of Shah of Iran, establishment of Islamic Republic under Ayatollah Khomeini
- Vietnam invades Cambodia expelling Khmer Rouge government
- Soviet army invades Afghanistan

1980

- Toshiyuki Kita: Wink transformable armchair
- Luigi Colani: prototype cameras for Canon
- **Alessi gets contemporary architects to design household products**
- Monospace Matra Espace motor car
- Voyager I transmits the first pictures of Saturn
- first trial launches of the European rocket Ariane
- **Minitel (France)**
- **Apple Macintosh personal computers**

- **birth of the Memphis group led by Ettore Sottsass Jr**
- Sandro Chia: *Incendiary*
- Georg Baselitz: *Der Brückichor*
- Martin Scorsese: *Raging Bull*
- Ronald Reagan is elected president of the United States
- in Poland, strikes in the shipyards at Gdansk and recognition of the Solidarity movement led by Lech Walesa
- start of the Iran-Iraq war
- second oil crisis

1981

- Ettore Sottsass Jr: Carlton bookcase

- **Daniel Weil: Bag radio**
- first solar-powered flight across the English Channel
- Andrzej Wajda: *Man of Steel*
- Ridley Scott: *Blade Runner*
- AIDS epidemic recognized
- in France, François Mitterand is elected president
- in Egypt, assassination of Anwar Sadat, Hosni Mubarak succeeds him
- SNCF's TGV service begins

- first flight of space shuttle (United States)
- death of Bobby Sands, member of the provisional IRA, on the sixty-sixth day of his hunger strike

1982

- Paolo Deganello: Torso armchair
- Elisabeth Garouste and Mattia Bonetti: Barbare chair

- Mario Botta: Prima chair
- Ernst Thonke, Jacques Müller and Elmar Mock: Swatch watch
- Fuji launches the disposable camera

- Endt and Fulton Design: terminal multifunction systems
- Joseph Beuys: *Grease Chair*
- Steven Spielberg: *ET, The Extraterrestrial*
- Wim Wenders: *The State of Things*
- William de Vries performs the first artificial heart transplant (United States)
- Falklands War

- in Nicaragua, a state of emergency is declared
- Israel invades Lebanon, expulsion of PLO from Beirut

1983

- Michele de Lucchi: First chair
- Elisabeth Garouste and Mattia Bonetti: Rocher table
- Honda VFR 750 motorbike

- Post-Graffiti exhibition at Caroll Janis, New York
- Bruce Nauman: Dream Passage
- Carolyn Carlson presents her choreography *L'Orso e la Luna*
- the compact disc is launched
- Pioneer 10 becomes the first spacecraft to leave the solar system
- American and French scientists identify the AIDS virus
- in the United States, Jane Fonda opens her aerobics club (California)
- Ronald Reagan announces the strategic defence initiative (SDI)
- *coup* in Grenada, the United States invades

1984

- Palais omnisports, Bercy, Paris
- Philippe Starck: Mister Bliss chair and Richard III armchair

- Martine Bedin: Charleston lamp
- **Roger Tallon: ski boot for Salomon**

- I. M. Pei selected to design the Grand Louvre

- Norman Foster: Hong Kong & Shanghai Bank
- Terry Gilliam: *Brazil*
- Jim Jarmusch: *Stranger than Paradise*
- Wim Wenders: *Paris, Texas*
- Milan Kundera: *The Unbearable Lightness of Being*
- Ronald Reagan is re-elected president of the United States
- Indira Ghandi assassinated

1985

- Enzo Mari: Tonietta chair

- Andrea Branzi: Gli Animali Domestici couch
- Sergio Cappelli and Patricia Ranzo: Plant Shelf wall console
- **opening of the Parisian gallery En Attendant les Barbares**
- Jean-Paul Gaultier fashion show, choreographed by Régine Chopinot
- Christo wraps the Pont-Neuf in Paris with 4 thousand square metres of material and 11 kilometres of rope

- Creation of the Pentagon group
- Cindy Sherman: series of self-portraits
- Barbara Kruger: series of poster-paintings
- Aldo Rossi: *Architecture of the Town*
- live transmission of the death of thirty-eight spectators at a football match in the Heysel stadium, Brussels
- in USSR, Mikhail Gorbachov is elected secretary general of the Communist Party
- Spain and Portugal enter the EEC
- civil unrest among blacks and coloureds in South Africa, state of emergency declared
- Great Britain and Ireland sign the Anglo-Irish Agreement

1986

- Ron Arad: hi-fi system
- Gaetano Pesce: plastic Vittel bottle

- Ron Arad: Well-Tempered Chair

- Shiro Kuramata: How High is the Moon armchair
- Sylvain Dubuisson: La Licorne lamp and T2/A3 clock
- Alternative Design develops in Europe
- NASA's Challenger spacecraft explodes with seven astronauts aboard
- launch of world's first permanently manned space station
- Richard Rogers: Lloyds Building, London
- opening of the MOCA (Museum of Contemporary Art) in Los Angeles, designed by Arata Isozaki
- Daniel Buren: *Les Deux Plateaux* (Palais Royal columns) create a scandal
- Jeff Koons: *Rabbit*
- David Lynch: *Blue Velvet*
- Margaret Thatcher and François Mitterand announce the Channel Tunnel project

1987

- Nestor Percal: fruit dish
- Frank Gehry: Little Beaver armchair made from pieces of cardboard

- a new supra-conductor material is discovered by IBM in Switzerland
- **Gaetano Pesce: Feltri armchair**
- Van Gogh's *Irises* are sold for $ 49 million
- Peter Greenaway: *The Belly of an Architect*
- Wim Wenders: *Wings of Desire*

- start of the intifada in the occupied territories
- world population reaches five thousand million

1988

- Elisabeth Garouste and Mattia Bonetti: Arc en Ciel table
- Sylvain Dubuisson: Lettera Amorosa vase

- Andrea Branzi: Axale sofa
- Olympus LSD 1000 camera
- Haim Steinbach: *Coat of Arms*
- B–2 stealth bomber (United States)
- first world conference on AIDS brings together one hundred and forty-eight countries
- the writer Salman Rushdie is condemned to death by Ayatollah Khomeini following publication of *The Satanic Verses*

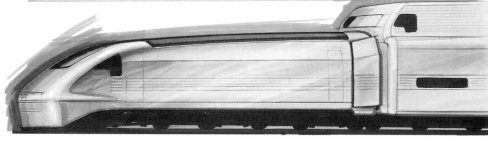

- reactor blows up at Chernobyl nuclear power station
- start of perestroïka and glasnost

- INF treaty between USSR and the United States provides for elimination of intermediate land-based nuclear weapons

- Stephen Hawking: *A Brief History of Time*
- Pedro Almodovar: *Women on the Verge of a Nervous Breakdown*
- global recognition that the ozone layer is being depleted
- in the United States, George Bush is elected president
- peace agreements in Cambodia
- in Pakistan, Benazir Bhutto becomes prime minister, the first woman to come to power in a Muslim country

1989

- André Dubreuil and Tom Dixon: neo-baroque furniture
- Sony camcorder
- Biodesign movement
- The TGV sets a new world record of 484 kmh
- Renault Twingo (conception)

- inauguration of the Arche de la Défense, designed by Otto von Spreckelsen
- Cady Noland: *Chicken in a Basket*
- A. S. Pons and M. Fleischmann announce that they have achieved cold fusion
- pro-democracy students occupy Tiananmen Square, Peking, but are violently dispersed
- in Czechoslovakia, Vaclav Havel becomes president

- the Berlin wall is demolished and the East European communist regimes collapse

- in Rumania, the government is overthrown and president Ceausescu and his wife are executed
- in Afghanistan, Soviet troops withdraw
- United States military intervention in Panama, arrest of President Noriega

1990

- Aldo Rossi: Parigi armchair

- **Philippe Starck: Fluocaril toothbrush**
- French and English Channel Tunnel workers meet up under the English Channel

- first pictures of Venus transmitted from the space probe Magellan

- Luigi Colani: briefcase
- Canon Q Pic still-video camera, records single-frame images onto floppy disc

- Christian Boltanski: *Inventaire des objets ayant appartenu à la jeune fille de Bordeaux*
- Mike Kelly: *Arena No. 10*
- David Lynch: *Wild at Heart*
- Krzysztof Kieslowski: *Dekalog*
- reunification of Germany
- in Poland, Lech Walesa is elected president
- Iraq invades Kuwait
- in South Africa, Nelson Mandela is freed after forty-eight years of detention
- global ban on chlorofluoro-carbons agreed, to come into effect by the year 2000

1991

- Norman Foster: Stansted Airport terminal
- Gulf war
- in USSR, collapse of the communist regime, Mikhaïl Gorbachov is temporarily deposed in a military coup
- founding of the CIS (Community of Independent States)
- start of civil war in Yugoslavia
- end of apartheid in South Africa

1992

- Philippe Starck: street lamp for Decaux

- Tom Dixon: Pylon furniture collection

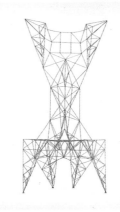

- Ron Arad: Soft Big Easy armchair
- Frank Gehry: furniture for Knoll
- Mathieu Bachelot: project for métro station entrances on the Champs-Elysées, Paris, for the RATP

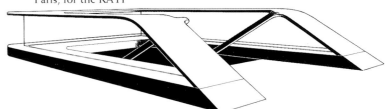

- **Lotus: racing bicycle for the Olympic games**
- Expo '92, Seville: Nicholas Grimshaw designs the British pavilion; Santiago Calatrava designs the Kuwait pavilion
- **Bertrand Voïnovitch: refuse towers**

- Spike Lee: *Malcolm X*
- signature of the Maastricht treaty, intended to bring about political and monetary union
- visit of emperor Akihito of Japan to China cements Sino-Japanese trade agreements
- Bill Clinton is elected president of the United States
- the UN decides on military intervention in Somalia to ensure relief supplies get through

1993

- Design: Mirror of the Century exhibition, Grand Palais, Paris (design by François Seigneur)

Italian Radical

Andrea Branzi

When we talk about Italian radical architecture, we are not referring to a defined cultural movement, but rather an energetic phenomenon, an experimental field which, from 1964 to 1974, stood at the very centre of 'the culture of the European project'. Such a long period nurtured contradictory experiences and brought forth both good and rotten apples. I do not propose, however, to provide a chronology of these events, nor a unifying approach to the various projects they promoted. I will rather seek to interpret their history as a kind of 'threshold', as a bridge across two differing periods, leading from 'classic Modernism' to its critical phase, or, if you prefer, across the two historical stages which split our century, leading from industrial to post-industrial civilization.

As in all transitional cultures, what is commonly called radical architecture contains novel elements as well as the remnants of the breakdown of old categories: a feeling for the new as well as an almost ferocious determination to be rid of the old. Heightened realism, combined with cos-mogonical utopianism. In general, the success of transitional cultures cannot be judged simply by measuring their pervasiveness. Other parameters should be employed, including their value as prophecy, as vague intuition and as a seedbed for the future. Even the fact that they are destined to fail forms part of their role – in the sense that this means they give rise to sons singularly unlike the father and to events not in the published programme: fracture, discontinuity, contradiction. In any case, all this does mean that what happens after will, at least, be very different from what happened before.

Radical architecture grew up at the beginning of the 1960s from the very first English avant-garde group (Peter Cook's Archigram) and spread to the new European youth culture, with the Austrians (Hans Hollein, Walter Pichler, the Haus Rucker, the Himmelblau Cooperative, the Saltz der Herde) and then to anti-design and nomadism, to street protest and the bright lights of the metropolis, to self-governing associations and ecological lifestyles.

It was in Italy that European radical

Architecture

architecture produced its most enduring fruit, through the work of groups like Archizoom Associati (of which I was a part), Superstudio, Ziggurat, 9999, or of individuals like Ettore Sottsass, Lapo Binazzi, Remo Buti, Gianni Pettena, Gaetano Pesce. The merit of Italian radical architecture lay above all in its capacity to outlast the initial instinctive outburst to which it was reduced in many other countries, and to seek to create a well-constructed and progressive 'long-lived movement'. It was capable of growing and maturing through different stages and sensibilities, becoming an international phenomenon with Nuovo Design (Alchimia and Memphis) and then, with the first real model of post-industrial design, Domus Academy, down to the most recent generation of young Italian designers.

All this could happen in Italy because there was already a fully-fledged political culture and an experimental and unconventional design environment. Italian design of the fifties had chosen to follow a road totally independent from the German experience and international rationalism, relying rather on a language of gestures, on an instinctive methodology, on small-scale production and on the re-evaluation of craft, placing its faith in the complexities of life and not on logics of scale. Not even between the wars was there a real and indigenous rationalist movement in Italy. Modernism arrived late, as an improbable consequence of late Futurism (Giacomo Balla, Fortunato Depero, Ivo Pannaggi). Italy then was the only European country where the rationalist movement was born directly of irrationalism (Futurism), from which our culture had inherited an idea of modernity based on scandals, factions and protest, and not on consensus, continuity and standardization. By the end of the fifties, this attitude led, by way of the Resistance, to reconstruction, to left-wing culture, which found in design a platform for public debate well beyond the confines of the profession, where theoretical reflection in journals such as *Domus* and

Casabella ushered in the cultural rebirth of the whole country.

From the outset, Castiglioni, Sottsass, Colombo, Munari and many other figures engaged with radical architecture in an intense, stimulating debate, based not on polemics but on overlapping dialogue. Equally, the newborn youth culture of design found a ready-made audience in the Italian industrial design sector, their heretical stamp corresponding perfectly to the experimental role that the Italian design industry was playing in the world market. So, in spite of its brief independent history, radical architecture could continue to grow, making an original contribution to the ever shifting history of Italian design, shepherding in the changeover from an industrial to a post-industrial European culture courageously and without illusions, uncompromisingly, yet without ever abandoning its leadership role. It became a culture made up entirely of transitions, crises and continual alarm bells, a way of leading history and the markets from the front, playing the part not of a spectator, but of a participant with a Latin sensibility – uneasy, uncertain, more ready to bring up new problems than search for solutions. A way of doing design using art for its constructive possibilities and technology for its artistic ones.

Radical architecture as a 'threshold' closes one age and opens another; and yet, paradoxically, it fits into the long Italian tradition of transitional phenomena. I will now try to outline a number of the principal themes of radical architecture which initiated what one might describe as the Period of Change (1968-88).

The discovery of complexity as the period's essential category

In 1966, Robert Venturi wrote his famous book, *Complexity and Contradiction in Architecture*. What does the 'discovery of complexity' mean? It means that, up until that point in time, modern culture had assumed that the chaos prevalent in human society – the contradictions, the discontinuity

I oppose to the mysticism of Hygiene, which is the superstition of
'Functional Architecture', the realities of a Magical Architecture rooted in the totality
of the human being, and not in the blessed or accursed parts of this being.

Frederick Kiesler, 'Magical Architecture', Le Surréalisme en 1947, 1947

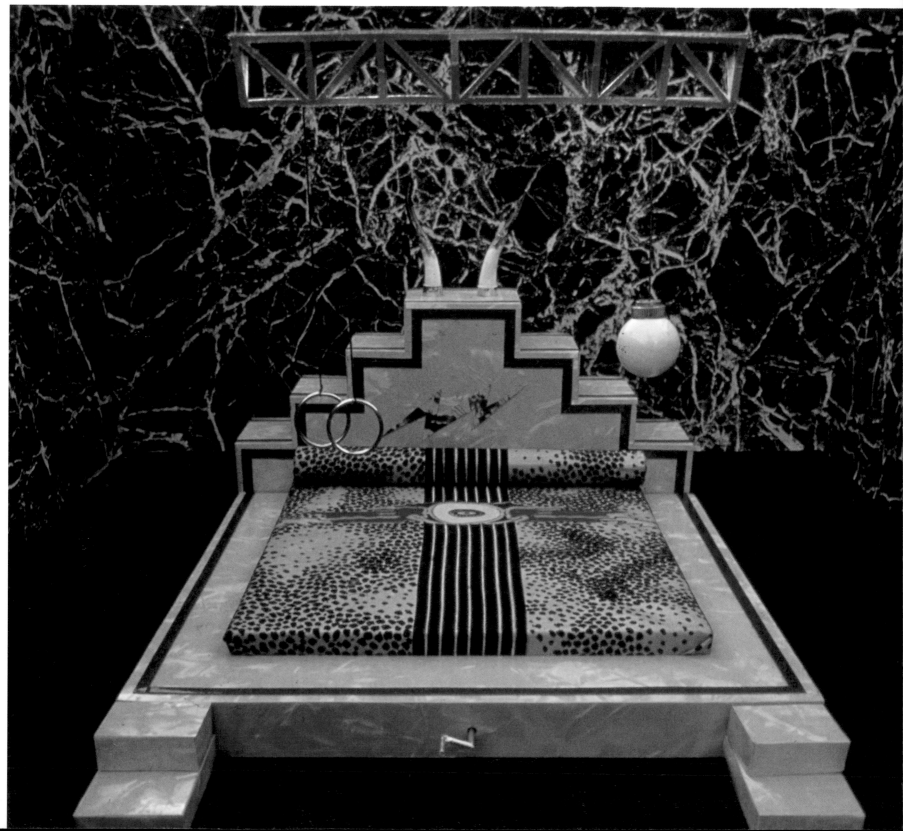

and irrationality of the physical world – constituted a provisional state of affairs, sure to vanish from the world within the growing industrial order. Chaos was envisaged as a consequence of the backwardness of modern industrial growth. According to the Modern Movement, in fact, industry had ordered the human and urban world along social, formal and cultural lines: a rational and logical universe in which both architecture and design foreshadowed from the outset linguistic and methodological unification.

In the sixties, however, the blueprint for reading that reality was inverted: because they are the latest fruits of the very processes of industrial growth, the complexity, discontinuity and contradictions inherent in the world are not bound to disappear in the harmony of industrial society. Chaos is not a temporary state of affairs at all, but a permanent one. It is not a legacy from the past, but a reality towards which this model of development tends. The avant-garde, however, must, as ever, endeavour to turn what was considered until recently as bad, as a nuisance, into something good and full of creative potential. So radical architecture took complexity as the period's primary category, and held that the multiplicity of languages and modes of behaviour contained in society and the marketplace was a boon and a richness.

Radical architecture took the logic of industry as an impetus for diversification, not standardization: the future would not be built up from a series of standards, robots and mass-produced goods, but from distinct production logics, where the one-off piece would live side by side with mass production, codes with anarchic languages, definitive products with throwaway ones, high technology with primitive processes.

And this is what has indeed happened.

Radical architecture proposed a renewed rationalism as a polemical alternative to the Modern Movement's rationalism of the sixties. This critical confrontation arose from the observation that the rational method was no longer capable of preventing an ever more complex world and an ever more contradictory society from slipping through its fingers.

Classical Modernism affirmed that history was powered by a few scientific laws of economics and that human behaviour should be directed towards rationality, functionality, seriality and other civic values of a similar type. Anything which could not be directly put into the service of these values was the product of irrationality and to be rejected *en bloc*. For radical architecture, however, the problem was not how to 'exclude' irrationality but rather how to provide for it and add it to the list of positive forces for historical growth. Radical architecture was not 'irrationalist', but engaged rather in the search for a renewed rationality which would allow for the understanding of irrationality, of the dreams and mistakes which themselves make up a large part of history and reality.

And this is what has indeed happened.

Radical architecture was one of those cultural movements – such as Pop Art, rock music, youth fashion and other expressive changes in art and behaviour of the sixties – which heralded the new, central position of consumer culture. Until then, modern culture had always deferred to the 'culture of production', that is to the rationality of construction processes, to technological certitudes, to a design mentality devoted to transferring the 'scientific model of manufacturing' to society and the whole physical world.

During the sixties attention shifted to the overarching consequences of industrialization: the society of the masses, business communications, consumer goods and all forms of creative behaviour. Intuition, emotion and persuasion replaced the analytical rationality of the Ulm school. Like all the visual arts, design began adopting all the aggressively secular signs of modern populism. Objects were designed with which the consumer could establish a 'complex' relationship, while mass markets fragmented into a series of specialized niches. It is impossible for design to think up neutral products that suit everybody. The product itself 'selects' its users or consumers, singling them out in the urban chaos like a flower or an insect in the forest which, using colours and smells to display its genetic code, attracts a mate.

And this is what has indeed happened.

Radical architecture established a new relationship between design and architecture, no longer in terms of co-operation, but in terms of competition. Composite, eclectic architecture is a culture which will never become a mechanism capable of transforming urban life. It is a culture incapable of surviving in an age which no longer provides the space and time for the metaphorical play architecture carries with it, which no longer has a place for the grand, unitary syntheses of which architecture feels itself the herald.

Today, in order to create a new architecture and new urban spaces, it is necessary to begin fur-ther upstream: one has to plunge one's hands into that vast planktonic soup of products, technology, pictures, signs and data which makes up the artificial universe in which contemporary man is totally immersed. It is an invasive and compromised artificial environment but none the less it does constitute the only real urban space. Design, bravely operating within the world of production and consumption, has gained its new-found supremacy through being the only planning entity able to transform reality. Composite architecture, on the other hand, is doomed to failure and marginalization.

And this is what has (more or less) happened.

On the basis of these main themes, radical design began its odyssey, through Global

Tools, Dressing Design, Design Primario, Nuovo Design, to the Domus Academy, which was to shape the first functioning model of post-industrial design. With each 'threshold' fitting in to the next like a telescope, this journey saw the development of a sustained and original period in post-war Italian design. None the less, not all the prophecies made by radical architecture have been realized. If the culture of complexity, a renewed rationalism, the new consumer culture and the new design metropolis have been the underlying characteristics of the decades we have called the Period of Change (1968-88), some of the most important agendas that youth culture drew up during that distant and prophetic period failed singularly to materialize.

These were not secondary schemes, but hypotheses which had their own strategic values, making up a sort of 'mega-trend' transforming society from top to bottom, and including certain specific design scenarios which only then would become meaningful. It might be said that all radical architecture's design machinery has during the formation of post-industrial society, in one way or other, been put into practice. On the other hand, the political machinery – with its context of radical social renewal in which the avant-garde was to search for legitimacy and synergy – has totally failed. I will give here a few examples of these failures.

The first is concerned with our certainty that radical architecture was to be the avant-garde of a 'liberalized society' in which a leisure society and 'intellectual production by the masses' was to have been based on electronic automation. That avant-garde movements ate away at the classic structures of our disciplines, at all the traditional codes of our profession, was seen as a process designed to bring culture into step with the creative freedom of both the individual and the masses, as a blow struck for the right of all to self-determination and to their own environ-

ment. 'Housing is easy,' affirmed Archizoom at MOMA in 1972.

Intellectual production by the masses was therefore the culmination of a process of social liberation where the age-old distinction between the 'professional intellectual' and the 'alienated consumer' would be transcended. The emancipation from work, brought about by the introduction of robots, was to have created a leisure society where everyone would produce and consume an individual culture, not within a universal value system, but as a free expression of personal creativity. Within

this new deconstructed system, the old professional categories in the worlds of culture and politics would dissolve, giving rise to 'intellectual production by the masses' made up of as many linguistic and behavioural models as there were active individuals in the society. This great utopic vision never came about. Its failure went hand in hand with the political inefficacy of that generation which, precisely for that reason scored such notable successes in the professional and cultural fields. In fact, that generation of 1968-88 sensed, understood and ushered in our century's

La Casa Telecomandata, designed by Andrea Branzi, 1986.

Grande Tapetto Ibrido, designed by Andrea Branzi, 1986.

Right-hand page: Labrador sauceboat, designed by Andrea Branzi for Memphis, 1982.

post-industrial society, following with great realism the shaping of the new, but letting drop as utopian all its radical political components. Success and failure are thus closely intertwined.

Such a statement might be made, not only of the generation of radical architecture, but equally of Western society in general. The collapse of true socialism has not meant the victory of democracy, but the breakdown of politics. The growth of consumerism and leisure has not led to a liberalized society, but to a more violent and less equitable one.

The culture of complexity has not corresponded to the construction of a really diversified society, but, on the contrary, to the application of a single model of global development – post-industrial capitalism – in which the only 'diversity' is to be found between rich and poor countries.

What parts of the methodological machinery and of the sensibility of radical architecture (Italian in particular) will remain useful in the short and long term? Certainly, its view that history is made from discontinuity and crisis and not from continuity and linear progression, and therefore that an industrial design culture must be ready constantly to problematize even its fundamentals and certitudes. A jerky continuity towards an incomplete and imperfect 'Second Modernity' in constant expansion.

Today we are faced by the necessity of having to reconstruct our culture in global and not regional terms: we can do it, but not if we base ourselves on a system of non-existent certainties. On the contrary, we must address the whole scope of the world's unresolved problems, all the unanswered questions.

Functional architecture has proved to be a wrong road, just like painting with a ruler. With giant strides we are approaching impractical, unusable, and finally uninhabitable architecture. . . And only after things have been creatively covered in mould, from which we have much to learn, will a new and wonderful architecture come into being.

Friedrich Hundertwasser, Mould Manifesto against Rationalism in Architecture, 1958

The Sacco chair

In Italy during the sixties, a counter-current known as 'radical design' or 'anti-design' emerged that was opposed to the alliance between design and the forces of capitalism and consumerism which flourished in post-war Europe. This movement set out to create cultural shocks, to question the role of design in industry and to provide an antidote, at least in theory, to the rule of capitalism.

Three tendencies brought these young designers together: American and British Pop Art; the return of a certain primitivism; and an economy of means (advocated by the artists of arte povera). This movement had a ready-made public made up of the growing numbers of people who were disgusted with consumer society and on the lookout for new forms and simple, modular furniture consistent with its views.

This new tendency did not produce a rupture between industrialists and designers; it led, instead, to the use, for the first time, of large businesses as design laboratories.

At the end of the fifties the Milanese company Zanotta abandoned traditional Italian techniques in favour of innovative research into questions of form, function and aesthetics. Accustomed to collaborating with designers on its furniture range, in 1968 Zanotta asked Piero Gatti, Cesare Paolini and Franco Teodoro to design a furniture line for mass production.

The Sacco chair was introduced in the same year as the Blow chair. The first was a large, amorphous sack made of plastic (or of leather in its more elegant version) half-filled with flexible expanded polystyrene balls; the second was made of transparent inflatable plastic. They were followed by the Joe Sofa, an enormous leather baseball glove inspired by the American Pop artist Claes Oldenburg.

The Sacco chair is a symbol of antiform, a radical, material refutation of formalism. The term should be taken here in its widest sense: the rejection of formalism is a rejection of conventions, of a conservative middle-class morality, which can only be successfully challenged by vehement utopian propositions. The standard Western notion of seating loses all meaning with this chair, which changes its form according to whether the user curls up, sprawls or sinks himself in its enveloping mass. Inspired by the hippie movement which took ideas from Eastern mysticism, the concept of being seated takes on a new meaning, akin to the Indian idea of 'living lying down', of ottomans and Persian carpets.

In fact, the Sacco chair was so successful that it was found in the lofts of young intellectuals as well as the homes of middle-class people who had discovered 'design' and felt obliged to follow the latest trends.

E. M.

Olivetti

In 1908, the Italian engineer Camillo Olivetti (1868-1943) founded a company specializing in office equipment. Convinced of the necessity of combining form and function, Olivetti began, in 1911, to manufacture the first Italian typewriter, the M1, using American machine tools. In 1932, the MPI, the first portable, was introduced. Designed by Aldo Magnelli in collaboration with his brother Alberto, an abstract painter, this was the first typewriter to be conceived as a consumer product in which the fusion of form and function was reinforced by the mark of an instantly recognizable style: the Olivetti style.

From 1933 Adriano Olivetti (1901-1960) played an active role in running the company. In 1934, he invited the architects Luigi Figini and Gino Pollini to design a new factory in Piedmont, to be built on the Olivetti family property. The Ivrea factory became an emblem of modernity for Italian architecture and industry during the years before the war.

Drawn to the graphics of the Modern Movement, Adriano Olivetti hired a designer from the Bauhaus, Xanti Schawinski, who gave the company's publicity material a new élan. At the same time the company launched a magazine, Tecnica ed Organizzazione, in which it laid out the key points of an industrial methodology that would subsequently be adopted by all of Italian industry.

Refining his new policy, Olivetti hired the designer Marcello Nizzoli as a consultant to revolutionize the image of his products. Adriano Olivetti's campaign to combine industrial design and the plastic arts assumed such importance that in 1952 the Museum of Modern Art in New York organized a large retrospective that would have a big impact on American design. He is still celebrated for his embrace of the avant-garde, from a social and political point of view as well as a cultural one, and for having invented a new discipline now known as design management. In 1955, the magazines Zodiac and Urbanisticà awarded him the Golden Compass, a new prize sponsored by the La Rinascente shops.

All the most prominent representatives of Italian design have collaborated with Olivetti: Franco Albini, Gae Aulenti, Mario Bellini, Michele de Lucchi, Vico Magistretti, Carlo Scarpa, Ettore Sottsass, Marco Zanuso.

Ettore Sottsass gave the company its trademark image, which became well known in Europe and the United States: 'In 1958, the engineer Adriano Olivetti invited me to design the first electronic typewriter to be made in Italy. For me, at that time, electronics were a kind of tragic, mysterious deity, and I designed machines that were completely enclosed with sheets of aluminium. And when after ten years the system was finally perfected, electronics became miniaturized and this system no longer served any purpose'.

At the end of the sixties, Ettore Sottsass wanted to 'decondition' man from his attitude to the consumer object. He wanted to 'defetichize' objects, to encourage man to have faith in himself rather than objects.

With the Valentine typewriter he managed to bring a vibrant sense of colour and form into a rejuvenated office landscape: 'Under the influence of American pop culture, which was beginning in those years, I designed a small typewriter called the Valentine that was red and had a very pop design.' The typewriter was a great success and remained in production for a long time. It was the first time that a product intended for the workplace was also perfectly adapted to the home, thanks to its size and colour, which masked the functionality of the design. Its smallness and brightly coloured plastic case made it the first easily transportable typewriter.

E. M.

Alessi

Founded in 1921 by Giovanni Alessi Anghini, in Bagnella d'Omegna, the Alessi company was initially nothing more than a modest sheet metal workshop producing hand-made objects in nickel silver and brass to order.

In 1924 the workshop began to produce its own trays and coffee pots. The following year it published the first mail-order catalogue of its products under the name FAO (Fratelli Alessi Omegna). In the thirties, as a response to the difficulties it faced in obtaining precious metals, Carlo Alessi, the founder's eldest son, launched a programme of research with steel and altered the structure of the business to adapt to the resulting technological developments. For more than 30 years steel dominated the company's output, most of which was exported.

In 1955, the company began to use outside designers (Luigi Massoni, Mazzeri and Vitale) and soon acquired an international reputation, notably in the hotel and restaurant business. At the beginning of the sixties renowned designers and architects like Richard Meier and Aldo Rossi, then Richard Sapper and Arata Isozaki were hired to design 'art-design' objects. In the eighties, Alessi became one of the central figures in Italian Post-Modern design and research.

The group was instrumental in reintroducing silverwork into the applied arts, linking it more to architecture than to crafts. In 1983 Michael Graves designed a silver service inspired by Viennese design from the beginning of the century, and Richard Meier designed another service that paid homage to Malevich's architectons. In 1984 Aldo Rossi designed a stainless steel coffee pot, which initiated an exercise in style for Alessi's designers centred on the theme of the coffee pot.

In 1982, the company established a new brand name, Officina Alessi, with the intention of producing objects that were still at the project or prototype stage and a studio was set up for the purpose. Even by the standards of experimental work, the results have been extremely innovative in terms of their form, production and function because of the absence of the usual constraints imposed by mass production.

These objects combine sophisticated industrial technology with craft working methods and are made from materials other than stainless steel, notably 'historical' ones like nickel silver, brass and copper, and also silver and tin. The Officina Alessi catalogue includes many re-editions along with its newly designed products, featuring work by Marianne Brandt, Christopher Dresser and Josef Hoffmann, as well as Achille Castiglioni, Andrea Branzi, Alessandro Mendini, Paolo Portoghesi, Michael Graves, Sylvain Dubuisson and Philippe Starck. Complementing the products offered by the original Alessi company, and manufactured in the same factory in Crusinallo, this brand is making its own mark in the increasingly complex contemporary market-place. It offers seven different lines, each of them quite distinct in terms of content, materials and price, and each bearing an evocative name: Antologia Alessi, Alessi d'après, Tea & Coffee Piazza, La Tavola di Babele, Archivi, La Cintura di Orione and La Casa della Felicità.

E. M.

Left-hand page: Detail of the La Cupola espresso coffee-maker, made from aluminium and polyamide, designed by Aldo Rossi, 1988-1989.

Background: Chimu centrepiece made from stainless steel, with feet in wood and aluminium, designed by Joanna Lyle, 1992.

Top, from left to right: Ti Tang teapot, made from white porcelain covered in aluminium coloured with epoxy resin, Philippe Starck, 1991-1992.

Stainless steel kettle with brass melodic whistle and handle covered with polyamide, Richard Sapper, 1983.

Stainless steel kettle with polyamide handle and bird whistle, Michael Graves, 1985.

Studio Alchimia

Proust armchair, designed by Alessandro Mendini, 1978.

Founded in 1976 in Milan by Alessandro and Adriana Guerriero, Studio Alchimia was a development of 'Alchimia, projection of images for the 20th century', launched two years before by Alessandro Mendini, architect, designer and editor of the magazine Domus. The name Alchimia evokes a return to Modernism coloured by the ambivalent effects of a chemistry which mixes mysticism with the banality of daily life. In 1979, the first furniture collections bore the ironic names 'Bau. Haus. uno' and 'Bau. Haus. due.' Both the furniture, which was highly expressive in form, and the objects were in warm, striking colours.

In addition to the dominant personality of Mendini, the theoretical pronouncements of Andrea Branzi and the experience of Ettore Sottsass provided a solid foundation for this group, which was awarded the Golden Compass in 1981 for its design research.

The studio's diverse activities have included exhibitions, seminars, objects, books, clothing, videos, experimental theatre sets, happenings, decoration and architectural projects. Alchimia's creations trace the passage between the radical design current of the late seventies and the subsequent neo-modern Italian tendency.

Decoration, banished from all theory after the Second World War, was reused by Alchimia for ideological ends. It symbolized the desire to provoke and subvert the meaning of objects, the ambiguity of whose sociological and political connotations was a feature of Mendini's work: 'We assumed the existence of a proletariat that, in actual fact, didn't exist; what does exist is the lower middle class. We anticipated a convergence between a cultured project and the underprivileged, whereas what exists is, on the contrary, a mass project, because the intel-

lectual is in the process of disappearing. And now the project developed by the masses has revealed itself to be an illusion, too... As it's become a generalized phenomenon, the avant-garde... is a phenomenon which I would call "banal", because in a certain sense quantity is banality'. For this 'banal' design, forms halfway between the common and decorative excess seem to be best suited to the post-industrial world in which Alchimia operates: a chaotic world whose governing principles transcend national boundaries, a world which needs to develop new reference points. In 1981, Sottsass set up his own studio, Memphis, and Alchimia gradually abandoned three-dimensional objects to express its political views with images, actions and artistic performances, still under the influence of Mendini's strong personality.

E. M.

The Feltri armchair

The architect and designer Gaetano Pesce was, from 1967, the principal protagonist of an alternative design that would prove influential in Italy, France and the United States. Thanks to his mastery of materials, Pesce was able to create totally new forms. His work reflects both a distinctive conceptual approach and a social concern, and his designs, which are made by the furniture manufacturer Cassina, have the quality of physical manifestos. Cassina collaborates with the designer in the search for unorthodox materials, concepts and structures that make for products that are unique in the field of furniture design.

In Pesce's view a piece of furniture must tell a story in which are indissolubly interlinked the tradition from which it issued, an innovatory content and technological research.

The Feltri armchair, designed in 1987, has a thick wool felt that brings to mind sculptures by Joseph Beuys and Robert Morris. Pesce here demonstrates his total mastery of the natural qualities of this traditional material which he combines with advanced technology to produce an original chair.

The felt is first stamped out by a powerful press. The lower part of the chair is impregnated with a thermosetting resin (polyester tinted to match the colour of the felt). Before the resin begins to polymerize, the impregnated felt is inserted into an appropriately shaped mould, which is then sealed and placed in an oven to accelerate the hardening process. The result is a rigid, self-supporting lower shell and upper part that remain soft and flexible. The seat itself, made with the same process, is fixed to the shell with cord and screws.

Pesce's experiments are the result of a very personal approach which does not conform to any system. It is an approach which gives him the freedom to create objects that generate meaning, in the anthropological sense of the term, objects – as Marc Augé emphasizes in his preface – which say something about human relations.

J. d. N. and E. M.

Industrial Design Today

Marion Hancock

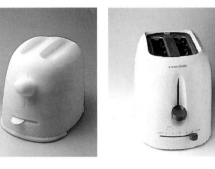

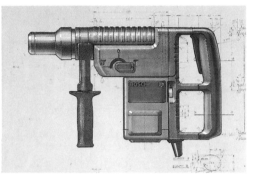

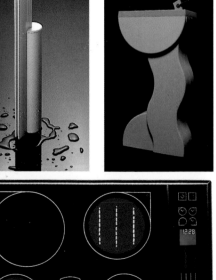

From top to bottom:
Autoprobe scanning microscope, by Lunar Design for Park Scientific Instruments, 1992.

Metropolitan toaster, model and final product, by Smart Design for Black and Decker.

Technical drawing of GBH 5-40 drill, by Slany Design for Bosch, 1991.

Window cleaning device, Ziba Design for Hanco, 1989.

Fountain (model), by Kenneth Wood, 1984.

TH 4500 vitroceramic hob unit, Scholtès, 1992.

Preceding pages, left: **Heart pump, by IDEO for Baxter;** *right:* **detail of the vase reproduced on p.273** *(background)* **and built-in oven, Scholtès, 1993.**

The manufacturer's dilemma

Japanese manufacturers have brought about a revolution in manufacturing in terms of the speed at which new products can be introduced and the number of variants that can lucratively be spun off from a core product. Brother, the Japanese maker of office equipment, takes only four weeks to bring a new product to market. Sharp develops about 2,000 products a year, of which perhaps two per cent contain some real innovation – the rest are simply re-configured or presented in some other way. Sony produces some 300 varieties of the basic Walkman alone. Awed by this cornucopia, manufacturing companies everywhere have tried throughout the eighties to accelerate the flow of new products. And just as Japan has shown that more products can be turned out more quickly than anyone thought possible, it has also shown that limited numbers of individual products can likewise be enonomically produced. Japan has computerized machines that can make a hundred products of one design, then switch to making, say, 50 of another. Industrial designers can be expected to interact with the production line on a visual, mechanical, engineering and product design basis. Flexibility is all.

We are also seeing a new attitude to innovation. Companies everywhere are tending to believe that innovation does not necessarily have to wait for random significant breakthroughs from unpredictable sources, but can be managed and produced.

But, just as many nations are beginning to catch up with the Japanese pace of production, environmental issues are raising difficult questions about the ethics and sustainability of production on this massive scale, and placing restrictions on manufacturing activities.

Companies also face the severe difficulty of distinguishing their products in what is now a very crowded market. When everyone has similar aims – to make products that are simple and convenient to use, with a high quality appearance – how can new products be individual and distinctive? The challenge for manufacturers grows ever more difficult.

The impact of technology on product aesthetics

Technological developments throughout the eighties and early nineties have not been the radical influence on style one might have expected. Rather, efforts have often been made to reserve aesthetic continuity with what went before. Household appliances incorporating the new technology of 'fuzzy logic' – machines like washing machines, vacuum cleaners and cookers that can analyse the task in hand and respond appropriately – look very much as their predecessors of recent years. New cooking technologies have not inspired strange and futuristic saucepans.

Microwaves look much like ovens. Bosch/Siemens is selling washing machines that use 50 per cent less detergent, 55 per cent less water and 45 per cent less electricity than their equivalents of ten years ago, but their appearance has not significantly changed in that time. Similarly, cordless appliances look much like their conventional predecessors – cordlessness was not seized on as an opportunity to rethink the style of the product. Computers look like hybrids of typewriters and televisions, videophones like telephones with an extra function – in market research, potential users had expressed a preference for the familiar. Consumers change their tastes more slowly than technology advances.

When, some years ago, efforts were made to make telephones extremely lightweight, manufacturers had not realized that 'heft' was traditionally associated with quality and stability in telephones, and that therefore weight was a positive attribute for these products. Miniaturization in general was for many people an unfortunate trend, resulting in such irritating details as 'buttons made by elves', as one designer put it. Nor have new materials had the dramatic impact one might imagine. Knowledge of materials is in many cases weak among designers. A survey of chief designers conducted in the mid-1980s established that more than half knew little or nothing about the applications of nylon, and their successors, the younger designers, were worse. In Japan, the material a product is made from changes on average every seven years. In the UK a change of material typically happens every thirteen years. In neither case does

this pace of change reflect the true pace of progress in materials development.

The impact of marketing

We forget how recent is the phenomenon of marketing. Even in 1983, a company as sophisticated as Braun was not really marketing its products. It was simply designing them well and trusting they would sell. Marketing and all of its concepts, 'market segmentation' in particular, have since become so much a part of industrialized society that even the average person, unconnected with the discipline, understands its basic precepts, blithely using such terms as upmarket, downmarket, middle market, niche market, and high end.

The roles of marketing and market re-

search have developed spectacularly in recent years, spinning off many sub-disciplines of interest to the designer. In Europe particularly, the advent of the single market has stimulated the study of national tastes and preferences. If you are a tableware producer, for example, it helps to know that some patterns will sell well north of the Rhine but badly south of it. Increased access to the findings of market research is a powerful influence on Industrial design today.

Marketing is also driving the increasing interrelationship of aspects of design. When marketing comes up with a new concept, often that concept will not fall neatly into one design discipline but cross the borders of several. What kind of designer, for example, would design slippers with torches in the toes – a trivial example and not the sort of product any industrial designer would think of, yet a fashion/industrial design hybrid which has been very successful in the Far East. Designers from different disciplines are being brought into closer contact through marketing, and all are watching with interest the predictions of an even newer profession, that of 'trend forecasting' – in fashion, cars and buildings, colours, textures and social habits.

So, more influential than new technology and new materials has been the way companies think about selling their wares. 'No companies sell products any more,' says Michael Wolff, a British corporate identity designer. 'A product is made up of 20 per cent production and 80 per cent marketing, concept, and advertising.' This view accords with that of many Japanese companies. Akihiko Amanuma at Sony believes that design is simply a function serving marketing, packaging and advertising – the whole cluster of image-creating elements which Sony terms 'software'.

Where once companies sold products that were ends in themselves, now they want to sell systems, concepts, 'lifestyle choices'. Apple sells flexible working methods, rather than computers. The makers of telecommunications equipment sell communication, not telephones. Office furniture makers sell efficiency, not chairs. And the makers of cars deal in dreams of status and escape, not in the technology they offer, important to them though this is. Ken Grange, a British industrial designer famous for his elegant and rational household products, remarks that in Japan (where he has many clients) the designers and manufacturers, having mastered functionalism, have a new buzz-word – *ambienza*, ambience.

Carrying this burden of symbolism,

modern products have shrugged off many of the early precepts of industrial design – of which 'truth to materials', and 'form follows function', were the leading principles. As the technology modern products contain becomes more anonymous and less understandable to the ordinary person, so it becomes less feasible that the form of those products should express their function. In any case, many people have little idea how their ordinary household products work. They may never have grasped fully how a television, a telephone or a camera works – what are their chances of understanding a videophone, a computer or a microwave? And anyway, how does a designer express the essence of the microchip?

Some design consultancies have coined alternative phrases to sum up this change. The German consultancy Frogdesign has said 'form follows fun', a philosophy visibly expressed in its witty and adventurous designs. British consultancy Seymour Powell has said 'form follows fashion', equally recognizable in its refined contemporary products.

Styling, concentration on form, is respectable again after some years out of favour. Visual playfulness and humour are now acceptable characteristics. The French consultancy Studio Naço aims to inject '90 per cent emotion, 10 per cent technology' into workaday products such as radios and calculators – this is the complete opposite of the philosophy which prevailed when both of these products were invented.

Individualism versus conformity

As metal bashing has given way to electronics, industrial design has moved (sometimes literally) from hard to soft. In terms of shape, this often means a shift from the straight-sided to the curvaceous and in terms of materials, from metals to plastics, resins and wood (occasionally even textiles – Emilio

Ambasz's 'soft tech' products embed calculators and telephones in leather pouches).

In moving away from what industrial designers now see as the sterile techno-solutions of the eighties, you could say that they have been liberated from a straitjacket. Not only do they now have computer-aided design tools, and production methods that can cope with short runs of individual products – thus increasing the chances of getting the unusual into production – but the old stylistic rules no longer apply. There is no one correct way for a product to look.

Despite this, however, we do not always see a great flourishing of very radical industrial design. We should perhaps not be surprised that, despite the current scope for individuality, designers everywhere are coming up with similar ideas and configurations, moving toward homogeneity. Products are rendered more uniform by two imperatives: first, the need for many products today to be saleable worldwide; and second, the desire that all manner of products should resemble consumer products.

Increasingly there is less to choose, stylistically, between the highly technical and the ordinary domestic product. There are heart pumps that look like Walkmans; insulin injectors that look like fountain pens; nautical instruments that look like TV remote controls. Recently, faced with pictures of a contemporary postal weighing balance, a medical product, a telephone and an electric razor, I found it difficult to tell which was which, so close were they in terms of their 'design language'. The consumer product aesthetic is spreading now even further to industrial machinery such as machine tools, weighing and measuring equipment, and heating and ventilation systems.

New branches of research, for example in interface design, information design

and ergonomics, equip designers with common information. If all designers are being fed the same information on how the human body works (how the average person absorbs information, sits in a car seat or handles a control panel), they naturally will tend towards comparable solutions to design problems. Common international safety and performance standards will dictate similar solutions, and product graphics are being standardized.

These are not the only factors contributing to homogeneity, there are also cultural factors. Japan, famous for mechanical precision, is beginning to backpedal on its ceaseless flow of new products, wanting to shift attention from the means of production to the more spiritual and cultural questions of how to imbue Japanese products with recognizably Japanese identity and values. In Italy, meanwhile, where flamboyant expressions of culture have never been lacking, the opposite is happening. At the last Salone del Mobile, the key cultural event in Italian design, style dealers were trying to shift the emphasis away from the studio and onto 'the factory', to real life, mass market goods and efficient production. In Spain, the fastest expanding economy in Europe and a country currently enjoying a tremendous reputation for innovative design, a similarly sobering influence is at work. The national plan for industrial reconversion is providing government incentives to bring products into line with international safety standards.

Eighties trends in form

Though the eighties may be remembered as the yuppie decade, the years of Braun calculators and Alessi kitchen gadgets, it did in fact encompass a wide variety of stylistic experiment. The decade began with a bang when Memphis, the Milan-based movement bringing radical experiment with form and colour to furniture, was first publicized. Products in sympathy with the Memphis movement began to acquire little Post-Modern details – that is to say, ornament began to be reinstated after years of exclusion from product design. Coffee machines, for example, acquired wiggly handles and bright pastel buttons. Meanwhile, 'product semantics' was being explored in the US – a mid-eighties trend whereby designers tried to design products whose appearance made literal their function. Lisa Krohn's Phonebook telephone was a key example of this trend. It proved short-lived, but was an interesting experiment along the escape route from Modernism.

Equally diverting were the 'punk' developments: Daniel Weil's 'bag radio', echoing developments in architecture, exposed the innards of the product. Meanwhile, designers such as Ron Arad and Tom Dixon were using industrial materials – medical equipment, old car seats – in the sculpting of furniture. Yuppie gadgets, designed to exist in sparse environments, were a late eighties trend that proved hard to live with in more ways than one. And now we are seeing the opposite trend. From ideas of exclusivity and novelty we have moved to folksiness and comfort, visible in the revivals of Shaker furniture, naïve art,

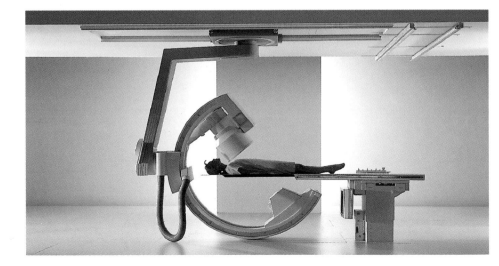

Microcomputer mouse, designed by Lunar Design for Alps OEM.

Right: **Sharp microwave oven, 1987.**

Integris C radiology machine for cardiovascular examinations, designed by Philips Corporate Industrial Design for Philips Medical System, 1991.

natural materials, and 'ethnicity'. Now, tables made of lashed-together twigs and sofas made of rattan sell in the high street.

The product designer today

It is difficult to envisage how product design, packaging ever more complex technology, will fit into homes that may be almost rustic in atmosphere. Five years ago the makers of kitchen equipment – kettles, toasters and so on – were predicting that individual purchases would give way to kitchen 'systems'. As yet there seems little evidence of this. While kitchen equipment manufacturers slave in laboratories on ever more sophisticated cooking methods, there has been a revival in the popularity of 'cooking stones' – the most basic way of cooking, on a lump of ceramic.

Though, in many ways, the product designer's sphere of influence has expanded to embrace the realms of modern technology, increasing homogeneity in the way new, technically advanced products are presented can mean that there is more scope for industrial design innovation in less technically impressive products. It sometimes seems, in fact, as though the industrial designer's palette has in reality contracted. And it is often the small changes that consumers appreciate the most.

German designer Hans Erich Slany, a specialist in capital goods design, succeeds in his aim of 'humanizing the world of work' and 'adapting machines and technical equipment to people'. One of his briefs, relating to a tool set for Witte, called for a conventional full-size screwdriver, with interchangeable bits stored in the handle. Slany suggested the alternative of six bits contained in a small case, a simple one-piece moulding also serving as a handle; the 'intelligent' packaging is not thrown away. Slany's Combit Box packaging thus becomes part of the product – the handle. A neat solution in several ways, though not a project on a major scale.

Senyera lighting system, designed by Perry King and Santiago Miranda for the Casa de Barcelona at the Olimpiada Cultural, made by Flos/Arteluce, 1992.

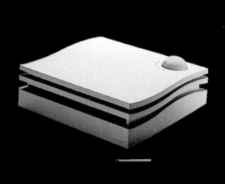

Similarly, British designer Geoff Hollington finds modest yet functional improvements where none might be thought possible. His cherrywood and nickel-plated candlestick has a flexible rubber flange at the top; flex it, and accumulated wax flakes off. Industrial designers around the world are engaged in the constant process of making small, incremental improvements to the performance of the things we use every day – adding small safety features and ergonomic and practical refinements to razors, toothbrushes, pens, clocks.

The future

Computer aided-design is likely to have a profound effect on the appearance of products. To name but one consequence, Bill Moggridge of international design group IDEO anticipates that the particular way in which computer-aided design tools draw a three point curve will introduce a completely new aesthetic in product design. The ability of computers to produce what he calls 'complex bulgy geometries' will, he believes, precipitate a move away from the Euclidean geometry of cones, spheres and rectangles (as examplified by Braun), and its companion trend, streamlining, which have together dominated the style of product design, in one way or another, for many years.

Virtual reality will also be a major influence. As yet still in its infancy, the simulation of product structures through virtual reality systems will enable designers to 'use' the products they design before they ever get to prototype stage, thus eliminating potential problems before they are ever incorporated into the design.

The eighties prediction that we would look back on that decade as years of surface glamour, with little spiritual content, has largely come true. Passing fashions still play a part in industrial design – in detailing such as the treatment of

buttons and switches – but for the most part, industrial designers today are working on the basis of a common, and longer term, agenda. Most of them want to design for the long term – the idea of built-in obsolescence is considered immoral by product designers, if not yet by all manufacturers.

Most designers want to design for the capabilities of the elderly and disabled. Just as architects, designing buildings for people with sensory impairment, are puzzling over how best to design a staircase so that its form stands out sharply from its environment, and how to make the route through a building understandable intuitively, so product designers too are trying to arrive at products which are 'transgenerational' – comprehensible and usable by all.

Most product designers also want to instil human qualities, some element of craftsmanlike skill, into their products. How they are doing this ranges from the literal use of craft materials and techniques – one new range of stationery includes a Filofax-like organizer made of papier mâché and many lighting designers are rediscovering the charm of paper and canvas – to efforts to redefine the role of technology in industrial design. In Italy, for example, Perry King and Santiago Miranda's Senyera lighting system employs a stretched fabric structure which hugs the wall, disseminating an impression of soft and sinuous light, integrated with the room – an approach in contrast with the prevalent focus on the hardware of the luminaire, never mind that it produces a flat and unmodulated light. Instead of focusing attention on the object itself, attention is focused on the creation of lighting effects through the melding of architecture with lighting design. And lighting itself is seen as a design task affecting perceptions of space, health and motivation – not just a simple matter of illumination. Designers trained in theatrical

lighting are forcing change on the producers of lighting hardware.

A sophisticated understanding of what technology can do to humanize design, combined with a craftsmanlike sensitivity to form, typify today's product designer. Whereas in the eighties, the talk was of achieving slick and 'well resolved' design solutions, now it is of products needing compassion and sensuality. Managers learning about the management of design are, at some institutions, learning by tactile methods – handling and taking apart their competitors' products, to absorb their subliminal as well as their obvious appeal. As Italy's architect/designer Mario Bellini has said: 'Industrial design means anything designed for the industrial process, but what does that mean? In architecture you don't distinguish between things that are built by an industrial process and things that are built by a traditional process.' The same breaking down of methodological barriers is evident in industrial design.

There are new factors influencing the consumer's choice of product. Fear is one – people are afraid of many products, sometimes rationally, sometimes irrationally. There have been cancer scares associated with microwaves. Blurred vision has been associated with the screens of televisions and computers, back strain with office chairs, breathing problems with the ozone emitted by photocopiers and vapours emitted by carpets and upholstery.

Green issues, and issues of quality, are major points of discussion. Together, these trends give today's industrial designers a seriousness of purpose which, combined with stylistic freedom and unprecedented production capability, should in theory augur well for product design. The role of industrial design in the economy is fairly well understood by the industrialized world. Now its role in society is the subject of scrutiny.

Candlesticks made from cherry wood, nickel-plating and synthetic rubber, designed by Hollington Associates, 1990.

Left-hand page: **Portable electric heater, designed by Ziba Design for Cadet Manufacturing, c.1990.**

The Apple microcomputer

The Apple Corporation was founded in March 1976 in Palo Alto, California, by two computer whiz-kids, Steve Wozniak and Steve Jobs. Six months later, the Apple microcomputer was placed on the market, priced at $666. The young entrepreneurs then announced boldly that Apple's sales would reach $500 million within ten years; as it happened, they achieved this result within five years.

The birth of the microcomputer was not simply a result of miniaturization of electronic components; it also marked a cultural revolution. As Philippe Breton[1] has emphasized in his history of computer technology, the microcomputer was born of a movement launched in the early 1970s, at the University of California, Berkeley, by young American radicals whose aim wasn't technical innovation but the democratization of information access. In 1972, the radical magazine People's Computer Company announced that computers were being used primarily to control individuals, and the article concluded: 'It's time to change this; we need a computer company for the people'.

It should be recalled that at the time the computer field was dominated by IBM, which had opted for the development of large systems intended to place centralized data banks at the disposal of corporate directors. In the military sphere – this was the era of the Cold War – centralized computer networks permitted the accumulation and manipulation of data about the private lives of millions of individuals in a completely undemocratic way. Interestingly, IBM's internal organizational structure functioned as a kind of cultural block, slowing down the irreversible tendency for information to be easily accessible and open to manipulation by all. Apple's founders were the first to design and manufacture a reliable product that was reasonably priced and easy to use. From 1985, all its computers were called Macintoshes and its publicity focused on a slogan affirming the universal vocation of microcomputers: 'The democratic principle as applied to technology is: one person, one computer.' The now familiar Macintosh hardware was designed by Frogdesign.

J. d. N.

Background: Microcomputer designed by Frogdesign for Apple Computer Inc.

Top: Powerbook 100 portable computer, designed by Lunar Design Inc. (Kenneth Wood and Matt Barthelemy) and Apple Design Group (Robert Brunner) for Apple Macintosh, 1992.

1. Philippe Breton, Histoire de l'informatique, Paris, 1987.

The Minitel

Initel, Intertel, Listel, Megatel, Memotel . . . It was Roger Tallon who, after considering numerous alternatives, came up with the name 'Minitel'. The product itself was invented by a group drawn from both the CNET (Centre National d'Etudes des Télécommunications) and the CCETT (Centre Commun d'Etudes de Télédiffusion et de Télécommunications).

The Minitel was tested between Rennes and Vélizy in 1972, but it didn't begin to appear in French homes until the early eighties. At first a simple decoder connected to a television, it has become a terminal for sending and receiving telematic messages and information. Plugged directly into a normal telephone line, its first function was as an electronic phone book. It has now become an accepted communications tool in France.

Using the Minitel, one can now make train reservations, find a flat to rent, carry out bank transactions and 'converse', via typed messages, with thousands of computers throughout the world. Keywords enable the user to access various services: 'mail-order' shopping, weather bulletins, horoscopes, sports information, film times, games, etc.

The eighties saw the start of a new sort of communication: the verbal cruising which the French have dubbed la messagerie rose. Who could have predicted that immaterial commodities such as information would evolve their own codes and systems of identification? Under cover of a pseudonym, hidden behind the screen, the Minitel user can maintain his or her anonymity.

The success of the Minitel has exceeded even the most optimistic projections – in 1990 there were five million in operation providing some 12,000 different services – and it is becoming increasingly widespread outside France. It has been interconnected with an Italian network and contracts have been signed with the United States (Videotel) and Japan (Nihon Philips and Mitsuji Knowledge).

In 1990, France Télécom successfully launched the M2, a new generation for which a password provides access to ten services. That same year the Matra company devised a portable Minitel with the dimensions of a sheet of paper and weighing less than four and a half pounds. Running off mains or battery, it can be used anywhere, at the office or in the car. Thus this 'network object' is part of the new tendency to create nomadic objects ideal for those who today regard the planet as a global village.

E. M.

The Walkman

From 1975, Japan started to establish itself as the leading manufacturing country for electronic goods, cars and motorbikes. Japanese companies offered reliable products at competitive prices. All these products were characterized by a sobriety of form. Electronic goods were designed according to the 'black box' aesthetic, which became established as the dominant international style. The components were enclosed within a cold, impersonal casing, while electronics and miniaturization accentuated the impression of immateriality.

At the beginning of the 1980s, action by the Japanese government, keen to improve the image of the country's industrial products, together with a new awareness on the part of companies essentially brought about by the Post-Modernist current, led to a gradual abandonment of the aesthetic language of the black box in favour of more subtle forms and colours.

The Sony group was formed, like Honda, just after the Second World War. After a trip to the United States in 1958, the company's founder Akio Morita changed the name from TTK (Tokyo Tsushin Kogyo Kabushikakika) to Sony, which alluded both to the Latin word 'son' and the familiar English term 'sonny'. Specialists in the manufacture of tape recorders, televisions and video recorders, Sony quickly became synonymous in the West with technological innovation and design quality.

The development of the Walkman was typical of Japanese products. This portable stereophonic cassette player, fitted with a light pair of headphones, was conceived by Akio Morita himself in 1979. Passionate about golf and music, Morita imagined a lightweight, easy-to-carry device which would enable him to indulge both these passions at the same time. Combining high technology with a slick appearance, Sony succeeded with its first model the TPS L2 in giving 245the jogger or adolescent on roller skates a flattering image and created a new market.

The styling of Sony's first Walkmans was smooth and cold, and these early devices only allowed for one set of headphones. To lessen the 'individualistic' side of the product – already a dominant feature of the decade – later models allowed for a second pair of headphones to be plugged in. In parallel with this development, from 1984, the styling became 'softer', more rounded, while the colours were of a more acidic and appealing hue. This evolution was in keeping with a new trend affecting all technological objects: user-friendly design, which demands that functional objects should no longer only perform well, but should also be man's friends. In 1988, Sony launched the first cordless Walkman onto the Japanese market. Weighing only 210 grams, it consisted of a cassette player, radio receiver and micro-transmitter. Sound is transmitted from the cassette player to the headphones by radio.

The figures testify to the success of a product which has come to symbolize its generation: in all some 50 million Walkmans have been manufactured.

E. M.

The Goupil toothbrush

Imagine an archaeologist of the future who, in the course of his excavations, finds the toothbrush designed by Philippe Starck for the Goupil Laboratories. Our archaeologist has already encountered other toothbrushes which appear to be ordinary tools. Why, he will ask himself, has this toothbrush been designed with such marked aesthetic intention? Starck's design is a free interpretation of the sculptor Constantin Brancusi's Bird, inserted in a perforated base shaped like a cone.

This toothbrush has become famous, and rightly so, for it tells us a story. The simple 'tool' toothbrush took its place in the bathroom at a time when it was a place of purification, a kind of domestic variation of the hospital. In this place of purity, it was only appropriate that hygienic measures to prevent germs should be enforced: one closed the door and prosaically performed one's ablutions.

The introduction of antibiotics in the fifties and the proliferation of health spas were not in themselves sufficient to stimulate a change in attitude towards this part of the house, which remained a temple of 'cleanliness and beauty' until the 1970s.

But then the notion of corporal expression took off in California and Jane Fonda catapaulted aerobics into the popular consciousness. The promotion of whirlpool baths proved wildly successful and the white ceramic tile bathroom gave way to a more colourful, convivial place, in which the body could indulge in ritual baths intended to restore its youth. This new space is not one of prohibitions; it is a place of pleasure and so it is only natural that beautiful objects should be found there. In this new, almost playful context, it is appropriate that the mundane 'tool' toothbrush be replaced by a 'sculptural' one.

The marketing department of L'Oréal (the parent company of the Goupil laboratories), aware of this cultural shift, called on a designer capable of conceiving a suitable new icon: Philippe Starck.

J. d. N.

Biodesign

Mike Jones

Mike Jones

Prototype of the CB 10 camera with automatic zoom, designed by Luigi Colani for Canon, 1982-1983.

Far left: Nikon M camera, 1950.

I n November 1985 *Design* magazine published three images with a single explanatory caption, entitled 'Frog prints'. The three biomorphically-styled cameras, modelled on the shapes of the human body, fish, animals and trees didn't even merit a page to themselves. Yet just a half decade later Luigi Colani's designs had come to represent the earliest evolutionary stage in a new family of product development – one which is taking Canon and a few companies like it into the new consumer-obsessed millennium – organic design.

As the crazy boom years of the eighties faltered and stumbled into the chastened, reflective nineties, and we argued about what exactly post-Post-Modernism, and 'good design' were – or even whether there could be such a thing anymore – organic design, or biomorphism, has been sprouting and multiplying all over the high street and under cover of the out of town superstore.

From the crustacean-inspired shells of cameras, to the mushrooming speakers of surroundsound audio equipment, the complex geometric curvatures of biomorphic design are a suitable bait for consumers jaded by the excesses of the sampling age. No more the simplicity of matt black, clean white and self-effacing brown boxes, nor even the baby toy primaries of deconstructed radios and fashionable electronic accessories. To sell off the shelf in the nineties it must not only be small, but personably formed, with the same fluidity of geometry as the fractal patterns which blossom in the virtual 3-D space behind the monitor screen.

Today, amid the bit-mapped cacophony of new age typography and microchip-propelled information technology, Colani's prototypes look almost mundane – hopelessly dated exercises in shaving off extraneous corners and awkward straight lines. Indeed, if it weren't for the global recession and the crisis of confidence in criticism it seems to have inspired, there would probably be a whole classification of organic and biomorphic design – the attempt to invest an inanimate object with a character of its own by using the forms and structures of the natural world. From there it would quickly progress through organic design, which might be construed as the mimicking of natural phenomena for marketing purposes, to soft touch, user-friendly and interaction design.

But even in the mid-eighties, after Ettore Sottsass had taken Milan's Salone del Mobile by storm with his Memphis collections, after architecture had gone resolutely Post-Modern, and long after Saarinen, Eames and Mollino had used organic forms in their work, Canon's prototypes seemed shockingly revolutionary, fantastical. The easy way in which they were dismissed at the time as attention-seeking oddities, marketing gimmicks unworthy of serious attention, belies the fact that virtually all consumer goods were still deeply entrenched in the black box, white box, brown box syndrome of global production for global markets, not by choice, but by necessity.

The new design of the eighties was dominated by luxury goods. Even the Italian furniture which was so strikingly portrayed in many magazines, was produced in far smaller quantities than the media images of it. It was batch produced or made as one-off pieces more for publicity purposes than for profit.

The makers of industrially produced consumer goods in Western Europe, the United States and the Pacific Rim, even when convinced of the merits of 'good design', were still competing largely on a combination of price and rapidly advancing technical performance. Whether buying new cameras, hi-fis or microwave ovens, only a tiny elite of privileged consumers based their choices on how a product looked. Instead, the majority bought because they took better pictures, gave a better quality of sound, or made their pre-packed meals

taste more like real food – and they did it at a price lower than last year's.

At the same time manufacturing technology was simply not capable of producing objects encased in complex geometric forms, as opposed to simple rectangular shapes (whether they be metal or plastic-based), at a price affordable on the global high street. And, as if these first two reasons weren't enough, 'good design', so-called, still demanded that form follow function with neat corners and trim lines. At the time articles about Sony's products, for example, talked lovingly of the young company's post-war roots in engineering and new technology. References were made to the excellence of its colour television pictures, the lightness of its matt black video cassette recorder and the ergonomic excellence of its hand held video camera.

Any glance at a shop window or warehouse shelf displaying consumer electronics in 1993 will reveal that the situation has clearly changed. It would be tempting to set responsibility for the sudden growth of organic design which has overrun the old order at the door of Colani Luigi, who, when searching for role models, rather ostentatiously selects Rodin. The sculptural forms of his biomorphically designed objects and his obsessively extreme, aerodynamically styled vehicles were a straightforward reaction against the strict, functionalist determinism of German design. After finally quitting his north German castle to travel in Japan, resettle in Bern, and meanwhile carry out an ill-fated commission from Sony to design a pair of headphones, Colani approached Canon in the early eighties through his Japanese agent, ODS Corporation.

For Canon, Colani was heaven sent. It had begun working on designs for the T-series, a completely new range of single-lens reflex (SLR) cameras in 1980, at a time when the international

market for SLR cameras was both lucrative and ferociously competitive. In 1983, recognizing a certain empathy between Colani's dictum that 'machines should conform to human beings' and its own corporate mission statement that 'Canon cameras are more and more approaching the shape of the human hand', Canon asked the designer to carry out a research project on the design of cameras for the future.

In the same year Colani presented five full-size models, illustrating proposals for different types of camera, which Canon decided to call, for publicity purposes, Five Systems. The results were quite unlike anything the high street had seen before. Making obvious references in their styling to the natural world, they look more like a series of strange aquatic life forms, unexpectedly washed up on the white page, than the classical geometry of cylinders, cubes and pyramids inhabiting Canon's production models at the time.

The models bear the same kind of resemblance to the rather obvious, biomorphically moulded cameras which followed in their wake as medieval drawings of beasts yet to be discovered do to the admittedly exotic but not quite so fabulous animals which awaited the geographical explorers who followed where imaginations had led.

The Hy-pro, for example, is a conch shell-cum-jet engine of an SLR camera with the barrel of its lens rudely emerging from a sinuously twisted plastic casing which also holds the LCD viewfinder, aimed at the professional photographer. There is the Lady, a pale and demure half-frame camera for beginners, with obvious grooves for inexperienced fingers, and the Frog, an amphibious SLR, mimicking its eponymous form, but also like a miniature submersible craft from a sci-fi cartoon, complete with deadly-looking protuberances on either side of its body.

There is not a straight line in sight and not a bad stab at what cameras were likely to look like in the future – though not even the visionary Colani could have foreseen how soon cameras would take on these biomorphic clothes.

Despite being pleased with the results of these initial concepts, Canon never put them into production. Instead, still in sympathy with Colani's philosophy, Canon commissioned him to design what was to be the top of the new T-series range, the T-90. At the same time Canon asked its own camera design team to come up with a competing design.

According to Wataru Nagasaka, the leader of that in-house team, there was no winner and loser in the competition: 'We decided to unify the excellent aspects of both designs,' he says, with the final, combined design being put into practice by the Canon team. 'The flowing form of the top cover originated from Mr Colani's proposal and the easy operational, practical grip part and the body design was taken from the Canon design team's proposal.'

In fact, stripped of its exuberant flourishes, it's not so much the 'flowing form' of the T-90 which departs from the standard buttons and lenses of previous SLRs, as its moulded handgrip and neat, inset buttons. The clean, flowing curves of the grip, with the shutter release button inset into its moulded, concave recess, are clear developments from Colani's much earlier Hy-pro prototype.

Subsequent cameras and other products which have adopted biomorphism developed the combination of rounded forms and highly 'touchable' controls. Videophones by Panasonic, Canon's own award-winning Epoca cameras, audio equipment from Yamaha, even Sony camcorders have since followed the Colani-Canon lead.

Luigi Colani's output is fascinating. On

Protector razor, designed by Kenneth Grange (Pentagram) for Wilkinson Sword Ltd, 1992.

the one hand the majority of his life's work – the bullet-nosed BMWs, the oil slick-styled Volkswagen Golfs, the impossibly massive hydrofoiled ships – are already beginning to look as dated as the futuristic cartoons of the thirties and fifties, all jetpack-backed citizens and cities in the sky. On the other, he is credited as being the visionary who changed the nature of mass-produced consumer goods, single-handedly ending the pre-eminence of the Bauhaus, Ulm and the all-pervading functionalism these schools spawned among the design-conscious manufacturers of the 20th century.

In fact, despite his international reputation, only a few of Colani's designs have been industrially produced. His planes, trains and cars remain resin shells, exotic one-offs motionlessly aping the function for which they were designed. The irony is that in the main body of his work – romantically elongated and impossibly aerodynamic transport designs – Colani's impact has been as a fantasist, not as a designer. Only when he turns his hand to small scale consumer goods – chinaware for Rosenthal, sanitaryware for Villeroy & Boch, cameras for Canon – does he get into production. And only with Canon has he scored a success on a par with the reputation engendered by his more fantastic creations.

Taken as a whole, Colani's work has to be seen as a failure. True, the eighties witnessed the emergence of Ford's 'jelly mould' cars and then the deluge of organically moulded, 'friendly' Japanese vehicles which have wiped the familiar boxes of the family saloon and the fleet car clean off the face of the city. But Colani can take little credit for that. He did not work for Toyota, Mazda and Nissan. And the companies he has worked for, such as BMW and Volkswagen, have not shared in the shapely successes of their competitors. Indeed, the designs being produced by the

likes of Toyota have more to do with the stylistic foibles of the fifties and with the new manufacturing realities of the nineties than they do with the concept cars of the seventies.

The emergence of biomorphic and user-friendly shapes in the eighties and its continued, perhaps unexpected, presence in the nineties has deeper roots than the stylistic preconceptions of a single designer.

Of course, the technology to make organic designs in natural, hand-crafted materials like ceramics, glass and wood had always been available. The forerunners of today's organic products were in furniture and tableware. It is no coincidence that Colani's early success was with sanitaryware and tableware, where the industrial production techniques already existed to make his designs feasible, if not functional. In the late seventies, however, the technology necessary to make seductively 'organic' products using computer-aided design, engineering and manufacture became available. Pioneered first in the aerospace and then in the car industry, CADCAM (computer-aided design, computer-aided manufacture) was at first a cumbersome and hugely expensive process suitable only for defence programmes and the long product cycles of the car industry. By the early eighties, however, fierce competition between, on the one hand, the authors and suppliers of the software and, on the other, the manufacturers of the computers used to run it, meant that not only were design programs getting much more sophisticated and easier to use, but also that their cost was plummeting. As a result, its use spread to industries where design and development served much shorter product lifecycles – like cameras, hi-fi, televisions, even white goods.

In Canon's case, the mechanical design, development and manufacture of the

Prototype of the Lady camera, designed by Luigi Colani for Canon, 1983. Designed for beginners, it has prominent grooves for the fingers.

Right-hand page: Roller skates, designed by Frogdesign for Indusco, c.1979.

tooling for the T-90 in 1983 was its first full use of CAD software, three-dimensional CAD software and numerically controlled, three-dimensional curved metal surface processors.

All of this tends to give the impression that biomorphism is simply the natural product of globally organized production and consumption. It would be wrong to assume that. Products with user-friendly shapes, as opposed to distinctively biomorphic products, were being designed and marketed for some time before Canon's foray into consumer goods. They tended to be aimed at babies' bottoms and disabled or geriatric fingers.

In the late seventies and early eighties, products like the Boots Babyware range and Gustavberg's ergonomic pens and water faucets were designed on something of a negative marketing premise – identifying the difficulty certain groups of people had using traditionally angular, everyday objects, such as sanitaryware, tableware and handtools, and then making them more user-friendly. This essentially meant more rounded and pleasant to touch, hold and use.

By 1985 the revolution in microelectronics, which had begun five years earlier, had started filtering into consumer electronics. That year Sharp launched its retro-styled 'fifties' QT50 radio cassette. Traditional high tech products like electronic calculators, SLR cameras and radios had become the new low tech, even if it was difficult to realize that at the time.

In an end-of-year review of design typical of the time, Peter Sampson, the then European marketing director of PA Design, caught the mood of change precisely. 'Thanks to refinements in thick film circuitry, these products (a solar-powered calculator, a credit card-sized radio, and a moulded digital watch) are actually more sophisticated technically,' he explained. 'But they're also less

pretentious and more user-friendly – they don't scream out "I am high tech" at you.'

He identified similar shifts in 35mm camera design. 'They've always been designed to look complex and technically advanced – even if they were fixed lens, fixed aperture models. But new Canon and Olympus ranges of fully automatic models are using much simpler styling, even though they've got all the state-of-the-art features, and they're much easier to use. I see products like these as the beginning of a happier relationship with technology, using it to express other than the traditional virtues, such as fun, fashion and comfort.'

Set against this background of rapid change and uncertainty, Canon's organic adventure was paralleled by a series of product developments which travelled the same marketing routes, albeit not necessarily using biomorphic styling. By the latter half of the eighties several of the most interesting of Western European and American product designers were exploring alternative avenues to the simplifications of form follows function, fantasy or fashion.

In the US, Bill Moggridge, a British designer who had moved to Silicon Valley from London in 1979, was becoming interested in what he has since termed 'interaction design' – the design of the process by which people interact with the complex electronics increasingly pervading even the most banal of everyday activities in homes, offices and public places. While a bank cash dispenser may well be as outwardly angular as anything designed by the German old school, the modern concern is with making machinery as comfortable to use as anything designed at Canon, through the use of screen graphics, and visual and audio prompts. Moggridge's teams at IDEO bring together the various skills of product designers, ergon-

omists, behavioural psychologists and specialists in human computer interaction like Bill Verplank.

In 1992, Emilio Ambasz unveiled his latest product proposal – soft tech – a series consisting of handkerchief TV, notebook computer, and portable radio/cassette player, all clad in soft leather cases, with circuitry which is held on a flexible membrane. Again, the hard angles and rigid cases of products were disappearing, making traditional concerns with design integrity irrelevant. The products were overtly friendly and imbued with the same sense of character as well-tailored clothes and the traditional craftsmanship of handmade objects.

The fact that the Japanese have a culture which leads them to find organically styled products attractive explains why there should be a domestic market for Canon's camera, but not why Japanese manufacturers and their designers should be so good at making them. The attention to crafted detail which comes from the cult of miniaturization – so apparent in bonsai – enables the designers to make products which win our hearts, not on technical advancement, nor on stylistic whim, but on their ability to feel comfortable in our hands as well as look good on our shelves.

Guy Dyas, a young British designer who has worked both at Matsushita – the vast conglomerate which owns the National Panasonic brand – and at Sony, tells of the fundamental difference between Eastern and Western culture. The latter is taught and practised on the premise of accurately visualizing product concepts in vivid two-dimensional colour renderings, displaying the artistry of the designer's hand as much as the appropriateness of the design itself. The former is based upon almost total disregard for two-dimensional work, with products refined in incredibly

short time by supremely accurate model-making, physical forms which can be turned and examined in the hand, buttons which can be metaphorically pressed, and the relationships between them and the fingers of the user tested. Handles might be broken off and repositioned again and again before a final design is reached.

It is this obsession with perfection in miniature and the importance of touch in Japanese culture which drives the Japanese design personality. What makes the combination of Colani and Canon significant is that it was the first conscious attempt to make products which were not self-consciously about technology, nor making life more comfortable, nor even slick marketing to an ever more sophisticated consumer. These products are not simply 'organic', which infers an exercise in American styling, nor are they just 'user-friendly', which implies the ergonomic efficiency of Scandinavian design. Rather, a better term is 'bio-friendly' and the fundamental cultural underpinning for them is, for the first time in industrial production, Japanese.

For Canon, and Japanese companies like it, there is nothing strange about organic design – indeed it represents the influence of Japan's own culture on the products they make and sell all over the globe better than any other aspect of Japan's incredible post-war modernization. While visiting Western eyes focus on the maelstrom of physical and, to use Ezio Manzini's phrase, semiotic pollution which greets them in Tokyo, Japan also has an ancient culture of designing small things which fit perfectly into the human hand. This makes organic design less a superficial styling opportunity, just another event in a rapidly moving sequence of product launches, and more a rediscovery of a cultural history.

'Organic design is extremely Japan-

oriented design,' confirms Wataru Nagasaka. 'The forms represented by the cups and tableware used in Sado (the Japanese tea ceremony) surely are examples of design fitting to the human hand. They are Japan's original organic design. Organic design is based on the ideology of harmonizing with nature, which is a typical characteristic of Japanese culture.'

Wataru Nagasaka is now the general manager at Canon responsible for, and the chief executive of, Tokyo Design Network, a joint design research project initiated by Sony, Nissan, NEC and Canon. His comments tend to confirm that the spate of organic design which followed the release of the T-90 was as much as anything a conscious reaffirmation of something submerged in Japanese design after the country's multinationals firmly embraced Western manufacturing technology in the aftermath of the Second World War. 'The organic design of Canon cameras represented by the T-90 has influenced the design of most other camera companies,' he adds. 'At the same time it influenced designs in the field of household electronics, audio products and office

machines. I would say these facts show the value of Canon's organic design.'

On the other hand, these products are successful not because they are better than before, nor even better looking, but because the computer technology which created them has also made many products 'immaterial'. We are moving into the virtual, computer-visualized world of the third millennium. Apartments aren't simply for living in, transport isn't necessarily just for getting from A to B, and physical transport isn't necessary anyway.

The products which fit into this landscape are not the obsolete square boxes of ten years ago: TV screens can be a few centimetres wide or be part of the actual material of an apartment wall; microwave ovens need to be 'crafted' like traditional silver serving platters if they are to find a place in our kitchens; cars need to symbolize the owner's mental image of his or her own self.

In this sense attributing significance to any one designer – or even any one style – is nonsensical. The whole premise on which we base our choice of product has changed: not utilitarian, not practical, not even emotional, but almost spiritual.

The current spate of organically styled products is probably as passing as any other preceding it, reflecting the current ecological, technical and spiritual obsessions with the fate of the planet, computer fractals and chaos theory. All of these things taken together probably do leave us standing on the edge of a material, spiritual, technological and philosophical threshold. But it is unlikely that biofriendly design is a symbolic representation of that.

It is much more likely that the design of artefacts, like the political forms of our societies, simply lags behind art, philosophy and science.

Like handkerchief TVs and user-friendly computers, biofriendly design is an indicator of the direction in which we are going. And it no more defines the culture of the 21st century than any one designer can be said to have been responsible for it.

Disposables

When it first appeared in the United States, shortly before the Second World War, plastic seemed to mark a significant technological advance. It was bound up with the utopian dreams of Modernism, offering the prospect of increased comfort. Valued for its practical advantages, plastic gave a special quality to mass-produced objects and signaled the increasing irrelevance of traditional materials.

In the age of plastics new kinds of objects saw the light of day and accelerated production rates led to disposables: the more that is manufactured, the greater the consumption, and, in turn, the more that gets thrown away. Wrapping – the plastic bag – was the first disposable object. While traditional materials could be retrieved and used again, in the post-war era we increasingly found ourselves dealing, for the first time, with everyday objects that could not be recycled. An array of products was linked to the waste of the fifties, corresponding to a way of life governed by new rules.

In 1953, baron Bich developed a process for manufacturing ballpoint pens that made it possible to reduce the retail price. The famous Bic was born. Some three billion of them are now bought each year. After his disposable cigarette lighters and razors met with similar success, Bic tried to market a cheap perfume, but the venture failed: consumers were not prepared to accept a perfume that did not express the idea of luxury.

Designers became increasingly interested in the ephemerality of disposable objects. Individual experiments, such as Peter Murdoch's polka dot paper chair (made from wood fibre), show that the principle of disposability could be applied to furniture. Other notable examples include Max Clendenning's puzzle furniture and Roger Dean's inflatable plastic chairs. The message was clear: functionalism was increasingly at odds with mass culture. Many English designers started to create pop-style objects. This new ephemeral consumerism seemed to demand loud colours and a new palette was created. Indeed, disposable cups, plates

and cutlery continue to be made in the bright colours which characterized the pop decade.

Unbridled consumption led to saturation, prompting a general re-evaluation of design. Influenced by the theories enunciated in Victor Papanek's book Design for the Real World (1972), which appeared at the time of the first oil crisis, designers of many different nationalities began to consider eco-design and to rethink the design of products for use in the third world and by the handicapped.

Today, disposable products allow for a new form of hygiene. AIDS has led to the growth of a new industry of disposables: condoms and syringes, the sad symbols of a new generation.

E. M.

The Yamaha Morpho II

The experimental motorcycle, which Yamaha has dubbed the Morpho II, marks a significant advance in bio-design, a trend launched by Canon in 1982 with a new range of cameras based on designs by Luigi Colani. Initially, biodesign was a reaction to the high tech, hard-edged geometric design of the seventies. Its promoters aimed to legitimize the idea of 'user-friendly' design and underlined their stance by saying that while in 1930 the dolphin was a symbol of aerodynamics, today it was considered a friend of man.

The Morpho II, designed by G. K. Dynamics for Yamaha, succeeds in creating the impression that one is in the presence of an organic machine, though not a 'friendly' one. In publicity material published by Yamaha in 1990, the designers of G. K. Dynamics declared that the contemporary motor-cycle was incontestably a 'sex object', but that the sexuality in question resembled that of the praying mantis.

The name 'Morpho' was prompted by a special feature of this vehicle: its con-figuration can be modified for either urban or motorway use. The choice of name was doubtless also influenced by the fact that the intense blue Morpho minelaus is one of the largest butter-flies of Southeast Asia.

The Morpho is a concept motorcycle that will evolve over time. Morpho I (1989) was an organic machine with skeletal frame and exposed motor, while the Morpho II's mechanical ele-ments bring to mind muscles covered by skin; in both cases the resulting 'look' is a bit unexpected. The classic control panel has been replaced by a blue cathode screen on which all the necessary information can be read.

This prototype is as much a product of marketing strategies intended to test future sales prospects, as it is the result of advanced technology and serious study in the realm of user-friendly technology.

J. d. N.

Leaving the 20th Century

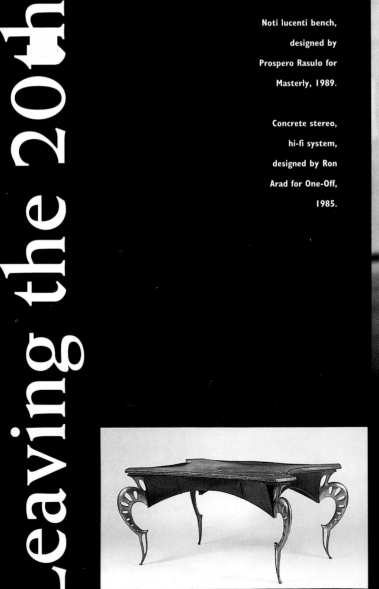

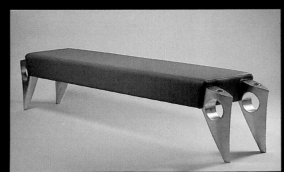

Catherine McDermott

Design has undergone a key cultural change in the last ten years: it has gone mainstream. Design is now an important issue on many different agendas, and figures in the political, economic and social arenas. Deciphering its role and significance for contemporary society has become increasingly complex and this essay will explore some of the important themes underlying design since 1980.

During the 1980s design was only part of an important transition in late 20th-century thinking with the cultural phenomenon of Post-Modernism. As a movement of widespread intellectual change, Post Modernism fundamentally altered approaches to science, philosophy, literature and critical theory, as well as strongly influencing design and architecture. Since the late 1970s, Post-Modernism has been used to describe cultural change in the widest possible sense and the name is itself a tribute to Modernism, and the ideas and designers of the Modern Movement who dominated 20th-century design from the 1920s to the 1970s. But in the post-war period a new generation of designers began to challenge Modernist principles. Quite simply they believed that Modernism's rejection of

decoration, popular taste and historicism was too limiting and restricted the idiosyncracies of human desires and dreams. Post-Modernism opened up a language of design that included a new way of working with imagery and materials that had been vetoed by the Modernists. What it produced was radical and exciting work from the new design superstar countries of Spain, the United States, Japan, France, Britain and Italy. It was an international language of design that has helped to shape our visual culture as we prepare to leave the 20th century.

Italy provided the first great shock of the new with the Memphis group. Established by the leading architect Ettore Sottsass, the group launched its first collection in 1981 to coincide with the September Italian Furniture Fair at a showroom in Milan just around the corner from the famous furniture firm Cassina, the bastion of Italian chic and good taste. Memphis was an overnight sensation. It premiered the work of an international group of collaborators which included Michael Graves, Hans Hollein, Terry Jones, Arata Isozaki, George Sowden, Michele de Lucchi, Matteo Thun, Martine Bedin and Nathalie de Pasquier. They showed objects and furniture with the simplicity and impact of children's toys, using a fresh, bright palette of colours and a new approach to decoration, mixing patterns from sources as diverse as 1950s coffee bars and 1960s Pop Art. The furniture challenged basic assumptions. Why couldn't you place cheap and cheerful plastic laminate finishes alongside expensive wood veneers? Why did the legs of a table have to be identical, or the shelves of a bookcase completely straight? The name itself, with its references to ancient Egypt and Elvis Presley was a mixture of irony, fun and ambiguity that reflected the new spirit of the whole group. Memphis was also the beginning of another 1980s design phenomenon, the focus of a new and massive media hype on the cult of design. The interaction between Memphis designers and the mass

media proved to be intense and immediate, and images of the group's work were featured in newspapers and magazines from Tokyo to New York.

Of course Memphis had its critics, who felt the work was an elitist avant-garde with little or no influence on the mainstream, but they were to be proved wrong. The influence exerted by the Memphis designers' use of colour and detail found its way into the high streets of Europe via companies such as Ikea and Habitat and in the new shop interiors of London, New York and Tokyo. Memphis also marked the rise of Milan as the international design capital of the 1980s. During this decade the city helped to launch on the international circuit the talented new Spanish designers, British furniture designers such as Ron Arad and Danny Lane, and Philippe Starck from France. The age of the designer as superstar had begun.

Underpinning these changes in design was the intellectual revolution brought about by Post-Modernism. One of the most significant shifts in attitude was due to the fact that these new theories and ideas did not come from the culture of design and designers, but from a group of intellectuals and scientists whose ideas interacted with design as part of the new climate of Post-Modernism.

Chaos theory is an interesting case in point. Chaos found its roots in the Harvard scientific community of the late 1970s and reached a wider audience in 1980, with the publication of Benoit Mandelbrot's book *The Practical Geometry of Nature*. The theory suggests that we have not begun to understand the complex and random chain of events in the natural world, and as a theory it presents an interesting paradigm to design, contrasting as it did the certainties of the rational Modern Movement with the uncertainties of Post-Modernism. Designers began to use the term creative chaos as a stance against a design process founded on a single and ordered approach. The resonance of creative chaos on an international

Dolcemare chest of drawers, designed by Prospero Rasulo, made by Masterly, 1988.

I like elements which
are hybrid rather
than 'clear', distorted
rather than
'straightforward',
ambiguous rather
than 'articulated'…
boring as well as
'interesting',
conventional rather
than 'designed',
accommodating
rather than
excluding…
equivocal rather
than direct and
clear. I am for
messy vitality over
obvious unity…I am
for richness of
meaning rather then
clarity of meaning.

Robert Venturi,
Complexity and
Contradiction in
Architecture, *1966*

level can be observed in the work of the Japanese architect/designers Arata Isozaki and Shiro Kuramata, as well as the American architect Frank Gehry. Britain also provides examples of the approach, in particular the work of Nigel Coates. Coates suggested that designers should mix sociological and architectural studies and that design should go with, and exploit, the cultural flow of ideas, indeed that chaos could be a much richer source of ideas than any attempt to impose order and structure. The results of his approach can be seen in a series of Tokyo projects, including the Metropole restaurant, the Cafe Bongo, and shops for the designer Katharine Hamnett and the fashion retail chain Jigsaw in London.

During the 1980s, Post-Modernism was part of a wider move to shift design away from being merely a practical problem-solving activity to the larger intellectual world of ideas. New and important ways of assessing visual culture came from France and the French post-war philosophical tradition. The most important figures for design were Roland Barthes, Michel Foucault, Jean Baudrillard and Claude Lévi-Strauss. In 1957, Barthes wrote a short collection of essays called *Mythologies* on subjects including cars, toys and advertising. For Barthes design was not interesting from a visual point of view but because it revealed the underlying framework of society while providing a rational, structuralist understanding of human conceptual activity. During the 1970s and 1980s designers felt that the analytical tools provided by Barthes, Lévi-Strauss and others, which included structuralism and semiotics, could be used to reveal the needs and wants of the consumer. Using these methodologies, objects could be deconstructed to reveal the complex layers of meaning by decoding social stereotypes relating to class, race and gender. And by reversing the process, designers could add onto design cultural signs that would enrich design objects for the consumer and the designer.

Jean Baudrillard was another key French

Study for
Totem,
designed by
Prospero
Rasulo.

Myths and rites are far from being, as has often been held, the product of man's 'myth-making faculty', turning its back on reality. Their principal value is indeed to preserve until the present time the remains of methods of observation and reflection which were (and no doubt still are) precisely adapted to discoveries of a certain type: those which nature authorized from the starting point of a speculative organization and exploitation of the sensible world in sensible terms.

Claude Lévi-Strauss, The Savage Mind, *1966*

Bohemia Jazz Club,
Tokyo, designed
by Nigel Coates
and the NATO
group, 1986.

Top: Tongue
armchair, designed
by Nigel Coates,
1989.

Centre:
Thinkingman's
armchair, designed
by Jasper Morrison
for Aram Designs,
1988.

Bottom left:
Glass table, chairs
and screen,
designed by Danny
Lane, 1986.

Bottom right:
Horns armchair,
designed by Ron
Arad for One-Off,
1986.

academic who explored the impact of consumer culture on society. Baudrillard highlighted a crucial issue for design in the 1980s, writing that with the era of new technology and the endless reproduction of images through television, film and fax the traditional view of originality had lost its potency. In this way he provided an important justification for the Post-Modernist interest in appropriating and retrieving imagery from sources including art history, film and video.

This view of design as a series of cultural signs that could be systematically analysed proved to be an important intellectual position that filtered into the design debate largely through the teaching at key international design schools, the most important of which were the Cranbrook Academy in America, the Architectural Association and The Royal College of Art in London and Les Ateliers in Paris. But while designers discussed and explored these intellectual areas, it is less easy to provide specific examples of their systematic application to the design process.

Other important cultural shifts that affected design and design thinking in the 1980s included new approaches to feminism. This has been particularly important in America were women academics have started to redraw the map of design history, seeking to reveal the way in which women's design work was produced and received, in order to challenge the accepted hierarchical and patriarchal view of design history. In the 1980s the feminist emphasis suggested that there has been no single feminist approach, just as there is no fixed feminine or masculine experience. But feminism during the last ten years has forced design to consider the simple fact that women's experience of the world as design practitioners and consumers is fundamentally different from that of men, but of vital importance in creating a balanced world for the future. Design without proscribed rules was the order of the day during the 1980s. Aspects of taste and visual culture that had previously been regarded as minority interests now entered the mainstream. Kitsch and camp, for example, were elements used to upturn the status quo in design. Designers began to exploit the crossovers between conventional good taste and the cheap, tacky and tasteless as devices to enrich the language of contemporary design. Perhaps the best known example of this is the pop icon Madonna. Her styling, using the clothes of Jean-Paul Gaultier, reflected a wider move in the design world towards bad taste and vulgarity. Designers started to use subculture references in their design work, exploiting and appropriating the coded signals used by Black hip hop, Los Angeles street gangs and the gay community.

Perhaps the most startling design transformation of the 1980s was found in Britain. In the late 1970s and 1980s Britain experienced an explosion of pop music, literature, club culture, fashion and design so powerful that many commentators compared it to the heady days of the swinging sixties. If

that comparison was over-optimistic what did emerge was a unique and strong British design identity, which exploited elements of anarchy, history, irony and the multi-layers of culture, inspiring new directions in design on an international level. This energy and talent was all the more amazing in that, firstly, Britain had virtually no manufacturing base to support these innovations or these new designers and that, secondly, this movement of change was not driven by Post-Modernist theory but by the British youth culture movement Punk. According to Malcom McLaren, youth culture remains Britain's most original contribution to post-war design and while this might be an exaggeration it has to be said that Britain's leading edge designers of the 1980s – Neville Brody, Peter Saville and Malcolm Garrett in graphics, Vivienne Westwood, John Galliano and Helen Storey in fashion, Ron Arad, Danny Lane and Tom Dixon in furniture, Nigel Coates and Ben Kelly in interior design – have all agreed

that their creative inspiration is rooted in British Punk culture.

One designer has come to represent this British approach: the fashion designer Vivienne Westwood. For nearly 20 years, in Britain and more importantly abroad, Vivienne Westwood has articulated a certain kind of Britishness. England made her. It is hard to think of another country with the rich and complex art school culture that shaped British post-war music and design. Westwood's early Punk persona has been well chronicled, most recently by Jon Savage's excellent book *England's Dreaming*, but it's worth pointing out that in the mid-1970s both she and Malcolm McLaren were older (they were in their mid-30s) than the Punk generation they inspired. They had both experienced art college life and, like other British designers in the 1970s, their work had an art analytical edge, influenced by Dada events and the French Situationist writings of the 1960s, and used the concept of the avant-garde as a touchstone for their

To carry and contain.
Every function has found its answer but as soon as this answer has been provided it become

To carry and contain. Every function has found its answer but as soon as this answer has been provided it becomes null and void before even being able to satisfy those who would have desired it. As Heraclides laconically said, looking and judging are elusive. Everything produced is soon thrown away and the marvels of technology are doomed to irremediable breakdown. The technological inventions of recent decades have only had a small impact on the creation and manufacture of daily objects (furniture) and simultaneously the tendency towards decoration can doubtless no longer be considered as anything more than a sign of recognition and privilege. Objects should no

longer be regarded in terms of their beauty or even functionality, but also in terms of intelligibility. This intelligibility is difficult to discern, for what has to be expressed is not ease but a state of consciousness relating to social and metaphysical questions. Paradoxically, it is sometimes preferable to give up speaking in order to express oneself more accurately. Function and use remain the incontrovertible foundations for the morality of design and of objects themselves. But, at the same time, every object represents the delimitation of a territory whose frontiers are not so much spatial as thematic. The key themes are: the void, metaphysics, inner quality, itinerancy, myths, the anodine, ambiguity, speech.

The material can only be grasped through the void. The void is the essential state of availability (in the sense described by Adolf Loos). The void is the ultimate experience. The void is what remains after we have consumed or accumulated. We learn about it on an everyday level.

The metaphysical may never be perceived, but no action is undertaken nor any object used that is not bound up with it. All the signs fostering this consciousness define the quality of our daily lives. The pretensions of the metaphysical go from the smallest presence to the most flagrant. The inner quality is the hidden face of the object, by turns its false bottom or double meaning, its secret. Technology

fashion innovations. Westwood's work captured the spirit, playing with the new signs of the times. Her clothes were charged with a vital life current that allowed the wearer to manipulate urban culture and street style and to participate in the counter-culture. Even for Britain, Westwood is a difficult, wayward and awkward talent. Unlike her peers abroad she does not run a multi-million pound empire. Her business, run from a converted schoolhouse in Battersea, is a modest one and so is her lifestyle (she lives in a small flat in Clapham). In spite of this, Westwood's influence and the mythology surrounding her personality and clothes is legend, although opinions on her divide into two camps: those who regard her as a genius and those who feel she is in part a creature of McLaren's making, part con-person and part of an uncertain Post-Modernism world that has upturned values and taste, and left few on certain ground. Recently there has been a significant turn around in the view of Vivienne as a perverse

and typically British designer, talented but hopelessly uncommercial, and interestingly this has come from America. John Fairchild, legendary editor of the American *Womens Wear Daily*, came out in her corner in his book *Chic Savages*. 'There are six designers today who are true twinkling stars, Yves Saint-Laurent, Giorgio Armani, Emanuel Ungaro, Karl Lagerfeld, Christian Lacroix and Vivienne Westwood. From them, all fashion hangs by a golden thread.'

So how can we assess Westwood as the example of the British design phenomenon? Is she one of the 20th century's great designers? Is she what the English call batty? What kind of analysis can we apply to her work and the British new wave? The first category where Britain has always scored well is in the areas of influential ideas and a quick checklist of some of her innovations makes for impressive reading: underwear as outerwear, boned corset bodies, baroque 18th-century prints, long skinny skirts and the mini-crini skirt. There is an exploratory

edge to Westwood's designs, a risk element that makes her work compulsive. Take for example her innovatory approach to the cut of clothes. This empirical approach goes back to the much copied ripped T-shirt of 1979. Westwood placed the neck opening under the arm so that when the T-shirt was worn it swung round touching certain parts but not others. This is because she believes that it is part of the function of clothes to slip off the body and allow the wearer to adjust the shape – a gesture of display that is an integral part of her attitude. Her clothes often expressed a robotic sense of movement, giving the feeling that different parts of the body could move in different ways.

A second area of assessment is the mass impact of her designs. Westwood does not reflect the themes and aspirations of the majority of British people and the time when you could interpret the world through what young people were wearing in London is now over. The fact is that the people who now shop at Worlds End include debutantes

---

ull and void before even being able to satisfy those who would have desired it.

sometimes acts as a mask to preserve, beyond functionality, the territory of inner quality.

Lightness and mobility, made possible by the recourse to new materials with their mechanisms of assembly and folding, would not be of much use unless they encouraged, in the first instance, itinerancy, that which reveals our difficulty in rendering, that which takes the form of the journey, considered as a wandering and the desire for knowledge – more than just escape, it is also the prefiguring of the ultimate metamorphosis.

Myths cut across history and countries like a common source of emotional recognition through which the role of dreams, of what is

indecipherable or inexpressible is expressed. The appropriation of myths by objects provokes exchange and makes them tend towards universality. Their reinterpretation is the sign of their vitality.

The everyday is made up of a succession of instants which pass by without us paying attention to them. Sometimes their disappearance is the guarantee of our availability. Sometimes an instant disrupts the flow of time or routine. The object carries within it this faculty to memorize the instant, functioning between the anodine and the primordial.

Functionality has promulgated the univocal side of objects, but the simplicity of service

has sometimes created a lack. Ambiguity is restored as a right, opening the field of perception and understanding: it brings the complexity of the question up to date and brings a response in suspension. The decoration of objects is, above all, no longer the accumulation of historical signs (evolving to determine the style of an epoch) of which we have lost the meaning, but a 'discourse' more or less audible, sometimes clear, sometimes tenuous, sometimes obscure, which transcribes the consciousness of our everyday life. Speech is contained within this. It is heard, either in an abstract way like the ideas which underlie the creation of form, or in a more obvious way like

writing, holding the effects both of decoration and meaning.

The boundaries of the objet are narrow, even though the fields of investigation are vast, because the charge of emotion or discourse can rapidly become transformed into a surcharge which can hinder the availability to live and act: the first finality of the object will always be carrying rather than containing.

Sylvain Dubuisson

who want a boned corset for a country house party, yuppies who want classic Westwood knitted twin-sets and some young clubbies who want to go classic. Westwood is no longer seen as lunatic fringe whose clothes cannot be worn. Now, for a certain kind of thinking woman a Vivienne Westwood outfit is a definite trump card and association with Westwood is an association with token intellectual values that feel daring but safe. The same coming of age theme runs through other areas of British design. For example, the radical typographic experiments seen in *i-D* and *The Face* magazines have now gone international mainstream, while the anarchic one-off furniture designs of Coates, Aras, Jasper, Morrison and Matthew Hilton are now in production and sold to museums and clients all over the world.

Westwood's work is quintessentially British, with its elements of irony, plunder and nostalgia. Her preoccupation with history and culture reflects the strengths and obsessions of the most creative forms of British design. For her, clothes and history are an aid to questioning and reappraising culture and her fixation on certain details, quotations and historical fragments represent for her something she describes as 'a charge of content'. This is a particularly British intensity and is expressed in her use of tartans, pinstripe suits, red fox hunting jackets and the image of the Queen as the perfect expression of fashion form and content.

Another British quality Westwood embodies is the old idea that Britain's creative tradition is a literary not a visual one. Indeed her starting points are words not pictures and she noted in an interview that 'the whole basis of my work is analysing what I do and building some sort of intellectual framework. The only possible effect one can have on the world is through unpopular ideas. They are the only subversion.' Westwood also represents another British tradition: she is an eccentric, a genuine naïve. She has no, what the British call, front and it's a disarming tactic. This lack of front is combined

with a monumental ego and certainty of purpose. If strength of creative obsession is a marker of quality in design, Westwood scores high. Her ego is virtually unshakeable and comes into the category the American writer Tom Wolfe describes as 'Papal'.

This ability to produce directional ideas which others pick up and use is another aspect of British design. Westwood has pointed out that over the last 20 years the idea has been the most important issue and execution a secondary point, a position she now feels strongly must change. She has said that 'the most terrible mistake of the 20th century has been to put creativity first,' and her recent collections are based on a return to craft and couture.

Of course, British attitudes, although interesting, are not the only priorities and new directions affecting design in the 1990s. In this context there are two hugely important innovations which have revolutionized design. The first is the development of new technology and the second is the impact of Green ecology attitudes. If Modernism was a response to the early 20th-century Machine Age, Post-Modernism is a response to the new age of information technology which includes two main areas, computers and telecommunications. The technological changes of the last ten years have been described as the Second Industrial Revolution and there is no doubt that they have transformed the process and production of late 20th-century design. In industrial design the microchip revolution has upturned the old idea that form follows function. In theory at least form has been liberated by the microchip. Technology has revolutionized design practice. In the West graphic designers have now dispensed with paper and drawing instruments to produce their work. They now work with Apple Macintosh computers which can talk directly to the client and printer, eliminating the need for hard copy and paste-up work. More recent developments include early research into artificial intelligence. Sometimes called 'fuzzy logic,' this allows the computer

programmer to key into industrial products a limited ability to make decisions, for example, washing machines that can assess how dirty clothes are and select a suitable programme. Meanwhile, the coming technological revolution is virtual reality, a fusion of multimedia including computers, video and television. As an educational tool VR will create real life experiences in which the viewer is no longer a passive but an active participant in a tactile and animated 3-D world. Soon students will be able to experience life in ancient Rome, and via VR visit museums and galleries all over the world.

The final important influence on design in the 1990s is the impact of the Green movement. The great triumph of the ecology movement in the 1990s is that it has gone mainstream. All designers are now asked to consider the long-term implications of their work, perhaps by avoiding the use of hardwoods or by using recycled products. The current Green buzz word is 'eco-balancing,' a method of evaluating materials on the basis of energy consumption, recyclability, raw materials used, pollution and waste. The European Community has moved Green onto a legislative level with an environmental policy that will introduce laws to curb both industry and the consumer. As a matter of course the major international manufacturing companies today have a Green policy. IBM has introduced a pioneering scheme to recycle old computers, BMW a scheme to dispose of old cars, while AEG has withdrawn its non-essential electric carving knife from the market. Developments like these are small scale but they mark an important change of attitude.

Design in the 1990s does not put forward a single idea about process or aesthetics and as we approach the end of the century design faces new challenges. The climate of Post-Modernism has helped to create a more sophisticated consumer and opened up design to a world of diverse and rich cultural references. Designers will have to respond to that and to the fact that technology looks set to reshape all our worlds in the 21st century.

The Bag radio

The first radios were cumbersome, fragile assemblages which comprised three basic parts – a transmitter, a receiver and an aeriel – together with, a battery.

At the 1931 Salon de la TSF, Philips presented the first compact model, which enclosed the various components within a single box. A lead made it possible to plug the radio into the mains. Liberated from functional constraints, the form evolved. The 'tin of ham' style of the earliest models was followed by extravagant designs in bakelite and plastic and, finally, the functionalist 'black box'.

In 1981, with his Bag radio, the Argentine Daniel Weil, who lives and works in London, reinvented the radio, which advanced technology and electronics had endeavoured to camouflage in a neutral, rectangular box. Were all the components enclosed to keep everyone but specialists away from them? Weil's response was simple: he replaced the black case with a transparent plastic film, thus rendering visible what had previously been hidden. He demystified the technology and made it aesthetic. The various electronic components within this soft, immaterial envelope evoke Cubist collages or Surrealist photomontages. They become so many plastic signs poetically forming an electrical home appliance, one that, in its new guise, becomes a cultural element in the domestic environment.

With its facetious, playful and resolutely impertinent appearance, the Bag radio is a rejection of the cold, impersonal 'black box' look which dominates audio and television design. It is a celebration of lightness and immateriality characteristic of much design in the early eighties. The Bag radio was, however, a commercial failure, remaining essentially a fashion accessory. The relevance of the principles which inspired it, however, has led to its inclusion in almost every major design collection.

Does lightness still have connotations of the cheap gadget, and is solidity, which is linked to the idea of weight, still unconsciously held to symbolize dependability? Does man need his everyday objects to have reassuring forms? Does this poetic design by Daniel Weil reveal the chasm that sometimes separates specialists from the general public?

E. M.

The VIA

One of the first objectives of the VIA (Valorisation de l'innovation dans l'ameublement) is to help young designers realize new projects and to encourage dialogue between industrialists, designers and the public.

As has been stated by Paul Jordery, the general secretary of the Comité de Développement des Industries Françaises de l'Ameublement (Codifa), the creation of the VIA was made possible by the introduction of new taxes in 1971. In 1977, the French minister for industry, after consulting with representatives of the profession, resolved to form a committee of experts under the auspices of Codifa and put Jean-Claude Maugirard in charge of implementing the project. The latter, president of the VIA, saw his job as that of 'issuing a standing appeal to professionals and non-professionals. . .in order to create a pool of the most important creative figures, on as open a basis as possible, offering its participants the widest conceivable range of expressive options'.

The establishment of the VIA fostered spontaneous associations between creative figures, much as the Union des Artistes Modernes (UAM, 1929-1958) had done earlier. Today, new companies interested in manufacturing novel products in small series are playing an increasingly important role: Academy, Ah, Artélano, Ecart international, En attendant les Barbares, Fenêtre sur cour, Fourniture, Neotu, Tebong, Xo, etc. Like Germany's Deutscher Werkbund before it, the VIA acts as a connecting link in the service of all.

Since 1980, young French designers have been able to benefit from the aid of the VIA. Notable beneficiaries include Francois Bauchet, Marc Berthier, Sylvain Dubuisson, Olivier Ganière, Garouste & Bonetti, Nemo, Jean Nouvel, Philippe Starck, Studio Naço and Martin Szekely.

Should the VIA remain open to all aesthetic tendencies or should it promote one tendency in particular? This question remains unanswered.

J. d. N.

Écart international

In 1958, after working as a journalist for the magazines L'Oeil du décorateur and Femina (later renamed Cahier de Elle) Andrée Putman started working for Denise Fayolle, who had just founded the chain of cheap department stores called Prisunic. She then collaborated with Maïmé Arnodin in setting up the agency Mafia, which specialized in furniture, and later, with Didier Grumbach, launched the display space Créateurs et Industriels, with the aim of making the work of talented young designers such as Issey Miyake and Jean-Charles de Castelbaljac better known.

In 1978, Putman created a place – more a laboratory than a showroom or design office – that was disconcerting or enchanting in its resolutely unconventional austerity. Here she and her team distilled the work of her favourite designers, bringing into the limelight forgotten personalities (Eileen Gray, Mario Fortuny, Robert Mallet-Stevens) or works that today are legendary but were then totally unknown. With a museum curator's tenacity and zeal, she used the tools of the past, working from original documents, rigorously respecting the creators' original drawings.

Far from being an exercise in nostalgia, Ecart international (à l'écart means 'apart' in French) was firmly anchored in modernity. This strategy of bringing up to date timeless objects rapidly won over the public. As an extension of this project of discovery, Ecart international manufactures the work of young designers (Sacha Ketoff, Paul Mathieu, Patrick Naggar), placing its prestige and commercial experience at their service. Each of Ecart's projects is carried out by a multidisciplinary team.

As for her own creations, Andrée Putman's approach stems from a vehement rejection of the decorative. She prefers the manipulation of volume and light to the saturation of space with 'decorative' details. Her originality lies in her eclecticism and her skill in devising arrangements of pure forms stated in neutral colours.

Her work extends into very diverse fields: museums, hotels, restaurants, theatres, ministries and private homes. On the company's headed paper, the word 'trace', an anagram of écart, appears in reflection. A recent design project for the popular Tati shops represented a new écart in Andrée Putman's career. And her 'trace' will now be visible in the sky: Air France has asked her to redesign the interior of Concorde. But Andrée Putman's adventure has left more than a mere trace, for it bears the stamp of a style which is synonymous with the 1980s.

E. M.

Background: Chairs designed by Andrée Putman for the Bordeaux CAPC.

Pentagon

In the German Federal Republic, amid a situation of creative chaos, disrupted by the turbulent political events, design asserted itself by casting off the heritage of the Bauhaus and the Ulm school. To break from their own past, some young designers sought inspiration from the example of Italian design, with its humorous and conceptual approach. But their search for a vocabulary of their own led them to replace the multicoloured with rawness and roughness. The beautiful finish gave way to the unfinished.

In 1985, five designers from Cologne came together to form the group Pentagon: Wolfgang Laubersheimer, Meyer Voggenreiter, Reinhard Müller, Ralph Sommer and Gerd Arens. In their opening statement, they declared: 'These days, the simultaneous mastery of the atom and the nuclear threat provide us with a model of relations for Post-Modern life. . .Design is no longer heading towards its predicted destination, but towards atomization, dispersal and disappearance. There will be no more Post-Modern design.' Two years later, after the creation of the Documenta café at Kassel had launched them, they became known world-wide and held numerous exhibitions in Germany and abroad.

This new concept of design was based on the immediate translation of ideas into reality: theoretically, no industrial constraint should come between the idea and its execution. Pentagon, therefore, does not offer products manufactured according to the classic norms of industrial design, but rather objects for habitation which give concrete form to a common idea. Made by the designers themselves or with the aid of one or two craftsmen, the objects incarnate the idea of opposing worlds which clash. Informal design is the new trend followed by designers who are not afraid of going beyond the limits, at the frontiers of art, philosophy and political commitment. In the 'inhospitality of our towns', hostile materials, generally industrial in nature, are used. Steel, often in its raw state, wire, sheet metal, inner tubes from the tires of tractors and cars, paving slabs, different kinds of plank, neon lights. . .all these materials were rediscovered in order to create heterogeneous items of furniture, in the image of industrial rock music which raged in a few disused Berlin factories. In a tense socio-political climate, an aesthetic of dissuasion sprouted. The designs created by Pentagon over the past seven years contradict Raymond Loewy's famous maxim: 'Ugliness doesn't sell.'

E. M.

En attendant les Barbares

**Topkapi sofa,
designed by
Elisabeth
Garouste and
Mattia Bonetti,
1989.**

'We are against design', declared Elisabeth Garouste and Mattia Bonetti in 1984. Frédéric de Luca, who shared their views, decided to use this manifesto phrase as the emblem of a new movement. Neither the triumph of functionalism, the aesthetic of the black box, nor standardized industrial design form part of their concerns. Running counter to industrial mass production, Garouste and Bonetti designed their first object: a lamp made from patinated bronze which seems to date from the mists of time. De Luca was to be both manufacturer and spokesman for a small circle of sculptors and interior designers which he brought together under the enigmatic name En attendant les Barbares (Waiting for the Barbarians).

'What are we waiting for, assembled here in the square?'

'The Barbarians are arriving today.'

'Why is our Emperor, who has been up since dawn, sitting solemnly under a canopy at the gates of the city, wearing his crown?'

These lines, translated from the Greek, are from the poetry of Constantin Cavafy. The people were assembled to present offerings to the noble Barbarians. De Luca, acting on the ideas of Garouste and Bonetti, called on creators weary with the prevailing functionalism. In response, Patrick Rétif designed a Carolingian mirror, Jean-Philippe Gleizes the Orque chair in patinated metal, Eric Schmitt the

Nostradamus standard lamp in rusted iron and perforated suede. All of them seek inspiration in the realm of magic, witchcraft and initiation rites, taking a fresh look at primitivism. Each has invented his own style, but all share the aim of bringing back a certain poetry to the applied arts. The decorative is a key element in their work.

After the Iron Age and the Bronze Age came ornament and colour. In 1987, the group developed a more baroque style, which was a logical progression of their work. The Topkapi sofa by Garouste and Bonetti, with its feet decorated in gold leaf, its volutes, its padding and red and gold damask initiated a new trend which today is widespread. The sofa was followed by the Jardin d'Orient et Jalousie carpet, which was acclaimed in the press, and then by the Marie-Antoinette range by Eric Schmitt, and candlesticks by Patrick Rétif and Migeon & Migeon. With the bicentenary of the French Revolution, the baroque became the symbol of 1989. Garouste and Bonetti's design for the interior of Christian Lacroix's fashion house reinforced the tendency.

This movement, which has sometimes suffered from excessive media attention, has brought a new decorative and poetic energy to French furniture design. Cavafy's poem ends: 'And now, what will become of us, without the Barbarians? Those people, they did offer a solution'.

E. M.

Contemporary Themes
in Industrial Design

Car Design

Gaston Juchet

From the wooden landaulet with an engine, to the 15 million Ford model T's, from steel plates cladding a wooden frame to the integral all-steel welded body, half a century has sufficed for the car to stage its revolution and become popular. After the 'streamlining' of the early designers, the car reverted to being a self-effacing near-cube in Europe and, after a lyrical and showy period in America, has finished up, following a continuous and rather reductive path of formal harmonization, as a protective, cushioned interior within an aerodynamic shell. The challenge for the new millenium is a car which is cleaner, agile rather than simply fast, characterful and easy to live with.

The evolution of the car

The metamorphosis from motorized horse-drawn cabriolet to today's 'supercar' will endure as one of the most instructive stories of our century. Nothing could halt the imperative demand for ever higher speeds which characterizes our civilization, even if, nowadays, we perceive more clearly its limitations and excesses and its negative social and ecological effects. The car (in the West at least) seems to be the best adapted and most popular way of fulfilling the apparently fundamental human need to go farther and faster.

This practical means of personal transport has moulded our way of life and the shape of our towns, has provided us with a new way of experiencing time and space and now makes up a large part of the world economy. It is also a diabolical machine possessed by speed whose praises were sung by the Futurists in 1922, which incited De Dion and Levassor in 1895 to inaugurate the Paris-Bordeaux-Paris race and which still weaves its spell on Formula One circuits.

The reasons for having a car are indeed complex and full of paradoxes: there is the need for mobility, for escape and for intoxicating speed, and for an overwhelming, roaring and somewhat mysterious power. On another level, the car satisfies more disreputable fantasies: pride, domination and aggression. Overtaking is as important as simply going fast. If he loses his self-control, the calm and courteous gentleman who gets into a car, joining forces with a machine full of energy, all reflexes and impulse, can easily be transformed into a dangerous and vindictive individual.

A car is not only in the image of its owner. It is also made in the image of its maker, each of whose products are part of an integral policy, a rallying cry which proclaims the conquest of the market by a particular marque and culture. Form and function, technology and style, mirror and symbol: these are the terms of reference for 'car design' and as such must remain at the forefront of the minds of all concerned (ignoring for the moment the semantic quarrels of the functionalist period and the disregard in which car design was held for so long).

From craftsmanship to industry

At the turn of the 20th century, coach-building was, in terms of its construction techniques and materials, a transposition of horse-drawn berlins, carriages, coupés, cabriolets, limousines, phaetons and buggies. Room had to be found for all the mechanical parts and this resulted in the development of a rear platform, a chassis supporting benches and a boot, and hoods and shutters to allow access to a still mysterious internal mechanism. Today we can still admire these somewhat hybrid vehicles in many museums: they bear witness to the extraordinary expertise of the craftsmen of the period.

The language of the cartwright and wheelwright (including such terms as louvres, valance, roof head, rear side panel) is curiously akin to that of the computer programmer and the structural technician.

A desire to imitate a kind of hermetically sealed drawing room, complete with cushioned seats, opening side windows, sliding roof or cleverly designed hood, quickly became established. The opulence of copper, brass, leather, woolen knit and fine

woods, each species carefully chosen, made the top-of-the-range cars of around 1910 into superbly finished masterpieces of refinement. Braid trimmings, wooden rails and delicately carved fillets offered the traditional coachbuilder the opportunity of personalizing every luxury car he made. Others had more ambitious ideas. Machine tools gradually replaced gouges, drawing knives and rabbeting planes. A belief in standardization, which was to reduce costs and enlarge the market, began to gain ground. Ford was soon able to make 15 million model T's between 1908 and 1926 thanks to his assembly lines. Wood was still king, however, and the body shape continued to owe much to the early carrioles. Many coachbuilders were to equip themselves to become suppliers for the 'constructors', who were more often than not simply mechanics. There was a resolve to standardize, but also to diversify and, even at this time, to offer a range. Firms like De Dion Bouton, Delage, Delahaye, Renault, Fiat, Peugeot, Olds and Dodge began researching into inexpensive chassis which could be used with different bodyshells.

Under the influence of aeronautics, a preoccupation with lightness and with profiling for improved aerodymanic qualities paved the way for a new concept: the torpedo body. The decorative and structural virtues of aluminium were discovered. The body now formed a single unit with the bonnet, with swelling curves for open-topped cars, streamlined with tapering tails in the 'sports' versions. Just before the First World War there was a revolutionary development: the advent of sheet steel. It first appears in the curved wings, the bonnets and the panels which cover the wooden frame and form a composite material bodyshell. This stage is quickly overtaken, however, in the United States, where the Dodge brothers – following experiments by the Budd Manufacturing Company – suggested a more generalized use of pressed steel and made progress towards the all-steel body made up from very rigid

Citroën 7CV traction avant, exhibited at the 1934 Salon de l'Automobile.

Bottom: Tatra V8, Hans Ledwinka and Paul Jaray, 1934.

Right-hand page: Monocoque bodyshells in the Citroën factory, 1948.

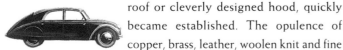

The automobile manufacturers have made, in the past few years, a greater contribution to the art of comfortable seating than chair builders had made in all preceding history.

Walter Dorwin Teague, 1940

welded sections. The advances made in reducing the weight of the all-steel body are so great that ground-breaking developments such as the flexible, ultra-light Weymann coachwork (made of stretched Leatherette) or the Vizcya all-aluminium body had no real future.

The beginnings of design

The years 1928-1930 mark the birth of modern bodywork design. The last glimmers of horse-drawn vehicles disappeared and the drawing together of disparate elements into a homogeneous whole started a long formal process which even today is rarely challenged. It was at this time that Harley Earl of General Motors set up the first styling research department, the Air and Colour Section. Its goal was to draw up plans for what might be marketed in the short term, but also to dream up products for the future.

Apart from a few individuals who were designing unconsciously, it was not until the years 1945-1950 that the new practice formed an official part of the car industry in Europe.

In about 1930, the car design landscape began to take shape. On the one side, coachbuilders were still making cars in one-offs or limited editions, with large amounts of manual work and without major investment. They employed highly-skilled craftsmen, heirs of the past but who now employed metal sheeting with the latest methods of soldering, painting (cellulose air-brushing) and chromium-plating (replacing nickel-plating). On the other hand, constructors had their eye on mass production, using die-casting and pressing of metals; their progress to the monocoque was rapid (Lancia in 1922 and the launch of the front-wheel drive Citroën in 1934). If the former were capable of great flexibility, inventing and realizing countless new ideas – many of them still rooted in tradition, however – the latter relied on heavy industry techniques and equipment. Happily, a few isolated forerunners were soon success-

fully disrupting the practices of both groups. It was research in aerodynamics which was the main stimulus behind formal evolution during this period. Pioneers like Camille Jenatzy (1899) and Carlo Castagna (1913) had already explored the 'bullet' and the 'tear-drop' body, but it was Paul Jaray's forward-looking Tatra V8 in 1934 which was decisive. With its 'pontoon' panels, its headlamps integrated into the front wing and its tapering rear end, it was a masterful premonition of the fifties and its drag coefficient (0,36) was worthy of the 1980s. It had an undeniable influence on the

Cisitalia coupé, designed by Giovanni Battista Pininfarina, 1947.

Lancia Flaminia, designed by Giovanni Battista Pininfarina. A development of the prototype the Florida (1955), it was manufactured in a limited series, 1958.

Right: Concept for a car of the future, designed by Raymond Loewy, 1943. This project foreshadows post-war developments which culminated in the Studebaker car of 1947.

American Streamline school, on the Chrysler Airflow, the Lincoln Zephyr and the Peugeot 402. When you think, in addition, of the 'pontoon' chassis of the Voisin Aerosport of 1936 and the flush doors of the Bugatti 57 of 1936, it is tempting to conclude that everything meaningful in bodywork design had been done before 1940.

It is indeed true that the first half of this century was a period of pioneering creativity while the second half has been devoted to the optimization of the following basic factors: reduction of cost price (through increasingly automated production), greater economy (through weight reduction, improved engines and better aerodynamics), handling, safety, and protection, quietness, reliability, durability and comfort (thanks to new materials and ergonomic seating).

The contemporary car

The next few decades brought with them important changes in design. Owing to their inability to adapt to either the monocoque or the pontoon body shape, the most prestigious names in French coachbuilding (in marked contrast to their Italian counterparts) gradually vanished from the scene, taking with them the equally renowned cars which bore their names (Talbot, Delahaye, Delage, Salmson and Hotchkiss).

The new wave came first from the USA. In 1947, at the onset of the rage for the chrome monsters made by the big three Detroit companies, Studebaker unveiled the Champion, a highly original design by Raymond Loewy. Italy soon followed, Giovanni Battista Pininfarina creating the Cisitalia in a style which, thanks to Michelotti, Scaglione of Bertone, Touring of Milan, Ghia and Frua, was to have a

A valve opening and closing creates a rhythm as beautiful, but infinitely newer, than an eyelid.

Umberto Boccioni, 1912

lasting impact on the European design scene. The two creations just mentioned are a successful rendition, with a still prominent rear wing, of the pontoon line which was to figure in a heavier form on the Hudson, Packard, Lincoln and the 1947 Keyser across the Atlantic.

During this time, the more democratically-minded European constructors increased their production of economy cars: the Citroën 2CV, the Renault 4, the Dyna Panhard, and the Volkswagen were followed by the Fiat 500 and the Austin Mini, none of which were designed in strict accordance with the general trends. In various guises, the pontoon shape was soon to become one of the main constants of contemporary car design. Also at this time, the European firms set up 'styling' studios (some 20 years after the Americans) and started to tap the 'modern' creativity of their Italian consultants.

The most emphatic statement of front-wheel drive, the Citroën DS 19, with its back wheels sunk into bulbous yet tapering rear wings and its sloping bonnet, similar to that of Loewy's Studebaker 53, transformed the design landscape. The very essence of high technology and advanced design, it has become one of the great cult cars of our time. It did not, however, have many successors, as a few years later it was the high cut-off tail which was to become popular. Simultaneously, Farina brought out the Lancia Flaminia which, with its rather American-style flanges, its wraparound windscreen and its new-found equilibrium between the front and rear, was to become a source of inspiration for, among others, the Peugeot 404, the Fiat 1800 and the Austin Morris.

In the 1950s American styling became increasingly extravagant, inspired by aeroplane design. New models were displayed in the famous Detroit motoramas. In 1959, however, in complete contrast, came the launch of the revolutionary rear-engined Chevrolet Corvair, with its clean lines. A dozen European models were inspired by

this car in which upper and lower shells were joined by a chrome band running right round the body. In fact, since the Chrysler Airflow, the American influence has been greater than is commonly held, even on Italian designers. It's not so much that the Americans actually invented sunken headlights, the pontoon body, tail-fins, wraparound windscreens and rear windows, self-locking doors and lights and radiator cowls which stretched across the whole breadth of the vehicle (these were all suggested by earlier lone inventors), but they were the first to have the resolve to apply them to mass-produced models. One should bear in mind that these watershed examples (the DS19s, Studebakers, Flaminias and Corvairs and, in 1968, the Ro 80s) are all commercial saloon cars, which is clear proof that a product brief with a long list of stringent requirements is more likely to produce original ideas than any 'show car'.

The stress on functionality characteristic of many French cars since the 2CV and the Renault 4 was again apparent in 1965 with the unveiling of the mid-range, five-door Renault 16, with its adjustable boot, folding back seat and its original roof assembly which improved accessibility. Though its design has been criticized, it was the first step in the direction of the five-door car, which today makes up 50 per cent of the market in this sector. From the end of the sixties date the most daring Italian models by Giorgio Giugiaro and Marcello Gandini: the wedge-shaped Mangusta, Miura, Marzal, Espada and Carabo with their narrow front end and squat, cut-off rear. This unmistakable shape – with its good drag-lift ratio – heralded the profile both sportscars and saloons were to have once aerodynamic considerations returned to the fore. A downthrust line (negative lift pushing into the ground) had replaced the upthrust line (which evoked take-off).

On a formal level, the oil crisis and a gradual awareness, encouraged by Ralph Nadar, of safety and ecological problems, were to bring about a change. Not everyone followed this new trend immediately: the Italians in particular carried on honing the sharp edges and crisp surfaces of the Maserati Boomerang, the Lancia Delta (by Ital Design), the Fiat Ritmo, the Fiat 130 Coupé (by Farina) and later Gandini-Bertone's Citroën BX. NSU produced the Ro 80 in a styling which heralded today's basic three-volume design; Farina, on Austin 1300 and 1800 prototypes, explored the square-backed profile soon to be seen on Citroën GSs and CX 200s; the Renault 5, the American Motors' Pacer and the Toyota EX III, on the other hand went back to curves. This trend was given further impulse by a psychological desire for soft, less aggressive shapes, together with progress in plastics technology and a concentration on low drag coefficients.

Synthetic materials

Thanks to synthetic materials which can be moulded, it is now possible to approach the problem of crashworthiness without reference to steel sections (the Renault 5) and the progress made in the study of collapsible materials has allowed the new safety requirements which so concerned designers in the seventies to be met. Rigid plastics, which are increasingly used for bonnets, wings and tail-gates are covered with the same lacquer as the steel sections. It remains rare, however, for the bodywork to be made entirely of plastics: for the most part, they are confined to forming panels which overlay a steel frame (Renault Espace). Interiors are a different matter. Plastics constitute the basic materials for the dashboard, door-panels, linings and flooring. In the guise of soft and giving foam rubber shapes, they also help to create a comfortable and welcoming cocoon for the passenger. Ergonomics research has made the instrument panel more accessible and easier to use, and has resulted in the design of fully adjustable seating.

The role of styling in the American motor car industry is, at once, the most exquisite refinement and the most regrettable despoliation of all that has directed the attentions of enlightened industrial designers.

Stephen Bayley,
In Good Shape, *1979*

Aerodynamics

In the eighties, aerodynamics led to the adoption of types of curve which had been forgotten for 30 years: they are still full, yet smoother than before, and are tested in wind tunnels on 1/5 scale models. Fared-in headlamps, glued and fitted rear windows and windscreens and flush wing-mirrors enable the Audi 100, the Ford Sierra and the Renault 25 to reach a CD of around 30. As many prototypes have shown, it is possible to reduce it to 20, but only to the detriment of other functions. It is a question of choice. The people carrier, or MPV, is one choice among many: even with a good drag coefficient, drag is still increased if one chooses to enlarge the main frame in this way. None the less, this type of vehicle has a bright future in leisure, sports and family contexts, as the success of the Chrysler Voyager and the Renault Espace shows, and very soon new competitors and variants in other sectors of the market (such as the Renault Twingo) will appear on the scene.

Japanese design

The astonishing emergence of Japanese design at the end of the 20th century has been crucial. By as early as 1980, the Tokyo Motor Show had became the main target for car designers, ousting the Turin show, which had been the benchmark for the industry since 1950. Ranging from revivalism to ultra-modernity, the diversity and eclecticism of these shows is remarkable. They are living proof of the vitality of an industry which, thanks to its extraordinary ability to satisfy the requirements of the market, has swept all before it. Countless ideas are presented, tested and, if the public reaction is positive, quickly developed on an industrial scale.

Japanese design has played a major role in the emergence of an international style, picking up from here and there whatever seems most fruitful at any particular time: the aerodynamics from Europe; power and solidity from Germany; American touches in the top-of-the-range models. Japan is also receptive to the growth of the kind of biodesign Luigi Colani has been advocating, which, reacting against the pure, yet repetitive lines of recent models, is a way of introducing style back into design and of recapturing elements of a lost expressivity and lyrical dynamism.

Early organic design has given way to a design of overall shape, of casing, made necessary by the requirements of higher speeds and all-weather protection. If one ignores the thirties fashion for long bonnets and the egocentric style of the sports coupés, the passenger compartment now extends as far as the outer edge of the wheels, thanks to the pontoon side-panels

Renault Espace, first European people carrier, designed by Matra-Renault, 1984.

Renault Twingo, one of a new breed of small urban cars, unveiled in 1992.

Bottom: **Matra Zoom, prototype for an urban electric car of variable length, 1992.**

and curved side-windows. As the windscreen and steering wheel move closer to, and eventually (as in the people carrier) above, the power unit, the passenger compartment also increases in length. It has become a hard shell inside which one feels safe, almost invulnerable.

In a few decades, the car body has been transformed (compelled by subconscious if not actual aerodynamic constraints and by the resulting formal unity) into a smooth and modelled one piece structure with a few air inlets, on which windows, headlamps, lights and scuttles are marked out. The profile is (and not only in the case of hatchbacks) neither two- nor three-volume. Integration has gone so far that it is often difficult to tell models and marques apart. Other factors, such as the multinational nature of car manufacture, designers' international training, the move towards a single market and the conformity

of technical schedules and marketing plans, have all had a role to play in the creation of this now familiar and somewhat unpopular standard. The saturation of the market has also resulted in some jaded palates and a smoothing out of aesthetic differences.

Luckily, from Jenatzy's Jamais-Contente to the Matra Zoom, the history of the car is peppered with unprecedented and exceptional creations, the fruits of the boldness of an engineer or the vision of a designer. It is to be hoped that others too will manage to turn the tide.

After the tumultuous birth of the concept of the car, after the unceasing outpourings of creativity and imagination which characterized it in the 19th century, the great challenge facing designers on the eve of the 21st century is how to preserve a characterful design industry instilled with new and progressive ideals.

Below left: Interior of Renault's Scenic concept car, with computer, 1991. The Scenic is a family car designed to provide maximum comfort and security.

Right: The key for the Twingo, reflecting the bright, youthful look that the designers wanted to give to the car.

The Process

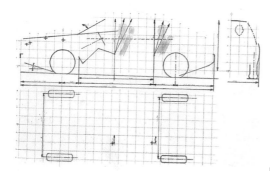

1

4

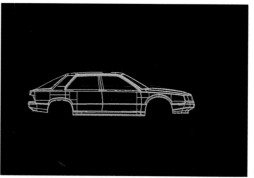

7

2

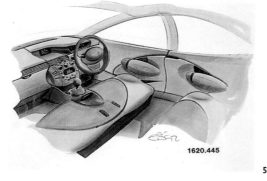

5

8

3

6

9

# of Car Design

Gaston Juchet

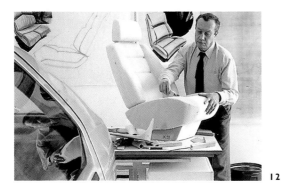

1. Bodywork plan.

2. Sketch.

3. 1/5 scale model made from clay.

4. Detail from a drawing made by a draughting machine.

5. Sketch of the interior.

6. Clay model of the dashboard.

7. Testing the driving position.

8. Computer-generated elevation.

9. Computer-generated image.

10. Full scale clay model and measuring apparatus.

11. Aerodynamic tests in a wind tunnel.

12. Model for a seat.

10

11

12

I n a context of rapidly changing social conditions, international markets and technologies (electronics and automation), drawing up plans for a vehicle five or six years before it goes on sale, to be manufactured for a five- or six-year period, is a perilous enterprise. A new level of ecological awareness, oil shortages, or a political upheaval such as the recent events in Eastern Europe can have important and sudden consequences.

During the development of a new car designers work in conjunction with sociologists, product 'forecasters' and, of course, research and product engineers. The development programme normally falls into two sections: the commercial 'product profile' and the technical 'specifications'. The decision to develop a new product can originate in either area and might have been the subject of exploratory proposals in collaboration with the 'advance design' department. They illustrate, through technical drawings, small- and full-scale mock-ups, the product concepts to be selected at the latest – 60 to – 57 months before the launch (the monthly timetable is calculated backwards from when the first production model is to be launched (month 0)).

The product profile

The product profile defines the vehicle in relation to the manufacturer's objectives on the one hand and the expected requirements of the consumers on the other. It situates the vehicle in its range and in relation to the predicted competition. It describes the vehicle's use, size and price, as well as its physical features and its more intangible, emotive qualities. It also defines the targeted buyers' social and professional marketing profile. Its aim is to create a well defined image of the future car. The words the product profile employs should have the same meaning and conjure up the same pictures for everyone working on the project, yet should leave the designer with some room for manoeuvre.

That special feeling, that blinding flash which gives one particular vehicle profile a crucial advantage over all the others cannot be created with a recipe book. Only a careful rendition of the spirit of the product through an understanding of the subtle way the driver relates to his car and decodes its design can do that. By what its bodywork expresses, the car has more connotations and symbolic meanings than any other consumer durable. The weight of tradition and the particular image of the marque combine in a complex way with a purely aesthetic conception and a desire to evoke vigour, dynamism or elegance, femininity or functionality in ways which can be immediately understood in widely differing cultures. The trick is to have a firm grasp of its most important characteristics, because trying to express too many (often incompatible) things, results in a bland neutrality. Compromise damages the strong expressive possibilities which come from having a central idea. The starting point is therefore crucial.

The technical specifications

Compiled by the technicians reponsible for the pre-planning stages, the specifications cover numerous technical aspects of the car and the dimensions of the interior. It asks whether the disposition of all the different components is compatible with the required overall dimensions, and whether the demands of the product are in accordance with the firm's industrial imperatives (the development of heavy components such as engines and gearboxes is not always in step with the design of new models). In the end, a plan of the dimensions, a bodywork plan, an outline of all the key points and constraints, together with an impressive documentation on all the international regulations, is given to the designers. Some points are negotiable, but discussions can be heated. There is both a desire for innovation and a desire to use existing techniques which have been developed over a long period and provide a guarantee of quality.

A typical planning schedule

Designers for whom the starting point is styling, put their trust in spontaneity and only later try to conform to the plan. Others have a more rational approach based on exploiting particular technical innovations and specifications. Whichever approach is adopted, the designers make their first sketches in a competitive atmosphere. These sketches are subjected to refinement and selection before serving as the basis for

1/5 or 2/5 models which are then made into full-scale mock-ups. This process takes place in the 'exploratory' phase (–57 months) mentioned above. Two schemas are chosen in the next, planning and development phase (from –57 to –45), and, after full-scale clay mock-ups, market tests, aerodynamic tests, other technical studies and early costings, a definitive and detailed specification and timetable are then drawn up. The third phase of the process (from –45 to –38), comprises hand-drawn and on-screen plans and 1/5 or 2/5 models (closely monitored by CAD technicians), allowing for the selection of three basic style types. These are then executed in full-scale clay mock-ups and then moulded for fibreglass bodies. The final selection is made on the basis of further product tests and aerodynamic tests by senior management at –38. Interior styling, using ergonomic models first alone then with the bodyshell, follows the same process, a few months behind.

The fourth and final stage, the feasibility phase, is the most exacting and technical. From –38 to –29, 50 to 80 per cent of the feasibility studies are executed on a clay model while 20 per cent are done on a fibreglass mock-up, which is programmed into a computer, becoming the final standard.

The project, then, has gone from the initial design office, in the exploratory preparatory phases 1 and 2, through to the department of computer-aided design in phase 3 and quality design department in phase 4. Obviously each project has its own life and each car manufacturer has its own working practices, and schedules can vary as much as several months from this programme.

Computer-aided design

When and to what extent computers enter the design process differs according to the manufacturers and practices concerned. Some designers claim they can create directly with computers and are able, using an infinity of permutations, to play with ideas and draw on screen or on a plotter. They can then examine in three dimensions

what they have just created by using numerically-controlled milling. Through a sequence of reprogramming, visualizations on screen and remillings, they gradually create the desired shape, which is simultaneously memorized by the computer. Others set tabulators and software to one side, believing that only the sensory relationship between hand and pen and the spontaneity of freehand enables the sensibility of an individual creator to 'come across'. In fact, certain style protocols (rigidly geometrical ones, for example) are better adapted to CAD than those with subtler and smoother lines. The choice of methods also depends on the deadlines dictated by each of the above stages: this practical consideration often pre-empts any prior philosophical considerations.

The most recent CAD development is computer-generated imagery. Completing or remplacing the static presentation of scale models by precise animated perspective drawings of the project is unquestionably useful. Ending a market test of a full-scale mock-up with a sequence showing the car in a realistic setting next to existing models, or driving along in a landscape, its various features shown in action, adds a dynamic dimension and brings the product to life, something which is essential for making a final judgement. It is also a fantastic working tool for concept designers, who are waiting for the time when prices will make a more widespread use possible.

Aerodynamic tests

The drag coeffcient, CD, an important factor in consumer choice, often appears in the specification, entailing preliminary tests in the wind-tunnel as soon as the small-scale clay mock-ups are ready. Experienced designers, modellers and aerodynamics experts can get to within an ace of the standard aimed at with little difficulty. It is those last few decimal points which are the problem: patient and methodical, nursing the surface joints, modifying the leading- and trailing-edges, they generally manage, fraction by fraction, with the odd unpleasant surprise on the way, to attain their objective. The methods employed today on scale models are generally reliable, but they always have to be verified on full-size mock-ups as modifications may be introduced at that stage.

Market tests

These tests were developed in the United States in the 1950s. Since the historic failure of the launch of the Ford Edsel, they have made great strides and today few companies do without them. Several hundred people, selected carefully for their socio-professional background, reply to a questionnaire about the future car during a secret test of an accurate mock-up. The devising and sorting of these surveys is contracted out to specialized firms. The key to a successful survey is to get social psychologists, semioticians, marketing personnel and designers to decode the results correctly. The members of the public taking part have to imagine themselves as future buyers and escape from the product image of the existing market leaders. Hence, it is not enough to follow in a crude way the simple choice indicated by the test: various arguments and alternatives have to be weighed up. Every company can cite examples of products which went on to be commercially successful after an unfavourable reception during these tests. In fact, history has shown that intuition and belief in the product remain crucial values in the final decision, though it is true that many designers do breathe a sigh of relief when the reaction to a product test is spontaneously enthusiastic.

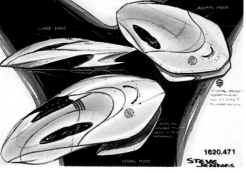

The designer competes not only with his colleagues but also with outside consultants who work in very different conditions and whose illustrious signature at the bottom of a design rarely fails to impress a board of directors. The decision process comprises a complicated series of subjective observations and comparisons which are, by their very nature, subject to discussion. The fact that only one project will be manufactured in millions and admired on the roads accounts for the incredible number of sketches, drawings and models eventually consigned to the storeroom. It's hard to have a design rejected without being upset about it. How is it possible to explain why a project has been shelved to a creator, an artist who has spent months passionately and enthusiastically working away on a product, thinking, in all good faith, that his could be the best? What is particularly frustrating for the designer is that, statistically speaking, this situation may well repeat itself many times. It is a job in which an almost obsessive passion for car design is required in order to overcome these disappointments.

Changing production techniques

This century has seen an astonishing transformation in car manufacture. Heirs of the medieval guilds, the wheelwrights, blacksmiths and ironworker-joiners, designers as well as constructors, slowly became sheet metal worker and often fitters who were assisted by chief tracers. The spread of the all-steel moulded body was to deal a mortal blow to the work of nearly all those fine craftsmen, whose well-made and brilliantly conceived creations can still be seen in museums and private collections.

'A well-made door, when it fits snugly, leaves just enough room to insert a one franc coin,' Henri Labourdette used to say. All our sophisticated machinery is not up to that. Have such virtues disappeared? Specialization, strict schedules and the profit incentive have all played a part in their slow erosion. If there is one place where they still have an indispensable role, however, it is in the design studio.

Not very far from the disembodied ballet of the robots and the tabulators labouring in response to speeding fingers, joiners and modellers with a special feel for their materials work in wood, resin and clay with all the sensitivity and precision of the craftsmen of old. During the most prestigious and rewarding part of the process – the stage of conceiving, researching and creating models and prototypes – they are the indispensable partners of the designers themselves. Specialization and ever-increasing technical complexities have led to the necessity for a conceptual and formal synthesis. This resulted in the appearance, in around 1930 in America and slightly later in Europe, of engineers and designers (known as 'stylists' at the time).

The desire to offer a range of models and to continually launch new products requires a continual search for new and varied concepts and possibilities. 'Styling' now takes place in impressive and constantly expanding centres of design. When these are based within a company, the designers, who have absorbed the cultural outlook of their firm, tend to cater for large-scale mass production, though their long-term planning departments also have an eye on the future. Outside design studios and bodyshell specialists, working for a large company account, are more like laboratories for free-flowing ideas, with workshops for their own, more craft-based, production. Yet things are changing fast: for example, the recent spiralling growth in the use of CAD and information science is effecting both types of studio.

Under market pressure, the already exceedingly complex design process for a new car has to function more effectively, rapidly and flexibly. This necessitates a constant optimization of the management of a huge number of factors and continual reassessment of existing production and evaluation processes.

The Jamais-Contente

'To see it drive past was an almost unreal sight and made a profound impression in the minds of those who saw this shell arrive and depart silently, almost without stirring up any wind or dust.' So wrote a journalist of the magazine La Locomotion éléctrique after having seen, in Achères (Oise), on 1 May 1899, the Belgian pilot and engineer Camille Jenatzy reach 65.8 mph (105.8 km/h) in his Jamais-Contente, a speed which set a new world record.[1]

In 1898, Jenatzy had obtained a 15-year inventor's patent to develop the motor car, and the result was the Jamais-Contente.

Being an engineer, Camille Jenatzy was the first person to understand that if speed records were to be broken, vehicles would have to be specially designed for the purpose. This gave him an important edge over his competitors, but he had also understood that a simple increase in power would not be sufficient to achieve the desired increase in speed, that it would also be necessary to reduce the vehicle's weight and give it an aerodynamic form.

Jenatzy set himself a tight specification and set out to design an electric car consisting of independent, interchangeable units which could be assembled on the vehicle's chassis.

He decided to do without differential gears and chains: his two electric motors would be directly linked to the back wheels. The problem then became one of finding a motor that was small but sufficiently powerful to turn the wheels. At the time, no such motor existed so Jenatzy designed one himself, had it built and tested it. It worked. At 600 rpm, the motor consumed 125 amperes under 200 volts, or 25 kilowatts. The two motors together provided 68 horsepower, which by the standards of the period was a great deal of power. The wheels were 55 centimetres in diameter and fitted with special Michelin tires.

The form of the body, which tapered at each end, makes us smile today, and is reminiscent of illustrations for works by Jules Verne, but by contemporary standards it was quite efficient. The vehicle's wheel-base was short (1.84 metres) and its front 1.4 metres wider than the back, a feature which anticipated aerodynamic cars like the Hotchkiss-Grégoire and the Citroën DS 19. The body was made of partimium, an aluminium-based alloy.

A replica of the Jamais-Contente is currently being constructed under the direction of Christian Wannyn, sponsored by the International Lions Club; it will be presented throughout Europe to promote electric-powered vehicles.

J. d. N.

Background: Camille Jenatzy in his electric car.

Top: The Jamais-Contente, Musée National de la Voiture et du Tourisme, Palais National de Compiègne.

1. This official record would not be broken until 1902, when Léon Serpollet reached 120 km/h under the same conditions using a steam engine.

The Ford model T

Assembly line at the Ford factory, 1913.

Top right: Henry Ford and André Citroën in April 1923.

Henry Ford built his first motor car in 1892 in Detroit, in a small rented workshop. It was a quadricycle driven by a two-cylinder, four horsepower petrol engine.

The Ford model T went into production in 1908, soon becoming the first popular motor car. Between 1908 and 1927, the Ford factories in Detroit would manufacture 15 million. The model T was one of the major innovations of the first quarter of the 20th century and new methods used by Ford in the production process led to the term 'Fordism'.

Between 1908 and 1926, the sales price fell from \$1,200 to \$290, while productivity levels and profits increased sharply. The reduction in cost resulted from several changes in the production process. Advances in casting, welding and assembly, as well as the introduction of less expensive materials, all helped lower the price. The resulting alterations to the car led to greater reliability. Electric headlights, enamelled bodywork, quieter motors and brakedrums incorporated into the wheel hubs were some of the changes that helped increase the model T's success in the market-place.

Production of the car was organized scientifically. When preparations were being made to put the model T into production, the industrial designers made detailed schematic drawings of all its components – drawings that could, if need be, serve as a reference in the case of disputes between workers and sub-contractors.

Other important factors in assuring the success of the production process were the establishment of 'families of operations', one for each part, itemizing the sequence of machining operations, the machine tools on which the part was to be made, and the gauges, fixed parts and diameters required.

Rigorous management and supervision of this organizational schema allowed Ford's production lines to turn out 3,000 vehicles per day. Each one of them had several hundred component parts, which means that millions of these elements were assembled on a daily basis.

The appearance of the model T, however, remained traditional, having a greater affinity with the aesthetic of the horse-drawn carriage than with that of the modern car.

J. d. N.

The Citroën 2CV

'A car that can carry two farmers in clogs, 100 pounds of potatoes, and a cask of wine.'

Pierre-Jules Boulanger, 1935

President of Citroën from 1935, Pierre-Jules Boulanger had the idea, new at the time, of a 'minimum' vehicle. The project was initially met with scepticism in the company's research department, but Boulanger remained committed to it.

The engineer André Lefèbvre, who had worked for Gabriel Voisin, was put in charge of the project and surrounded himself with a strong team, one of its most notable members being the designer Flaminio Bertone, who had overseen the design of the 11CV front-wheel drive vehicle.

The engine of the future Citroën was a two-cylinder, water-cooled, 375cc design. There was no self-starter – the car was started with a cable, like an outboard motor. The first trials took place in 1937, with prototypes that then underwent substantial modification.

The 'high tech' aspect of these 1937-1939 prototypes brings to mind the 1928 designs for the Maximum vehicle by Le Corbusier and Pierre Jeanneret.

The question as to whether Citroën knew of these sketches has never been definitively settled. But it is certain that Le Corbusier knew Gabriel Voisin; it is possible that André Lefèbvre saw them in the offices where he was employed at the time.

Research continued during the war. The body was judged to be unattractive and so was redesigned, while the interactive suspension system and inertia dampers that would figure in the final product were introduced.

The Citroën 2CV was first presented to the public at the 1948 Salon de l'Automobile, 12 years after the project had been initiated. The vehicle was a success from the start, becoming the object of a veritable cult. The 375cc engine of 1948 would become a 600cc one in 1963. Perhaps the most impressive characteristic of this astonishing car was the way it held the road, even at high speeds.

The styling of the 2CV is widely admired today; some designers have gone so far as to call it the finest piece of design ever. But for those who shaped its design, aesthetic considerations were of secondary importance.

J. d. N.

The Morris Mini Minor

Background:
The Mini in the
Monte Carlo
rally, 1967.

Top right:
Alec Issigonis.

It was after the Suez crisis, in 1956, that the president of the British Motor Corporation (BMC), Sir Leonard Lord, decided to create a small, economical vehicle primarily for urban use.

He entrusted the project to the corporation's head designer-engineer, Alec Issigonis, famous for having designed the Morris Minor, which had been successfully introduced in 1948. Issigonis opted for a box-like shape of 3 x 1.2 x 1.2 metres, with 80 per cent of its volume being set aside for passengers and baggage. To save space, he had the ingenious idea of using a transverse motor driving the front wheels through an intermediary gearbox and an axle near the crankcase. Unfortunately, this configuration took up too much space in the centre, so Issigonis finally decided to place the gearbox underneath the engine, using an intermediary sprocket wheel.

The Mini was not very successful when it first appeared – its characteristics and size were too novel. But gradually the public grew to like it. In 1960, 100,000 of them were manufactured. The figure reached one million in 1965 and five million by 1985.

The success of the Mini resulted from a conjunction of several factors:
– It was the first small urban vehicle and, given the particular advantages it offered in heavy traffic and areas where parking was difficult, it had no real competition for a long time.
– It appeared at the beginning of a period of prosperity unprecedented in Western economic history.
– Its seductive design had broad appeal, proving equally attractive to the fashion-conscious, women and the British royal family.

The introduction in 1961 of the Mini Cooper and, in 1963, of the Cooper turned the car into a viable competitor on the racing circuit and Minis carried drivers to victory in the Monte Carlo rallies of 1964 and 1965.

Today, more than 33 years after its birth, the Mini is still being sold and none of its would-be imitators have yet managed to duplicate its successful combination of qualities. Perhaps the Twingo, introduced in 1993, will prove to be the first one-passenger Mini of an entirely new generation of such vehicles.

J. d. N.

The Citroën DS

At the 1946 Salon de l'Automobile in Paris, 'well informed' people were amazed to find that there was nothing new on the Citroën stand. Certain people who were in the know were aware that, since 1932, the designer Flaminio Bertoni had been making a number of studies for a new streamlined, aerodynamic car. The general public, however, had to wait nine years before discovering Citroën's replacement for their famous 11CV traction avant car. They were not disappointed when they saw the DS19 for the first time at the 1955 Salon. During these years of gestation for the car, originally baptized the VGD (voiture à grande diffusion), Citroën was working on a number of innovations.

Apart from its motor and its four wheels (and even these are different in diameter to allow for larger tyres at the front than at the back), the DS (which is pronounced like déesse, meaning goddess) does not have much in common with other cars of the period. For visitors to the Salon, the first surprise came from the car's bodyshell, with its streamlined front, honed and angled for maximum aerodynamic effect, and its tapering rear. When they took a look inside, the visitors saw a dashboard which was reminiscent of the control panel of a spacecraft; the steeering wheel was mounted on the end of a long steering column; there was a gear lever which also activated the starter; and the seats were covered in a material then unknown. On the floor, there was a sort of mushroom, which was in reality the brake pedal, and there was no handbrake. Under the bonnet, the first thing that one saw was the spare wheel, underneath which was the motor, surrounded by an impressive array of tubes, pipes and components.

The leaflet about the car described a range of features which were completely new at the time: hydropneumatic suspension; clutch control; disc brakes for the front wheels (the first time disc brakes were used on a production car); wheels held in place by a single bolt; foot-operated parking brake; large capacity boot designed for easy loading.

During the first months of its existence, the DS suffered from a number of teething troubles, often aggravated by the incompetence of the mechanics called upon to repair a car which bore little resemblance to other cars and for which the least error could have catastrophic repercussions. Electrical circuits became part of car technology for the first time.

After this difficult start, the DS, considered to be the most 'intelligent' vehicle of its time, proved to be a marvellous touring car. A simpler version was produced, the ID 19, which was exhibited at the 1956 Salon de l'Automobile, while Henri Chapron made a DS cabriolet. In November 1967, Citroën created yet another version: a presidential DS for General de Gaulle.

In all, Citroën manufactured, between October 1955 and April 1975, 1,456,115. The DS was a revolutionary car, breaking new ground in the areas of styling, comfort, braking technology and roadholding.

E. M.

The American motor car

The whole of American mass culture was centred on the motor car. It was a catalyst that profoundly changed the daily lives of consumers. It was also a key aesthetic influence, a constant stylistic reference that assured a certain continuity. Thus in the United States the car developed in a context quite different from the European one. In the fifties, belles américaines, as they were dubbed in France, were not merely a means of transport but objects of desire cast in Dionysiac, baroque forms. After the Second World War Americans approached life with a new enthusiasm, seeking to express their individuality through consumer goods, notably the motor car.

In 1958 General Motors, then at the height of its power, started to look for ideas which would arrest the attention of a clientele demanding not only new vehicles but, above all, a style which reflected the energy of a people looking

optimistically to the future.

It was at this point that Harley Earl entered the picture. In 1928 he had been named director of the Art and Color Studio at General Motors, the first integrated design department in the history of the car industry. In 1938 Earl designed the Buick Y-Job, a very low-slung vehicle by period standards that is regarded as the ancestor of American dream cars. Its lines were to influence the Cadillacs of the post-war years.

Harley Earl was more an artistic director than an industrial designer. He started work in Hollywood, where he devised custom bodies for the cars of film stars. He was the first to use clay, a material which enabled him to create models – a decisive advance over the two-dimensional plans used up until then. Earl's method was later adopted by the whole industry. Shortly after the war he came up with the idea of the 'motorama', which was intended to stimulate the taste for beautiful vehicles. These circus-like shows, complete with orchestra, moved from city to city presenting General Motors' cars to an appreciative public.

The belles américaines were designed in the immediate post-war period. They reflected the ideas of stylists and

marketing specialists as to what the public would want when production hit full stride once more. They gave concrete form to new ideas about the architecture of cars – not just body forms, but also interior fittings.

Until 1940 Harley Earl had been under the influence of the Hispano-Suiza car, which had been tailored to satisfy the European luxury market. But from 1943 he became increasingly enamoured of airplanes. In 1951 he created the Buick Sabre, whose lines were clearly influenced by aircraft design, as were those of the various Cadillacs up until 1959.

His mentor was Clarence 'Kelly' Johnson, a specialist in structure and aerodynamics, who was known for having designed the Lockheed P-38 warplane, which had a double fuselage. The Lockheed's two directional rudders proved to be a source of inspiration for the American car industry for an entire decade, notably on the Cadillac Eldorados of 1957-1959.

Harley Earl's career came to an end in 1959 with the Cadillac Cyclone, in which he abandoned flamboyance in favour of lines influenced by intercontinental missiles.

J. d. N.

The Lotus 78

It was the English designer and engineer Colin Chapman (1928-1983) who was responsible for the Formula One racing car as we know it today. He was also the first to master the effect of drag close to the ground. His name will always be linked with the Lotus,342 which he helped create.

The key to Chapman's success was his understanding of the difference in aerodynamic behaviour between bodies moving close to the ground and those moving freely through the air, like wings. This is connected with the effect of Bernoulli's law, which states that when air is made to move faster by reducing the space through which it flows, its pressure is lowered. This diminution of pressure occurs on the underside of the car's chassis as well as along the surface of the ground, but as the latter cannot move up the body of the vehicle is sucked down. The shape of the Lotus reduces this drag by a factor of two, which is a considerable reduction.

In the past, the shape of Formula One cars meant that they tended to lift up: the fuller the profile of the body, the lower the pressure between car and ground and the greater the lift. With the greater engine power that became possible in the sixties, fins were introduced

to increase traction, making it possible to take bends at higher speeds.

The Lotus 78 was the first anti-drag racing car. Its sides were shaped like upturned airplane wings and air flow was channelled by 'skirts' close to the ground. This innovation improved performance on curves but resulted in lower speeds along straights. And it produced a serious problem: if a vehicles lost contact with the ground during an accident it jerked upwards violently. In an attempt to minimize the risks, strict rules governing the use of 'skirts' were introduced in 1981. The Lotus 78 won the world championship in 1979 and all Formula One racing cars since have copied it.

J. d. N.

Armchair, designed
by Giuseppe
d'Amore for
Play-Line, 1992.

Right: Moonkey
glasses, designed
by Vitrac Design for
Alpha Cubic, 1989.

Colour, Design
and Mass
Consumption

Michel Pastoureau

The History
of a Difficult Encounter
(1880 - 1960)

The history of the role of colour in design has yet to be written. Until recently, historians have had little interest in colour generally and its place in daily life in particular. The prolonged tyranny of black and white over documentation and publications has played a role in this lack of interest. But one could point to other reasons as well. These are linked to the very essence of design, which has always been more a strategy of form than of colour.

A detailed examination of the way colour has been used in design reveals that, in general, it has not been used very inventively. The achievements of the Bauhaus (contrary to a preconception dear to art historians) and its imitators with regard to colour have been extraordinarily limited. There was, above all, a failure to grasp the importance of ethical considerations and of fashion which, in the west, condition ll social uses of colour: there was recourse to a rudimentary kind of symbolism and a haphazard aesthetic which aimed to 'establish harmony' between the colour and function of objects; there was a more or less naïve belief in the scientific truthfulness of colours and in optical and chemical laws permitting mastery of them; and, finally and above all, there was a refusal to admit that colour is essentially a cultural phenomenon which resists generalization, if not all analysis and all discourse.

A moral barrier

What is striking when looking at domestic objects produced in large quantities in the late 19th and early 20th centuries is the poverty and uniformity of their colour schemes. Almost all their colours fall within the axis black-grey-white-brown. Bright, vivid colours are rare, and the juxtaposition of highly contrasting colours is rarer still. The first explanation for this penury of colour that comes into mind has to do with the chemistry of industrial dyes. Could it be that these were not suited to the mass production of objects in bright, fresh, luminous, saturated, and varied colours? In fact this was not the case. From the 18th century, western man was able to use precisely nuanced colours in industrial manufacture and from the mid-19th century he was capable of greatly multiplying these nuances and fixing colours on any and every object.

In truth the problem was neither chemical nor technological. If the first household appliances, fountain pens, telephones and cars were black, grey, white, or brown as opposed to apple green, bright red, or lemon yellow, the main reasons were ethical. By the standards of the industrial society of the 19th and early 20th centuries, bright, vivid colours, warm colours, colours which attract the eye and hold the attention were dishonest colours. They were to be used with the greatest restraint. By contrast, more neutral and sober colours, those belonging to the range of greys and browns or the universe of black and white, were held to be dignified, virtuous, and efficient. Considerations of social ethics encouraged their use for clothing, domestic objects and everything to do with daily life.

This moralizing attitude towards colour was the result of both middle-class values and, above all, the Protestant ethic underlying capitalism. One need not embrace Max Weber's views in their entirety to admit that there are close ties between industrial capitalism and the Reformation. Undeniably the manufacture of products intended for mass consumption went hand-in-hand with moral and social considerations rooted largely in the Protestant ethic. In the matter of colour, the great captains of industry held the same views as the great reformers of the 16th century: every honest citizen, like every good Christian, should free himself from aggressive, immodest, gaudy colours; polychromy was to be banished, as were all vivid hues; white, black, and grey are the ones best suited to all circumstances because they are the most discreet, the most humble. The most

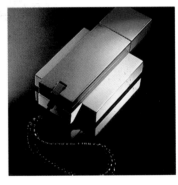

From top to bottom: Portable television sets, Sharp, c.1980.

Enorme telephone, designed by Sottsass Associati, 1988.

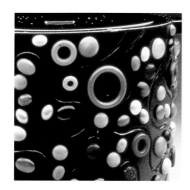

famous adherent of these precepts was Henry Ford, a puritan preoccupied by the ethical implications of everything. Despite repeated public demands and the colour strategies of his competitors, he insisted for most of his life on selling only black cars.

The evolution towards pastel hues

It would be hard to exaggerate the effect on early design of the constraints imposed by the social ethics of colour. For several decades they made it impossible to match an object's colour to its function (already a goal with regard to its form), thereby impeding the development of a true code of functionality and limiting the aesthetic ambitions of designers and manufacturers. As a result, there was a strong resistance to rethinking the proprieties governing the use of colour on products. The brighter, fresher, more varied palette intro-duced into the marketplace shortly after the First World War – due in large part to the artistic revolutions taking place at the time – was often greeted with ridicule by the public. The colours were not only deemed eccentric, but also some-times even obscene. As a result these devel-opments remained marginal (a fact too often forgotten), and had no effect on mass culture.

This same conservative, ethical bias against colour recurs in many other areas of society and culture. Commercial colour films, for example, would probably have appeared in cinemas earlier if it had not been for such moral pressures: moving images in colour for the general public was a bit much for society's moral arbiters. Here too the ob-stacle was ethical rather than technological or financial. But it was in the area of dress, the social code *par excellence*, that the moral resistance to colour had its strongest, most lasting impact. It was only in the second half of the present century that the general range of colours employed in men's and women's clothing became brighter and more intense.

In the realm of design and of clothing the values which facilitated the erosion of the old black-grey-white-brown moral system were pastel or demi-colours (colours 'which dare not speak their names', in the happy expression of Jean Baudrillard). More decent than bright, saturated colours, but more seductive than greys and browns, they have played an important, and misunderstood, role in the colour mutations of the 20th century – far more important than that of the radical revolutions advocated by artistic movements like Futurism, Cubism, Constructivism, Dadaism, and Surrealism. For it was these poor pastel colours – sky blue, pale yellow, faded green, pink, mauve, beige, and so on – which, between 1880 and 1950, made possible the explosion of 'real' colours – dense, luminous, joyous, tonic, and occasionally aggressive – in mass culture. Where are the historians, sociologists, and artists willing to do them justice?

A utopian semantics

Faith in science and the positivist quest for colour truth must also bear some responsibility for the naïve, insufficiently anthropological approach to colour which has prevailed in design. Seeking to unify the power, colour and function of objects, designers were, until recently, inclined to believe in the natural and physiological reality of colour, as if there really were colours which were pure and impure, hot and cold, related and unrelated, dynamic and static, exciting and calming. Oblivious to the cultural nature of perception and the utterly conventional character of colour symbolism, design has several times attempted to construct a universal code around colour's supposed 'ontological truth'. Not only do these codes and their accompanying explanations now make historians and anthropologists smile, they

Ornament from a harness, 14th century. Engraving from the *Dictionnaire raisonné du mobilier français*, by Eugène Viollet-le-Duc, 1874.

have always been off-putting to consumers and so have got in the way of the desired objective: harmony between practical and aesthetic satisfaction. Everything relating to water cannot be blue; everything relating to fire, red; to nature, green; to the sun, yellow. All hospital rooms cannot be white; all speedy cars cannot be red; all children's toys, yellow or orange.

By the same token, excessive confidence in the scientific theory (should we say pseudo-scientific?) of primary colours (yellow, blue and red, the last two having been monstrously renamed cyan-blue and magenta) and complementary colours (green, violet, orange) has restricted and even misled the colour aspirations of industrial designers. It should be emphasized that this theory, first put forward by scientists in the late 18th century and taken up by artists in the 19th and 20th centuries, has no foundation in the social and cultural realities of colour. What is more, it is inconsistent with the use of colour in previous eras. Given this, it's not surprising that it has conflicted with beliefs and value systems which have been solidly established in the western sensibility for centuries, and so has been poorly received by a hostile public.

The case of green provides us with a typical example. First science and then contemporary art refused to grant it the status of a primary, basic colour; they demoted it to the rank of a complementary colour, a sort of second generation colour, because for them green represented simply a mixture of yellow and blue (which was not the case in antiquity and the middle ages). But the devalued status of green, which was em-braced by design early on – to the point of making it a second-level colour – was inconsistent with all ancient usages and traditions. In the West, since feudalism, traditional knowledge and popular culture has recognized not three primary colours but four: red, blue, yellow, and green. To these four colours must be added black and white, which for centuries, even millenia, were understood to belong

to the order of colours, and were essential poles in all colour systems.

A slave of the spectrum and of colour classification, industrial design has often been misled into refusing to acknowledge black and white as colours, going so far as to posit a systematic opposition between the world of colour and that of black and white. In doing so it has been at odds with taxonomies far more ancient than the spectrum, ones whose anthropological roots go far deeper. Here again the sensibility of the public has been jostled, bruised, and led astray.

Incomprehensible fashions

Fashion is the third factor that has limited the ambitions and achievements of industrial designers in the use of colour. Fashion's shifting patterns amply demonstrate how difficult it has been, as far as colour is concerned, to impose tastes and predilections. These predilections are ephemeral, subtle, and incomprehensible, not really individual but not really collective either, and they are resistant to both psychological and sociological analysis.

For the designer as a producer and encoder of colours, the most difficult parameters to master are those of innovation and convention. In effect, a colour or association of colours is attractive and value-enhancing only when it diverges from other colours and other colouristic associations, from established habits and practices, from that which is available, ubiquitous, plentiful, and not, as the design agenda would have it, when these are in harmony with the object's form and function. Extensive use of a given colour or combination of colours in a great many products – the very goal of industrial design – will result in a success which is slight or ephemeral. In the world of fashion shifts of the pendulum are rapid and capricious, especially, perhaps, where colour is concerned. When all cars were black, it was considered chic to have one that was red, blue, or green; and when brightly coloured cars became the norm, owning a black car

It is the dyer who will doubtless see our work with a favourable eye. Dyers were the first and, for a long time, the only people to notice the inadequacies of Newton's theory of colours. . .For attitudes can vary greatly according to the threshold that one crosses when discovering knowledge. The real man of practice, the craftsman, the maker who experiences every day the laws of phenomena, for whom putting convictions into practice results in profit or loss, for whom the time or money that he loses are not matters of indifference: this man feels the emptiness and falseness of a theory much more quickly and more deeply than the man of science, for whom the formula is correct even if the physical phenomenon to which one applies it does not conform to it.

Goethe, Zur Farbenlehre, *1810*

became the ultimate in sophistication. Despite their best efforts and sustained reflection on the laws of mass production, designers have never been able to devise a way out of this trap, all the more formidable and tortuous because in any given time and place each social milieu, each age group, each social or professional class or sub-class has its own values which are difficult to grasp from the outside, impossible to channel, much less secure, and prone to react to the tiniest stimuli with reversals, disavowals, and transformations that are totally unpredictable.

This is why the historian has reason to assert that almost all of design's attempts to master this fashion dynamic through colour have led to disappointing results. True success has been achieved only by flying in the face of the ethics and exigencies of industrial design, by renouncing mass production and low retail prices – two basic constraints in true design – and introducing into the market-place domestic objects conceived from the beginning as class signs. Caught up in a whirlwind of shifting fashions, economic laws, and the caprices of snobism, design, like every other contemporary creative field, has never been able to emerge from it with increased stature. To be sure, 'ugliness doesn't sell' (Raymond Loewy), but isn't it ugliness of another kind to make beauty in order to make money?

Despite the gloom – and necessary reductionism – of this picture of the relationship between design and colour from the late 19th century to the 1960s, it is obvious that there have also been a few genuine successes. The stylists formed by the Bauhaus, for example, after settling in the United States in the thirties, introduced into the mass market-place many products with simple, seductive, and 'functional' colour schemes (but who can really define this last term?) which were well received by the public.

But as I see it, the great merit of industrial design lies elsewhere, in its having known how to enunciate the primary social function of colour: that of classifying. Whatever use is made of it, whatever the codes employed, colour is above all a means of classifying, ordering and labelling, of opposing, associating, and establishing hierarchy. The taxonomic function of colour affects men as well as ideas, places as well as objects, texts as well as images. It has figured in the West in every epoch and every culture. For this very reason, it underlines the vanity of any narrowly scientific or purely artistic approach to colour. Colour can only be properly defined, comprehended, and studied in relation to the social uses to which man puts it. In other words, the history of colour must be a social history.

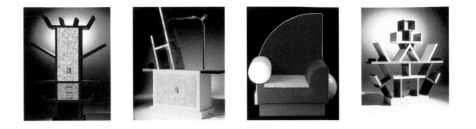

Memphis

Memphis was not an avant-garde movement publishing theoretical texts and manifestos. Created in Milan in 1981 on the initiative of Ettore Sottsass and the Italian industrialist Ernesto Gismondi, the group was formed to counter a functionalist design aesthetic that seemed unable to renew itself. Its own aesthetic agenda is interesting from several points of view.

It used a vocabulary of colours and forms in accordance with a simple heraldic code, one that was sufficiently distanced from specific traditions to transcend national boundaries. Colours in particular were always used to maximize contrast.

The relation between forms and colours in Memphis designs is complex and reflects a wide array of influences, all of them rooted in mass culture: advertising, toys, pop art, comics, commercial packaging, computer graphics, construction games, and so on.

Certain of their forms are reminiscent of totemic signs: this influence is apparent above all in objects by Ettore Sottsass himself, such as his Carlton bookshelves and Casablanca buffet. Here it's a question of an influence removed from its context but which nonetheless integrates perfectly with another formal idiom. The same goes for the palpable influence of toys on numerous objects designed by Michele de Lucci and Peter Shine.

The systematic use of laminated plastic materials, always decorated with patterns close in style to those of popular graphics, gives certain articles of furniture a stylistic unity suggestive of fairgrounds and festivals.

Memphis was the first coherent design movement since Art Deco to have explored the question of decoration and to have understood that the decorative arts implies the creation of objects intended to generate meaning and whose forms could be said to be more important than their function. Barbara Radice,[1] in her book on Memphis, writes: 'Memphis furniture, especially that designed by Sottsass, Sowden and de Lucci, is conceived exclusively in terms of decoration; this decoration is always abstract and suggests the development of a motif in every conceivable direction; its asymmetrical aspect has the effect of introducing ruptures and of rendering the form more dynamic and unstable.'

The influence of Memphis has been considerable and its impact between 1981 and 1986 is indisputable. According to the group, a new language appears when the prevailing cultural system becomes so radically transformed that the old language can no longer satisfy its requirements.

Ettore Sottsass played a key role in creating the visual language used by Memphis; hints of it can be detected in his work for Olivetti as early as 1961.

J. d. N.

Right-hand page: Zambia chintz fabric, Nathalie Pasquier, 1982.

Top, left to right: Beverly wardrobe, Ettore Sottsass, 1981.

Casablanca buffet, Ettore Sottsass, 1981.

Bel Air armchair, Peter Shire, 1982.

Carlton bookshelf, Ettore Sottsass, 1981.

1. Barbara Radice, Memphis, London, 1985.

The Voice of Things

Louis Dandrel

Objects, though they lack souls, have voices. Discreet or intrusive, they say what they do and what they are. Our daily universe is full of them. Material voices, motorized voices, electrical voices, they construct a reality, that of time, and give the world of 'things' its interiority. It might also be said that objects lacking a voice have a noise (the song of the earth is sweeter than that of plastic. . .). But that does not matter, providing that we are prepared to admit that their sonorous presence carries meaning.

The door of a Cadillac sedan shuts with a velvety sound bespeaking luxury. The Vespa scooter is a Mediterranean insect which for a long time heralded spring, the 2 CV a hard-wearing, rickety alarm clock. The Singer sewing machine clicks dryly and the Frigidaire closes with an opulent 'clunk' which inspires confidence. What would all these 'objects' be without their distinctive voices? Here begins the history of sound design, a curious history indeed since sound design does not exist. In 1933, the Bell company perfected the telephone, a masterpiece of technology. When it was time to give this marvel a body, Bell called upon one of the most celebrated designers of the moment, Henry Dreyfuss. Thus was born *the* tele-phone of modern times. And what musical genius, what skilled violin maker, piano maker or ironmaster was summoned to develop its ring? Judging from the sound of it, no doubt some obscure engineer who made do with an ordinary bell found at the bottom of a drawer. For quite some time there was a curse hanging over the voice of the telephone, one which seems especially perverse in light of the fact that Alexander Graham Bell, who died ten years earlier, had started out as a musician.

Wherever one trains one's ears, the message is equally disastrous. Most of the aural signals in the industrial world are impoverished, not to say downright ugly. In two centuries, there has not been a single instance of collaboration between composer and industrialist. The first, who deals in outpourings of the soul, and the second, of matter, have encountered one another only beneath Venetian lamps, and hymns or symphonies in praise of machinery have done nothing to close the yawning gap between them. Blame for this must be shared by both parties. Serious engineers have seen their work ennobled by visual artists. But what value could musicians possibly add to it? They shut the door on a new world of sound inaccessible to their own imaginations, satisfying themselves with functional responses to their needs for sounds. For their part, musicians grasped that at best their role would be marginal, their takings slim. Pro-noise manifestos and other such gestures were but poor excuses for not undertaking anything. But history is curious, because sound design *did* come into existence in the end. Certain sounds changed in the course of use, either because they became part of our heritage or because they were actually modified. Boat horns, train whistles and car horns have acquired strong, unmistakable emotional overtones.

The virtuosity of engine drivers who knew how to make their locomotives 'speak' has become legendary. Some modulated the whistle's tones by manipulating its control valve. The famous American engine driver Casey Jones invented a special five-note whistle adaptor that he carried about with him. Mr Klaxon was somewhat less inspired in his first creations, but his invention of the two-note car horn, which came to symbolize the beautiful American car, made the people and filmmakers happy.

In fact, it was the film industry that first revealed the full capacities of sound design. It was not only the actors who were given voice in the 'talkies', but the sets as well.

Within the concentrated expanse of the screen, things could be made to speak. And it was discovered that actual sound was worthless. The first sound designers were the sound effects men; they created a sound world that was more 'real' than reality, that was calculated for dramatic effect. The lavish science fiction productions of today are veritable paradises of sound invention, from the closing of a door to the electronic voices of robots. The sound effects men became sound directors or designers, and were respected as artists rather than handymen.

Alas, everyday life lags far behind films, but there are a few encouraging signs. Car manufacturers, for example, are beginning to pay serious attention to the quality of sound produced by their vehicles. For some time now the Germans (Mercedes above all) and the Japanese (Toyota, Nissan) have been studying the noise of their cars with regard to acoustic comfort. But there's a new tendency to treat engine noise as a constituent element of the product. At Renault, a motor hum that would be ideal according to the marketing catechism is simulated in a recording studio and then handed over to engineers to be reproduced mechanically. The head of the studio is an acoustician-musician. And the developers of household electrical appliances have finally understood that the domestic sound environment should be respected. They boast of the 'silence' of their products – a significant first step towards sonorous creativity. In fact, a new level of activity can be observed today in almost all areas concerned with sound design: communications (sound logos, following the example of graphic logos and associated products); signalling (in airports, stations and shopping centres); ergonomics (sounds produced by computers, calculators, etc.).

The accumulation of sounds in daily life has made the intervention of 'sound shapers' – or alternatively, musicians willing to apply their skills to ordinary objects – a matter of some urgency. The necessary conditions already exist: the technical means, both acoustic and electro-acoustic, are available; public demand is increasingly demonstrative; and a few pioneering businesses have already opened the way. What will the new designed sounds be? The answer to this question can be found within the history of Cadillac, Vespa and Singer. . .sounds that are rich, distinctive, ergonomic and meaningful. Sounds that will reduce the useless signals now clogging our sonorous environment to silence. Is that so very utopian?

Ornament and

Ascetic aesthetics
and the eloquence of ornament

The role of ornament in design has been fuelling the flames of debate ever since the mid-19th century. This often vituperative discourse has been dominated by two opposing ideologies. The first embraces notions of a rational, functional aesthetic with roots in scientific positivism, and is associated with the clean, machine-like forms of the international style in design and architecture which emerged in Europe in the 1920s and 1930s. The second ideology expresses a greater commitment to the exploration of metaphor, symbolism and meaning through the use of ornament and decoration. The latter sees the use of ornament in design as an expression of status, power, or wealth, whether on the part of an individual or an organization, as a way of embracing associations

Hommage à
Madonna fork,
covered in gold-
plated silver with
plastic handle,
designed by
Matteo Thun for
Würtemburgische
Metalwarenfabrik
(WMF), 1986.

with national or regional identity, or of resonating a warm and secure domesticity far removed from the ardours of the workplace. Fashionable ornament has also been used by designers and manufacturers seeking to boost sales figures, whether through the exuberant celebrations of technical ingenuity and stylistic encyclopaedism mass-produced by the mid-19th-century manufacturing industry, the baroque, space age, chromium

Industrial Design

Culture, Status and Identity

Jonathan M. Woodham

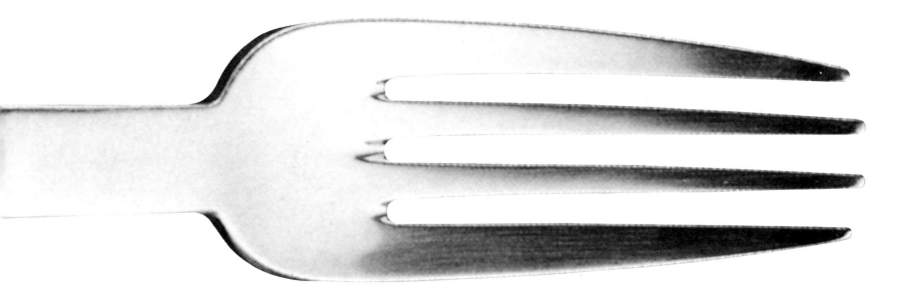

fantasies of radiator grilles and dash-boards common in American cars of the 1950s,[1] or the more refined forms of the neo-Georgian coach lamps which have adorned the porches of the socially aspirant in many British suburban housing developments since the 1960s.

However, the battle over ornamentation has also been bound up with issues of taste and cultural elitism. The Austrian architect and writer Adolf Loos, in his

This Post-Modern cutlery has a style and cultural status which override utilitarian considerations.

widely cited essay *Ornament und Verbrechen* (Ornament and Crime) of 1908, went so far as to dub the 'modern ornamentalist' as either a 'cultural laggard or a pathological case', one who was out of tune with what the avant-garde saw as the true style of the 20th century. This style looked to new materials and processes and saw standardization and rationalization in modern industry as a means of providing an aesthetic in which form and

function happily co-existed. Allied to this outlook was the belief that the abstract, undecorated forms of this First Machine Age[2] were wedded to a democratic ideal whereby the majority would be able to enjoy a better living standard in a hygienic, healthy and modern environment. This ideal underpinned the spirit of progressive Modernism in the work of avant-garde designers in the 1920s, particularly in Germany, France,

Holland, the USSR and Scandinavia. However, with the spread of fascism in Italy and Germany, set against a wider backcloth of political and economic uncertainty in the rest of Europe, there was a nationalistic and conservative reaction against the internationalizing tendencies of the avant-garde, which were often tinged with notions of cultural Bolshevism.

In such a context ornament was seen – as it still is – as a potent means of communicating particular social and cultural resonances, whether through the *völkisch* spirit pervading many designs manufactured during the Third Reich, the overt references to the power and grandeur of ancient Rome in Mussolini's Italy, or the historicizing styles in the declining years of the British empire.

Cultural elitism, taste-forming and the battle against ornament

Many of those who promoted the Modernist cause during the years leading up to the Second World War were motivated by a desire to 'improve' taste, and to promote a gospel of 'good design' among manufacturers, retailers and consumers. In reality, these advocates of design reform were often drawn from a very narrow social spectrum. In Britain, for example, the development of Modernism in the late 1920s and 1930s has been attributed to 'school, class and family ties'.[3] The Board of Trade's own Council for Art and Industry (like its ideological offspring the Council of Industrial Design, later the Design

Council),[4] which first met in 1934, reflected the effete, metropolitan values of south-east England, as well as the considerable influence of gentlemen's clubs in St James's Street and Pall Mall, with their proximity to the civil service in Whitehall and the Houses of Parliament. The Council's outlook was also compatible with the moral didacticism of the recently-founded British Broadcasting Corporation (BBC).[5] Stripped bare of superfluous decoration, the aesthetic of Modernism has, until fairly recently, dominated the kind of industrial design represented in museums, themselves powerful agencies of cultural conditioning. Such collections have reflected a linear history of design reform, which might be summarized as follows: following the critical rejection of ornamentation for its own sake in the 19th century, designers explored the possibilities of establishing an emphatically 20th-century Machine Age style, particularly in Germany during the 1920s. This culminated in the internationalization of 'good design', illustrated by the products of such 'enlightened' companies as Braun in Germany, Olivetti in Italy, IBM in the United States and the furniture manufacturers Hille in Britain.

One of the chief culprits responsible for perpetuating a faith in Eurocentric puritanism (or products without 'decadent' ornamental clothes) was the Museum of Modern Art (MOMA) in New York. Founded in 1929, it did much to promote the Modernist cause through its

department of architecture and industrial art, established in 1932. Its outlook was epitomized by the celebrated Machine Art exhibition of 1934 organized by Philip Johnson, one of a series of didactic shows promoting the Modernist cause held during the 1930s. The series culminated in the museum's tenth anniversary retrospective of 1939, in which the section devoted to industrial design was extremely small. The moral disapproval of American streamlining – ornamentalism in tune with the wider social preoccupations, with speed, technological progress and science fiction – was reflected in the selection of only one American product – Richard Buckminster Fuller's highly rationalized Dymaxion bathroom. Marginally more room was devoted to the less commercial, culturally more 'elevated', chairs by Le Corbusier, Marcel Breuer, Mies van der Rohe and Alvar Aalto. This commitment to the symbiosis of form and function at the expense of ornament and decoration continued into the 1940s under Eliot Noyes[6] and the Good Design shows of Edgar Kaufmann Jr. in the 1950s.

After the Second World War there was also a frenetic burst of energy to further the spirit of Modernism on the other side of the Atlantic. In Britain, the Council of Industrial Design, financed through the government's Board of Trade, spearheaded a campaign to 'improve' standards of design in both industry and the market-place.[7] With its own Design Centre in central London,

opened in 1956, it started to bestow Good Design Awards on products which conformed to the Modernist canons of taste. Similar awards were being bestowed elsewhere. In the United States a Good Design label could be conferred by MOMA in conjunction with the Merchandise Mart of Chicago. In Italy there was the Compasso d'Oro award by La Rinascente department store in Milan and in France the Beauté-France award conferred by the Ministry of Commerce.

Multinational companies, Modernist enterprise and the globalization of 'good design'

It was not merely the lobbying of the cultural and design reform agencies which promoted a Modernist aesthetic in the face of a changing consumerist climate. After the Second World War, multinational corporations emerged as a dominant economic force, penetrating world-wide markets as traditional markets and trading cartels were broken down. In his book *The New Industrial State*, the American economist J. K. Galbraith declared: 'Power in the modern industrial society resides with the large producing organizations – the large corporations. So, far from being safely and resignedly subordinate to the market, as the neoclassical argument holds, they fix prices and go on extensively to accommodate the consumer to their needs. And they also obtain from the state such further action as is needed to ensure a benign and stable environment for their operations.'[8]

As part of their visible presence (their business environment) in the public arena, such organizations adopted a clean, Modernist aesthetic, with its connotations of efficiency and rationalism, rather than one which hinted at unseemly indulgence in ornamentation or featured intrusive decorative motifs, characteristics which might be seen to betray qualities of individuality, and thus fallibility, or the simple out-datedness of ephemeral styling. The resulting corporate identities happily embraced the design of office equipment produced by Olivetti in Italy, of electronic equipment manufactured by IBM, and furniture by Herman Miller and Knoll in the United States and by Hille and Race in Britain. Companies' business and organizational profiles, however, were often at odds with the products for which they were renowned, as for example with General Motors, whose profits were based on vehicles whose extravagant, fashionable ornamentation ensured speedy obsolescence.

As a means of furthering their efficient, progressive identities, a number of leading corporations also participated in debates about improved standards of design in industry, particularly through the international design conferences held in Aspen, Colorado. Concerned with the role of design in the changed conditions of the post-1945 era, these colloquia were conceived to 'promote a better understanding of the value of first-class design to industry and incidentally improve public taste'.[9]

However, such debates were double-edged in their consequences: having convinced many manufacturers of the commercial benefits of involving designers in the production of new designs, many designers soon became increasingly concerned about their relative impotence in design decision-making in the face of overwhelming commercial pressures – styling, ornamentation and obsolescence were the everyday weaponry of the designer.

Although MOMA made a number of purchases outside the purist confines of a Bauhaus-dominated aesthetic, many critics were moved to mount swingeing attacks on the museum's design collection. Even as late as 1975, one critic characterized its outlook as a 'promotion for the takeover of Modernism in architecture in the 1940s and 1950s by a highly corporate conventionalization of the International Style'.[10] The collection was seen as reflecting a sense of 'good taste' which was thoroughly Protestant, 'as much in its mercantile secularism as in its intolerance of spontaneity and vitality, its distrust of pleasure and its distaste for the body; as much in its attempt to invest commodities with ethical value as in its appeal to vanity and pride and its view of prosperity as a sign of salvation.'[11] Its embrace of design was also seen as very limited in sociological terms. 'While social developments have thus radically impinged upon design, the Museum of Modern Art has dug in its heels and collected what it seems to think is the 20th-century equivalent of Meissen and Boulle: the next supremely lovely mix-master or the coffee table of tomorrow.'[12]

Revisionism and the Modernist aesthetic
A new transnational breed of product appeared, typified by Gerd Alfred Müller's Kitchen Machine for Braun of 1957, which earned plaudits from the advocates of 'good design'. Braun appliances were celebrated on both sides of the Atlantic, winning critical acclaim at the Milan Trienali of 1957 and 1960, the Brussels World Fair of 1958 and at MOMA, New York in 1959. The austere appearance of Müller's appliance betrayed a spiritual ancestry rooted in the Modernist aesthetic of the inter-war years. Its design, however, represented a move away from a reliance on artistic intuition towards problem-solving methods derived from management theories, especially those propounded at the Harvard Business School. These methods had roots in the use of scientific techniques for problem-solving during the Second World War, and this more rigorous and systematic approach to design was deemed appropriate in the complex scientific and technological climate of the 1950s. Much of the impetus for this approach came from the Hochschule für Gestaltung at Ulm in West Germany with which Braun had close links. There were also close affinities with the contemporary Design Methods movement which was concerned with the application of scientific methods and knowledge to solving particular problems, an approach in which ornament had little or no place. In the closeted world of the progressive professional designer, ergonomics, cybernetics, marketing and management science were deemed the more appropriate bedfellows for enlightened design thinking.

Ornament as expression: obsolescence and mass consumption
This partisan (if not dominant) cultural account of industrial design has tended to predominate. At places like the Design Museum in London, the Boymans van Beuningen Museum in Rotterdam, and the Centre de Création Industrielle at the Centre Georges Pompidou in Paris, its icons, with their austere aesthetic, are put on display as culturally and artistically significant.

Such a view of industrial design culture, however, ignores the social and cultural realities, not to mention potency, of ornament in the context of the emergence of commercial radio and television, the global impact of American popular culture and the increasing erosion of regional, and national, patterns of taste and style.

Between the 1930s and the late 1950s increasing sociological, cultural and literary attention was paid both to the nature and impact of mass culture. A widening intellectual chasm opened up between the self-appointed guardians of high culture and those that damned 'the culture industry'. Writing in America of the 'cultural class war' in 1960, Eric Larrabee declared: 'This is what mass culture most often means to the highbrow – the quintessence of all the stuffed dolls, jukeboxes, outlandish architecture, scatological postcards, comic books, roadside pottery stands, adenoidal singers with duck-tailed haircuts.'[13]

The design establishment fulminated against the 'moral dangers' of such unbridled self-expression on both sides of the Atlantic. Edgar Kaufmann, not content with the task of stemming the tide of highly stylized products in the United States while Director of Industrial Design at MOMA, warned about the undesirability of ornament for its own sake in the British magazine *Architectural Review*.[14] He attacked the vogue for streamlining, typified by the indiscriminate application of chromium speedwhiskers to all kinds of industrial products from pencil sharpeners to jukeboxes. He considered it 'the jazz of the drawing board', unwittingly condemning its ornamental characteristics as decadent and impure in much the same way as the National Socialists in Germany had condemned its musical namesake in the 1930s. In Britain, those connected with the official bodies promoting 'better standards of design' were equally condemnatory of any ornamental exuberance, whether relying heavily on historicizing styles or drawing on the chromium-plated fantasies of American mass production. A similar position was adopted by key figures in the French design world. Jacques Vienot, who had established the influential design research consultancy Bureau Technès in 1948,[15] was opposed to ceaseless change and obsolescence as a means in itself. He wrote: 'we should not feel obliged to change the design of typewriters or engines each year, as women change their hats, in order to please manufacturers who want to force this change upon us under the heading of "new fashions". This continuous change cannot possibly be indefinitely an improvement.'[16]

In the mid-1950s, he was seeking to found a centre devoted to *conjoncture morphologique*, a centre which should not be concerned with 'commercial processes, but should rather anticipate the evolution of technology and psychology, of social needs and aesthetic ideals, in order to prepare the designer for certain directions, which he should follow regardless of the consumer's dictates but for the consumer's ultimate satisfaction'.[17] This 'designer knows best' approach echoed the attitude of the 'improvers of taste' in the 1930s.

Referring to the science fiction-inspired gadgetry of many 1950s domestic appliances, John Blake, writing in *Design* magazine, the official mouthpiece of the British Council of Industrial Design, warned of 'the growth of a new mythology, comparable to that of ancient Greece. . .the more dials and controls we possess, the more we can identify ourselves with our space heroes'.[18] This fascination for goods which expressed participation in the glossy, technologi-

cal consumer world of the United States as portrayed in film, television programmes and magazines, found articulation in the symbolic ornamentation of products which drew heavily on contemporary motor cars. Another contemporary writer drew attention to the use of language accompanying the 'chrome spears, speed lines and similar fragments of [appliance] iconography. . .References to 'aquamatic action', 'jet spray', 'centrifugal clutch drive', in the washing machine, figure well with General Electric's new cooking range names – the Stratoliner and the Liberator.[19]

Despite the widespread fears expressed by many critics[20] that it would lead to the erosion of national characteristics, regional identity and the homogenization of culture, the values of the new ad-mass society – disposable incomes, expendability and fun – began to find expression in products catering for the vibrant market of the pop era.

'Less is a bore': the Post-Modern ethos

In the late 1950s, a number of critics, theorists and designers became interested in the relationship between visual and 'linguistic' signs. Writers such as the French critic Roland Barthes, the Italians Umberto Eco and Gillo Dorfles and the Amercian Robert Venturi[21] began to explore the semiotic possibilities of design and architecture. This was allied to advances in electronics technology – the minimalist scale of the microchip had rendered the Modernist adage 'form follows function' obsolete.

The contribution of the Italian avant-garde within this new approach has been particularly important, through the work of groups such as Archizoom and Superstudio in the 1960s through to Studio Alchimia and Memphis in the 1980s. The new, rich syntax of form and meaning, which explored a wide range of

cultural references (both popular and esoteric) could, at its most telling, witty or ironic, be read intelligibly. By the late 1980s, however, surface decoration and ornamental motifs were often blended with as little thought as changing television channels with a remote control handset.

The critiques made of the mindless application of heavy ornament to industrial forms at the height of 19th-century eclecticism were also applicable to the indiscriminate surface decoration of what was termed Post-Modernism in the late 1980s. In Germany, Volker Fischer was highly critical of what he saw as the 'simplistic, reach-me-down formulae', feeling that, at three or four removes, they may degenerate into a new form of kitsch, easy on the eye and tailor-made for the suburban bungalow, with oriels and columnettes adorning façades across the land. Post-Modernism is basically characterized by the rediscovery of ornament, colour, symbolic connections and the treasure trove of the history of form. . . The Post-Modern look is becoming increasingly popular in product design, as exemplified in the field of 'table culture' and 'living environments'.[22]

However, just as the social and political critiques implicit in the 'free love' and LSD sub-cultures of the late 1960s or in the affirmation of an alienated urban working class in the punk years of the mid-1970s were rendered impotent by their appropriation and marketing by commercial concerns, so Post-Modern designers rendered merely fashionable iconographic references which, in their original contexts were at least interesting or unsettling. Mattheo Thun's Hommage à Madonna cutlery designs, for example, can be seen to hint at the sexual frisson engendered by the pop star's penchant for heavy jewellery and sadomasochistic trappings, but as place-settings for the rich or museum exhibits

As it manifested itself in the field of industrial design, nostalgia was an important ingredient of the times. However, like many aspects of Post-Modern imagery, it often consisted only of the obvious outward trappings of style and cultural reference, such as the wholesome images of agricultural workers dressed in smocks scything corn on the sides of electric toasters, or the roses or hedgerow flowers evoking rural life which adorned the sides of tea cups. Nostalgia was often very broad in its general application across the cultural spectrum. One writer referred to the historical mess seemingly accurate films could generate when creating a period atmosphere. For example, with regard to the film *The Sting*, he wrote that 'the problem of hyper-naturalism's artificiality is compounded by the cavalier imposition of pre-First World War ragtime music and "big store" con games onto the chic gangsterism of the twenties and the social protest of the thirties'.[23]

It was this sense of a non-specific past, devoid of any precise social, cultural or aesthetic reference, that pervaded the ornamentation of so many industrial products.[24] Indeed, in Britain the rise of the 'heritage industry'[25] has been widely seen as the consequence of a shift of thinking which has endorsed the replacement of the heart of the British manufacturing industry with theme parks and leisure 'experiences' devoted to promoting and marketing those notions of the past which society wishes to preserve.

Heritage has also been associated with the years under Mrs Thatcher, one of whose aims was to 'restore national pride and other old values back to the country at large'.[26] This is still a current preoccupation judging by the displays in the British pavilion at Expo '92 in Seville, which were dominated by the very 'British' companies of Royal Doulton

they become little more than dated conversation pieces.

Nostalgia, heritage and homage to the past

Ever since the early years of the Industrial Revolution there has been a tension between the implications of mass production processes and considerations of artistic integrity. In the late 18th century, the English visionary poet William Blake felt that the constricting world of science and reason was shackling the liberating world of the imagination, just as William Morris and the adherents of the Arts and Crafts Movement were to cry out against the harmful social, creative and spiritual consequences of the division of labour in industry. Similarly, nearly a century later, in the technology-conscious

1950s and 1960s, the supposedly functionalist aesthetic was seen as a threat to individual expression and the creative impulse.

There has been a long-standing belief that hand-made goods were inherently superior to the machine-made, both in terms of aesthetics and function. Goods which are hand-made – or appear to be – are often felt to exhibit better techniques of construction than those that are mass-produced, perhaps because they were perceived as part of a heritage of traditional (and thus 'better') culture and long-established values which were fast disappearing. In Britain, particularly in the years following the Second World War, the development of industrial archaeology, and the new interest in folk songs and oral history, testified to this retrogressiveness.

evident in the light fittings, gas fires and tableware which resonated the traditional values of warmth, elegance or status associated with domestic life, and in the molecular globules featured on clocks and coat stands or the feet of plant pot holders and chairs. These reflected a widespread vogue for ornamental form which allied itself to popular interest in scientific progress on both sides of the Atlantic. Nor do ornamental motifs conform to simple period classification as the historians of style suggest. Many designs from before the First World War are still in production. The world's best-selling tableware design, *Old Country Roses*, was designed by Harold Holdcroft for Royal Albert (Royal Doulton) in 1962, selling more than 90 million pieces in many different countries. Drawing on 'country garden' motifs introduced by the company in the late 19th century, it reveals the enduring appeal of particular forms, patterns and ornament which transcend the vicissitudes of ephemeral fashion.

In conclusion, the use of ornament in industrial design may be seen for the consumer as an important means of communicating social and cultural beliefs, but, as a readily marketable commodity, it is also something which can be controlled and exploited by commercial interests. As a result, ornament often loses the original conviction of the messages it was intended to convey, becoming a means of making profit rather than the potent bearer of a particular ideology.

Vacuum cleaner designed by James Dyson for Apex Inc., 1986. This sculptural, Post-Modern design has a high tech form softened by the use of colour. From the 1950s onwards, this type of domestic appliance was designed to be seen rather than put away in a cupboard.

and Marks & Spencer, and by the government's instantaneous decision to restore Windsor Castle to 'its former glory' in the wake of the recent fire. Europe has undergone many changes since the death of Franco in 1975, with, recently, the demolition of the Berlin Wall, the constantly shifting economic priorities of eastern Europe and moves towards smaller national and regional groupings. Despite the drive towards a federal Europe, the question of national identity has re-emerged as a central concern to a number of EEC countries. Conversely, the power of the large multinational corporations to market products across national boundaries remains undiminished. For those countries struggling to develop free market economies the form and style of these industrial products may be seen to symbolize progress: the af-

fectations and idiosyncrasies of Post-Modern styling have a glittering allure for the interiors of an aesthetic largely conditioned by state monopolies.

Ornament as a form of social and cultural communication

If one were to believe the rhetoric of the design press over the past 25 years or more, the widespread deployment of ornament and decoration was due to the Post-Modernists. That the Post-Modernists have provided a theoretical justification for an enriched visual syntax, drawing on a wide-ranging aesthetic vocabulary which embraces popular culture alongside more esoteric references, is not in question. However, the use of ornament as a mediator between individuals and their environment has always been a conspicuous feature of 20th-century life. In the 1950s, it was

Still from the feature film *The Day the Earth Stood Still*, directed by Robert Wise, 1951.

Beyond a
Semiology of Objects

....

Henri Pierre Jeudy

The object is not a Medusa's head. It can fascinate but it does not turn us to stone. Its uses and uselessness alike testify to its presence. It transforms itself gradually without ever renouncing the parenthood of its forms. Its functions create the impression that it has always been necessary, despite its novelty. The object can sometimes unnerve us – it seems to have a life of its own that is quite distinct from the intentions which shaped its conception. Even when it has no internal mechanism it often evokes the automaton through its strange capacity to dispense with man, its putative master. Its autonomy was once magical and has now become technological. The object remains in the service of man, but it creates the impression of exercising its own power. From Leonardo da Vinci's flying machines to the robots of the future, the object plays with chronology, blurring the distinction between history and science fiction. Everything is done to guarantee that it will be as perfect as possible. We devise its ideal form, we select the appropriate materials, we anticipate its fu-

ture, but in the end it resists both time and obsolescence by establishing its own timelessness. Put on exhibition, it represents the great epochs that have succeeded one another in terms of stylistic evolution, without violence, without conflict, in a serene sequence of forms and tastes which have always gone hand in hand with extravagance and incongruity. What would a museum without objects be, if man himself couldn't figure in it? If human history is a rather bloody tragedy, that of objects seems to transcend death.

When we visit the bedroom of Louis XIV at Versailles, the armchairs, the commodes and the bed evoke a presence for us as vividly as if they were ghosts. Museology increasingly favours images over objects and modern technologies which allow us to construct every imaginable prosthesis are creating a virtual universe where the image becomes real. Thus our perception of objects can transform itself into a perpetual *déjà vu*, as though the dead were no longer really dead since the image became our reality principle. But the object remains an

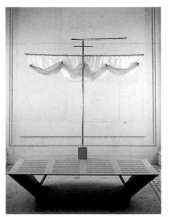

Bed exhibited at the Great Exhibition in London, 1851.

Mechanical headboard of the Testeria bed, designed by Denis Santachiara for Domodinamica s.r.l., 1991. The middle of the headboard comes down to form a small table, with the vase taking up a position at the end of the table.

L'Inconscient bed, designed by Sylvain Dubuisson for Fourniture, 1987.

indestructible witness. It is always there as a sacred store of human invention. In the realm of the virtual, is the object still king? Its enigma still radiates because, even with all its strategems, the image cannot exhaust it. This eternity of objects is reassuring, constituting a gigantic museum of the world in which each creation has its own place – a symbolic universe which appeases the uncertainties of a history whose meaning is indecipherable. Instead of making it disappear, the image confers upon the object a multiplicity of lives, it engenders imaginary metamorphoses and so increases its mystery. Are we to believe that man's dream is to become an object among objects? At the dawn of the 21st century, our strange passion for the museography of the lived suggests the irresistible temptation of a petrification of the world in which the subject becomes object, by the redoubtable means provided by the image.

When Bulgakov's dog begins to speak does he do so as a man? Anthropomorphism permits every sort of affective and intellectual projection, and if this dog has a heart it can only be that of a man. The object does not speak, it seems to have a secret which discourse cannot penetrate. It often seems to be saying something we can't quite hear. Sometimes, during little fits of madness, we are led to believe that it has just expressed something we dare not express ourselves. Very young children don't hesitate to treat objects and people in the same way: they hit a chair they've run into, even if it was 'designed' by Charles Eames. As the object is the silent witness of our existence, we also imagine that it looks at us and we sometimes call it to account by moving it or breaking it to escape its presence. If we talk about it, we attribute a certain history to it which distinguishes it from others, which ascribes to it an autonomy outside the space in which it has been placed and over and above its uses. When it defies us we implore it to continue working and when it seems to exceed its capacities we offer thanks for its courage. Even the most functional of objects is the

recipient of injunctions and reprimands, as though it were capable of deceiving us, of playing a role inconsistent with its intended function. Despite its docility, despite its tendency never to contradict the signs exalting its 'being there', the object seems to have a freedom which disconcerts us. In the end we don't much care for the distinction between the animate and the inanimate. And we never cease attributing life to the world of objects because the play of signs goes beyond the limits established by uses and functions.

We sometimes speak of a language of plants, of insects, of birds. . .What of the language of the objects we use every day? In the name of scientific objectivity, we distrust our anthropomorphic tendencies, our way of projecting our intentions and meanings onto things that don't speak. In doing this we apprehend objects as necessary extensions of our own bodies and as the proximate mirror of our acts and thoughts. Their language seems to constitute a system of symbols of our intentions and the goals determining our actions. Hence the world of objects, like a world of signs, provides support for the dynamic system of our representations.

Jean Baudrillard, in his book *The System of Objects*, describes this relation between the staging of social life and the symbolic combinative of objects very well. His analysis was based on semiology – the science of signs – which is founded on linguistics. But the real question is that of determining whether the world of objects forms a system comparable to that of language. The classification of objects, the recognition of their use or function and the values we attribute to them seem to suggest that the world of objects is an ensemble of signs that is rigorously normative. And the banalization of forms adds further support to such a view. Roland Barthes, in his *The Empire of Signs*, offers a 'semiotic' description of the use of chopsticks in Japanese cooking which combines a poetic approach with rigorous sign analysis. The semiology

Bianca M radio,
designed by
Studio Naço,
1991.

Left-hand page:
Ciminiera lamp,
designed by
Denis
Santachiara,
1987. Indoor
chimney with
light which
produces
perfumed
steam, for
humidifying the
home or office.

Corkscrew,
designed by
Smart Design
for the Good
Grips® range
of kitchen
utensils by
OXO, 1993.

of objects succeeds in creating the impression that there is a veritable language of objects. On rereading these pages, however, which are certainly very beautiful, we are struck by the fire power of semiology: the system for analysing the gestures involved in manipulating objects precedes and guides perception. Japanese culture, in a sense, is used here to illustrate semiology, with Barthes being deeply moved by this scene of the 'trembling of the signifier', just as in the seventies a campaign was mounted to 'liberate the signifier'!

Semiology seems to be a discourse imposed upon the social and cultural practices associated with the object. This discourse has its own dynamic modelled on the system of language, and in this sense its richness can seem inexhaustible. Social distinctions, cultural identities, moral values all manifest themselves in the world of objects, which legitimizes exhaustive study of man's relation to them. The move to explore and discover signs runs the risk of being determined beforehand by such an interpretive system, which is readily available to anyone who would apply it. If the world in which we live is a universe of signs, it retains its mystery despite all our attempts to decode it. The 'trembling of the signifier' of which Barthes spoke is, paradoxically, at odds with the semiotic enterprise: the empire of signs is not reducible to the power of semiology. On the contrary, the infinite play of sign combinations only accentuates the enigma of the object. It's not a question of defending the animism present in our relations with objects, but rather of our grasping that the semiotic transparency of the object is overly dependent upon an arbitrary system of reading borrowed from linguistics.

The paradox facing the designer – not unrelated to that of the actor as described by Diderot – is that of conceiving an object without being able to talk about it. To be sure, the craftsman remained silent, but a glance at his actions while he was working provided sufficient basis for a subtle description of how, where and why an object was produced. The designer knows perfectly well what he's doing, but he can speak of the object only as a technician, by explaining the various phases of the realization of his project. He finds himself constrained to turn over all power to make the object speak to those in charge of publicizing it. For the designer, even if semiology influences his conception of it (consciously or unconsciously), an object is shaped by a set of economic, functional, cultural and aesthetic parameters, but intuition always plays a role in his activity. He doesn't use the science of signs as a work charter, and the semiology of the object comes into play only *a posteriori*, like discourse about how the final product is used and perceived. So it would seem the object becomes a sign only after its conception. If we could reverse the process such that the science of signs, in alliance with technical knowledge, determined the object's conception, then we might be able to imagine the creation of the perfect object. Now the object's optimal character only corresponds to a specific moment and does not transcend the time during which the object was in use, even if subseqent generations continue to admire it. The infinite progress of technology will not suffice to explain the present imperfection of objects, because those from the past can come to be regarded as 'ideal objects', to be gazed at in museums. The quest to optimize objects is at the heart of their conception, and at the same time endows them with mystery. In order to create an object that is a sign must one forget the science of signs?

In the sixties, semiology was for Roland Barthes a 'critical adventure'; it had nothing to do with 'conceptual legitimation'. It was the focal point of ideologies or, at least, it was hoped to be. But it has become, in the world of the production and consumption of objects and images, a vast mechanism of signification and legitimization. For the creative minds involved in shaping objects, space, the image. . .it precedes and delimits the product like an envelope of the idea. In

T2/A3 clock,
designed by
Sylvain
Dubuisson,
1986.

a very real sense, it is the intellectual packaging which gives the object its conceptual legitimacy. Barthes distinguished three levels of meaning: informational, which corresponds to communication; symbolic, which corresponds to signification; and that of a meaning which remains harder to decipher.[1] Self-evident meaning is produced by the intentions of the author of an object or image, presenting common signifieds which permit the avoidance of any uncertainty. An object's function represents a self-evident meaning. Sign meaning, on the other hand, corresponds to that which is not self-evident, being the very expression of meaning's uncertainty. In principle, the functional object should leave no room for sign meaning because it excludes all semantic equivocation, at least in its ideal form. But that is a paradox: how can a sign be created if we remain exclusively within the order of signification and information?

The designer Philippe Starck put it this way: 'Our profession is in no way that of the artist, and certainly not that of the aesthetician, but rather that of the semanticist. . .Objects must give off signs, like children, animals and forest fires.' That which is of the order of sign meaning encompasses a great deal more than just artistic creation. When I look at an object I can use I don't perceive it the same way I do a painting or a photograph, and yet I lend it meaning not exclusively defined by its form and function. The play of projections it permits is not inscribed within a prior structure of meaning. I retain a freedom of meaning like that of the conceiver himself, whose intuition was largely responsible for its creation. Does the role of signification become more restricted because the object is conceived in industrial terms? On the surface of it, this is certainly the case. If a functional object allowed for an infinite play of signifiers it would become an aesthetic object. But we are forgetting the magical universe of objects: an object's meaning as a sign

derives from a confrontation between different imaginations. The more an object is hemmed in by information and signification, the more that signification becomes an expression of the closeness of the relation between subject and object. Often an object's creator says he doesn't know what to say about it. He can explain the parameters which shaped its conception, but he is unable to make the object speak about its non-functional significance. His creative intuition remains mute and he delegates responsibility for talk about the object to publicity agents able to make consumers dream. And he resents the power of these publicity agents, who devise language to suit an object that they did not themselves conceive. The intimacy of their creation is obscured, or at best is publicly invoked as the sign of their inventive genius. Thus the spheres of sign meaning and signification do not really meet; it's as though the functional and symbolic stereotype of objects constituted the very principle of their semantic transparency.

At the dawn of the 21st century, the banalization of objects imposes a symbolic formalism that is not based on the play of appearances. It is the symbol itself which becomes the object's envelope. It will always remain possible to demonstrate an object's symbolic references, but these have now become elements in a purely formal combination. Should box-like appliances (Walkmans, remote controls, television sets) be given rounder forms, we can continue to think that that is a feminine symbol and that the necessity to make them rounder is imposed in an arbitrary way. Cultural identities end up being used as stratagems. The Japanese have become masters at this. Their basic principle is that it's up to others to discover the 'Japanese-ness' which characterizes their objects. Japanese design has shown itself to be capable of absorbing and then perfecting the technology of western products, and it has developed according to a cultural pluralism which makes it possible to go beyond the very

Double Soft Big Easy sofa, designed by Ron Arad, manufactured by Moroso, 1992.

idea of an original authenticity of an object. Therefore, cultural difference must be determined by others because it no longer corresponds to an initial intention. The game is subtle: cultural identity is determined not by the object's creator but by those who look at it and use it. And this otherness becomes purely formal because it lends itself to an aleatory distribution of the object's cultural attributes. The Japanese designer is happy to see the 'Japanese-ness' of what he has created determined by Westerners! Thus the trick is worked: this symbolic formalism allows for a plasticity of universal symbols without threatening cultural integrity. Any crisis of object symbolism is resolved: sign and symbol finish by becoming one and the same, signs no longer refer to symbols, they are sustained by the symbolic formalism. And we are all the more inclined to accept this state of affairs if we consider the universe of objects of communication as representing a universal culture beyond specific cultural identity. There will always be a stratagem for attributing a 'national' character trait to any given category of objects. But the Japanese are more clever – they themselves do not think about their 'Japanese-ness', but rather receive it as a homage offered to their otherness. This capacity to integrate all cultural signs seems to be based on a cultural integrationism shaped by the ritual defence of tradition. On the one hand symbolic formalism is a principle of absorption of all cultural signs, on the other the rigidity of symbols in Japanese daily life remains a device for protecting cultural identity. The stronger the cultural identity, the more encompassing can be the dynamic of expansion of symbolic formalism.

This is not an exclusively Japanese phenomenon. A nostalgia for the symbolic values of the past, even if it sustains the traditional perception of the world of objects, finds satisfaction in the *trompe l'oeil* of modernity. From now on standardization and the contamination of signs will be the starting point for the adventure of the object.

The Polaroid camera

Background:
Polaroid
model 95,
1948.

Vignette:
Edwin Land
in 1947.

When it comes to the number of patent applications filed in the United States, the inventor Edwin Herbert Land rivals Thomas Edison: Land's patents number 533 and Edison's 1200. In 1937, at the age of 28, Edwin Land founded the Polaroid Corporation, which specialized in the manufacture of sunglasses and polarizing filters. In 1948, he launched the first camera capable of developing and printing a photograph in a few seconds, the Polaroid 95. The Kodak company didn't take the Polaroid seriously, regarding it as a gadget, and took no interest in Edwin Land's new invention.

In 1972, Land filed an application for a patent, indexed under the code SX-70, which was the name of the Polaroid. The Polaroid camera was rather strange in appearance, but apart from its automatic focusing mechanism, its features were the same as those of traditional cameras. In the face of the success of the Polaroid, Kodak decided, in1976, to

manufacture its own range of Polaroid cameras. The Polaroid company sued for an infringement of rights and, after ten years of legal wrangling, won the case which accorded them exclusive use of the process and $909.5 million in damages and interest.

The magic of the instantaneous image, bordered in white, and the distinctive sound the camera made as the photograph came out have become mythical elements of the Polaroid. It is not widely known that, since 1978, another detail distinguishes this camera from others: an ultrasound transmitter-receiver, a radar which, in a thousandth of a second, sends a high frequency note towards the subject, picks up the echo, calculates the distance with the aid of a minute digital computer and automatically adjusts the focus. That is why, on family photographs, pets, which are sensitive to these frequencies, seem to be posing, their gaze fixed on the camera lens.

The Polaroid Vision system provided another occasion for the company to demonstrate its ingenuity. The camera was the result of an impressive series of optical, electronic, mechanical and chemical innovations. A market survey was conducted to assess the potential demand for the new system, which was then applied to a whole series of cameras, such as the Photokina, launched in September 1992. This model was particularly innovative in its design and the chemical composition of the film required. It consists of a lightweight, folding single-lens reflex camera which is entirely controlled by a microprocessor and uses an unusual colour film format. For the first time in the 50-year history of Polaroid cameras, the user is able to take continuous photographs. The pictures are conserved in a storage chamber with a window through which the user can see them develop in about one minute.

E. M.

The credit card

In his Discourse on Banks, *Isocrates (436 – 338BC) described the system of the 'bill of exchange' which made it possible for people involved in commerce to travel without having to take large sums of money. Merchants and travellers went to the banker in their home town who drew up a bill of exchange to be given to the banker in the town they were going to. These bankers gave depositors receipts inscribed with the depositor's name – forerunners of the cheque. Money had started its dematerialization.*

The first bank to issue banknotes was the Stockholm Rijksbank in 1658, followed by England. In France, in 1803, the Banque de France was accorded the privilege of issuing banknotes.

American Express, taking up the idea of the bill of exchange used by travellers, invented the traveller's cheque. The first of these was issued on 5 August 1891 and the system was rapidly adopted in Europe, contributing to the de-velopment of tourism and international exchanges at the beginning of the century. The first credit card organization was created in 1950 by the American Ralph Scheider. When the scheme started, 27 New York restaurants adopted the Diner's Club as it was called and the first two hundred members were able to dine on credit.

In 1958, capitalizing on this initiative, which had been highly popular with the New York jet set, the Bank of America issued the first bank credit card: the Bankamericard. In the same year, the famous American Express card was launched. One year after its creation, 235,000 people owned one. Today the number is 15 million. Originally violet, the same colour as the traveller's cheques, the card became green in 1969, like the dollar bill.

The card is only an imitation of money, but it is this very imitation which emphasizes its symbolic function. When using one, the reality of money becomes blurred, the act of buying something is no longer linked to a specific point in time. Thanks to 'plastic money', the fact of having to pay out the sum demanded is put off to some later date. At the end of each month, the money is debited from the account of the owner of the said card.

In France, the first card featuring a magnetic strip was introduced in 1971 by the Carte Bleue organization. In the same year, magnetic coding made it possible to withdraw money from the bank via automatic cash dispensers installed by the Bull company. In 1984, the setting up of a unified system of payment rendered all bank cards in France compatible. The term monétique was coined in 1982 in a report by the Conseil Economique et Social to describe the various electronic, computer and magnetic systems which now make it possible to carry out transactions without paper.

E. M.

The mantelpiece and the television set are often used for the commemoration of family memories.

Opposite page: Mère Denis, who featured in advertisements for Vedette washing machines in France, 1977.

The Domestication
of Objects

Martine Perrot

....

What is there in common between the farmer from the Haute-Lozère region who one day fashioned the bin of his washing machine into an unusual sort of electric churn, the worker from Mende who hand-crafted a television table identical to a mass-produced one sold in department stores and the Parisian designer who declared one day that 'African art is a form, a function, a need, even the very essence of design'?[1] The first effected innovation through the transposition of technology, with the result that his family could make home-made butter like they used to in the past. The second copied a mass-produced object creating what was in effect a prototype. The third appropriated an exotic symbolic language to create a new style of furniture.

At root, these undertakings scarcely differ from one another; they all reveal a certain attitude towards material culture, understood to be complex and rebellious. Nor are these three examples exceptional. One need only take a close look at what each of these individuals did with an object and exactly how they domesticated it. It is perfectly

We are living the period of objects: that is, we live by their rhythm, according to their incessant cycles.

Jean Baudrillard,
'Consumer Society', 1988

legitimate to see them merely as exhibits proving social distinctions and alienated, alienating, consumption, but that fails to illuminate a whole set of relations fundamental to ordinary life. However, if we examine not only the object itself with its signifying armour, but also, and above all, what goes on between the object and its user, we are likely to obtain more satisfactory results. This approach tends to weaken certain prejudices about standardized lifestyles, modernization and patterns of consumption. The object is resistant – nothing produced by man is more 'stubborn' – but childhood memories, family ties, people's know-how, the transmission of knowledge from one generation to another, the need for shelter and the desire to make a favourable impression are even more so. Having had occasion to pursue my investigations in rural areas, notably in several villages in Haute-Lozère, where certain household 'machines' entered general use much later than elsewhere, I can testify to the progressive intrusion and sometimes the warm reception – as with a freezer which arrived in 1975 – of some of them into the domestic universe. I use the word 'universe' advisedly here, for in such circumstances the new object comes into contact with an entire interior cosmogony.

Household equipment

Simultaneously guests and intruders, household appliances are not always placed where one might expect. Washing machines, which are fixed to the floor and need their own space, can still play the itinerant. Installed in the kitchen along with the dishwasher, refrigerator, gas

blatant in certain rural homes, where an archaic domestic regime was maintained until quite recently. Here the arrival of these bulky guests overloads, literally and figuratively, the space, that is to say creates disorder and inexactitude in the use made of it. Come to think of it, the term 'equipment' is well suited to describe this confrontation. We equip ourselves to go skiing, mountain-climbing and bike-riding. It used to be that the house was furnished and decorated; today it is above all 'equipped'. Statistics are quite revealing on this point:

dent on the factory, on the world of work, if only through the instructions supplied for operating the appliance. Such instructions perform a crucial intermediary function in the transmission of new usages. Often fastidious, mostly incomprehensible to the majority of us, the summarized or pictorial versions on the inside of the refrigerator door and under the hatch of the washing machine are supposed to permit a faster understanding of how the appliances work. In any case, these instructions are only relevant when we first operate the appliance.

Council housing interiors, 1981. The most trivial objects can be imbued with history, in fragmentary form like anecdotes, or linked to family events. Each object or piece of furniture tells a circumstantial story which is distinct from its style or its epoch.

cooker and spin drier, they become part of that 'machine room' which is the modern kitchen. They can also settle in the bathroom, benefiting from the hygienic linkage of bodily care to clothing care, or in the laundry room, if there is one.

But they can also simply be displayed. Since show takes precedence over function some washing machines on farms in Margeride occupy a place of honour in what used to be the communal room, a place never previously used for washing clothes. The availability of pipes and electrical fittings, as well as constraints of space, may have had something to do with this eccentric practice. In fact, few of us live in homes which are contemporary with these objects; space was not set aside for them, hence their conquest of the home has differed from one household to another.

Thus one of the primary functions of these objects, paradoxically, has been to break up the domestic order they were intended to create. This state of affairs is particularly

refrigerators, television sets and washing machines, those basics of domestic comfort, are becoming more and more widespread.[2] This rapid evolution brings with it increasing parity between rural and urban areas. Freezers, which were once considered rural appliances, are now installed in two-thirds of French households.

Some observers think that this irrepressible proliferation has brought about a radical transformation of domestic space, whose function has shifted from production to maintenance.[3] The home comes to resemble a ship, with a machine room which must be kept in good repair if it is to set out each day from the family port. In the event of technical problems, repair men are urgently summoned. Cooking, freezing and laundry appliances are all vulnerable to breakdowns which few of us know how to put right. Symptomatically, the spare parts departments of department stores are gradually losing their clients. Thus the private home is becoming increasingly dependent

Once we've learned how to do that, there's nothing more to master. This makes appliances very different from craft objects, which we become more adept at operating with time. Advertisers revealed how thoroughly they understood this when they invented the character of mother Denis and her traditional 'know-how' in the publicity campaign for the Vedette.

Ongoing technological advances accentuate this state of affairs: today's washing machines, for example, last on average seven years! Rapid obsolescence reinforces the idea of an indifference to the object itself, while at the same time the general tendency is to buy furniture for life.[4]

In view of this, can we still maintain that household appliances are 'domestic'? Do they produce anything other than a limited, repetitive set of gestures, the art of pushing buttons and 'programming' the desired service, as many analysts maintain? Our current relation to the domestic environment is schizophrenic. Somewhere between memory and forgetting, production and maintenance, private and public, it is characterized by this ambivalence, this paradox. In an attempt to escape from this situation, some endlessly reinvent a symbolic aspect, wherever symbolism is threatened. From this point of view the rural milieu is revealing, because there the processes of 'domestication' of household appliances are incomplete. Practices passed down through time, which are well adapted to the space of the communal room, put up a token resistance while machines insinuate themselves

veniently be left on the cast iron hot plate of the wood-burning stove. In this unexpected way, the industrial object continues to be linked to the rhythm of the seasons. These practices still go on in the Lozère region, but examples can also be found in cities. Many city dwellers, for instance, still prefer to see a flame when they cook their meals and distrust electric stoves, which have existed in France since the thirties.[5] Force of habit, or *habitus*, some will say. That would appear to be probable, but *habitus* precisely because it is 'incorporated'

of ashes and hot coals. We play with fire when its symbolism is on the wane.

The third perverse effect of the adoption of certain appliances is the reversion to traditional practices. It is the freezer that's most in question here, for it facilitates the partial return to a self-sufficiency that seemed to be gone forever. In effect, far from having eliminated traditional forms of conservation, the freezer proposes an additional one. It participates in domestic production and makes possible, in both rural and urban areas, a rediscovery of the rhythm of the

quite rapidly into this space which was never conceived for them. One could easily establish a simple typology of domestic strategies adopted to integrate a new appliance. There are three: cohabitation; misappropriation; and, finally and most surprisingly, reversion to traditional practices.

Cohabitation is the most frequently encountered, especially where cooking is concerned, for this activity involves practices handed down from mother to daughter, as well as local resources still closely linked to older household appliances. Even in late 20th-century France, the gas cooker has not managed to eclipse the symbolic power of the venerable wood-burning stove. The mistress of the house heats things and seals meat on the former, while on the latter she stews and simmers them. Pots on the stove do not need to be closely watched – while a dish slowly cooks, the milking can be done in the stable, next door to the house. Likewise, electric irons are 'economized' in winter because the old iron can con-

and because it implicates the body, demands from each of us identical, unchanging repetition and so hardly makes it possible to 'embroider' those functional and decorative motifs offered by production and imposed on us by advertisers. And this 'symbolic embroidery', these variations on a theme are constantly at work in the everyday practices linking us to domestic objects. Misappropriation is a frequent and exciting illustration of this. Within each master and mistress of a household there lurks a slumbering situationist. The fireplace is one of the most valuable indicators of this, given the considerable symbolic and emotional charge it carries. How many kitchens still feature wood stoves, or gas cookers, or both together? How many blocked chimneys have been reopened so that a stove could be put in? And then there's a more recent development: the gas fireplace with unvaryingly identical flames, marketed to nostalgic Parisians as guaranteeing warmth and fire without the inconvenience

seasons by encouraging the conservation of fruits, vegetables and poultry. It revives old practices fallen into disuse, such as the making in summer of a butter richer in fat than that prepared in the winter, something which has enabled some farmers to revive ancient patterns of autarky. The freezer has also created new kinds of inter-generational exchange: children living in the city introducing their parents, still residing in the village, to frozen dishes, while the parents offer meat or vegetables from the garden on their Sunday visits.[6] In the city, where such equipment became common in the sixties, despite the proximity of shops selling frozen dishes, home cooking prepared in ample portions and in advance has not been abandoned. The freezer has made its owners more attentive to seasonal produce for purchase and conservation, but taken them outside the seasonal cycle when it comes to consumption.

Thus there is a subtle interaction between the economy of time and the economy of the weather. In some regions, harsh weather conditions such as snowstorms lead to occasional power failures. Then the food thaws and cannot be consumed. To avoid catastrophe in such situations, freezers are sometimes loaded onto tractors and carted to a neighbour's house where the current is still running, or simply taken out into the snow to slow the thawing process. Here we have an example of a machine being subject to the caprices of the weather, unexpectedly reinforcing the sense of local community. Another object which must be taken into account, because it has now become emblematic, is the television set. A lot has been written about this 'image box'. So much, in fact, that one would think that writing about it was an almost magical way of protecting oneself from it; and yet the television can no longer be, as the computer can, 'a mythic guest in the household'.[7] Its presence is no longer held to be a mark of social distinction; indeed, its absence today is more likely to have this privilege. It has been accepted as a member of the family and, as such, is treated with care and respect as well as familiarity.[8] However, the reactions and changes that it prompts in the household are linked to differentiated social practices. Its location is especially important in this regard. Placed high up, it creates in the domestic environment a rather public aesthetic associated with bars and hotel rooms. Placed on the floor, it becomes suggestive of a bohemian sixties or adolescent lifestyle. We should also mention its admirable gift for ubiquity, which allows it to migrate from the bathroom to the bedroom by way of the kitchen. But what is most interesting is the role of decorative substitute often assigned to it. The new family altar covered with knick-knacks and family photographs, it functions like a surrogate mantelpiece. This open window onto the outside world no longer warms the body but it captures the gaze, and, for the duration of a programme, it re-establishes the family circle around it. Family unity is now forged in the

reflections of images from the outside world. Yet this much-criticized object, this scapegoat for the loss of sense of community, childhood laziness and the alienation of the masses has a no less essential role to play when it is turned off. It can be covered by a cloth to protect it from dust, garlanded in the Christmas season, camouflaged within a piece of furniture whose doors are opened only when it's in use, or hidden away, preferably where it's difficult to get at, so that the force of its attraction is weakened by the effort required to install it. So there are many ruses which govern the use of this piece of equipment, which is an article fraught with risk for family ties, communality and even the souls of children. Because it puts the loss or survival of domestic life at stake, the television is regarded with genuine ethical and aesthetic concern.

The return of the symbolic

Having examined all the various ways of using and placing domestic objects, must we conclude that there is always some sort of symbolic compensation when an artisanal object is displaced by an industrial product, after the engineer and the designer have performed their intermediary functions and how-to-use instructions have obviated the need for know-how? An ethnographic approach to these practices, to the *bricolage* so dear to Michel de Certeau,[9] suggests that there is still room for guile and poaching. It is a sign of our times that numerous creative figures are trying to rediscover this symbolic necessity. Certain design tendencies confirm this, such as a recent emphasis on 'objects infused with nature, in which the work of the human hand and the effects of time are visible'.[10] A similar approach has left its mark on the so-called 'primitive' inspirations of Garouste and Bonnetti, transformed into works of art by their being issued in limited series. In this context, the practice of issuing limited series is significant; it imposes rarity where there might easily be proliferation. It restores to the multiple object a certain artistic value. A

Three emblems
of comfort:
the television,
the refrigerator
and the
combined
refrigerator and
freezer.

Left-hand page:
Containers,
designed by
Terence Conran
for Airfix, 1964.

Japanese
domestic
appliances,
1980s.

dealer will always insist on telling you that this lamp by Emile Gallé was produced in a very limited number. On the other hand, mass production, being the drama and strength of industrial objects, identifies and dates these objects as much as their form does. That series number that the repair man requests to identify your computer constitutes the product's technological and historical certification. It is a discreet means of classifying and distinguishing an object for connoisseurs and technicians. The notion of the unique object has no place here, unless all the other examples have disappeared and even then the last would only be a survivor. Copies can be made by hand, whereas mass-produced series standardize and multiply a prototype. Such is the primary regime under which the industrial object comes into being. So it is not difficult to understand why limited editions increase commercial and artistic value. Or why it is that today's designers seek inspiration outside industrial societies, where the concept has no sense.

When the kind of symbolization provided by an artist's signature, a limited edition or even a numbered series is no longer à possibility, what happens? What are we to make of the myriad of objects 'without qualities', falling short even of kitsch, which has now been granted a certain legitimacy? I'm thinking of snow scenes and other such holiday souvenirs, of plastic statues of the Virgin and Bernadette of Lourdes, of vases, candle-holders, clocks, flowerpot holders, ash-trays and cigarette lighters, all of which are liable to mass production. How can these pariahs of distinction take on a symbolic function when the models and the way they are used are themselves codified and forced on us through magazines, shop windows and catalogues? One way is by means of stories, of the narratives they carry with them and within which they are set. Even the most insignificant objects are bearers of history, fragmented like the anecdote, linked to events like that of the family. In effect, almost all such objects are connected in some

way with marriages, baptisms, mother's day celebrations, or other of those special moments which punctuate family life. When we examine closely the conditions influencing the acquisition and circulation of objects, we see that they form a tight network of family and friendship ties. Each object, each piece of furniture has a circumstantial history that is separate and apart from its style and period of origin.

The television set that's been co-opted to serve as a mantelpiece provides us with a good example of the exercising of family memory, of a kind of topography of affection. The objects arranged so carefully on top of it evoke rituals and reinforce private ties of affection, whether family or professional (as with a gift from one's boss) and attest to their strength. There is nothing gratuitous about this prominent display, which has been shaped by an imperious necessity which is both emotional and decorative in nature. The objects in question permit a daily ritual of commemoration because they must be cleaned and maintained. These famous 'dust traps' add to the atmosphere of domestic warmth, for they form the household 'epic'.

In the past, objects have consistently served as boundary markers for the family and played an important role in its privatization, and the advent of industrial production has done nothing to break down this capability. On the symbolic level, they can sometimes function as scapegoats or as domestic idols, but their narrative capacities remain intact. It even seems as though this quality is more readily acknowledged today than in the past. While specific places seem less and less capable of registering memory, history and sense of community, the object is increasingly sought after as a means of creating community and domestic bonds. From this perspective, while it will probably continue to be one of the most 'stubborn' of human creations, as I suggested at the beginning of this essay, it will surely also continue, paradoxically, to be one of the most easily domesticated.

Knick-knacks
and religious
artefacts form a
kind of domestic
epic.

Left-hand page:
Evergreen
wardrobe,
designed by
Patricia Ranzo
and Sergio
Cappelli for
Lapis, 1988.

CAD

and the Conception of Objects

Jean Zeitoun

In an industrial society as complex as ours, the design and manufacture of objects and systems, material or immaterial, necessitates a conceptual phase of ever increasing importance. To a great extent, a product's feasibility, quality and capacity to satisfy expectations are determined by the initial concept. The designer, by his very existence, is proof of the importance of this early stage in the development process.

The computer has had a considerable impact on all phases of product development and manufacture. Research departments, whose task is to assess the feasibility of a product concept, quickly came to depend on computer programs to make plans and other technical documents. New computer drawing techniques, first used simply as a computer-aided drawing board, gradually became of interest to designers.

Computer programs, which became simultaneously more powerful and more user-friendly, made possible new kinds of technical expertise. Likewise, management tools and databases, once only employed at the

administrative and manufacturing stages of product development, are now readily available to designers, who are beginning to exploit their possibilities. First used only in the most technical and concrete phase of an object's manufacture, the computer is gradually being used in all stages of development, from original idea to final product.

Use of the computer at the conceptual stage has fostered the development of a wide variety of CAD (computer-aided design) software. This software provides designers with a variety of tools, the most obvious of which is three-dimensional 'drawing', which allows objects to be visualized while they are still just concepts. Computer-generated models can be manipulated on a screen, enabling the designer to analyse them, look at how they function and explore possible operational problems, something that, in the past, he would only have been able to do with the aid of a prototype.

Simulation of this kind, which makes it possible to evaluate a model's performance under almost any conditions, greatly reduces the pressure to avoid making mistakes early on and so encourages a level of experimentation previously unheard of. Another advantage of the computer is that it enables the designer to communicate his ideas, drawings and information easily to colleagues, clients and other people involved in the project. Thanks to the computer, the projected product can be seen, calculated, tested and shown well before it is manufactured. Computer animation techniques have added a new dimension to the designer's visuals.

After a decade or two of use, what diffe-

meters, but none the less sufficient to carry out the initial phase of his work without constraint.

All this still remains something of a dream. The first aims of CAD were threefold: economic, because it was supposed to increase productivity; functional, because it increases the capacity for analysis, manipulation and experimentation; and cultural, because information technology is omnipresent and has become an integral part of communications. CAD is one of the designer's links to the modern day production process, where cost-effectiveness,

honoured manual skills such as drawing and modelling, as well as all forms of plastic expression generally, retain a certain value in the conceptual process and so continue to be used by designers. Technology cannot replace these skills, but it can extend them and, in certain cases, improve the conditions under which they are exercised. Although creativity plays an important role in design, it is only one component of the design process and must be seen in the context of the constraints and technical considerations involved.

The designer can never be completely in-

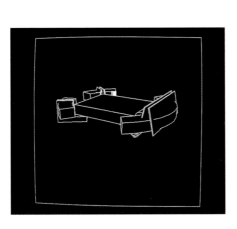

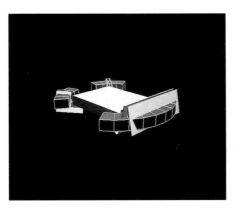

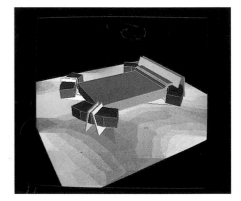

rence has CAD made to the various aspects of the design process? What conclusions can be drawn about the impact it is having on design practice?

Technology brings about a change in ideas

Initially, CAD was a technological dream: a sophisticated tool, capable of relaying the designer's noble work to a machine equipped to solve all manufacturing problems. The main aim behind the use of CAD was to be the creation of a product under the best possible conditions. CAD would offer the designer a means of visualizing, controlling and providing specifications for every aspect of the product in question. Apprentice, assistant, engineer, manager, administrator and user all in one, this fantasy machine would also provide the designer with a new, computerized working environment, limited by certain para-

speed and efficiency are key factors.

Before assessing the impact of CAD on industrial design, it is important to understand the importance of the conception phase (whether it be carried out with a computer or without) as a basis for the transformation of needs, potentialities and ideas into products or systems. It is important to understand the various dimensions of this profession which appeared in our society quite recently. What does 'industrial design' mean today and how might it evolve in the future?

The development of the design profession is just one aspect of a general trend to identify and reconcile the technical sophistication and complexity of products with the way they are used and the way they are perceived culturally.

To avoid all ambiguity concerning what might reasonably be expected of technology, it should be remembered that time-

dependent of his tools and the use of CAD has a number of implications for the products concerned and imposes certain constraints. Total mastery of a particular technology is a designer's best guarantee that he will end up using it correctly, and this brings us to the key question. How does CAD influence the designer's output and working methods? Or to put it differently, how has design changed now that design practice takes place in a sophisticated technological environment, within a society which gives pride of place to information and communications?

CAD creates a new form of representation and modifies the status of the object

With the hardware and software available to him, the designer has new and varied tools with which to approach, develop and test a design. CAD provides a real extension to the designer's material capacities – it is a toolbox that he can adapt to suit his needs and abilities.

To simulate, understand, question, become informed: these are the basic activities which make up his work and his way of communicating with other people involved in the design and production process. The conception of any object, whatever its nature, requires preliminary preparatory work. It must be represented, in one way or another, at each successive stage of development, to allow for modification and evolution, before being made into a prototype.

propriate choices and objectives. In short, one must clearly define the problem and home in, by a process of investigation and verification, on the right solution.

Choices lead to specifications. The brief, once established, will serve to define the work and validate the product. At this stage, computers are of considerable help because they allow a number of the brief's requirements to be analyzed, for example dimensions, properties of resistance or behaviour in materials, functional and operational characteristics. This research calls for tools capable of simulation and

to digital files, it is also possible to transmit images through telecommunications networks.

The designer's work consists, increasingly, of integrating diverse requirements and postponing experimentation with real objects for as long as possible. This is to limit the expenditure of both time and money entailed in making models and prototypes. These computation and simulation tools, some of which are useful to engineers as well (it is possible, for example, to make precise calculations of the rate at which fluid passes over a given form, or how a material

From left to right: **CAD images by Campenon Bernard SGE– Eurograph for a bridge in Normandy: cutaway of the top of the tower; view of the tower; general view.**

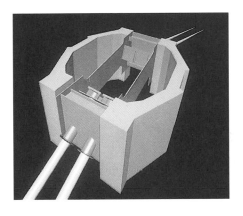  

This observation holds true for any work which, through reflection, analysis and imagination, leads to the production of an object, a product or an action. To conceive means to manipulate ideas and forms present only in the mind and give them concrete form by converting them into drawings, models or texts.

This work rarely proceeds *ex nihilo*. The designer usually has a set of requirements, a brief, formulated by the client or person in charge of the project. Guidelines of some sort, written or oral, are essential in order to establish the characteristics of the product and its parameters. This is already an important task which ensures that the design concept meets the basic requirements. To answer a need, one must try to understand it fully, analyse it and identify the context – commercial, social or otherwise – which has led to it. One must proceed by investigation and then determine the ap-

computation. In the case of a mixer tap, for example, the design would have to be visualized, measured and weighed, and its operation and assembly would have to be tested, much as though one were X-raying or dismantling a real mixer tap.

Simulations, as the term suggests, release the designer from the obligation of having to produce a prototype. This working procedure, where the concept of 'life size' is replaced by 'simulated size', is the very essence of contemporary industrial production. To produce is above all to conceive.

It is desirable to maintain contact with objects (something, as we shall see, that is not always possible) and the designer has at his disposal the facility to transform the virtual model on the screen into a physical object with the aid of digital machines which sculpt the required sections out of the desired material. Given that everything the designer produces is reducible

will bend under certain stresses) creates a world of simulation which the designer must adapt to in two important respects. First, a computer representation corresponds to certain attributes of the object but not necessarily all the attributes the designer envisages. Second, the use of computers provides information about the performance and properties of materials which he will have to take into account in the development process – the basic design cycle of proposal-evaluation-modification.

The designer's work is part of this cycle and is also implicated in the larger cycle of data exchange between those responsible for commission, conception, technical assessment, manufacture and final evaluation. This latter cycle is increasingly a 'virtual', or computer-generated one. At the extreme limit, the designer could converse with his client entirely through computers and computer-generated images and information. The tendency to rely on CAD becomes more pronounced every day. We have come a long way since the time when engineers paid occasional visits to craftsmen working in the isolation of their studios.

Drawing, generating, capturing

Much more spectacular, but ultimately less original than its computational functions, is CAD's capacity to generate images. Computer-generated images are becoming increasingly widespread in all professions, especially those that are visually based. My argument about design applies with equal force to the techniques used for constructing three-dimensional objects, and for the synthesis and processing of digital images.

Drawing is an act whose origins are lost in time. Apart from a few mechanical devices, ours is the first era in the history of civilization in which drawings can be produced by a machine. Machine drawings are not the automated reproduction of an individual's gestures and draughtsman's skills. Rather they are virtual objects in three dimensions. They are sculptures which inhabit a space produced with mathematically-based functions more or less simple to use. All these functions constitute a range of genuine practical, manual skills.

The drawing of plans is now nothing more than the processing of a model generated by particular functions. The construction of an object proceeds on the basis of a functional language which can generate surfaces on the basis of a few selected points, deform, transform and fuse elements, make them hard or soft, animate their moving parts, alter their mechanical parameters, and change the elasticity of materials. As opposed to geometry, this sculpture constitutes a virtual universe whose physical properties are variable, but which, it is hoped, bear some resemblance to reality.

Drawing is now just one part of CAD. The designer can generate forms and structures by means of gestures, formulas, or languages. Such images no longer function on the level of representation, as in perspective renderings, but as actual objects, with the caveat that they exist only as pure data. The more closely this on-screen form parallels the technical, geometric and reactive properties of the projected object and the materials from which it is to be made, the more successful is its 'computerization'. It will be easily simulatable and its dynamic will be a product of underlying computation models.

Another important aspect of computer drawing is the facility to make use of existing computer images and models for reference or inspiration. In the case of the mixer tap, for example, the designer can first of all consult catalogues of similar products and study their form and how they function. If these catalogues have been recorded digitally on a database or on CD-ROM, the information can be easily assimilated into his own CAD project. If he has a real mixer tap to hand he can photograph it and digitize the image by laser scanning. This will give him a three-dimensional computer model which can be used as a starting point for his work. He will thus have taken a real object and integrated it into his field of investigation. The assimilation of data in this way is a function which allows the designer to work with an existing object which becomes material or a guide for his own project. Although this type of activity is just emerging, it is indicative of a tendency which is becoming established in design practice.

These new developments, which are already being exploited in some quarters, offer some indication of the way computer equipment and new technology will influence design practice in the future. The current trend suggests an ever increasing availability of objects, data and tools, in a virtual working environment which is accessible through a workstation or network of workstations.

Computer-generated image of a motorway structure, created using Model View software on an Intergraph computer. Jean Muller International, 1992.

Towards a new workplace

How far has CAD progressed and what direction has it taken? How is design evolving under the influence of computer technology and what might the next steps for designers be?

The first steps for CAD were extremely close to the automating of gestures, the making available of mathematical toolboxes. At first, it was intended to be a conceptual aid, if not a means of resolving microproblems. CAD is undoubtedly prized by those involved in industrial design, but its initial promise has yet to be fully exploited. Certainly, the ability to generate images and create simulations has given a new impetus to the role of computers, enabling better communication. The fact that designers work in these spheres has given them a place in the production process, from the point of view of digital information and the sharing of resources such as databases and tools of expertise.

From the point of view of design itself, that is to say production, computers have made their mark in several ways. The flexibility and control offered by computer programs and systems, and the ability to generate lines and mathematically correct layouts have certainly had a significant influence on design.

A particularly important tool is the one which enables designers to define a surface by means of a number of points in space which are automatically created by mathematical calculation. These points – points of control or positioning – serve as a guide for the creation of the desired surface. By moving them, the designer modifies the surface interactively. The position of the points is determined by series of algorithms, that is to say mathematical rules, which not only function in this way as tools, but also as potential stylistic forms with distinctive visual characteristics.

For sure, designers are using, and will continue to use, elementary models for generating forms and procedures. In the

The computer and the human mind have quite different but complementary abilities. The computer excels in analysis and numerical computation, the human mind in pattern recognition, the assessment of complicated situations and the intuitive leap to new solutions. If these different abilities can be combined, they amount to something much more powerful and effective than anything we have had before.

Mike Cooley, 'From Brunelleschi to CAD-CAM', Design after Modernism, 1988

past, the ruler and the compass played a similar kind of role, so there is nothing really new about this aspect of CAD. Gradually, designers will extend their use of CAD. Firstly, the possibility of dealing with other aspects of product design such as technical calculations of properties of resistance and behaviour and what one could call the technical simulation of mechanisms, materials and performance, has compensated for the abuse of the facilities induced by the manipulation of computer modelling tools. This technical capacity, which enables the designer to test his design more effectively and is now increasingly available at computer work stations, will probably play an increasingly important role in years to come. The creation and manipulation of forms through CAD will often be highly logical, thanks to information processing programs. Technical knowledge of all kinds will be used in product development, with particular reference to technical and functional characteristics.

A further development in the conception process will stem from a new type of dialogue between experts through telecommunications networks which link images, voices and information. These networks of co-operation reflect the same trend towards the computerization of working practice and the gradual creation of 'immaterial', virtual workplaces. The increase in expertise brought about by these networks will create new working procedures for the designer who, increasingly, will be able to work in real time and in a more complex and more realistic environment. Expertise will then be brought into play through this 'delocalization' of the workplace. In this case, people will be used rather than software, even if these people use their own specific computer tools.

At the same time, the capacity for simulation provided by new technology will spread to other areas due, again, to information technology. Once the simulation workshop has been set up for diverse reasons, whether industrial or military, it will become available to everyone and people from all domains will try to use it to improve their performance and to try new things. The new material spread by this workshop will be first and foremost virtual. It consists of information in all forms and from all sources. The design of an object will become the design of the virtual, for which the only form of representation, apart from simulation itself, is simply repetition or narrative text.

Thus we have witnessed a double movement in the relationship between the material and the immaterial. On the one hand, the aim of CAD was to develop systems of concepts and tools capable of carrying out the tasks delegated to it by designers. This ambitious, immaterial function changed by the force of things, and CAD was used as a toolbox along the lines of the traditional techniques of drawing, measurement and cataloguing. On the other hand, we have gradually acquired a multitude of information processing techniques and networks which have opened up new fields of investigation.

Design of the virtual

The term 'design of the virtual' designates the new work environment in its entirety, a work environment in which design innovation is still possible. Most of today's new industrial products, for example, include an informational dimension. Whether it be a household electrical appliance, a machine tool or some kind of technical device, it is not unusual for machines to contain a microprocessor or computer data. In other words, appliances are enveloped in a kind of software or informational layer. This suggests that a new conceptual field is emerging in design, based on the relationship between man and machine, a dialogue which necessarily exploits this informational component of products. The design of the virtual consists in particular in designing this informational component in the most general sense. In order to do this,

Computer-assisted design, computer-assisted writing, computer-assisted living. . . What do these imply? . . . Instead of being made to concentrate on very recent memories, of what it is that has to be done and how to do it correctly, I can now forget all that, trusting the process to sort it out later. The forced memorizing of intentional actions . . . is gone. Instead the spontaneous memory, as in laughter or conversation, the joy or terror of living, can return to 'industrial' action.

John Chris Jones, 'Softecnica',
Design after Modernism, *1988*

CAD tools become tools for simulating processes containing and processing information. Thus a scene will be simulated in which a person, computer-generated or real, will try to communicate with a machine. The designer will analyze, in real time, how he attempts to understand or use this machine for which the informational envelope has to be designed.

Machines of this kind are actually very common. One example is the sophisticated photocopier which is equipped with control screens and maintains a dialogue with the user, or even a cash dispensing machine or a teaching method using multimedia computers. In the case of these examples, the user enters into a dialogue with the machine which behaves like an electronic service whose forms and virtual functions have to be designed, as indeed does the way the user is intended to perceive and interpret it. This will result in a sort of style or rhetoric of the virtual. To simulate these scenes down to the smallest detail is to construct, play out and explore this scene, varying the different characteristics of the object being conceived, which here consists of a flux of information, and this in a virtual workshop operated by machines. This workshop in the end, is just an extension of the previous CAD workshop. Beyond dialogue, the virtual object can still take other forms, like service in general or like the procedures which make up different areas of professional, domestic or social life.

Design or designer?

During the last ten years of use, CAD has become an established part of the working practice of designers (as well as architects and engineers) without causing a metaphysical revolution. Certainly, the first step was to master these new tools which made modelling and simulation a practical proposition in terms of exploitation and know-how, but which demanded a new state of mind and a process of adaptation. CAD and its derivatives, such as computer graphics, have become powerful but commonplace tools. The stylistic effects created by algorithmic facilities and options have not disappeared, but they have gradually been tamed, even if computer graphics have reinforced the tendency to play with the variation of parameters. The manipulation of parameters has engendered a combinatory state of mind which tends to look for a solution to a problem of form or func-tion by varying the available parameters of the software. The role of creativity and imagination has changed and is now a question of exploring the possibilities of hardware and software.

That is fair enough and is in fact simply the technological equivalent of traditional pen and paper methods, but in a more powerful and sophisticated form.

The question of whether CAD has had a bigger effect on the designer or on design is not as strange as it sounds, for CAD has acted on the two in different ways. For the designer, equipment has become more powerful, more technical and easier to integrate. The designer who works normally with a CAD system uses it in the same way as an engineer or a manufacturing technician. He is no longer regarded as a peripheral figure addressing stylistic questions, but as a link in the production chain. For design, the question is different. The move towards the simulation of processes and immaterial objects such as services, communication with machines and virtual spaces in general, is a significant development. That is why CAD and product design maintains links in both directions.

Design is tackling new objects that CAD can simulate. There resides the real challenge for designers. Indeed, virtual objects – objects of communication – and networks, to which we could add the creation of new unexplored territories, which we could call 'telespaces', offer the designer an immense field of invention and creativity. The quest to give virtual objects quasi-form will inevitably lead to a new type of design.

The Lockheed Stealth Bomber

Advances in radar technology and infrared detectors have made military aviation and long-range missiles particularly vulnerable. To render planes stealthier and more discreet, it has become necessary to diminish the strength of the standard radar signal generated by conventional aircraft by a factor of a thousand.

Making a plane like the Lockheed F-117A 'stealthy' entailed a complete redesign of its form. If an object like an airplane is struck by an electromagnetic wave, part of this is absorbed and transformed into heat, while the balance of its energy is radiated and dispersed in various directions and can be picked up on a radar.

The amount of echo power registering on a radar receiver tracking an object is called the object's radar surface equivalence (RSE). To calculate a plane's total RSE, it must be considered as a heterogeneous collection of 'hot spots' correlating with the fuselage, the fins, the engines' air intake ducts, electrical discontinuities resulting from abrupt changes of surface materials, etc. The key to reducing the radar signature of an airplane is, then, the reduction of the number of these hot spots.

The shape of the F-117A startles because it was devised to achieve maximum stealth potential, even at the expense of aerodynamic efficiency. It is a great flying wing, crisply geometrical, all of whose elements have been integrated as fully as possible. Its form is especially disconcerting because, by definition, it is intended to remain invisible. This means that we can only understand the plane's unusual form by means of a 'secret', non-expressive, visual code. It is hardly surprising, then, that the Lockheed F-117A, nicknamed the 'block jet', strikes the layman as strange and is often misunderstood, even though its appearance is the result of rigorously functionalist principles.

J. d. N.

Enlargement of the inside of a hypertexture, created by Stephane Deverly, Centre de Recherches Image Numérique, Université de Paris 8.

Opposite page: Eat, a virtual restaurant created by Michael Naimark. Virtual objects call into question the very concept of the object, and, beyond that, of matter, if not reality itself.

Time-objects
Beyond Form

Edmond Couchot

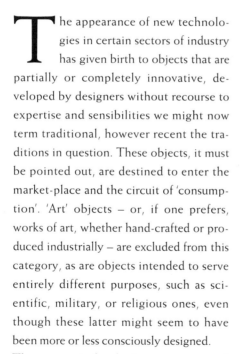

The appearance of new technologies in certain sectors of industry has given birth to objects that are partially or completely innovative, developed by designers without recourse to expertise and sensibilities we might now term traditional, however recent the traditions in question. These objects, it must be pointed out, are destined to enter the market-place and the circuit of 'consumption'. 'Art' objects – or, if one prefers, works of art, whether hand-crafted or produced industrially – are excluded from this category, as are objects intended to serve entirely different purposes, such as scientific, military, or religious ones, even though these latter might seem to have been more or less consciously designed.

These new technologies are many and varied, but two of them present problems radically different from the ones with which design is usually confronted, and for which new kinds of answers must be devised. The first is biotechnology. We are now capable of operating at the level of the gene, something which makes possible the 'industrial' production of animal and vegetable hybrids, which figure increasingly in the current consumer circuit. In the laboratories where these genetically-altered animals and vegetables are perfected, concern about colour and form is far from absent. The creation of a new variety of rose – within our reach for some time now – calls for a refined sense of shape, for the form in question remains uniquely well suited to its decorative function. But the improvement of a variety of courgette, or better yet the creation of a new vegetable in which features of the courgette and cucumber are combined, means assuring not only that this vegetable has an agreeable taste – that its gustatory 'form' is pleasing – but also that it is beautiful, that both its shape and its colour are appealing. What is required is a form adapted to the specific dietetic function of vegetables. To succeed, a 'designer' vegetable must come across unequivocably as a vegetable, while stimulating the appetite.

Biotechnologies seem to have the same goals as agriculture and breeding, which have always aimed at improving the quality of their products, aesthetic quality included. In reality, however, we are witnessing an unprecedented qualitative change in the possibilities of manipulation. By acting directly on genes, the smallest components of life, biotechnologists are becoming involved in the very heart of the life process. The field of genetic combinations that are now possible, or soon will be, is seemingly infinite. The boundaries established by nature, which in a certain order of things impose a pervasive aesthetic 'by default', are becoming blurred, leading to a fantastic increase in possibilities. Traditional techniques of hybridization and cross-breeding have given us a great many fruits, vegetables, flowers and races of domestic animals which fall comfortably within the natural continuum; but the new ones might well facilitate the development of products effecting a complete break with this continuum: blue tomatoes, cubic eggs, chickens with four thighs, green beans by the metre, even hybrids of jellyfish and peas.

So far as I know, currently there are no designers specializing in the development of these new products, presumably not due to any technical impediments, but because of the difficulty of distinguishing between aesthetic and biological areas of activity. But it's not unlikely that the future will see the emergence of new categories of creative professionals: 'zoodesigners' and 'phytodesigners'. However that may be, the developers of hybrid species, anxious to give their products a pleasing appearance, are now, perhaps without realizing it, inaugurating a new kind of design which breaks completely with tradition. In effect, while the central preoccupation remains the conception of form, the material with which the zoodesigner would work would be profoundly different. For he would deal with genes, in other words with coded information that's living but quasi-abstract, reduced to chains of molecules without tangible form, and the effects produced by his work would only become apparent as the being harbouring them

Above right:
Visualization headset and data glove, VPL.

Virtual Reality, **image created by Warren Kovinetti, University of North Carolina. In the same way that photography gave birth to the 'imaginary museum', interactive technology makes it possible to create a 'virtual museum'.**

Right-hand page: **Poster designed for the Industrial Design conference organized by the Centre de Recherche Busnelli, 1973.**

By the late 20th century, our time, a mythic time, we are all chimeras, theorized and fabricated hybrids of machine and organism; in short we are cyborgs. The cyborg is our ontology; it gives us our politics.

Donna J. Haraway, 'A Cyborg Manifesto', Simians, Cyborgs, and Women: the Reinvention of Nature, *1991*

develops. He would operate with potential forms, processes, and futures – in a way,
with time.

A redefinition of the concept of the object

The science of genetics, it is true, is still in its
infancy and we cannot predict its future with
any certainty, but computer technologies
have already had an enormous impact on the
world of industry. They, too, produce all
kinds of objects, some of which are totally
new and will radically alter design methods
and types of project. Computer-aided design,
or CAD, for example, has permitted a flexible
and economic way of working on numerous
industrial products, from the car to the refrigerator by way of furniture and clothing. The
advantages of computer visualization are
countless: with the aid of, for example,
tightly controlled mathematical curves,
the most complex forms can be generated
with great speed and manipulated in real
time, 'seen' from any point of view, under
whatever lighting conditions might be
desired, and the results can be duplicated
or altered with the greatest precision and
without encountering the slightest material
resistance.

Mastery of the smallest constituent element
of the image on the computer monitor,
namely the pixel, has made it possible to
create objects *ab nihilo*, without recourse to
some exterior reality, object or reference
material. CAD has become a precious tool
for the designer. Likewise, in publishing,
computers have been of great service to
graphic designers and layout artists – the designers of the print world. There has even
been talk of using CAD in the retail clothing
market. A 'computer-aided tailor' would
make it possible to automatically cut a garment to the client's measurements: these
could be taken by electronic scanners
capable of generating a digital mannequin
in the body's image, which would then be
used to guide a laser to cut out the bits of
material, which would be glued as opposed
to sewn together. The entire operation

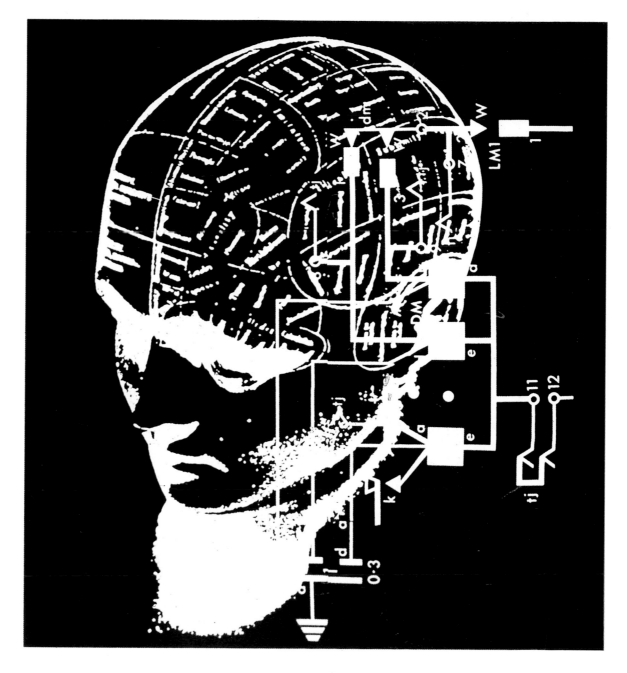

The micro-processor, already invisible,

has about it a quality which eludes appearance –

a quality, Kant might perhaps of said, of formlessness.

Also of the sublime.

Thierry Chaput, 'From Socrates to Intel: the Chaos of Micro-Aesthetics',
Design After Modernism, *1988*

would require only a few moments. What's more, each garment would be a personalized variant of a model conceived by a great couturier (not available for purchase), and so in a certain respect would be unique.

In any event, most designers use CAD as an extension of current practice, without changing it radically – only the methods change. This is remarkable, given that the introduction of automatic calculation capacities radically modifies the design of forms. But there are other objects designed with computers which are very different and pose unexpected questions. These objects – which exist only inside the computer and so have been dubbed 'virtual' – put in question the very concept of the object, and beyond that the concept of material and even of real-

ity itself. For the moment, it is impossible to give them physical form, not because of their virtuality *per se* (even coffee makers and cars exist only as virtual objects at a certain phase in their development) but because there are no extant materials, either natural or artificial, which correspond to their form. But even simply in their visual, virtual form they are of great interest. 'Hypertextures', for instance, make it possible to create virtual objects halfway between solids and surfaces (and thus distinct from fractal objects), sponge-like entities of indeterminate identity which none the less have gradients of existence. 'Particle systems' permit the generation of three-dimensional forms controllable from within which can be transformed into other forms without the

slightest break in continuity. And 'behavioural procedures' make it possible to set a multitude of real or imaginary entities in motion through space and time in a quasi-autonomous way, without having to describe their individual trajectories in detail. Certain interactive mechanisms in real time permit the viewer to take part himself in the creation of signs and figures and to be involved in their development. In this way time becomes an essential constituent of an object's form.

Some audio-visual products such as interactive videodiscs and compact discs, and certain electronic games have introduced other strange categories of 'time-objects'. Museums are beginning to use interactive databases to present their reserve collec-

Microcosm Virtuality System linked to an Apple Macintosh 900 Quadra computer, designed by Ideo for VPL, 1992. Inside a virtual, three-dimensional space, the spectator's eye moves according to the movements he imparts to the seat. The spectator is thus free to choose his own visual itinerary.

tions in the form of on-screen images to the public. A simple gesture – a finger placed on the tactile screen, the press of a key, the movement of a small ball, or even the movement of the eyes – enables the stationary 'visitor' to travel through the museum's rooms, moving from one work to another, from one painter to another, from one school or period to another in any order desired, compare paintings and drawings, ask for a closer look at specific details, or call up critical texts and information (written or oral) about the painters and the works. Jeffrey Shaw takes the spectator, who remains seated comfortably in an easy chair, inside a three-dimensional virtual museum. The visitor's eye moves about – advancing, pulling back, turning, scanning the walls or the paintings themselves according to the movements he imparts to his chair. Nothing in these types of journey is predetermined, for the viewer has total freedom to choose his visual itinerary. It goes without saying that in such circumstances certain important physical characteristics of the paintings are lost, and with them the pleasures of lingering in front of a canvas, of smelling its odour, but they give birth to a new kind of scrutiny, a new kind of pleasure of seeing, similar to the 'serial appreciation' already observed by George Kubler.

Diamorphosis

What, then, becomes of the object and of form, in these time-objects? What is or will be the designer's role in their design? In the case of the interactive museum, the visible objects remain the points of reference and the designer of the videodisc or interactive compact disc software does nothing to alter this. Rather, his work consists of imagining possible routes according to schemas which are rather like trees, knots or branchings consisting of combinations and various associations. He doesn't create forms that are fixed and stable; rather, he plots the possible courses, journeys and ways of accessing the image. He becomes involved at the level of time, the process of 'reading' and

visualizing. He becomes involved upstream, as it were, working on the conditions which shape interpretation and, consequently, meaning. He creates an entirely new way of consulting, he enlarges our perception of the works of art, he makes it possible for us to see them with new eyes. Just as photography gave birth to what André Malraux termed an 'imaginary museum', so these techniques of interactive consultation are giving birth to a 'virtual museum', to a new sort of memory. We can expect to see a whole new set of time-objects appearing in the years ahead. Wherever there is an interactive exchange of information, through images, sounds, or text, between a database and a user through the intermediary of a computer program (which are becoming more and more sophisticated every day), a time-object is produced. And the forms of all these time-objects – whether tools for teaching and communication or simple games (individual or arcade games) – must be adapted to their various functions, in other words, must be better adapted to their function; in short, designed by true designers specialized in this new domain.

Henceforth we must think of form – of *Gestalt* – as something in the process of formation or becoming over time; we must think of it as *Gestaltung*, to use Paul Klee's term. Our notion of form must be re-examined and completed; a temporal dimension must be added to it. In the virtual space-time continuum of computers, forms tend to become deployments of particular instants, assemblages of itineraries, 'accidents', if you will, detached from a matrix in perpetual gestation. It is crucial that the designer – and, more generally, the artist – find some way of thinking beyond form or even simple metamorphosis, that he begin to reflect in terms of diamorphosis – in other words, what happens between forms. It is a question not of inventing new forms, but rather of controlling the passage of these forms from one state to another – not setting these forms in motion, but exploring the power of the intervals separating them and the time

spans in which they are steeped. Whether computer technologies or biotechnologies are used, the essential project remains the same. Mastery of the fundamental small component elements of the image (the pixel) and the life process (the gene) demands that the designer work with virtualities constantly in a state of becoming. It would appear that the technologies of virtuality do nothing to undermine conventional design practice. The means they offer creative professionals can prove invaluable to those who see design primarily as a question of function and efficiency, to the exclusion of all decorative ornamentation. And they can be just as helpful to those strictly interested in the wishes of the user, with the previously utopian project of a unique product (the 'computer-aided tailor' offers a good example). For them, the computer is an ideal tool. Drawing and design are fused when the designer begins to work with the smallest component elements of the image (and one day, no doubt, of life itself). They can also be used to fulfil the Bauhaus ambition to transcend the adaptation of the object to its instrumental use and introduce it into a vast signifying system of elements which are mutually-referential like the words of a language. Likewise, the theories of informational design, such as those developed by the Ulm Hochschule für Gestaltung, now seem relevant once more. Communications theory can help us to conceptualize the object and its function as bundles of messages, which is important given that time-objects have become the stock-in-trade of communications networks. Partisans of design concerned primarily with codes of construction, with plastic and operational codes as opposed to form in the narrow sense, linked to robotized industrial production, will find in the technologies of virtuality the means suited to their objectives.

Opportunities to be seized

However, the technologies in question introduce new elements which might well oblige us to reformulate the entire design problematic. Mastery of the pixel – and of the gene – as virtual entities necessitates a rethinking of time-objects in fluid as opposed to static terms, as diamorphosis. But the 'process aesthetic', which encompasses much of the art produced throughout the present century, has run its course. It is no longer a question of making visible the interior of objects and machines, of emphasizing their structural elements, but rather of penetrating the innermost recesses of this space-time 'interior' so as to control the latter's possible evolution. The goal of rendering process visible, of exhibiting certain fixed images of its various phases, has given way to that of seizing all its adjacent parts in their very virtuality. This project is extremely difficult, and clearly ambiguous.

Our having gained access to the smallest constituent element of form – notably the pixel – is not an unmitigated blessing for the designer. The latter doesn't manipulate them individually like the knots in a carpet, he exercises control over vast ensembles. To define a curve, construct a volume, or set a form in motion, he asks the computer to engage a programme to arrange, rapidly and without error, the various points where they ought to be on the monitor. Each such operation entails reference to a mathematical, logical model which the programmer has borrowed from any one of various scientific disciplines: geometry, topology, physics, and optics among them, of course, but also chemistry, botany, biology, and, increasingly, the cognitive and neuro-sciences. These models propose interesting ways to generate certain forms, certain relations between forms, or certain potential evolutions of forms – 'form' being understood here as designating not only fixed, non-evolutionary forms but also diamorphic ones, such as the forms with variable identities specific to certain virtual objects (on the increase) – program reading itineraries, branchings of possible choices, etc. The designer no longer works directly with pen-

cils and erasers, or does so but rarely; he is aided by abstract formal models, by a programmed technical language developed by techno-science of extraordinary power but which he finds disconcerting; but he must thoroughly familiarize himself with it and master its hidden effects if he is to retain control over the decisions confronting him – which is no small task.

Such an endeavour will strike many as exceedingly difficult, perhaps even impossible. The power which computers give us should not be allowed to obscure the fact that automation of technical operations

demands that the designer approaches the creative process in a new way – and this also holds for the visual arts and music. We must not forget that design itself was born of the need to compensate for the absence of art in the forms of industrially-produced products. The need to use calculus and the continual borrowings from techno-science (factors in even the most basic software) will implicate design that much more in the 'manipulation of signs' characteristic of the logic of consumption (see Jean Baudrillard's critique of design). Doubtless a new mythology of time-object is now

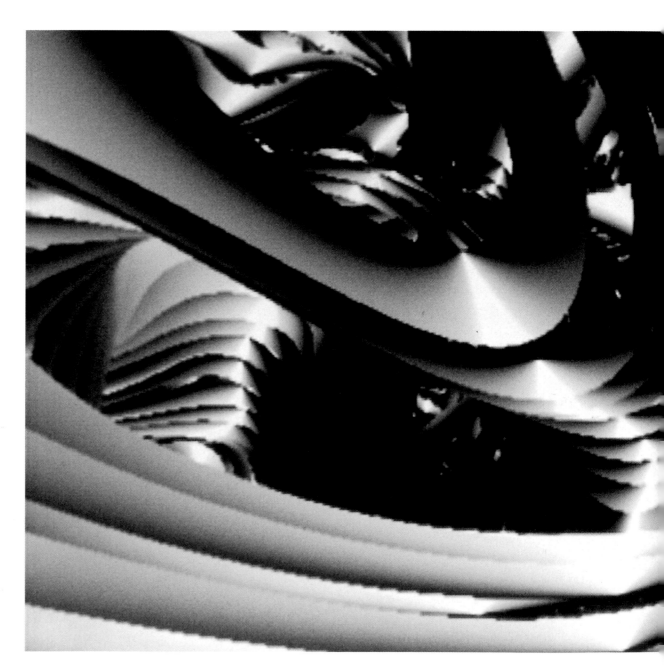

emerging. The heavy media coverage of 'virtual reality' provides confirmation of this. But the radical change in modes of visualization effected by virtual technologies (digital simulation having rendered optical representation obsolete), in the relations between art and techno-science as well as between the real and the imaginary, is so great and so radical that we might well ask whether the prevailing notions of communication, consumption, and even of the sign ought to be re-examined. And whether the 'production' of meaning at the heart of advanced technological societies doesn't proceed in accordance with a set of laws and principles which ought to be redefined. Nothing allows us to conclude, *a priori*, that the development of these technologies will only aggravate the decline in values deplored by so many, or, conversely, that they make it possible for us to realize our wildest utopian visions. What is certain, however, is that the striking novelty of the questions they raise and the terrible ambiguity of the answers hold out the prospect of new possibilities, uncertainties and faults in the world around us: so many opportunities ripe for the seizing.

Enlargement of the inside of a hypertexture, created by Stephane Deverly, Centre de Recherches Image Numérique, Université de Paris 8.

New Materials

in the Industrial Age

Raymond Guidot

Detail of Air
Titanium
spectacles,
designed by
Lindberg Optic
Design and Dissing
& Weitling
Architectes.

Below left:
Construction of
the Menai Bridge,
in England, 1826,
designed by
Thomas Telford,
architect and
engineer.

Below right: View
of the workshop
for making
locomotive wheels
at the factory
belonging to
Arbel, the
Desflassieux
brothers and
Peillon. From
L'Illustration,
1862.

I n addition to the image of the steam engine it inevitably brings to mind, the Industrial Revolution evokes mass production and the repetitive cycle of machine finishing. It also raises the issue of appropriate materials. For the Industrial Revolution to have been possible it was necessary to have materials that were not only available in large quantities but were also statistically homogeneous, because machines, at least early ones, were incapable of making distinctions, choosing and adapting. As a result, most natural materials traditionally used by craftsmen were, for quantitative or qualitative reasons, inappropriate.

This was the case, notably, with fibrous vegetal materials like wood, whose properties vary significantly depending upon whether it is approached along or against the grain: wooden planks cut along the grain can be quite long but not very wide; what's more, they inevitably feature irregularities deriving from their origin as living organisms. Most of these flaws result from the existence in the trunk of concentric zones that are more or less soft depending upon whether they are composed of inner sapwood or outer deadwood, but there can be other flaws, too:

curls, gnarls, splits and cracks, as well as the forking of branches, which creates knots. These many structural irregularities escape machine control and are detrimental to the proper functioning of tools. The potential for conflict between material and fashioning tool increases when mechanization is augmented by automation. For all these reasons one of the oldest materials used by man was constrained, if it was to be of industrial use, to alter its nature, to metamorphose.

Thus planks cut from tree trunks were replaced by artificially reconstituted wooden panels that were wider, more homogeneous, and produceable in large quantities. The most obvious example is plywood. Its production process – which consists of glueing thin wooden strips peeled from tree trunks on top of one another in multiple layers such that the grain doesn't always run in the same direction – was first developed in the middle of the 19th century, but it was perfected only when the military needed it for the cabins of fighter planes in the First World War. Subsequently developed was the fibreboard or particle board, still more homogeneous than plywood, which entered widespread use in the fifties. Fibreboard is a composite material (a category which now represents the avant-garde current in new materials, as we shall see). The wood

becomes a mere component used only because of its low cost: the panel's resistance is determined more by the binding substance than by the fragments of wood used. The Industrial Revolution, then, demanded materials which were homogeneous and lent themselves to mass production. The most exceptional materials of this kind, ones which enabled industrial civilization to expand and extend its hegemony over the entire world, are ferrous metals.

Ferrous metals and the Industrial Revolution

At the dawn of the 19th century the novelty of these materials – which had been known of since earliest antiquity – was due to the fact that for the first time they could be produced in massive quantities. This was thanks to the steam engine, which made it possible to force large quantities of compressed air into the base of a blast furnace, as well as to the use of a combustible, porous material in the furnace: coke (this process was perfected at the beginning of the 18th century by the British industrialist Abraham Darby). The massive production of cast iron, which started some 70 years before the construction of the Coalbrookdale Bridge – the first large-scale cast-iron construction in history – brought with it the massive production of iron made possible by decarbonization of the smelting process, thanks to the technique of puddling invented in 1784 by the Englishman Henry Cort.

Once it became feasible to produce these materials in large quantities, it was possible to devise and manufacture a multitude of 'products' (works of art, buildings, vehicles, objects for everyday use), giving physical form to the idea of the applied sciences and in the process radically transforming modern man's way of life.

Of these new objects and machines, the one which generated the most profound changes, because it simultaneously brought about the conquest of space and of time, was the steam locomotive. Once George Stephenson had made the locomotive a practical proposition, it became, with its capacity for transporting merchandise and travellers, an essential arm of industrial civilization. It made possible the annexation of entire continents and the gradual subjection of populations to the law of the strongest.

The railways represent a remarkable technological loop, for the same steam engine that contributed so much to the mass production of ferrous products (by furnishing compressed air to blast furnaces, facilitating the extraction of water from coal mines, and assuring the rapid conveyance of combustible materials, ore and pig iron) became, with the advent of steel railway tracks, the principal consumer of puddled iron. And this consumption occured through a process that itself set metallurgy on a new course.

The iron rails used in railway tracks, with their uniform profile, led to the idea of half-finished products, which in turn led to rolling mills becoming one of the crucial factors in technological progress. Thanks to them, iron beams shaped like T's, I's, U's and similar configurations came into being, generating new building construction methods, which permitted larger buildings. They opened the way to a vast domain in which the talents of engineers trained to serve the Industrial Revolution – many of

them in schools established for precisely this purpose in the early 19th century – would produce magisterial results.

Among these technicians of a new age, we should mention Henri Navier for his important role in perfecting, towards the middle of the century, methods for calculating the resistance levels of various materials. With this development the inspired empiricism guiding the execution of the first great projects of the engineer-builders gave way to projections calculated in design offices. In the matter of sectional iron, such projections eventually made it possible to order from a catalogue materials with the desired standard dimensions and resistances, which then had only to be cut to the proper lengths and assembled by rivets (and later by soldering) to obtain a structure consistent with a theoretical image established by means of calculation and working drawings.

At the end of the 19th century, the array of iron forms was considerably enriched thanks to Henry Bessemer's converter, invented in the middle of the century, in which molten pig iron is converted into steel. This steel was successfully used to construct large, skeleton-frame buildings, such as the department store The Fair in 1890, by the architect-engineer William Le Baron Jenney, a leading figure of the Chicago school. Like cast iron, steel was

perfected and used on an audacious scale only after a prolonged period of reflection and experiment. In the epic story of the beginnings of modern technology, it was in the chapter devoted to construction that 'new materials' made their mark. The great precursors in this field, include the Englishman Thomas Telford, who, in his 1801 project for a bridge over the Thames and his gigantic suspension bridge over the Menai Strait in 1826 brilliantly exploited the compressive and tensile strength of iron. A comparable knowledge of the performance levels of materials was possessed by Joseph Paxton, who built his immense Crystal Palace out of a few basic, industrially prefabricated elements manufactured in huge quantities, using for each one the material best suited to its particular function. This approach made it possible for him to meet the challenge of erecting one of the largest structures ever built in the space of a few months.

The theorist Eugène Viollet-le-Duc, in his *Entretiens sur l'architecture*, written between 1863 and 1872, took the dreams of the builders of the great Gothic cathedrals to their logical conclusion, ascribing to cast iron the role of a 'super-stone' permitting maximum reduction of sections made of compressed elements, and to steel that of 'nerves and bands', thanks to which it had become possible to 'bind vaults that

are very flat and quite wide'. Even so, he was only extending work done by builder-engineers in the earlier part of the century, in particular Jean Barthélemy Camille Polonceau, who, in 1847, invented a truss that now bears his name, consisting of laminated iron or wooden rafters, iron posts and tie-beams, together with cast-iron angle-braces.

Giving new materials an identity in the world of mass production

The technical knowledge which consists of breaking down a finished object into an ensemble of constituent elements and choosing the material best suited to each of them, had no bearing on the design of furniture. Cast iron, which could be moulded to imitate architectural elements from antiquity or the middle ages which were originally executed in stone or wood, was initially only a substitute material, used for the duplication of past models. New synthetic materials resulting from chemical treatment of natural organic macromolecules would play a similar role. The vulcanization of rubber, for example – discovered by the American Charles Goodyear and perfected by the Englishman Thomas Hancock in 1842 – would make it possible to obtain an elastic material as well as a hard one: ebonite. In wide industrial use because of its resistance to chemical agents and its suitability for electrical insulation, ebonite would also be used in moulding a wide range of fancy goods (boxes, combs, penholders, buttons, knick-knacks).

Other new materials would also be used in the manufacture of small objects: celluloid, developed in 1870 when John Hyatt managed to plastify cellulose nitrate with camphor; and galalith, which Spitteler and Krische made in 1897 by condensing milk casein with formaldehyde, and which was used as a substitute for celluloid, ivory, and so on.

All new materials produced by industry, it would seem, first had to pass through

a kind of purgatory, and synthetic materials, which differed from their predecessors in having been conceived independently of pre-existing materials, followed the same path. Such was the case with bakelite, which was invented and perfected in 1909 by Leo Hendrik Baekeland, a Belgian chemical engineer who had migrated to the United States. Searching for a product that might be a substitute for the shellac used as varnish, he happened upon a synthetic substance which, while satisfying his original requirements, was also extremely well suited to being cast into resistant objects. It was soon taken up for use in the production of commercial products, but before long it became clear that bakelite's properties were even more exceptional than had originally been thought and it came to be known as 'the material with a thousand uses'. Furthermore, it appeared at an especially propitious moment, a time when, as a consequence of the Industrial Revolution, many mass-produced objects issuing from the applied sciences were entering everyday use. As many of these were electrical appliances, bakelite – a remarkable insulator – became the preferred material, being clearly preferable to aluminium for the casting of casing elements, on condition these were not subjected to excessive strain and abuse.

In addition to the manufacture of moulded elements, bakelite could also be used to impregnate wood and paper to produce plates for use in electrical mounts rivalling those made of ebonite. Its resistance to heat was also a distinct advantage, but it was bakelite's remarkable suitability for moulding, with the only heat required being that necessary to induce an exothermic chemical reaction, that opened the way for the era of synthetic materials. In the inter-war period, thermosetting resins would have an enormous impact on the form and finish of everyday objects: first the phenoplasts (bakelite), then, beginning in the thirties, the aminoplasts (melamine), which unlike phenoplasts

From top to bottom: WF 400 water filter, designed by Kenneth Grange for Kenwood, 1992.

Sansone table made from coloured polyester resin, designed by Gaetano Pesce for Cassina, 1980.

Algol II television, designed by Marco Zanuso and Richard Sapper for Brion Vega, 1964.

Right-hand page: Stackable chairs made from moulded plastic, designed by Joe Colombo for Kartell, 1968 (detail).

could be dyed in bulk. From this point on, in numerous domains – principally those involving moulding – metal would give way to plastics.

Casting the man-made world

In taking on the project of one day being able to cast, if not the entire material world at least most of the objects produced by man, industrial civilization had at its disposal a choice material in cast iron. A source of other ferrous metals whose capacities, with the development of 'special' alloys in the 19th century, became increasingly spectacular, cast iron has not yet ceased to surprise us. Thus iron made from spheroid graphite today possesses mechanical properties – notably elasticity and tensile strength – quite close to those of steel. All the same, a significant handicap affects the casting of iron and other ferrous metals: temperatures of 1200-700°C are required for fusion. This necessitates the use of highly refractory materials (smelting sands rich in silica) for the actual moulds, which are destroyed in the course of each operation. Unable to resist the effects of shrinkage while the piece cools, the sand moulds unavoidably entail large dimensional tolerences and the defective surfaces of newly cast pieces necessitate their undergoing extended and costly processes of polishing or coating.

This explains the presence on 19th-century cast iron of 'decorative' elements (ornate cast reliefs or painted decoration): these were a response to the difficulty of obtaining simple forms free of flaws. One thinks of the iron columns of cast-iron architecture, but also of the frames of old sewing machines, whose swan's neck shapes, dictated by technical considerations, were covered in painted decorations (often floral designs) intended to mask their manufacturing defects.

When casting temperatures permit, it is possible to replace the highly refractory materials with metal blocks. In such cases the material can be used repeatedly and adapted to mass production (as was demonstrated during the bronze age, when hatchets and iron spears were made with stone blocks from which the shapes to be moulded had been hollowed out, a method allowing for the production of many pieces). The use of non-ferrous metals such as copper, zinc and aluminium alloys, whose fusion temperatures fall between 400-900°C, permitted the use of 'steel dies' in the casting process, which gradually evolved towards the injection method. Thus in 1965 the Peugeot 204 and the Renault R16 were equipped with block motors made of an alloy of aluminium silicon and copper moulded under pressure, with cast-iron water-jackets.

Moulding with reusable casts is the natural process for thermosetting plastics, as well as thermoplastics, both of which involve low temperatures (less than 200°C). Thanks to low moulding temperatures, numerous materials can be used to make the moulds; but when working a press, the effort expended and, in the case of the injection method, the opening and closing of the apparatus, make it necessary to use steel – a high performance metal in which the polished casts are cut to facilitate the removal of the cast from the mould; these casts result in products whose exterior appearance resembles that of ceramic or glass objects.

The aesthetic of moulded plastic

Throughout this century we have seen the development and proliferation of objects with perfectly smooth surfaces, which they acquire from the brilliant polish of their casting moulds. In bakelite, American 'streamline' objects of the thirties found a material ideally suited to all kinds of aerodynamic fantasies. Modest or luxurious, these invaded everyday life and created a new style. At the same time, improvements in techniques for pressing metals were developed in order to meet the new demands of the aesthetic, notably in the area of car manufacture.

Thermoplastic synthetic resins were initially of considerable importance in the textile industry. The discovery of polyamides made possible the appearance on the market of the famous nylon fibres produced by Wallace Hume Carothers and his team in the Du Pont laboratories. And the perfecting of the various thermoplastic resins, which was accelerated by the war effort, led in the late forties to massive production of objects of all sorts through pressure moulding. In a parallel development, advances in the techniques for compressing and then transferring thermosetting resins (phenoplasts and aminoplasts) made possible production rates close to those obtainable with thermoplastic injection. And in any case, the dimensional precision attainable with pressure moulding eventually rendered unnecessary costly machine finishing, which was beginning to seem like a kind of heresy in the world of advancing technology. Thanks to their many belatedly acknowledged qualites, the new 'ersatz' materials were finally enjoying a brilliant triumph.

Programmed research by companies played a crucial role in the creation of polyamide fibres and these days many companies employ large teams of researchers. This has resulted in a significant acceleration of the pace at which new synthetic materials are discovered. These materials conform more and more closely to specific chemical, physical and mechanical properties sought. The aeronautics and space industries, significant players in the game of demand and supply, subject new materials to stringent testing procedures. The research connected with their prestigious projects is not without impact on the realm of everday life, another realm which gives significant impetus to technical progress. This is evident above all in the appearance and durability of materials now being used in the manufacture of everyday objects. Thus the polysterene of the fifties, which was fragile and aged poorly, was displaced by ABS (acrilonitrilebutadiene-styrene), a robust and seductive successor in the sixties.

To a large extent, it was this material that launched the era of beautiful plastics – as exemplified by the remarkable products of the Braun company, conceived in accordance with rationalist-functionalist criteria and developed in conjunction with research carried out at the famous Hochschule für Gestaltung in Ulm. And it was ABS that became the preferred material of the dynamic Italian school of industrial design, which saw creative figures such as Marco Zanuso and Richard Sapper working as a duo for the Brionvega company, and Ettore Sottsass and Mario Bellini producing designs for Olivetti. And then there is Joe Colombo, whose famous furniture designs, such as the 1965 Universale chair manufactured by Kartell, made it easier for the general public to accept a material that is solid and capable of retaining its brilliance and rich colours for quite some time.

The spread of objects made of thermoplastic resins moulded by high speed machines – objects produced at the lowest possible cost – imposes certain contraints on form (beginning with those entailed by the process of automatic removal of the cast). These technical constraints have important and long-lasting implications for the appearance of our everyday environment. The depreciation of tooling results in a preference for simple volumes adapted to straightforward turning operations. Injection moulding has become the spearhead of mechanical production, with objects of modest dimensions dominant. As for larger ones which, through imitation or because of the use of simple manufacturing techniques, have also taken on the simple forms of the sixties and seventies, these could only be moulded by using other techniques and materials. In the case of thermoplastics, for example, the technique employed is that of rotary moulding, which makes it possible to spread large quantities of material of uniform thickness into moulds. And then there is thermoforming, in which a flat sheet softened by heating and then applied to a model by means of blasting or suction, permits complex surfaces suitable for use in a wide range of contexts. The technique produces shapes with rounded corners and had stylistic repercussions in the late sixties as important as those previously triggered by the sheet metal stamping process developed by the car industry in the thirties, which also exploited that material's malleability.

The age of composite materials

Thermoplastic resins, ideally suited to the production of utilitarian objects on a massive scale, have succeeded in conquering everyday life. Yet thermosetting resins have also played an important role. And if we are looking for techniques and materials which have led to a global rethinking of the everyday environment – housing (architecture, interior design, furniture), street furniture, car bodies, etc. – then moulded polyester reinforced with fibreglass takes the prize hands down. A miraculous material that also served in the war – used, among other things, for radomes on aeroplanes – it leads us to the important subject of composite materials. We might begin with a celebrated episode in the history of industrial design: that of the winning project in the Organic Design in Home Furnishings contest organized in 1940 by the Museum of Modern Art in New York. This project, and its subsequent development by its creators Charles Eames and Eero Saarinen in the late forties, led to two kinds of 'composites'. The second composite represented a simple solution to a problem incompletely resolved by the first. Development of the two was separated by an interval of several years, and involved both different constituent materials and

Plastics in modern tableware

Of all the materials used to make modern tableware, only plastics can claim to be an entirely 20th-century phenomenon. The earliest plastics in use – celluloid and bakelite – were not considered suitable for products in which moisture, taste and smell were considerations. It was only when Beetle moulding powders were introduced for light-coloured resins in the mid-1920s that designers at last had a new medium in which to produce tableware. The results included the famous Ban-

dalasta picnic sets and vacuum flasks of the late 1920s and early 1930s.

Then, in 1932, an improved material called urea formaldehyde arrived, destined to supplant the mottled colours of Bandalasta in the homes of the 1930s. But the big breakthrough came in 1939, when the American Cyanamid Company made melamine commercially available for the first time. After the Second World War, melamine was widely used by tableware manufacturers, its colour, lightness,

cheapness and durability making it highly suitable for domestic use.

The first melamine tableware was designed by the American Russel Wright for Cyanamid in 1949 under the name Meladur. But although this was used by a New York restaurant chain it never found favour in the home. Then, in 1953 Wright created the Residential dinnerware range in melamine for the Northern Industrial Chemical Moulding Company of Boston: this achieved a breakthrough in domestic

acceptance and was widely imitated.

In Britain the Melaware range of 1959 designed by A H Woodfull and the Fiesta range of 1961 designed by Ronald Brookes demonstrated the versatility of melamine. But it was the Italians who seized on the new possibilities in plastics tableware. Plastics enabled a more freeform use of shapes and encouraged stackability and inter-lockability.

Jeremy Myerson and Sylvia Katz,
Tableware, 1990

production techniques, but the formal aims were the same. It was in 1940, that the use of plywood for the manufacture of seat shells met with certain difficulties in the cutting and shaping of the superimposed sheets of wood. Polyester reinforced with fibreglass turned out, in 1945, to be an ideal solution.

The notion of the composite, an essential element of advanced research, brings us back to natural materials, most of which are in fact composites. Some of them, like granite, have a grainy character, and are statistically homogeneous but incapable of sustaining mechanical interventions other than compression, others, such as wood, have a texture which is consistent and runs in one direction and thus are pliant and have great tensile strength. It is to materials of this kind that we should compare 'intelligent' artifical composites, in which the qualities of the constituent substances are combined to achieve a better response to exterior stimuli.

In construction, concrete – an artifical conglomerate of rocks, gravel and sand pressed together hydraulically, a kind of reconstituted stone – has surprising tensile strength and flexibility when given a steel reinforcement, and even more so when, by stretching the latter, the combination is prestressed. The procedure is similar when, in the shell of a part mechanically subjected to heavy stresses, a variety of materials are used, here one that can be twisted, there one that can be bent, and elsewhere one that can be compressed, with a polymerizable resin linking them all together. In doing this we are applying to structures which can be microscopic in size, theoretical, macroscopic models which have been used by man for quite some time, as in the bow with its wooden or metal stick and its cord made of dried animal tendons.

This example brings to mind another, one intimately linked to the heroic period of the Industrial Revolution, the Polonceau truss metioned earlier, in which each of the various components plays a specific

role according to its particular properties. But adaptation of these composites and sub-composites on a smaller scale can sometimes imply a heterogeneity incompatible with the industrial objective. Composites like honeycomb web sandwich or panels of synthetic foam with metal covering (stratified, laminated, etc.), semi-finished products subject to subsequent shaping and fitting, can be perfectly manufactured automatically in great quantities, but such is not always the case for objects in which the composite must fit a shape which has been precisely calculated beforehand. The moulding which results can indeed be of an industrial nature. Such is the case when textiles pre-soaked in thermosetting resins are pressed, or when resin-soaked threads are rolled, or a high-resistance thermoplastic resin and short fibres or trichites with a very high mechanical resistance are simultaneously introduced into an injection press. But very often when making a part that must sustain considerable mechanical wear and tear and has an eccentric shape – the blade of a helicopter rotor, for example – the production process inevitably becomes artisanal.

By way of conclusion

Industrial progress unfolds as a sequence of dialectical exchanges in which diverse lines of thought and opposing tendencies finally result in a fruitful synthesis. And as paradoxical as this might seem, forward movement can sometimes occur through a return to the past. Today we sometimes see the most advanced technology (laser cutting, for example) being used in tandem with skilled handiwork to produce particularly high performance objects, ones we will not be able to produce industrially for quite some time. The aeronautics and space industries find themselves caught in this strange contradiction, because they use the most advanced materials and the most sophisticated technology in a manufacturing process that does not conform to the principles and constraints of mass pro-

duction and that must often involve artisanal techniques.

In the light of this, it is interesting to consider the fact that small, dynamic, flexible enterprises with an artisanal approach are increasingly becoming, in Italy especially, a breeding ground for experiment and development from which are emerging the most promising models and protypes in every domain – those destined for industrial mass production at some future date, to be sure, but also those of a more experimental nature which form the focus of technicians' and designers' development of the man-made world of tomorrow. Freed from the constraints of mass production, companies and designers, working at the limits of feasibility, here accord themselves the right to make mistakes. Thus certain businesses, such as Italy's Cassina, have established, alongside their studios designing for mass production, departments committed to purely experimental research. It is in Cassina's laboratory that Gaetano Pesce, in particular, has for decades been allowed to give free reign to his imagination in developing projects oriented towards the unconventional use of materials and manufacturing techniques, as well as, through the introduction of chance elements into the manufacturing process, creating an element of differentiation among mass-produced objects. This experimental work will, without any doubt, figure importantly in the future preoccupations of those industries currently implicated in mass production, which is increasingly coming under attack for its dispiritingly repetitive character.

Computer science, which has made such astonishing progress recently, will prove a crucial ally in the quest for a less uniform approach to mass production. The programming of manufacturing equipment will enormously increase flexibility, making it possible to vary two objects within a series without adversely disrupting the production rate at all.

Polonceau truss (named after its inventor Jean Barthélemy Camille Polonceau), Gare du Nord, Paris.

Left-hand page: **Section of a helicopter rotor blade.**

Micromachines

Background:
Micromotor next
to a human
hair.

Vignette:
Micromotor
(diameter:
0.1mm) of
variable
capacity,
photographed
with the aid of
an electronic
microscope.

The first micromotor became an experimental reality in 1988, when Professor Richard Muller and his team at the University of Berkeley succeeded in making cogged wheels out of selenium that were less than 150 micrometres in diameter (one hundred micrometres is roughly equivalent to the diameter of a strand of hair).

Since then this technology has been copied and perfected. Today, the Japanese corporation NEC is capable of manufacturing an experimental micromotor in selenium with a diameter of less than 50 micrometres and a thickness of 12 micrometres that is capable of turning at a rate of more than 1,000 rpm over a period of several hours.

These marvels of miniaturization can only be seen with the aid of a microscope. We can only conceive or deduce the existence of such objects: their presence is difficult to detect.

Many problems remain to be solved before widespread use of micromachines will be practicable. If they are to be viable and sufficiently long-lived, it will be necessary to reduce their friction levels markedly and increase their efficiency. But once these problems have been solved, micromachines could prove useful in domains as varied as medicine, audio reproduction and electronics. *In a few years it might be possible to put together a true micro-robot consisting of a tool, a sensor and a microprocessor that could be introduced into the body's circulatory system to destroy a blood clot obstructing a coronary artery. Microstructures might make it possible to improve control over the functioning of laser-disk readers.*

This research is a collaborative effort involving Japanese as well as American companies, such as the California-based SRI International, which makes artificial muscle fibres consisting of electrostatic micromachines.

When integration of microelectronics and micromechanics becomes both achievable and economically viable, it will be possible to make a machine capable of hovering in the air and performing microsurgery in real time. Such a machine would also be able to move small objects, for example on an assembly line. Perhaps electronic micromachines will perform the genetic manipulations of tomorrow.

For more information, the reader should consult an article by Gary Stiy, 'Le micro-usinage', in Pour la science, no. 183, January 1993, pp. 84-90.

J. d. N.

High speed multihulls

A capacity of 500 passengers and their vehicles, a speed of 50 knots, a length of 100 metres, and a five-hour cruising range: such will be the characteristics of the high speed ferry vessels of the future on which naval engineers are now at work.

On 10 November 1992, a hybrid catamaran-hovercraft, the Agnes 200, an experimental French 50-metre vessel, reached a speed of 43 knots during a test run off Cherbourg.

At the end of the 19th century, Nathaniel Herreshoff and his sons Francis and John inaugurated what was to be a brilliant racing future for the catamaran. They were the first to understand that multihulled vessels would be capable of much higher speeds than traditional monohulls. Naval architects demonstrated that their theories were correct by constructing small experimental catamarans about ten metres long that could exceed 18 knots. But new materials, of an unprecedented strength and lightness, would be required to build large vessels and these became available only in the 1960s.

Today a multihulled racing vessel can make the crossing from New York to Lizard Point in less than eight days. While we should not underestimate the skills of the crews on these ocean-going Formula One's, we must also acknowledge the role played by the engineers whose innovations made such results possible. Thanks to them and to new advanced composite materials, hulls can now be made which have the strength of steel but are four or five times lighter.

The strategy of the designers and builders working on the boats of the future is to experiment with forms and materials. According to Jean-Pierre De Loof, Director of Research at the Institut Français de Recherche pour l'Exploitation de la Mer (IFREMER), it is still too soon to make a definitive choice among the design concepts now under consideration: too many technical problems remain unsolved. Three options are being explored: catamarans riding over the surface on air cushions, much like the Agnes 200; extremely slim single-hulled vessels such as the Italian Acquastrada (101 x 14 metres); and catamarans of the Swath type, with two submerged hulls shaped like torpedoes that are linked by two supports to a cabin raised above the water.

For the moment, energies are focused on refining the design of the Eole, which will mark an advance on the Agnes 200.

J. d. N.

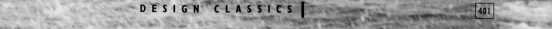

The Lotus pursuit bicycle

It was thanks largely to this new bicycle that British cyclist Chris Boardman became an Olympic champion in Barcelona against all expectations. The bike was the result of a collaboration between a young English inventor, Mike Burrows, and Lotus Engineering.

Using Burrows' prototype, Lotus, after several months of research, succeeded in perfecting a machine that was significantly faster than existing pursuit bicycles. It had a one-piece aerodynamic frame made of oriented carbon fibres in an epoxy resin matrix. The pedals and handlebars were made of titanium. The back wheel was attached to the frame via an integrated suspension system, while the front wheel was held by a one-piece fork made of carbon fibre. Lotus Engineering is now developing a new bike for an attempt on the world speed record.

The use of advanced technology in the design of sports equipment often leads to spectacular improvements in performance. Notable examples include fibreglass vaulting poles, sailboards, hang-gliders, javelins, jogging shoes, and ski boots and clothing. When such articles are mass produced for the general public the financial gains can be substantial.

J. d. N.

The modern ski boot

The evolution of ski boots offers a striking example of the extent to which new materials can affect the look of a consumer product.

Before 1960, ski boots were made of leather and were closed with laces, very much like walking boots. It was not until 1966 that plasticized leather and snap-hooks appeared.

Obviously, traditional boots were not well suited to improving one's performance. Modern ski boots have to meet several basic functional requirements: First, their inner design must be ergonomic, allowing for maximum comfort and security. Second, the boots must be fixed to the skis by grippers and must be waterproof.

Given that ski boots are consumer products intended for amateur as well as professional skiers, styling could not be left to chance. Manufacturers' marketing specialists commissioned designers to come up with forms which took into account the tendency of weekend sportsmen to identify with champions.

The modern functional boot became reality when it became possible to inject durable plastic materials (such as polymers and polyesters) into steel moulds under pressure, thus obtaining ultra-resistant outer shells. To guarantee comfort, it was necessary to make an autonomous inner shoe of polyurethane foam lined with velvet that would provide great stability as well as a snug fit.

The use of these new materials, in tandem with the development of ergonomic models created with the aid of CAD (computer-aided design), led to the following characteristics: access from the back; a rigid sole with a flexible shaft toward the front connecting with an articulated joint; a tight fit at certain points to ensure both support at the heal and a certain freedom of movement for the foot; the possibility of adjusting the boot from memory such that it can be done instinctively.

Despite these constraints, the designer retains a considerable freedom when it comes to designing the outer form of the ski boot. Possibilities range from high tech to biodesign, and all the colours of the rainbow can be used.

J. d. N.

Background:
Salomon boot,
c.1960.

Top, left to right:
Evolution of the
Salomon boot :
c.1970, c.1980,
c. 1992.

Throughout history, every society has devised arms with which to defend its territory and, on occasion, to appropriate territory from others. This family of objects is just as much a part of a people's culture as those devised for use in religious rites or the practice of a craft. One has only to walk through the galleries of the Louvre to realize that the artists of Egypt, Greece and Rome, as well as painters from the Renaissance to the Empire left many works in which the military aspect of their cultures figures prominently. Today, it is film rather than painting that most conspicuously resorts to images of war in representing our age – from Napoleon by Abel Gance to Apocalypse Now by Francis Ford Coppola.

The army as an institution has always used theatrical effects to impress the people, maintain troop morale and deter enemies. One need only read The Radetzky March by Joseph Roth to understand the prestige associated with military uniforms in the Vienna of Emperor Franz Joseph.

As is the case for other types of object, a particular weapon can take different forms from one culture to another. As André Leroi-Gourhan, in Le Geste et la Parole (1964-1965), has shown us, one of the most striking examples is that of a dagger 'specifically intended to pierce coats of mail and the joints of armour. Accordingly, this weapon had to have a blade between 30 and 40 centimetres long with an extremely sharp, square- or lozenge-shaped, piercing end. This functional ideal was reached between the 14th and 18th centuries in Europe, the Middle East and Japan. In the quality of the steel used and the penetration of their blades, the daggers of these great civilizations have almost identical properties, but the European ones take the form of a short double-edged sword while those of the Middle East resemble straight knives and those of Japan short sabres. Clearly it would

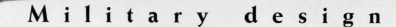

Military design

be possible to demonstrate that none of them conforms exactly to the theoretical penetration ideal. This is due to the notion of functional approximation which characterizes their differing responses to the contradictory requirements of mechanical efficiency and the need for each milieu to leave its mark on the object.'

Armament industries, today as in the past, are situated in a politico-economic context of great urgency, which explains why military material is often in advance of civilian material. Designers working for the military are dealing with a unique client that knows what it wants and is capable of drafting coherent and very ambitious briefs. The military also has the wherewithal to pay for research at a reasonable price and to carry out any trials that might be necessary before production.

Designers and industrialists can find such challenges and working conditions highly stimulating and the most interesting fallout in the civilian sector is often indirect. Those working on military projects usually accord greater importance to research, which enables them to accumulate a reservoir of discoveries capable of future exploitation. The development of air transport and telecommunications, and the use of transistors in microcomputers resulted from the transfer of technologies from the military sector to civilian life. The same goes for the development of advanced composite materials. Many objects developed for military use become models for future civilian products. The Jeep, for example, served as the basis for the very popular Land Rover.

In the seventies, many household electrical appliances were given forms and colours evocative of military hardware – to such an extent that marketing professionals spoke of the 'military look'. And countless military objects have inspired toymakers, writers of espionage and science fiction, filmmakers and cartoon artists. War continues to exert a strong fascination over the popular imagination.

The Cold War and the arms race resulted in an unprecedented proliferation of material and weapons systems. At the same time, the development of telecommunications and the media has brought war into our living rooms, giving us access to live coverage of the bloodiest, most spectacular encounters from around the world. Coverage of the Gulf War on CNN offers a prime example of this and the excesses to which it can lead.

J. d. N.

New Questions

The Fluidification of Matter, the Acceleration of Time and Production of Meaning

Ezio Manzini

Objects can be seen as a system of physical references which we enter into relationships with, base our biological existence on and from which, culturally, we construct our images of the world. This essay will examine three main themes. The first is concerned with how the very materiality of things has undergone a historical transformation and how, in the last decades of this century, this transformation has resulted in the production of a man-made environment radically different from anything we have confronted in the past. It is an environment in which we can perceive both an acceleration in time[1] and a saturation of space,[2] and in which matter appears both fluid[3] and contradictory. In some ways matter has become ephemeral (in the virtualization of human experience), but it has also become more burdensome (in the accumulation of waste products). Allied to this state of affairs is the question of the particular physical characteristics of new

Tank suitcase, designed by Alberto Meda for Mandarina Duck, 1990. The structure is made from ethylene-propylene polymer. Scientific research is yielding new materials endowed with sophisticated properties, adapted for specific technical applications.

materials and their potential, which is both extraordinary and problematic.

Our second theme, intricately bound up with the first, concerns human 'doing', that is all the activities through which man engages with matter, taking possession of it and manipulating it to his own ends. It is both a design and a production enterprise, born of a complex interweaving of technical and cultural factors from which things emerge in all their physicality and meaning. What we call design is the specific form this interweaving has adopted at a time when the pace of innovative change on both the technical and socio-cultural levels is accelerating. Today's explosive environmental upheavals (that is to say, the ever faster transformations of the materiality of things) resurface in the guise of an increased 'demand for design' and, as a consequence, an increase in the 'responsibilities of design'.

The third and last theme relates to the role of design faced with the new-found and extraordinarily malleable material nature of objects. If, on the one hand, technically speaking, everything is possible, on the other, for a number of primarily environmental reasons, it is abundantly clear that not everything can be realized.

The role of design is to operate within the terms of that contradiction: if everything is now possible but not everything can be done, one has to identify with a strong degree of certainty what is to be done in the future. This essay will explore this line of thought and outline some areas of research.

The fluidification of materials and the realm of the possible

1) The essential core of man's 'doing', of his actions, of all his productive and project-based activities, has always been the dialectic between ideas and matter. In this struggle, the 'ideas' pole is always envisaged as dynamic and mobile while the 'material' pole is seen as static, inert. It is always matter which is pictured as constraining the free play of ideas.

Traditionally, the 'culture of doing' has been built around the concepts of effort and compromise: effort expressed as the work required to bend matter to our will; compromise arising from the unavoidable obligation to take account of matter's inertia in shaping the outcome.

So, for centuries, it has been material inertia which has set the limits on forms and reduced the number of viable alternatives. In the last analysis, inertia has simply slowed down the introduction of novel solutions, refining rather those possible within the given bounds. On the other hand, this very inertia has given rise to the dream that there might exist a world where everything is possible, where new forms – and therefore new applications – would be available without effort and without compromise, a world in which the old dialectic between ideas and matter would be resolved into a monologue for ideas alone, where ideas would simply replicate themselves. A world of the materialization of ideas. This dream has never come true, and will forever remain a dream.

None the less, with the amazing evolution of materials in the last few years, it has indeed moved ever closer. Today, indeed, matter itself has lost much of its traditional ponderousness and resistance, and has become far less unwieldy and more malleable than in the past. Matter is now fluid, able to produce any type of shape, fulfil any use and mould itself to any conceivable human purpose.

2) If by the expression 'material system', we mean the entirety of all the technological processes potentially available for modifying matter, it would not be unfair to state that recent years have witnessed a veritable revolution. From the realms of electronics and space technology, as well as from consumer production, there flows an unending stream of innovations. As a result, products can be made smaller than ever, can do things quickly which previously required a considerable amount of time and effort, and can be made in single units when before

they were mechanically elaborate. In short, innovation has increased and varied to infinity the forms of objects and images produced.

At the root of all these changes lies the synergistic effect arising from the recent integration of the science of materials with information science. This has created a wide-ranging and profound transmutation in the way in which matter is now available for human use. This transformation is wide-ranging because it involves not only the recently evolved materials like advanced composites or those used in optoelectronics, but also older, traditional materials, like wood, ceramics and marble. In fact, in the contemporary atmosphere of intense competition between alternative technical options, older materials have been given a new lease of life and today all materials are in some way or other 'new materials'. The transformation is a profound one because the very notion of matter has changed.

If historical materials have always been *a priori* components of a project, the situation is very different with the new 'designer materials', whose characteristics are evolved *ad hoc* according to a set of performance requirements. Furthermore, if historical materials are susceptible to a limited range of uses, in the case of the new materials the scope of applications appears ever wider and more sophisticated. Thus, these new materials have become 'intelligent', solid-state operators, capable of performing extremely complex tasks simply on the basis of the intrinsic properties of their molecular or atomic structure.

3) Such then are the 'new materials': hyperplastic and offering hyperperformance, capable of assuming various forms and fulfilling a multiplicity of functions, expanding the realm of the possible as never before.

These materials, with their unique characteristics, in a social and manufacturing environment driven by large-scale development imperatives, have invaded the so-called 'system of objects', carrying to their logical conclusion the values of what we

Relitech lamé, designed by Andrea Branzi for Abet, 1978. Plastic lamé with tactile qualities. In the 1970s and 1980s, certain designers began to explore a new design field: the design of materials.

might call the 'culture of quantity', defined by increased production, cost reduction, accelerated product life-cycles and a plurality of product forms.

An artificial environment has thus been created, distinguished both by an extraordinary proliferation of economically and functionally beneficial goods and by an equally large mass of ephemeral and culturally vacuous products. It is a world in which all products can be reduced to disposable gadgets.

The general picture suggests that these new materials have enjoyed 'excessive success' at the heart of a culture of quantity. This culture, as I have described, grew up through a confrontation with the 'inertia of matter' (with its attendant consequences of reducing, stabilizing and perfecting the formal characteristics) and it therefore has not been able to learn how to control matter once it loses its traditional characteristics, loosens its bonds and becomes fluid. In other words, the 'culture of quantity', faced with a new form of matter which allows itself to be transformed (in much the same way as in the old dream where 'everything is possible'), finds itself bereft of the relevant cultural tools for making effective choices. It is only now that we can finally get to grips with the problems brought about by such a loss of control, now that we have become aware, precisely at the moment that 'everything is possible', that this does not mean that everything is worth doing. It is now being recognized that it is imperative to know how to decide unambiguously what is worth doing and to develop new values and quality criteria capable of steering production and consumption on a different course.

The acceleration of time and the role of design

1) What we call design has only recently made its appearance in the long story of man's 'doing', the history of man's endeavours to master matter. Design was also limited solely to western culture and has only

recently had an impact in, and been reinterpreted by, other cultures. The advent of design coincides more or less with the realization of a break in the linear progession of technical and social-cultural evolution. We talk of design only after the breakdown of the age-old cultural conventions which governed not only the identity of materials and the social system but also the meaning the former has always possessed within the latter.

To speak about design has been, and still is, to speak about human activity in general wherever it is confronted with new materials. These materials no longer form part of the technical and cultural trappings of society. They are no longer governed by specific conventions as to their uses and meaning within that culture. If it is the case that the history of design is one which, at its very inception, is bound up with the problem of giving a social significance to 'new materials' (meaning not only the materials themselves but also the conversion processes they undergo), t is still true that more recent times have seen a change, and the relationship between design and materials should refocus attention on the nature of the present situation.

2) The initial stage in this evolution is that of pre-modern society and the long timescales of change which created it. In such a society, the history of objects – the evolution of materials, of the techniques to transform them and of the resulting products with their social and cultural significance – was slow enough for its consequences to go unnoticed. In this almost static situation, objects derive their significance from immediate and involuntary semiotic mechanisms. The meaning of things is built up through an accumulation of repeated experiences, while a series of cultural conventions consolidates their meaning within any one social group.

In this situation, the materials then available (often dating from the dawn of time) had acquired meaning and spoke a lan-

guage which, within a given social grouping, was sufficiently rooted in the culture to be transparent. From stone to wood, from iron to gold, a stable system of signifiers was established corresponding to a precise system of signifieds. In short, one might speak of a semiology of materials and, in general, of products which were assembled spontaneously, evolving slowly within a language game in which everyone unconsciously participates. In other words: the 'language' of materials and products is understood just as naturally as members of a social group understood human language.

Yet for this to happen two conditions must be fulfilled: the materials posited as signifiers designating signifieds must be invariable with respect to time and must be of a limited number, distinguishable one from the other. For as long as this was the case, for as long as the history of objects evolved slowly and evenly, there was no need for design.

The history of design begins with the rupture of that continuity, when the totality of the social, economic and manufacturing factors which grew out of the Industrial Revolution led to an exceptional increase in the pace of change. In other words, design arrives on the scene just as the 'new' enters the fray, rendering obsolete all the traditional technical and cultural conventions through which materials and products had up until then acquired their meaning.

3) The second stage shows European society as it was at the beginning of the 20th century, by which time engineers had already planned and built bridges and other structures, and designed and produced machinery hitherto unheard of. They had been responsible for the introduction of something radically new: a world of objects whose social signification derived spontaneously from their very novelty. If, however, the social signification of a locomotive lies in its power and that of an aircraft in its ability to fly, what is the signification of a steel chair? Similarly, if there

were never any cultural problems in contextualizing a train or an aircraft (when both the object and the context are equally new), how is a new piece of equipment such as a washing machine to be absorbed into the cultural space of a house, into an environment with such a profound historical tradition? Such questions, it seems to me, mark the beginning of the history of design.

Essentially, design begins to take on cultural and practical forms whenever appliances formerly designed by technology for other areas are introduced into the sphere of the everyday – whenever they are, so to speak, domesticated. Within this framework, the great 'stage sets' designed by the masters of the Modern Movement were devised to function as a cultural context in which the new products and materials industry made available might gain a semantic resonance and meaning. Design's role was to explore the expressive potential of the new materials of the time – of steel and plywood, of industrial glass and early plastics – and to consolidate this potential into a formal language identifiable and readable in a modern context.

The semantic charge of historic materials derived from centuries of accumulation. This was no longer so in the case of the new materials, so the effect of design and the images it generates and the culture it develops has been to 'accelerate' the social production of meaning. Design was born to give meaning to the new.

This analysis emphasizes the novel aspects of the relationships between materials, purpose and meaning which were characteristic of the birth of design. Looking back on such events almost a century later, however, it is possible to discern elements of continuity between this phase and the one immediately preceding it.

During the initial stage of the advent of design, the new materials concerned were very different from earlier ones, but they did possess a number of shared characteristics: their number was still limited and the forms they could be made into were limited

by the relevant technologies. The two conditions necessary for the generation of a viable semiotic of materials still basically applied. Design was able to develop its role of 'accelerating' and of clarifying a semiotic process which was anyway guaranteed by the stability and the limitations of the technologies of the period. It was in this ambit that design itself could execute that piece of cultural gymnastics known as the aesthetics of the 'sincerity of the materials'. Materials could only be beautiful if they presented an honest face, as closely as possible allied to the dominant technology of the time.

4) The third stage is represented by our present day situation, where, as has already been observed, the 'system of materials' has evolved to a point where traditional technical limits have broken down. At the same time, industrial society has changed radically and today is undergoing a dual transition. Firstly, there is the on-going shift from a 'classic industrial society' to a 'late industrial society'. Secondly, early but significant signs of a passage from a 'society of economic growth' to a 'society of sustainable development' have, in recent years, become more pronounced.

For industrial designers, such a situation poses a host of new questions. As hyperplastic materials can fulfil any function or take any form, what possible links can be established between the form of a product and its function? What signification does the functionalist principle of the bond between form and function take on in this case? Such perplexing questions are still grounded in the traditional debate on design culture. They are now accompanied, however, by other, less familiar questions, related to the contradiction between what is technically possible and the emergence of new problems, above all environmental. These, too, are essentially reducible to the question we have already put: if, technically, anything seems possible, what ought we to do?

5) This last decade has seen such questions

permeate the culture of design in the form of a series of 'discoveries' of themes ordered not in any hierarchical manner – separating what is fundamental from what is secondary – but in a heuristic one. The culture of design has drawn into discussions of its nature and praxis those elements of which its protagonists – theoreticians and designers working in rich industrialized societies – have tentatively become aware. Since the beginning of the eighties, a series of gradually understood phenomena has modified our view of reality, asking us new questions and pointing to new lines of research into our relationship to raw materials.

With regard specifically to the connections between design and these materials, the problems which have slowly surfaced are derived from the inversion of the traditional relationship between intention and matter. Historically, it was the latter which imposed limits on the former, but today, in many respects, the contrary is the case. Design's new purpose, confronted by both the disappearance of the system's internal limits – namely, of the traditional technical boundaries – and the appearance of new external limits of an environmental and socio-cultural nature, should be to select, reinforce and give cultural value to a reduced number of technically feasible alternatives. This new role should be exercised on two different but complementary levels, the first focused on the reinterpretation of the semiotic environment and researching into the 'identity of materials', while the second, whose research concerns the 'sustainability of materials', refers to a reinterpretation of the physical environment.

Production of meaning and design research

1) Planning for the identity of matter, or towards an interpretation of the semiotic environment.

In the last ten years it has been gradually understood that, in our late industrial society, the joint evolution of production

Aging Pen fountain pen, designed by Nic Poulten, made from a new material with a long technical and cultural lifespan.

Left-hand page: Folia lamp, designed by Andrea Branzi for Memphis, 1988. Electroluminous material by Sinel.

systems and of materials alters both the nature of the products and the part played by the producers. It has become clear that both have increasingly become simple operators acting within a cultural space which now acts as a framework of competition.

The culture of design has, from the outset, manifestly grasped this state of affairs and the communications role that the new materials, owing to their hyperplasticity and hyperperformance, can play in such a context. The 'language revolution' in design in the eighties (encapsulated in the catchphrase 'towards a liberalization of forms and of dignity') is without doubt a significant expression of that awareness. On the other hand, the subsequent proliferation of the languages has in part swept away the very culture of design which promoted and legitimized it.

It has been apparent in fact that this cultural space has rapidly become saturated and that the plethora of applications available has had the effect of banalizing products, confusing signifieds, and, in the end, creating an overall 'noise'. Research centered around the 'new qualities', undertaken recently by a section of design culture, has attempted to address the following contradiction: how is it possible to give cultural weight and permanence to products immersed in an environment saturated with images and in a state of continual flux? How can one invest materials which can be produced in any form, with an identity, with a fixed mental image of genuine cultural weight?

For those who have investigated these questions, two particular lines of research have opened up: one is centered on the linguistic and poetic potential of new materials, while the other is linked to the promotion of new identities.

The first research area has been an experimental activity. Leaving to one side the diversity of the new materials, it pursues the traditional role of design in 'domesticating' the technologies and materials developed in other fields and for other uses. The alter-

native line, however, is more recent and specific to our third stage: faced with a crisis in the processes of the semiotization of materials, more deliberate choices have to be made to give them a cultural identity. If, as has already been observed, matter is at present in a state of flux and can give rise to any type of image whatsoever, it is necessary in some way to stabilize the situation.

The identity of materials is, in fact, already in the nature of a relative stabilization. We need to select the most significant modes of existence and advance them within a system of cultural reference. By laying down the conditions of the identification of materials we will construct their potential significance. Today, this is not simply a research area but has already given rise to a sustained methodology and praxis: in every respect, the 'design of materials' identity' is a totally new aspect of design.

2) Planning for the sustainability of materials, or towards a reinterpretation of the physical environment.

Recently, the environmental question has changed and has changed us. Not only have its attendant problems become more obvious and pressing, but also the question has shifted from being a rallying cry for a minority to being a concrete and daily concern for everyone, crying out for solutions not just analysis and protest. Although it is now universally accepted that the only development worth considering is sustainable development, it is far more difficult to imagine what life would be like in a sustainable society.

What is required is a new industrial design outlook comprising both an overall view and concrete proposals based on new quality criteria. As far as design and new materials are concerned, the question is to discover how to combine their potential with the environmental imperatives that are currently on the agenda. Though the new materials can be employed in pursuit of the most varied objectives, the question of what 'sustainable' objectives should be pursued in the area of reduced con-

sumption of raw materials and energy remains to be solved.

The answer is neither simple nor one-sided – and cannot at all be reduced to the essential yet simplistic question of recycling: the discovery of the environment is also the discovery of its 'complexity', of the irreducible complexity of the systems in which we have to operate, and of the need for elaborate and articulated solutions to problems if and when they arise. In our late industrial society, the sustainability of materials must be the subject of research at many levels, built upon a complementary logic, the principle of articulation guaranteeing against 'monological' solutions.

Three possible scenarios form the context for any possible solutions to the problems of waste and the over-exploitation of the Earth's natural resources:

– The 'minimum matter' scenario, in which effort is made to reduce to a minimum the physical size of a product or to replace it with a service. [4]

– The 'eternal matter' scenario, in which we research products with a greatly extended lifespan. [5]

– The 'average matter' scenario, in which objects with a short lifetime are produced, but within a system offering the maximum possible recycling, thereby ensuring the survival of the raw materials used in the various products. [6]

It should be said that technological potential (that is, the potential of the materials) is today better suited to realize the objectives proposed than is the deeply entrenched culture of production, industrial design and consumerism.

So, what is required is a 'design research project' capable of developing quality criteria which allow these scenarios to be not only environmentally sustainable but also acceptable socially and attractive culturally. So doing, they would also become 'pivotal points' within a vast dynamic of social change, transforming the late industrial society we have today into a sustainable late industrial society.

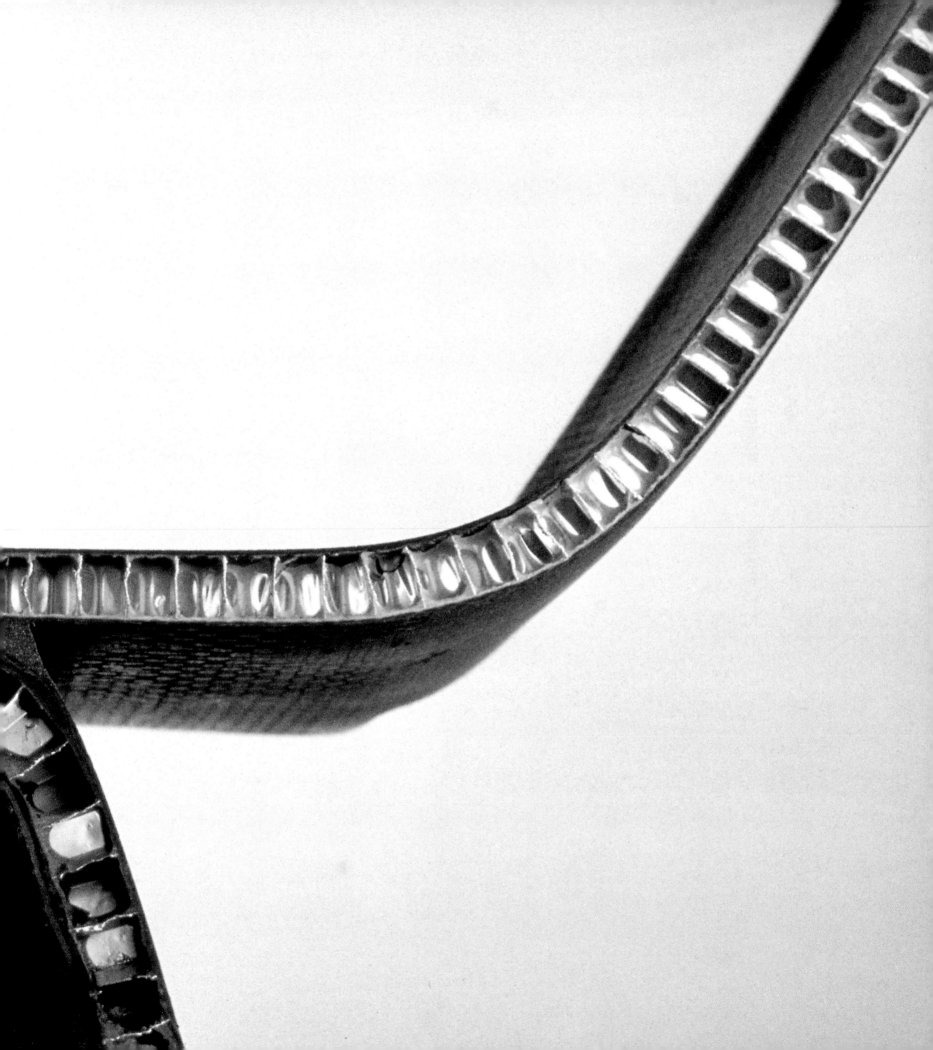

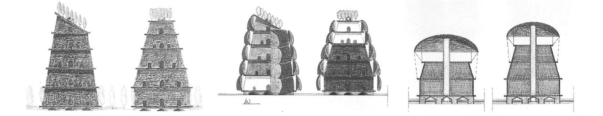

Monuments to waste disposal

Drawings based on a study made by Ademe (Agence de l'Environnement et de la Maîtrise de l'Energie), involving INSA, CETE in Lyon and QUADRIC, 1992.

In France a law is currently under study that would prohibit further use of traditional dumping grounds from the year 2002. But the problem of stockpiling stabilized waste remains.

Once purchased and used by consumers, many industrial products made of new materials should simply disappear; but others are not biodegradable and some will pose a threat to the environment. A way of dealing with this waste has to be found.

Surprisingly, architecture and design could prove useful in solving this problem. Many non-recyclable, non-biodegradable products can be pressed into bricks (or some other form) which could then be made into stockpiles. Simply burying them would not be feasible due to the problem of monitoring them, not to mention the increasing concern over the environment. There is already widespread opposition to burial, so new solutions have to be found.

The Angers office of Ademe, got the Institut National de Sciences Appliquées in Lyon, as well as some architects, to look at the problem. In the light of this research, Ademe then started working on an idea based on an analogy with living organisms. We know that organisms use membranes to isolate all undesirable or non-assimilable foreign bodies they may have inside them. The same principle could be applied to consumer waste and it should be possible to compact the waste into any form. Techniques for the long-term stockpiling of non-recyclable waste would make it possible to create surface dumps of a novel kind. The architect Bertrand Voïnovitch has conceived of these as huge monuments, works of art as vast as conventional dumping grounds, with colossal towers about a thousand feet high, vividly-coloured ziggurats of waste condensed into bricks that bring to mind the temples of ancient empires, replete with terraced roof gardens that could be brightly illuminated by night.

These 21st century 'funerary monuments' would be fitting symbols for a civilization that had decided to expose its waste in transformed, stabilized form in order to safeguard its precious, vulnerable environment.

From the moment a society resolves to make environmental protection a civic priority, it becomes legitimate to celebrate waste disposal. In a similar spirit, it would be only natural for the design of dustbins and recycling centres to reflect this new symbolism.

J. d. N.

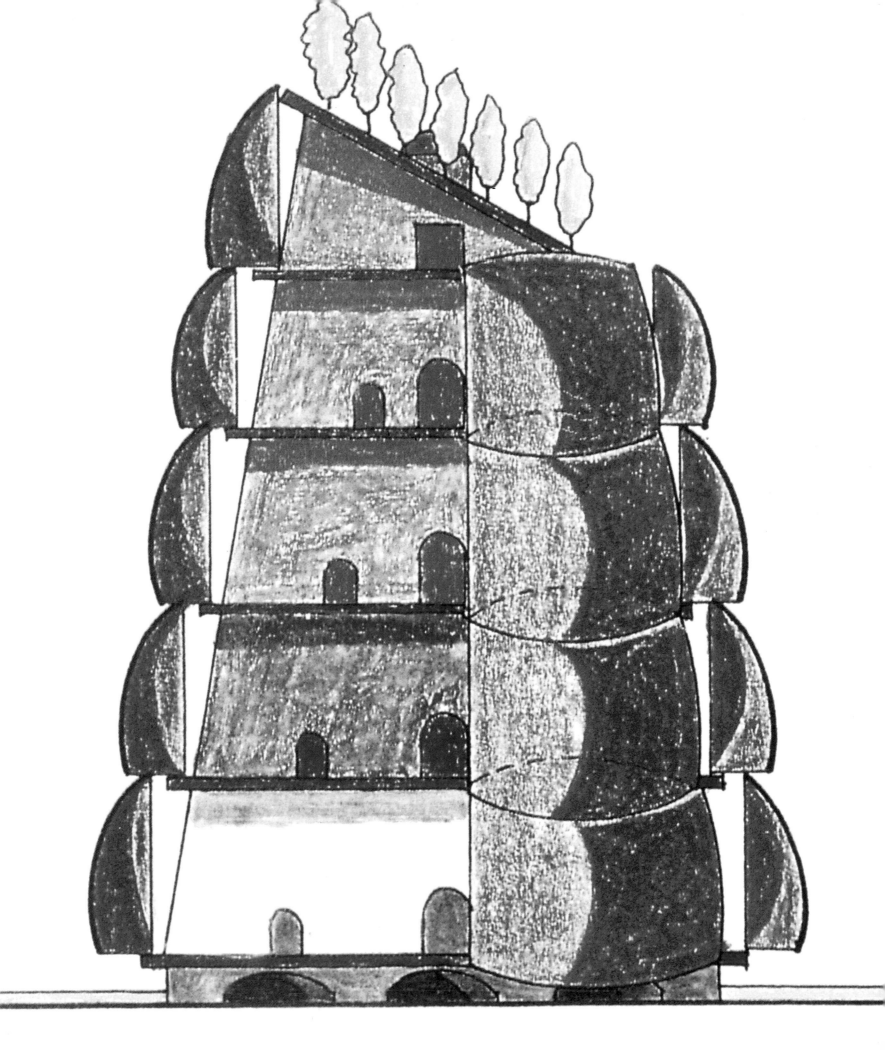

Towards the 21st Century: Design in Quest of an Identity

Anne-Marie Boutin

Design, a human activity centred on the conception of everyday objects, is doubtless one of the world's oldest occupations. But it was only with the advent of industrial production and, later, the Modernist movement that the profession began to structure itself and develop in an autonomous way. The fifties saw the appearance of its first international institutions. The International Council of Societies of Industrial Design, or ICSID, was founded in Paris in June 1957. Then came its sister organizations, the IFI[1] for interior design and ICOGRADA,[2] in 1963, for graphic design. Recognized as non-governmental organizations, or NGO's, by UNESCO and UNIDO,[3] from the beginning they saw their mission as that of promoting design, defining the profession's various areas of activity and establishing its theoretical foundations and code of professional ethics.

Today, in most countries and in each of these three areas, there are professional organizations, centres for the promotion of design, and (more rarely and more recently) design councils, whose character is political and strategic.

Thus design is in the process of becoming a profession like any other, with its own territory, institutions, spokespersons, prizes, schools, rites and pilgrimages reserved for the initiated, as well as its own debates.

Today the situation of this profession, in the Post-Modern era and on the threshold of a post-industrial society, is fraught with paradox. It is evolving towards a new model well suited to the present moment, forming bridges between culture and technology, art and science, economy and human behaviour; it is increasingly involved in the emergence of values associated with quality and responsibility, and finds itself in the position of being able to propose creative visions of the future that are full of significance.

At the same time design is in the fragile position of a profession that has not yet reached maturity, one whose relations with its partners in the innovation process have not been fully mastered and which is still in search of its identity.

Today the world of design is experiencing a crisis of expansion for which it is ill prepared. Without doubt it is at a crossroads.[4]

The creative century

Today, the future seems uncertain and causes for concern numerous: the limited natural resources of our earth, now turned 'global village'; the demographic explosion; the development of the megapolis and its suburbs, which are turning into jungles ruled by violence and gangs; the problem of social alienation.

Some historians compare the period in which we live to the Renaissance. It is characterized by a crisis of values, profound changes and a questioning of our relationship with technological progress. Never has man had so much knowledge, so many scientific and technical tools at his disposal. But he must learn how to find his way around this vast reservoir of knowledge and how to share it. He also needs, in order to make wise choices, a philosophy and a vision, a relation to meaning and being.

For traditional approaches and models, which leave little room for non-rational approaches and creativity outside the field of art, have reached their limits and have revealed themselves to be ineffectual. Only after the shock of successive economic crises and the emergence of the idea that they might signal a profound transformation did we begin to question the view that reality should be broken down into separate disciplines linked by objectively comprehensible relations.

Reality is complex and evolving; it should be understood globally. It is no longer sufficient to be interested in individuals or objects, we must also think in terms of systems in which objects, persons and relations have a dynamic function. Factors rooted in the irrational and the imagination must not be forgotten. They can be approached through holistic methods, which is to say ones in which material, intellectual and emotional components all play a role.

The transition from an industrial to a post-industrial society, from an expanding society to a stable, mature one will be accompanied by changes that are slow-moving but profound.

Competition is giving way to co-operation: the alliances of IBM and Apple, General Mills and Nestlé, Coca-Cola and Lipton are revealing in this regard.

Physical expansion is no longer possible. The elimination of an enemy no longer brings a new freedom, but rather deprives the world of a bit of its richness. The world will not survive, according to Michel Serres, unless it manages to function as a set of distinct cultures 'sewn together like a Harlequin's costume'.[5] For diversity is a necessary part of life.

Thus standardization and differentiation, the internationalization of markets and a quest for identity now seem to be complementary rather than conflicting values.

This new schema can encompass simultaneously the rise of individualism, pluralism and collective responsibility, and the search for meaning and identity. Philosophical arguments are converging with economic imperatives. If advertisers have begun to play on the idea of collective responsibility, for example with regard to the environment and even cultural identity, this is because individuals now find such ideas reassuring.

The philosophy of quality has displaced the myth of quantity. Today, quality is a central concern of political and economic leaders, the media and intellectuals, and for all those who refuse to be regarded as just citizens or consumers. What is in question, of course, is not only the quality of products and services but that of our relation to objects, of our personal, social, intellectual and cultural lives, and that of the environment.

After years of unbridled consumption, an ethic of consumerism is emerging, as evidenced for example by the recent vogue for long-lived and multifunctional products, the consequence both of the economic crisis and concern over the limits of our natural resources.

Hierarchical organization is giving way to more flexible structures. The business world has not escaped these changes, as Michel Crozier has stressed in his book *L'Entreprise à l'écoute*.[6] After a period devoted to the management of technological resources, over-organization, centralization of decision-making and increasing procedural complexity in response to ever-increasing technological complexity, we are now entering an era of simplification, in which the dominant concern is with human resources, with the establishment of a decentralized management structure based on responsibility in which a business's culture and identity act like a glue holding everything together.

The functions of decision-making, conception and production are becoming increasingly integrated. The simultaneous search for quality and speed has brought the segregation of the design and production phases into question, and as a result specialists are beginning to work together much more closely during the development process. The value of this team approach has become even more obvious with the introduction of the amazing Canon EOS, and numerous businesses are developing research and training practices along these lines.

The future of design

In 1971, Victor Papanek wrote: 'Design can and should become a means for young people to participate in the evolution of society.'[7] Design will play an even more important role in the future if it can assume its identity, if it accepts fully its human and cultural responsibility as well as its prospective dimension. This implies continuity and renewal, and a synergy with other economic and social agents. For what is important first of all is to define what exactly the designer's function is. In its quest for status, the profession often tends to value know-how and mastery of tools at the expense of intuition, creativity and vision.

Some would go so far as to regard design as a discipline

like any other, which is exactly what it is not. Design is cross-disciplinary. It is a permanent source of questioning and provocation for other disciplines, and the undeniable success with which designers have integrated into research and development teams will encourage further efforts along these lines rather than through the development of independent design research. Can design afford to forget that a certain indiscipline is one of the sources of creativity? If design were set up as a distinct discipline, it would become isolated, fixed within set parameters and it would lose its cross-disciplinary character.

If designers are to help reinvent the world, they must find – or recover – the courage to place themselves in relation to the important issues of society: the philosophy of quality, the limits of our natural resources, cultural identity, biotechnology, demographic imbalances, relations between developed countries and the Third World, a code of ethics.

The question of the designer's role, or rather roles, immediately arises, for he is also an originator, and it is important to preserve the diversity of modes of expression, creative talent and professional activities.

At the moment, the designer fulfils one of three basic roles. The first is that of mediator. Anxious to ensure good communications with their partners, designers seek a minimum common language and even go as far as to adopt the dominant one, whereas their role ought to be that of an integrator who, through sensitivity, intuition and the diversity and specificity of his means of expression, can manipulate different languages and modes of thought with mastery, giving each its due. But the designer also plays the role of intermediary between the world of objects and that of scientific specialists in various disciplines. This mediating role can be assumed by any designer, whether he works for a small consultancy, a manufacturing company or as a freelance.

Many designers assume design management responsibilities, making no distinction between these functions and executive control. Managers try to assure that the means are adequate for the objectives and the processes involved. They are responsible for ensuring that the system functions smoothly. A director defines objectives and gives a sense of direction. It is not managers that are lacking today, but charismatic and courageous individuals, capable of spearheading a project and persuading their partners. It is the role of design direc-

tor that designers might legitimately claim for themselves. Clarifying this issue is at the heart of the debates taking place on the Design Leadership course at the University of the Industrial Arts in Helsinki.[8]

The third area that should not be neglected, above all in this period of crisis, is that of the work of independent designers, who are often in a position to look further ahead than many of their colleagues. This doesn't mean that they should work alone, but rather that places should be created from where they can build links between different disciplines and fields of knowledge. Some design courses and educational establishments could also play this role, much as the Bauhaus did, a place where craftsmen, artists and architects lived and worked together.

We expect designers to teach us anew to be attentive to things, as well as to the beings around us.

Along with a preoccupation with quality, there has also been a reawakening of the desire to establish relations with objects, learn their histories and measure their cultural impact. As part of the international Ways of Eating project,[9] students visited an old woman in a village in India; she had laid out in front of her door a variety of objects from her kitchen which had long been a part of her existence. They asked her, 'In your view, what have been the consequences of the change from earthenware vessels to plastic ones?' and she replied, 'They are perhaps the reason mothers are more negligent of their babies.' She went on to explain: 'If you must take care of things then it becomes natural for you to take care of everything.'

We expect designers to help sensitize the general public to these issues. For the life of objects – their history, use and function – is a largely neglected subject in education throughout the world. Consumer education simply does not exist. The designer has at his disposal communication tools that could enable him to make an intelligent and sensitive contribution to such education. It should be possible to educate people from childhood, by showing them by means of real projects, the integration of disciplines and their interrelationships.

We expect designers to offer us visions and make us dream. In the past it was engineers and scientists who, through their discoveries, permitted man to realize his dreams. Perhaps this role will be taken up by the designers of tomorrow. Certainly it will fall to them to offer visions touching the deepest part of our being.

List of Design Classics

by Jocelyn de Noblet and Éric Mézil

Notes

Design in Progress
by Jocelyn de Noblet

1. An association between industrials, artists, experts and entrepreneurs created to develop the quality of industrial products.
2. Alfred Sloan, director of General Motors from 1923 to 1947.

Design in the First Machine Age
by Jacques Guillerme

1. Gérard-Joseph Christian, *Vues sur le système général des opérations industrielles ou Plan de technonomie*, Paris, 1819, p. 146.
2. Jean-Jacques Bachelier, *Discours sur l'utilité des écoles élémentaires en faveur des arts mécaniques*, Paris, 1792, p. 2.
3. *Ibid.*, p. 6.
4. Robert Morris, *Select Architecture*, 2nd ed., London, 1757.
5. Joseph Priestley, *A Course of Lectures on Oratory and Criticism*, London, 1777, p. 66.
6. *Ibid.*
7. Peter Jeffrey Booker, *A History of Engineering Drawing*, London, 1963.
8. Christian, *Vues sur le système*, p. 54.
9. Jean-Baptiste Say, *Cours complet d'économie politique pratique*, vol. 2, pp. 151-154.
10. Damas Hinard, *Napoléon, ses opinions et ses jugements*, Paris, 1838, vol. 2, pp. 306-310.
11. Gribeauval, *La Correspondance de deux généraux*, Paris, 1801, pp. 150-52.
12. Jean Charles Baptiste Migout and Claude Lucien Bergery, *Théorie des affûts*, Metz, 1840, p. 272.
13. Ennio Concina, 'Une lettre de Vettor Fausto', in *Amphion 1*, pp. 150-52.
14. Gérard-Joseph Christian, *L'Industriel*, June 1826, pp. 93-98.
15. Karl Marx, *Das Kapital*, vol. 2.
16. Franz Reuleaux, *Cinématique*, French trans. by A. Debize, Paris, p. 553.
17. Pierre Alexandre Forfait, *Traité de la mâture*, 2nd ed., Paris, 1815.
18. Archibald Alison, *Essays on the Nature and Principles of Taste*, Edinburgh, 1790.
19. Antoine Chrysostome, known as Quatremère de Quincy, *Essai sur la nature, les buts et les moyens de l'imitation*, Paris, 1823.
20. Auguste François Silvestre, *Essai sur les moyens de perfectionner les Arts économiques*, Paris, year IX, p. 79.
21. See Jean Da Silva, 'Une critique des Arts décoratifs par Joris-Karl Huysmans', *Amphion 4*, 1992, pp. 289-296.
22. A phrase coined by Abraham Moles.
23. Translator's note: Guillerme

uses the word *stylème* to signify a reduced and paradigmatic symbol that represents a literary or aesthetic style.
24. See 'Le style dans la conception', *Amphion 2*, 1988, pp. 177-191.
25. Jean Baudrillard, *Le Système des objets*, Paris, 1968, p. 223.
26. Alain Findeli, 'De l'esthétique industrielle à l'éthique…', *In-formel*, summer 1990.

Abolish Bric-à-brac
Profusion and Confusion in 19th-Century Industrial Art
by Michel Vernes

1. Henry Havard remarked that it was not unusual for a family to redecorate four times in less than thirty years.
2. C. A. Oppermann, *Album pratique de l'art industriel*, Paris, 1866.
3. Henry Havard, *L'Art dans la maison*, Paris, 1890.
4. Madame Alquié de Rieupeyroux [Louise d'Alq, pseud.], *Le Maître et la maîtresse de maison*, Paris, 1882.
5. Léon Verleye correctly observed that during the 19th century the industrial arts 'piled up styles by implanting one upon the other'. See *La Composition décorative et la pratique industrielle*, Paris, 1928.
6. Léon de Laborde, *Travaux de la commission française sur l'industrie des nations*, VIᵉ groupe, XXXᵉ jury. Beaux-arts, Exposition universelle de 1851, Paris, 1856.
7. Charles Laboulaye, 'Art industriel', in *Dictionnaire des arts et manufactures*, 5th ed., 5 vols., Paris, 1881.
8. Édouard Didron, *Exposition universelle internationale de 1878. Rapport d'ensemble sur les Arts décoratifs*, Paris, 1882.
9. Philippe Burty, *Chefs-d'œuvre des arts industriels*, Paris, 1866.
10. Pierre Bourdieu, *Distinction. A Social Critique of the Judgement of Taste*, London, 1985.
11. Alexandre Du Sommerard, *Notice sur l'hôtel de Cluny et sur le palais des thermes*, Paris, 1834.
12. Ernest Bosc, *Dictionnaire de l'art, de la curiosité et du bibelot*, Paris, 1884.
13. Gustave Flaubert, *Dictionnaire des idées reçues*, Paris, 1923.
14. *Ibid.*
15. Didron, *Exposition universelle internationale de 1878*.
16. Joris-Karl Huysmans, *À rebours*, Paris, 1884.
17. Cécil Sorel, *Les Belles Heures de ma vie*, Paris, 1946.
18. Before becoming a curio cabinet, these were tiny rooms where the mistress of the house could conceal herself from indiscreet eyes. With the Age of Enlightenment they were filled with books and rare objects.
19. Henri de Noussanne, *Le Goût dans l'ameublement*, Paris, 1896.
20. Huysmans, *À rebours*.
21. Victor Segalen, *Essai sur l'exotisme. Une esthétique du Divers*,

Paris, 1978.
22. E. Guichard, *De l'ameublement et de la décoration intérieure de nos appartements*, Paris, 1866.
23. C. A. Oppermann, *Album pratique*.
24. Eugène Viollet-le-Duc, *Entretiens sur l'architecture*, XVᵉ entretien: Décoration intérieure et extérieure, Paris, 1863-1872, 2 vols. and 1 album.
25. Henry Havard, *Dictionnaire de l'ameublement et de la décoration*, Paris, 1887-1890, 4 vols.
26. Mⁱˡˡᵉ Dufaux De La Jonchère, *Le Savoir vivre dans la vie ordinaire et dans les cérémonies civiles et religieuses*, Paris, 1883.
27. Marcel Proust, *À la recherche du temps perdu. Albertine disparue*, Paris, 1925.

Comfort
by Roger-Henri Guerrand

1. Charles Nodier, *Examen critique des dictionnaires de la langue française*, Paris, 1828.
2. Charles Fourier, *Traité de l'Association domestique-agricole*, 1829. See also Victor Considérant, *Destinée sociale*, 1834.
3. Roger-Henri Guerrand, *Une Europe en construction*, Paris, 1992.
4. Adeline Daumard, *La Bourgeoisie parisienne de 1845 à 1848*, Paris, 1963.
5. Monseigneur Pie, *Easter sermon on the spirit of renunciation and sacrifice*, 1853.
6. Ernest Renan, *Journal des débats*, November 1855.
7. Roger Henri Guerrand, *Les lieux, histoire des commodités*, Paris, 1985.
8. *La Vie heureuse*, 1913.
9. Christine Frederick, *The New Housekeeping: Efficiency Studies in Home Management*, New York, 1913. Part of this work appeared in French translation in 1918 and a complete edition was published in 1927 under the title *L'Organisation Ménagère Moderne*.
10. Paulette Bernège, *Si les femmes faisaient les maisons*, Paris, 1928.
11. Letter written in April 1946, published by the Société des amis de Georges Bernanos in June 1950.
12. Frédéric Hoffet, *L'Impérialisme protestant*, Paris 1948.
13. *Cahiers de la Pierre-qui-vire*, October 1952.
14. Jean and Françoise Fourastié, *Les Arts ménagers*, 1950.
15. *Encyclopédie française*, vol. XIV, 1954, chapter 4, 'Les Arts ménagers au service de la civilisation quotidienne'.

Dandyism: From Luxury to Immateriality
by Françoise Coblence

1. François René de Chateaubriand, *Mémoires d'outre-tombe*, book 27, ch. 3, Paris, 1951, p. 77.

2. Stendhal, *De l'amour*, chapter LXI, 1822 edition. The passage is deleted in subsequent editions.
3. Honoré de Balzac, *Les Illusions perdues*, *La Comédie humaine*, vol. 4, Paris, 1952, p.809.
4. Jacques Boulenger, *Sous Louis-Philippe. Les dandys*, Paris, 1932, p.180.
5. Anne Martin-Fugier, *La Vie élégante ou la formation du Tout-Paris 1815-1848*, Paris, 1993, p. 355.
6. Eugène Marsan, *Les Cannes de M. Paul Bourget et Le Bon Choix be Philinte*, Paris, 1923, p. 5 and pp. 77-81.
7. Charles Baudelaire, 'Le peintre de la vie moderne', *Œuvres complètes*, vol. 2, Paris, 1975, p. 711.
8. Joris-Karl Huysmans, *A Rebours*, Paris, 1975, ch. 1, pp. 61-62.
9. Jacques Boulenger, *Sous Louis-Philippe*, p. 8.
10. Honoré de Balzac, 'Physiologie de la toilette', *Théorie de la démarche et autres textes*, 1978, pp. 130-131.
11. William Jesse, *The Life of Beau Brummell*, London, 1886, vol. 1, p. 63.
12. Immanuel Kant, *Critique of Judgement*, Oxford, 1978.
13. Jesse, *Beau Brummell*, p. 130.
14. Jules Amédée Barbey d'Aurevilly, 'Du Dandysme et de George Brummell', in *Œuvres romanesques complètes*, vol. 2, Paris, 1966, p. 690.
15. Edgar Allan Poe, 'Philosophie de l'ameublement', transl. Charles Baudelaire, *Œuvres en prose*, Paris, 1951, p. 974.
16. Barbey d'Aurevilly, 'Du Dandysme', p. 1435 (preface to 1861 edition).
17. James Laver, *Dandies*, London, 1968, p. 34.
18. Honoré de Balzac, *Traité de la vie élégante*, Paris, 1911, p. 38.
19. Walter Benjamin, *Charles Baudelaire, A Lyric Poet in the Era of High Capitalism*, New Left Books, New York, 1977.
20. Baudelaire, 'Salon de 1846', *Œuvres complètes*, vol. 2, p. 494.
21. Barbey d'Aurevilly, 'Du Dandysme', p. 674.
22. *Ibid.*, p. 675.
23. Yves Saint Laurent, quoted in *Le Nouvel Observateur*, December 1983.
24. Yves Saint Laurent, quoted in *Le Monde*, 8 December 1983.
25. Marcel Duchamp, 'A propos des "ready-mades"', *Duchamp du signe: Ecrits*, Paris, 1975, p. 192.
26. Paul Valéry, 'Introduction à la Méthode de Léonard de Vinci', *Œuvres*, vol. 1, Paris, p. 1162.
27. Friedrich Hölderlin, 'Anmerkungen zur Antigonä', *Werke und Briefe*, vol. 2, Frankfurt, 1969, pp. 783-790.

The Survival of the Craft Ideal
by Gillian Naylor

1. See the following recent

publications: Isabelle Anscombe and Charlotte Gere, *The Arts and Crafts in Britain and America*, London, 1978; David Brett, *C. R. Mackintosh: The Poetics of Workmanship*, London, 1992; Alan Crawford, *C. R. Ashbee: Architect, Designer and Romantic Socialist*, London, 1985; *Encyclopedia of Arts and Crafts: The International Arts and Crafts Movement, 1850-1920*, London, 1989; Gillian Naylor, ed., *William Morris by himself*, London, 1988; Werner J. Schweiger, *Design in Vienna 1903-1932*, London, 1984.
2. Nikolaus Pevsner, *Pioneers of the Modern Movement*, 1936; see also *Pioneers of Modern Design*, Harmondsworth, 1960.
3. Nikolaus Pevsner, *Pioneers of Modern Design*, pp. 39 and 54.
4. *Ibid.*, p. 16.
5. From an untitled text on the 'work programme' for the Wiener Werkstätte, 1905, quoted by Schweiger, *Design in Vienna*, p. 42.
6. Nikolaus Pevsner, *Pioneers of Modern Design*, p. 169.
7. *Ibid.*, p. 175.
8. Schweiger, *Design in Vienna*, p. 113.
9. *Ibid.*, p. 118.
10. *Studio Year-Book of Decorative Art*, p. 94.
11. Walter Gropius, *The New Architecture and the Bauhaus*, London, 1935, pp. 53-54.
12. See the following recent publications: Gillian Naylor, *The Bauhaus Re-Assessed*, London, 1985; Anna Rowland, ed, *Bauhaus Source Book*, London, 1990; Frank Whitford, *The Bauhaus*, London, 1984; Frank Whitford, *The Bauhaus: Masters and Students by Themselves*, London, 1992.
13. Eckhardt Neumann, ed., *Bauhaus and Bauhaus People*, New York, 1970, p. 98.
14. Herbert Read, *Art and Industry*, London, 1934, pp. 63-64.
15. Quoted in *Scandinavian Domestic Design*, E. Zahle, ed.), London, 1963, p. 10.
16. *Ibid.*, p. 56.

Art for Everyone
by Lionel Richard

1. Dʳ Foveau de Courmelles, *L'Esprit scientifique contemporain*, Paris, 1899, p. 1.
2. *Ibid.*, p. 145. Artist and writer, Albert Robida (1884-1926) was a contributor to *Le Journal amusant*, *La Vie parisienne* and *La Caricature*. He published *Electric Life of the Twentieth Century* in 1883.
3. Dʳ Foveau de Courmelles, *L'Esprit scientifique*, p. 196.
4. *Ibid.*, p. 65.
5. Léon de Laborde, quoted by Paul Léon, in *Art et artistes d'aujourd'hui*, Paris, 1925, pp. 64-65. Laborde's writings inspired the organization of an exhibition in Paris in 1863 by the Union centrale des Beaux-Arts appliqués à l'Industrie. Founded

by the architect-decorator Guichard and eleven industrialists, the Union Centrale was devoted to development of artistic culture in France and to the promotion of 'Beauty in Utility'.
6. See Robert de La Sizeranne, *Questions esthétiques contemporaines*, Paris, 1904.
7. See the comments by Fernand Weyl in *L'Art décoratif*, no. 13, October 1899. See also in the same article G. M. Jacques, 'Les limites du décor', no. 16, January 1900, pp. 141-144, and 'L'intérieur rénové', no. 24, September 1900.
8. Louis Lumet, *L'Art pour tous, conférences*, Paris, 1901, p. 15. Lumet was also a regular contributor to the magazine *L'Enclos*, founded in 1895. He was involved in the adventures of the 'théâtre social' at the turn of the century, and most notably was in charge of the Théâtre civique. Actor and novelist, Lumet also contributed to *La Revue naturiste* and to *La Plume*.
9. Lumet, *L'Art pour tous*, p. 34.
10. Marius Vachon, *Rapports à M. Edmond Turquet, Sous-Secrétaire d'État, sur les Musées et les écoles d'art industriel et sur la situation des industries artistiques en Allemagne, Autriche-Hongrie, Italie et Russie*, Paris, 1885, p. 80.
11. Dr Foveau de Courmelles, *L'Esprit scientifique* p. 138.
12. Camille Mauclair, *Trois Crises de l'art actuel*, Paris, 1906, p. 165. In *Essai sur l'art décoratif français moderne*, Paris, 1921, p. 6, Gabriel Mourey published an excerpt from a similar text by Alfred Picard, General Commissioner of the 1900 Paris Exposition universelle: 'The cult of the past has been carried to an extreme, it absorbs all intelligence, all science and all the entrepreneurs and draughtsmen who restrict themselves to copies. Furnishings cannot be adapted easily to a certain social class without immediately becoming the object of severe criticism. The audacious one who trys to is an ignoramus and a sacreligious person. These days we can only find Henri II, Louis XIV, Louis XVI furnishings. New and original ideas are proscribed.'
13. Camille Mauclair, *Trois Crises de l'art actuel*, p. 167.
14. *Ibid.*, pp. 168-169.
15. *Ibid.*, p. 172.
16. Waldemar George, 'L'art décoratif moderne', in *La Revue mondiale*, no. 5, 1925, pp. 82-85.
17. Paul Léon, *Art et artistes d'aujourd'hui*, Paris, 1925, p. 64. See also the comments by Georges Auriol quoted in Émile-Bayard, *Le Style moderne*, Paris, 1922, p. 85: 'During recent years we have used the terms Art, Decorative Art, Art Industries and Art Workers wrongly and mistakenly, and we have also forgotten the only concern that should have inspired us, which is to embellish or to modify even the most insignificant utensils, all the while respecting and even improving their practical value. This abuse too often has led us to produce unique and exceptional objects for curio cabinets and collectors. This is an error! We should not try to create showpieces. It is through selection that a salt-cellar becomes the hostess of a museum. But first, it must contain salt'.
18. Paul Léon, *Art et artistes*, pp. 65-66.
19. Frantz Jourdain, 'L'art populaire', in *La Revue*, no. 24, 15 December 1913, pp. 453-461.

Art Deco Nostalgia and Post-Modernism during the First Machine Age
by Suzanne Tise

1. See Charles Jencks's definitions in *What is Post-Modernism?* London, 1986.
2. Parisian manufacturers of furnishings complained to the city council that after the Universal Exposition of 1900 they were apparently left with large stocks of Art Nouveau-style furnishings that they could not sell. See discussion in Conseil municipal de Paris, *Procès-verbaux*, 1912, Paris 1913, no. 1782, p. 1018.
3. For example, the comments of Frantz Jourdain: 'It is high time we abolished the symbolist theories, those unwholesome dreams, conventional types, women without sex, androgynous men, all the inept nonsense with which they have tried to cloud the clarity of the French genius! . . . We have not escaped the Roman chariots only to ensconce ourselves in nightmarish ivory towers!' Frantz Jourdain, 'Les meubles et les tentures murales aux salons de 1901,' *Revue des arts décoratifs*, vol. 21, 1901, p. 212.
4. See Lionel Richard's article 'Art for Everyone' in this volume.
5. Roger Marx, *Notes sur les arts*, 1911, pp. 73-74.
6. Charles M. Couyba, 'Rapport portant sur la fixation du budget général de l'exercice de 1907,' Ministère de l'Instruction Publique des Beaux-Arts et des Cultes, Paris, 1906.
7. At the time when Couyba made his declarations in the Chamber of Deputies, several forces had come into play that made his suggestions both propitious and attractive to a wide range of interest groups. He presented his report in a climate of social crisis, marked by the increased militancy of the trade union movement and a wave of strikes that had been rocking the nation since 1904. In 1906, the building and furnishing industries also went on strike. Couyba's project was proposed during the first year of Clemenceau's ministry (1906 to 1909). Upon forming his government, Clemenceau had announced an ambitious programme of social reforms and created a Ministère du Travail to prepare them in accord with workers' organizations. Alongside these, a major international exhibition of decorative and industrial arts organized on the scale of the Universal Expositions could supplement such measures by providing employment for workers in the building and furniture industries, while the social content of the programme could allay class tensions.
8. See *Idées modernes*, vol. 1, January 1909, pp. 46-57. For more on Roger Marx (who became editor-in-chief of *Gazette des Beaux-Arts* in 1911) see Madeleine Rebérioux, 'De l'art industriel à l'art social: Jean Juarès et Roger Marx,' *Gazette des Beaux-Arts*, February 1988, pp. 155-158. See also Camille Morineau, *Roger Marx*, DEA thesis, Paris 8, St.-Denis, 1988.
9. 'Nous voudrions aussi qu'elle fût moderne, que toute reminiscence du passé s'en trouvât exclue sans pitié, les inventions de l'art social n'ayant d'interêt et de raison d'être que dans la mesure où elles s'adaptent rigoureusement au temps qui les voit paraître.' *Notes sur les arts*, p. 73.
10. Following the reception of a French delegation from the city of Paris at the 1908 Munich exhibition of industrial arts, Frantz Jourdain, president of the Salon d'Automne, invited the Munich decorators to Paris to display their work. Ken Silver was the first to discuss the impact of the exhibition on the Parisian art world. See Kenneth E. Silver, *Esprit de Corps, The Art of the Parisian Avant-Garde and the First World War, 1914-1925*, Princeton, 1989, p. 171.
11. *Les Marches de l'Est*, 15 November 1910, cited in *Apollinaire on Art*, pp. 119-120.
12. From the Salon d'Automne, the Société Nationale de l'Art à l'Ecole, and the Société Nationale des Beaux-Arts Appliqués à l'Industrie.
13. René Guilleré, *Rapport sur une exposition internationale des arts décoratifs modernes, Paris, 1915*, Paris, 1911, Archives François Carnot, bibliothèque des Arts décoratifs, Paris. See also *Avis présenté au nom de la commission du Commerce et de l'Industrie sur le projet de loi concernant L'Exposition internationale des arts décoratifs et industriels modernes*, Chambre de Députés, session de 1923, no. 5849, 2. The project is also explained in H. Roblin, *Rapport fait au nom de la commission du commerce et de l'industrie chargée d'examiner la proposition de loi de M. François Carnot et plusieurs de ses collègues tendant à organiser en 1915 à Paris une exposition internationale des arts décoratifs modernes*, Chambre de Députés, 1 July 1912, no. 2078.
14. See 'Enquête', *L'Art décoratif*, supplement, April 1911, n.p. The following responses are taken from this non-paginated article.
15. 'Enquête,' n.p.
16. See 'Puvis de Chavannes et la peinture d'aujourd'hui', *L'Art décoratif*, January-June 1912, p. 37. It should be noted that Puvis was on the editorial board of the review *Art et Décoration*.
17. André Vera, 'Le Nouveau style', *L'Art décoratif*, January 1912, pp. 21-32.
18. Vera, 'Le Nouveau style', p. 32.
19 On Süe see Susan Day, *Louis Süe, Architectures*, Brussels, 1986.
20. Day, *Louis Süe, Architectures*, p. 51.
21. The critic Fernand Roches called Süe a *coloriste*. See *L'Art décoratif* n. 28, 1912, p. 304.
22. On the Salon d'Automne see Fernand Roches, 'Le Salon d'automne de 1912', *L'Art décoratif*, 1912, pp. 281-328. See also Marie-Noëlle Pradel, 'La Maison cubiste en 1912,' *L'Art de France*, 1961, pp. 177-186.
23. On Marinot, see *Maurice Marinot*, exhibition catalogue, Musée de l'Orangerie, Paris, 1989.
24. Mare ended the letter by telling Marinot to consult the article by André Vera in *L'Art décoratif* for indications. Letter from André Mare to Maurice Marinot, artist file 'André Mare', Musée des Arts Décoratifs, Paris.
25. Pradel, 'La Maison cubiste en 1912,' p. 180.
26. *Le Passage à niveau* by Léger, *Femme avec faon* by Metzinger, *Les Joueurs de cartes*, by La Fresnaye, and *Le Jugement de Paris* by Paul Vera. See Pradel, 'La maison cubiste en 1912', pp. 184-185.
27. This painterly approach led critics to call Mare and his group *coloristes*. Evelyne Possémé, 'Le mobilier des années 1910', in *Le mobilier sort de sa réserve*, exhibition brochure, Musée des Arts Décoratifs, Paris, 1990, p. 5.
28. See Apollinaire's comments in *L'Intransigeant*, 3 October 1912, in *Apollinaire on Art*, p. 250
29. Unpublished manuscript quoted in Pradel, 'La Maison cubiste', p. 79, note 6.
30. Paul Valéry, 'Sur la crise d'intelligence', (1925) reprinted in *Oeuvres*, vol. 1, Paris, (1960), p. 1044.
31. On modernity and tradition see Jürgen Habermas, 'Modernity – An Incomplete Project', in *The Anti-Aesthetic, Essays on PostModern Culture*, Hal Foster, ed., Port Townsend, 1983, pp. 3-4. See also Gladys Fabre, 'Why this exhibition?' in *Antiguitat/Modernitat en l'art del segle XX*, exhibition catalogue, Fundació Joan Miró, Barcelona, 1990, pp. 299-300.
32. The word was a neologism in decorative arts terminology that summed up the contemporaneous demands for collective action and encompassed the notion of the artist as a creator of unified decorative environments or a director of a team of artists working collaboratively.
33. Jean-Louis Vaudoyer, 'Le Salon d'automne', *Art et décoration*, 1919, p. 181.
34. Lucien Dior and Charles de Lasteyrie, 'Projet de loi concernant l'Exposition internationale des arts décoratifs et industriels modernes', Chambre des Députés, no. 5825, session de 1923.
35. Léon Riotor, 'Proposition relative à la participation de la Ville de Paris et du Département de la Seine à l'Exposition internationale des arts décoratifs et industriels modernes en 1923', *Bulletin du Conseil Municipal*, no. 71, 1920, p. 1. Léon had been one of the founders of 'l'Art à l'Ecole', see Chapter 2, note 63.
36. André Vera, 'La Doctrine décorative de demain', *Le Matin*, 21 November 1918. The article also appeared in *La Grande Revue*, 1918, *La Belle France*, 1919, *Le Petit Messager*, May 1919, *Les Arts français*, 1919. On André and Paul Vera, see Janine Hébert, *Mémorial des Frères Vera*, Pontoise, 1980.
37. The celebration of *métier* also assumed an important role in discussions of a post-war order in painting, as Jean Laude has shown. Before the war, the fragmentation of Cubism, for example, was attacked by certain artists and critics as a sign of artistic decadence and a refusal of the fundamental laws of artistic craft. In the context of the *retour à l'ordre*, the style underwent a process of rehabilitation that accommodated its analytic approach to the ancient laws of the craft of painting to arrive at a more mature, synthetic result. Laude, 'Le Retour à l'ordre', in *Le Retour à l'ordre dans les arts plastiques et l'architecture*, Saint-Etienne, 1975, p. 46.
38. André Vera, 'Modernité et tradition', *Les Arts Français*, 1919, pp. 95-96. See also 'Précisions sur la tradition', *La Douce France*, January 1920, pp. 244-249.
39. Gerard Monnier, 'Un Retour à l'ordre: architecture, géométrie, société', in *Le Retour à l'ordre*, p. 52.
40. Gance's *La Roue* (1924) was a hymn to the locomotive; L'Herbier's *L'Inhumaine* (1924), with sets designed by Robert Mallet-Stevens, celebrated the benefits of the scientific advances of the 1920s over the decadence of the pre-war years.
41. 'Les Arts décoratifs ne sont pas des arts mineurs, dit M. Chaumet', *Bulletin de la Chambre syndicale de l'ameublement*, no. 397, May 1925, p. 199.
42. See 'Exposition internationale des arts décoratifs et industriels

modernes', *L'Hôtel d'un collectionneur*, preface by Léon Deshairs, Paris, 1925.
43. See G. Remon, 'Nos artistes décorateurs, Süe et Mare', *Mobilier et Décoration*, vol. 6, January 1926, pp. 9-21. See also G. Remon, 'Le meuble', in *Exposition internationale des arts décoratifs et industriels modernes Paris, 1925*, (special issue of *L'Art vivant*), 1925, p. 32.
44. *Bulletin de la vie artistique*, 15 November 1925, p. 494.
45. R. Craig Miller, *Modern Design, 1890-1990*, New York, 1990, pp. 17-25. See also Jean-Paul Bouillon, *Journal de l'Art Déco*, Geneva, 1988, pp. 241-252.
46. It worked so perfectly that there were serious discussions about prolonging it. See the notes on the continuation of the exhibition in the October and November 1925 issues of *Bulletin de la vie artistique*.
47. Becker and Bernstein, *Victoire et frustrations: 1914-1929*, Paris, 1990, p. 178.

The Bauhaus and the Theory of Form
by Elodie Vitale

1. Wassily Kandinsky, 'La valeur de l'enseignement théorique en peinture', *Ecrits complets III*, Paris, 1975, p.147.
2. E. Vitale, *Le Bauhaus de Weimar, 1919-1925*, Liège, 1989, p. 48.
3. Inaugural Bauhaus manifesto, first published Weimar, April 1919.
4. Reprinted by Hans Wingler in his documentary collection *Das Bauhaus 1919-1933, Weimar, Dessau, Berlin und die Nachfolge in Chicago seit 1937*, Bramsche, 1968, p. 64.
5. Johannes Itten, *Werke und Schriften*, Zürich, 1972, p. 211.
6. Johannes Itten, *Le Dessin et la Forme*, Paris, 1970, p. 81.
7. Vitale, *Le Bauhaus de Weimar*, p. 54.
8. J. Itten, *Art de la couleur*, abridged edition, Paris, 1971, p. 7.
9. *Ibid.*, p. 27.
10. *Ibid.*, p. 14.
11. *Ibid.*, pp. 94-95.
12. In the course of its existence the Bauhaus would be closed down three times due to the political opposition of the right. Created in 1919 in Weimar, it closed there in 1925. Welcomed by the city of Dessau, it closed once more in 1932. After becoming established in Berlin as a private institution, it was definitively closed by the Nazis in 1933. See the article by E. Vitale, 'Le Bauhaus et la République de Weimar: trois fermetures', in *Art et Fascisme*, edited by P. Milza and F. Roche-Pezard, Brussels, 1989.
13. Laszlo Moholy-Nagy, *Von materiel zu architektur*, Mainz-Berlin, 1968 (facsimile of the 1929 edition), p. 94. This book contains outlines of the classes

taught in the Bauhaus preliminary course (Weimar-Dessau) from 1923 to 1928, when Moholy-Nagy left the Bauhaus.
14. Vitale, *Le Bauhaus de Weimar*, p. 236. See also Josef Albers, 'Werklicher Formunterricht', *Bauhaus*, no. 2-3, 1928.
15. For Moholy-Nagy, man has an objective relation with his fellows and his universe is rooted in his biological make-up. He felt it was this which provided the objective foundation of art.
16. On Gestalt theory see Paul Guillaume, *La Psychologie de la forme*, Paris, 1979.
17. Hannes Meyer succeeded Gropius as director of the Bauhaus in 1928. He reinforced the tendency, already present under Gropius, towards functionalism. He was removed by the right in 1930 and replaced by Mies van der Rohe, who occupied the post of director until the Nazis closed the Bauhaus in 1933.
18. The passages quoted are from Paul Klee, 'Schöpferische Konfession', *Tribune der Kunst und Zeit*, no. 13, Berlin, 1920 (English translation by Norbert Guterman: 'Creative Credo', in *Theories of Modern Art: A Source Book by Artists and Critics*, edited by H.C. Chipp, Berkeley, 1968, pp. 182-186 [trans. slightly altered]).
19. The quotations in this section come from a manuscript by Klee, *Beiträge zur bildnerischen Formlehre*, facsimile edition Basel and Stuttgart, n.d.
20. It would be impossible within the framework of the present article to discuss this aspect of Klee's colour theory in depth, or even to provide more than a summary treatment of his rich, suggestive teachings, which remain difficult to synthesize. For more extended analysis, see Vitale, *Le Bauhaus de Weimar*, chapter VII.
21. Kandinsky, *Concerning the Spiritual in Art*, trans. by M. T. H. Sadler, New York, 1977, p. 37, note 16.
22. G. Muche, 'Arts plastiques et formes industrielles', in Vitale, *Le Bauhaus de Weimar*, p. 300, appendix 14.
23. Interview with Marianne Brandt in 1979, *Form + Zweck*, March 1979 (special Bauhaus issue).
24. Until this time the Bauhaus, which held architecture to be the supreme aim of its teaching, none the less did not have an architecture studio *per se*. The economic circumstances of the post-war period had made it difficult to obtain commissions, and Gropius did not want to sponsor a studio devoted exclusively to projects with no hope of realization.
25. Giulio C. Argan, *Gropius et le Bauhaus*, Paris, 1979, p. 92.

Streamlining 1930-1955
by Jeffrey L. Meikle

1. See Robert R. Updegraff, *The New American Tempo*, New York, 1929, one of a series entitled 'The Little Library of Self-Starters'.
2. Helen Appleton Read, 'The Exposition in Paris', *International Studio*, no. 82, November 1925, p. 96.
3. Edward L. Bernays, *Biography of an Idea: Memoirs of Public Relations Counsel Edward L. Bernays*, New York, 1965, p. 225.
4. Ralph Abercrombie, 'The Renaissance of Art in American Business', *General Management Series*, no. 99, American Management Association, New York, 1929, pp. 6-7.
5. Roy Sheldon and Egmont Arens, *Consumer Engineering: A New Technique for Prosperity*, New York, 1932, p. 55.
6. Carbon copy of a letter from Egmont Arens to Industries' Sales Committee, 23 November 1934, Arens Collection, Box 19, George Arents Research Library, Syracuse University, Syracuse, New York.
7. Letter from Alfred H. Barr Jr. to Norman Bel Geddes, 4 December 1934, File 296, Norman Bel Geddes Archive, Humanities Research Center, University of Texas at Austin.
8. From official announcement of the National Alliance of Art and Industry exhibition, *Advertising Arts*, January 1934, p. 48.
9. Loewy as paraphrased in 'Streamlining – it's Changing the Look of Everything,' *Creative Design*, no. 1, Spring 1935, p. 22.
10. William J. Acker, 'Design for Business,' *Design*, no. 40 November 1938, p. 12.
11. 'San Francisco Golden Gate Exposition 1939,' *Architectural Forum*, no. 70, June 1939, 464. The comment appeared in a comparison of the New York and San Francisco World's Fairs.
12. Egmont Arens, 'Next Year's Cars,' *The American Magazine of Art*, no. 29, November 1936, 736.
13. Siegfried Giedion, *Mechanization Takes Command: A Contribution to Anonymous History*, Oxford, 1948, p. 611.
14. This sense of vertigo appears as the major psychological component of modernity in Marshall Berman's convincing study, *All That is Solid Melts into Air: The Experience of Modernity*, New York, 1982.
15. J. Gordon Lippincott, *Design for Business*, Chicago, 1947, p. 20.

Design for the Happy Days: The 1950s
by Jocelyn de Noblet

1. Thomas Hine, *Populux*, New York, 1989, a study of mass culture in the United States.

2. Jean Fourastie, *Les Trente Glorieuses*, Paris, 1979.
3. Quoted in Didier Pasamonik, *L'Expo 1958 et le style atome*, Brussels, 1983.
4. *Ibid.*
5. *Ibid.*
6. Le Corbusier, *Poème éléctronique*, Paris, 1958.

Modernity and the Ulm School
by Bernd Meurer

1. 'What does the Scholl School want'? Typewritten text, unsigned, undated. HfG-Synopsis, Ulm, 1986, leaflet: prehistory 3.
2. Quoted from *Output*, no. 1, March 1961, p. 4 and *Archithese 15*, 1975, p. 263.
3. Tomas Maldonado, 'New industrial developments and the training of product designers', *Ulm*, no. 2, 1958, p. 40.
4. *Ibid.*, p. 34.
5. Anonymous, *Ulm*, no. 6, 1962, p. 2.
6. Tomas Maldonado, 'The training of architects and product designers in a world in the making', *Ulm*, no. 12-13, 1965, p. 4.
7. Tomas Maldonado, 'Jolting the contented design education system', *Ulm*, no. 17-18, 1966, p. 15.
8. *Ibid.*, p. 18.
9. Theodor Adorno, 'Funktionalismus heute', *Ohne Leitbild*, Frankfurt, 1971.
10. See Wolfgang Fritz Haug, *Kritik der Warenästhetik*, Frankfurt, 1971.
11. Tillman Rexroth, *Warenästhetik - Produkte und Produzenten*, Kronberg, 1974; Bernd Meurer and Hartmut Vincon, *Industrielle Asthetik*, Geissen, 1983.
12. *Ibid.*
13. Jürgen Habermas, 'Modern and postmodern architecture', *Die Neue Unübersichtlichkeit*, Frankfurt, 1985.
14. The Ulm school tried to find a way of using the theory of probabilities to solve complex methodological design and planning problems. Methodology, the theory of science and functional analysis were taught at the school by Horst Rittel from 1958 to 1963.

Ornament and Industrial Design Culture, Status and Identity
by Jonathan M. Woodham

1. In the 1950s George Walker, Ford's chief designer, was nicknamed 'The Benvenuto [Cellini] of Chrome'.
2. See Reyner Banham, *Theory and Design in the First Machine Age*, Architectural Press, 1960, especially Chapter 7, 'Adolf Loos and the Problem of Ornament'.

3. H. Lipstadt, 'Polemic and Parody in the Battle for British Modernism', *AA Files*, January 1983, pp. 68-76.
4. The Council of Industrial Design (COID) was set up under the Board of Trade in 1944 and was reorganized in 1972 as the Design Council.
5. See especially D. L. LeMahieu, *A Culture for Democracy: Mass Communication and the Cultivated Mind in Britain between the Wars*, Oxford, 1988.
6. He had studied at Harvard under Gropius and Breuer, further consolidating the modernist outlook, and was appointed Consultant Director of Design at IBM in 1956.
7. In Germany, there appeared to be significant movement through the founding of the Stuttgart Design Centre in 1949, the Rat für Formgebung (Advisory Board for Design) in Darmstadt in 1951, and the Haus Industrieform (House of Industrial Form) at Essen. In Holland the Stichting Goed Woenen (Good Living Foundation) was set up in 1946, followed by the Instituut voor Industriële Vormgeving (Institute for Industrial Design) in 1951, the same year as the Institut d'Esthétique Industrielle in France.
8. John K. Galbraith, *The New Industrial State*, London, 1974, p. 12.
9. For further reading on this area see J. S. Allen's *The Romance of Commerce and Culture*, Chicago 1983, especially Chapter 9, 'The Aspen Muses and the Twilight of Modernism'. Links with the pre-war ideology of the modernists were consolidated through Philip Johnson's membership of the steering committee for the setting up of the Aspen Conferences in the United States in the 1950s.
10. J. Mashek, J., 'Embalmed Objects: Design at the Modern', *Artforum*, February 1975, p. 50.
11. *Ibid.*, p. 53.
12. *Ibid.*
13. E. Larrabee, 'The Cultural Class War', *Horizon*, January 1960, pp. 4-11.
14. Edgar Kaufmann, 'Borax, or the Chromium-plated Calf', *Architectural Review*, August 1948, pp. 88-93.
15. He also founded the Institut d'Esthétique Industrielle in 1951 and the Chambre Syndicale des Stylistes Industriels in 1954.
16. Jacques Vienot, 'The Design Outlook in France', *Print*, August 1956, p. 44
17 *Ibid.*, p. 45
18. J. E. Blake, 'Space for Decoration', *Design*, no. 77, 1955, p. 12.
19. J. McHale, 'Technology and the Home', *Ark*, no. 19 (Royal College of Art), 1956, p. 25.
20. In Britain see, for example, R. Hoggart, *The Uses of Literacy*, London, 1957; in France the

intellectual outcry against Americanization and its 'civilisation des gadgets' was more prominent in the following decade, when concern was also expressed about the pervasive new meta-language 'franglais'.
21. See, for example, Robert Venturi, *Complexity and Contradiction in Architecture*, New York 1966; R. Venturi, *et al.*, *Learning from Las Vegas*, Cambridge, 1972.
22. Volker Fischer, *Design Now, Industry or Art*, Munich, 1989, p. 87.
23. F. Davis, *Yearning for Yesterday: A Sociology of Nostalgia*, New York, 1979, p. 90
24. In this context it is worth referring to Eric Hobsbawm, and Terence Ranger, eds., *The Invention of Tradition*, Cambridge, 1992, for ways in which tradition has been manufactured in a number of fields, several bearing upon design.
25. Robert Hewison, *The Heritage Industry*, London, 1987.
26. Patrick Wright, *On Living in an Old Country: the National Past in Contemporary Britain*, London, 1985.

Beyond a Semiology of Objects
by Henri Pierre Jeudy

1. Roland Barthes, *Essais critiques*, vol. 3: *L'Obvie et L'Obtus*, Paris, 1988, pp. 43-44.

The Domestication of Objects
by Martyne Perrot

1. See the remarks of Nelly Rodi in *Marie Claire Maison*, November 1992, p. 181.
2 In the spring of 1988 they were found (respectively) in 98 per cent, 94 per cent, and 84 per cent of French households, as opposed to 94 per cent, 88 per cent, and 72 per cent in 1979. INSEE, *premiers résultats*, November 1988.
3. See Pierre Belleville, 'Pour une nouvelle économie domestique', *Culture technique*, no. 3, special issue, 'Machines au foyer', September 15, 1980.
4. In France, people rarely replace furniture and just as rarely dispose of it, even when it's quite old and they have had plenty of time to grow tired of it. Only on one out of four occasions do they replace a piece of furniture when they get rid of something. *INSEE, Premiers résultats*, Ameublement 1988, 'Des Meubles pour la vie', no. 166, December 1988.
5. See Yves Stourdze on two examples of the persistence of archaic practices, in *Culture technique*, no. 3, special issue, 'Machines au foyer', September 1980, p. 43. Electric stoves began to be mass produced outside France in 1920.

6. A. Guillou and P. Guilbert, 'Le Froid domestiqué: l'usage du congélateur', *Terrain*, April 1989, pp. 7-15.
7. The title of an article by Michel Bozonnet on the advertising for, and rationale behind, domestic computer link-ups, *Terrain*, 'Du Congélateur au déménagement', April 1989, p. 15.
8. In 1988, 94 per cent of French households had televisions, 80 per cent of which were colour sets. Thus this appliance ranks second as an element of comfort for the French, after the refrigerator and ahead of the washing machine. *INSEE, Premiers résultats*, no. 158, November 1988.
9. Michel de Certeau, *L'Invention du quotidien*, vols. I and II, Paris, 1980. An English-language edition of volume I has been published as *The Practice of Everyday Life*, translated by Steven Rendall, Berkeley, 1984.
10. A remark by Nelly Rodi, *Marie Claire Maison*.

New Questions
by Ezio Manzini

1. Acceleration of time: the reduction, almost to zero, of the time required to transform matter, to transport people, to circulate and process data.
The implications are: the development of 'real time', wherein the system responds immediately; the spread of interactive systems with their conversational ties to devices, together with a universal reduction in product lifetime in the production and consumption cycle and the dominance of a throwaway relationship to objects.
2. The saturation of space: the saturation of physical space (both in the country in general and in the home), of the economic space (or of the market-place), of the semiotic space (or of mental space).
The implications for products are: on the one hand, a great standardization of uses (the main applications being already totally catered for); on the other, a widespread search for formal variety (a variety which none the less tends to peter out into background noise).
3. Fluidification of matter: the disappearance of technical limits, the diversification of production possibilities, an ever more intensified use of materials, the miniaturization of components, the flexibility of manufacturing processes.
The implications are: the gradual dematerialization of certain products, the increase and diversification in their proposed uses, the spiralling of choice (with the escalation in available product variants).

4. The 'minimum matter' scenario: here, the reduction in the physical size of the products – or their replacement by services – is closely linked to the availability of high-performance materials which allow the production of a new generation of 'dematerialized' goods and services.
This is the highly complex industrial design and manufacturing theme of how matter is supplanted by information: from the replacement of physical goods with information products (telematic data systems replacing telephone books), to that of replacing the physical motion of things and people with data transfer (fax and videoconferencing rather than letters and business trips); from a reduced consumption of materials and energy allowing better control of all processes (not only in large-scale industries but also in the case of 'little processes' like the programme cycles of a washing machine) to – and here we employ the term 'dematerialization' in its widest sense – the general reduction in all physical motion, with the resulting decrease in energy use (from trains and cars right down to moving machine parts).
In the area of materials, this will make for the replacement of low- with high-performance materials, not only in the field of electronics but more generally in all domains where the reduced inertia of lighter materials produces energy-conserving products.
5. The 'eternal matter' scenario centres on the manufacture of longlife products linked to the availability of materials which 'grow old with dignity'. This model implies a change in the concept of product (for example as to their maintenance and lifecycle) both within the economic system (how can one encourage an economy based on longlife products?) and in the consumer imagination (how can the lifetime of a product be developed into one of its quality criteria?).
As regards materials in this scenario, there are no major problems to overcome, though some additional research needs to be done. As has already been observed, many raw materials have an extended intrinsic lifetime. The problem is rather how to design them so that the unavoidable wear and tear they suffer is reduced to a minimum and, by adding value to the materials concerned (as in the ageing of wood, leather and copper), made 'culturally acceptable'.
6. The 'average matter' scenario focuses on the manufacture of short-lived yet highly recyclable products which allow for the

recovery of raw materials so they can be re-utilized in the making of new products. In this case also – and perhaps more so than in the other two scenarios – a complete overhaul of the cultural, technical and pragmatic components of the entire production system is necessary. In fact, since we work within an economic system, we have to make the whole recycling process financially viable. This requires a number of different factors and agencies working together: the industrial designer has to think up products which are easily and economically recyclable; the authorities have to introduce an environmental policy and draw up 'rules of the game' favouring recycling; and the public has to facilitate the smooth operation of such a complicated system with new behaviour patterns.

Postface: Towards the 21st Century
Design in Quest of an Identity
by Anne-Marie Boutin

1. International Federation of Interior Designers.
2. International Council of Graphic Designers Associations.
3. United Nations Industrial Development Organisation.
4. 'At the Crossroads' was the theme of the ICSID congress in Slovenia, May 1992.
5. Interview published in *Le Monde*.
6. Michel Crozier, *L'Entreprise à l'écoute*, Éditions d'organisation, 1991.
7. Victor Papanek, *Design for the Real World: Human Ecology and Social Change*, London, 1985.
8. Thesis by Peter McGrory for the Master of Arts in Design Leadership: *The Role of Design as Integrator in New Product Development Teams*.
9. 'Ways of Eating', recherche sur l'identité culturelle, 1987-1990. Les Ateliers - Studio international, Ministère de la Culture.

Bibliography

Josef ALBERS, *Interaction of Color*, New Haven, Yale University Press, 1964.

C. Edson ARMI, *The Art of American Car Design*, Pennsylvania State University Press, 1987.

Rudolf ARNHEIM, *Vers une Psychologie de l'Art*, Paris, Seghers, 1973.

Art Into Life, Russian Constructivism, 1914-1932. The Henry Art Gallery, New York, Rizzoli, 1990.

V. ARWAS, *Art Deco*, London, Academy Editions, 1980.

Marc AUGÉ, *Non-Lieux, Introduction à une Anthropologie de la Surmodernité*, Paris, Seuil, 1992.

Reyner BANHAM, *Design By Choice*, New York, Rizzoli, 1981.

Reyner BANHAM, *Theory and Design in the First Machine Age*, London, Architectural Press, 1970.

Roland BARTHES, *Mythologies*, translated by A. Lavers, London, Paladin, 1973.

Jean BAUDRILLARD, *La Société de Consommation*, Paris, Denoël, 1970.

Jean BAUDRILLARD, *Le Système des Objets*, Paris, Gallimard, 1968.

Stephen BAYLEY (ed.), *Taste*, London, The Conran Foundation, 1983.

Stephen BAYLEY, *The Conran Directory of Design*, London, Conran Octopus, 1985.

Norman BEL GEDDES, *Horizons*, 1930, New York, Dover Publications, 1977.

Walter BENJAMIN, *Illuminations*, translated by H. Zohn, New York, Schocken, 1969.

Philippe and Martyne BONNIN, 'Le décor domestique en Margeride', in *Terrain*, no. 12, April 1989, pp. 40-54.

Pierre BOURDIEU, *Distinction: A Social Critique of the Judgement of Taste*, translated by R. Nice, London, Routledge, 1990.

Andrea BRANZI, *The Hot-House: Italian New Wave Design*, London, Thames and Hudson, 1985.

Yvonne BRUNHAMMER and Suzanne TISE, *French Decorative Art, The Société des Artistes Décorateurs*, Paris, Flammarion, 1990.

Lucius BURCKHARDT, *Le Design Au-delà du Visible*, Paris, CCI-Centre Georges Pompidou, 1991.

Donald BUSH, *The Streamlined Decade*, New York, G. Braziller, 1975.

J. CAMPBELL, *The German Werkbund – The Politics of Reform in the Applied Arts*, Princeton, Princeton University Press, 1978.

Serge CHERMAYEFF and R. PLUNZ, (eds.), *Design and the Public Good*, Cambridge, Mass., MIT Press, 1982.

Robert JUDSON CLARK, (ed.), *The Arts and Crafts Movement in America 1876-1976*, Princeton, Princeton University Press, 1972.

Françoise COBLENCE, *Le Dandysme, Obligation d'Incertitude*, Paris, PUF, 1988.

Ulrich CONRADS, *Programs and Manifestoes on 20th-century Architecture*, Cambridge, MIT Press, 1975.

Michael COLLINS, *Towards Post-Modernism*, London, British Museum Publications, 1987.

Philip COLLINS, *Radios, The Golden Age*, San Francisco, Chronicle Books, 1987.

Michel COLLOMB, *La Littérature Art Déco*, Paris, Méridiens Klincksieck, 1987.

Edmond COUCHOT, *Images: de l'Optique au Numérique*, Paris, Hermès, 1988.

François DAGOGNET, *Pour une Théorie Générale des Formes*, Paris, J. Vrin, 1975.

Sylvie DENÈFLE, 'Tant qu'il y aura du linge à laver...', in *Terrain*, no. 2, April 1989, pp. 7-15.

Bernard DENVIR, *The Early Nineteenth Century, Art Design and Society 1789-1852*, London, Longman Group Ltd., 1984.

Andrea DINOTO, *Art Plastic, Designed for Living*, New York, Abbeville Publishing Group, 1984.

Norbert ELIAS, *Society of Individuals*, Oxford, Blackwell, 1991.

Jean-Pierre EPRON, (ed.), *Architecture, une Anthologie*, vol. 1, Liège, Pierre Mardaga, 1992.

Volker FISCHER, (ed.), *Design Heute: Masstabe, Formgebung Zwischen Design und Kunststuck*, Prestel-Verlag, Munich, 1988.

Adrien FORTY, *Objects of Desire*, London, Thames & Hudson, 1986.

Hal FOSTER, (ed.), *Postmodern Culture*, London, Pluto Press, 1985.

Pierre FRANCASTEL, *Art et Technique*, Paris, Éditions de Minuit, 1956.

Mildred FRIEDMAN, (ed.), *De Stijl: 1917-1931, Visions of Utopia*, Oxford, Phaidon, 1982.

Jean-Charles GATÉ and Jean-Pierre VITRAC, *Design, la Stratégie Produit*, Paris, Eyrolles, 1993.

Siegfried GIEDION, *Mecanisation Takes Command*, Oxford, Oxford University Press, 1948.

Siegfried GIEDION, *Space, Time and Architecture*, rev. ed., Cambridge, Mass., Harvard University Press, 1967.

Clement GREENBERG, *Collected Essays and Criticism*, Chicago, University of Chicago Press, 1988.

Walter GROPIUS, *The New Architecture and the Bauhaus*, Translated by P. Morton Shand, Cambridge, Mass., MIT Press.

Roger-Henri GUERRAND, *Les Lieux, Histoire des Commodités*, Paris, La Découverte, 1985.

J. HESKETT, *Industrial Design*, London, Thames and Hudson, 1980.

Kathryn B. HIESINGER and George H. MARCUS, *Design since 1945*, London, Thames and Hudson, 1983.

Thomas HINE, *Populux*, London, Bloomsbury Publishing Ltd, 1987.

Henry-Russell HITCHCOCK and Philip C. JOHNSON, *The International Style: Architecture since 1922*, New York, Norton, 1966.

Johannes ITTEN, *Design and Form: the Basic Course at the Bauhaus*, rev. ed., London, Thames & Hudson, 1975.

Charles JENCKS, *What is Post-Modernism?* London, Academy Editions, 1986.

R. JENSEN and P. CONWAY, *Ornamentalism*, London, Allen Lane, 1982.

Sylvia KATZ, *Classic Plastics*, London, Thames and Hudson, 1984.

Le Corbusier, *The Decorative Art of Today*, translated by J. Dunnett, London, Architectural Association, 1987.

Le CORBUSIER, *Towards a New Architecture*, translated by Frederick Etchells, London, Rodker, 1927.

Agnès LEVITTE and Margo ROUARD, *Cent Objets Quotidiens Made in France*, Paris, APCI-Syros Alternative, 1987.

Lucy R. LIPPARD, *Pop Art*, London, Thames and Hudson, 1966.

Bernd LÖBACH, *Industrial Design, Grundlagen der Industrieproduktgestaltung*, Munich, Karl Thiemig Verlag, 1976.

Christina LODDER, *Russian Constructivism*, New Haven, Yale University Press, 1983.

Raymond LOEWY, *Never Leave Well Enough Alone*, New York, Simon & Schuster, 1951.

Adolf LOOS, *Spoken into the Void: Collected Essays, 1897-1900*, translated by J. O. Newman and J. H. Smith, Cambridge, Mass., MIT Press, 1987.

Edward LUCIE-SMITH, *A History of Industrial Design*, Oxford, Phaidon, 1983.

Jean-François LYOTARD, *The Post-Modern Condition, A Report on Knowledge*, translated by G. Bennington and B. Massumi, Manchester, Manchester University Press, 1986.

Ezio MANZINI, *The Materials of Invention*, Arcadia Edizioni, 1986.

Catherine McDERMOTT, *Street Style: British Design in the 80s*, London, The Design Council, 1987.

Jeffrey L. MEIKLE, *Twentieth Century Limited*, Philadelphia, Temple University Press, 1979.

Daniel MILLER, *Material Culture and Mass Consumption*, Oxford, Basel Blackwell, 1987.

William MORRIS, *News from Nowhere*, London, Penguin, 1984.

Lewis MUMFORD, *Future of Technics and Civilization*, London, Freedom Press, 1986.

Gillian NAYLOR, *The Arts and Crafts Movement*, London, Studio Vista, 1971.

Jocelyn de NOBLET, *Design et Succès Industriel*, Paris, CRCT, 1989.

Jocelyn de NOBLET, *Design, Introduction à l'Histoire de l'Évolution des Formes Industrielles de 1820 à nos jours*, Paris, Stock-Chêne, 1974.

Jocelyn de NOBLET, *Design, le Geste et le Compas*, Paris, Somogy, 1988.

Erwin PANOFSKY, *Perspective As Symbolic Form*, translated by Christopher S. Wood, New York, Zone, 1991.

Michel PASTOUREAU, *L'Étoffe du Diable*, Paris, Seuil, 1991.

Nikolaus PEVSNER, *Studies in Art, Architecture and Design*, London, Thames and Hudson, 1968.

Nikolaus PEVSNER, *The Pioneers of the Modern Movement*, London, Faber, 1936.

Danièle QUARANTE, *Éléments du Design Industriel*, Paris, Maloine, 1984.

Barbara RADICE, *Memphis*, London, Thames & Hudson, 1985.

Herbert READ, *Art & Industry*, Bloomington, Indiana University Press, 1961.

Lionel RICHARD, *Encyclopédie du Bauhaus*, Paris, Somogy, 1985.

Jacques ROUAUD, *Soixante ans d'Art ménager, 1923-1939: le confort*, vol. 1, Paris, Syros-Alternatives, 1989.

Herwin SCHAEFFER, *The Roots of Modern Design*, London, Studio Vista, 1970.

Penny SPARKE, *An Introduction to Design and Culture in the Twentieth Century*, London, Allen & Unwin, 1986.

Walter Dorwin TEAGUE, *Design The Day*, New York, Harcourt Brace, 1940.

John THACKARA, *Design After Modernism*, London, Thames and Hudson, 1988.

Nancy TROY, *The De Stijl Environment*, Cambridge, Mass., MIT Press, 1986.

Gianni VATTIMO, *End of Modernity: Nihilism and Hermeneutics in Post-Modern Culture*, translated by J. Snyder, Oxford, Polity Press, 1988.

Thorstein B. VEBLEN, *Instinct of Workmanship and the State of the Industrial Arts*, Transaction Publishers, 1990.

Robert VENTURI, *Complexity and Contradiction in Architecture*, New York, Museum of Modern Art, 1966.

Robert VENTURI, *Learning from Las Vegas*, Cambridge, MIT Press, 1977.

Elodie VITALE, *Le Bauhaus de Weimar, 1919-1925*, Bruxelles, Pierre Mardaga, 1989.

WHITNEY Museum, *High Styles: Twentieth-Century American Design*, New York, Summit Books, 1985.

Hans M. WINGLER, *The Bauhaus, Weimar, Dessau, Berlin, Chicago, Boston*, MIT Press, 1978.

Tom WOLFE, *From Bauhaus to Our House*, London, Cardinal, 1989.

Jonathan M. WOODHAM, *Twentieth-Century Ornament*, London, Studio Vista, 1990.

Photographic credits

Pp.12-13 Agence François Seigneur /Flammarion; pp. 18-19 SNCF; p. 20 Jean Marquis; p. 21 Renault; p. 22 Roger Tallon – Honda; p. 23 Washington Smithsonian Institution – From the Collections of The Henry Ford Museum & Greenfield Village; p. 24 Philippe Starck; p. 25 Denis Santachiara; p. 26 Plan Créatif; p. 27 Thonet brothers – Marie-Magdalène Chatel de Raguet de Brancion Collection/Flammarion – Vitra Museum; p. 28 CRCT; p. 29 CRCT; pp. 30-37 Evert Endt Collection; p. 33 Norman Bel Geddes Fund, The Humanities Research Center, The University of Texas with the authorization of Edith Lutyens Bel Geddes; pp. 38-39 Michael Freeman; pp. 40-41 Kodak; pp. 42-43 The Coca-Cola Company; pp. 44-45 Centre National de la Photographie; p. 46 Société Française de Photographie; p. 48 All rights reserved (1779, 1782, 1849) – Jean-Loup Charmet (1808) – *Les Merveilles de l'industrie* (1812, 1847) – *Les Merveilles de la science* (1819, 1835, 1850) – Smithsonian Institution, Washington, D.C. (1844); p. 49 Evert Endt Collection (1851) – *Les Merveilles de la science* (1852, 1854, 1859¹) – *Les Nouvelles Conquêtes de la science* (1852, 1859²) – *Le Magasin pittoresque* (1853) – Saint-Gobain Collection (1855) – All rights reserved (1857) – Thonet brothers (1858); p. 50 *Les Merveilles de l'industrie* (1860¹) – *La Science française* (1860²) – *Le Magasin pittoresque* (1861¹) – Musée de Compiègne/Jean-Loup Charmet (1861²) – CRCT (1863) – Paris, Musée d'Orsay/RMN (1864) – *Les Merveilles de la science* (1865); p. 51 Dite (1869) – *Les Nouvelles Conquêtes de la science* (1871, 1875) – CRCT (1872, 1876) – *La Nature* (1873) – *Les Merveilles de l'Exposition* (1878); p. 52 All rights reserved; p. 53 CRCT; pp. 55-56, 58-59 Jacques Guillerme; p. 57 CRCT; pp. 60-61 Électricité de France; pp. 62-63 CRCT; p. 64 All rights reserved; p. 65 Flammarion; pp. 66-67 CRCT; pp. 68-69 Photothèque des Musées de la Ville de Paris; pp. 72-73 H. Roger-Viollet; p. 74 CRCT; p. 75 AEG; p. 76 CRCT; p. 77 CRCT – London, Design Council; p. 78 CRCT; p. 79 London, Design Museum; p. 80 CRCT – AEG; p. 81 Calor; p. 83 CRCT; pp. 84-85 CRCT; pp. 86-87 Jean-Loup Charmet; p. 88 MBD Design; p. 89 All rights reserved; p. 91 Frédéric Dumas/Hermès; p. 92 Giraudon – Louis Vuitton; p. 93 Flammarion; p. 94 Guerlain – Yves Saint Laurent; p. 95 Lalique; p. 96 *Les Nouvelles Conquêtes de la science*; p. 97 *La Nature* – Swatch; p. 98 CRCT; p. 99 Louis Vuitton – Hermès – Samsonite; pp. 100-101 H. Roger-Viollet; p. 102 Boyer-Viollet; p. 104 CCI (1879¹) – Lauros-Giraudon (1879²)

– Cl. Vignal/SNCF (1880) – *La Nature* (1882) – CRCT (1884¹) – *Les Merveilles de la science* (1884²) – London, National Gallery/Bridgeman-Giraudon (1884³) – *La Nature* (1886, 1892²); p. 105 *La Nature* (1888) – All rights reserved (1889¹) – L'Illustration/Sygma (1889², 1890) – American Express (1891) – Stuart Davis, *Odol*, 1924. Cincinnati Art Museum/Edimedia (1892¹) – Flammarion (1894¹) – Jean-Loup Charmet (1894²) – Gillette (1895¹) – Assistance publique/Centre de l'image, Paris (1895²) – Cassina S.p.A. (1897) – CCI (1899¹) – *La Nature* (1899²); p. 107 CCI (1900, 1902, 1904, 1905) – Meccano (1901); p. 108 All rights reserved (1907¹) – New York, Museum of Modern Art (1907²) – CRCT (1908) – L'Illustration/Sygma (1909) – Michelin (1910) – CCI (1911); p. 109 Edimedia (1912) – Donald Bush Collection (1913¹) – P. Hinous/Edimedia (1913²) – L'Illustration/Sygma (1914) – The Coca-Cola Company (1915) – Roger Schall/Chanel (1916); p. 110 Courtesy of Sotheby's London – All rights reserved; p. 111 All rights reserved; p. 112 CRCT – Haslam & Whiteway Ltd, London – Victoria & Albert Museum, London; p. 115 Haslam & Whiteway Ltd, London; p. 117 Victoria & Albert Museum, London; p. 119 All rights reserved; pp.120-121 CRCT; p. 122 All rights reserved; p. 123 CRCT; p. 124 All rights reserved; p. 125 All rights reserved – CRCT; p. 126-129 All rights reserved; p. 130 Marc Aumonier Collection – Meccano; p. 132 Roger-Viollet; p. 133 Musée des Arts décoratifs, Paris/Laurent Sully-Jaulmes; p. 135 All rights reserved; p. 136 Alessi S.p.A. – Flammarion – All rights reserved; pp. 138-139 Flammarion; pp. 140-141 Musée Albert Kahn, Département des Hauts-de-Seine; p. 144 CCI – Cassina S.p.A.; p. 145 Flammarion; pp. 146-147 Musée des Arts décoratifs, Paris/Laurent Sully-Jaulmes; p. 148 CRCT; p. 150 CRCT (1918) – All rights reserved (1920, 1923) – Chanel (1921) – International Olympic Committee (1924) – Knoll International (1925); p. 151 All rights reserved (1926) – L'Illustration/Sygma (1927) – Opel (1928) – CRCT (1929, 1932¹) – Knoll International (1930) – CCI (1932²); p. 152 Guerlain (1933) – Cassina S.p.A. (1934¹) – Citroën (1934²) – CRCT (1935) – La Cinémathèque (1936¹) – L'Illustration/Sygma (1936²) – Dite (1937) – All rights reserved (1938); p. 153 Walter Dorwin Teague (1939) – CCI (1940) – Dite (1941) – Serge Bellu Collection (1942) – Jean Lemaire/Keystone (1944) – Daniel Legendre (1945); p. 154 All rights reserved; pp. 155-156 Bauhaus Archiv Berlin; p. 157-158 All rights reserved; p. 159 London, Design Museum – All rights reserved; pp. 160-161 CCI;

p. 163, 165 Bauhaus Archiv Berlin; p. 167 Vitra Museum; p. 168 Flammarion; p. 169 VAG; pp. 170-171 Opel; p. 172 Musée National d'Art Moderne, Centre Georges Pompidou; pp. 173-176 All rights reserved; p. 179 Musée National d'Art Moderne, Centre Georges Pompidou – All rights reserved; p. 180 Musée National d'Art Moderne, Centre Georges Pompidou – Lauros-Giraudon ; p. 181 Musée National d'Art Moderne, Centre Georges Pompidou – Vitra Museum; p. 182 Evert Endt Collection ; p. 183 All rights reserved; p. 184 Jonathan Woodham Collection– Norman Bel Geddes Fund, The Humanities Research Center, The University of Texas with the authorization of Edith Lutyens Bel Geddes; p. 185 CCI; pp. 186-189 Evert Endt Collection; pp. 190, 192 Jonathan Woodham Collection; p. 193 SNCF – CRCT; pp. 194-195 Robert Patterson/From *Radios: The Golden Age* by Philip Collins, Chronicle Books; p. 196 CRCT; p. 197 Dite; pp. 198-199 Citroën; p. 200 Willy Ronis/Rapho; p. 202 Forney Library, Paris (1946¹) – Renault (1946²) – CCI (1947) – Polaroid Corp. (1948¹) – L'Illustration/Sygma (1948²) – Olivetti (1950¹) – All rights reserved (1950²) – Braun (1951); p. 203 Knoll International (1952) – Seb (1953) – Ampex (1954) – McDonald's (1955) – Citroën (1955) – All rights reserved (1955) – Knoll International (1956); p. 204 Renault (1956¹) – CRCT (1956²) – Serge Bellu Collection (1958¹) – All rights reserved (1958²); p. 205 Zanotta S.p.A. (1959) – Dite (1960¹) – CRCT (1960², 1965) – *Paris-Match* (1961) – Kodak (1962) – Airborne (1964); p. 206 Sottsass Associati (1966¹) – Studio Artemide (1966²) – Zanotta S.p.A. (1968¹) – *Paris-Match* (1968²) – Aérospatiale (1969¹) – Gaetano Pesce (1969²); p. 207 Dite-Nasa/Dite (1969-1970) – Terraillon (1971¹) – Zanotta S.p.A. (1971²) – Renault (1971³) – Gaetano Pesce (1972) – Olivetti (1973); p. 208 All rights reserved; pp. 208-209 McDonald's; pp. 210-211 CRCT; pp. 212-213 CCI; p. 213 London, Design Museum; p. 214 Calor; p. 215 CCI; p. 216 CCI – CRCT; p. 217 CCI – Belgian Embassy, Paris – All rights reserved; p. 218 Seymour Powell – Gaffarel Musique – All rights reserved; p. 219 Piaggio; pp. 220-221 Archives Christian Dior; p. 222 Vitra Museum; p. 223 Stadt Aachen-Ludwig-Forum für Internationale Kunst/Anne Gold – Burdick Group; pp. 224-225 Flammarion; p. 226 Stadtarchiv Ulm/HfG-Archiv; pp. 226-227 Bernd Meurer; pp. 228-229 Zanotta S.p.A; p. 229 Stadtarchiv Ulm/HfG-Archiv; p. 230 ninaber/peters/krouwel; p. 231 Tom Newhouse Group; p. 232 Alexander Neumeister – Bernd Meurer; pp. 232-233

Bernd Meurer; pp. 235-236 Erco Leuchten; pp. 238-239 CRCT; p. 240 Gillette – Braun; p. 241 Lego; p. 242 Roger Tallon – Renault; p. 243 Musée de Radio-France/All rights reserved; p. 244 André Courrèges – Mary Quant; p. 245 Habitat; pp. 246-247 Aérospatiale/Plan Créatif; p. 248 Harry Gruyaert/Magnum; p. 250 Innovation Group (1974) – Bic (1975) – Cassina S.p.A. (1976¹, 1979) – All rights reserved (1976², 1977); p. 251 Apple Computer France (1980) – Memphis (1981¹) – Michel Henri/SNCF (1981²) – Neotu (1982) – Honda (1983) – Les Trois Suisses (1984); p. 252 Flammarion (1984) – Zanotta S.p.A. (1985) – CRCT (1986¹) – Vitra (1986²) – DCA Design Consultants (1986³) – Vitra (1987¹) – François Lehr/Agence Sipa (1987²) – Sylvain Dubuisson (1988); p. 253 Renault (1989¹) – Raymond Depardon/ Magnum (1989²) – Unifor (1990¹) – Eurotunnel (1990²) – J. C. Decaux/ P. Starck (1991²) – Cappellini (1992²²) – RATP (1992³) – François Seigneur (1993); p. 254 CCI; pp. 254-258, 260 Andrea Branzi Collection; p. 261 Memphis; p. 262 Zanotta S.p.A.; p. 263 Olivetti; pp. 264-265 Alessi; p. 266 Alessandro Mendini; p. 267 Cassina S.p.A.; p. 268 IDEO Product Development; p. 269 Scholtès; p. 270 Lunar Design Inc. – Smart Design – Slany Design – Ziba Design – Kenneth Wood – Scholtès; p. 271 Lisa Krohn; p. 273 Aldo Cibic – M. Ceramic; p. 274 Lunar Design Inc. – Sharp – Philips Medical System; p. 275 King Miranda Associati; p. 276 Ziba Design; p. 277 Hollington Associates; p. 278 Lunar Design Inc. – Frogdesign; p. 279 Alcatel Business Systems; p. 280 Sony; p. 281 Goupil Laboratories; p. 282 Nikon; pp. 282-284, 286 Canon; p. 285 Pentagram; p. 287 Frogdesign; pp. 288-289 Nissan; p. 291 KID – Nissan – Renault; p. 292 Bic – Durex; p. 293 Yamaha; p. 294 Catherine McDermott Collection – All rights reserved – Prospero Rasulo; p. 295 Peter Marlow/Magnum (cropped photograph) – One-Off; pp. 296-297 Prospero Rasulo; pp. 298-299 NATO; p. 299 Nigel Coates – Jasper Morrison – Danny Lane – One Off; p. 303 Daniel Weil; p. 304 VIA; p. 305 All rights reserved; pp. 306-307 All rights reserved; pp. 308-309 En attendant les Barbares; pp. 310-311 John Batho; pp. 312-313 All rights reserved; p. 313 CRCT; pp. 314-315 Citroën; p. 314 All rights reserved; p. 316 Serge Bellu Collection – Lancia; pp. 316-317 Evert Endt Collection; pp. 318-319 *Paris-Match*; p. 318 Renault – Donald Bush Collection – BMW; pp. 320-321 Renault; pp. 322-323, 325-326 Gaston Juchet Collection; p. 327 All rights reserved – RMN;

p. 328 Dite; p. 329 From the Collections of The Henry Ford Museum & Greenfield Village; p. 330 Citroën; p. 331 Marc Aumonier Collection; pp. 332-333 Citroën; p. 334 CRCT – London, Design Museum – Dite – Serge Bellu Collection; p. 335 Serge Bellu Collection – Presse-Sport; p. 336-337 Giuseppe d'Amore; p. 337 Vitrac Design; p. 338 Sharp – Sottsass Associati; p. 339 ninaber/ peters/krouwel – ACH Stefano Giovannoni – Ziba Design – Olympus; p. 340 CRC; pp. 342-343 Memphis; p. 344 Ircam – SNCF; p. 345 H. Dreyfuss Associates; pp. 346-347 WDK; p. 348 London, Design Council – Jonathan Woodham Collection – The Good Housekeeping Institute – Jonathan Woodham Collection; p. 349 Jonathan Woodham – London, Design Museum – Astral Telecom Ltd – Jonathan Woodham Collection; p. 352 London, Design Museum; p. 353 Apex Inc.; p. 354 All rights reserved – Denis Santachiara – Sylvain Dubuisson; p. 356 Denis Santachiara – Oxo International; p. 357 Studio Naço; pp. 358-359 Sylvain Dubuisson; p. 361 Ron Arad; p. 362 Polaroid Corporation; p. 363 American Express; pp. 364-365 Philippe Bonnin; p. 365 All rights reserved; pp. 366-367 CRCT; p. 368 Jonathan Woodham Collection; p. 370 Patricia Ranzo & Sergio Capelli; pp. 369-371 Philippe Bonnin; pp. 372-373 Campenon Bernard SGE-Eurograph; p. 373 MBD Design; p. 374 Fred Baier; p. 375 Campenon Bernard SGE-Eurograph; p. 377 Jean Muller International; pp. 380-381 Lockheed Corp.; pp. 382-383 Centre de Recherches Image Numérique, Université de Paris 8; p. 383 Ezio Manzini Collection; pp. 384-385 All rights reserved; p. 386 IDEO Product Development; pp. 388-389 Centre de Recherches Image Numérique, Université de Paris 8; pp. 390-391 Lindberg Optic Design; p. 391 All rights reserved; p. 392 Kartell; p. 393 CRCT; p. 394 Kenwood – Cassina S.p.A. – Brion Vega; p. 395 Kartell; p. 398 J. C. Planchet/CCI; p. 399 Flammarion; p. 400 All rights reserved; p. 401 DGA-DCN; p. 402 Lotus; p. 403 Salomon; pp. 404-405 GIAT AMX-APX; pp. 406-408, 411-413, 415 Ezio Manzini Collection; pp. 416-417 Ademe.

We would especially like to thank Dominique Lemoine, Jean-Pierre Piton and Raymond Guidot (CCI, Centre Georges Pompidou), Marc Aumonier (Lotus France), Serge Bellu (*Automobiles Classiques*), Andrea Branzi, Philip Collins, Evert Endt, Ezio Manzini, Maurice Magnien (Électricité de France) and Jonathan Woodham for all of their help with the illustrations in this work.